Deviance and Deviants

An Anthology

Richard Tewksbury
Patricia Gagné
University of Louisville

Foreword by
Martin D. Schwartz
Ohio University

Roxbury Publishing Company
Los Angeles, California

Library of Congress Cataloging-in-Publication Data

Tewksbury, Richard
   Deviance and Deviants: An Anthology/Richard Tewksbury, and Patricia Gagné.
    p. cm.
   Includes bibliographical references and index.
   ISBN 1-891487-27-2
   1. Deviant Behavior. I. Tewksbury, Richard. II. Gagné, Patricia.
   HM811.D49 1999
   302.5'42—dc21   99-36595
                                     CIP

DEVIANCE and DEVIANTS: AN ANTHOLOGY

Publisher and Editor: Claude Teweles
Copy Editor: Jackie Estrada
Production Editor: Cathy Yoo
Production Coordinator: Renee Burkhammer and Anne West
Production Assistants: Remy Goldsmith, Josh Levine, and Dawn VanDercreek
Typography: Synergistic Data Systems
Cover Design: Marnie Kenney

Printed on acid-free paper in the United States of America. This paper meets the standards for recycling of the Environmental Protection Agency.

ISBN: 1-891487-27-2

ROXBURY PUBLISHING COMPANY
P.O. Box 491044
Los Angeles, California 90049-9044
Tel: (310) 473-3312 • Fax: (310) 473-4490
Email: roxbury@crl.com
Website: www.roxbury.net

Contents

Part I: Substance Use and Abuse

Weisheit draws on interviews with commerical marijuana growers to explain non-economic motives for
criminal behavior.

In this article, the author interviews a sample of
women–crack-cocaine dealers in Detroit, Michigan,
then examines their coping strategies in a male-dominated world.

VanNostrand and Tewksbury report on interviews with
street-level drug dealers as to how they organize their
business operations, emphasizing ways in which an illicit business is similar to a legal business.

McCormick and Ureda employ survey data to examine
how and when students put themselves at risk for
drunk driving accidents and how they rationalize driving drunk or riding with a drunk driver.

Part II: Sexual Deviations

Part III: Medicalized Forms of Deviance

Part IV: Intimate Forms of Violence

Part V: Deviant Sports

Part VII: Deviant Subcultures

Acknowledgments

We thank Mark Richard and Matthew Sargeant for their assistance in the preparation of this manuscript. We are also grateful to the reviewers who provided us with commentaries regarding the content and organization of this collection: David Curry, University of Missouri-St. Louis; Janet Hankin, Wayne State University; Robert F. Meier, University of Nebraska-Omaha; Alex Piquero, Temple University; Chris Rasche, University of North Florida; Martin Schwartz, Ohio University; Michael Stein, Lindenwood College; and Richard A. Wright, Arkansas State University. Finally, we also thank the staff at Roxbury Publishing Company for their commitment to this project. ✦

About the Contributors

Georgia J. Anetzberger is affiliated with the Benjamin Rose Institute in Cleveland, Ohio.

Edward Brongersma is the founder of the Brongersma Foundation, A Dutch institution devoted to the study of sexuality of youth.

Thomas C. Calhoun is associate professor of sociology and African-American Studies, and Director of the Institute for Ethnic Studies at the University of Nebraska.

Meda Chesney-Lind is professor and director of women's studies at the University of Hawaii at Manoa.

Collin Clark is member of the faculty of the department of sociology at the University of Reading, England.

Gloria Cowan is professor in the department of pyschology at California State University, San Bernardino. Her research is centered on issues in social psychology and women's issues—including pornography, rape, and hate speech.

Laura Craig is a faculty member in the department of sociology at the University of Calgary.

Todd W. Crosset is assistant professor in the sport management program at the University of Massachusetts at Amherst. He is primarily concerned with social problems in sports organizations.

Dean Dabney is assistant professor in the department of criminal justice at Georgia State University. His research focuses on white collar crime in the health care industry.

Donna Darden is professor in the departments of sociology and philosophy at Tennessee Technological University. Her primary interests are in the areas of deviance and social psychology.

Cliff English is head of the department of sociology at Luther College. His research interests include deviant behavior and social problems.

Mark Fenster holds a Ph.D. in communication and a law degree. He is an independent scholar living in Denver.

Patricia Gagné is associate professor of sociology at the University of Louisville. Her research interests include domestic violence, gender identity management, and public health sex education campaigns.

Jane F. Gilgun is professor in the school of social work at the University of Minnesota. Her research interests include child welfare and child sexual abuse.

Jack Glascock received his Ph.D. from the mass media program at Michigan State University.

Robert Hale was assistant professor of sociology and criminal justice at Southeastern Louisiana University. His research focused on violent offenders and the death penalty. He passed away in 1998.

John W. Heeren is professor of sociology at California State University, San Bernardino where his research focuses on issues of deviant behavior, religion, and sociological theory.

Columbus B. Hopper is professor emeritus of sociology at the University of Mississippi.

Elizabeth Hottle received her Bachelor's degree from the department of sociology and anthropology at Washington and Lee University. Her paper in this volume won the undergraduate student paper competition from the Virginia Social Science Association.

Rick Houlberg is professor of broadcast and electronic communication arts at San Francisco State University.

Karen A. Joe is assistant professor of sociology at the University of Hawaii at Manoa. Her primary areas of interest are in criminology, deviance, and sociology of law.

Liz Kelly is a faculty member in the child and woman abuse studies unit at the University of North London.

Susan E. Kelly is assistant professor of Sociology at the University of Louisville. Her research interests center on the ethics of genetic research and social policy.

Suzanne J. Kessler is professor of psychology at the State University of New York at Purchase. Her central focus is in the psychology of gender.

Jill E. Korbin is professor of anthropology at Case Western Reserve University. Her primary areas of interest are cultural and medical anthropology as well as cross-cultural family studies.

Mary Kreger is a licensed clinical social worker in private practice.

Robert LaRose is professor in the department of telecommunication at Michigan State University where his research focuses on the uses and effects of information technology.

Carole Lee earned her bachelor's degree from the department of psychology at California State University, San Bernardino.

Daniella Levy earned her bachelor's degree from the the department of psychology at California State University, San Bernardino.

Becky Marrujo holds a masters of social work and works in Pine Hill, New Mexico.

Donald L. McCabe is professor in the department of organization management at Rutgers University.

Laura K. McCormick is assistant professor of behavioral sciences at the University of Texas, Houston school of public health.

Mark A. McDonald is assistant professor of sport management at the University of Massachusetts at Amherst where he teaches sport management and strategic management of sports organization.

Charlene E. Miall is associate professor of sociology at McMaster University. Her primary areas of research interest are in social psychology, deviance, and family studies.

Tom Mieczkowski is professor of criminology at the University of South Florida, St. Petersburg. He is the editor of the *Journal of Drug Testing*.

Jody Miller is assistant professor of criminology and criminal justice at the University of Missouri-St. Louis. Her research interests include women and crime and feminist criminology.

Johnny Moore is a staff member at the University of Mississippi, where he earned his Bachelor's degree.

Trevor Pinch is a professor in the department of science and technology studies at Cornell University.

James Ptacek is assistant professor at Suffolk University, working in the sociology and criminal justice programs.

Steven P. Schacht is a sociologist at Montana State University.

Martin D. Schwartz is professor of sociology at Ohio University. His research is in areas of criminology, feminist theory, and gender and crime.

David Shichor is professor of criminal justice at California State University, San Bernardino. His research is primarily in the areas of corporate crime, corrections, and victimology.

Debra Snyder earned her bachelor's degree from the department of psychology at California State University, San Bernardino.

Richard Tewksbury is associate professor of justice administration at the University of Louisville. His research focuses on urban and rural drug markets, gender identity management, institutional correctional programming, and men's studies.

Nancy Theberge is professor with a joint appointment in the departments of sociology and kinesiology at the University of Waterloo.

Susan K. Tomita works in the school of social work at the University of Washington.

John Ureda is on the faculty of the department of health promotion and education in the school of public health at the University of South Carolina.

Lise-Marie VanNostrand is a probation officer with the Kentucky department of probation and parole. Her research focuses on the illicit drug industry and institutional corrections personnel.

Neil Websdale is associate professor of criminal justice at Northern Arizona University. His research is centered in issues of policing, gender and crime, and domestic violence.

Ralph A. Weisheit is professor of criminal justice at Illinois State University where his research interests are in the areas of alcohol and drugs, women and crime, and rural crime and justice.

Steven Worden is associate professor and director of undergraduate studies in the department of sociology, social work and criminal justice at the University of Arkansas.

Kevin Young is associate professor of sociology at the University of Calgary. ✦

Foreword

Martin D. Schwartz
Ohio University

What do people look for when they look at new anthologies in deviant behavior? If the answer is a run through the classics, a view of the same articles that the professor read when she took the course herself years ago, then there are several multi-edition books already on the market that should serve these purposes very well.

What Tewksbury and Gagné have to offer is a completely new and fresh approach. Their approach is new and interesting from several different directions. First, they do not organize their articles around the themes of different sociological and psychological theories. Although there is a long and hoary tradition in this organizational scheme, it is one that seems to appeal to fewer and fewer professors. It never did appeal much to students. Rather, the organization here emphasizes the various topics and subtopics within the study of deviance. It is the way many of us teach the course today, the way that many of the main textbooks are organized, and certainly a useful way to organize a book.

When I first read this book I wondered about the relative youth of the two editors here, although both are prolific and brilliant scholars. It then occurred to me that the articles that they have chosen are the very ones that a younger generation of deviance scholars is particularly interested in discussing. While my generation virtually memorized Howard Becker's description of learning to smoke marijuana, there are other related issues on the minds of people today, not least of which is crack cocaine.

One of the great strengths of this book is the mix of articles here between the familiar and the unfamiliar. Too many books seem to me to be catalogs of titillation, seemingly driven by exposing students only to materials that shock and disrupt their comfortable lives. As it so happens, I think that this is a good way to teach and strongly approve of that goal. Yet, there are disadvantages of leaving the impression that deviance consists of cross-dressing, transgender behavior, exotic sex acts in exotic countries, and the like. Students often learn more when they have at least some vague familiarity with the subject matter, or when at least they can identify with what is being studied. It is too easy to dismiss sexual deviance as things that rich Asian businessmen do on vacation in Thailand and Sri Lanka. It is harder to dismiss articles about your own familiar life.

Thus, Tewksbury and Gagné include here material on a variety of topics that might be far from the world of the typical college student, except for their exposure to TV specials. This might include the problems of street prostitutes, skinheads, or motorcycle gangs. Few students will come into deviance classes with deep knowledge of the behavior of men who cruise the streets looking for sex either as purchasers or sellers. Few will know about the world of cockfighting. Many will know much less than they should about elder abuse or child abuse.

Yet, the study of deviance and deviants includes the study of many people who are close at hand, and may in fact even include some of the very students in the course. College sports provides a rich set of examples of students who sexually objectify women and are supported in this endeavor by their coaches and schools. Nothing could be more stereotypical college behavior than sexual and physical violence against women.

There are many other topics where the students in any college class will immediately identify with the material at hand and will no doubt have much to add. For example, drunk driving is epidemic at many college campuses. Moreover, most students will know at least something about stuttering, dieting, childlessness, and telephone pornography.

Thus, a particular strength of the book is the mix of articles here. This includes not only the mix of materials from familiar to unfamiliar topics, but also a mix from top journals to articles that appeared in periodicals less likely to come to the attention of many teachers. All of the pieces are well-written, and the whole is significantly greater than the parts. ✦

Preface

At one time scholars believed that deviance was the result of biological or psychological abnormalities found in individuals. However, sociologists have since seriously questioned these approaches, largely by showing how power and social arrangements contribute to definitions of deviance. As the social construction perspective argues, deviance is what society labels as deviant.

In this anthology, we have assembled a collection of highly readable and compelling articles that highlight sociological concepts key to the study of deviance. The articles examine a wide range of specific types of behavior.

Our book is unique. We have arranged the readings by subject matter, rather than theoretical perspectives or concepts. The book features articles that look at drugs, sex, medicine, relationships, sports, work, and deviant subcultures to provide students a basis for grasping central sociological ideas. These include labeling, rationalization processes, motives and the experience of deviance. We also provide articles that offer students insights into the role that power plays in the definition and perception of deviance. We believe that this approach will assist students in understanding these readings—both theoretically and substantively.

These articles provide students with real-world examples of the concepts and perspectives that we believe are key to the study of deviance. We have found that this approach facilitates active learning, classroom participation and a desire to connect what might otherwise be dry concepts to the real world and students' experiences. ✦

Part I

Substance Use and Abuse

Every year, millions of Americans abuse alcohol and drugs. When we think about substance abuse, all kinds of associated problems immediately come to mind—crime, violence, poverty, accidents, and injuries, suicide, health problems, and a general loss of productivity. From a sociological perspective, it is interesting that most people think of drug and alcohol abuse as deviant, yet this is behavior most people engage in at some time in their lives and that many practice regularly. Despite the prevalence of substance abuse, we know that it can cause substantial personal and social problems.

The articles in this section take a sociological perspective on alcohol and drugs. Rather than looking at the personal effects of using, growing and manufacturing, or distributing these substances, the authors consider how drugs and alcohol influence the way people organize their lives. Whether looking at the abuse of alcohol or the sale of drugs, all of the articles in this section point out ways that individuals who engage in deviant behavior rationalize their deviance, equating it with practices that are necessary or normal.

The first three articles look at how drug dealers organize their daily activities and avoid arrest. Like all businesspeople, drug dealers have costs and benefits associated with their careers. Unexpected rewards can come from growing and selling illegal substances, and Ralph Weisheit's article on marijuana farmers focuses on the sense of personal pride and public status that growers who cultivate high-quality crops can experience. However, rewards are not universal, and problems are common. Tom Mieczkowski's article about women crack-cocaine dealers shows us that drug dealers can find themselves in unanticipated and highly dangerous situations. But, like all good entrepreneurs, women crack dealers develop creative ways to deal with unexpected circumstances. To them, it's just a job, similar to the careers that Lise-Marie VanNostrand and Richard Tewksbury examine in their article on street-level drug dealers. In that article, they show how drug dealers organize their businesses and work to avoid police detection. Dealers argue that selling drugs is similar to legitimate business operations, and they explain that they go into business for the same reasons as other entrepreneurs: to be able to buy necessities and luxuries and because they enjoy the work.

Finally, Laura K. McCormick and John Ureda look at the reasons college students give for drinking and driving. As a form of deviance, drinking and then driving is a dangerous activity; nevertheless, it may also be a "regular" part of college life. The fact that students know this behavior is dangerous may influence their decisions; however, feeling as if they have no choice but to drive home drunk seems to have an even greater impact. After attending parties or going to bars to drink, for example, many students find that they have no other way home. Thus, we see that with some forms of deviance, people may feel they "must" engage in the deviant acts. This thinking not only rationalizes the deviant behavior but also results in illegal and dangerous practices.

These articles show us that deviant behaviors can be quite similar to many nondeviant activities. Although some people think that those who participate in deviant acts are different, particularly when it comes to using and selling drugs, these articles show us that this may not always be the case. Some of the activities that deviants engage in certainly differ from those of nondeviants. But, in many respects, both the actions themselves, and the reasons people have for engaging in them can be very similar for both deviants and nondeviants.

The articles in this section show us that we need to think carefully about the specific aspects of a particular activity that make it deviant. As you read the articles, think about what it is that makes an act "deviant." Is it the situation? Is it some characteristic (such as the age, gender, or race) of the individual? Is it the reason for engaging in the action? Or, is it the effect the action has on others that makes it deviant? ✦

1

The Intangible Rewards From Crime: The Case of Domestic Marijuana Cultivation

Ralph A. Weisheit

This article looks at how the world of American marijuana farming and distribution operates. Marijuana farmers share many similarities with other farmers and often grow and sell marijuana along with other crops. The experiences of these farmers vary widely, depending on how much time and money they devote to marijuana cultivation. This tells us that people find different ways of engaging in similar forms of deviant behavior and that their rewards can vary greatly.

Studies of the drug business in the United States have had an evolving focus, generally paralleling shifts in the explanation of crime more generally. Early studies depicted street-level dealers as irresponsible and poorly adjusted addicts who use drugs to escape the demands of the social world around them (e.g., Chein, Gerard, Lee, and Rosenfield 1964). They expected, and were granted, little respect by members of their community.

In 1969, Preble and Casey challenged this view, noting that addicts were anything but passive. The addicts in their study were active, busy people, working to maintain a steady income from drug sales and associated hustling activities:

> The brief moments of euphoria after each administration of a small amount of heroin constitute a small fraction of their daily lives. The rest of the time they are aggressively pursuing a career that is exacting, challenging, adventurous, and rewarding. They are always on the move and must be alert, flexible, and resourceful (Preble and Casey 1969, p. 2).

Since then, research has continued to focus on the "business" of drugs. By the 1980s, studies were examining street-level organizations in which the drug sellers were not addicts, often were not allowed to use drugs while working, had a strong commitment to the work ethic, and viewed their activities as a career (Mieczkowski 1986; Williams 1989; Fields 1986). Increasingly, drug dealing has come to be defined within the context of "drugs as work" (Manning and Redlinger 1983).

These studies have provided valuable insights into the drug business, but like previous views, the focus on economic factors and the business of drugs has drawn attention away from other important aspects of the phenomenon. In particular, the drug business can provide rewards other than the drug high and financial gain. It is ironic that Preble and Casey's article, which set the stage for over 20 years of research on the economics of the drug business (see Johnson et al. 1985), both began and concluded by highlighting rewards which were neither economic nor pharmacological:

> The quest for heroin is the quest for a meaningful life, not an escape from life. And the meaning does not lie, primarily, in the effects of the drug on their minds and bodies; it lies in the gratification of accomplishing a series of challenging, exciting tasks, every day of the week. (Preble and Casey 1969, p. 3)

> [Heroin use] provides a motivation and rationale for the pursuit of a meaningful life, albeit a socially deviant one. The activities these individuals engage in and the relationships they have in the course of their quest for heroin are far more important than the minimal analgesic and

euphoric effects of the small amount of heroin available to them. If they can be said to be addicted, it is not so much to heroin as to the entire career of a heroin user. The heroin user is, in a way, like the compulsively hard-working business executive whose ostensible goal is the acquisition of money, but whose real satisfaction is in meeting the inordinate challenges he creates for himself. (Preble and Casey 1969, p. 21)

This study examines the rewards from the drug business which are neither monetary nor psychopharmacological. The findings are based on interviews [in Illinois] with 31 commercial marijuana growers, 30 law enforcement officials familiar with domestic cultivation, and about a dozen others with connections to marijuana cultivation. . . .

The Growing Operations

Growers in this study had been in the business for an average of 5 years, with one grower having been involved for 18 years. The largest operation had over 6,000 plants, and the median size of operation was 75 plants. Nearly all of them cultivated sinsemilla, a technique of cultivation in which only female plants are grown and only the flowering buds are harvested (the product is considerably more potent than that from only leaves). Most expected to harvest from 1/2 to 3/4 of a pound of marijuana from each mature plant. Though growers were reluctant (and usually unable) to provide details about their income from marijuana growing, most expected to receive between $700 and $1,500 a pound for their crops. During periods when the domestic marijuana was scarce, they could receive as much as $2,000 a pound. A conservative estimate of $750 for each mature plant would mean the median operation in this study could expect a gross income of over $56,000 per year from their operation. Further, an operation of this size could be run with little or no hired help and, if grown outdoors, at an almost negligible operating cost. (The elaborate irrigation systems reported in some California operations are seldom necessary in the Midwest).

Six of the 31 growers grew all or part of their crops indoors, which made detection more difficult and which allowed them to harvest crops year round. Because of the expense of equipment and utilities, indoor operations are usually much smaller than outdoor operations. . . .

Types of Growers

Understanding the rewards from commercial marijuana growing requires an understanding of the types of people involved in growing and the factors which motivate them to enter the business. Elsewhere I have identified three types of marijuana growers: the hustler, the pragmatist, and the communal grower (Weisheit 1990b, 1990c). A brief description of these groups will facilitate understanding the discussion of rewards.

Hustlers

These marijuana growers are entrepreneurs by instinct. They may have used marijuana and may have engaged in some dealing for the challenge of it, though neither activity is a necessary prerequisite for their involvement in growing. Some use farmland they already own, others purchase or rent farmland for the explicit purpose of growing marijuana, and still others enlist the aid of land owners who are having financial problems. For some, the risks associated with growing are themselves part of the appeal of growing. Although the money they make may serve as an indicator of success, they are generally less motivated by the money itself than by the challenge of being a successful entrepreneur. They could just have easily set up business in any one of a dozen legitimate or illegitimate enterprises and once the challenge wears off, they are likely to move out of marijuana growing. . . .

Numerically, hustlers probably represent a very small proportion of growers, though their grandiose schemes push them to large growing operations. Thus, they have a disproportionately large impact on the marijuana market (Weisheit 1990a). . . .

Pragmatists

These growers are driven to marijuana production by economic necessity. Importantly, they approach marijuana with no moral or philosophical righteousness. They often see what they are doing as both legally and morally wrong, but feel they have few options. Unlike hustlers, they are in the marijuana business to help themselves through tough economic times, not to become wealthy.

> G04: I didn't plan on getting rich or anything, I just wanted to hang on to what I had. I had no illusions of buying a yacht or anything like that. I was just trying to hang on to what I had. . . . I believe most of the people who are trying to make money off of marijuana are doing it because they're broke. And, they are usually like me, I was faced with foreclosure, even though I was not a farmer. A lot of the farmers around here, you know, lose 10 to 15 thousand a year growing corn and make it up growing reefer.

***

> G29: I was laid off at the coal mine, and hell, had house payments and everything else coming in. And, I just couldn't make it farming and stuff, and I couldn't find a job. So I thought I'd try that [marijuana growing] first. . . .

Pragmatists are a particularly interesting group, for they demonstrate that growing requires no commitment to a drug lifestyle or even a "liberal" or tolerant attitude toward drugs in general. Potter, Gaines, and Holbrook (1990) note that in Kentucky, marijuana growing is most common in regions which are both impoverished and characterized by conservatism. . . .

Although more common than hustlers, pragmatists are, in most regions, probably not the most common type of grower. The size of their operations varies greatly, depending primarily on their economic need. . . .

Communal Growers

These persons probably represent the single largest category of grower, though their operations are often very small. They cultivate marijuana as part of a larger lifestyle, of which marijuana use is often an important part. Some seek to retreat from society by living in remote areas, and others are active mainstream members of society for whom marijuana growing is a personal statement of rebellion or independence. For many, growing makes a social statement. They have little interest in the business side of marijuana or in accumulating money from growing marijuana, although the money may help them through short-term financial problems. A few are holdovers from the late 1960s and early 1970s, but more commonly they are indistinguishable from "ordinary" citizens in their outward appearance and involvement in conventional activities. In the current study, several were involved in volunteer work with such groups as the Red Cross and the Special Olympics. . . .

As their comments indicate, a number of the growers interviewed for this study could be classified as communal growers:

> G07: I probably grew about 10-15 pounds per year and about three of those pounds were for me personally. Another 4-5 I would give away, and I'd save five pounds every year and around Christmas time I sold it to the same guy every year, and I used that money to buy presents, something we couldn't otherwise afford. . . . I sold it well under commercial prices. Because you see, that's one of the main reasons I got into it in the first place, because commercial prices were ridiculous, and plus I don't believe in supporting organized crime that's into all this other shit, too. There's a philosophical argument about smoking marijuana that could go on for days, but personally I think it's a person's—if somebody wants to, it's no big deal, if you are an adult. I don't think kids should, of course, but I think if you are an adult and you want to, it's no different than drinking a beer, or whisky, or wine, and whatever else. And, it's none of the damn state's business. . . .

The idea of simply giving away marijuana is common among communal growers, but would be unthinkable for hustlers, unless it was to attract future business. Several communal growers also saw their activities as having political and economic implications. They felt that domestic marijuana growing helped the overall balance of trade with other countries, benefited the local economy, and kept money from going to organized crime—which they were certain would happen if they bought marijuana through an importer. . . .

These economic and political issues were secondary considerations, and may have been nothing more than rationalizations to justify their illegal activities to themselves. Nevertheless, these arguments cannot be dismissed as irrelevant to the process if the growers truly believed them, and it appeared they did.

Approaching production as they do, communal growers view other growers as kindred spirits rather than threatening competitors. When communal growers get together they often enjoy sharing experiences and technical information about growing, and "war stories" about their brushes with the law and with marijuana thieves. Similarly, this group is less likely to engage in the violence sometimes associated with marijuana growing, such as setting booby traps and guarding crops with automatic weapons or dogs (Lawren 1985; Warner 1986; Raphael 1985).

The Rewards of Growing

Growing marijuana can be a lucrative business, depending on the variety grown, whether the product is sinsemilla or commercial grade, and current market conditions. The value of the crop to the grower tends, everything else being equal, to be directly related to the amount of effort and technical expertise the grower applies to the process. At the bottom of the scale are those who only harvest wild growing marijuana, also known as ditchweed. This practice takes little effort and can yield as little as $50 per pound. At the other extreme are those who cultivate potent strains and grow the plants as sinsemilla, which can yield as much as $2,000 per pound. Most growers in this study focused on sinsemilla and expected to receive an average of $1,000 per mature plant. Although demanding and time consuming, it is possible to develop operations which gross over $1,000,000 per year. By their sheer size, such operations are at higher risk of detection and usually require hiring help, which itself increases the risk of arrest and of theft. These large operations are generally undertaken only by the most ambitious (such as a hustler) or the most desperate for money (such as the pragmatist).

Although money is important, and perhaps the most important reason for commercial growing, it is not the only motivating factor. This is particularly true for communal growers who are less likely to be driven by internal (hustlers) or external (pragmatists) forces to use growing to make large sums of money. For many growers in this study, the expected cash return from growing was modest, and the intangible rewards of growing rivaled cash benefits as motivating factors.

Intangible Rewards

Aside from cash benefits, there were at least three ways in which the process of growing was itself rewarding and satisfying. Growers tended to emphasize either the spiritual, social, or intrinsic rewards from growing.

Spiritual Rewards

Several spoke of the spiritual rewards from growing, using religious or almost religious descriptions of their feelings. The process of growing, as distinct from the money or the effects of using marijuana, was something they spoke of with great passion.

Q: Aside from the money, was there anything else about growing marijuana that you found satisfying or enjoyable?

G03: This plant of all the Lord's plants is the most intriguing plant that I know of. Yes, I would grow this plant as some people grow roses. I think roses are dumb even though I grow them and like them. Bananas are a lovable plant and so is papaya, but marijuana is in a category all by itself. I would class it as one of the more sophisticated plants. Yes I took great pride in producing a high quality product for my fellow man to enjoy. I have brought much happiness and well being into this world. To me this is one of the miracles of this world that the Lord has given us such a worthy plant for us to enjoy.

***

G02: There is something about growing a marijuana plant, unless you do it you don't understand it, because it is a beautiful experience. I'm talking from a spiritual sense in that you nurture, you work, you learn, and then you—I tell you, I used to go out late at night, and lay down under my plants and watch the moon pass through those beautiful buds and just smoke one and lay there and watch the moon pass through them, just amazed. You know there are moments in that period that I just, I loved, I just loved it.

It is ironic, perhaps, that in several ancient civilizations marijuana was treated as a mystical plant provided by the gods (Chopra 1969; Abel 1980). Similarly, the contemporary hemp movement seems to grant such mystical qualities to the plant, seeing it as a solution to a variety of problems, from global warming to faltering rural economies. Perhaps the most explicit statement of this position is Jack Herer's book *The Emperor Wears No Clothes* (1990) which is subtitled: "The Authoritative Historical Record of the Cannabis Plant, Hemp Prohibition, and How Marijuana Can Still Save the World."

Social Rewards

More common was the emphasis on social rewards from growing. Many enjoyed impressing their friends with the quality of their crop and there was often friendly competition among growers. What was important was not the fact of their growing, but the quality of the product they grew and the status from having others recognize a job well done. . . .

Q: And, you felt a lot of pride in the quality of plants you were growing?

G1O: Yeah. In the plants I got caught with in the house. I had budded those out in mid-summer in the house and we had been smoking it all summer. And I was letting other people smoke, friends of mine. They said, "Oh, this is the best pot we've ever smoked." You know, I had this great feeling of accomplishment. When you get done, come out back and look at my vegetable garden, and you'll see. I've got radishes and onions, and all that, ready all ready. Yeah, well, you see, that year I didn't grow any garden, cause I was obsessed with growing pot.

I go out for the awards. I want to be the best. The same thing happened to me with the pot. I got obsessed with growing it. I wanted to outdo all those guys. I wanted to have the best pot, you know.

When you grow a garden you want to have the biggest tomatoes or whatever. As a hobbyist, you know how hobbyists get involved, so sometimes they were obsessed with their hobbies too. Well, that was my hobby that year, and I thought at the same time I could have enough stashed to last me a year or two. And, I even had in my mind that I could make some money, cause things were financially tough because I went through a bankruptcy.

***

Q: You felt a lot of pride in the quality of the plants you were growing?

G09: Oh, yeah. You take a big pride, especially when people get it, you got better than anything else, than somebody else around, I don't know how to put this tactfully. I mean, you're not a woman, you can't satisfy someone in that way, but no matter if they're a whore on the streets, some people are going to be, cause they need that relief, that satisfaction. You give them a form of relief and they're kind of grateful to you for it, even if they are paying a ridiculous price for it.

Q: So, aside from the money, you were helping people out?

G09: Oh, yeah, in a way.

Q: Did you use hydroponics or anything?

G09: Oh, yeah, I used hydroponics. When I first got into it, I did a lot of experiments. I learned how it works. Yeah, it was great it was fun, it was a blast. And of course, I wasn't worried about getting busted. Then all of your friends get into it, you know. It's something everybody starts getting into. Something to sit around and talk about. Some people get into cars, some people get into plants. . . .

Similarly, Adler's (1985) study of upper-level cocaine dealers recognized the importance of social relations and informal networks which both reinforce and facilitate involvement in the drug business.

Intrinsic Rewards

Finally, a number of growers reported that growing provided them with intrinsic rewards. For these growers the process provided the kind of self-satisfaction that many people find in hobbies with which they become deeply enmeshed.

Q: Aside from the money, was there anything about growing that you found enjoyable or satisfying?

G22: I was growing a high quality product. It was kind of rewarding to see all your work turn into something that was going to be nice. . . .

***

Q: Aside from saving money on buying and all that, is there anything else about growing marijuana that you found satisfying or enjoyable?

G08: Oh, yeah, I liked to grow it, it's just like growing a nice patch of sweet corn and getting kind of proud of it. Maybe you have a friend come over who enjoys smoking a little marijuana, and you say "Hey I grew this," and he says "Oh wow, that's nice shit." You know that's just like taking a nice bunch of tomatoes to your grandma's. So, I guess I more or less took pride in a good job, everybody does that, whether it be building a bird house, or growing something. Well I like just being a nature person, you know I enjoy it, whether it be pot or some other plant. I just seemed to always be growing things and I'm kind of a green thumb, you know, a horticulturist I guess. My grandmother had flowers of every variety. I used to help her, so maybe that's where I got the interest. I've got all kinds of house plants, it's just another plant to me. . . .

***

G16: Well, I enjoy doing it. Yeah. It's just like I grow a big garden. We have a garden out here with sweet corn, all kinds of stuff. I like growing things, always have. We farmed all our lives. . . .

Intrinsic rewards are not simply the product of putting a seed into the ground and watching it grow, but also of the fact that growers can take a simple "hobby" and make it as complex as they wish. The nature of the marijuana plant makes it particularly suited for this (Weisheit 1990a). . . .

The complexity of these operations often went well beyond what was needed to simply make money. Several growers used technical how-to books for marijuana growing, but quickly found them inadequate and moved on to general books and magazines about horticulture and plant botany. One grower shared his technical skills with others to help them deal with plant diseases, insects, and general problems with growing marijuana. He did not charge for his services, although it was common for growers to show their appreciation by sharing samples of their marijuana.

Pragmatists Versus Communal Growers

Positive experiences with growing were common, but the level of enthusiasm shown in these illustrations does not mean that every grower felt this way. Pragmatists, in particular, were more likely to be motivated by little more than money. They were also likely to define cultivation as work, an unpleasant task which had to be done, rather than an interesting challenge. Compared with the views expressed by communal growers, the following quotes illustrate how very differently pragmatists approach the process:

Q: Aside from the money, was there anything else about growing marijuana that you enjoyed or found satisfying?

G29: Ha-ha. No, not really.

Q: Did you feel any pride in the plants or their quality?

G29: No. I mean, quality I guess, but you know I don't smoke. It didn't do me any good. The only thing I was in it for was the money.

***

Q: Other than the money, was there anything you liked about growing marijuana?

G01: No, it was hard work. Well, I guess you could compare it to a weedy garden. It was a real pain in the neck, and I'd go through a 72 tablet container of Rolaids every three days. It just killed me. I *hated* it, the guilt, you know, of this stuff maybe getting in the hands of kids, or just being illegal. I love this country passionately, and just doin' something under Uncle Sam's nose, I hated it. It even had a physical impact on me.

***

Q: Aside from the money was there anything else you found enjoyable or interesting about growing?

G30: Just dollars. Just the money.

Q:Did you feel any pride in the plants you were growing?

G30: Only if it brought money. Only if I could sell it.

This group, for whom marijuana was nothing more than a source of income, was very much in the minority. Understanding what motivates most growers requires an appreciation of the rewards from growing which go beyond cash profits. Another way to illustrate how communal growers approach marijuana growing is to contrast them with people who harvest wild marijuana, or ditchweed.

Harvesting Wild Marijuana

Without understanding the pride and satisfaction that some growers feel from producing a potent product, it is difficult to understand the attitudes of these growers toward the harvesting of wild marijuana. In general, those growers who took pride in their product had nothing to do with harvesting or using wild marijuana, defining that as the province of kids, rank amateurs, or unprincipled opportunists.

There are only two reasons for harvesting wild marijuana, either (1) for direct use or sale, or (2) for mixing with more potent marijuana to increase the profits of the seller. Professional growers in this study seldom did either. For them, it would have been analogous to the maker of an exclusive fine wine selling a cheap imitation, or using a cheap wine to dilute high quality stock.

G20: If anybody mentions ditchweed, their noses turn right up, like ugh. As if that's like going out and eating dirt. You don't do that.

Q: So it's something you'd sell to someone who doesn't know any better?

G20: Yeah. . . .

***

Q: Did you ever harvest any of the ditchweed, the wild marijuana?

G21: Yeah, a long time ago.

Q: For selling or for using?

G21: Not for selling. Everybody knew what that was. You know, ditchweed, whatever. When things were real dry, when there wasn't any pot for one reason or another, everybody got the idea to get some ragweed just to have something to smoke. Nine times out of ten it was just a waste of time.

Q: Is that something that is very common, harvesting it?

G21: Ragweed? No. I'd say that's just something for young people, like teenagers, high school kids.
Q: It's not something a professional grower would do?

G21: No, no, not at all. . . .

Money can be made from harvesting wild marijuana, but the $50 to $100 a pound it yields is small when compared with the $700 to $2000 a pound from cultivated sinsemilia. Several factors make harvesting wild marijuana a bad deal for professional growers.

First, the legal penalties are the same for wild and cultivated plants, but wild marijuana is far more bulky, increasing the risk of detection. And because it is less lucrative, the seller must deal with a larger pool of buyers to make a comparable income, and this also increases his risk of arrest.

Second, the seller of wild marijuana is forced to deal with less discriminating users, often teenagers. As a group they are a less dependable outlet, requiring a larger pool of customers—customers who are generally unable to appreciate the "craftsmanship" of the professional grower. These customers are also less likely to have any personal ties to the harvester and will quickly "roll over" on the seller if picked up by the police. Thus, they present a greater risk of official detection than a smaller group of friends who are seasoned and selective consumers.

Third, harvesting ditchweed often means selling to young people who know little or nothing about marijuana. This is something which many professional growers find abhorrent (Weisheit, forthcoming). Although the professional's crop may be consumed by teenagers, this is not their intended market and many take elaborate steps to at least rationalize to themselves that kids are not obtaining their product. Such pretexts are almost impossible for the harvesters of ditchweed.

Finally, harvesting wild marijuana offers none of the opportunities for pride in growing skill or for experimenting with growing. The concern with producing a "quality product" makes little sense for marijuana which is so low in potency that the user is more likely to receive a headache than a high. The harvester of ditchweed has no personal stake in his final product.

As an alternative to dealing with teenagers, the harvester may sell bulk quantities to smugglers who use it to "cut" imported commercial grade marijuana. This separates the harvester from the final consumer and means providing a product *because* it is cheap (and of poor quality). Both factors serve to undercut any sense of pride or accomplishment in their work. . . .

Conclusion

This study has shown how a crime which on the surface appears to be a purely economic enterprise, can also provide a strong level of personal enrichment. The business of drugs has been examined from a number of perspectives. Early studies viewed dealers as pathetic addicts who were little more than passive reactors to their environment. More recent research has shifted the focus to dealers as hard-working entrepreneurs who share much of the drive and motivation of the legitimate businessman. This study has drawn attention to yet another aspect of the issue, the drug business as a means of personal enrichment and satisfaction. Rather than some manifestation of pathology, these nonmonetary rewards are directly comparable to those

which derive from legitimate hobbies. Like the enthusiastic sports fan or the dedicated gardener, these marijuana growers are addicted (if that is the right term) to the experience of growing marijuana. The "high" comes from a process rather than a chemical substance, in a manner consistent with Peele's (1985) conception of addiction. . . .

References

Abel, Ernest L. 1980. *Marihuana: The First Twelve Thousand Years*. New York: Plenum Press.

Adler, Patricia A. 1985. *Wheeling and Dealing. An Ethnography of an Upper-Level Drug Dealing and Smuggling Community*. New York: Columbia University Press.

Chein, Isidor, Donald Gerard, Robert Lee, and Eva Rosenfeld. 1964. *The Road to H*. New York: Basic Books.

Chopra, Gurbakhsh S. 1969 "Man and Marijuana." *The International Journal of the Addictions* 4:215–47.

Fields, Allen B. 1986. "Weedslingers: Young Black Marijuana Dealers." Pp. 85–104 in *Teen Drug Use*, edited by G. Beschner and A.S. Friedman. Lexington, MA: D.C. Heath.

Herer, Jack. 1990. *The Emperor Wears No Clothes*. Van Nuys, CA: HEMP Publishing.

Johnson, Bruce D., Paul J. Goldstein, Edward Preble, James Schmeidler, Douglas Lipton, Barry Spunt, and Thomas Miller. 1985. *Taking Care of Business: The Economics of Crime by Heroin Abusers*. Lexington, MA: D. C. Heath.

Lawren, Bill. 1985. "Killer Weed." *Omni*, 7:16, 106.

Manning, Peter K. and Lawrence J. Redlinger. 1983. "Drugs as Work." Pp. 275–300 in *Research in the Sociology of Work*, edited by I. Harper Simpson and R.L. Simpson. Greenwich, CT: JAI press.

Mieczkowski, Tom. 1986. "Geeking Up and Throwing Down: Heroin Street Life in Detroit." *Criminology* 24:645–66.

Potter, Gary, Larry Gaines, and Beth Holbrook. 1990. "Blowing Smoke: An Evaluation of Marijuana Eradication in Kentucky." *American Journal of Police* 9:97–116.

Preble, Edward and John Casey, Jr. 1969. "Taking Care of Business—The Heroin User's Life on the Street." *International Journal of the Addictions* 4:1–24.

Raphael, Ray. 1985. *Cash Crop: An American Dream*. Mendocino, CA: Ridge Times Press.

Warner, Roger. 1986. *Invisible Hand: The Marijuana Business*. New York: Beech Tree Books.

Weisheit, Ralph. 1990a. *Cash Crop: A Study of Illicit Marijuana Growers*. (Draft of report for grant

#88-IJ-CX-0016). Washington, DC: National Institute of Justice.

——. 1990b. "Domestic Marijuana Growers: Mainstreaming Deviance." *Deviant Behavior* 11:107–29.

——. 1990c. "Marijuana as a Cash Crop: Drugs and Crime on the Farm." Pp. 17–35 in *Criminal Investigation: Essays and Cases,* edited by James N. Gilbert. Columbus, OH: Merrill.

——. Forthcoming. "Drug Use Among Domestic Marijuana Growers." *Contemporary Drug Problems.*

Williams, Terry. 1989. *The Cocaine Kids.* New York: Addison-Wesley.

2

The Experiences of Women Who Sell Crack: Some Descriptive Data From the Detroit Crack Ethnography Project

Tom Mieczkowski

Mieczkowski examines the role of women in the crack cocaine industry. By looking at women's experiences, we can see how a drug business operates and how other social-structural issues (such as gender) influence deviant worlds. This research reveals for us that although many people may be involved in the same deviant activities, their individual status and other nondeviant activities can be important influences on how they engage in deviance and on how they experience the deviant world.

Introduction: Women, Drugs, and Drug Dealing

In the large literature on drugs, drug addiction and drug-focused criminality, data on women is relatively small. Drug selling in particular evokes images of largely "a male problem" (Datesman 1981: Henderson 1991). This situation is both a particular as-

pect of the construction and presentation of the drug subculture. It is also an analog to the larger and longer-term issue of the neglect of women in the general study of criminology and deviance (Warren 1981: Pohl and Boyd 1992). The Detroit Crack Ethnography Project (DCEP), sensitive to these critiques, gathered data on women crack cocaine sellers.

In general, the DCEP found that women in the study sample were actively involved in distributing crack cocaine and other drugs. They carried out these activities in a variety of organizational formats and also worked at many different levels within drug distribution organizations. As sellers of illegal drugs they experienced problems common to all persons involved in drug dealing. But, as women, they also faced unique aspects of those problems that were linked to their gender. Consequently, female dealers often coped in unique ways with their problems.

The objective of this article is to present findings on the female dealers by providing relevant sociodemographic data on these women, and examining and reflecting on descriptions of their experiences as crack dealers. The objective is to add to the slender amount of information available about female crack sellers, and to address several issues raised in the traditional literature regarding the roles women play in drug distribution systems. These issues are developed in the review of the literature.

The Literature on Women, Drugs, and Drug Dealing

In general, writers on women's involvement in the drug subculture have emphasized three types of criminality. One is women as users who must secure substantial funds for drugs. Traditionally, this has emphasized female involvement in prostitution as a means to secure either cash for drug funds or drugs-in-kind for sexual services (Inciardi et al. 1991; Mieczkowski, 1990; Rosenbaum 1981). A second theme is women users who commit property crimes to secure money for drugs, primarily larceny, forgery, shoplifting, burglary, and robbery (Inciardi and Pottieger 1986; Hser et al. 1991). The third theme, which has been least emphasized, is women's involvement in entrepreneurial drug sales. These selling activities are sometimes described as solo entrepreneurial efforts, but more often they are in roles cast largely as assistants to male drug sellers. In this third thematic view, women have been described as adjuncts who work for males or male-controlled organizations (James et al. 1979; Lyman and Potter 1991; Mieczkowski 1986; Adler 1985). In this context, it has been argued that male perceptions of women's "appropriate" involvement in entrepreneurial criminality affects the objective opportunity structure for women in organized criminal subcultures (Steffensmeier 1983).

However, while male attitudes, it is argued, tend to exclude or marginalize women in organized criminal enterprises, some studies (Inciardi et al. 1982: Pettiway 1987) have suggested that women's criminality in the drug subculture is more multifaceted and diverse than has historically been recognized, and women may effectively transcend these limitations, at least under some conditions. Some women may be independently active in many categories of crime, switching back and forth between various earning opportunities as entrepreneurs in search of capital (Sanchez and Johnson 1987). While women may not replicate the roles of males, they create substantive independent roles that cannot be considered passive, dependent, or accessory to male operatives. Indeed, Datesman (1981) argued a decade ago that, in spite of the prevailing belief that women's drug activities are heavily linked to male partners, women are on their own involved in a variety of independent criminal enterprises, including drug sales. Furthermore, women are more likely than the current literature indicates to be active in securing their own independent sources of drugs and in making independent sales of drugs. Recent research by Hser and associates (1991) supports the belief that drug dealing is a major source of income for women who are defined as addicted (daily drug use for more than thirty days); and Datesman's (1981) Miami data supported that same conclusion. Also, Hser and associates research suggests that for women who were not dependent on others, drug dealing was a major source of support for their own drug use. Pettiway (1987), looking at this issue, reported that women can attain independent roles in the drug subculture and that black female opiate users (as opposed to other race/ethnic groupings) have a higher probability of forming a mixed-sex crime partnership "which is not dependent on sexual or romantic intimacy." Also, it is interesting to note that Deschenes and Anglin (1992)—in comparing a sample of Anglo and Chicana females—report that women involved in dealing drugs are "less active" than men, but that the difference is especially large when "for profit" drug dealing is reported as distinct from "general" drug dealing. The implication is that if women deal, they are more likely to be dealing to support their use. Men also frequently deal to support their use as well, but they are nearly twice as likely in the DCEP sample (and it is true regardless of ethnicity) that they are also dealing "for profit." This lends support to a characterization of women as "hustlers who commit a wide variety of crimes" although these criminal acts can be characterized as "feminine crimes" that occupy the "low status end of the criminal hierarchy" (Pettiway 1987).

Research Questions

The literature supports the contention that the nature and complexity of female drug dealing is not fully understood or documented. Focusing specifically on crack cocaine, the statement takes on an even stronger emphasis. Several important questions stand out.

- What do we know about the women crack sellers in terms of their basic sociodemographic character? Are they youngsters, teens, or "older" adults? Are they well or poorly educated? Are they heavily drug involved? Do they make money or not? Are they linked to male partners in non-business and business relationships? What are the ranges of these variables among this group?

- If it is true that women "deal" crack more frequently than is popularly perceived, how are their experiences similar or different from men crack dealers?

- Can a generic model of dealing be equally or even approximately applied to both male and female participants? What similarities and differences exist in models which are based on female as opposed to male samples?

The body of accumulated qualitative research on female crack selling is slender. Some arguments have been made for a distinct set of female theories, based on studying relationship patterns with opposite-sex partners (Anderson and Braunstein 1992). . . .

The need to examine in more detail the actual life experiences of female dealers is necessary for developing better conceptualizations of drug selling as a social activity. This article provides data whose aim is to increase qualitative and quantitative data on women's involvement in crack dealing. . . .

Method

The DCEP Group: Users and Dealers in Treatment

The group examined in this article is derived from the Detroit Crack Ethnography Project (DCEP), funded by the Bureau of Justice Assistance (Contract # OJP-88-M 39J). This project was conducted during 1988 and 1989. The data base on this group consists of two separate components: responses to a structured questionnaire, and taped, open-ended interviews. . . . We will examine the twenty-three subjects who are females, of whom sixteen were dealers of crack cocaine. All the female crack dealers were black. The volunteer informants, who were clients at a treatment facility, were interviewed anonymously. . . . Once a member of the center had volunteered to participate, they were scheduled for an interview. . . . They were also informed that they would receive a $25 stipend upon completion of the interview. Interviews varied in duration, but generally lasted from one to three hours.

Findings: Aggregate Descriptive Information

This first section provides basic information on the age, education, marital status, work, and criminal history of the sample. All twenty-three females had been crack users who considered themselves "addicted" to crack and were at the time of the interview residents of a therapeutic community. All had been heavy crack users in the recent past.

Age and Education

The mean age of the females was 30.04 years of age (s. d. = 6 years) and the median age was 29 years. The youngest person was 21 years of age and the oldest was 50. The subjects were relatively well educated. Ten of the twenty-three had completed some college, and one was a college graduate. Eleven had some post high school education, and one had a bachelor's degree in social work. The lowest attained educational level was the ninth grade. Seven subjects quit school by the eleventh grade. The mean years of formal education is slightly greater than twelve and a half years and the median is thirteen years.

Relationships

. . . It is generally true for this sample that female involvement in drugs use is typically bound up with opposite-sex relationships. . . . The female component of the DCEP study group was comprised of women who were typically single. As *singles* we mean that they were not involved in stable, ongoing, opposite-sex relationships at the current time. Almost three-quarters of the group were not and had never been legally married. Only two were married at the time of the study and three were legally divorced. Two subjects had vaguely articulated relationships which did not fit the three dominant forms.

One consequence of this, perhaps, is a relatively high level of legitimate employment, considering this is a heavy cocaine-using sample. Although the majority of the women were not working at their time of admission to the therapeutic community, it was only a slim majority. Approximately 43% were working either full or part-time when admitted. Relatively well-paid and even professional work was represented among the fulltime workers.

Criminal Charges

A majority (fifteen of twenty-three) of the subjects admitted to engaging in criminal acts above and beyond the use of drugs themselves. About half (eleven out of twenty-three) of the interviewees reported being arrested and charged with a crime, and nine reported being convicted of a criminal offense. The most common crimes were property offenses. Generally, the charges were serious. Of the eleven charges lodged against these women, eight were felonies and three were misdemeanors. However, only two of the women reported actually serving time in prison for a criminal conviction. The subjects also reported a substantial amount of illegal behaviors in their interviews for which they were never apprehended.

Drug Involvement

First Use of Crack

All twenty-three females in this study used crack and all twenty-three considered themselves dependent on crack. The age of first exposure to crack varied considerably, from nineteen to forty-six years of age at the time of first use. Eight respondents had used crack within the last month. . . . The average age of first use was approximately twenty-six years (26.65, s.d. = 6. 11 years). The median age was 26 years.

The average age of initiation to crack and the average of crack dependency differ by approximately one half a year (with a similar standard deviation). While the mean age of first use is 26.6 years, the age of first dependency is 27.2 years (s.d = 6.33 years). This demonstrates that, on average, for these persons it took roughly six months from their initiation to develop a self-admitted crack dependency. . . .

Alcohol, Marijuana, and Heroin

Almost all the interviewees had experience with alcohol. Twenty-two of the twenty-three females had used alcohol at some time in their lives. The earliest use of alcohol re-

ported was ten years of age and the latest was twenty-one years. The average age for first alcohol use was sixteen years of age (s.d = 2.8 years), and the median age was sixteen years as well. . . .

Marijuana

Ninety-six percent (twenty-two of twenty-three) of the subjects used marijuana. Thus the group was as equally marijuana-exposed as it was alcohol-exposed. More than half of the group (twelve out of twenty-three respondents) reported a dependency on marijuana at some time in their lives. It is interesting that while only three women self-report as alcoholics, twelve self-report as marijuana dependent. What is also interesting is the onset age of this marijuana dependency was reported relatively early in their lives when compared with alcohol. While the earliest reported age of alcohol dependency was twenty-six, the earliest marijuana dependency was thirteen years. Approximately 58% of the marijuana users reported being dependent by age 15 years or younger.

Heroin

Nine of the interviewees had used heroin. The mean age of onset for heroin use is 21.3 years, and the median age is twenty years. Only three women reported having been heroin dependent at some time in their lives. For these three, the age of onset of heroin dependence was respectively 18, 20, and 21 years of age.

Cocaine and Crack Selling

Dealing and Career Longevity

Nearly 70% of the subjects (sixteen out of the twenty-three) had sold drugs. These experiences ranged from informal, infrequent, "dabbling" to more professional, profitable, and well-organized enterprises. Of the twenty-three subjects, sixteen had sold cocaine. Of these sixteen cocaine sellers, two sold powder cocaine and the fourteen others sold "rocked up" crack. Eleven of the subjects had sold crack within the last twelve months of the interview.

On average the interviewees had about two years experience in the drug trade, but the range of values is very broad (mean = 24.27 months, s.d. = 27.76 months). . . . The range was a considerable 89 months. Nine of the interviewees had been involved in selling for at least one year or more, and seven had been involved two years or more.

The primary drug of use and of sale for this group was crack. But they did not necessarily confine their selling activities to crack alone. Marijuana was the second most popular drug of sale, followed by cocaine (which in this case means powdered cocaine as distinct from crack). . . .

This group was almost exclusively user/dealers. . . . Some became involved with crack because they "ran with" male dealers who initiated their use, while some had vaguely defined "goals" of being a profit-oriented seller, but had never realized those goals. Many became involved in dealing to supplement a source of funds that, early in their use history, was derived from other, often legal, sources. We shall characterize these changes as role transitions. The complexity of these roles transitions is demonstrated in the case selections in the following section.

Life with Crack: Women's Experiences and Voices

Opportunity and Entrepreneurial Drug Models

. . . For most of the women in the DCEP study, becoming a drug dealer was an opportunistic extension of their life experiences. Thus, their experiences reflect Datesman's contention that female drug dealing is not as exceptional as one might believe. Drug dealing, for these subjects, was a mode of surviving that represented a variation on a class of "hustling" activities they had pursued. Driven by choice, necessity, or a combination of both, to be independent, to make one's own way in life, led to the decision that, like many other hustles, drug dealing was simply a good way to "get over." In this regard the women reflected a choice pattern that was indistinguishable from the males in the study.

Quite often the women in this study operated within a range of sex-linked roles that included elements of dependence upon, interdependence with, and sometimes dominance over males. Furthermore because of their gender, these women faced some unique problems and had to develop specific coping strategies. The degree of systematic and organizational independence from males varied from almost none (a woman who simply stood by or handed out drugs for a boyfriend or employer) to complete autonomy and the operation of multiple drug selling sites. . . .

Describing Role Types

We begin by describing the relative degrees of independence from or dependence on males partners or associates, as well as the particular type of dealing activity that the subjects report. The objective of this section is to document the variety which the data reveal, and to show the complexity of these typologies, and the degree to which they are "mixed" in the experience of the subjects of the study. . . .

Relative Independence

We start with subject #10, a thirty-three-year-old black female. She represents a relatively independent seller who marketed, at different times, both heroin and crack.

Subject #10 manifests a relatively high degree on entrepreneurial action and an absence of dependence on an opposite-sexed relationship in her business activities. This is demonstrated in three different ways. First, she organized and operated her own business on her initiative once she received an opportunity to sell. Second, she employed males—teenage "runners" to carry out retail street transactions. Third, she entered into an arrangement with another woman to secure a selling locale—using her residence in exchange for supplying the occupant with drugs. She was dependent on male suppliers. She did not conceptualize her selling activity as exceptional. She viewed it purely as a sensible, efficient, and even necessary means for funding her heroin habit, and later her crack habit.

Interview: Subject #10

(Tell me how you started selling drugs)

How I got into selling heroin? Well, I used to hang around a lot of people that uh sold drugs. It was easier to sell it and that way you would always have some although it never really worked out like that. I was thirty-one when started selling it (crack). Sold it in the rock form for $20 hits and $10 hits basically. I did that on my own. At someone's house they said I could sell it outta there and all I'd do was give em like $20 or a $20 rock. I bought my own drugs, but they gave me a place to stay. . . . This lady let me sell drugs outta her house. She had teenage kids that did the running, you know. They would go down and get the money. I never really came in contact with the people.

Subject #19, like subject #10, viewed her drug selling as "a job," an instrumental means to obtain income either in the absence of other sources of income, or at higher rates than any legitimate employment could provide her. Subject #19 was a small-time crack seller, twenty-four years old, never arrested or charged with a crime. She was a small-scale user/dealer, primarily interested in funding her own crack use. She did not experience any extraordinary violence or problems during her selling activities. She did not realize she was dependent on crack until "the money ran out," and primarily focused on the interference the drug caused with her ability to maintain her regular employment as a secretary. She relied upon males as her source for cocaine, but she paid for her drugs in advance ("up front") and was primarily interested in selling enough to support her own crack use. She did rely mainly on male friends to "rock up" for her. She also sold primarily to men, but reported no serious problems in dealing with male customers. . . .

Moving Away from Independence: Female Rollers

"Rollers," as the term is typically used, are people who sell drugs as salespersons for others. Such persons are not independent entrepreneurs, but rather act as selling agents for a larger organization. The roller does not typically pay in advance ("up front") for their drug consignment. They sell it and then pay back the consignee with the cash pro-

ceeds. . . . "Rollers" mostly work in groups, involving at least one "boss," and sometimes full-time security personnel. Several female subjects in this sample worked as rollers. These rollers worked as crew in crack houses, retailing crack from occupied dwellings or abandoned buildings. Subject #94 is a good illustration of female rolling.

Interviewee #94 was twenty-one years old and a black female who rolled for a male crew boss. She was a user/dealer, one who just worked to "get high." She first began by selling powder cocaine provided on consignment to her by a male friend (with whom she got high). She typically received cocaine powder for which she would have to pay $100, and was able to sell it for about $300 at retail. She "never had any problems doing this" because she sold to people she knew — "most of the people who came over I grew up with."

However, she began smoking crack cocaine and became in her words "quickly dependent, the first time I did it" She became a heavy user and experienced a number of difficulties because, although she was supposed to be selling crack for her male friend, she typically would smoke up large portions of the consignment, resulting in her being "fired." She also lost conventional jobs as a cashier for pilfering cash, or else would pilfer cash and quit before she was discovered and move on to another job. She eventually entered a nonresidential treatment program, but upon release began using again. She reentered a one-month residential treatment program, but relapsed quickly and began to fund her drug use via prostitution. . . .

Interview: Subject #94

I sold crack for a guy and sold it in a dope house. There would be a person at the front door, a person at the window with a gun and you come to the side door or window. And I would be there and sell the crack. The customer stayed outside. You pass through the window. The money comes in first and then the crack goes out. I was paid $10 off of every $50. I would make about $80 – $100 a day. I took it in cash and spent it on rock, so eventually we took it in rock. We really didn't make no money. I was just working to get high.

Some crack houses I worked in paid $75 a day and some gave you a $1 off of every $10.

The statement here of "not really making any money" should be understood as describing a result not an intent. At least superficially, all "rolling operations" are supposed to be profitable. Generally, crew bosses do not care if the crew wants its pay in drugs. However, they are not generally permitted to use those drugs while "on duty." Note, for example, how violence ensues as a result of smoking in the "house."

Interview: Subject #94

Once in the crack house I got beat up. This one guy that I was staying with, I had his dope and he gave me so much for myself and the workers in the crack house. This one girl was really begging me for one. I told her that I would give her some, but it would have to come out of her pay. He was sleeping and I had the dope, so I gave her one. While she was smoking, he woke up and he automatically jump on me because they weren't suppose to be smoking. He stomped me in my back and threw me down a flight of stairs, sprang my arm and I was in the hospital for about two days.

Further Complex Role Transitions

In addition to rolling out of a crack house, some female subjects transited through several types of different selling circumstances. In the following case, subject #33 acted early in her selling involvement in very much a dependent role. . . .

Subject #33, an attractive and articulate young women, was thirty years old. After completing her high school education, she worked as a seamstress and tailor for a custom clothier. She had some post-high school education and was trained in both fashion design and upholstery design.

Interview: Subject #33

(Interviewee #33 stated that she started dating a man who was a "big time dealer" and he had given her the first powder cocaine she ever had for a birthday present.) I'm very much attracted to material things. He had a lot of money, nice car, nice house and we weren't living together at the time. He had a lot of money and that

sucked me right in. Right after that I was selling it pretty good to my co-workers.

Notice here, that when she refers to being "sucked in" she means that her boyfriend had succeeded in recruiting her to work for him by vending cocaine to her co-workers. She became increasingly involved in helping market cocaine for her boyfriend, spending long periods of time with him at his house (from where he sold), assisting him with various aspects of the business. Eventually she became a trusted stand-in for him, doing some of his business.

Interview: Subject #33

A lot of his associates would come to his home and if he wasn't around, then I would take care of the business. Still no one is coming to *my* house.

(What quantities were you selling it in?)

We would break it down into grams, $125 to $150. This went on on a consistent basis. I wouldn't work that many hours there because he knew that I had to be at work at 9:00 a.m., so after I got off in the evenings, I would go and stay sometimes to 12:00 midnight and he would make sure that I got home.

It is interesting that she comments so directly on his provision of protection and security, for example, "making sure" she got home. . . . [I]t is interesting that although she apparently was trusted to manage some aspects of his business, she did not consider herself a "lieutenant" in the sales organization. . . .

This person's account is quite a contrast to the first two examples. This woman is involved in this situation not simply as some instrumental mechanism to acquire drugs. She initially is in an emotional relationship that takes on increasing functional aspects. She also evidences various components of dependency. She readily admits her attraction to the male's financial resources, her requests for and acceptance of his money, and her dependence on him for physical security.

Eventually, after struggling with increasingly problematic crack addiction, she broke up with this boyfriend and went to Narcotics Anonymous at the encouragement of her mother. She was "clean" for about one year and resumed working in tailoring and clothes making. Then her sister was murdered in a drug-related incident and her life began again to experience major difficulties. This resulted in a return to crack and alcohol involvement, but now in a very different fashion from her first experiences. Also, her life became increasingly involved in violence.

Interview: Subject 33 (continued)

I quit my job and left home. I got my own place after we buried my sister. I met this guy and asked him to move in with me and he was a crack user too. We didn't get along very well. He jumped on me and I left the house with him. I moved out some of my things, the main thing was that I left there and started roaming the streets, living here and there, sleeping in crack houses, sleeping on the streets. The last couple of weeks I was sleeping in a truck on 8 Mile Road. I didn't care where I slept.

(Did you try and sell any drugs?)

Yea, it was crazy. Depending on how many "dates" ("tricks" or prostitution-customers) I would turn. Sometimes I would make $200–$300 a night, depending on how I wanted to work. I would get a motel room and stay where I knew they didn't have any crack. I would go and sit and try to sell some. Like if they were out, I would go there and try and sell mine.

(The people operating the crack house didn't mind?)

No, because they knew me and they would say when we get back on, you got to go. That was okay as long as I could keep a supply for me. Even though I was still smokin', I managed to keep some to sell and money to buy me some more crack later on that night.

Subject #33 was operating in an independent, entrepreneurial mode here, and was not acting subordinate to a male, that is, a pimp, procurer, or boyfriend. However, "independence" in this regarding has a rather circumscribed meaning, since it could not be characterized as a happy or fulfilling situation for her. The transformation from her early experiences were profound.

Interview: Subject 33

(You were turning over $200–$300 a night selling crack?)

No, not that much maybe $100. In selling my body, I would make $200 to $300.

(So, total income is $300–$400?)

Yes.

(How did you find the time to turn the tricks?)

$50 a trick, but then it got down to $20 – $15 a trick.

(Were you working the street?)

Yea, and I had regulars, pay $50 and pay for the room so I didn't have to worry about a place to sleep for that night.

(Where did you sleep literally?)

Sometimes I wouldn't go to sleep for four or five days and just stayed high on crack all day long and all night until my body couldn't take it anymore. I'd go to an associate's or girlfriend and lay down for a couple hours, wash up. My clothes were scattered by the way. I would change clothes and go right back out.

(Did anybody ever pay you in drugs for tricks?)

No. I had to have the money, I made that clear.

(You didn't have a pimp?)

No.

(Because you didn't, did you ever have any problems?)

Yea.

(How did you deal with customers who wouldn't pay?)

I threatened them, lied, and told them that my boyfriend was watching when I really didn't have anybody. I tell them that he was behind us in a car and had their license plates. I wouldn't date black guys because they were really street smart.

Subject #33 invokes a fictive boyfriend as a means of protection. This action demonstrates a unique strategy opportunity for females. Males create security by grouping, by arming themselves, and by trying to cultivate a "scandalous" reputation, a reputation defined primarily by irrationality in the use of violence and volatility of temper. These are designed to control problem behaviors by overwhelming physical force. Females rarely use these devices, instead employing guile, sometimes arranging male protection, and only rarely carrying weapons. It is also interesting that she preferred white customers simply because she found them to be more gullible regarding the various defenses she could use to help enhance security, given her situation.

Danger and Violence

. . . Female dealers in this study rarely used physical force unilaterally, or rarely threatened it, though it is not unreported completely. For example, subject #33 reported carrying a weapon along with her boyfriend. But her statement about her feelings toward the weapon are purely symbolic and non-functional from a damage-infliction point of view — "I felt real powerful because I wasn't using it."

Females in this project (in contrast to many male subjects) generally do not report pulling out guns, shooting people, or ostentatiously carrying weapons. Yet they do not infrequently report having to cope with violence or the threat of violence, or are the objects of violence on the part of others. Recall that subject #94 reported her supplier "jumped on her" and then "stomped" her and threw her down some stairs for permitting smoking of the inventory. And recall that subject #33 reported the need to refer to an imaginary "boyfriend" or "pimp" to deal with prostitution customers who could only be controlled by insinuation of violence.

A few women report repeated violent confrontations, which they occasionally resisted with force themselves. Interview subject #26 was a twenty-nine-year-old black female who began using crack with a boyfriend and whose crack use "eventually got totally out of control." The result was that she turned to street prostitution in order to raise money for crack. She, like subject #33, worked without a pimp or protector. She experienced violent encounters with customers. The circum-

stances for these violent encounters included a variety of factors. One was simply a desire by the customer to receive the sex for free and the belief that he could so exploit her and "get away with it." Another was the customer's attempts to coerce the prostitute into performing sex acts that she did not wish to perform. Consider the following excerpt:

Interview: Subject #96

I had borrowed all the money I could and couldn't pay back anything, so I started hustling. I stood on Woodward Avenue prostituting. On the weekends I could make $50 or $60 and on a slow day $30. Sometimes I would run into trouble where a trick may want to take his money back or (want me to) do it for free. They say "yes" (to the prostitute's proposition), take you to a place, and pull out knives and use different things or use physical force to make you do things. So some nights I might run into one of them.

However, she was also victimized because of the resentment of "tricks" who themselves were previously victimized by another prostitute who "burned" them for their money. It was not unusual that a prostitute wanted to get her money "up front" in order to purchase and consume her crack prior to providing sexual services to her "trick." This meant that the trick/prostitute relationship can become extended over time. Thus, the conceptualization of street sex as a brief and fleeting interlude ("wham, bam, thank you, [ma'am]") is not necessarily accurate. The relationship can become extended in time while the female goes to a crack source and makes a purchase. Since the "trick" has fronted money to the prostitute, he is going to accompany her in order to protect his money. They then would consume the crack, and if the "deal" went well, they would then have sex while smoking crack or right after the crack was consumed. This extended involvement of prostitute and customer meant opportunities for other scenarios to play out, and in many ways increased risk for the prostitute. Subject #96 speaks to this possibility in the next excerpt. She begins by gesturing to a prominent scar on her forehead.

Interview: Subject #96

(How did I get) this scar on my forehead? This guy had picked up a lady before picking me up and she ran off with his $20. And he didn't get what he paid for. So when he picked me up, he was already mad, but I didn't know this. So, I wanted a rock bad, I am desperate by now and trying to talk him into it. I finally do get him to go along with me and when he is about there he pulls out a knife cause I was asking for the money up front. He said "no." (I said) that is okay. I said I will meet you half way and do this and that, and if you don't like it you don't have to give me the money or you can just take your money back. Just when I am getting ready to say forget it, I don't want to do it, he pulls out a knife. I kept trying to explain to him that I am not the one that ran off with your money and that I am not trying to hurt you. Why are you trying to hurt me? I said to myself that if I don't go on and fight this motherfucker back, he is going to hurt you anyway, so go and fight. I fought my way up out of the car.

In a later encounter subject #96 told of having to jump out of a moving car to escape a "trick" in similar circumstances. She was once again attempting to secure money prior to providing sex in order to smoke crack before "servicing" her customer. She injured herself quite severely and walked with a limp as a result of the injury she sustained.

Interviewee #28 illustrates another type of violent confrontation with yet another alternative coping strategy. This subject was a twenty-seven-year-old black female who was introduced by a relative to selling crack. She also used the common technique of working out of another's dwelling in exchange for providing the tenant with drugs. She was savvy and experienced, a relatively independent dealer who showed considerable initiative in establishing her business. She had been a live-in girl friend for a prominent heroin dealer. He was eventually imprisoned. Using contacts established through her relationship with him, she was able to establish a cocaine distribution business. . . .

Another reported strategy for female dealers is to surround oneself with hired male security. This is most feasible in relatively highly organized selling circumstances (e.g., a crack house operation). In these conditions one can, if successful, generate enough income to employ armed "security guards." These conditions may also allow additional "fortifying" of the selling location, which can also enhance physical protection against any violence. However, this will not work if there are lapses in the security services performed, the security personnel are not trustworthy, or one leaves the secure circumstances, or allows breaches of the security system. Case #29 demonstrates these points. This subject was the most successful of the female dealers, in terms of income, operations size, and longevity. She operated and maintained a profitable multi-site marijuana selling and crack selling organization.

Interview: Subject #29

(So you had a successful business. What did you do with the money?

Partying. Spending it on myself and my son and made sure he had everything and.... eventually I got me a house and then I was selling like big time out of my house.

(So, what was your weekly income?)

I would make something like $1,500 a day and that was on a slow day. I had so much money I couldn't keep track of it. I started hiring people to work my door. Sell the weed for me and I stayed there with my son at the time and so much money that it all went to my head. I was bringing it out of another house and had people running out of there.

(So you were working two places?)

Yeah. The fascination was, that I was a woman. It was my own and I wasn't selling it for nobody and I had the big head cause it is like everybody respected me. It's the action and the game, you know.

The next segment documents a violent robbery she experienced within her home at the hands of a male predator. A robber gained access to her house because she broke her own security rules by staying "open" past operational hours, and permitting a customer entrance when there was no security on the premises. Also, quite interestingly, the robber, reacting to her position and her gender, chastised her for being in a "man's" business. He made no attempt to sexually assault her.

Interview: Subject #29

(I'm sure that it must have occurred to you that other men out there dealing must of said hey this is a woman, we can go take this woman out. Weren't you worried about that?)

Yeah, at first it didn't dawn on me like that until I got stuck up in the house.

(Tell me about that.)

It must have been at about 12:00 midnight, and I went to the door . . . I usually close at 11:00 p.m. And I let these people in and I usually never let nobody in, but this particular time I let somebody in.

(A man?)

Yeah, and he said let me get a dime and I said I ain't got no dime. He said let me see what your ounces look like. I grabbed an ounce out the bag and when I was grabbing the ounce, he pulled a gun out and he said get on the floor. So I got on the floor and he held the gun to my head and said I don't want no sex, I want all your money. Where is your money, where is the weed at? I said I ain't got no money, I ain't got no more weed. This is it in the bag. He said I want you to know that you are a woman and we have been watching it. We set you up, we been watching you for about two weeks. We know your program, when you come and when you go. . . . My nephew was asleep in the house. I said don't hurt my kids. Are you going to hurt my kids cause I wanted to know cause if you was I would have tried something. He said no. I ain't going to hurt you, I just want all your money and want you to know that you are a woman and you can't be playing this game. Who is you to be rolling, you ought to have a man like me to roll for you. I said how am I going to let you roll for me and you stickin' me up? He said put your head to the floor. He started searching the house and asking where the gun at, where the gun at. So he never found the gun, he kept finding money in my drawers.

(Did you have a gun in the house?)

Yes, he kept finding (money), like $10 or $20 here. But all the money was on me, in my pocket.

(How much did you have on you?)

About $3,000. I had about five pounds of weed upstairs under the chair. I stapled it back. He said if I find some more money, I am going to kill you. What kept running through my mind is whether I should go in my pocket and say here. Cause he never searched me. I had on a nightgown. I had just got through playing baseball and my jersey was real low and I had on baseball sweats, but you couldn't tell that.

(So, he didn't think about you having a pocket?)

Right, that's why he kept sayin' I don't want no sex.

(So, he wasn't worried about you having a gun?)

Yeah, he was saying where the gun, where the gun, he was looking all around for the gun. I said ain't no go. He never found the gun. The gun was up under the seat. He searched everywhere, he pulled my rugs up, my drawers in the kitchen, the refrigerator, everywhere and he never found the weed or nothing. He took my son's jar of money and said I'm going to fuck you up if I find some more money. So after he searched all these places and kept moving me from room to room while he searched. So finally one time he turned his back and I reached in my pocket and threw all the money up under this chair he had already searched just in case he searched me, but he never did and he told me to turn my face and put it in the corner and to count to ten and he ran out of the door.

As traumatic as it was for her, the robbery experience did not drive this woman from the drug trade. Ultimately, she lost her business due to her very high levels of personal crack use. This incident illustrates, however, how a male predator was conscious of and upset by the reality of a woman "rolling" in what he considered a "man's business."

Summary

The information gathered as a part of the DCEP project shows that women are involved actively in distributing crack cocaine, as well as other drugs, and appear to work at many levels within distribution systems. While they face problems common to all illicit drug dealers, they also face unique aspects of those problems tied to their gender. As a consequence, they cope in unique ways with those problems.

Considering these women as a group, they are young, relatively well educated, quite likely to be employed, and typically have been involved in using various drugs, especially alcohol and marijuana. These women are likely to report dependencies on marijuana much more frequently than alcohol. The usual route by which they become involved in drug selling is via associations with males, although these associations may range rather widely, from casual and instrumental to intense and emotional. Women can become deeply, and even dominantly, involved in drug distribution processes, and may work in roles ranging from "gofers" for males to the "chief executive" of operating distribution syndicates. Most importantly, many of these women transited through multiple roles, each role quite distinct in characterization and content. . . .

While women dealers experience distinctive aspects of the world of drug distribution, they also encounter in many ways the same general problems with which male drug dealers must grapple. These "generic" problems center around violence and its consequences, the problems of order maintenance while conducting business, and the need to exert self-control around the drug inventory.

Women crack dealers obviously encounter unique circumstances and problems related to their gender. A central and overwhelming problem is the potential for exploitation by males, either through manipulation of a "trusted" male, or the possible predation by males who view women as weak and inappropriate in a "man's business" of selling cocaine (Adler 1985). Women in this regard, have ambiguous and sometimes hostile feelings for men, reciprocating the ambivalence and hostility of males toward them. Females often invoke the protection of males (either real or fictive). But the use of that "protection" can be itself risky. These male protectors may be lovers, relatives, friends, or business associates but their "protection" can be exploitive. . . .

These data show that women face a host of problems as dealers. In spite of this, some women became considerably self-reliant, and were successful in curtailing violence. But the vulnerability that women feel in these circumstances and the concomitant stress is also quite telling. Women do feel a special sense of vulnerability in the crack world, and that vulnerability, while tied into the general risks *all* crack users face, is amplified by their gender. Subject #100, in reflecting back on her sales to male customers, noted that

> They said "Look at this young lady. She is getting over, why can't I do it? So why not take it from her and go start off like she has done?" As a result it is nothing but total madness. The scene is total madness and that is why I am here. . . .

References

Adler, P. 1985. *Wheeling and Dealing*. New York: Columbia University Press.

Anderson, M. and M. Braunstein. 1992. "Concepts of Therapy: Personalized nursing LIGHT model with chemically-dependent female offenders." In *Drugs, crime and social policy*, ed. T. Mieczkowski. Boston: Allyn and Bacon.

Boyd C. and T. Mieczkowski. 1990. "Drug use, health, family and social support in "crack" cocaine users." *Addictive Behaviors*, 15:481–5.

Datesman, S. K. 1981. "Women, Drugs, and Crime." In *The drugs-crime connection*, ed. J. Inciardi. Beverly Hills, CA: Sage.

DesChene, L. and M.D. Anglin. 1992. "Effects of Legal Supervision on Narcotic Addict Behavior: Ethnic and Gender Influences." In *Drugs, crime, and social policy*, (ed.) T. Mieczkowski. Boston: Allyn and Bacon.

Henderson, D. 1991. *Sexuality, relationships, and self-Correlates to women's crack cocaine use*. Unpublished Master's Thesis. University of Michigan.

Henderson, D., C. Boyd, and T. Mieczkowski. 1992. "Women's sexuality, relationships, and use of crack cocaine: A content analysis." *Journal of Research in Nursing and Health*.

Hser, Y., M. D. Anglin, and C. Chou. 1991. "Narcotics use and crime among addicted women: Longitudinal patterns and effects of social interventions." In *Drugs, crime and social policy*, ed. T. Mieczkowski. Boston: Allyn and Bacon.

Inciardi, J. and A. Pottieger. 1986. "Drug use and crime among two cohorts of women narcotics users: an empirical assessment." *Journal of Drug Issues* 2:56–64.

Inciardi, J., A. Pottieger, M. Fomey, D. Chitwood, and D. McBride. 1991. "Prostitution, IV drug use, and sex-for-crack exchanges among serious delinquents: Risks for HIV Infection." *Criminology* 29(2):221–36.

Inciardi, J., A. Pottieger, and C. Faupel. 1982. "Black women, heroin, and crime: Some empirical notes. *Journal of Drug Issues*, 4:241–250.

Gosho, J. and R. Wohl. 1979. "The relationship between female criminality and drug use." *International Journal of the Addictions,* 14:215–229.

Johnson, B.D., P. Goldstein, E. Preble, J. Schmeidler, D. Lipton, B. Spunt, and T. Miller. 1985. *Taking care of business: The economics of crime by heroin abusers*. Lexington, Mass.: Lexington Books.

Johnson, B. D., A. Hamid, and H. Sanabria. 1991. "Emerging models of crack distribution." In *Drugs, Crime, and Social Policy*, ed. T. Mieczkowski. Boston: Allyn and Bacon.

Lyman, M. and G. Potter. 1991. *Drugs in society*. Cincinnati, Ohio: Anderson Publishing.

Mieczkowski, T. 1986. "Geeking up and throwing down: Heroin street life in Detroit." *Criminology* 24(4):645–66.

Mieczkowski, T. 1989. "The Economic Concepts of Crack Dealers in Detroit.: An Examination of Market Dynamics." Paper presented at the American Society of Criminology Annual Meetings, Reno, Nevada.

Mieczkowski, T. 1990. "The operational styles of crack houses in Detroit". In *Drugs and violence, NIDA Research Monograph no. 103.* Washington, D.C.:National Institute on Drug Abuse.

Pettiway, L. 1987. "Participation in crime partnerships by female drug users: The effects of domestic arrangements, drug use, and criminal involvement. *Criminology* 25(3):741–66.

Pohl J. and C. Boyd. 1992. "Female addiction: A concept analysis." In *Drugs, crime, and social policy*, ed. T. Mieczkowski. Boston: Allyn and Bacon.

Reuter, P., R. Macoun, and P. Murphy. 1990. *Money from crime: A study of the economics of drug dealing in Washington, D.C.* Santa Monica: The RAND Corporation.

Rosenbaum, M. 1981. "Sex roles among deviants: The woman addict." *International Journal of the Addictions*, 16:859–877.

Sanchez, J. and B. D. Johnson. 1987. "Women and the drugs-crime connection: Crime rates among drug-abusing women at Riker's Island." *Journal of Psychoactive Drugs*, 19(2):205–216.

Steffensmeier, D. 1983. "Organization properties and sex-segregation in the underworld: Building a sociological theory of sex, differences in crime." *Social Forces*, 61:1010–1032.

Warren, M., ed. 1981. *Comparing female and male offenders*. Beverly Hills, CA: Sage.

3

The Motives and Mechanics of Operating an Illegal Drug Enterprise

Lise-Marie VanNostrand
Richard Tewksbury

This article discusses the ways drug dealers operate their businesses. How drug dealers set up and conduct their businesses and the reasons they give for selling drugs are very similar to those of legitimate businesses. This indicates that people who engage in deviance may not see their actions as very different from those of nondeviants. The authors show us that motives for deviant activities can include a feeling that no legal alternative is available and a belief that a fine line exists between how legal and illegal actions are conducted.

. . . The domestic drug trade has become a booming business throughout the latter part of the 20th century. For example, between 1985 and 1994, nationwide arrests of drug law violators (including both possession and sale) increased by over 60% (Bureau of Justice Statistics 1996). More specifically, between 1980 and 1987 adult arrests for drug manufacturing and selling increased by an estimated 113% (Tunnell 1993). As a result of the increased efforts of policing and law enforcement, drug traffickers are now apprehended, convicted and imprisoned at greater rates than at any [other] time during this century (Tunnell 1993).

Although such data may suggest a measure of success from the last several decades' wars on drugs, the increases in arrests and convictions of drug traffickers have been commensurate with increases in drug use. With an ever-increasing demand for drugs, one can inevitably conclude that there will be an increase in drug trafficking to supply that demand. The demand for drugs has been steadily increasing since the 1960s, and though drug dealers are now arrested more frequently than in the past, they still make up only a small percentage (27%) of total drug arrestees (Bureau of Justice Statistics 1996).

With the apparent failed attempts to control the supply side of the drug economy, research has emerged investigating drug dealers' motives and their methods of operating illicit drug businesses. Included among the reasons that dealers sell drugs are financial gain, and an alternative to low paying jobs, a desire for status and power, hedonism, and the need to support a drug habit (Biernacki 1979; Flores 1981; Adler 1985; Mieczkowski 1986, 1990, 1994; Murphy, Waldorf, and Reinarman 1990; Faupel 1991; Lyman and Potter 1991; Weisheit 1991b; Myers 1992; Dembo, Hughes, and Jackson 1993; Tunnell 1993; Hagedorn 1994; Hafley and Tewksbury 1996; Shover 1996; Curcione 1997). Were there merely one factor that motivated drug dealers, it would be relatively simple to curb the domestic supply of drugs. As it stands, similar motives drive both illegitimate and legitimate businesspersons. Drug dealing serves as an alternative method of realizing socially valued goals.

Like other businesses, drug dealing often takes on the form of a career with similar methods of entry, levels of advancement, and retirement stages found in both legitimate and other illegitimate work environments (Adler 1985; Skolnick, Correl, Navarro, and Rabb 1990; Dunlap, Johnson, and Manwar 1994; Hafley and Tewksbury 1995, 1996; Johnson and Natarajan 1995; Maher and Daly 1996; Shover 1996).

Both urban and rural drug trafficking organizations reflect some degree of hierarchical structure similar to that found in legitimate businesses (Adler 1985; Murphy et al., 1990; Weisheit 1991; Hafley and Tewksbury

1995, 1996; Curcione 1997). Each level of the hierarchy has a definitive job description and level of responsibility to assure smooth operation. Like those in legitimate businesses, drug dealers rely on their knowledge to train new recruits and tend to organize, plan, and execute their ventures in ways similar to legitimate businesspersons. Those with the highest degree of responsibility earn the most profit. . . .

Crack Cocaine Distribution

Crack cocaine has some of the more prominent negative effects of commonly abused drugs and has been linked to increasingly high rates of violent crime (Fagan 1989; Mieczkowski 1992; Dembo et al. 1993; Johnson, Golub and Fagan, 1995; Dunlap and Johnson, 1996). . . . With the introduction of inexpensive crack cocaine in the 1980s, systems of distribution have emerged as a consequence of the market demand that vary from methods used when dealing in other substances (Dembo et al. 1993; Inciardi, Lockwood, and Pottieger 1993; Chitwood, Rivers, and Inciardi 1996). . . . Consequently, a highly lucrative market for drug dealers has been established (Miller 1995).

Murphy et al.(1990) defined a cocaine dealer as someone who is "fronted" drugs (given drugs on consignment to be paid for when sold) or who buys drugs to sell. To become a dealer one must (a) have one or more reliable suppliers, (b) make regular purchases in amounts of 1/8 ounce or greater, (c) maintain regular supplies for sale, and (d) have a strong network of customers who purchase drugs regularly. For many drug dealers, initiation of a dealing career involves determining the demand for a specific drug in the area and the feasibility of either cultivating, producing, and selling that substance. The methods a dealer employs will determine the success or failure of a drug trafficking organization.

Dealers typically purchase wholesale amounts of crack and make multiple retail doses in bags, bundles, or vials that are sold or consigned to lower level street sellers (Adler 1985; Inciardi et al. 1993; Johnson and Natarajan 1995; Chitwood et al. 1996). Due

to the brief duration of the crack high, most sellers must offer services 24 hours per day to cater to customers repeatedly returning for varying amounts of the drug (Inciardi et al. 1993; Johnson, Natarajan, Dunlap, and Elmoghazy 1994; Chitwood et al. 1996; Jacobs 1996). Although some research suggests that most crack sales occur on the street (Skolnick et al. 1990; Pettiway 1995), others contend that crack sales occur primarily indoors and that crack houses are generally the primary retail outlets (Mieczkowski 1990, 1992; Inciardi et al. 1993; Chitwood et al. 1996; Knowles 1996).

Since crack dealing has become a lucrative market within the drug economy, it has become a primary focus of law enforcement to detect, arrest, and incarcerate drug dealers. However, the domestic law enforcement crack-down on drug trafficking does not appear to have resulted in a decrease in the supply of drugs to the domestic market. Although drug markets may be displaced temporarily, in actuality dealers may simply be developing new strategies to avoid detection rather than being eliminated by increased police pressure (Caulkins 1992; Johnson and Natarajan 1995; Jacobs 1996).

Several researchers have found that drug dealers are often able to employ tactics to avoid police detection and are able to identify law enforcement officers through both verbal and non-verbal cues (Mieczkowski 1986; Skolnick et al. 1990; Caulkins 1992; Jacobs 1992; Johnson and Natarajan 1995; Knowles 1996). Dealers are careful when selecting buyers and locations for transactions and often believe they are able to identify law enforcement officers by how they look, what they wear, what they drive and how they engage verbally when making transactions. In addition, when one adds the constitutional restraints governing police drug buys, arrests and seizures, the likelihood of arrests of dealers appears very modest (Caulkins 1992; Myers 1992; Johnson and Natarajan 1995).

The current research offers an expansion of this literature and focuses on the motivating factors that influence individuals to deal drugs and the means of operating a drug business while avoiding detection. [Drawing on in-depth, semi-structured interviews with

20 dealers participating in a drug court diversion program]. These issues, furthermore are explored from drug dealers' perspectives. Finally, based on these findings this research offers suggestions regarding future drug war policy. . . .

Findings

Analysis of dealers' accounts suggest three primary motives to deal drugs: financial gain, greed, and a desire for the lifestyle itself. Additionally, dealers identified their methods of selecting buyers, arranging transactions, avoiding detection and identifying law enforcement officers. Through explanations of how dealers structure and conduct business transactions, we can move toward better understandings of the dynamics that facilitate the proliferation of dealing enterprises. The discussion that follows first examines the specific motivations that draw individuals into a drug-dealing career. Second, we outline and examine the mechanics of operating a successful drug business.

Motives to Deal Drugs

Subjects in the current study identified three primary motives that lead them to begin dealing. Some were motivated by a perceived need to earn either a primary or supplemental income. These individuals perceived few or no lucrative, legitimate employment opportunities available to them. Others began dealing strictly due to greed and a desire for luxury material items. Still others were motivated by the fast lifestyle perceived to accompany a career in drug trafficking. In essence, although not chemically addicted, some dealers are addicted to the lifestyle of a drug dealer. Although most subjects began dealing based upon a single motive, these motives frequently evolve and vacillate over time, serving to support a continued involvement in the drug trade.

Financial Need. Some subjects began dealing drugs primarily due to financial need. Commonly reported is an absolute financial need and perceptions of blocked opportunities for substantial, gainful employment. The majority of subjects (80%) reported having children, and although at the time of the interview only 30% were married, many had been previously married. As such, those who most often reported dealing to fill a financial need had families for whom to provide. These dealers saw drug dealing as the quickest, and often only, method of gaining financial survival and stability. As described by Shane, a high school graduate and former military serviceman, lack of employment opportunities and familial responsibilities lead to his involvement in the drug trade:

> I came home from the service in 1991 and got married out of high school. Perfect little life. When I came home, my wife was pregnant and I couldn't really find a good job to get all the baby stuff I needed. . . . I got caught up in it. I didn't get caught up in the lifestyle, it was the money I was into.

Similar motives were expressed by Sid, who reported that after dropping out of college, he was unable to achieve the "American Dream" through legitimate means:

> I got a job now. You know, it's decent, but it's not anything for a house payment, car payment, two kids. You know, the money just ain't enough. . . . That's probably the biggest reason today for most people out there selling dope.

Richard agreed, and reported that although he tried legitimate means of achieving financial security, he found that the income derived from drug dealing far outweighed his earnings from a legitimate job.

> The money is one reason that got me motivated because I wasn't working and I was trying to make ends meet. Trying to take care of my responsibilities. Then, I started to work. It was like, "I don't have to work. I can make more in a day [dealing] than what I would for a whole week doing this."

After seeking financial independence and security through conventional means, failures and obstacles pushed many to seek alternative, illicit opportunities. They were married, had children, sometimes continued their educations and worked in the hope of achieving a measure of personal success. However, they were unable to effectively manage the stressors associated with their familial responsibilities and as a result of either desperation or the attraction of drug dealing, turned to selling drugs.

In this respect, this research supports previous literature that suggests that drug dealing may sometimes be motivated simply by a need to supplement incomes for those persons categorized as "economically depressed." Yet, unlike some previous research (Flores 1981; Weisheit 1991a, 1991b; Hafley and Tewksbury 1995, 1996) subjects in the present study did not necessarily live in economically depressed or rural areas. Recognizing drug dealing in their communities as a prosperous enterprise, these individuals opted for illegal pursuits rather than the few paying jobs that were available to them (see also Mieczkowski 1986; Murphy et al. 1990; Myers 1992).

Greed. In addition to perceptions of financial need as an initial motive to sell drugs, other subjects reported little need to supplement their incomes and were motivated strictly by greed. Although not believing it necessary to sell drugs to make ends meet and provide basic life necessities, dealers motivated by greed sought supplemental income to attain luxuries. Previous literature identifies the profit motive as a major incentive for drug dealing; however, much of the research does not separate financial need from issues of greed. Instead, a profit motive comprised of several variables is typically employed (Dembo et al. 1993; Mieczkowski 1994; Tunnell 1993). Still, there is a distinct difference between dealing motivated by necessity and dealing motivated by greed alone.

Several of the dealers in this study reported little or no need for supplemental incomes. Simply put, they expressed a desire for fast and easy money that drug dealing afforded them. These subjects often maintained conventional employment and/or operated profitable legitimate businesses. As explained by Joel, his greed for money was described as "madness," since he already had significant income earned through legitimate means:

> I was doing construction work and making a lot of money, so I was able to buy the stuff (cocaine) in quantity and sell it. And, you know, one thing lead to another. . . . I

didn't need the money because I had plenty.

Like sentiments were expressed by Andy, who very candidly reported that he perceived himself as spoiled and that his sole motivation to deal drugs was based on greed:

> I can't say that I was forced. My family always had money. I was never broke, I was never hungry. . . . The people I hung around with kind of caught on to me. I guess I was just a spoiled brat, or whatever. I started hanging around guys that was dealing and they would show me all this money and all this stuff. . . . Money started coming so fast!. . . . It just grabs you, takes you.

Most dealers reported earning an average of $2,000 to $5,000 per day on drug sales. For many, the earnings potential for drug sales was unparalleled to that of the legitimate opportunities available to them. As described by Dwain, while he could easily obtain legitimate employment, this would pay little more than minimum wage. Therefore, drug sales offered a much more attractive opportunity:

> I couldn't find a good job. I got a job paying $5.50 an hour, but after I started making so much money [dealing], I just figured I was making four times that amount.

The desire to earn "fast money" was overpowering. Although their incomes from dealing meant they had little need for legitimate work, some operated and maintained successful businesses not only as a "front" for their dealing operations, but because they wished to have "something to fall back on" in the event their drug businesses were exposed. These subjects tended to be operating at the middle and upper levels of the drug hierarchy and were often able to avoid detection at the height of their careers (see also Curcione 1997).

It is important to mention here that several respondents who initially dealt drugs because of a perceived financial need eventually achieved stability, but continued dealing to enhance their lifestyles. Though initial motives may vary, after achieving lucrative financial rewards, those seeking merely supplementary income often described the money as "very difficult to give up." Here we see "motive shifts," as described by Adler (1985), that often lead to dealers' involvement in the drug trade far beyond the time needed to secure financial stability.

Addiction to the Lifestyle. Although financial need and greed motivate many to embark upon a career in drug selling, there are additional factors that also may motivate individuals to deal drugs. The drug dealing lifestyle tends to be very fast paced and for many, provides social popularity, status and power not otherwise realized in legitimate work environments (Adler 1985; Weisheit 1991; Dembo et al. 1993; Inciardi, Horowitz, and Pottieger 1993; Tunnell 1993). The fast pace, money, recognition, and power all combine to make the drug dealing lifestyle attractive, and as described by several dealers, addicting in and of itself. This was clearly expressed by Sharon, a 31 year old mother of two:

> I was working at the hospital and I used to ask myself, "How come I'm not satisfied with this?" Then, I realized, it's not as fast paced. . . . To me, it wasn't always about profit . . . It's just like using because you're addicted to the money, recognition, and the fame.

. . . Like a "rush," drug dealing provided many with an opportunity to achieve status unlike any they had ever known. The luxuries and power associated with dealing gave many the freedom to pursue a measure of social status that other career choices would not have provided.

Numerous dealers described the attainment of recognition and fame as an addicting part of the lifestyle. The dealers in this study sometimes resided in less affluent neighborhoods and perceived themselves as possessing few skills or attributes that would earn them respect. Once becoming dealers, however, they found themselves both respected and envied within their communities for having seemingly unlimited supplies of cash and material luxuries. As described by one young woman. . . .

> It seemed that the more I tried to do better (legitimately) somebody was always trying to put me down. People gave you more respect (as a dealer). They looked at you better. You could just feel the difference. . . . It's a real big difference.

Shane, who initially began dealing to support his family, related similar feelings. He described his addiction to the lifestyle as a result of his feelings of superiority over others within the community, and explained that the perceived sense of respect motivated him to continue dealing.

> I didn't think you could be addicted to selling drugs. I found myself doing the same things a user would do. Crazy stuff! . . . A lot of people get hooked to putting them on a level and feel like, higher than other people.

Perceptions of respect and power held many dealers in the drug trade. Being admired and respected by many made their chosen career path a very personally and socially rewarding one. Like many who choose legitimate means of employment, status attainment may be a motive for entry and continued pursuit of a particular career. The prestige and recognition, coupled with money and material possessions, lead many dealers to believe that there were no other means for attaining such prosperity and "control" over their fates. This addiction to the lifestyle itself served as a strong motivator for continuing to deal, as fears of losing monetary and personal gains held dealers' commitments.

A notable difference between subjects in this study versus subjects in previous research (Biernacki 1979; Mieczkowski 1990; Murphy et al. 1990; Reuter, MacCoun, and Murphy 1990; Faupel 1991; Tunnell 1993; Hagedorn 1994) is that none reported being motivated by the need to supplement a personal drug habit. Although all subjects reported some use of illegal drugs, most did not use the drugs that they sold. The few who did report using what they sold self-identified as recreational users and tended to use only after an extended period of time dealing. These reports vary from most previous research that suggests dealers often begin selling to maintain access to drugs (however, see also Hafley and Tewksbury 1995, 1996). This may be attributed to the fact that the majority of dealers in this study sold primarily crack cocaine, not heroin or marijuana. . . .

In some circumstances subjects reported a shift in motives over time. What may begin as a financial need may lead to one becoming accustomed to the monetary and personal rewards of dealing. Like continuous use of an addictive substance, the lifestyle itself may also become addicting. As a result, the original motives for entering the drug trade may evolve over time as those involved become addicted to the money, power and prosperity identified with the illicit drug economy.

Mechanics of Drug Dealing

In addition to the motives that lead individuals to deal drugs, the mechanics of drug dealers' activities also provide important insights to how and why drug dealing continues to proliferate. This insight can most effectively be gained through examinations of dealers' selectivity when choosing buyers, how drug transactions are arranged and means for avoiding and detecting law enforcement.

The hierarchical structure of the drug dealer's world is clearly evident in both the means by which careers are initiated and how, when identifying and assessing potential drug buyers, dealers focus on perceptions of buyers' abilities to pay. Potential buyers that are perceived as likely to not have enough cash with which to purchase drugs are actively avoided. Typically, those types of buyers are described by dealers as "addicts" and will offer merchandise rather than cash in exchange for drugs. After selecting buyers, dealers must also determine effective and efficient ways of arranging transactions that not only protect them from violence by customers, but also protect them from detection by law enforcement.

Methods of Entry and Levels of Advancement. As with any legitimate business opportunity, there are ways to gain entry and levels of possible advancement within the drug industry. For the subjects in this study, it was not a simple matter of deciding to sell drugs and then going out and buying a supply, but rather a matter of exploiting (or being exploited by) connections with others already involved in the drug industry. Most com-

monly, dealers were recruited and trained to operate successful drug businesses by other, higher-level dealers. As illustrated by Leroy, his initiation to the drug industry was by way of a friend's "schooling process."

> Basically, what got me into it was there was this guy that was running with me and he was dealing . . . He was real cool and we were just kickin' it . . . One night, it just hit me. I was like, "man, I want to see what this is all about. . . ." It's more like a schooling process and he was just showing me.

Other dealers described a similar training process by friends or family members who were dealing (see also Hafley and Tewksbury 1996). In this way the subjects were able to establish reliable reputations, facilitate connections with suppliers and acquire a regular customer base. These steps not only can draw one into dealing but can also facilitate advancement to higher levels of dealing. As Richard recalled, he was able to advance from a low-level seller to a mid-level dealer primarily because of his connection with an upper-level dealer.

> I was at the bottom of the tree. He [a friend] was right there with the big guys and he had more access to it [cocaine], more than I did . . . He pulled me into it and the opportunity came on. So, I went from a crumb to a big block of bread.

Dwight reiterated this experience, explaining how his connections allowed for rapid advancement within the drug market.

> I started at the bottom and worked my way up. It's not what you know, it's who you know. Somebody I knew, knew somebody and they hooked me up. I was now part of their program.

Much like those operating legitimate businesses, drug dealers in the present study tended to enter and advance in the drug industry in the same ways as legitimate businesspersons pursue careers. Having the right connections with an experienced dealer allowed many easy entry and rapid advancement in the drug industry. Without such connections, dealers would have been less likely to enter the drug trade and would have realized even fewer opportunities for career advancement.

Selection of Buyers. All dealers in the study were very selective in terms of those to whom they were willing to sell. In addition to a general consensus that they would not sell to persons unknown to them, most dealers expressed a significant degree of selectivity, preferring affluent buyers rather than lower-class "junkies" (see also Mieczkowski 1992). Lucratively employed middle- or upper-class businesspersons or professionals were reported to be "easier to deal with" and are the buyers of choice. Transactions with such buyers have both a lower degree of threat of violence (or "hassle") and also ensure that buyers will have adequate cash resources.

Dealers' descriptions of transactions with addicts commonly emphasized "stressful" and "nerve racking" qualities. Addicts as customers were typically described as generally dishonest and untrustworthy people who tended to offer excuses for a lack of cash. Furthermore, addicts were seen as "slaves to the drugs" they used, as evidenced by their offers of nearly anything (including sex) in exchange for drugs. Buyers without lucrative employment were perceived as less likely to offer cash transactions and therefore were most often avoided. As one dealer explained,

> I basically dealt with people that had good jobs. . . . Someone with a good income where I'd know if they came, it [money] was exact and there were no excuses and there were no long run stories.

In essence, dealers expressed pride in their ability to deal with "high class" people and tended to lack respect for those perceived as under the control of drugs (see also Mieczkowski 1986). It appears that in dealers' minds, to sell to "respectable" persons is not only more desirable because it is "easier," but transactions with such customers also grant more status to dealers. Similar to Goffman's (1963) idea of "courtesy stigma," dealers who regularly transact business with addicts share in the stigmas granted to addicts. In addition to believing it riskier to sell to less-respectable customers (see below), dealers widely believed it to be less prestigious and indicative of lower status to be known as a

dealer catering to a lower class of users. As described by Garrett, who reported dealing primarily with middle and upper class professionals, not only was it less likely to confer status to deal to addicts, but doing so also served to further others' life problems.

> I stayed away from junkies because to me, they didn't need it. Believe it or not, I actually had a conscience about who I sold to. People that couldn't afford to and wanted me to front it, I didn't sell to because I knew that they was goin' too far with it.

Other dealers reported that when they began dealing drugs they initially sold to street addicts, but only because this was the most easily accessed pool of buyers. Dealing with middle and upper class buyers—and sometimes other dealers (see also Adler 1985)—was something one had to "work into." As Andy described his ascent in the dealing hierarchy,

> In the beginning, I sold mostly to addicts . . . They got to be a real nuisance . . . I didn't like dealing with them. They'll try to snatch your stuff. Then I started dealing with dealers. . . . I would buy from a big dealer and sell to a smaller dealer.

What is interesting to note is that although many of the dealers in this study lived in the lowest income areas of the inner-city, the majority did not sell to the abundant array of street people in their neighborhoods. Through their reputations among dealers and consumers, these individuals became attractive to more affluent customers. This not only afforded a larger array of customers, but assured access to buyers who could and would pay higher prices.

In addition to selecting buyers on the basis of status (both social and economic), dealers also tended to prefer dealing with male rather than female customers. Male buyers were described as more direct, more trustworthy, and more likely to be satisfied that they received fair exchanges of drugs for cash. Dealers' experiences suggested that men were more likely to buy for cash, and less likely to offer payment in goods or offers of sexual activities. As succinctly explained by Joel,

Men had more money. Women always wanted credit. I tried not to deal with it [and] mostly dealt with men.

Interestingly, one female dealer also preferred dealing with male buyers, since she believed female buyers tended to be untrustworthy and manipulative.

I've never really liked to deal with a lot of women. They were different because they're more spineless, more conniving, full of games. You can never tell when you can trust them. A man will be more straight up. With women, it was always a lot of bullshit. Always trying to get over.

Male (and occasionally female) dealers also report female customers frequently offered sex in exchange for drugs. Offers of oral, vaginal and anal sex in return for drugs are rather commonplace among (especially addict) female customers. Male buyers may on rare occasions offer sex in exchange for drugs; however, no dealers in the current study reported accepting such offers from men. Furthermore, most dealers offered some variation on the declaration that men "can't proposition you." [Dealers did, however, accept offers of sex from women.] As described by Sid, who did sometimes accept sex in exchange for drugs, such exchanges are not only readily available, but also generally an accepted behavior in the drug economy.

I'd be in a hotel room with two or three women, you know. Not bragging, but that's just how it was. It's sickening what they would do for their drugs. You know, anything goes.

A more graphic illustration was described by Richard, who also admitted to having accepted sex in exchange for drugs.

Women would give me a sob story or tell me they would, excuse my French, give me a blow-job, or "I'll fuck you for this or that". . . . The statement I would always hear is, "What does a bitch have to do to earn a piece?"

Although a majority of dealers on occasion accepted sex for drugs, most expressed a desire to avoid regularly doing so, as a drugs for sex trade was not seen as a financially wise

transaction. However, it is not only the financial costs that discourage dealers, but also their strong expressions of disgust for crack-dependent women. The sex-for-drugs exchanges reported by these dealers were not typically in crack house environments as described in previous literature (Inciardi, et al. 1993), but rather occurred in private locations, such as hotels or homes. . . .

Arranging Drug Transactions. The dealers in this study had preferred methods and locations for arranging drug transactions. Some arranged their sales primarily through word of mouth, with transactions often taking place in their homes or the homes of their buyers. Dealers in this group perceived risks of detection and violence as greatest when dealing outside their homes and therefore confined transactions to locations they considered to be "safe". Tending to live in suburban communities, where they believed they were subject to less scrutiny by police, these dealers acquired a regular customer base by word of mouth, and completed transactions that required little or no negotiation (see also Curcione, 1997). As explained by one dealer, it was his reputation that made transactions virtually effortless.

I wasn't small time. . . . I had a place, they came to me. Nobody brought anybody to me. They [buyers] just heard my reputation.

Another dealer who operated out of his home reported that he too made little effort to contact buyers and that transactions were usually arranged when customers dropped by.

I had this one room in my house that I had my tools in, sorta' like a junk room. . . . That is where I did all my drug work. . . . I always did it at home. They [buyers] always came to me, I didn't have to go to anybody. Ninety percent of the time, they just came by.

In contrast, a second group of dealers perceived the risks of detection as much higher, were they to sell from their homes, due to the constant flow of customers in and out. These dealers typically resided in inner-city neighborhoods known for heavy drug sales. Consequently, it was standard practice for these dealers to be constantly developing new means for avoiding detection by frequent police patrols. Because of the neighborhoods in which they lived, they perceived less risk associated with discreet deals in public areas, since law enforcement officers were reported to frequently park across the street from homes of suspected dealers. Therefore, most transactions were arranged by pagers, cell phones and car phones and were scheduled to take place discreetly in public areas (including stores, parking lots, and at pay phones). When Richard described how he arranged drug transactions, he noted the use of three separate pagers that allowed him to estimate the amount of cocaine a buyer wished to purchase. Additionally, he believed he could operate more discreetly if he segmented his customers in this manner.

> I had three different pagers. One for people that wanted small stuff like an 8 ball or something. The second one was for people that wanted a half ounce or so. The third one was for those people that wanted quarter kilos or half kilos...If the person didn't page me, I would not deal with you because I only gave my pager number to certain individuals.

Richard also described a rather simple method for arranging actual cash-for-drugs exchanges in public places, emphasizing his efforts to be discreet.

> We had certain places and certain people we would meet to make it not look so curious. We [seller and buyer] might go into a store, same store, and be in the same aisle buying something. Well, I would bend down and he would bend down . . . I would go to the same department he was looking at and there was the money. And he would go to the department I was looking in and there was the product. We would go up and buy a candy bar or a pop or beer. We would just walk out.

Other common methods for completing exchanges varied from being paged and arranging to meet a buyer in an abandoned lot, to exchanging drugs for cash stashed in the change slot of a pay phone. Drug transactions could be arranged in a wide range of ways and could take place in almost any location. Although dealers are easily categorized by

their preferred methods of completing transactions, both those dealing from inside their homes and those dealing in public places report having successfully avoided detection for extended periods of time.

Avoiding and Identifying Law Enforcement. The mechanics of a drug dealing business will determine how successful that business may be. One of the primary reasons that drug dealing can remain undetected is the ability of dealers to become knowledgeable about the mechanics of law enforcement. Along with careful attention to arranging transactions, dealers develop strategies to elude police detection. Strategies used by dealers in the present study included dealing exclusively with known, trusted customers, choosing locations for transactions known for infrequent police patrols, keeping money and drugs in separate locations, and sometimes operating legitimate businesses as a front to deter suspicion. These strategies add to the existing literature that describes common techniques dealers use to avoid detection (Johnson and Natarajan 1995; Jacobs 1996).

A common theme found throughout all interviews is that dealers avoided potential detection by limiting sales to persons whom they knew and trusted. In this way, dealers were often able to avoid detection by law enforcement. . . . When approached by strangers, dealers typically feigned ignorance about the potential buyer's request. As Blaire described, acting ignorant to a stranger's request for drugs was the only way to safeguard against exposure by undercover law enforcement.

> People that walked up to me and said something like, "You got that?" I would be like, "What do you mean, got what?" I was like, "No, I don't." You know what to say.

Other dealers reported that in addition to knowing the individuals they sold to, the location of transactions was critical to avoiding detection by law enforcement. Although several subjects reported arranging transactions to take place in public places, they were very discreet when arranging actual exchanges and strove to give the appearance of being involved in regular, everyday activities. There were, however, particular public behaviors, such as standing idly on street corners that were widely acknowledged as triggering the suspicions of law enforcement. As explained by one dealer who had previously been arrested selling drugs on the street,

> This time I ain't gonna' be too careless. I ain't gonna' be standing in the open. If I'm standing in the open, they (police) know I'm doin' something, selling drugs or something.

Thoughts such as this were rather common sense issues to most dealers, for street level sales were largely avoided. Such high visibility (and therefore high risk) activities were considered stigmatizing as well as being likely to lead to detection.

. . . Dealers believed that if they were to be arrested (based upon reasonable suspicion), it was important not to have drugs or money on one's person. There would be little concrete evidence to support a conviction if these rules were carefully followed. As recounted by Leroy. . . .

> I was always the type that if I made some money, I'd go and put it up. I would never keep no drugs on me.

[Another rule was to avoid keeping records.] Garrett, who believed dealing from his home limited his risk of detection, believed that banking profits and keeping records of drug transactions were two of the strongest forms of evidence that could ultimately lead to conviction. . . . As he explained:

> I never had any records I'd go by. I kept a lot of stuff over the years, but I didn't keep any kind of legible records . . . That's how they get you hooked a lot of times. . . . You can't bank your money. No way! I mean, how many people make ten to twenty thousand dollars a week? . . . You know, I made everything look good. You had to watch what you were doing. You had to bury your money.

Additionally, some dealers operated profitable, legitimate businesses or held legitimate jobs that also served as fronts to their illegal drug businesses (see also Fields and Walters 1985; Johnson and Natarajan 1995; Curcione 1997). For one dealer, his lucrative

business as a barber allowed him to operate a successful drug business that was never detected. Two other dealers operated successful construction companies that not only provided ready-made customer bases, but also served as fronts throughout their dealing careers.

In summary, dealers employ several methods to avoid suspicion and detection and to protect themselves against conviction if arrested. Dealing with known customers, choosing safe locations, effectively managing drugs and money and operating business fronts, [are strategies] of avoiding suspicion, detection and conviction. Dealers perceive these techniques as general common sense, and because they believe these techniques have been successful their efficacy is reinforced.

Not only did dealers carefully restrict the visibility of their transactions, but they also heavily relied on their skills of detecting specific factors or clues that they believed allowed them to expose undercover law enforcement officers. As seen in previous literature (Mieczkowski 1986; Skolnick et al. 1990; Jacobs 1992, 1996; Knowles 1996), dealers often believe they are able to (and in fact often may) identify law enforcement by how undercover officers look, dress, what they drive, how they engage verbally when making transactions and by way of informal street networks. Dealers in the present study described some of these same factors, as well as personal "vibes" that they believed tipped them of law enforcement.

For several dealers, a potential customer's race could arouse suspicion. Similar to other research (Jacobs 1992), whites were often associated with law enforcement. As the majority of subjects in the study were African American, white buyers tended to raise considerable suspicions, especially among those who resided in primarily African-American neighborhoods. As illustrated by Sid, an African-American crack dealer:

> If you was white, I wouldn't deal with you. Wouldn't deal with you for being white in that environment. . . . I just didn't sell to white people.

In addition to the factor of race—whether correctly or incorrectly interpreted as a cue to identifying law enforcement—dealers also commonly rely on cues in potential buyers' verbal and non-verbal behaviors to identify undercover law enforcement officers. Said to appear uncomfortable, ask too many questions, and attempt in-depth involvement in the dealer's operations, undercover officers are believed to be fairly easily detected. As Joel believed, law enforcement officers tended to give themselves away by a demonstrated (or feigned) lack of knowledge as to how drug transactions take place.

> I never had any trouble picking them out. It's just the way they act. They tried to be too much involved. People will tell you that people that deal with drugs don't do much talking about the drugs. They [narcs] front too much, wanting to know how you run your operation.

The inappropriate behaviors of potential buyers signalled to dealers that buyers were likely law enforcement officers. By having the ability to recognize these behaviors as atypical to the drug using population, dealers avoided what they believed were attempted buys by undercover police.

Other factors relied upon for exposing law enforcement officers were the feelings dealers would get indicating to them that something was "not right" with a situation. They perceived these feelings or "vibes" (or as Faupel (1991 p. 82) refers to such, "intuitive skills") as very reliable cues and did not pursue transactions when these feelings persisted. As Shane recalled, not respecting his intuition and suspicions lead to his detection.

> I got like this gut feeling in a situation. I used to count on that…I really didn't have much worry. When I went against the rules I went by, it cost me some trouble.

Numerous dealers described such intangible cues and knew to discontinue their dealing activities until such feelings subsided. At times they would cease all dealing activities for short periods until they felt safe enough to resume. However, the financial and lifestyle motivations lead them to curtail these periods of inactivity in relatively short order.

A final means dealers relied upon for identifying law enforcement officers was a gathering of information from street networks that funneled intelligence into and throughout neighborhoods. Community networking is not unique to these dealers (Hafley and Tewksbury 1995; Johnson and Natarajan 1995). Through cooperation among dealers, buyers, residents, and allegedly some individuals inside law enforcement agencies, dealers in the current study identified suspected police and subsequently avoided interaction. As one dealer succinctly explained, the street grapevine served as a valuable information system to identify law enforcement officers to dealers.

> They [police] are real well known. People can see. Through the grapevine out on the street, I found out.

These informal networks among drug industry participants (sometimes including informants within law enforcement agencies) were very highly respected and valued. Dealers almost universally cited such networks as invaluable aids in identifying and avoiding law enforcement. Especially valued contacts in this study were those inside law enforcement. As alleged by one dealer,

> You would be surprised who at the [police] station tells you what is going on. You know they are coming over here next.

Drug dealers firmly believe they are able to successfully elude law enforcement detection, if they are careful and consistent in their practices. Dealers also believe they can identify law enforcement officers by appearance, behavior, and informal street networking. Thus, dealers in the present study believed they had extended their dealing careers by detecting and avoiding law enforcement officials.

Summary

It has been shown by this analysis of drug dealing that dealing tends to be characterized by similar motives, economic goals, and business problems as are found in other illegitimate enterprises, as well as legitimate economic pursuits. Like those seeking lucrative, legitimate employment, drug dealers choose dealing on the basis of economic need, greed, or a desire for a particular lifestyle. Additionally, in order to develop and maintain a prosperous business enterprise they must be able to learn all aspects of the drug business and effectively manage the inherent obstacles encountered in criminal occupations. In short, we suggest that to be a successful drug dealer requires a variety of resources, a savvy business sense, intelligence, and perhaps a bit of luck.

The drug dealers in the present study initiated dealing careers as a result of three general motivating factors. For some, absolute economic need facilitated entry to the drug economy. Dealers so motivated perceived themselves as unable or unlikely to obtain substantial, gainful employment and saw dealing as an opportunity for considerable financial gain. Others maintained lucrative, legitimate employment and had little need for supplemental income. As such, their integration within the drug economy was based primarily upon greed or a desire for a lifestyle not attainable through legitimate avenues. Finally, some dealers perceived the lifestyle of a drug dealer as exciting, luxurious, and empowering. These aspects of the lifestyle itself, then, tended to draw and hold these individuals in the illicit drug economy.

Once motivated to enter the drug trade, dealers had to learn the mechanics of operating a successful drug business. The first priority was to acquire a regular and safe customer base (see also Faupel 1991). Dealers developed individual ways to screen and select customers, and dealt almost exclusively with known, trusted buyers. A second aspect to operating the business was to determine locations and methods of arranging transactions. Dealers either dealt primarily or never from their homes. Varying with perceptions of how law enforcement efforts were structured and focused, dealers made conscious choices about how to limit the visibility of their activities. A third critical factor was the ability to identify (and subsequently avoid) buyers suspected of being law enforcement officers. Dealers believed they could identify law enforcement officers by assessing both verbal and non-verbal cues. These perceptible cues, as well as informally gathered information, were perceived as critical to extending their dealing careers. . . .

References

Adler, Patricia. 1985. *Wheeling and Dealing: An Ethnography of an Upper-Level Drug Dealing and Smuggling Community*. New York: Columbia University Press.

Bureau of Justice Statistics. 1996. *Sourcebook of Criminal Justice Statistics*, 1995. Washington, DC: U.S. Government Printing Office.

Caulkins, J. 1992. "Thinking About Displacement in Drug Markets: Why Observing Change of Venue Isn't Enough." *Journal of Drug Issues*, 22:17–30.

Chitwood, Dale D., James E. Rivers, and James A. Inciardi. 1996. *The American Pipe Dream: Crack Cocaine and the Inner City*. Fort Worth, TX: Harcourt Brace.

Dembo, R., P. Hughes, L. Jackson, and T. Mieczkowski. 1993. "Crack Cocaine Dealing by Adolescents in Two Public Housing Projects: A Pilot Study." *Human Organization* 52:89–96.

Dunlap, E., B. Johnson, and A. Manwar. 1994. "A Successful Female Crack Dealer: Case Study of a Deviant Career." *Deviant Behavior* 15:1–25.

Fagan, J. 1989. "The Social Organization of Drug Use and Drug Dealing Among Urban Gangs." *Criminology* 27:633–663.

Faupel, C. E. 1991. *Shooting Dope: Career Patterns of Hard-Core Heroin Users*. Gainesville: University of Florida Press.

Fields, A. and J. Walters. 1985. "Hustling: Supporting a Heroin Habit." Pp. 49–73 in *Life with Heroin: Voices from the Inner City*, edited by B. Hanson, G. Beschner, J. Walters, and E. Bovell. Lexington, MA: Lexington Books.

Flores, E. 1981. "Dealing in Marijuana: An Exploratory Study." *Hispanic Journal of Behavioral Sciences* 3:199–211.

Goffman, Erving. 1963. *Stigma: Notes on the Management of Spoiled Identity*. Englewood Cliffs, NJ: Prentice-Hall.

Hafley, Sandra Riggs and Richard Tewksbury. 1995. "The Rural Kentucky Marijuana Industry: Organization and Community Involvement." *Deviant Behavior* 16:201–221.

Hafley, Sandra Riggs and Richard Tewksbury. 1996. "Reefer Madness in Bluegrass County: Community Structure and Roles in the Rural Kentucky Marijuana Industry." *Journal of Crime and Justice* 19:75–94.

Hagedorn, J. 1994. "Homeboys, Dope Fiends, Legits and New Jacks." *Criminology* 32:197–219.

Inciardi, James A., Ruth Horowitz, and Anne Pottieger. 1983. *Street Kids, Street Drugs, Street Crime.* Belmont, CA: Wadsworth.

Inciardi, James A.., Dorothy. Lockwood, and Anne Pottieger. 1993. ,*Women and Crack Cocaine.* New York: Macmillan Publishing Company.

Jacobs, Bruce. 1992. "Drugs and Deception: Undercover Infiltration and Dramaturgical Theory." *Human Relations* 45:1293–1309.

Jacobs, Bruce. 1996. "Crack Dealers and Restrictive Deterrence: Identifying Narcs." *Criminology* 34:409–431.

Johnson, B., A. Golub, and J. Fagan. 1995. "Careers in Crack, Drug Use, Drug Distribution and Non-Drug Criminality." *Crime and Delinquency* 41:275–295.

Johnson, B. and M. Natarajan. 1995. "Strategies to Avoid Arrest: Crack Sellers' Response to Intensified Policing." *American Journal of Police* 14:49–69.

Johnson, B., M. Natarajan, E. Dunlap, and E. Elmoghazy. 1994. "Crack Abusers and Non-Crack Abusers: Profiles of Drug Use, Drug Sales and Non-Drug Criminality." *Journal of Drug Issues* 24:117–141.

Knowles, J. 1996. "Dealing in Crack Cocaine: A View From the Streets of Honolulu." *FBI Law Enforcement Bulletin* 65:1–8.

Lichtenstein, P. 1914. "Narcotic Addiction." Pp. 67–69 in *Yesterday's Addicts: American Society and Drug Abuse*, 1865–1920. edited by H.W. Morgan. Norman: University of Oklahoma Press.

Lyman, M. and G. Potter. 1991. *Drugs in Society: Causes, Concepts and Control.* Cincinnati, OH: Anderson Publishing.

Maher, L. and K. Daly. 1996. "Women in The Street-Level Drug Economy: Continuity or Change?" *Criminology* 34:465–491.

Mieczkowski, T. 1986. "Geeking Up and Throwing Down: Heroin Street Life in Detroit." *Criminology* 24:645–666.

Mieczkowski, T. 1990. "Crack Distribution in Detroit." *Contemporary Drug Problems* 17:9–30.

Mieczkowski, T. 1992. "Crack Dealing on the Street: The Crew System and the Crack House." *Justice Quarterly* 9:151–163.

Mieczkowski, T. 1994. "The Experiences of Women Who Sell Crack: Some Descriptive Data From the Detroit Crack Ethnography Project." *Journal of Drug Issues* 24:227–248.

Miller, Jody. 1995. "Gender and Power on the Streets." *Journal of Contemporary Ethnography* 23:427–452.

Murphy, S., D. Waldorf, and C. Reinarman. 1990. "Drifting Into Dealing: Becoming a Cocaine Seller." *Qualitative Sociology* 13:321–343.

Myers, S. 1992. "Crime, Entrepreneurship and Labor Force Withdrawal." *Contemporary Police Issues* 10:84–97.

Pettiway, Leon. 1995. "Copping Crack: The Travel Behavior of Crack Users." *Justice Quarterly* 12:499–524.

Potter, Gary and Larry Gaines. 1992. "Country Comfort: Vice and Corruption in Rural Settings." *Journal of Contemporary Criminal Justice* 8:36–61.

Reuter, P., R. MacCoun, and P. Murphy. 1990. *Money from Crime: A Study of the Economics of Drug Dealing in Washington, D.C.* Santa Monica, CA: RAND Corporation.

Shover, Neil. 1996. *Great Pretenders: Pursuits and Careers of Persistent Thieves.* Boulder, CO: Westview Press, Inc.

Skolnick, J., T. Correl, E. Navarro, and R. Rabb. 1990. "The Social Structure of Street Drug Dealing." *American Journal of Police* 9:1–41.

Tunnell, Ken. 1993. "Inside the Drug Trade: Trafficking From the Dealer's Perspective." *Qualitative Sociology* 16:361–381.

Weisheit, R. 1991a. "Drug Use Among Domestic Marijuana Growers." *Contemporary Drug Problems* 18:191–217.

Weisheit, R. 1991b. "The Intangible Rewards From Crime: The Case of Domestic Marijuana Cultivation." *Crime and Delinquency* 37:506–527.

4

Who's Driving? College Students' Choices of Transportation Home After Drinking

Laura K. McCormick
John Ureda

This article looks at the choices made by college students about whether to drive after drinking or to ride with someone who has been drinking. Many students report that they drive themselves home after drinking at bars or parties, and many more ride with friends who have been drinking. They say they do so because they have no other options. This finding suggests that instead of making informed decisions, people who engage in deviant acts often do so because they feel they have no alternative but to do something dangerous or deviant.

Introduction

... The major cause of death for youth aged 15 to 25 is automobile crashes; forty to sixty percent of all fatal crashes involving a young driver are alcohol-related (U.S. Dept. Health, Education & Welfare, 1979). A growing body of evidence suggests that the probability of crash involvement increases with increasing blood alcohol concentration (BAC), and that for young drivers, risk begins to increase at very low BAC's (Anda, Remington, and Williamson 1986; Farina, 1988).

Legislative age restrictions do not appear to have a significant impact on adolescent drinking. National surveys have shown that alcohol consumption has remained relatively stable over the past decade with approximately 92 percent of college students reporting having ever consumed alcohol (Johnston, O'Malley and Bachman, 1991; NIDA, 1987). Generally, underage students do not have difficulty obtaining alcohol. The most common sources for obtaining alcohol are from friends, although 25% of underage drinkers report using falsified identification (Vaughn, 1983).

Alcohol consumption among adolescents, especially college students, continues to be the norm rather than the exception (Maddox, 1970). Drinking has been an integral part of college socialization for decades. Students have reported drinking at parties, bars, restaurants, residence halls, and the homes of friends and family. In 1953, college students reported drinking most often at bars, restaurants or pubs (Straus and Bacon, 1953). After forty years, this general pattern has not changed (Perkins and Berkowitz, 1986; Vingilis and Salutin, 1980). . . .

Young male drivers are reported to be at greater risk than young females for drinking-driving (Farrow, 1985), although more recent studies have found no significant gender differences in adolescent DUI behavior. Individuals are also at risk for alcohol-related fatalities from riding with an alcohol-impaired driver. At least two thirds of high school students have ridden with an alcohol-impaired driver on one or more occasions (Nusbaumer and Zusman, 1981; Swisher and Bibeau, 1986). Few studies have addressed gender differences among riding with alcohol-impaired drivers, although Sarvela and colleagues (1987, 1990) found that among [those] rural secondary school students females were slightly more likely to ride with an intoxicated driver.

Legal and educational interventions have been generally ineffective in reducing alcohol use among college students (Bangert-Drowns, 1988; Goodstadt and Claeekal-John, 1984; Moskowitz, 1983, 1989). The majority of college students drink alcoholic beverages regardless of the legal drinking age. Policy changes resulting from the increase in the legal drinking age may reduce drinking opportunities available to students on campus. Therefore, students will drink off-campus. College students returning from off-campus drinking events will be forced to decide how to return home after drinking.

The purpose of the study was to determine how college students were returning home after attending bars and parties off-campus, and to determine the frequency at which they placed themselves "at-risk" for alcohol-related traffic fatalities as a result of their decision.

Methods

Subjects

. . . This population was chosen for several reasons. Students living in on-campus housing were assumed to have relatively equivalent opportunities for drinking, both on- and off-campus. Students living in on-campus housing are generally younger than those living off-campus, providing a sample population which better represents adolescents. Lastly, drawing from the residence hall population eliminated the possibility of interviewing students who live with their parents, which might limit their drinking activity or self-reports of their drinking activity.

Sample Selection

A non-purposive quota sampling technique was used to select subjects. A list of 1200 on-campus housing student telephone numbers was provided and randomized by the university computer center. The final list contained only the listing of telephone numbers, with no individual names or identification of any type. The desired sample size was approximately 400, based on a campus population of 16,000 and expected frequency of drinking and driving of 15% (Bradstock et al., 1985).

Instrumentation

The survey instrument was a 52 item questionnaire which was administered over the telephone. The survey had numerous skip patterns and varied in length of administration from 3 to 10 minutes, dependent upon whether the subject drank alcohol, had attended a bar or a party off-campus in the previous 5 to 6 weeks, and if so, which method of transportation was used to return home.

Interviews were conducted weekday afternoons and Sunday through Thursday evenings for a two-week period. Friday and Saturday evenings were excluded because it was assumed that the students who attended bars and parties off-campus were more likely to be away from their residences, resulting in potential selection bias. . . .

Because drinking and driving behavior is illegal and perceived as a threatening topic, several steps were taken to lessen the threat to the respondents. Before receiving consent for the interview, the anonymity of responses was assured. Respondents were told that their telephone number had been selected at random, and that the number would be discarded after the interview was completed. Respondents were told that the purpose of the study was "to learn about some of the health practices of college students," rather than the explicit purpose of learning about their drinking and drinking-driving behaviors. Students who reported that they were not currently living in on-campus housing were ineligible for the survey, and interviews were ended when this information was provided.

The next section of the interview consisted of questions regarding general drinking behavior; if the subject ever drank alcohol, and if so, the most frequently attended off-campus drinking location. Previous studies, as well as preliminary data collection for this study, have shown that the most frequent off-campus drinking occurs in bars or at parties. Therefore, subjects were asked about drinking behaviors at these two events. The subject was asked the number of times s/he had been to a bar since Spring Break. Spring Break was chosen as a reference point because it was a time-linked event that all students were familiar with and because of its relative recency, 5 to 6 weeks before the survey period. Also, students tend to drink more during Spring Break, and this would not be a representative indicator of drinking-driving behavior.

Following a series of questions about the most recent bar attendance, the same questions were asked about the most recent party attendance. The final section contained demographic items including college class, age, race, weight, and sex.

Operationalization of Key Variables

Alcoholic drink. Subjects were asked "How many alcoholic drinks did you have at the bar and/or party?" An alcoholic drink was defined as 12 ounces of beer, 4 ounces of wine or a shot (1 1/2 ounces) of distilled spirits.

Alcohol impaired. A subject was defined as alcohol-impaired if his/her Blood Alcohol Concentration was calculated to be 0.05% or greater. BAC was derived from the standard BAC equation based on an individual's body weight, the number of alcoholic beverages consumed and the length of the drinking period (Winek, 1983).

"At-risk". Subjects were determined to have placed themselves at-risk for an alcohol-related traffic fatality by returning home from a bar or party in a car with an alcohol-impaired driver. There were two ways that a respondent could have been defined "at-risk"; by driving a car while alcohol-impaired (DWI) or returning home with a driver who was perceived to be alcohol-impaired (RDWI).

The BAC of respondent drivers was calculated from a mathematical formula based on self-reported length of time at the event, number of drinks consumed, and the individual's body weight. This indirect method lessened the possibility of under-reporting driving while intoxicated. . . .

The measurement of frequency of riding with alcohol-impaired driver had greater opportunity for bias, however. Unlike the calculations of the BAC of the respondents, this measure was obtained based on the respondent's *perception* of the impairment of the driver and therefore many not have represented an accurate picture of alcohol-impairment. . . .

The respondents who were categorized as driving while alcohol-impaired (DWI) and those who were classified as riding with an alcohol-impaired driver (RDWI) from each drinking location were combined to form the total [number of respondents] "at-risk" for an alcohol-related traffic fatality. . . .

Survey Response

One thousand, one hundred fifty-three telephone calls were made in order to obtain 402 useable surveys. The majority of the calls were unsuccessful in making contact on the initial attempt; 58% of the attempted calls resulted in no answer or reaching an answering machine. Once students were contacted they were generally willing to assist with the survey; only six percent of the students contacted refused to answer the survey questions. Four hundred six interviews were conducted, and four surveys were discarded due to incomplete or uninterpretable answers.

Results

. . . The sample characteristics matched those of the university population on gender (p>.10), but not on age. . . . This was expected, since students living in on-campus housing tend to be younger than those living off-campus. . . .

Of the 402 respondents, 80.1% (n = 322) reported that they "ever drank alcohol." There was no association between age and ever drinking . . . and the association between gender and ever drinking was weak. . . . Since the focus of the study was on off-campus drinking at bars and parties, more specific questions about "current use" of alcohol (past 30 days) were not addressed.

As predicted, bars were the most frequent choice for off-campus drinking (48.1%), followed by friend's houses (27.1%), parties (15.0%), and parent's houses (1.9%). Two respondents most frequently drank at fraternity houses, and one was most likely to drink in a car. Seven percent said that they did not drink off-campus. Respondents were asked how many times they had attended a bar or party off-campus in the previous 5 to 6 weeks; responses ranged from 0 to 30 times.

Total 'At-Risk' for Alcohol Related Traffic Fatalities

In order to determine the total number of respondents who were "at-risk," four groups were created: students who attended at least one party but no bars, students who attended at least one bar, but no parties, students who attended neither, and students who attended both. Table 4.1 shows the distribution of each of these four groups.

Table 4.1

Student Attendance at Potential Drinking Events

		BAR ATTENDANCE		
		NO	YES	
PARTY	NO	73	50	123
ATTENDANCE	YES	73	206	279
	TOTAL	146	256	402

In total, 329 or 81.8% of the study population reported attending a potential drinking event in the 5 to 6 weeks prior to the interview. Of these 329, 176 left the setting alcohol-impaired. This represents 53.5% of the subjects who attended a potential drinking event, and 43.8% of the total sample population. Males were significantly more likely to be alcohol-impaired than females . . . and students under 21 years old were significantly more likely to be impaired than older students. . . .

The total at-risk group represents 15% of the total sample (n = 402), 18% of all respondents who reported attendance at a bar or party off-campus (n = 329), and 27% of all students who were estimated to be alcohol-impaired after attending a bar or party off-campus (n = 225). Eight subjects placed themselves "at-risk" following both their most recent bar and their most recent party attendance. The total "at-risk" group was 55% male, 92% white, 5% black and 75% under the age of 21 years old. There were no significant associations between these demographic characteristics and being "at-risk."

Regardless of whether the respondent drove or was driven home, most of the drivers were male. Males were reported as being the driver of 62.9% of the sample of bar attendees and 66.0% of the sample of party attendees.

Attendance at Bars

In response to the question, "Since Spring Break, how many times have you been to a bar off-campus?", 63.7% (n = 256) of the sample responded that they had been to a bar one or more times. There were no differences in bar attendance by gender, age or race. Less than half (45.7%) left the bar alcohol impaired.

More impaired subjects (84.8%) reported being driven home by someone else than by driving themselves home. . . . Twenty-eight percent (n = 10) of respondents were estimated to have a BAC of .05% or greater and reported that they drove themselves home (DWI). Seventy-two percent (n = 26) were RDWI: they reported being driven home from the bar by someone they perceived to have had too much to drink to drive safely.

Attendance at Parties

The same series of questions were asked about party attendance. In response to the question "Since Spring Break, how many times have you been to a party off-campus?", 69.4% (n = 279) of the sample responded that they had been to a party one or more times. Forty-six percent (n = 129) of party goers were alcohol-impaired upon leaving the party. Impaired party goers were more likely to be male (55.8%) than female. . . . Alcohol-impaired party attendees were more likely to return home in a car (58.9%) than by other means.

More alcohol-impaired subjects were driven home (81.6%) than drove themselves home from a party. Five percent (n = 14) of party goers were estimated to have a BAC of .05% or greater and reported that they drove themselves home (DWI). Seven percent (n = 19) reported being driven home from the [party] by someone they perceived to have had too much to drink to drive safely (RDWI). . . . Males were significantly more likely to engage in "at-risk" behavior (DWI or RDWI) than females. . . .

Discussion/Conclusion

This study was cross-sectional in design and therefore reflected drinking-driving behavior for only the *most recent* party or bar attendance. For the majority of respondents, the potential drinking event occurred on a Friday or Saturday evening. Therefore, this study provides evidence that, on a given weekend, one in six college students who attend a bar or party away from their campus residence place themselves at-risk for having an alcohol-related traffic fatality by driving while impaired or riding with an impaired driver. Although higher incidence of both riding with an alcohol impaired driver and driving while alcohol impaired have been reported in other studies (Beck and Summons, 1987; Farrow, 1985; Swisher and Bibeau, 1986) the results represent lifetime prevalence and are therefore not comparable. . . .

Males were more likely than females to report that they had consumed a sufficient number of drinks over a specified time to reach an estimated BAC of at least 0.05%. Males were also more likely than females to drive themselves home from a party while impaired (DWI). Parenthetically, male respondents were more likely to drive home from either bars or parties than were females, who often reported being driven home by a male. Prevention efforts should focus on males, not only as a population targeted to receive education, but as a focus for peer resistance strategies. Normative prescriptions demonstrate that males tend to be the primary drivers, particularly in dating situations. Young women may be reluctant to assert themselves in drinking-driving situations. Thus, it appears that education in peer resistance strategies for women, specifically related to gender issues in drinking and/or driving situations is warranted.

A larger number of students rode home with someone who they perceived to have been impaired (RDWI) than drove home while impaired (DWI). This suggests that students may be more concerned about personal legal risks (i.e. being arrested for driving under the influence of alcohol), than the prevention of injury to self or others. It has been suggested that intervention or assistance by others may be helpful in preventing drinking-driver situations (Monto, et al., 1992). In addition to education regarding the dangers of riding with an impaired driver, students need to learn skills and techniques to avoid RDWI situations.

When asked why they returned home with an impaired driver, many students remarked that they felt there were few, if any, alternatives. One of the most common responses was "because that is how I got [to the event]". . . .

A continuing debate among college and university administrators, as well as citizens of college towns, is the issue of restricting bars to a location beyond a one to five mile radius of the campus. The findings from this study do not support such a policy, particularly as an attempt to reduce the number of alcohol-impaired drivers. The majority of students who walked home from a bar or party reported doing so because it was close and convenient, and many who rode home in a car did so because it was either too far to walk or they saw no other alternatives. A distance policy would be likely to increase rather than decrease the prevalence of alcohol-impaired driving injuries and fatalities.

A weakness of this study is the non-random sampling techniques that [were] used to select subjects. Although the telephone numbers were randomly selected from all student telephone numbers, only those students who were in their dormitory rooms at the time of the telephone calls were included. It is possible that students who were not at home were attending off [campus] drinking events, resulting in an underestimation of at-risk behavior. There are many reasons for students not to be in their dorm rooms that are not alcohol related, however. . . .

References

Anda, R.F., P.L. Remington, and Williamson, D.F. (1986). A sobering perspective on a lower blood alcohol limit. *Journal of the American Medical Association*, 256, 3213.

Bangert-Drowns, R.L. (1988). The effects of school-based substance abuse education—a meta-analysis. *Journal of Drug Education*, 18, 243–264.

Beck, H.W. and Summons.T. G. (1987). The social context of drinking among high school drinking drivers. *American Journal of Drug and Alcohol Abuse*, 13, 181–198.

Bradstock, M.K., J.S. Marks, M.R. Forman, E.M. Gentry, G.C. Hogelin, and F.L. Trowbridge.

(1985). The Behavioral Risk Factor Surveys: III Chronic Heavy Alcohol Use in the United States. *American Journal of Preventive Medicine*, 1, 15–20.

Farina, A.J. (1988). *Effects of low doses of alcohol on driving skills: A review of the evidence.* (Technical Report, DOT-HS-807-280) National Traffic Safety Administration.

Farrow, J.A. (1985). Drinking and driving behaviors of 16- to 19-year-olds. *Journal of Studies on Alcohol*, 46, 369–374.

Goodstadt, M. and A. Claeekal-John. (1984). Alcohol education programs for university students: A review of their effectiveness. *The International Journal of the Addictions*, 13, 1307–1317.

Johnston, L.D., O'Malley, P.M. and Bachman. J.G. (1991). *Drug use among american high school seniors, college students and young adults, 1975–1990.* (DHHS Publication No. ADM 91–1835). Rockville, MD: National Institute on Drug Abuse.

Maddox, G.L. (1970). *The Domesticated Drug: Drinking among Collegians.* New Haven: College and University Press Publishers.

Monto, M.A., Newcomb, M.D., Rabow, J., and Hernandez, A. C. R. (1992). Social status and drunk-driving intervention. *Journal of Studies on Alcohol*, 53, 63–68.

Moskowitz, J.M. (1983). Preventing adolescent substance abuse through drug education. *National Institute on Drug Abuse Research Monograph Series*, 47, 233–249.

Moskowitz, J.M. (1989). The Primary prevention of alcohol problems: A Critical review of the research literature. *Journal of Studies on Alcohol*, 50, 54–88.

National Institute on Drug Abuse. (1987). *National trends in drug use and related factors among American high school students and young adults, 1975–1986.* (DHHS Publication No. ADM 87–1535). Washington, D.C.: U.S. Government Printing Office.

Nusbaumer, M.R. and Zusman, M. E. (1981). Autos, alcohol, and adolescence: Forgotten concerns and overlooked linkages. *Journal of Drug Education*, 11, 167–178.

Perkins, R. and P. Berkowitz. (1986). Perceiving the community norms of alcohol use among students: Some research implications for campus alcohol education programming. *International Journal of the Addictions*, 21, 961–976.

Sarvela, P.D., Newcomb, P. R., and Duncan, D. F. (1988). Drinking and driving among rural youth. *Health Education Research: Theory and Practice*, 3,197–201.

Sarvela, P.D., Pape, D. J., Odulana, J., and Bajracharya, S. M. (1990). Drinking, drug use, and driving among rural midwestern youth. *Journal of School Health*, 60, 215–219.

Swisher, J.D. and Bibeau, D. (1986). Who's driving home? Assessing adolescent drinking and driving." *Journal of Alcohol and Drug Education*, 32, 25–30.

Straus, R. and Bacon, S. D. (1953). *Drinking in College.* New Haven: Yale University Press.

U.S. Department of Health, Education, and Welfare. (1979). *Healthy People: The Surgeon General's Report on Health Promotion and Disease Prevention.* (DHEW Publication No. ADM 79-55071A). Washington, D.C.: U.S. Government Printing Office.

Vaughn, M. (1983). The normative structures of college students and patterns of drinking behavior. *Sociological Focus*, 16, 181–193.

Vingilis, E. and Salutin, L. (1980). A prevention programme for drinking driving. *Accident Analysis and Prevention*, 12, 267–274.

Winek, C.L. (1983). Blood alcohol levels: Factors affecting predictions. *Trial: The national legal magazine*, 19, 38–47.

Reprinted from: Laura K. McCormick and John Ureda, "Who's Driving? College Students' Choices of Transportation Home after Drinking." In *The Journal of Primary Prevention*, 16(1), pp. 103–115. Copyright © 1995 by Human Sciences Press, Inc. Reprinted by permission. ✦

Part II

Sexual Deviations

Sex is a part of most people's lives. It is something people think about a lot, even if they know little about alternative forms of sexuality or sexual activity. Although they see and hear about sex all the time—on television, in music, in advertising, even on the news—most Americans have a limited view of the range of sexual behaviors that exist in the world. And, they hold strong opinions about what constitutes "normal sex."

The articles in this section all look at forms of sexual activity frequently thought of as deviant, even though research shows that some of these behaviors are quite common. Whether the behavior involves anonymous homosexual encounters, pornography, prostitution, sexual violence, or sex with children, all of the articles in this section point out ways that people's assumptions and definitions of sex and deviance vary.

In the first article, Richard Tewksbury examines how men "cruise" public parks to find other men with whom to have sex. The article suggests that many forms of deviance are carried out in everyday settings. But, unless a person knows about how such activity is transacted or how people who practice such behavior communicate with each other, he or she might never know explicitly what is going on. Tewksbury shows us that subcultures are based on shared definitions and on how people interpret specific behaviors and signals.

The next two articles look at the content of two commonly used forms of pornography:

recorded telephone fantasies and X-rated videos. Both articles question whether common assumptions about the content of these media are accurate. The authors have found that, in some respects, these assumptions are accurate, but in others they are not. Of course, the same is true for almost all forms of deviance.

In the first article, Jack Glascock and Robert LaRose examine the content of dial-a-porn recordings. Contrary to common belief, they find no evidence of violence against women. Instead, in cases where violence is portrayed, the woman is dominant. In the second article, Gloria Cowan and her colleagues examine the content of X-rated videos and find that over half contain violence against women. Although the two sets of researchers found different levels and styles of violence, these two articles suggest that different forms of pornography cater to men with different interests and tastes. That's how most of the world works, though, so we shouldn't be surprised for it to be the case with pornography as well.

The role of definitions in establishing what is deviant is central to Jody Miller and Martin D. Schwartz's article on the sexual violence experienced by street prostitutes. Most prostitutes find their work fraught with violence, including sexual assault. Even though most people think of rape and sexual assault as deviant, they also think of prostitution as deviant. The result, as Miller and Schwartz explain, is that most people, including law enforcement officials, react to prostitutes' claims of rape on the basis of the fact that these women are prostitutes. Consequently, they refuse to define the victimization as rape. The myth that promiscuous women cannot be raped clearly guides most people's views of a prostitute's claim of having been sexually assaulted.

Finally, the last article in this section questions common assumptions and "knowledge" about sexual forms of deviance. Edward Brongersma challenges many of our ideas about adult men who have relationships with young boys. Brongersma argues that an objective understanding of boy-lovers is difficult to achieve, in part because of the stigma attached to the topic. The facts are that most people think sex with children is wrong and that every state has outlawed such activity. But, Brongersma contends that our biases make it difficult for us to see aspects of sex with children that boy-lovers think are positive. Brongersma raises an important issue about the scientific study of deviance: If science is, in fact, objective, why is it that those who study boy-lovers focus solely on the negative aspects of the relationships? Whether you agree or disagree with what Brongersma has to say about sex with children, he does raise important issues about

social definitions of deviance and the ways they can influence objective understanding of the social world. When we look at any type of deviance research, it is important to consider whether it is objective or biased by cultural beliefs.

Taken together, these five articles reveal some of the intricacies of various forms of alternative sexualities and sexual behaviors, and they clearly show that people's assumptions and definitions of "normal sex" and deviance are important factors in how they view the world. As you read these articles, think about how shared ideas and definitions influence your thinking about deviance. For example, what behaviors count as "having sex"? Is anything involving the genitals of two or more persons a sexual experience? What role should sex play in people's lives? Are there normal and abnormal reasons for having sex? What are the advantages and disadvantages of expressing one's sexuality in different ways? Is there really one "best" way to express sexuality? You may find that your answers to these questions change as you read the articles in this section. Or, perhaps you'll gain a better understanding of why you believe as you do. Either way, these articles offer important lessons about deviant and nondeviant behavior. ✦

5

Cruising for Sex in Public Places: The Structure and Language of Men's Hidden, Erotic Worlds

Richard Tewksbury

Tewksbury provides a look at members of one common, often-overlooked deviant subculture—men who seek anonymous male sexual partners—and how they go about engaging in sexual acts in public places. Many deviant worlds have their own modes of communication, based on a need to avoid detection by outsiders. This article shows that the study of deviants and deviance can help us understand that all social actors structure interactions.

To date, studies of interpersonal, especially sexual, attraction have focused almost entirely on heterosexual relationships (but see Ross and Paul 1992). Although these relationships are important to understand, such studies are too narrow for practical use in contemporary society. Understanding how and why men may be attracted to other men, or women to other women, can lead to important conclusions regarding social structures, public health, marketing, legal implications, and daily work and leisure activities.

The mere fact that some sexual settings are homosocial necessarily leads to expectations for varying sexual scripts based on differing values, desires, and expectations. Men are re-

puted, and shown in the research literature, to be more likely than women to have engaged in casual sex (Herold and Mewhinney 1993) and to be more willing to accept a sexual invitation from an unknown other (Clark and Hatfield 1989; Clark 1990). With this in mind, an examination of the means by which men who have sex with men (MSMs) pursue and carry through with casual sexual encounters via cruising—seeking sexual partners, often in public places—becomes an important and socially relevant topic of research.

The Study of Sex Between Men

The study of MSMs is not necessarily a study of gay culture, but simply the study of . . . men who happen to engage in sex with other men (whether or not they are sexually active with women as well). There is a well developed body of literature that has documented that men of varying sexual identities . . . do engage in sex with other men (Kinsey, Pomeroy, and Martin 1948; Humphreys 1970; Sundholm 1973; Corzine and Kirby 1977; Delph 1978; Donnelly 1981; Weatherford 1986; Gray 1988; Desroches 1990; Earl 1990; Tewksbury 1990; Doll et al. 1992).

Although we know that large numbers of men do engage—at least at some point in their lives—in sex with other men, we have only limited knowledge regarding how men initiate such encounters. What research we do have available typically focuses on one specific type of sexual arena; the present research adds to this aggregation by explicating the processes and perceptions of participants in a previously overlooked sexual arena—the urban public park.

The present research also expands our current understandings by drawing on a research method not yet fully implemented in investigations of public sexual arenas: formal, in-depth interviews. Earlier researchers have examined male-male, public, and anonymous sexual encounters but have typically approached such topics from a detached position. Humphreys's (1970) classic work stands as one exception among these pieces; however, Humphreys's means of obtaining interview data on involved men was covert and as such did not directly address men's experiences in casual, same-sex sexual encounters. Other important exceptions to the norm of detached observation and analysis are Lee's (1979) and Kamel's (1983) reflections on gay sadism/masochism (S&M) and Styles's (1979) and Brodsky's (1993) analyses of social organization in gay bathhouses and sex clubs. Most common among the other approaches to the topic have been the utilization of law enforcement surveillance techniques (Gray 1988; Desroches 1990; Maynard 1994), observations supplemented with informal interviews (Ponte 1974; Weinberg and Williams 1975; Corzine and Kirby 1977), and simple observation (Delph 1978; Tewksbury 1990).

The discussion that follows relies on indepth interviews with eleven men who have had sex with men in public, anonymous encounters. . . . The following discussion yields an advanced understanding of the behaviors and strategies men employ while cruising in public places. . . .

Cruising for Sex Partners

In order for an individual to participate in public cruising activities it is, of course, first necessary for him to know that such activities occur, and to know where, when, and how such activities occur. Within urban gay communities, the fact that cruising and public sex occur is relatively common knowledge. Locations where cruising takes place are basic kernels of subcultural knowledge, often including specifics about particular "types" of men one may expect to find in particular settings (Lee 1979; Brodsky 1993). However, in the rare instance that a man does not know where or when he may find cruising activity, there are annually published guides to public sex locations for most American urban areas. Therefore, the where issue is addressed, leaving a man to answer only when and how.

Both sexual scripting (Gagnon and Simon 1973; Simon and Gagnon 1986) and imaging (Kamel 1983) are important means by which individuals manage presentations of self, which in turn shape and direct interactional (especially sexual) possibilities. . . . Depending on the imaging practices and scripts pursued by setting participants, the encounters among men vary in form, degree, intensity, and success.

The playing out of sexual scripts and imaging practices occur everywhere in society, but [is] most common (and obvious) in subcultural locations known for cruising and sexual activity. The process of cruising has a long history in gay male communities. The perpetuation of such behavior is so well known, and so commonly practiced, that one theorist has been lead to critique cruising as a "ritual" (Pollack 1993).

Cruising can be a dangerous activity. Media and anecdotal accounts abound about violence and blackmail arising from public sex and the search for it. Consequently, many MSMs seek out protected environments for casual . . . sex, places where access can be controlled and victimization potential limited. Such controlled environments—sex clubs, baths, and some gay bars—not only function to provide a sense of protection from invading cultural outsiders, but also allow for transformations of sexual and sex-seeking activities within the controlled boundaries. . . . [T]he virtual absence of access control and less authoritative means of enforcing situational norms [in public parks] means the structure and process of cruising public places is significantly different from the sex-seeking behaviors of other, more restricted, cruising locales. Understanding the men who cruise for sex with other men in public places, and how the ritual is performed, are the next topics of this discussion.

Learning the Ropes

Once a man seeking to locate other men interested in anonymous sexual encounters identifies a location, all that he needs to do is go to the location and, as Steve succinctly explained, "just start walking, it'll be there. At least somebody there is waiting to service your every need." In other words, even the naive, inexperienced cruiser can expect to engage a willing sexual partner. Where the individual encounters challenges and has a need for subcultural knowledge is in the area of facilitating his likelihood for achieving a successful and safe encounter. As Lee (1979) has elaborated, concerns about finding structured and protected settings and establishing means to negotiate encounters are central to the experience of sexual encounters with anonymous or casual-acquaintance others. These are abilities and skills that must be learned.

Although public park cruising locales are widely known within the subculture of an urban area's MSMS, such locations cannot be approached as if everyone found there [were] interested in sex with everyone and anyone else. Obviously, not all individuals or even everyone in public parks are in search of sexual encounters. Despite the apparent openness and unrestricted nature of the sexual activity, there are norms that regulate activities. Many of these norms may appear to be simple courtesies, maintaining a sense of civility within the setting. Additionally, and more importantly, norms structure activities and foster avenues by which men may screen potential partners for safety and enter into familiar negotiation patterns. As Kirk, a well-practiced cruiser, explains,

> You don't walk straight up to someone and put your hand in their crotch, that's for sure. That's a little forward. You don't assume that just because the other person's there to have sex, that they want to have sex with you .

It should be noted, however, that many men do report norm-violating experiences including things such as having another simply walk up and place a hand on their crotch. Such instances, where sexual receptiveness is assumed and contact is immediately initiated, do occur. However, typically men methodically seek out and negotiate sexual interactions, and only then perhaps enter into a sexual exchange. Regardless of whether an encounter is methodically negotiated or a surprise contact, both men are allowed to withdraw quickly, easily, and without negative consequence, at any time (Weinberg and Williams 1975; Brown 1976; Lee 1979; Tewksbury 1990; Brodsky 1993). Simply because sexual contact is initiated does not mean that it will necessarily result in both men's (or either individual's) ejaculation. When a man wishes to remove himself from a sexual interaction, he does just that. Replacing one's clothing and walking away are acceptable, although not always desirable, to one's anonymous sex partners.

How does one learn the norms of a public sex arena? Explicit instruction from a friend who is knowledgeable may be one way for some men to learn how to cruise. Or, simply being present and observing the actions and interactions of others may be the most fruitful method. Or, as has been the case for some, learning may occur as a result of violating the unknown norms and being subsequently sanctioned. To successfully learn via observation, and to successfully complete a sexual encounter, the trick is, as Vince puts it, to "look inconspicuous."

Meticulous scrutiny of co-present others is generally believed not only to be the key to locating desirable, willing sexual partners, but also to serve as a screening device to assess the situation for risk. Such a practice is by no means unique to public sex arenas. What may be unique here, though, is that the use of such an activity serves both to facilitate seeking and to assess the setting for possible threats to safety. If such a canvassing reveals the presence of men of dubious appearance, activities can be restricted, or the individual can safely retreat from the perceived threat.

Characteristics of Men Found in Public Sex Arenas

The men found in public cruising areas are, according to Steve, "just your average build, average body, average hair, average, average. Very average-looking." In short, the men in public sex arenas run the full spectrum from highly unattractive to attractive, old to young, poor to wealthy, short to tall, and so forth. Stating this position more completely is Matt, who says cruising men are not stereotypical gay men, but rather:

> You're finding trolls, you're finding young adults, you're finding married men, you're finding truckers, you're finding the whole spectrum. I mean, that's who you would find in any cruising spots, I guess. . . These are often people that don't want to admit their homosexuality yet.

Standing on the edge of social acceptability, and on the edge of being "out," the men who cruise in public parks (and in other public sex arenas) do not fit common stereotypes of gay men. Neither do men in public cruising areas adorn themselves in "costumes" common to other gay settings (Lee, 1979; Kamel, 1983; Brodsky, 1993). Cruising men are not necessarily feminine, highly fashionable, flamboyant, or hypermasculine. If anything, it can be expected that cruising men fit more closely with stereotypes of "traditional masculine" presentations of self. This is clearly seen in Jack's definition of men in the park:

> They are not your average queen. They're not the little faggot down the street with the loose wrist and the lisp and the high heels that walks like they're stepping on eggshells. You will very seldom find that person in the park, because the park intones to them more masculinity.

For some, the more masculine nature of cruising for sex outdoors might suggest a parallel with ideals of heterosexuality. This may stand as one reason, together with the setting's norms of anonymity and quick sexual consumption, that all men interviewed believed a significant percentage of those who cruise in public are self-identified heterosexuals. Such "men who have sex with men" are more likely to venture into the more easily permeable setting of the public park than they are to cross the boundaries that maintain more recognizable gay settings (such as gay bars and baths).

This evidence suggests, then, that cruising public parks is something that is looked upon as, at best, marginal to the gay community. Although a sizable minority (or, perhaps a slight majority) of gay men may at one time or another seek out anonymous sex in a public sex arena, this is not an activity that is commonly discussed openly and honestly among gay men. Rather, to be known as a man who cruises in the park is to be, as Albert claims from personal experience, severely stigmatized. In his experiences, Albert says he has learned, "Oh God, everybody that goes to the park, if you are seen at the park you are automatically tagged a scuzz. You are a real slut."

All of the men interviewed for this project believe that most, if not nearly all, MSMs at one time or another cruise in public sex arenas. This universality accounts for the perception of participating men as both diverse and "average." Within the gay community, however, such activity remains stigmatized. Due in part to the increasing awareness of the health risks of having multiple anonymous partners, gay community norms have moved toward lower levels of acceptance of multiple anonymous sexual contacts. Rather than adhering to the very expressive sexual freedom perspective that characterized many urban gay communities in the 1970s and early 1980s, gay men in the 1990s are less apt to embrace sexual excesses. Consequently, those men who regularly engage in anonymous public sex are likely to be stigmatized.

When Is Cruising Most Productive?

Knowing that cruising in public sex arenas is not a highly respected or respectable activity, men clearly guide the temporal aspects of cruising by a combination of utilitarian and self-protective interests. The utilitarian interests are seen in efforts to be present when other, similarly interested men will also be present. The self-protective interests are the efforts not to be present when "outsiders" are present; in this way, men seek to maximize the effects of screening procedures and to provide opportunities for sexual encounters that are not likely to be interrupted by the "unwise." In practice, most cruising activity in public parks occurs at night. Although men do visit the park during daylight hours, and may meet and leave with other men, actual consummation of relations most often is an after dark activity. This is a practical practice, for, as Kirk says, "If you're intent on having sex in the park, yes, it is at night. . . . That's your cover; people don't see you." Darkness facilitates the anonymity of the setting and thus the sexual activity.

Minimizing the likelihood of intrusions (including arrest) means that cruising rarely takes place during hours when large numbers of "straight" people are using the park. Often referred to as "family time," these hours (afternoons, early evenings, weekend daylight hours) are perceived as both too dangerous for sexual activity and simply inappropriate. Marc explained this saying, "A bad time is when, well, family time. . . . It's our criteria. Family time is kind of an etiquette, you just don't do it. There is etiquette out there."

Even during the hours when supposedly "polite" men do not have sex where they may be detected, cruising does occur. Such hours host sex between men, but in more secluded areas, places where "straight" people are unlikely to venture. Daytime sexual relations, when they occur, are most likely to be consummated deep in the woods, or in locations removed from the easily accessed regions of the park. In other words, especially when running increased risks of detection, active attempts are made to "hide" sexual activities. Delph (1978), discussing how men transform innocuous public settings into erotic oases, described prime locations as those having distinct boundaries and structural features that help acknowledge the approach of others. Out-of-sight, deep-in-the-woods locations offer these same attractions to men who transform public parks into erotic oases.

Therefore, both time of day and season (in most climates) influence the structure and amount of cruising that occurs in public parks. In the Midwest, late fall through early spring is a very slow time for cruising; weather turns cold, leaves fall from trees, and the setting loses its veils of secrecy. However, even on cold, sunlit days, at least a few men are likely to be cruising in the park. The setting, both physically and temporally, may facilitate or complicate cruising, but it does not strictly govern the who, when, where, or how.

Contacting and Contracting With Anonymous Sexual Partners

As outlined above, cruising for anonymous sexual partners in public sex arenas is a subcultural phenomenon that requires knowledge of locations, comprehension of norms, and often a period of time during which skills are acquired and refined. However, what remains to be discussed is the crux of the matter: the process by which men actually identify mutually interested others and the ways they communicate and negotiate sexual interactions. The "information game" (Goffman 1959) is a process by which individuals carefully seek to negotiate a mutual understanding of the situation: involved others and mutual needs, wants, and expectations. It is this process that cruising men recreate each and every time they return to the park and pursue a new sexual partner.

What is perhaps the most notable characteristic of interactions in pursuit of sexual relations in public sex arenas is the lack of verbal communications. As seen above, cover of darkness, bushes, and other obstacles to visibility are desirable elements of an erotic oasis, in part because they provide means to shield identities, as well as activities. Nonverbal communications are also, at least partially, a shield against identity disclosures. When one speaks, one conveys more information than the mere content of one's words. If the verbal aspects of communication are removed, so too may some of the additional identity elements be removed from an individual's interactions. Consequently, the great majority of cruising activities found in public sex arenas are conducted under the veil of silence.

Because verbal conversations are severely limited, and due to the subcultural stigmas associated with cruising public parks, men interested in other men they find in the park have restricted means to learn of others' sexual and social reputations. Whereas in other settings men may ask their associates about particular others, this is not generally possible in the arena of the public park. Additionally, because of both the very fluid nature of the park's patrons and their preference for after-dark cruising, identifying others can often be a very difficult task. Therefore, there may be only minimal assurances that a sexual partner is not prone to violence or to exposing others to social and physical dangers.

On those rare occasions when verbal conversation is used to establish contact, it is brief and presented in ambiguous fashion. One man may greet another, or make a simple request (ask for the time, a match, or directions to a landmark). Such opening comments allow for a quick appraisal of another man, in a very low-risk form of contact. Once a man is deduced as willing to speak, the conversation starter will ask some type of leading, or double-meaning, question. This is the way that Adam makes initial contact with men in the park. Adam says he likes to feel as if he knows *something* about the men with whom he has anonymous sexual encounters, so he always asks others a few questions.

> I might say something about any subject that I knew would be of common interest . . . or, I'd ask if you were driving through enjoying the day, or looking? Everybody knows what that means! If you're driving through enjoying the day, or you're not interested, you'll tell me. That's a comfortable way out, and not being rude. If you are interested, you're going to tell me that you are—you are looking.

As explained earlier, withdrawing from an unwanted interaction is acceptable, and provided for, in men's homosocial, sexual environments. Ambiguous questions not only facilitate the negotiation of sexual encounters but can also provide for easy withdrawal from undesirable potential encounters.

The way that men communicate their interest in other men, and contact and contract with others, is via five primary modes of non-verbal communication: eye contact, use of personal space, body language, subtle forms of touching (of both themselves and others), and movement through the park in pursuit or in tandem with other men. Non-verbal communication is the rule in erotic oases (Delph 1978; Donnelly 1981; Weatherford 1986; Tewksbury 1990). The "language" of such a subcultural location is well summarized by Ted, who explains the way men who cruise public parks communicate, saying,

> It has its own language, and you don't—well, I'm sure I don't know all of it. But what I have come to learn and be able to recognize is that there is a subliminal language to it that is not words. It's certain actions, certain movement. . . . This is something I've never really put words to until now.

To understand the language is to use it while not needing to think consciously about it. It is only when one develops a fluency in the "subliminal language" of the public sex arena that successful cruising is likely to occur. The way men communicate while cruising is indeed a language in its own right, just as is any patterned form of communication that requires study, skill, and practice. . . .

With verbal communication essentially absent, men need to have means of getting the attention of others, as well as a means of acknowledging the call for attention of another. This is the principal function of eye contact. As Goffman (1977:309) believed, "the male's assessing act—his ogling—constitutes the first move in the courtship process." Eye contact is the main means by which contact is made. Contact is not simply looking at a man, but looking consistently into his eyes and holding his gaze. The "prolonged" look, directly into the eyes of another, which might be considered deviant in ordinary, daily interactions, is the means by which men greet one another and quickly determine whether sufficient mutual interest exists to continue with increasingly intimate contact.

. . . Duane, who knows that police regularly visit the parks undercover, says that when he is cruising in the park,

> Eye contact for me is ultimate. By being able to catch a person's eye and the way that—well, I can tell whether they're really comfortable or not. Even cops aren't comfortable enough to hold your gaze, you know—I mean 'cause they are just not to the point of doing it. That's one of the biggest clues for me.

Another way of looking at the functions of eye contact while cruising is offered by Matt, a self-described "long experienced" public sex arena cruiser: "Eye contact is the way you invite someone to participate with you. . . . It's not just looking at someone, but like *really* looking at someone, and them really looking at you."

Eye contact is the contact point, the initial way to investigate another man's subcultural experience, and perhaps motivations. Eye contact can open the door to continued, increasingly focused, sexually directed interactions. The eyes serve as the filter for determining which others in the setting may be appropriate, interested, and suitable partners, with whom one may wish to move into the initial contracting stage. As amount and intensity of eye contact increase, so too do interactants' personal investments in continued interactions (Iizuka 1992).

There are two general, and related, means by which increasingly focused interactions are pursued. Communicating an interest in contracting is put forth either through one man entering another man's "personal space" (see Hall 1959) or through body language signaling a sexual interest.

Body language—positioning oneself within the setting, posing in the line of another's vision, and contorting the body so as to present or emphasize certain parts of it—can communicate meaningful messages. Many men maintain that even though they don't speak with others, "body language says a lot." Or, more specifically, as Ted explains it,

> There are several forms of body language. If a person is standing facing toward you and they're moving about in place. . . . Fondling himself, making it apparent that they're interested in some kind of sexual contact. Maybe by fondling themselves directly at you, so that is something that they perceive is what you're looking for. Their intention is pretty clear and very tight. Then that followed with a smile.

Body language often involves motions and signals. As attention is maintained between men, these signals frequently involve touching oneself. Touching, stroking, and massaging parts of one's own body are taken to communicate interests (often specific sexual interests). Rubbing one's chest or lips, or stroking the inside of one's thighs or, most obviously, stroking, massaging, or caressing one's genitals (usually, but not always, through one's clothing) communicates sexual interest, and for most men is taken as an invitation for sexual contact. Body rubbing is done in conjunction with eye contact. To create the most direct message possible, a man moves, rubs, or serially poses while maintaining what he hopes is a mutually held gaze.

Body language also means presenting one's body in what is self-perceived as an at-tractive manner. Often, especially during warm weather, careful attention is given to the apparel a man wears to the public sex arena. Clothing not only functions as costume, but ideally for the cruising man also provides easy access to critical sexual body parts. Ease and speed of removal and replacement are important. More important, though, is the way that clothing accentuates what a man perceives as his appearance strengths. On occasion men will be seen in cruising areas wearing very revealing clothing (e.g., bathing suits, leather accessories, workout clothing). The intention of men so attired is presumably obvious to others, both those cruising and not. Among many men in public sex arenas, "there's this whole mentality of putting yourself on display," says Duane. Being on display can be dangerous, though; this is why many gay men prefer cruising in controlled access environments (e.g., bars, baths, and clubs) where costuming can be beneficial to one's displays but only minimally dangerous (Brodsky 1993).

In addition to the presentation of oneself, communicating a sexual interest in another man involves personal space invasions and perhaps subtle, "accidental" forms of contact. When one man allows himself to be touched in any way by another man and does not indicate a dislike or unwillingness to have it continue or occur again, an agreement to progress in the form and intensity of touching is presumed. Vince explained that when he cruises for a sexual partner in the park, after making eye contact with a man he next moves to

> invasion of personal space. Another thing after that is accidentally brushing up against him and neither one of you moves away. That's important, 'cause that dude not moving shows a willingness to be touched.

Touching, posing, placing oneself in another's line of vision, gazing at and receiving a return gaze: these are the tools of communication men in public sex arenas use to replace verbal exchanges when contacting and contracting for exchanges.

Intervening between the initial eye contact and an eventual sexual contact are a period of time and a series of interactions in which men pursue each other (both literally and figuratively). The pursuit involves men following each other through the park, whether on foot or in their automobiles, testing one another's resolve and commitment to an exchange. For many men, this phase takes on the quality of a game, or becomes a literal "hunt" and conquest series of interactions. Jack, who believes himself to be among the most skillful and experienced public park cruisers in his city, related the following description of "the chase":

> It's more like playing a game. Basically, that's what it is with a lot of them, it's a big game. You see somebody, you walk by, they'll take off and you follow them from one end to the other, chasing each other. If you give up and turn around, then they'll start chasing after you. That will happen as much as seven or ten times; it's a two-way game, until the connection is made.

The rules of the "chase" game are fairly simple. If you make initial contact with someone that you are interested in, you either follow him or position yourself so that he can easily follow you. The chase is not supposed to be simply one man following another to a location where they have sex, however. Rather, the chase is a test of each man's dedication to the process and the possibility of a sexual encounter with his chosen other.

Many times the chase lasts for extended periods of time, perhaps 2 hours or more. During the course of this time, men report, they are consistently strategizing ways to read the intentions of the other and to seek ways to draw the other man into making a more assertive advance. Adam, a friend who often goes to the park with Jack, but who always cruises alone, describes how his mind is constantly at work strategizing while playing the "chase game." According to Adam, after making an initial move to follow a man with whom he has already made contact, his mind turns to:

> The next move is his, what will he do? Will he go back the other way? Will he at that point take the initiative and come up to me, or will he pass me and go down the path 10 or 15 feet and stop? If he does that, it's quite obvious he knows how to play the

game. He's interested. He knows that second stop on his part has told me something. . . . Then I know. He already knows, because I've already stopped. I was first following him, and I stopped to give him a chance to follow me. If he's not interested, he'll do something else. He'll go the other way or do something that will tell me that. It's all just a game!

In the game, the role with the greater degree of both control and prestige is the role of the pursued. To be followed is to be complimented. Men who are sought after may, in fact, experience situations when more than one individual follows them. In such a situation the matter is complicated when only one of the others involved in the game is desirable to the sought-after man.

Throughout the chase game, communications remain on the non-verbal level, and they may often include heavy doses of eye contact. Whenever a man is being followed, he needs to be aware constantly of whether his pursuer is still in pursuit. This means both visually checking behind him and carefully listening for the other man.

Obviously, to be successful at the chase game requires skills, yet not every man in the park possesses these skills. They can be learned but frequently may require numerous futile (and therefore discouraging) forays. However, with time, dedication, and careful observation (if not direct instruction from a friend) . . . a man can become a skillful player of the game.

Conclusion

The processes employed by men who have anonymous sexual encounters with men in public places are culturally created and reinforced phenomena. The idea that men seek out and consummate sexual relationships with anonymous others, while perhaps shocking or disturbing to some, actually carries many similarities to the processes by which men and women seek out both sexual and long-term relationship partners.

Regardless of the gender of those involved, partner-seeking activities require that an individual be aware of the locations where potential partners can be located, have a sense of when others are likely to be in these locations, understand the basic scripts for normative interactional patterns, and be at least somewhat fluent in the language and dialects of cruising. Where differences become apparent is in the fact that gender-based roles are altered, and only men are present. Rather than having attraction based on gender differences, these men must establish differences in roles, expectations, and desires among potential partners. Communication among and between those seeking partners must be clear and complete.

However, because men who cruise for male sexual partners in public settings must be ever attentive to the possibilities (and likely negative consequences) that other men present may not be seeking sex, common communication modes present obstacles. Therefore, the process of communication is tracked into a (typically) prolonged, carefully navigated cruise through double-entendres and ambiguous non-verbal statements. Communication modes include body language, movement throughout the setting, eye contact, and subtle forms of gestures and touch. In essence, men seeking male sex partners in anonymous public settings employ some of the traditionally feminine means of communication. The homosocial nature of the interactional environment necessitates reconfiguration of gendered interactions.

The language of cruising serves as a gatekeeping mechanism for the subcultural setting of the public sex arena. As an open, yet carefully guarded, subcultural setting, a closed set of discreditable (Goffman 1963) men are provided an environment that meets their needs and desires. Although open, the setting does provide some degree of territorial bounding as well as a potential "cover" for men's presence.

References

Brodsky, Joel I. 1993. "The Mineshaft: A Retrospective Ethnography" *Journal of Homosexuality* 24:233–251.

Brown, Rita Mae. 1976. "Strangers in Paradise." *Body Politic* (no volume):23.

Clark, Russell III. 1990. "The Impact of AIDS on Gender Differences in Willingness to Engage in Casual Sex." *Journal of Applied Social Psychology* 20:771–782.

Clark, Russell III, and Elaine Hatfield. 1989. "Gender Differences in Receptivity to Sexual Offers." *Journal of Psychology and Human Sexuality* 2:39–55.

Corzine, Jay, and Richard Kirby 1977. "Cruising the Truckers: Sexual Encounters in a Highway Rest Area." *Urban Life* 6:171–192.

Delph, Edward. 1978. *The Silent Community: Public Homosexual Encounters*. Beverly Hills, CA: Sage.

Desroches, Frederick. 1990. "Tearoom Trade: A Research Update." *Qualitative Sociology* 13:39–61.

Doll, Lynda, Lyle Petersen, Carol White, Eric Johnson, John Ward, and the Blood Donor Study Group. 1992. "Homosexually and Non-homosexually Identified Men Who Have Sex With Men: A Behavioral Comparison." *The Journal of Sex Research* 29:1–14.

Donnelly, Peter. 1981. "Running the Gauntlet: The Moral Order of Pornographic Movie Theaters." *Urban Life* 10:239–264.

Earl, William. 1990. "Married Men and Safe Sex Activity: A Field Study on HIV Risk Among Men Who Do Not Identify as Gay or Bisexual." *Journal of Sex and Marital Therapy* 16:251–257.

Gagnon, John, and William Simon. 1973. *Sexual Conduct: The Social Sources of Human Sexuality*. Chicago: Aldine.

Goffman, Erving. 1959. *The Presentation of Self in Everyday Life*. Garden City, NY: Doubleday.

Goffman, Erving. 1963. *Stigma: Notes on the Management of Spoiled Identity*. Englewood Cliffs, NJ: Prentice-Hall.

Goffman, Erving. 1977. "The Arrangement Between the Sexes." *Theory and Society* 4:301–331.

Gray, Jane. l988. *The Tearoom Revisited: A Study of Impersonal Homosexual Encounters in Public Setting*. Unpublished PhD dissertation, The Ohio State University, Columbus.

Hall, Edward.1959. *The Silent Language*. Garden City, NY: Doubleday.

Herold, Edward, and Dawn-Marie Mewhinney. 1993. "Gender Differences in Casual Sex and AIDS Prevention: A Survey of Dating Bars." *The Journal of Sex Research* 30:36–42.

Humphreys, Laud. 1970. *Tearoom Trade: Impersonal Sex in Public Places*. Chicago: Aldine.

Iizuka, Yuichi. 1992. "Eye Contact in Dating Couples and Unacquainted Couples." *Perceptual and Motor Skills* 75:457–461.

Kamel, G.W. Levi. 1983. *Downtown Street Hustlers: The Role of Dramaturgical Imaging Practices in the Social Construction of Male*

Prostitution. Unpublished Ph.D. dissertation, University of California, San Diego.

Kinsey, Alfred, Wardell Porneroy, and Clyde Martin. 1948. *Sexual Behavior in the Human Male.* Philadelphia: W.B.: Saunders.

Lee, John Alan. 1979. "The Social Organization of Sexual Risk." *Alternative Lifestyles* 2:69–100.

Maynard, Steven. 1994. "Through a Hole in the Lavatory Wall: Homosexual Subcultures, Police Surveillance, and the Dialectics of Discovery, Toronto, 1890–1930." *Journal of the History of Sexuality* 5:207–242.

Pollack, Michael. 1993. "Homosexual Rituals and Safer Sex." *Journal of Homosexuality* 25:307–317.

Ponte, Meredith. 1974. "Life in a Parking Lot: An Ethnography of a Homosexual Drive-In." In *Deviance: Field Studies and Self-Disclosures*, edited by J. Jacobs. Palo Alto, CA: National Press Books.

Ross, Michael and Jay Paul. 1992. "Beyond Gender: The Basis of Sexual Attraction in Bisexual Men and Women." *Psychological Reports* 71:1283–1290.

Simon, William, and John Gagnon. 1986. "Sexual Scripts: Permanence and Change." *Archives of Sexual Behavior* 15:97–120.

Styles, Joseph. 1979. "Outsider/Insider: Researching Gay Baths." *Urban Life* 8:135–152.

Sundholm, Charles. 1973. "The Pornographic Arcade: Ethnographic Notes on Moral Men in Immoral Places." *Urban Life and Culture.* 2:85–104.

Tewksbury, Richard. 1990. "Patrons of Porn: Research Notes on the Clientele of Adult Bookstores." *Deviant Behavior* 11:259–271.

Walsh, Debra and Jay Hewitt. 1985. "Giving Men the Come-On: Effect of Eye Contact and Smiling in a Bar Environment." *Perceptual and Motor Skills* 61:873–874.

Weatherford, Jack McIver. 1986. *Porn Row.* New York: Arbor House.

Weinberg, Martin, and Colin Williams. 1975. "Gay Baths and the Social Organization of Impersonal Sex." *Social Problems* 23: 124–136.

6

Dial-a-Porn Recordings: The Role of the Female Participant in Male Sexual Fantasies

Jack Glascock
Robert LaRose

This article looks at themes found in recorded dial-a-porn telephone messages. Instead of the expected emphasis on violence and rape, the authors found the most common scenarios to involve women dominating men. As might be expected, most recordings featured women relating a sexual fantasy. The authors found the level of sexual explicitness to be low on 900 numbers but high on 800 numbers. This suggests that some important differences exist in types of telephone pornography and that these types of fantasies do not necessarily fit with popular assumptions about pornography for men.

The number of new media offering pornographic materials has grown in recent years. New technologies and recent policy decisions have given rise to a host of media, such as home videos, videotext, and audiotext services, that have made pornographic materials more readily available to the general public. Recent investigations into the content of pornographic materials have focused primarily on sexually explicit videos and magazines (Cowan, Lee, Levy, and Snyder, 1988; Dietz and Evans, 1982; Garcia and Milano, 1990; Palys, 1986; Scott and Cuvelier, 1987; Thomas, 1986; Winick, 1985; Yang and Linz,

1990). One medium that has not yet been studied systematically is pornographic audiotext services or "dial-a-porn."

Much of what has been reported about dial-a-porn content has come from anecdotal evidence presented by conservative politicians or representatives of anti-pornography groups (Helms, 1987; Specter, 1989; Swindell, 1988; Vander Ark, 1988). For example, in its final report, the Attorney General's Commission on Pornography (Meese Commission) asserted that dial-a-porn might include "lesbian sexual activity, sodomy, rape, incest, excretory functions, bestiality, sadomasochism and sex acts with children" (U.S. Department of Justice, 1986: 1431). The commission's assertion was apparently based upon the testimony of one witness, a federal attorney relatively active in prosecuting dial-a-porn services (Ward, 1988).

The objectives of this study are to systematically analyze the content of dial-a-porn, compare the findings to other content analyses of pornography, and evaluate the findings in terms of policy initiatives.

Pornographic Content

Pornographic videos exhibit a wide range of sexual behaviors. For instance, Palys (1986) reports a prevalence of oral sex (72% of all sexually explicit scenes), fondling breasts/genitals (64%), intercourse (52%), masturbation (27%), and anal intercourse (10%). Garcia and Milano (1990) found that intercourse and oral sex were the most typical sexual activities in erotic videos, with fellatio being twice as common as cunnilingus, indicating a "male bias."

Most content analyses of pornographic materials have found some evidence of sexual violence against women and male dominance. Palys (1986) found sexual aggression in 12% of all sex scenes in pornographic videos, with males most often the perpetrators and females the victims. Yang and Linz (1990) found rape to be the predominant sexually violent theme (42% of sexually violent scenes) in pornographic videos, followed by sadomasochism (21%). Cowan et al. (1988) found domination (28% of all sexually explicit scenes) and exploitation (26%) as major themes in x-rated videos, with males doing most of the dominating and exploiting. Smith (1976), in his analysis of adult paperbacks, found force or coercion used against females in a third of all sex episodes.

Potential effects of pornographic audiotapes have been studied in a series of experiments by Malamuth and Check (1980, 1983, 1985). One of their more significant findings was that subjects exposed to a "rape-arousal" depiction, in which the female is perceived as becoming aroused during a rape, perceived less trauma for a rape victim and believed that a greater percentage of men would rape than did subjects who heard a "mutually-desired" story in which both participants consented to the sexual act (Malamuth and Check, 1980).

For the most part we would expect dial-a-porn to be similar to other types of pornography in terms of depicting explicit sexual activities with themes including male aggression and dominance. These themes have fueled much of the research probing the effects of pornographic materials (Linz, Donnerstein, and Penrod, 1984; Malamuth and Check, 1980, 1983, 1985; Zillmann and Bryant, 1982, 1988) and have been strongly criticized as reinforcing sexist attitudes toward women (Longino, 1980).

Dail-a-Porn Services

Interactive 900-number services were implemented by long-distance carriers in the 1980s, allowing customers to access information, complete transactions, and answer questions with touch-tone phones (LaRose and Atkin, 1992). By 1991 when customers were spending $975 million calling 900-number services ("900 Services Reach," 1991), 6% of 900-number services offered messages describing or suggesting sexual acts or body parts (Glascock and LaRose, 1992). In response to public criticism, carriers for 900 numbers announced in 1991 they would no longer bill and collect for adult services ("MCI Stops," 1991; "Sprint TeleMedia Shuns," 1991). This was not good news for an industry already plagued by a high percentage of uncollectables (Harper, 1992). In fact, when a local exchange carrier, Pacific Bell,

stopped billing telephone subscribers for adult services in December 1991, 75% of these providers either discontinued their services or changed their program content ("Pacific Bell Stops," 1991).

In December 1991, the Federal Communications Commission (FCC) adopted rules requiring a preamble for most 900-number services disclosing the price of the call, a short description of the program content, a warning to minors, the name of the service provider, and an allowance for the caller to hang up without being charged for the call (Federal Communications Commission [FCC], 1991). (Services with less than a $2 flat rate are exempted from the preamble requirement.) Preambles had been opposed by industry groups due to predicted consumer annoyance and increased costs, and some industry spokespersons estimated that such messages would reduce the number of calls to 900-number services by over 70% (Fogel, 1991). Such fears, while perhaps exaggerated, seem somewhat legitimate given the impulsive nature of many 900-number callers (Dalton, 1990). Finally, in January 1992 the Supreme Court upheld a 1989 law, known as the Helms Amendment, requiring telephone companies that provide billing and collecting for adult services to restrict access to subscribers who request it in writing (*Dial Information Services Corporation of New York v. Barr*, 1992). . . .

Method

Sample

We began with 771 dial-a-porn numbers, drawn from issues of six widely circulated, sexually explicit men's magazines on February 4, 1991: *Cheri, Gallery, Hustler, Oui, Playboy, and Penthouse*. From a random start, this list was then systematically sampled, yielding 217 numbers which were called. Included in this sample were 16 additional numbers from a second sampling of 900 number services. This was done to obtain a comparable number of 900-number fantasies for comparisons to 800 and long-distance-number fantasies.

Thirty-two numbers (14.7%) were eliminated due to lack of access (not in service, wrong number, etc.). Of the remaining 185 numbers, 64 offered recorded fantasies. The rest offered either live-only services and/or other types of recorded messages. Once it was discovered that a number offered only live services, the call was terminated. The process of explaining the purpose of the call, gaining permission to record it, and then obtaining a representative recording comparable to a prerecorded fantasy was deemed too problematic to include live services in this study. Because only one long-distance number offered recorded fantasies and the content was similar to 800 numbers, this category was combined with that of 800 numbers in analyses comparing services.

The recording time for most numbers was the first five minutes. Exceptions were made to allow for the recording of a fantasy in its entirety. If a fantasy was less than three minutes in duration a second fantasy was recorded from the same number. While this may have weighted some numbers more than others within a service, the objective was to compare fantasies between services. In sum, two fantasies were recorded for 20 numbers, 10 from each type of service (900 number and 800/LD number). In all, 84 fantasies were recorded. Two of these were found to be inaudible and were not included in the analysis. . . .

Themes

The type of pornography that was predominant in each fantasy was used to categorize the theme of that fantasy. In contrast to other content analyses, these themes are characterized from the female's perspective. There were two reasons for this. During the recording phase of the study, it became apparent that recorded dial-a-porn fantasies are described almost exclusively by the female voice. Thus, the female's role was the most obvious and easiest to identify. Second, the concern of some feminist writers has been with the female role, specifically the portrayal of women as "anonymous, panting playthings, adult toys, dehumanized objects to be used, abused, broken and discarded" (Brownmiller, 1980, p. 32). Coding definitions for the themes are provided below.

Dominance/submission refers to a situation in which the scene is dominated by one person who verbally controls or commands the action of others (Cowan et al., 1988). This person typically uses derogatory or patronizing language ("That's a good little boy").

Reciprocal is characteristic of a situation in which each participant in the sexual activity has an equal role (Cowan et al., 1988). Each participant is described as giving and receiving satisfaction and pleasure during the sexual activity.

Subservience occurs when one party is portrayed as actively encouraging or soliciting sexual behaviors primarily for the satisfaction of others (Zillmann and Bryant, 1982). Zillmann and Bryant (1982) argue that this type of portrayal of women in pornography is preponderant, although such characterizations have not been specifically investigated in previous analyses of pornographic materials.

Reluctance/coercion is similar to a category used by Garcia and Milano (1990) to refer to instances in which one party is hesitant or reluctant to engage in sexual activity, but is coerced, either by persuasion or seduction into participating.

Violence is characterized by the use of force against another to gain sexual favors. A violent theme would include acts such as rape, bondage, or sadomasochism. While a rape depiction would certainly characterize a recording as violent, acts of bondage or sadomasochism would not necessarily result in a recording being coded as violent unless they were considered predominant.

Explicitness and Inequalities

Explicitness was characterized by the language used to describe the sexual activity. A high level of explicitness is defined as using profane or graphic words to describe sexual activity or body parts. A medium level of explicitness includes descriptions of sexual activity or body parts without the use of profanities or graphic words. Expressions such as, "Touch me down there," would fit into this category. A low level of explicitness refers to wording that only alludes to sexual activity or body parts, usually through the use of symbolic expressions such as, "He filled my deepest desires." The mere mention of activities such as kissing or touching would fit into this classification. Messages with no reference to sexual activity or body parts and offering only general or romantic conversation were recorded as having no explicit language. Given the FCC's (1990) definition of indecency as "the description or depiction of sexual or excretory activities or organs in a patently offensive manner" (p. 4927), presumably recordings characterized by highly explicit language would be considered indecent or pornographic.

Status inequalities such as those documented by Cowan et al. (1988) were also examined. Feminist authors have contended that such inequalities used in a sexual context are indicative of pornographic materials (Steinem, 1980). Indicators used in this analysis, which depended on non-visual cues, included differences in age, wealth, occupation, and nudity. Examples might include older man/younger woman or boss/secretary relationships. Occupational status was rated according to average salary (*American Salaries and Wages Survey*, 1991).

Reliability

Two coders, one male and one female, independently coded all numbers offering recorded fantasies for the content categories. Intercoder reliability levels (Scott's pi) were .70 for pornographic themes, .81 for sexual activities, .71 for initiation of sex act, .67 for inequalities, and .85 for explicitness.

Results

Typically, a dial-a-porn recording consisted of a female voice guiding the caller, presumably a male, through a series of sexual activities in which both parties are imagined as participants. The male was rarely heard in dial-a-porn recordings, whereas the female voice was present exclusively in 94% of all fantasies. In 79% of 800/LD recorded fantasies, the speaker referred to the caller in the second person, using such terminology as "You turn me on" or "Your touch feels so good." Very few 900-number fantasies used the second person (5.7%).

No sexually violent themes were found in this sample of dial-a-porn numbers (see Table 6.1). Even though instances of violence

were found, they were not considered to be predominant in any recording. Subservience and reciprocal behaviors were the two most common themes for 800/LD numbers, each describing over a third of all 800/LD fantasies. Dominance/submission was found to a lesser extent and only on 800/LD numbers. Both 800 and 900 numbers offered a small percentage of recordings with themes of reluctance/coercion. In dominant/submission recordings, the female was always the dominant party while in reluctance/coercion recordings the female was always the reluctant party. The dominant/submission recordings took the form of a "mistress-slave" relationship in which the male was subjected to various indignities, ranging from being told to stand in a corner to being urinated on. Most 900-number fantasies had no sexual theme, primarily because few or no sexual activities were described.

"Hard core" sexual activities, such as intercourse, oral sex, anal intercourse, fondling of breasts/genitals, and masturbation, were much more likely to be found in 800/LD fantasies (see Table 6.1). As for oral sex, cunnilingus and fellatio were found in comparable quantities. Other less common forms of sexual activity such as fetishism, use of accessories, coprophilia, and urophilia were infrequent and found only on 800/LD numbers. No instances of male homosexuality or bestiality were recorded while descriptions of lesbianism and group sex were found in relatively small amounts. Mild sexual activities such as kissing and touching were more prevalent on 900-number fantasies. A little over half of 900-number fantasies described no sexual activity at all. Violent acts were very rare, especially in 900 fantasies.

The predominant themes were subservience and reciprocal, especially in 800/LD numbers (see Table 6.2). In general the language used in 800/LD-number fantasies was highly explicit while no explicit language or language that only alluded to sexual activity was found on 900 numbers. Status inequalities were found in greater frequency on 900-number fantasies than 800/LD-number fantasies. When inequalities were present, the female participant was most often portrayed as having less status (80%). The most fre-

Table 6.1

Percentage of Recorded Fantasies Depicting Various Sexual Activities

Sexual Activity	900 Numbers		800/LD Numbers		Chi
	%	n	%	n	Square
No sexual activity	51	18	0	0	23.0**
Kissing, touching	40	14	13	6	6.7**
Fondling breasts, genitals	0	0	53	25	24.3**
Intercourse	3	1	51	24	19.8**
Anal intercourse	0	0	15	7	3.9*
Oral sex					
Cunnilingus	0	0	36	17	13.9**
Fellatio	3	1	43	20	14.6**
Masturbation	3	1	47	22	17.1**
Lesbianism	6	2	8.5	4	<1.0
Male homosexuality	0	0	0	0	——
Group sex	6	2	8.5	4	<1.0
Violent acts					
Spanking, slapping, etc.	3	1	13	6	1.4
Sadomasochism[a]	0	0	11	5	2.3
Bondage	0	0	0	0	——
Rape	0	0	0	0	——
Fetishism	0	0	8.5	4	1.6
Use of accessories such as dildo and vibrator	0	0	6	3	<1.0
Coprophilia, urophilia	0	0	4	2	<1.0
N of recorded fantasies		35		47	

Note. Degrees of freedom for all chi-square scores equal 1. All chi squares utilize Yates's correction factor. Each fantasy was coded for various types of sexual activities. [a]Consists of acts of spanking deemed sadomasochistic. *$p < .05$; **$p > .01$.

quent type of status inequity was occupation (67%), followed by nudity (20%) and age (13%). Instances of wealth inequity were not found.

More sex acts per recording were reported on 800/LD-number services (M = 3.36) than on 900-number services (M = 0.66), $t(80) = 8.80$, p<.001. As expected, sexual acts initiated by females were more frequent than those initiated by males. This disparity was most pronounced on 800/LD numbers, with females initiating 2.77 sexual acts per fantasy and males 0.60, $t(46) = 5.64$, p<.001. There was no significant difference between male-initiated (M = 0.26) and female-initiated (M= 0.40) sexual acts per fantasy on 900 numbers, $t(34) = 0.82$, p = .419.

Discussion

Given the FCC's definition of indecency, it seems reasonable to assert that 900 numbers are no longer pornographic (including indecent or obscene materials) while many 800 numbers are. What remains on 900 numbers can best be described as general conversation containing infrequent references to mild sexual activity. On the other hand, fantasies offered by 800 or long-distance numbers include hard-core sexual activities, often described using graphic or profane language. In light of this, the ensuing discussion of dial-a-porn will be limited to 800/LD numbers.

Perhaps most notable among the findings was the absence of violent themes and the nature of sexually violent activities on dial-a-porn recordings. While other studies have not examined violent themes per se, in-

Table 6.2

Percentage of Recorded Fantasies Characterized by Themes, Levels of Explicitness, and Inequalities

	900 Numbers		800/LD Numbers		Chi Square
	%	n	%	n	
Themes					
Subservience	6	2	36	17	8.8**
Reciprocal	11	4	36	17	5.2**
Dominance/submission	0	0	13	6	3.1*
Reluctance	6	2	13	6	<1.0
None	76.5	27	2	1	46.9***
Explicitness					
High	0	0	83	39	52.1***
Medium	6	2	13	6	<1.0
Low	34	12	4	2	10.7***
None	60	21	0	0	34.8***
Inequalities	20	7	13	6	<1.0
N of recorded fantasies		35		47	

Note. Degrees of freedom for all chi-square scores equal 1. All chi squares utilize Yates's correction factor. *$p < .10$; ** $p < .05$; *** $p < .01$.

stances of rape, which in itself would constitute a violent theme, have been uniformly reported. For example, Yang and Linz (1990) found rape to be the predominant form of sexual violence in pornographic videos. The frequency of sexually violent acts was similar to that found by Palys (1986). However, in contrast to Palys and other investigators, the violence in dial-a-porn was typically suggested and, more often than not, carried out by the female. Violent acts in dial-a-porn were primarily found in fantasies characterized by dominance, typically involving a "mistress" demanding to spank or be spanked by her male "slave."

In themes of dominance, the female invariably assumed the dominant role, frequently subjecting the male to various forms of degradation, mental as well as physical. This differs from previous studies in which the female has most often been found in the submissive role and the male in the dominant role (Cowan et al., 1988; Palys, 1986). This more assertive role of the female might be expected from a medium in which the female is called upon to (1) present the fantasy and (2) instigate most of the sexual activity. Additional insight, in terms of the appeal of this type of portrayal, is offered by research employing a technique known as guided im-

agery. This method requires subjects exposed to it to assume a first-person, present-tense orientation to experiencing a fantasy, which can be structured according to experimental objectives (Mosher and White, 1980). Using this technique, Sirkin and Mosher (1985) found that male subjects who imagined a female initiating sex and being assertive during intercourse experienced more arousal and enjoyment than subjects exposed to a tape where men showed more initiative and assertiveness.

Other differences found in dial-a-porn might also relate to the mode of presentation. While Garcia and Milano (1990) found fellatio twice as common as cunnilingus, the frequencies of these two activities were about the same for dial-a-porn recordings. Because dial-a-porn fantasies are described primarily by the female voice, any feelings and euphoria associated with the sexual activity must be articulated by the female, a condition favoring the presentation of cunnilingus. Masturbation was found in almost 50% of dial-a-porn recordings compared to 27% of all sex scenes in pornographic videos (Palys, 1986). Since the caller typically plays the role of the male participant in dial-a-porn, additional references to masturbation seem logical considering the ways in which the caller might participate. Inequities, primarily against females, were found in dial-a-porn recordings, but to a lesser extent than in pornographic videos (Cowan et al. 1988). The lack of visual cues in dial-a-porn makes inequities such as age and nudity much less apparent and more transitory than in more visual media such as x-rated videos.

Similarities to other pornographic materials included the frequent depiction of such hard-core sexual activities as intercourse, fondling breasts/genitals, oral sex, anal intercourse, and masturbation. These activities were found in frequencies comparable to Palys (1986). Themes of reciprocation and reluctance/coercion were roughly parallel to similar themes found by Cowan et al. (1988). Subservience, identified as a common theme in videos, was also frequently found in dial-a-porn. The relative scarcity of kissing and touching in dial-a-porn recordings lends support to criticism of pornography in general as lacking sensuality and warmth (Steinem, 1980). Also evidence of lesbianism but not male homosexuality concurs with similar findings by Garcia and Milano (1990).

Considering the absence of pornographic services on 900 numbers, it seems likely that industry and governmental regulation has prompted dial-a-porn services to move to 800/LD numbers. The decision by 900-number carriers to stop billing and collecting for adult services, together with the FCC preamble regulations and the Supreme Court's affirmation of the Helms Amendment appears to have resulted in dial-a-porn providers finding a safe harbor, at least for the time being, in credit card billings via 800/LD numbers.

The portrayal of women in dial-a-porn recordings as more assertive may have implications for future research into the potential effects of such media. The research by Malamuth and Check (1980, 1983, 1985), which was done well before the advent of dial-a-porn, used audiotapes of a male voice describing a rape scene. But rape is rare in dial-a-porn. It is much more common to hear fantasies about non-violent sex. Future research needs to examine the effect of this type of content on the telephone as has already been examined concerning the effect of this type of content on video (Zillmann and Bryant, 1982, 1988).

References

American salaries and wages survey. (1991). Detroit, MI: Gale Research.

Brownmiller, S. 1980. Excerpt on Pornography From *Against Our Will: Men, Women and Rape.* In L. Lederer (Ed.), *Take back the night: Women on pornography* (pp. 30–34). New York: Morrow.

Cowan, G., Lee, C., Levy, D., and Snyder, D. (1988). Dominance and Inequality in X-Rated Videocassettes. *Psychology of Woman Quarterly,* 12, 299–311.

Dalton, L. C. (1990, September). Saatchi and Saatchi's In-Depth Study of Audiotext Users. *Infotext,* pp. 44–47.

Dial Information Services Corporation of New York v. Barr, 112 S.Ct. 966 (1992).

Dietz, P. E., and Evans, B. (1982). Pornography Imagery and Prevalence of Paraphilia. *American Journal of Psychiatry,* 139, 1493–1495.

Federal Communications Commission. (1991). Interstate 900 Telecommunications Services, 56 Fed. Reg. 56,160.

Fogel, B. (1991, January). The Murder of the Information Age. *Infotext,* p.34

Garcia, L. T., and Milano, L. (1990). A Content Analysis of Erotic Videos. *Journal of Psychology & Human Sexuality,* 3(2), 95–103.

Glascock, J., and R. LaRose, R. (1992). A Content Analysis of 900 Numbers: Implications for Industry Regulation and Self-Regulation. *Telecommunications Policy,* 16, 147–155.

Harper, S. (1992, February). "Selective Blocking Will Stop Caller Fraud." *Infotext,* p.64.

Helms, J. (1987, December 1). *Congressional Record,* pp. S16, 794–S16, 795.

LaRose, R., and Atkin, D. (1992).Audiotext and the Re-Invention of the Telephone as a Mass Medium. *Journalism Quarterly,* 69, 413–421.

Linz, D., Donnerstein, E., and Penrod, S. (1984). The Effects of Multiple Exposures to Filmed Violence Against Women. *Journal of Communication,* 34(3), 130–147.

Longino, H. E. (1980). Pornography, Oppression and Freedom: A Closer Look. In L. Lederer (Ed.), *Take Back the Night: Women on Pornography* (pp. 35–39). New York: Morrow.

Malamuth, N. M., and Check, J.V.P. (1980). Penile Tumescence and Perceptual Responses to Rape as a Function of Victim's Perceived Reactions. *Journal of Applied Social Psychology,* 10, 528–547.

Malamuth, N. M., and Check, J. V. P. (1983). Sexual Arousal to Rape Depictions: Individual Differences. *Journal of Abnormal Psychology, 92,* 55–67.

Malamuth, N. M. and J.V.P. Check. (1985). The Effects of Aggressive Pornography on Beliefs in Rape Myths: Individual Differences. *Journal of Research in Personality, 19,* 299–320.

MCI Stops Adult 900 Billing. (1991, June). *Infotext,* pp. 16–17.

Mosher, D. L., and B.B. White. (1980). Effects of Committed or Casual Erotic Guided Imagery on Females' Subjective Sexual Arousal and Emotional Response. *The Journal of Sex Research, 16,* 273–299.

900 Services Reach $975 Million in Billings. (1991, December) *Infotext,* pp. 50-52

Pacific Bell Stops Billing for Porn. (1991, December). *Infotext,* p. 14.

Palys, T. S. (1986). Testing the Common Wisdom: The Social Content of Video Pornography. *Canadian Psychology, 27,* 22–35.

Scott, J. E., and Cuvelier, S.J. (1987). Sexual Violence in *Playboy* Magazine: A Longitudinal Analysis. *Archives of Sexual Behavior, 16,* 279–288.

Sirkin, M. I., and Mosher, D.L. (1985). Guided Imagery of Female Sexual Assertiveness: Turn On or Turn Off? *Journal of Sex and Marital Behavior, 11,* 41–50.

Smith, D. D. (1976). The Social Content of Pornography. *Journal of Communication,* 26(l), 16–24.

Specter, A. (1989, November 16). Congressional Record, p. S15, 796.

Sprint TeleMedia Shuns Most 900 Services. (1991, November). *Infotext,* p. 14.

Steinem, G. (1980). Erotica and Pornography: A Clear and Present Difference. In L. Lederer (Ed.), *Take back the night: Women on pornography* (pp. 35–39). New York: Morrow.

Swindell, W. D. (1988). Statement of William D. Swindell, President, Citizens of Decency Through Law, Inc. *Telephone Decency Act of 1987: Hearing on H.R. 1786 Before the Subcomm. on Telecommunications and Finance of the House Comm. on Energy and Commerce,* 100th Cong., 1st Sess.

Thomas, S. (1986). Gender and Social-Class Coding in Popular Photographic Erotica. *Communication Quarterly, 34,* 103–114

U.S. Department of Justice. (1986). *Attorney General's Commission on Pornography. Final Report.* Washington, DC: Author.

Vander Ark, D. (1988). Statement of Dar Vander Ark, President, Michigan Decency Action Council, Inc. *Telephone Decency Act of 1987: Hearing on H.R. 1786 Before the Subcomm. on Telecommunications and Finance of the House Comm. on Energy and Commerce,* 100th Cong., 1st Sess.

Ward, B. (1988). Statement of Brent Ward, U.S. Attorney, District of Utah. *Telephone Decency Act of 1987: Hearing on H. R. 1786 Before the Subcomm. on Telecommunications and Finance of the House Comm. on Energy and Commerce,* 100th Cong., 1st Sess.

Winick, C. (1985). "A Content Analysis of Sexually Explicit Magazines Sold in an Adult Bookstore." *The Journal of Sex Research, 21,* 206–210.

Yang, N., and D. Linz. (1990). "Movie Ratings and the Content of Adult Videos: The Sex-Violence Ratio." *Journal of Communication, 40*(2), 28–42.

Zillmann, D., and J. Bryant. (1982). "Pornography, Sexual Callousness, and the Trivialization of Rape." *Journal of Communication, 32*(4):10–211.

Zillmann, D. and J. Bryant. 1988. Pornography's Impact on Sexual Satisfaction. *Journal of Applied Social Psychology, 18,* 438–453. ✦

Reprinted from: Jack Glascock and Robert LaRose, "Dial-a-Porn Recordings: The Role of the Female Participant in Male Sexual Fantasies." In *Journal of Broadcasting & Electronic Media*, pp. 313–324. Copyright © 1993 by Broadcast Education Association. Reprinted by permission. ✦

7

Dominance and Inequality in X-Rated Videocassettes

Gloria Cowan
Carole Lee
Daniella Levy
Debra Snyder

This article examines the prevalence of themes of domination and inequality in X-rated videos. The authors found that a majority of sexually explicit scenes in these videos focus on domination or exploitation, usually with men dominating women. These findings suggest that men, as the primary viewers of X-rated videos, have sexual fantasies that center on control, not intimacy.

Linking hard-core pornography with sex crimes, the Attorney General's Commission on Pornography (1986) recommended a crackdown on pornography. The report by the Commission, however, did not meet with unanimous acceptance. Some of the members of the Commission itself—J. Becker and E. Levine—found fault with the evidence presented at the hearings, including the concern that the Commission focused on the most extreme material. The present study focused specifically on the content of X-rated videocassettes. The Motion Picture Association of America (MPAA), a private organization, rates films "x" on the basis of the presence of explicit sex. The Commission defined pornography as "material predominantly sexually explicit and intended for purposes of sex-

ual arousal" (pp. 228–229) and subdivided these materials into four categories: (a) nudity, (b) nonviolent and nondegrading materials, (c) nonviolent materials depicting degradation, domination, subordination, and humiliation, and (d) sexually violent materials. Using this definition, X-rated videos would fit within the general rubric of pornographic materials. Whether the sexually explicit X-rated videos contain significant amounts of sexually violent and degrading imagery are the questions asked in this study.

Eroticized violence and, secondarily, themes of degradation have emerged as potentially the most harmful types of sexually explicit material. In general, laboratory studies have shown that male exposure to eroticized violence affects attitudes toward rapists and rape victims and acceptance of rape myths, and produces an increase in aggressiveness toward a female target (Linz, Donnerstein, and Penrod, 1987). Malamuth and Brier (1986) proposed an indirect model in which portrayals of sexual violence interact with and mutually influence other factors, such as personality characteristics, in determining sexual aggression. Donnerstein, Linz, and Penrod (1987) further suggested that it is the violence, not the sexual explicitness, that has the most significant effect on attitudes and behavior. Regarding degrading, but nonviolent sexually explicit material, the evidence regarding harm is less consistent.

Feminists have objected to the degrading and abusive aspects of pornography rather than to its sexual explicitness. Steinem (1983), for one, distinguished pornography, defined as an imbalance in power—"images of sex in which there is force, violence, or symbols of unequal power" (p. 219)—from erotica or sexual desire involving choice and equality. At the most fundamental level, feminists have objected to material that supports an ideology of sexual inequality (Longino, 1980; MacKinnon, 1985). Thus, both blatant inequality (e.g., rape, bondage, torture) or more subtle images (e.g., the use of authority, class, or other inequalities) may be seen as pornographic in a sexual context. In a feminist analysis, any combination of these characteristics constitutes an attempt to present women as subservient and submissive to dominant males. Furthermore, feminist authors have argued that violent and degrading pornography is a reflection of our patriarchal society, where the power to dominate is vested in men, by men, and expressed as hostility toward women (Brownmiller, 1975; Dworkin, 1985; Griffin, 1981; Killoran, 1983; MacKinnon, 1985; Morgan, 1978). Thus, the impact of pornography as so defined for feminists includes, but is not limited to, sexual violence, physical aggression, and attitudes toward rape. What is objectionable, then, is the maintenance of a political system in which women are unequal.

With the advent of the affordable videocassette recorder, pornographic movies are no longer confined to the adult book store or specialty theaters and are now available at the same outlets where general movies are rented. . . . Data cited in the Attorney General's report indicate that videocassettes are now the dominant mode of pornography production. . . .

In a story of adults-only paperback fiction, Smith (1976) found a repeated pattern of male dominance in sexual acts and a perpetuation of the "rape myth," wherein the woman initially resists forcible sexual intercourse but enjoys it in the end. Of the 4,588 sexual episodes depicted in 428 paperbacks, a full 20% involved rape, 91% of which were rapes of a female by a male. Less than 3% of the attackers were reprimanded for their crime. A study of adult magazine covers from 1970 to 1981 found an increase in domination and bondage (Dietz and Evans, 1982). In 1981, bondage and domination imagery was featured in 17.2% of the magazine covers.

Malamuth and Spinner (1980) studied the sexual violence contained in *Playboy* and *Penthouse*, two popular erotic magazines. Over a five-year period (1973–1977), the amount of sexual violence in these magazines significantly increased. In 1977, a reader of these two magazines was exposed to sexual violence in 10% of the cartoons and 5% of the pictorials. However, a more recent analysis (Scott and Cuvelier, 1987) of violence in cartoons and pictorials in *Playboy* magazine from 1953 through 1983 found violence rare and on the decline in recent years.

Palys (1986) studied the content of triple-x and adult videocassettes available in Vancouver, Canada, focusing primarily on the extent of sex, aggression, and sex combined with aggression. Contrary to expectations, more aggression and sex combined with aggression were found in the adult videos than in the triple-x videos. Men were portrayed as the perpetrators and women the victims of sexual aggression in the majority of sexually aggressive scenes.

The present study was designed to analyze the sexual content of X-rated videocassettes from a feminist perspective. The focus of this research was on the extent of domination and inequality found in the sexually explicit scenes in X-rated videocassettes. This videocassette medium was chosen in acknowledgment of the impact cassette rental has had on the distribution of sexually explicit materials. It was expected that X-rated videocassettes reflect the ideology of sexual inequality and male dominance, as well as contain significant amounts of eroticized sexual violence.

Method

Sample

In order to establish a list of widely available X-rated movies in southern California, catalogues from seven rental stores with a family orientation in the Riverside/San Bernardino, California area were examined. The catalogues listed videos by category, such as children, comedy, horror, action, and adult. Adult films were not categorized according to "x" versus the less explicit adult label (e.g., *Playboy films*) or according to specific types of sexually explicit films. In the seven stores sampled, the display of X-rated videocassettes was alphabetical and, like the catalogues, did not separate different types of material. The great majority of materials, however, in the adult section are X-rated or sexually explicit. To be considered widely available, a movie's title had to appear on at least four of the seven lists from the adult section of the catalogue; availability ranged from four to seven. A list of 121 titles that met the availability requirement was derived. Of these, 48 of the 121 titles were randomly assigned to the four coders (12 each). Three tapes were defective and were subsequently eliminated from the data analysis; as a result, 45 movies were included in this analysis. These movies were all "X-rated" films. A number of the videocassettes analyzed were recognized as classics in the field (Holliday, 1986). Copyrights ranged from 1979 to 1985. . . . Most sexually explicit videocassettes are distributed on a national scale (Attorney General's Commission on Pornography, 1986), and therefore, it is not likely that the videocassettes analyzed were regionally specific. . . .

The Coders

The coders were psychology majors enrolled in a senior psychology advanced laboratory in social psychology. These four coders chose to work on this project rather than a number of other possible projects and were given the opportunity to change projects if they found the material too disturbing. All four coders had limited previous exposure to pornography. Coder 1 was a single, Anglo feminist female, 21-year-old, who was born Jewish but considers herself agnostic. Coder 2 was a 34-year-old married male, who is a Catholic Hispanic and considers himself apolitical. Coder 3 was a 26-year-old single Anglo Catholic female, who considers herself liberal. Coder 4 was a married 35-year-old Anglo female feminist with teenage children, who is also Catholic. The two feminists had taken a psychology of women course.

Coding Categories and Reliabilities

Four coders developed the categories employed in the content analysis from the subsample of three tapes: "Insatiable," "Taboo," and "Debbie Does Dallas II." The overall theme or mood of each sexually explicit scene was coded as Dominant, Reciprocal, Exploitative, or Autoerotic. In addition to categorization of the overall theme, the following specific indicators were coded for their presence in each sexual scene: Physical Aggression, Verbal Aggression, Verbal Dominance, Submission, Rape, Bondage, Incest, Inducements, Status Inequalities, Verbal Inequalities, Transformations, Voyeurism, and Verbal Reciprocation. Thus, coding of the primary

theme was based on the coders' judgments of which theme appeared to predominate in each sexually explicit scene. The specific indicators, however, were scored on the basis of presence rather than predominant mood of the scene and any number of indicators could appear in a given scene.

Three additional videotapes were used to establish reliability. Reliability was calculated as percent agreement. The formula used was 2 times the number of exact agreements on presence of the category in a scene divided by the number coded as present by both of two coders. The percent agreements between sets of two coders (six sets) were averaged. The overall mean interceder reliability was $r = .89$. Only explicit sexual scenes, those in which physical sex acts were clearly identifiable, were timed and coded ($r=.97$ for explicit content). Timing of sex episodes began with foreplay and concluded when sex acts were completed or a scene's focus shifted ($r = .94$ for scene length). The overall theme or mood of each scene was coded as Dominant, Reciprocal, Exploitative, or Autoerotic.

Each scene was assigned to only one of the four categories based on the predominant theme (average $r = .84$). Although a scene could include elements of more than one theme, the coders coded only the predominant theme in the scene. Dominant scenes depicted one participant controlling the sex act, either physically or verbally. Exploitation involved participant(s) clearly using one or more participants without consideration of the used person(s). Aside from an overall theme of one person(s) exploiting another or others, exploitation typically included inducements of various types (alcohol, hypnosis, aphrodisiacs, money, blackmail) and inequality (status, age, occupation, and clothing differences). Reciprocity involved mutual consent and mutual satisfaction, including both verbal and nonverbal expression of reciprocity or mutual satisfaction. Autoerotic scenes depicted masturbation or self-stimulation.

The remaining specific categories were coded for their presence in a scene; frequency within a scene was not counted. Physical Aggression, identified by the use of clear force (e.g., whips, pinching, slapping, hairpulling, bondage, kicking) (r = .98 for physical aggression), showed the recipient in apparent pain or discomfort. A scene was not coded as physically aggressive if any of these indicators were employed in a mutual, reciprocal context (i.e., a consenting context in which no pain cues were apparent). Bondage, Incest, and Rape as indicators of non-normative sexuality were separately identified. Bondage occurred with the use of external restraints, such as tying up a person. Incest was scored when the scene clearly indicated that the participants were related. Rape was defined as an attack, in which the victim did not stimulate the rapist, the attack was unexpected, and the victim was an unwilling participant. Hence, the coding of rape did not include those scenes that portrayed the rape mythology that women provoke and enjoy rape.

Status Inequality was scored when a scene presented a participant as a subordinate with regard to his or her status during a sexually explicit scene. Specific indicators of Status Inequality included age, wealth, clothing, occupation, and race (when used explicitly to indicate differential status) (r = .94 for Status Inequality).

The Submission and Transformation categories consisted of overt, marked change in a participant(s). In Submission, one or more of the participants initially resists a sexual advance, is coerced or induced into participation, and eventually cooperates and/or enjoys it. Submission most likely reflects rape mythology. Transformation depicted one actor as originally innocent or virginal, who is then transformed into an insatiable, sex-driven person (r = .71 for Submission and Transformation). Voyeurism involved scenes in which undetected character(s) watch either a sexual act or the disrobing of a person (r = .99).

Verbal indicators were used in several categories. Derogatory, abusive language was coded as Verbal Aggression (r = .90). An example would be: "You were asking for this, bitch." Verbal Aggression also included an abusive, derogatory tone of voice. Language that reflected inequality and consisted of any patronizing or infantilizing language (e.g., "good girl," "Daddy likes it") was identified as Verbal Inequality (r = .87). Language that indicated differential status was included here, such as "Your job depends on your performance." Verbal demands and commands, such as commands to assume a particular body position or perform a particular act, were recorded in the Verbal Dominance category (r = .93). If a statement was made whereby a profane command was given, it was categorized in both the Verbal Dominance and Aggression categories. Verbal Reciprocation consisted of actual terms of mutual appreciation and gratification (r = .95). For all the verbal communication categories, language not occurring within the sex scene was not coded.

In addition to the four themes and specific categories, the sex, race, occupation, and sexual orientation of the characters were also noted. Notes were used to indicate any elaboration of the categories, for example, the use of full frame genitalia shots—shots of the vulva or close-ups of fellatio, penetration, sodomy, etc., that filled the entire space of the screen. In addition, coders noted instances of infantilization of the woman, through use of clothing (barrettes, bows in hair) or tone of voice.

Procedure

For the analysis, the coding units were the explicit sex scenes with no sampling within films. Scenes not containing explicit sex were not coded for content. The sexual scenes, then, were the units of analysis, not the films. A checklist was devised whereby the presence of indicators of the coded categories could be noted. Movies were coded in random order to control for selection biases, and no more than two per day were viewed to control for habituation effects. Coders also noted the presence of other information besides the specified categories.

Results

Data were collected for 3,577 minutes of adults only, X-rated films. Within this sample, 60% (2,131 minutes) [were] composed of explicit, graphic depictions of sex acts. The movies averaged 78 minutes in length, of which an average 47 minutes contained explicit sex. A total of 443 sex scenes were coded, averaging about 10 per film. Of these 347 (78%) were heterosexual, 47 (11%) were homosexual, 8 (2%) were bisexual, and 40 (9.1%) were autosexual or masturbatory. None of the films sampled were targeted at a gay population. The distribution of sexual orientation in scenes was 86% heterosexual, 12% homosexual, and 2% bisexual. Male homosexuality or bisexuality was never represented; these orientations were only portrayed by women. Of the female characters, 57% were heterosexual, 35% bisexual, and 8% homosexual.

Table 7.1 presents the percent occurrence of each of the primary themes and specific indicators. Dominance and exploitation as major themes comprised 54% of the sexually explicit scenes, compared with 37% judged to be reciprocal in mood. An additional analysis of the number of movies containing dominance and exploitation indicated that dominance occurred in 35 (78%) and exploitation in 37 (82%) of the films.

Men did most of the domination and exploitation. Of the 124 scenes characterized by dominance, 78% were commanded by men; only 22% of the dominant scenes were female-dominated, and of these, 37% were depictions of women dominating other women. In 68% of the exploitation scenes (77), a man exploited one or more women. Women appeared as exploitative in only 26 scenes (23%), and of these, 38% represented women exploiting other women. Of the total of 40 autoerotic scenes, 38 depicted women and 2 depicted men.

The data for the specific indicators, as well as the themes, are presented in Table 7.1. Physical aggression occurred in 101 scenes (23%). Physical aggression appeared in a much greater percent of the films (33 films or 73%) than the specific sexual scenes.

Gender was not noted for every specific category. All inducements, however, were directed toward female characters. Interestingly, father-daughter incest was never observed in this sample. Types of incest presented were mother-son, sister-sister, brother-sister, aunt-nephew, and uncle-niece. Of the 14 bondage scenes, 10 showed female bondage, whereas only 4 presented a bound man.

When a man was bound it was done so in a playful tone. The mood of these scenes was coded as reciprocal; however, when a female was bound, it was done in a violent, abusive manner and was associated with a mood rating of dominance. A rape occurred in 23 (51%) of the 45 films. All rape scenes were rapes of females; of these, 25 scenes (90%) presented a man raping a woman. Three scenes depicted homosexual rapes. Evidence of submission occurred more frequently (14%) than rape.

Table 7.1

Frequency and percent of themes and specific content coded as a percentage of all sexually explicit scenes (n = 443)

Category	Frequency	Percent
Theme		
Dominant	124	28%
Exploitative	113	26%
Reciprocal	166	37%
Autoerotic	40	9%
Specific indicators of dominance and inequality		
Physical Aggression	101	23%
Verbal Aggression	90	20%
Verbal Dominance	126	28%
Submission	62	14%
Rape	28	6%
Bondage	14	3%
Incest	14	3%
Inducements	43	10%
Status Inequalities	174	39%
Verbal Inequalities	79	18%
Transformations	41	9%
Voyeurism	128	29%
Verbal Reciprocation	48	11%

Status inequalities were also indicated by the demographic and occupational distribution of male and female characters. Of the 282 main characters identified in the 45 movies, 124 (44%) were men, of whom 96% were white. Sixty-two percent of these men were identified as professionals or businessmen. Of the 56% women (158), 93% were white. The professions of the women, when identified, were traditional: 58% were clerical/secretarial workers, students, or housewives.

Indirect evidence suggesting objectification of women included voyeurism, masturbation, and full-screen genitalia shots. Voyeurs appeared in 128 (29%) of the 443 scenes: 101 (79%) were men and 27 were women (21%). Of the 40 autoerotic scenes, 95% were of a woman masturbating. Only one coder kept track of full-frame genitalia shots. She observed a total of 790 genitalia shots, in which 205 were solely female, 91 solely male, and 494 both male and female. Regarding the genitalia full-screen exposures of one participant, 69% were female shots and 31% were male shots.

Typical Scenario

In general, the majority of the heterosexual scenes followed a definite format. The scene usually began with the woman performing fellatio on the man who then performed cunnilingus on the woman. Intercourse then followed with the man in a dominant position over the woman, either standing while the woman was on her back on a bed (or different surfaces such as tabletop) or kneeling in an upright position on the bed. Very rarely did the upper bodies touch during sexual intercourse, and kissing occurred infrequently. The man typically remained in this position until right before ejaculation, at which time he would withdraw his penis and ejaculate on the woman's stomach, face, breasts, or back just above the buttocks if he moved to a rear-entry position. Notes kept by the coders indicated that 97% of all heterosexual sex scenes showed a man ejaculating on a woman. In some scenes, anal intercourse would follow, but more frequently, the woman performed fellatio on the man a second time. The scene would end with the man ejaculating on the woman a second time, and the woman would either lick it up or rub it over her body. In most of these scenes, the man was expressionless and the woman moaned with pleasure.

General Observations

Status and clothing were two of the most overwhelming inequalities in the videos. The man, usually more powerful and wealthier than the woman, usually had on some piece of clothing. The woman was almost always nude except for the ever-present garter-belt and high-heels (usually black). Interestingly, when a woman was an inexperienced innocent, she had on (white) garter belts and high heels.

One recurring theme noted by the coders was that of infantilization. Although the women who portrayed young girls were obviously not adolescent, they were frequently dressed in youthful attire, such as school uniforms with socks and barrettes or bows in their hair, and portrayed high school girls or younger sisters. The female character often spoke in a childlike voice and had no pubic hair.

Discussion

A significant amount of dominance and sexual inequality was found in videocassettes commonly available for rental in video stores. Dominance and exploitation were primary themes in the present sample, comprising together the core of over half the total number of sex scenes. In addition, domination and exploitation were primarily directed toward women; women were infrequently portrayed as dominating or exploiting men.

The more blatant indicators of abuse—a full 23% of the scenes containing at least one act of physical violence—were directed toward women. Reinforcement of the rape myth, that women enjoy being forced to engage in sex, occurred in 14% of the scenes, which showed women submitting to dominant, often coercive, acts and ultimately responding with acceptance and/or fervor. Women seldom vocalized discomfort. Thus, the fusion of sex and aggression present in these videotapes, including the portrayal of rape, bondage, female submission, and verbal abuse, supports the ideology that sexuality includes domination and abusive treatment of women.

A secondary count of themes of domination and exploitation, physical aggression, and rape in sexually explicit scenes by movie indicated higher percentages than the analysis of scenes. Domination themes were scored in 78% and exploitation in 82% of the movies. Specific acts of physical aggression appeared in 73% and rape in 51% of the movies. From the perspective of probability of exposure, a viewer has a higher likelihood of seeing sex and abuse linked than the analysis of scenes would suggest. In a number of these movies, one rape or one sadistic/masochistic scene was presented in the context of fantasy.

The more subtle indicators of unequal power were pervasive as well. The male characters were likely to be professionals or businessmen, always heterosexual, typically in control, physically or verbally, and rarely expressive. The female characters were likely to be secretaries, housewives, or students. The women appeared in less clothing than the men. Objectification of women is seen in the more frequent close-up shots of female genitalia, including masturbation scenes. Filming of male ejaculation on the surface of the woman's body might be defended as specific to films because ejaculation as a component of intercourse occurs unseen. In our opinion, however, the almost total portrayal of heterosexual sexuality in this way demeans and degrades women's bodies.

The recent study of pornographic videocassettes by Palys (1986) comparing adult pornographic material with triple-x materials found a decrease in the presentation of violence and sexual violence in triple-x (identical to the type of pornography analyzed in the present study), but not in adult videos. Additionally, a larger percent of aggressive, sexually aggressive, and male-dominated (in general and as perpetrators of sexual aggression) scenes occurred in the adult than the triple-x videos. It is difficult, however, to compare our data directly with Palys's because his percentages were computed relative to the total number of scenes, sexual and nonsexual, or the total number that included sex, aggression, or sexual aggression, whereas our percentages were calculated relative to the total number of sexually explicit scenes. Furthermore, the data he presented included percentages of specific aggressive and sexually aggressive indicators relative to the overall frequency of aggressive and sexually aggressive scenes respectively, not to the total number of sexually explicit scenes. Also, our categories were developed from a feminist perspective which holds that pornography portrays women as willing victims of domi-

nation and rape, as objects to be used, and as a sex diminished, immature, and unequal to men in subtle as well as in obvious ways.

Our findings are similar to those obtained by Smith (1976) in his analysis of adult paperbacks. Women in pornographic movies are treated with the same inequality and in the same violent manner as women in pornographic novels. Smith concluded that pornography is a man's world. X-rated videocassettes are also made for men. The message men receive from these videos, however, is a distorted characterization of both male and female sexuality that is especially degrading to women. Comparison of gay and lesbian sexually explicit films with those aimed at the heterosexual male market would be instructive. . . .

References

Attorney General's Commission on Pornography (1986). Washington, DC: U.S. Department of Justice.

Brownmiller, S. (1975). *Against our will: Men, women, and rape.* New York: Bantam Books.

Commission on Obscenity and Pornography. (1970). *The report of the commission on obscenity and pornography.* New York: Bantam.

Dietz, P. E., and Evans, B. (1982). Pornographic imagery and the prevalence of paraphilia. *American Journal of Psychiatry,* 139, 1493–1495.

Donnerstein, E., Linz, D., and Penrod, S. (1987). *The question of pornography.* New York: Free Press.

Dworkin, A. (1985). Against the male flood: Censorship, pornography, and equality. *Harvard Women's Law Journal,* 8, 1–29.

Griffin, S. (1981). *Pornography and silence: Culture's revenge against nature.* New York: Harper & Row.

Holliday, J. (1986). *Only the best.* Van Nuys, CA: Cal Vista.

Johnson, P., and Goodchilds, J. (1973). Comment. *Journal of Social Issues,* 29, 231–238.

Killoran, M. M. (1983). Sticks and stones can break my bones and images can hurt me: Feminists and the Pornography Debate. *International Journal of Women's Studies,* 6, 443–456.

Linz, D., Donnerstein, E., and Penrod, S. (1987). The findings and recommendations of the Attorney General's Commission on pornography:

Do the psychological "facts" fit the political fury? *American Psychologist, 42*, 946–953.

Longino, H. E. (1980). Pornography, oppression, and freedom: A closer look. In L. Lederer (Ed.), *Take back the night: Women on pornography* (pp. 40–54). New York: William Morrow.

MacKinnon, C.A. (1985). Pornography, civil rights, and speech. *Harvard Civil Rights-Civil Liberties Law Review, 20*, 1–70.

Malamuth, N. M., and Brier, J. (1986). Sexual violence in the media: Indirect effects on aggression against women. *Journal of Social Issues, 42*, 75–92.

Malamuth, N. M., and Spinner, B. (1980). A longitudinal content analysis of sexual violence in the best-selling erotica magazines. *Journal of Sex Research, 16*, 226–237.

Morgan, R. (1978). Theory and practice: Pornography and rape. In R. Morgan (Ed.), *Going too Far: The personal chronicle of a feminist* (pp. 163–169). New York: Random House.

Palys, T. S. (1986). Testing the common wisdom: The social content of video pornography. *Canadian Psychology, 27*, 22–35.

Scott, J. E. and Cuvelier, S. J. (1987). Violence in Playboy magazine: A longitudinal analysis. *Archives of Sexual Behavior, 16*, 279–287.

Smith, D. D. (1976). The social content of pornography. *Journal of Communication, 26*, 16–24.

Steinem, G. (1983). Erotica vs. pornography. In G. Steinem (Ed.), *Outrageous acts and everyday rebellions* (pp. 219–230). New York: Holt, Rinehart, & Winston.

8

Rape Myths and Violence Against Street Prostitutes

Jody Miller
Martin D. Schwartz

This article looks at the sexual violence experienced by prostitutes. Most people do not believe that someone who sells her body can be raped. A prostitute is perceived as so deviant and stigmatized that people believe she cannot be a victim. This article suggests that definitions of deviant behavior are often dependent on who is involved and whether the person is considered deviant already. In short, some acts are not considered deviant if they are done to "disreputable" persons.

"It is unlikely that any occupation or lifestyle exposes a woman to the threat of assault and gratuitous violence as constantly and completely as prostitution" (Fairstein 1993, p. 171). This is true for a number of reasons; and an important one is a combination of powerful ideologies that define women (and prostitutes as an extreme example) as sexual property. . . .

Throughout Western history women who were not considered male property (divorcees, sexually active women) had more difficulty in obtaining legal protection than women who were considered male property, such as married women and virgin daughters (Clark and Lewis 1977). This is still true today (Hatty 1989; Vachss 1993). For example, the criminal justice system is commonly accused of basing its treatment of rape victims on the extent to which they are white, middle-class and reasonably chaste (Estrich 1987; Her-

man 1988; Frohmann 1992). Worse yet, as Andersen (1988) points out, those very women who are less likely to be defined as male property are simultaneously the most likely to be victimized by rape in the first place.

In recent years, there have been many studies of various types of sexual assault, with an emphasis on the different types of victims. Stranger rape is different from acquaintance rape, and the latter can be differentiated into marital rape and date or courtship rape (Young 1992). Shotland (1992) even argues that there are strong reasons to treat courtship rape itself as being of several different types. Perhaps the least studied has been the assault and rape of street prostitutes: the women traditionally viewed as the most likely to be outside the protection of society's values, if not laws.

This paper investigates the experience and meaning of this violence against street prostitutes, exploring how and why prostitutes are particularly vulnerable to violent physical and sexual attacks, and how they feel they are treated and perceived when they are victimized. It is now commonplace in the literature to argue that the ideologies prevalent in society commonly called "rape myths" describe the justifications for sexual assault of women. Here, the argument is extended to suggest that rape myths also explain much of the physical violence against marginalized women in society.

Interestingly, even though the nature of their work may make prostitutes more vulnerable to violent attack than other women (Bracey 1979; Silbert and Pines 1982; Hatty 1989; Perkins 1991), prostitutes are essentially invisible in criminological studies of violence and rape (J. L. Miller 1991). Yet, it is part of the thesis here that sexual violence in the context of street prostitution illuminates the functions and meanings of violence against women generally in American society. Likewise, street prostitutes' treatment within the criminal justice system illustrates societal definitions of appropriate female sexuality, of worthy victims, and of the "unrapeable." Much of this can be explained, we suggest, by a mechanism like the techniques of neutralization described by Sykes and Matza (1957).

History

. . . Most classic works on prostitution ignore violence completely. Those that mention the subject, such as Bullough and Bullough's *Women and Prostitution* (1987), or William Sanger's mid-19th century *The History of Prostitution* (1937), tend to take for granted mob violence or the fact that for thousands of years some women have been sold into sexual slavery. Sanger does periodically mention some surprisingly modern sounding situations, such as a problem in Toulouse, France, where the prostitutes in the early middle ages were plagued by young men who both were violent and "refused to pay for their pleasures" (1937, p.100). Other works, such as Corbin's (1990) study of prostitution in late 19th century France, and Connelly's (1980) study of the responses of early 20th century American Progressives to prostitution, take for granted the fact that prostitutes suffer violence and occasional slavery, but are more concerned with violence by prostitutes, and in fighting the excessive claims of the white slave trade literature.

In the U.S., we do not know enough to speak of the universal experience of prostitutes, but we know that violence against them dates back to the country's beginnings. For example, there are the well known episodes of "whorehouse riots," as early as in the 17th century, where gangs demolished houses of prostitution (Connelly, 1980). . . .

Although violence against prostitutes has not been a common criminology theme, when scholars began to look for violence against prostitutes, they found an enormous quantity of it. Cohen (1990) cites an 1836 survey of 22 brothels on one block in Manhattan that turned up 20 deaths, some of them violent, in only a 3-month period. Hill's (1993, p. 229) examination of New York City newspapers and court records in the mid-19th century is a catalog of acts of personal violence: "prostitutes were beaten, stabbed, stomped, kicked, burned, bludgeoned, stoned, cut, bound, raped, seared with acid, shoved down stairs, and, finally, murdered." Things had

not changed by the early days of the 20th century (Rosen 1982, p .83):

> Working the streets was considered by many prostitutes to be the most dangerous and brutal form of prostitution. . . . The dangers of customer and police harassment made street prostitution a particularly formidable and degrading occupation.

As a general rule, the literature on modern prostitution is uninterested in violence against prostitutes or takes it for granted (J. L. Miller 1991). Weisberg (1985), for example, is as concerned with violence *by* prostitutes as violence *against* prostitutes. This study of juvenile prostitution suggests that violence occurs partially because girls are smaller than women, and partially because girls do things to bring the violence upon themselves. . . . We will hear from prostitutes later regarding how they view these "factors," but those who have looked at the physical and sexual victimization of prostitutes claim that "prostitutes can be raped with impunity" (Weisheit and Mahan, 1988, p. 96), and that such victimization is characterized by very high violence, which leads prostitutes to fear for their lives. . . . Generally, however, how and why this violence occurs has not been an area of great interest among criminologists.

Methodology and Demographics

. . . [T]his research is based on in-depth interviews with 16 street prostitutes who engage in sex for money, although in most cases a significant portion of this money is used to purchase crack cocaine. . . . The sample [for this study] was drawn from women who were incarcerated at the county jail in a Midwestern city during December 1990 and January 1991. . . . Interviews were held in the "lawyer's booth," a small soundproofed room containing a table and two chairs, where the interviewer explained the purpose of the interview in depth. The voluntary nature of interviews was stressed, and the women were told that they could stop an interview at any time. Of the 17 women, one later found that discussing her experience with violence was too emotional an experience to continue, and she asked for her interview to be stopped. The other 16 completed the interviews. . . .

Prostitutes' Experiences With Violence

Women who engage in street prostitution face widespread physical and sexual violence. Some sort of sexual assault had been experienced by 93.8% of the women; 75% had been raped by one or more tricks; and 62.6% had been raped in other contexts on the streets. In addition, 56.3% had had money stolen from them by tricks after their sexual transactions were completed.

Most of the women (87.5%) were also victimized by physical assaults, which ranged from being punched or kicked (31.3%) to being beaten up (61.2%), stabbed or slashed (31.3%), or being hit with an object like a baseball bat or brick (25%). Additionally, 37.5% had been kidnapped and held captive. Two reported having been choked, three had suffered serious injuries such as broken bones, one had had her head rammed through a glass door, and one had been tortured with electric shock.

Unfortunately, standard quantification techniques do not capture the dynamics of violence on the streets. These women were simply incapable of answering questions on how often they had been beaten, kicked or raped. Cissy said she had been raped or robbed in the context of turning tricks "at least once a week—once a week, twice a week." She continued, "That's just part of the business. That's just part of working; that's just what happens." According to Candy, "You know, this happens so many times, um, it's just, a lot of times men just grab you, like I said, grab your hair or whatever, and make you do shit. You can't get away from 'em."

Lacy gave a variety of answers indicating that her experiences were uncountable. "All the time, all the time. It happens to us girls all the time . . . I could tell you, we could sit here all day and talk about it. Like I said, it happens so much." When asked if she had ever been stabbed, she held out her arms and said, "Yeah, take your pick," referring to the numerous scars on her arms. She further stated:

We have a lot of really sick people out there, you know, and when they get a hold of you, they do a whole bunch of crazy stuff to you. I've been in the hospital before and I been shot, I been stabbed eight times, I been kidnaped, I been tied up, all kinds of crazy things. There's just some really sick people out there.

Often the violent encounters the women spoke about in detail were the ones they said stuck out in their minds because, as Lacy said, "I really thought I was gonna die." Jessie said she was able to look at some violent incidents "lightly" because "I know what it was like to be in those death situations." Veronica talked in detail about a brutal rape that went on for two hours. These interviews reveal that violence is seen by these women as an ever-present part of street prostitution, something that is constantly expected or experienced.

Rape Myths and Violence Against Prostitutes

A central argument of this paper is that the arguments commonly termed rape myths can be of value in understanding the nature of violence against prostitutes in American society. . . . These ideologies about rape and women's sexuality serve to institutionalize and perpetuate violence against street prostitutes by rendering this violence invisible and unimportant.

A central component of such belief systems are rape myths, which Burt (1980, p. 217) defined as: "prejudicial, stereotyped, or false beliefs about rape, rape victims, and rapists." These myths allow "normal" men to engage in what would otherwise seem forbidden behavior, because they are able to rationalize it as being outside the usual definition of wrong or forbidden (Weis and Borges 1973). Since their victims are not "real" victims (Estrich 1987), these men can conclude that they have not committed a moral wrong (Brownmiller 1975).

Their unique position as women who openly sell sex to men makes prostitutes face a conglomeration of rape myths even stronger than those faced by other women. What is exceptional about the myths that define violence against prostitutes is that they include ideological beliefs that are normally thought to apply only to acquaintance, date or marital rape situations, as well as ideologies about stranger rape. While some of the myths involve subtle contradictions of one another, all involve a fundamental belief that prostitutes are public property and that their bodies are open territory for assault.

In our examination of these interviews, we found that we were able to identify four themes embedded within the women's comments that shed light on the ideologies that circulate about prostitutes' assaults: that prostitutes are unrapeable; that no harm is done; that prostitutes deserve to be raped; and that all prostitutes are the same. . . .

Prostitutes Are Unrapeable

One of the strongest myths in the American rape-supportive ideological system is that prostitutes cannot be raped; they are public sexual property. Interestingly, the strongest comparison to this myth is the tradition of a marital exemption within rape law, whereby married women are considered to be the private property of their husbands. Such women are deemed to, have given unrevokable consent to sex by their marriage vows, making them unrapeable by their husbands (Schwartz 1982; Finkelhor and Yllo 1985; Russell 1990). Somewhat comparable is the American myth that a woman who has sex with a number of partners is implying her consent to have sex with any man. . . . Certainly, prostitutes offer a strong example of women who violate these standards. Prostitutes are considered to be public property and to have given consent to any sexual acts by participating in promiscuous commercial sex (Rubin 1984).

This myth is still powerful throughout society. For example, Gilmartin-Zena (1988) specifically found that her sample of college students still accept the myth that prostitutes cannot be rape victims. The problem with this myth, of course, is that it confuses sex with violence, and it denies that prostitutes, just like other women, fear both rape and violence (including murder) within rape (J. L. Miller 1991; Perkins 1991).

Further, because they are seen as unrapeable, the legal system too often does not pro-

vide an avenue for prostitutes when they are the victims of crime (P. Miller and Biele 1993). For example, Frohmann (1992) found in her study that prosecutors typically do not prosecute cases involving prostitutes, while Fairstein (1993), a Manhattan sex crimes prosecutor herself, claims that many communities even today automatically dismiss all complaints brought by prostitutes.

The women in this study provided many examples of times when they felt that the criminal justice system did not take them seriously. Kay Kay, for example, was very bitter. She was held captive, stabbed numerous times and raped repeatedly, but the man she accused was released despite previous rape convictions, mainly because of her lack of credibility because she was a prostitute. After she was attacked, she "was out for three days. I couldn't even—they said I lied about rape because I was asleep for so long [and they hadn't collected physical evidence during that time]." Kay Kay was angry that prostitution is criminalized—she was serving time when we spoke—yet the man who stabbed and raped her was not convicted of the crimes. "He tried to make me look like I'm a liar. . . . They just let him out. I see him all the time, he said hi to me. Ain't that some shit?" She continued, "Oh, just because I'm a ho' I don't have rights? They just let him loose and I'm a ho' and I get time?" As Kay Kay's experience indicates, the stigma prostitutes face for selling sex defines them as untrustworthy, as women who lie about being raped, and therefore as "unrapeable." From their perspective, the crime of selling sex may be treated as a more serious offense than a rape or violent attack against the woman who sells it.

In addition, others may see prostitutes as unrapeable in certain specific contexts. Once a prostitute has consented to any exchange of sex for money, these women see many men as assuming that she has given up the right to refuse consent in any situation. Once her sexuality has been "purchased," her body "belongs" to the purchaser to use. This was a constant theme in the interviews. Many women encountered men who treated their agreement to engage in some form of sex as permission to abuse the women's bodies in any way they wished, as long as they gave the women monetary compensation. . . .

Tammy's description was typical of the type of experiences many women had that they considered life threatening, but which were justified by a man because he "paid" for it:

Well, a girlfriend brought a date over to a friend's house where we was stayin' . . . And, uh, she was gonna go out with him but instead he saw me and he wanted to date me. Ok, so I said yeah. And, uh, we went back and got in his car, and as we was leavin' he pulled a knife out and stuck it to my throat with one hand and drove with the other one . . . And he drove me all the way to ***, and on the way there, he stopped on the side of the freeway and he tied my hands behind my back, and tied my feet together, and put a thing around my mouth so I couldn't scream or nothin' no more. And, uh, after that, we got to *** in this field and he put a rope around my neck and tied it to the steering wheel. He blacked both my eyes, he busted two ribs, and busted up my back real bad. He beat me for like four hours. And he was gonna kill me, if it weren't for my friend havin' his—the color of his car and stuff was and all that, he would've killed me I think. And then he gave me twenty dollars and put me out in the field. Told me to find my own way back home.

No Harm Was Done

In perhaps the strongest confusion of sex with violence, many people believe that the greater acquaintance a person has with consensual sex, the less harm is done by rape. In a date rape situation, for example, sexually experienced women, or women who had previously had consensual sex with the aggressor, are often considered to have been involved in a less serious event (Warshaw 1988). In some ways, this can be compared to the belief that some people have that rape of a prostitute is just a bad business deal, to be compared to an instance of someone sneaking into a movie theater without paying admission. Much more serious is a variant of this myth that does not question whether prostitutes can be raped. Rather, it puts forth the notion that prostitutes' lives are not valu-

able enough for violence against them to be taken seriously.

This latter myth was critiqued by a number of the women in this sample. Blondie insisted that, "Being prostitutes, we still know the difference between rape and uh, you know, not gettin' raped. Just because we do it for a living doesn't mean we want it, you know?" She claimed that prostitutes "get raped all the time and it doesn't matter to the police because you're a prostitute, you know. You don't really have a case against them." Similarly, Ginger explained, "I don't care, just because I'm working the streets, it's not casual to me, it's still a traumatic thing. You know."

These women had rarely gone to the police. When Jane was gangraped, she believed she couldn't go to the police "because they don't have no pity for no prostitutes. They figure if you out there whoring you s'posed to take what's coming to you . . . you get some that's so nasty and mean to you out there." Those who had filed reports felt they were not taken seriously. Sugar went to the police after she was thrown out of a man's truck, but was disturbed when the officers' response "was laughin' about it." Pepper was beaten in the head by a trick who tried to rob her. She managed to escape, ran to a nearby children's hospital, and called the police:

And they was like, "Well, these things always happen, if you wanna go to the hospital we'll take you," you know, and they really wasn't concerned so I said forget it. Just drop me back off on Main Street . . . I was mad [at their response] because I was, you know, I was hurt. But I just said fuck it . . . wasn't no use. They didn't really care. . . .

Lacy, the only woman in the sample who reported having a good relationship with police, still believed that "police won't really do much about [violence] . . . 'cause they consider us just a statistic . . . They figure like, well, maybe if we do die at least they won't have to fuck with us no more." Her voice was echoed by that of a city vice officer, interviewed as part of this study, who said it was a common belief among local police that when a prostitute was found dead: "Who really cares? Who really cares? [You're dealing with] a girl who's zero.". . .

Prostitutes Deserve Violence Against Them

Amir (1971) suggested that a woman who cursed in public, dressed suggestively, or otherwise stepped out of her "proper" gender role could be seen as having "precipitated" the crime against her. Rapists generally have argued that there are a wide range of such behaviors, including hitchhiking, being out alone at night, or using drugs, that make the victim deserving and the rapist excused (Estrich 1987; Scully 1990; Frohmann 1992). To at least these men, there is a powerful discourse in this society that legitimizes sexual attacks on ordinary women who reject any of these sexually repressive norms, such as going out alone (Schwendinger and Schwendinger 1983). Prostitutes, who violate gendered sexual expectations so greatly, seem from the stories of these women to expand also the level of anger and moral indignation expressed by the men who attack them.

One reflection of this anger is the constant verbal harassment that goes with being on the streets (Perkins 1991). The public harassment of women functions to define public space as male, and to remind women of "their roles as sexual beings available to men . . . " (Bernard and Schlaffer 1989, p. 387). This verbal abuse labels and stigmatizes the women, creating contexts in which violence against them becomes legitimized.

Verbal harassment was perceived by the women in the sample as something that "comes with the territory" of being a street prostitute. According to Veronica, "you get that all the time. Just, you might have some young kids going out on the street, you know, bitch, prostitute, shit like that." It was common for people riding by in cars to "cuss you out. 'Go home ho'.' You know, 'Go take a bath, bitch.' " Jessie explained:

> Mostly it'd be teenagers that they're probably in high school, and you know that, they got on brand new tennis shoes that their mom just bust her ass to buy, you know, or their dad, and they're riding high. You know, they don't understand what it's like. You know, to be out there.

According to Lacy, it "runs your self-esteem down real low . . . you don't have no self-respect for yourself." Sugar said, "It upsets me sometimes, makes me kinda depressed, but I just keep goin' on." In addition, sometimes women faced verbal abuse at the hands of tricks, who used the verbal assaults to justify their violent behavior. A man who was physically abusive to Lisa before she managed to jump out of his car told her, she reports, "Well, if you wasn't a whore you wouldn't be out here; if you wasn't, if you couldn't handle these things, and you're a tramp anyway."

All Women (Prostitutes) Are the Same

The women in this sample strongly felt that men viewed them all as being the same. They were perceived by men as belonging in a stigmatized category, identified as interchangeable sexual objects. Of course, the ideology of women as disposable, usable objects of male consumption is pervasive in American culture (Schur 1984; 1988), with many men feeling entitled to domestic and sexual services from women as a class (Russell 1984). Black (1983) popularized the notion of "collective liability" to suggest that all people in a particular category are held responsible for the actions of any of their counterparts in that category. A woman who is raped may be the victim of a rapist who thinks this way: "A man's intent may not be to punish the woman he is raping but to use her because she represents a category to him" (Scully 1990, p. 138). For the prostitutes in this sample, this ideology was acutely present and literally placed them in danger. They were typically responded to on the streets as members of a category of devalued women, rather than as individuals.

For example, it was not uncommon for these women to report that a man who was angry at one prostitute picked up another woman and took out his aggression on her. Lacy explained, "A girl might rip him off, and he might come around the block and see you and pick you up and beat you up. You know what I'm saying? That's because they just, they think we're all the same." Jessie related a similar story. She got in the car with a trick who "pulled out a gun and he made me have sex with him, 'cause someone had just robbed him, he said. And he was mad." Another time, Jessie was forced to have oral sex with a man after "he had smoked all his dope out with this girl, who didn't give him any sex. So he dropped her off, he's mad at the world, and he wants his things off, so he just, you know, grabbed somebody." The prostitutes believe that this perception of them as members of a category further allowed them to be blamed for their own victimization. Lacy repeated a similar theme that people see any or all prostitutes as not only the same, but also as uniformly publicly available for any sort of attack:

> We get beat up all the time . . . I mean, we're the objects of everybody's anger it seems like, you know. The dope man's had a bad day, and we just happen to come along at the wrong time, you know. Or dates, you know, get picked up by stupid dates. Ex-boyfriends, and people who are on crack. . . .

Neutralization or Learned Behavior?

One difficulty of the above analysis is that it is a description of women's perceptions of men's behavior. Even if it is also an accurate description of men's attitudes, there still remain several problems. They can be highlighted through the use of Sykes and Matza's (1957) theoretical model on techniques of neutralization and the controversy surrounding this explanation. Simply put, these theorists are interested in how youths who seem to endorse so many of society's values can at the same time engage in delinquent behavior. There are some overlaps between rape myths and the specific techniques Sykes and Matza suggest that delinquents use, particularly in the notion of *denial of injury* (I didn't really hurt anyone), or, if that is untenable, *denial of the victim* (the victim deserved it). Their main suggestion, however, is that youths take attitudes and values already present in the main society (such as rape myths) and extend them into neutralizing attitudes before committing a criminal act to loosen the constraints upon them of societal values and norms.

This argument is fairly similar to the one being made here. We have argued that in a rape-supportive culture, attitudes and values that degrade women and make rape possible are in existence and learned at some level by all men. If Sykes and Matza are correct, some men choose to accept these values, integrating them into their own, and create neutralizations that allow them both to maintain their self-image as law-abiding citizens and also to victimize women. As the women at the extreme end of a continuum of stigma, prostitutes are the most likely to be victimized—and the most likely to have rape myths applied to them.

. . . Certainly there is a level of discourse available in society that suggests that prostitutes are unrapeable, that no harm is actually done in forced sex, that women who violate gender norms deserve to be treated poorly, and that all women are the same, or collectively liable. A person looking to neutralize societal norms certainly can find these excuses easily, whether they are rapists or assaulters of prostitutes, or whether they are criminal justice system officials looking for a reason to turn a blind eye on the complaints of prostitutes.

The techniques of neutralization theory are particularly useful in the case of violence against prostitutes, because they are so often the victims of men who look, act, and generally probably are prosocial in most ways. Most street prostitutes have strongly developed protection schemes that keep them from entering a car unless it is decent, driven by a respectable-looking man. Many prostitutes look for class and race cues based on societal stereotypes of who is more safe. If these women do not date men who "look" dangerous, the violence described in this paper has been committed for the most part by men the women identified as unlikely to be criminals. If these women and their stereotypes are in any way correct, then their victimizers are men who have found some way to convince themselves that prostitutes are acceptable victims. Sykes and Matza (1957) suggest that a primary element of their theory is that young boys learn that some people are legitimate to victimize and some are not. . . .

Conclusion

It is common in the rape literature to argue that violence arises from rape myths that define women as sexual property, where rape is defined as the sexual assault of a woman who is not your own (Scully 1990). This discourse, damaging as it is for a great many women, has specifically left prostitutes in a position where many consider them unrapeable. They are publicly available for male consumption; they belong not to one man but to any man. Rape ideologies that typically apply to marital, date, and stranger rapes are uniquely combined in the case of prostitutes to circulate the powerful message that prostitutes are open territory for assault.

The women in this study faced an enormous amount of violence: 14 had been physically attacked, some in the most brutal fashions imaginable. For some women, violence was so widespread as to be immeasurable.

Ideologies concerning who "asks for" rape, who "deserves" it, and why appear to have been played out in the treatment of street prostitutes. Based on the victims' reports, it appears that for some men the fact that these women were in the social category of prostitutes meant that they were available for verbal, physical, and sexual abuse. The women reported that other men seemed to assume that once a woman agreed to some form of sexual transaction, she was then available for any further assault. Sometimes, even the most violent attacks were apparently "purchased" by men when they paid the women they had just raped or beaten. Prostitutes saw men as treating them as women who had no right to resist, as having no individuality; they believed they were treated as members of a category. The apparent assumption of "collective liability," that all prostitutes are the same, may have led men to act as though they were justified in assaulting one prostitute in order to vent their anger or get revenge on another. The women felt as though they were "the object of everybody's anger" on the streets. As devalued and stigmatized women, they perceived themselves as having been defined as legitimate and deserving targets of male abuse. Further, their experiences with police and prosecutors led these women to believe that representatives of the criminal justice system would often show that they agreed with these assessments by failing to find criminal acts against prostitutes as an actionable problem, or else denying prostitutes the right to file complaints as reputable citizens.

It is not only the general myth in society that prostitutes are unrapeable that harms these women. The general myths on rape—that no harm is actually done, particularly if the woman is sexually experienced or sexually active; that all women are the same; that women who violate gender norms "deserve" to be treated with violence (or at least it is less of a problem if it happens to them)—all seem to work more strongly in the case of these prostitutes.

Violence against street prostitutes is an extreme case of sexual exploitation. Its patterns and handling reveal deeper meanings attached to women's sexuality in American culture. The fact that prostitutes, are perceived and treated as unrapeable, as having forfeited their right to consent by choosing to participate in promiscuous, commercial, public sex (Rubin 1984), reveals generally the extent to which women are still expected to adhere to narrow standards of appropriate sexuality and are still defined as the sexual property of men. Prostitutes' victimization and mistreatment are a clear example of the embodiment of these beliefs.

References

Amir, Menachem. 1971. *Patterns in Forcible Rape.* Chicago: University of Chicago Press.

Andersen, Margaret L. 1988. *Thinking About Women: Sociological Perspectives on Sex and Gender.* New York: Macmillan.

Bernard, Cheryl, and Edith Schlaffer. 1989. " 'The Man in the Street': Why He Harasses." Pp. 384–387 in *Feminist Frontiers* 11, edited by Laurel Richardson and Verta Taylor. New York: Random House.

Black, Donald. 1983. "Crime as Social Control." *American Sociological Review* 48:34–45.

Bracey, Dorothy H. 1979. *Baby Pros.* New York: The John Jay Press.

Brownmiller, Susan. 1975. *Against Our Will.* New York: Simon and Schuster.

Bullough, Vern, and Bonnie Bullough. 1987. *Women and Prostitution: A Social History.* Buffalo: Prometheus.

Burt, Martha R. 1980. "Cultural Myths and Supports for Rape." *Journal of Personality and Social Psychology* 38:217–230.

Clark, Lorenne, and Debra Lewis. 1977 *Rape: The Price of Coercive Sexuality.* Toronto: The Women's Press.

Cohen, Patricia Cline. 1990. "The Helen Jewitt Murder: Violence, Gender, and Sexual Licentiousness in Antebellum America." *NWSA Journal,* 2:374–389.

Connelly, Mark Thomas. 1980. *The Response to Prostitution in the Progressive Era.* Chapel Hill, NC: The University of North Carolina Press.

Corbin, Alain. 1990. *Women for Hire: Prostitution and Sexuality in France After 1850.* Cambridge, MA: Harvard University Press.

Estrich, Susan. 1987. *Real Rape.* Cambridge, MA: Harvard University Press.

Fairstein, Linda A. 1993. *Sexual Violence: Our War Against Rape.* New York: William Morrow and Company.

Finkelhor, David, and Kersti Yllo. 1985. *License to Rape: Sexual Abuse of Wives.* New York: Holt, Rinehart and Winston.

Frohmann, Lisa G. 1992. *Screening Sexual Assault Cases: Prosecutorial Decisions to File or Reject Rape Complaints.* Doctoral Dissertation, University of California, Los Angeles.

Gilmartin-Zena, Pat. 1988. "Gender Differences in Students' Attitudes Toward Rape." *Sociological Focus* 21:279–291.

Hatty, Suzanne. 1989. "Violence Against Prostitute Women: Social and Legal Dilemmas." *Australian Journal of Social Issues* 24:235–248.

Herman, Dianne. 1988. "The Rape Culture." Pp. 260–273 in *Changing Our Power: An Introduction to Women's Studies,* edited by Jo Whitehorse Cochran, Donna Langton, and Carolyn Woodward. Dubuque, IO: Kendall/Hunt Publishing Company.

Hill, Marilynn Wood. 1993. *Their Sisters' Keepers: Prostitution in New York City, 1830–1870.* Berkeley: University of California Press.

Miller, Joann L. 1991. "Prostitution in Contemporary American Society." Pp. 45–57 in *Sexual Coercion: A Sourcebook on Its Nature, Causes, and Prevention.* Edited by Elizabeth Grauerholz and Mary A. Koralewski. Lexington, MA: Lexington Books.

Miller, Peggy, and Nancy Biele. 1993. "Twenty Years Later: The Unfinished Revolution." Pp. 47–64 in *Transforming a Rape Culture,* edited by Emilie Buchwaid, Pamela R. Fietclier, and Martha Rotli. Minneapolis: Milkweed Editions.

Perkins, Roberta. 1991. *Working Girls: Prostitutes, Their Life and Social Control.* Canberra: The Australian Institute of Criminology.

Rosen, Ruth. 1982. *The Lost Sisterhood: Prostitution in America, 1900–1918.* Baltimore: The Johns Hopkins Press.

Rubin, Gayle. 1984. "Thinking Sex: Notes for a Radical Theory of the Politics of Sexuality." Pp. 267–319 in *Pleasure and Danger: Exploring Female Sexuality,* edited by Carol S. Vance. London: Pandora.

Russell, Diana E. H. 1984. *Sexual Exploitation.* Beverly Hills, CA: Sage.

Russell, Diane E. H. 1990. *Rape in Marriage, expanded and rev. ed.* Bloomington, IN: Indiana University Press.

Sanger, William W., M.D. 1937 [1897]. The *History of Prostitution: Its Extent, Causes and Effects Throughout the World.* New York: Eugenics Publishing Company.

Schwartz, Martin D. 1982. "The Spousal Exemption for Criminal Rape Prosecution," *Vermont Law Review* 7:33–57.

Schwendinger, Julia R., and Herman Schwendinger. 1983. *Rape and Inequality.* Beverly Hills, CA: Sage.

Schur, Edwin. 1988. *The Americanization of Sex.* Philadelphia: Temple University Press.

Schur, Edwin. 1984. *Labeling Women Deviant.* New York: Random House.

Scully, Diana. 1990. *Understanding Sexual Violence: A Study of Convicted Rapists.* Boston: Unwin Hyman.

Shotland, R. Lance. 1992. "A Theory on the Causes of Courtship Rape: Part 2." *Journal of Social Issues* 48:127–143.

Silbert, Mimi H., and Ayala M. Pines. 1982. "Victimization of Street Prostitutes." *Victimology: An International Journal* 7:122–133.

Sykes, Gresham M., and David Matza. 1957. "Techniques of Neutralization: A Theory of Delinquency." *American Sociological Review* 22:664–670.

Vachss, Alice. 1993. *Sex Crimes.* New York: Random House.

Warshaw, Robin. 1988. *I Never Called It Rape.* New York: Harper & Row.

Weis, Kurt, and Sandra Borges. 1973. "Victimology and Rape: The Case of the Legitimate Victim." *Issues in Criminology* 8:71–115.

Weisberg, D. Kelly. 1985. *Children of the Night: A Study of Adolescent Prostitution.* Lexington, MA: Lexington Books.

Weisheit, Ralph, and Susan Mahan. 1988. *Women, Crime, and Criminal Justice.* Cincinnati: Anderson.

Young, Vernetta D. 1992. "Fear of Victimization and Victimization Rates Among Women: A Paradox?" *Justice Quarterly* 9:419–441.

Reprinted from: Jody Miller and Martin D. Schwartz, "Rape Myths and Violence Against Street Prostitutes." In *Deviant Behavior: An Interdisciplinary Journal*, pp. 1–23. Copyright © 1995 by Taylor & Francis. Reprinted by permission. ✦

9

Boy-Lovers and Their Influence on Boys: Distorted Research and Anecdotal Observations

Edward Brongersma

In this article, the author looks at the research and assumptions about adult men who have emotional and sexual relationships with boys. He concludes that most of our knowledge about such men is in error because it confuses issues of sexuality. The author argues that research usually does not distinguish between men who are attracted to boys and those who are attracted to children in general, and he points out that research is generally biased and inaccurately assumes that man-boy relationships are based only on sex. This article calls into question the usual assumptions about some forms of deviance, and provides a chance to understand one of the most strongly stigmatized forms of deviance from the views of those who engage in such behaviors.

Sources of Knowledge

The influence a man may have on a boy in a man/boy-relationship is a difficult subject to broach: empirical research is conspicuous by its virtual absence and theory has been highly distorted by social prejudice and the seeming inability of most investigators to make proper distinctions. Thus an outsider who wishes to gain some insight into what really happens in a sexually expressed relationship between a man and a boy has very little to go on. This paper, then, can pretend to do little more than clear the path of a few obstacles which will be faced in later scientific research; of necessity it must remain somewhat anecdotal.

The author himself has met over 500 boy-lovers of 17 different nationalities over the past 35 years. He met only a small minority of them in his official role as counsel for defense in criminal trials. In most cases the contact was on an informal, even footing in his own home or visiting them in their homes, which is certainly an advantage when one is trying to gain an accurate impression of a human phenomenon. Included among these boy-lovers were members of virtually all the professions, and also men who lived on a very modest social level. In addition, the author had the opportunity to interview 45 adolescents and young men and ask them questions about the intimate details of their sex lives. Most, during their childhood and teenage years, had had sexual contacts with adult men, either on a casual basis or within a more lasting relationship.

In all these meetings, conversations and interviews, including letters exchanged before and after, there was little that confirms the image developed in the scientific (or pseudo-scientific) literature on pedophilia. Most papers and books on the subject—the work of Pieterse (1982) and Sandfort (1982) are notable exceptions—seem to have been born in another world where laboratory and theory remain aloof from living reality. In this difficult area of human interaction, fiction writers, with their unique ability to identify with their characters, have often been more successful in giving us an accurate picture than the men [and women] of science. By reading books like those of Michael Davidson, Alan Edward, Isabelle Holland, Iris Murdoch, Fritz Peters, Jean-Michel Prigny, Christiane Rochefort, Angus Stewart and Gerald Tesch (listed in the references)—to mention only a few—the intelligent non-pedophile may get a better impression of what goes on, for good or evil, during intimate man/boy-relations than by studying a large number of academic treatises.

Inadequate Research

It is inherent in intimate human relations that both partners can exercise a profound influence upon each other. Where the status of the partners is very unequal, as in any relationship between an adult and a much younger person, people tend to attach special importance to the influence which the older, who is perceived as being the most powerful, has over the younger. To judge what might be the benefits or the dark sides of such a relationship it is essential to know more about "the" boy-lover. Is it true that he has special characteristics, and, if so, what are they?

Up until now, however, research has conspicuously failed to answer this question. It is important to understand why it failed and how it failed in order to discover why and how the public image of the boy-lover, and the influence he is supposed to have upon the boy, has become so amazingly distorted. I will first consider the errors which have been made in research and examine what effects they have had on how people judge the boy-lover's impact on his young friends.

First Source of Error: Sexual Activity As the Decisive Test

The first error is using sexual activity as the decisive indicator of sexual preference. It is the same error which permeated older studies of homosexuality. "Pedophiles" were sought among inmates in psychiatric hospitals and people sentenced by the courts. Everyone who had committed an "indecent assault" upon a minor was labelled "pedophile," just as in the past everyone who had had intercourse with a partner of his own sex was called "homosexual" (Bullough, 1979; Taylor, 1981; West, 1977). Implicit is the assumption that sexual behavior is always indicative of sexual desire: in other words, a pedophile act rather than the configuration of a man's erotic appetite defines him as a

pedophile. Sexologically this is an untenable simplification.

There were periods in the past of our own cultural heritage, such as Greek antiquity (Buffiére, 1980; Dover, 1978; Foucault, 1984; Patzer, 1982) and today in certain other cultures (Bleibtreu-Ehrenberg, 1980; Cline, 1936; Herdt, 1981 and 1982) when it was or where it is considered normal for adult males to have sexual relations with boys. This shows that sexual attraction to youthful individuals of his own sex is present to a greater or lesser degree in every human male, and this makes it possible for every man to have sex with a handsome boy. As Geiser (1979), puts it, "Surprising as it may seem, otherwise normal adult males who work with young boys can often, quite inexplicably, find themselves becoming sexually aroused." We should "face the fact that quite normal men can be aroused sexually by young boys. That they are is not evidence of homosexuality, but may even be evidence of their humanness and sensitivity" (pp. 93–94).

As boys physically have certain things in common with women (the smooth skin, the red lips and rosy cheeks, the rounded forms, the brilliant hair), adult heterophile men, when no women or girls are available, will tend to find greater sexual satisfactions with a substitute boy than with a substitute man. The non-availability of females can be for either internal or external reasons. Externally: females are not to be found in certain social settings and institutions, and so we see predominantly heterophile men satisfying themselves from sheer necessity with boys on ships, on scientific expeditions into wilderness areas or in prisons, and then, once back home, resuming their contacts with females. Internally: some males because of personality peculiarities are abnormally unable to establish intimate contact with the adult partners they would prefer. They may turn to children because these are more easily approached and less exacting in the sexual area than an adult woman or man would be. Thus a man might have sexual contacts with a boy even though his ideal erotic mate would be an adult. We should best call such a man a pseudo-pedophile in order to distinguish him from real pedophiles, i.e., adults having a pronounced and conscious dominating sexual preference for boys and/or girls.

Sexual activity with a minor (pedosexuality) tells us little in itself about a man. Pedosexuality is hardly an infallible indicator of pedophilia, a term which should only be applied to persons for whom children are the most important elicitors of sexual arousal. Among true pedophiles, then, are individuals having frequent and extensive sexual relations with children, and others who for one reason or another never touch a child and so avoid being labelled as a pedophile (Pieterse, 1982).

In their detailed investigation of a large number of male sexual delinquents incarcerated in American prisons, Gebhard et al., found very few pedophiles among those sentenced for offenses with children. Among 244 males found guilty of sexual activities with children under twelve, only two declared they really preferred a partner this young. Among 269 males found guilty of sexual activities with children from 12 to 15 years, only 17 declared they preferred a partner in this age bracket. Gebhard and his co-workers conclude that the problem "is not so much one of a predilection for youth as it is one of lack of discrimination against youth" (1965, p.66, p 681).

One could raise the objection that the study dealt with prisoners, and prisoners are subject to greater than normal temptations to give the "socially desirable answer." But considering the number of cases in which Gebhard's subjects admitted having committed other crimes which had gone undetected, or in which subjects not serving sentences for crimes against children admitted feeling sexual attraction to children, it seems unlikely that the pressures to give "socially desirable answers" distorted these remarkable figures enough to invalidate them.

The problem of the "socially desirable answer" was avoided by the sociologist Charles H. McCaghy (1967) whose sample consisted of 181 males convicted of "child molesting" in the state of Wisconsin. He categorized his subjects "measured by the range of interaction which adults had with children: the extent to which their life patterns were occupied by contacts with children"—that is,

through occupational and leisure time activities, etc. By doing so he established substantial differences between those in the group where social contacts with children were frequent and enriching and those in other categories. The men who had many social contacts never used any form of coercion to obtain sex: a non-sexual relationship usually preceded the sexual activities which were usually restricted to active fondling of the genitals. These were the men whose lives were deeply interwoven with those of children: in other words, they were the pedophiles.

The important distinction between pedophiles and pseudo-pedophiles was not made until a few decades ago, but today it is stressed by most researchers in the field: Albrecht (1964), Baurmann (1983), Bendig (1979), Crawford (1981), Fisch (1971) Freund (1981), Gagnon and Simon (1970), Gebhard (1965), Geiser (1979), Haeberle (1978), Hart de Ruyter (1976), Howells (1980), Kerscher (1978), McCaghy (1967), Möller (1983), Newton (1978) O'Carroll (1980), Pieterse (1982), Righton (1981), Rouweler-Wuts (1976), Sandfort (1980), Schillemans (1983), Schorsch (1973), Sengers (1970), Socarides (1954), Swanson (1968), West (1980), Wyss (1967), Yaffé (1981), Zeegers (1977). Groth (1978) makes a similar distinction but blurs the issue by defining those with a sexual preference for children as "fixated pedophiles" and pseudo-pedophiles as "regressed pedophiles."

Trying to Avoid the Error: Samples of Pedophiles

An opportunity to carry out investigations using samples consisting entirely of true pedophiles seemed to arise in the early 1970s when pedophiles in various countries started to form pedophile organizations and come out into the open. Pioneer work was done by Dutch psychologist Frits Bernard who in 1973 distributed a printed questionnaire during an international symposium and continued to repeat this procedure at subsequent meetings. Rouweler-Wuts (1976) and Pieterse (1982) also distributed different kinds of questionnaire among members of

Dutch pedophile work groups and their acquaintances. In England the Paedophile Information Exchange (PIE) carried out a "Survey of Members," and in France Léonard des Sables made an enquiry among boy-loving members of Arcadie, a male homophile group (published 1976–1977). In Belgium the Centre de Recherche et d'Information sur l'Enfance et la Sexualité distributed in 1984 a questionnaire among 300 subscribers to its monthly magazine and a French gay weekly magazine, as well as their acquaintances. All the groups mentioned here, as well as the German DSAP and AKP, the Swiss SAP and the American NAMBLA, are made up, almost without exception, of male boy-lovers. Pieterse's sample was less one-sided, but even here 79% of her subjects were drawn to boys exclusively. It seems that women are less interested in legalizing pedosexual contacts than men and therefore less inclined to join such groups.

But even for male boy-lovers these associations are not totally representative. People fighting against discrimination and for the abolition of laws directed against their activities are not average citizens. Moreover, the man who has a great deal to lose if his essential erotic tendencies are discovered will be reluctant to join such a group, and will be even less inclined to show up at its meetings. Fear of discovery, however, sharply diminishes after one's cover has disappeared upon police arrest. Studying the members of a pedophile association (a selection) having the courage to present themselves at a meeting (a selection of this selection), Bernard (1979) found—no wonder!—an extremely high percentage (54%) who had been convicted in a court of law.

In their introduction to their report on male sexuality, Pietropinto and Simenauer (1979) share the view of Alexander Pope that the proper study of man is man: he who wants to study mankind should go to common man, not just to psychiatric patients, to members of specific organizations or to people who write letters to him. Weinberg's statement (quoted in Levine, 1980) that public stigmatization makes it impossible to compose a representative sample of homophiles is even more applicable to pedophiles, living as they do under a far heavier burden of stigmatization. Taylor (1981) points out that one simply cannot generalize from a sample taken from a pedophile work group. The several research studies mentioned here may have taught us something about the membership of pedophile organizations but little about pedophiles.

Second Source of Error: Mingling Boy-Lovers and Girl-Lovers

It wasn't just the impossibility of obtaining a really representative sample of boy-lovers which mitigated against the work of professional researchers: in most studies *everyone* who had sex with children was regarded as belonging to one homogeneous group in which no distinction was drawn between those mainly attracted to girls and those mainly attracted to boys.

The reactions of boys to sexual approach by an adult are strikingly different from those of girls. Boys are less inclined than girls to talk to their parents about their sexual adventures with grown-ups (Landis, 1956; Rennert, 1965). Boys tend to take the initiative in such acts more often than girls (Churchill, 1967; Gebhard et al., 1965; Giese, 1964; Reiss, 1967; Wyss, 1967). They are less likely to reject advances by an adult and more likely to cooperate in any sexual acts which ensue (Gerbener, 1966). Boys are more receptive to advances made by strangers (Gebhard et al., 1965). They are more interested than girls in sexual activities and seem to be much more open to involving themselves sexually with an adult partner. Thus it is hardly coincidental that violence in sexual contacts between men and boys is quite exceptional, while it is a frequent occurrence in sexual acts between men and girls (Gebhard et al., 1965; Jersild, 1964; Landis, 1956; Rennert, 1965).

This may largely explain the findings of Baurmann (1983) who studied all 8058 cases which came to the attention of the police in the German state of Lower Saxony during 1969–1972 in which females below the age of 20 and males below the age of 14 were sexual "victims." Six to ten years after the event he made an additional follow-up study of a random selection of these victims. He found that while a number of the females had sustained a greater or lesser degree of injury, in not one single case injury could be detected in the males.

Conclusions based on studying sex between men and girls should never be applied to sex between men and boys. Research concerning pedophiles which mixes the two categories together is quite simply unacceptable.

Third Source of Error: Bias

Many investigations are conspicuously distorted by researcher bias. In labelling the sexual activity "abuse," "offense," "indecent assault," "molestation" or "rape"; calling the adult partner "actor," "perpetrator," "delinquent," "offender," "criminal," "abuser" or "molester," and the child "victim," authors betray the fact that they are operating upon premises which have yet to be proven.

We might justly ask what is the reason for this absurd violation of one of the first principles of scientific investigation: to remain objective. Herek (1984, p. 45) quotes Ferenczi, Marmor, Cory, MacDonald and Weinberg as authorities for "the often-advanced hypothesis that many people are hostile toward homosexuals because they fear their own unarticulated homoerotic impulses." The research of such sexologists as Stekel (1922), Gordon (1978), Geiser (1979), Schorsch (1973) and Freund (1981) led them to believe that sexual attraction to children is a universal phenomenon, and—as we have already observed—the existence of cultures where every adult man is supposed to have sex with boys (Ancient Greece, Siwa, Keraki, Big Namba, New Guinea) suggests that sexual attraction to boys is more or less present in every human male. But as this tendency collides so strongly with the standards of sexual morality which for centuries have dominated Western culture, it is of course, in most males energetically suppressed and denied. Utilizing the above hypothesis concerning homophobia, we might suggest that many people—quite apart from their concern over boys' mental and moral health—exhibit such violently emotional hostility toward boy-lovers because they fear their own unarticulated pedophile impulses.

In a number of countries (including many states in the USA) every sexual activity with a minor under the age of consent is, in the language of the law, "rape" because the minor is considered unable to give a legally valid consent. Blindly following such legal niceties of terminology hardly contributes to scientific knowledge. Moreover, a number of very important questions are evaded: (a) to what extent are these minors really unable to "give consent" and how does the validity of their consent differ with age? (b) is there a difference between a man who scrupulously limits himself to those intimate acts which the minor evidently enjoys and eagerly requests and the man who selfishly, even violently, pursues the satisfaction of his lusts upon an obviously unwilling minor?

Absence of Violence

While professional research has contributed little to our knowledge of boy-lovers, we have learned a bit more about their sexual relations with boys. First of all, as we have already seen, the use of violence is exceptional. In the case of real sexual abuse it makes little difference to the victim, compelled to submit by violence, threats or abuse of authority, whether the offender is a pedophile or a pseudo-pedophile. But if violence is a common complaint in man-girl relations, it is much rarer with boys.

This can clearly be seen in court statistics. One should always keep in mind when examining these figures that they apply to only a minuscule sample of adult-minor sexual acts which take place day in, day out in our society. Brongersma (1971 and 1975) and des Sables (1977), using quite different methods of calculation, independently arrived at an identical estimate: one unlawful sexual act with a minor in three thousand is discovered, tried and results in a sentence: the rest are "dark numbers." Since instances in which violence takes place are more likely to lead to a complaint being lodged with the police and to detection, there will always be more violence among reported cases than in these which go undetected.

Gebhard et al., studying 888 male sexual offenders sentenced to prison terms (including 232 imprisoned for sexual contacts with boys 0-15 years of age), drew a distinction among heterosexual offenders between "aggressors" and non-violent men. Force and threat, however, proved to be "minimal in homosexual offenses and accordingly has not been made the basis for separate categories" (1976, p. 45, p. 272). Baurmann, studying cases of illegal sexual activities involving 8058 minors (including 877 boys under the age of 14), writes, "Boys rarely experience sexual violence (1983, p. 157, p. 221). He suggests that the reason for this may be that boys approached sexually by a man tend to behave passively or even compliantly, while girls are much more inclined to reject such advances (1983, p. 322, p. 430). Wolters (1982) also stressed the fact that sexual aggression against boys is rare. The statistics upon which these conclusions are based do not differentiate between pseudo-pedophiles and pedophile actors, but on this point there is little need to differentiate, as it may be assumed that all aggression is traumatizing and nefarious.

The argument put forward by some authors (for example Sonenschein, 1983) that a real pedophile never will use violence because he loves children is not valid. Individuals such as Haarmann (Lessing, 1925), Corrl (Gurwell, 1974; Olsen, 1974), Bartsch (Föster, 1984) and other sadistic torturers and mass murderers of boys were certainly pedophiles according to the definition adopted here, since they preferred sexual contacts with young males. The same can be said about some pedagogues advocating severe discipline in education: they are at least suspect.

The difference between pseudo-pedophiles and pedophiles becomes important when we consider their respective ways of approaching boys or reacting to sexual advances from boys. We have seen that it is impossible to claim that all cases of sexual violence and brutal treatment must be ascribed to pseudo-pedophiles, that pedophiles are always gentle and tactful. We can easily imagine instances of a boy being better off with a kind-hearted pseudo-pedophile than with a coarse and dominating pedophile. But on the whole there is more risk for him with

a pseudo-pedophile who takes the boy only as a second-best solution for the satisfaction of sexual desires mainly directed toward women. Baurmann concluded from his research that "most pedophiles behave strikingly gently and tenderly with children: they try to establish a mutual relationship with them, to act like children when they are with them." And he quotes Schorsch: "The pedophile wants to introduce himself to the boy's world as an equal, a participant, to be as a boy is, to feel as boys feel. Thus with these pedophiles we will almost never find them using aggression. Aggressive activities are much more frequent in substitutive sexual contacts with children. The group of sexual delinquents (. . .) who abuse children for sexually substitutive activities seems to have little in common with the group of pedophiles and more in common with rapists" (1983, p. 304).

Differences in Sexual Practices

In the context of the pedophile's desire "to be as a boy is, to feel as boys feel," it should be noted that the sexual contacts, especially with younger children, will mostly "resemble the sexual behaviour that goes on between children" (West 1977, p. 214). Intimacies with small boys are mainly limited to those activities which Mohr and Turner (1967) described as "pregenital sex play such as looking, showing, touching, kissing and fondling." After some time masturbation will be added to the pregenital play. There is almost no question of the boy acting as insertee in oral or anal intercourse, unless, (1) he has grown bigger and older, (2) he has a longer lasting steady relationship with the man and (3) he insists on these practices himself. With a stranger, in casual meetings, a boy will rarely want to go so far and he habitually limits the play to touching of his naked body or being masturbated or fellated by the older partner (Baurmann, 1983; Gerbener, 1966; Ingram, 1979; Landis, 1956; McCaghy, 1971; Potrykus and Wöbcke, 1974; Righton, 1981).

This stresses the importance of differentiating between casual meetings and longer lasting relationships. It may be supposed that the casual meeting will be sought more by the pseudo-pedophile with his lesser interest in the boy as such, while steady relationships will be more congenial to pedophile boy-lovers.

Rouweler-Wuts (1976), approaching the phenomenon from the standpoint of a social worker, questioned 60 pedophiles. She quotes Plaut to make the point that the majority of girl-lovers have casual, passing contacts whereas boy-lovers work harder to achieve long lasting relationships. In a later investigation (N = 148) Pieterse (1982) found that half of her respondents expressed the desire for extended friendships, and where they succeeded the average duration was as long as 33 months. There are two factors which tend to work against longevity, however: (1) society's rejection of man-boy contacts makes a steady relationship more difficult and more dangerous than casual secret meetings with strangers; (2) since boyhood is a transitional phase of life, the erotic attraction fades away as adulthood is approached.

Casual Contacts

The impact upon the boy of a casual contact is, of course, different from the effect of a long lasting relationship. For a number of boys the casual meeting may be the kind best adapted to their stage of evolution. Hart de Ruyter (1976) writes that from a boy who, during the course of his adolescent development, has not yet attained a degree of self-assurance, we can expect little more than attempts at sexual intercourse and a direct discharge of impulses. He cites anthropological evidence that in many cultures which live in closer harmony with nature a period of promiscuity precedes marriage. Kentler (1970), in his book on sexual pedagogy, makes a similar observation, adding that the casual, short-lived sexual liaisons prevalent among some groups of Western youth seem to him age-appropriate.

To demand that a boy make his first sexual contact a declaration of love is asking perfection of a beginner. For him it will rather be a matter of hygiene, of exercising a new bodily function, of getting rid of physical tension. It is a first step forward from masturbation.

Some boys emphatically do not want to move beyond the casual contact. An Austrian pedophile told me he once got to know a 14-year-old boy at a swimming pool in Vienna. They had sex on several occasions and slowly the man found himself falling in love with the boy. And so one day he invited him to the movies, to be followed by a good meal at a restaurant. But the boy flatly refused. "Oh, no. I don't want any of that. I come here to get fucked and nothing else!" Erskine Lane (1978) relates a most curious adventure in the same vein with a Guatemalan boy.

Where it is adapted to the boy's phase of development, the casual meeting may mostly pass by as an incident of little importance, a variation on the routine of masturbation. Thrusted without tact upon an unprepared boy, we might suppose it could shock him profoundly and permanently, but research concerning the lasting traumatic effects of sexual confrontations with adults does not support this hypothesis (Bender and Grugett, 1952 quoted by O'Carroll, 1980; Landis, 1956; Brunold, 1962; Lempp, 1968; Bernard, 1979; Corstjens, 1975; Ingram, 1977; Burton, 1968; Baurmann, 1983). On the other hand, in some cases the casual sexual meeting is remembered by the boy as a very positive experience, affirming his personal worth.

A Swedish man in his forties told me about an unforgettable incident which happened to him when he was eleven. One day during his summer holidays he met a man sunning himself on the side of a swimming pool. They began to play-wrestle with each other; both got erections which each could feel inside the other's trunks. "Wouldn't it be nice to do this completely naked?" the man asked. The boy enthusiastically agreed and eagerly accompanied the man to his home where they continued their wrestling games, this time on the man's bed and without their swimming suits. Suddenly the man hugged him very tightly in his arms, thrust with his hips, moaned with pleasure and sperm spurted out of his penis. "I can still remember," my informant told me thirty years later, "how I ran home skipping and singing, enormously proud and happy that my little body could elicit such a strong passion in a grown-up."

In their book of sexual information for adolescents, the New Zealand authors Felicity Tuohy and Michael Murphy (1976) quote the words of a boy who, at a birthday party for one of his teachers, got talking with a man who seemed to have an erotic interest in him. "He gave me his name and address and said, 'Ring me.' I rang him Sunday night and he told me to come in and meet him at his flat in town. I went in about eleven o'clock in the morning. We got into bed and he screwed me and then let me screw him. He was so good. He treated me so well and he was really good at screwing. It was an incredible thing for me because at home everyone was hostile to each other and at school I had no friends. Here was this guy showing me kindness and gentleness and it was an amazing experience I went back Tuesday, Wednesday, Thursday, Friday and that was the last week of the school holidays. Then I went back to school and never saw him again" (p. 212).

Wilson (1982) talked with an adult Australian who, as a boy of fifteen, was taken for a drive by Clarence Osborne and masturbated by him. "I enjoyed talking to him and I enjoyed the sex as well. He's the only man I've ever had a relationship with before or since. As you know I am married now with two kids, but at times I still think back to when he did those things to me and get excited by the thought of it. All I know is that I wanted some sex then and I got it, even though before I could never have imagined myself having it off with another guy, let alone a man who was about thirty years older than myself" (pp. 39–40).

Lasting Relationships

Whatever the impact of such casual meetings upon the boy's developing sexuality and his self-image, it is only through a more lasting relationship that the "pedagogical eros" can come into play and so influence his character and behavior. It has long been recognized that during those years when a boy's character is forming and he is developing a personal philosophy of life and his attitudes toward society and humanity, a close, warm friendship with one or more adults can be of great importance. If physical intimacy occurs

as well the influence of that adult can be even greater, for it is just then that the boy's body and its capabilities are of paramount importance to him.

An educator interviewed by Sandfort (1984) said that boys of fourteen and fifteen are preoccupied with sex the whole day through. The same observation was made by an Austrian teacher (Archives of the Brongersma Foundation). The mystery with which our society cloaks sex leaves boys with many questions unanswered and important problems, some amounting to obsessions, unsolved (De Boer 1978 and 1979; Hass 1979; Sorensen 1973). Kerscher (1977) attributes a high percentage of adolescent suicides to inadequate sexual information, or no information at all. While the popular press and professional literature ignites scandals around the theme of child victims supposedly sacrificed to the sexual lusts of men, we would do better to turn our attention to the enormous number of children who are more or less permanently traumatized by and sacrificed to sexophobia. Parents and teachers are often unable to discuss sex with children as a result of their own upbringing and many teachers are prohibited from doing so by law. In this connection, as Krist (1976) pointed out, shared intimacies with an adult, a shared delight in resolving fascinating physical tensions, initiation into a whole new level of existence—all become deeply significant to the boy. Here is a grown-up who is not only willing to discuss sexual problems with him and answer honestly all his questions but who also reveals and shares with him his own sexual desires. In giving confidence he evokes confidence.

The powerful influence which an adult may thus acquire is in itself neither good nor bad: it all depends upon what he does with it. Adults have a greater capacity than children for good as well as for evil (O'Carroll 1980).

For evil: In the archives of the Brongersma Foundation there is a set of notebooks in which a 30-year-old man kept a careful record of shoplifting committed by him and his 13-year-old friend. In the man's mind these thefts solidified and proved the boy's affection, their close alliance, their mutual love of adventure, their cleverness and courage. Thus he encouraged the boy in his share of the criminality. The total value of the goods stolen over the course of two years was substantial. When they were eventually caught the court, quite rightly, blamed the man for his role in recruiting the youngster into crime. Other instances of evil are men binding boys to them by providing them with drugs, spoiling them by excessive gifts or luxuries, keeping them from their work, isolating them from their peers.

For good: Rossman (1976) gives several examples of social workers achieving miracles with apparently incorrigible young delinquents—not by preaching to them but by sleeping with them. Affection demonstrated by sexual arousal upon contact with the boy's body, by obvious pleasure taken in giving pleasure to the boy, did far more good than years in reformatories. A French author with close contacts with gang adolescents in Paris, Jacques de Brethmas, wrote, "Show me the juvenile judges or pedagogues who have managed to disengage boys from criminal gangs, made them willingly throw away their stilettos, as have many men labelled 'molesters' and 'moral corruptors' by society!" (1980, p. 42).

There are judges who admit the truth in such assertions. Amsterdam juvenile judge Cnoop Koopmans openly advocated this form of social therapy in a public speech (1982). I personally know of cases brought before this man. In one, a boy who had been arrested several times for shoplifting, who had been a terror at home and a failure in school, suddenly turned over a new leaf, gave up crime, started getting good marks at school and became a national champion in his favorite sport. All of this occurred after a boy-lover had been asked officially to take care of him. Their friendship survived the termination of its erotic aspect and, with the boy now an adult, continues today.

Likewise, in Berlin a test program was instituted in which young delinquents were put under the supervision of boy-lovers. The results were totally successful, but unfortunately the fear of public reaction soon closed the program down (Schult 1982).

The French poet Paul Verlaine told of his love for working-class boys, and this is a pref-erence which is rather frequently encountered (Abraham 1969; d'Arch Smith 1970; Barrington 1981; Oskamp 1980; Tripp 1975). If the man takes pleasure in sharing his enthusiasms with his young lover, the boy himself may develop interests in culture, science and technology, learn to appreciate good music and art and so receive a kind of supplemental education he never would have got at school or in his parental home.

Importance of Sex

Where a lasting relationship has been established between a man and a boy it would be wrong to assume it exists only for its sexual pleasures. The investigations of Rouweler-Wuts (1976) among adult pedophiles, of Sandfort (1979 and 1982) among boy-lovers and their boys, as well as documents in the Brongersma Foundation and my own experience, demonstrate that neither for the older nor for the younger partner is sex usually the most important aspect of their friendship. For some men and boys it is a very important element; for virtually none is it the *most* important. Among the pedophile subjects of Rouweler-Wuts (N = 60), 86% felt that friendship with a boy was more important than having sex with him, while only 11% thought sex more important; 73% had had friendships without wanting to introduce sex into them; 19% said, for them, this was impossible. Only 5% said they would definitely terminate a relationship if the boy refused further sexual contacts; 81% said they definitely would not, while 14% were uncertain (Rouweler-Wuts, 1976, pp. 94–95).

One of my correspondents put it this way: "If I had to choose between a steady friendship without any sex and casual sex with a beautiful boy I would not hesitate a second before choosing the former." Rouweler-Wuts described the meaning of the relationship as "fostering the character development of the child, accompanying the child on his way to adulthood, improving his social skills, his financial conditions and his physical development" (1976, p. 60).

Boy-Love Emancipation

"Accompanying the child on his way to adulthood" assumes great importance during those years when he is liberating himself from parental authority. The inevitable misery which accompanies all emancipation processes arises from the tendency of the individual emancipating himself to try to rush things, while the authority from which he is breaking away is simultaneously putting on the brakes. This can lead to those continuous and bitter conflicts which characterize both the political emancipation of a colony and the social emancipation of an adolescent. Puberty rites and manhood initiation ceremonies in other civilizations may well serve to reduce or eliminate such conflicts.

In our culture the boy tries to lift the yoke of parental control and forge ahead with his own independence faster than his stage of maturation generally permits. He still needs protection and guidance but can no longer comfortably accept them from his father. He becomes unsure of himself. As Schlegel (1966) observes, he needs the help of someone else. He is looking, then, for an authority he can trust, but his striving for independence will only permit him to tolerate an authority of his own choice, to whom he submits of his own free will—an authority, moreover, which he can shake off the moment it becomes too much of a burden. At this point the loving pedophile may for some years fit the description, giving the boy a kind of companionship, a security and a protection which his peers cannot provide.

A 28-year-old Italian announced his marriage in a letter to the man with whom, as a 14- to 18-year-old boy, he had carried on a sexually expressed friendship: "I'm working hard at my job, and I think you must take a lot of credit for this. If now things are going well for me it is because of everything you taught me with so much patience and love. I'm so grateful to you, all day and all night; I'll never forget you!" (Archives of the Brongersma Foundation).

Sexual Education

In such a lasting relationship, affection, care and tenderness can flower and fuse together. A boy of seventeen whom I interviewed about his five-year relationship with a middle-age man said, "He taught me the meaning of love." This experience of integrating lust and love may keep the boy from developing our culture's infamous madonna/whore complex. In a Dutch broadcast about pedophilia a few years ago a 15-year-old boy told the following story. At thirteen he had begun to have sex with girls, and that to him meant a girl on her back, him climbing on top of her, shoving his penis in her and thrusting it back and forth until he came. That was all. Then at a football game he met an attractive forty-year-old man. The boy accepted the man's invitation to accompany him home, well aware that the man was sexually interested in him but curious about what might take place. They had sex that afternoon, but the way it happened was a revelation to him. He had never experienced such tenderness, such concern for his feelings, so much respect, even reference [*sic*]. He finished his story by saying, "I'm really 100% heterosexual. After a couple of years of making love with this man I'll be too old for his tastes and then I'll certainly go back to girls again. But when that happens I'll treat them completely differently than I did before, when all I cared about was my own physical satisfaction. I've now learned that sex is so much better if you do it with love and consideration for the other person.' In the event, things turned out exactly as he had foreseen. Just as in the case of the 17 year-old described above, he is now a happily married man—and neither have ever forgotten their former lovers, who have remained their close and trusted friends.

Attitude of Parents

Society seems determined to overlook these positive aspects. It makes it impossible for most men to build a steady relationship with a boy without putting themselves and their young friends at great risk. Sexual history tells us that laws never succeed in subduing the sexual impulse. As Wheeler (1967) correctly observes, "The history of legal control of sex conduct is largely one of failure" (p. 84). The laws may be unable to stop all sex between men and boys; their effect is rather to encourage the less risky casual anonymous contacts, which are usually pedagogically worthless and sometimes even objectionable, at the expense of closer relationships with their manifold opportunities.

Unless a boy's parents care little about his well-being, where he spends his time and with whom—in other words, neglect him— an undisturbed relationship, especially with a younger boy, can only proceed in deep secrecy, or with their consent.

A relationship outside the family, and certainly one involving sexual intimacies, is often perceived by parents as a challenge to their authority. In this they probably are wrong. Parents who look upon the man who loves their son (and is loved by him in return) not as a rival or competitor, not as a thief of their property, but as a partner in the boy's upbringing, someone to be welcomed into their home, will see, on the contrary, a strengthening of the ties which bind them to their son. The boy can relax without ambivalence in his affection for a father and mother who understand and approve of these deep feelings and desires of his. Parents actually retain more influence over their son if they are involved in this relationship, take their share of responsibility for what happens within it. They can then exercise some control over it and, when necessary, help or advise the boy, or even intervene when things go wrong (Möller 1983).

A French father, speaking of his son's erotic friendship with an adult man, put it rather well: "You can tell right away the difference between a man who gives and a man who takes. All you have to do is look at the boy—because he is your child. You'll know immediately whether he is happy or is feeling on edge" (Hennig 1979, p. 159).

The 40-year-old mother of a 12-year-old boy, Menno, was quoted in a widely-read Dutch weekly as saying, "I may seem to a lot of people like a degenerate mother, but I don't care; I'll keep on doing what I'm doing. Look, I don't urge him to do anything; I don't forbid

anything; I leave it all up to the boy. This man, Kees, with whom my son has his relationship, was once in prison but I have trust in his friendship. So why should I break it up? I've known Kees for two years, now. After my divorce I had the feeling I was losing contact with Menno. He had become completely alienated from me. One day I told Kees this, and he said, 'Send the boy to me—I'll talk to him. He can spend the weekend with me.' I thought, well, now, that will be good for Menno, to have a change of scene. I hoped Kees would have a good influence on him. The first time Menno went for the day, then for a weekend—and the next weekend, too. (. . .) Well, since that day Menno has gone off nearly every weekend to Kees. I could see that a wonderful affection had grown up between them; it seemed perfectly normal that they spend a lot of time together. And then I noticed that Menno was becoming more and more open with me. He started to tell me things again. It was amazing how he changed. My oldest boy noticed it, too. Menno had lost his trust in people, and he regained it through Kees. I haven't the faintest idea what goes on between them sexually. Quite frankly, I've never asked questions about it. But if something is happening, then I believe it is a great advantage for a boy to have someone like Kees to guide him. It seems to me like a sort of natural development. If it's based upon tenderness and friendship it can't be wrong, can it? I think it can be a great protection for a child. A security" (Berkel 1978).

On the other hand, parents who react with hostility, or who the son imagines will react with hostility, may very well lose their control. As the boy grows older it becomes increasingly difficult to know everyone he has contact with. If he feels it is necessary to be secretive, his parents have no say in the matter at all and are thus unable to help him or intervene when there are tensions or troubles, as may arise in any intimate relationship.

Secrecy, often adopted out of necessity because of social hostility to this kind of relationship, is seen by some psychologists such as Burgess and Holmstrom (1975) as traumatizing; others like Bernard (1979) view it more positively. Perhaps this tells us more about these psychologists themselves than about the children. Open, talkative children who take great delight in relating all that happens to them (especially nice experiences) usually find secrecy difficult. Reserved, taciturn boys may find it easy. A secret can be nursed as something beautiful; the fact that "only he and I know about it" may actually increase a boy's self-esteem. On the other hand, the knowledge that the relationship is forbidden, the intimacies thought dirty and despicable, may give rise to all manner of guilt feelings. Moreover, having to maintain secrecy may necessitate systematic lying with all its concomitant risks of encouraging a bad habit.

The Dominant Partner

While these latter risks could be ameliorated by parents showing more understanding, many people are convinced that undesirable consequences are inevitably linked with all man/boy relationships. The partners, they claim, are unequal: the boy is the weaker, less experienced one; he will thus be completely dominated by the physically and socially more powerful man.

This objection is really only brought to bear because the sexual aspect of the relationship (wrongly, as we have already observed) is thought to be the only, or at least the most important, element in it. For no society objects to children being dominated by older individuals: parents, teachers, priests, etc. It is assumed that such adults have good intentions towards the children in all their dealings, will protect them and help them—at least until the contrary is established. Adult/child relationships are only suspect if it is supposed that sex is involved. Then and only then is adult domination supposed to be disastrous; the child's sexual freedom must be protected from the overpowering dominating pedophile.

Now, it is at this point that one must use a bit of psychological caution. In any relationship between human beings he who needs the relationship most has the least power and the greatest dependence upon the other. Thus in boy-love if the boy is the one who most strongly desires the sex the man will be the dominant partner in this area—he can grant sex or refuse it, but whenever sex takes place it will be in accordance with the boy's wishes and thus—as empirical research by Baurmann (1983) and Constantine (1981) [has] shown—it will not traumatize him. If, on the other hand (and as public opinion generally assumes), it is the man who most strongly desires the sex, then the boy will be the dominant partner in this aspect of their relationship.

A number of cases examined by Sandfort (1982) points in this direction. A heterosexual adult using the name of "Jack Ryan" wrote a fascinating article (1986) in which he told how from his 13th to his 18th year he had many sexual contacts with quite a large number of men. Even though many of them were well-to-do, socially prominent people, he always felt in these contacts that he was the more powerful, dominant party. During those same years he had legitimate (non-sexual) jobs in a supermarket and as a messenger boy, and *there* he did feel exploited, powerless and dominated by others. Thorstad wrote about man/boy sex, "The boys usually control these relationships.(. . .) They control what kind of sexual acts are performed, they control when the sex will take place, and they have just as much control as the man over when the relationship will end" (Thorstad 1980, p. 21). My own information confirms this. . . .

The first true sexual relationship with a partner is a milestone on the road of a boy's emancipation. Most parents know this intuitively and so want to delay that moment. Other developmental advances are welcomed, but puberty generally is not. . . . Hanry (1977) wrote that he was often consulted by parents worried about their children showing sexual interests which they considered precocious, but never by parents worried by a lack of sexual interest, which he felt was much greater cause for concern.

A good sexual education should aim to ennoble and refine the sexual function in order to humanize it, just as good up-bringing should refine the functions of eating and drinking. But it is only possible to refine the sexual life of a boy if you are happy he has one. Here the boy-lover has an advantage. "For children, the proper way of learning something is through touch rather than hearing" (Schérer and Hocquenghem 1976, p. 60).

When accused of corrupting boys, Nobel Prize winner Andre Gide exclaimed, "Corrupting youth? As if initiation to sexuality is corruption! Mostly it is exactly the opposite. People forget, or, better, they don't know, what accompanies the caresses, out of what feelings of trust, loyalty and nobel competition such friendships originate and develop" (Last 1966, p. 34).

It is certainly not by chance that so many "primitive" people make homosexual intercourse part of their initiation rites (Brongersma 1987). Hanry (1977) believes that homosexuality poses many more problems to young people if they try to suppress it than if they experiment with it. Davidson (1962) saw this confirmed in the behavior of Southern Italian youth. Giese and Schmidt (1968) found heterosexual mobility and refinement in intercourse slightly higher among students with homosexual experience.

What Happens in Pedophile Friendships

Just as in a boy/girl love affair, sexual activities occupy a man and a boy for only a small part of the time they spend together (Hass 1979; Righton 1981). Case histories presented by Berkel (1978), Ingram (1977), Pieterse (1982) and Sandfort (1982) illustrate this point vividly. Together man and boy go to movies, theater, museum exhibitions, the zoo, carnivals. They camp, swim, fish, sail, make bicycle and boat trips. At home they romp and rough-house together; there is backgammon, chess, music, television, woodworking, photography, reading, drawing, stamp collecting. And then there is homework. In short, they do what a boy likes to do; the man talks with him about personal and social problems; they do everything which might help him find the right solutions to the problems peculiar to his age and the particular situation in which he finds himself.

The real risk in boy-love relationships lies not in the sexual activities. From my own experience with boy-lovers and their young partners I would rather say that the greatest danger is of the man spoiling his friend with gifts (and later cigarettes, alcohol and other drugs) and being too permissive about the boy's aggressive and destructive impulses. An environment too permissive in this sense is pedagogically nefarious (Hart de Ruyter 1976). The pedophile here can be compared with the over-generous uncle or the spoiling grandfather. Unwise indulgence can lead to character distortion, encouragement of the boy's greed, parental jealousy or the malevolent attentions of the people surrounding him.

The picture which all careful investigations has left us of man/ boy relationships (Bernard, Ingram, Pieterse, Rouweler-Wuts, Sandfort, my own research) has little or nothing in common with the usual image the public has of it, and of the view of investigators, approaching the phenomenon only from its criminal or psychopathic expressions. In their view the sexual element is not only overstressed, it is the only aspect that is ever taken into account. One hardly need prove that society, as a result of its condemnation and punishment, renders the sexual element in man/boy relationships all the more problematic and more obsessive for the boy-lover.

Gabriel Matzneff, a French author who openly confessed his attraction to boys and girls under sixteen, once wrote (1974, p. 65, p. 109), "I'm no pedagogue, but I do know that the youngsters with whom I had more lasting relationships came out of them happier, more free, more 'realized,' as the Indians say. To love a boy only makes sense if this love will help him develop himself, fulfill himself, realize himself completely, to burst the gates of the family cage, to easily reject the false obligations society tries to impose upon him. Our love must not be vampire-like, egoistic love, burdening him with a yoke, oppressing, dominating, jealously controlling, suffocating—the love of the wolf for the lamb. No, this love should be fertilizing, liberating, life-bestowing, as the Byzantine liturgy affirms the Holy Spirit." (. . .) "What a pity it is that the boy-lover must mostly limit himself to secret, casual meetings which don't give him the opportunity to benefit the boy as much as he would like. To a boy growing up nothing is as beneficial and salutary as meeting an older person who loves him, who takes his hand and helps him to discover the beauty of Creation, to understand people and what they do, to acquire self-knowledge. If I were a father I wouldn't hesitate for a moment to entrust my 13-year-old son to one of these 'wicked strangers.'"

References

Abraham, F. (1969). *Les perversions sexuelles.* Paris: Productions de Paris.

Albrecht, O. (1964). *Die Unzucht mit Kindern.* Keil: Universität.

Arch Smith, T. d'. (1970). *Love in Earnest.* London: Routledge & Kegan Paul.

Barrington, J. S. (1981). *Sexual Alternatives for Men.* London: Alternative Publishing.

Baurmann, M. C. (1983). *Sexualität, Gewalt und psychische Folgen.* Weisbaden: Bundeskriminalamt.

Bendig, B. (1979). *Résumé.* Neuss: Privatdruck.

Berkel, M. (1978). De pedofielen. *Haagse Post,* 65 (11), 26–31.

Bernard, F. (1979). *Padophilie-Liebe mit Kindern.* Lollar: Achenbach. English edition (1985): *Paedophilia, a Factual Report.* Rotterdam: Enclave.

Bleibtreu-Ehrenberg, G. (1980). *Mannbarkeitsriten.* Frankfurt: Ullstein.

Boer, J. de (1978). *Gevoelige kwesties omtrent seksuele kontakten van jongeren.* Deel 2. Zeist: NISSO.

Brethmas, J. de (1980). *Détournement de majeur.* Paris: Perchoir.

Brongersma, E. (1971). Homosexualiteit en strafrecht. In Psychiatrisch Juridisch Gezelschap, *Homosexualiteit.* Amsterdam: van Rossen.

Brongersma, E. (1975). *Over pedofielen en 'kinderlokkers.'* Amsterdam: Intermediair.

Brongersma, E. (1987). *Loving Boys.* Volume 1. Elmhurst, N. Y. : Global Academic Publishers.

Brunold, H. (1962). Beobachtungen und katamnestische Feststellungen nach im Kindesalter erlittenen Sexualtraumen. *Praxis,* 51 (39): 965–971.

Buffiére, F. (1980). *Eros adolescent.* Paris: Les Belles Lettres.

Bullough, V. L. (1979). *Homosexuality.* New York: Garland.

Burgess, A. W. and Holmstrom, L. L.(1975). Sexual Trauma of Children and Adolescents. *Nursing Clinics of North America,* 10 (3), 551–563.

Burton, L. (1968). *Vulnerable Children.* London: Routledge & Kegan Paul.

Churchill, W. (1967). *Homosexual Behavior among Males.* New York: Hawthorne.

Cline, W. (1936). *Notes on the People of Siwah and El Garsh in the Libyan Desert.* Menasha: Banta.

Cnoop Koopmans, A. J. (1982). Forumdiscussie. In Nationale Raad voor Maat-schappelijk Welzijn (Ed.), *Waar ligt de grens?* 's-Gravenhage: Nationale Raad voor Maatschappelijk Weizijn.

Constantine, L. L. (1981). The Effects of Early Sexual Experiences. In Constantine, L. L., and Martinson, F. M., *Children and Sex.* Boston: Little, Brown & Co.

Corstjens, J. M. H. (1975). *Opvoeding en pedofilie.* Doktoraalskriptie Katholieke Universiteit Nijmegen.

Crawford, D. A. (1981). Treatment Approaches with Pedophiles. In Cook, M., and Howells, K., (Eds.) *Adult Sexual Interest in Children.* London: Academic Press.

CRIES (1984). *Rapport des responses reçues suite á la premiere diffusion de notre questionnaire sur l'attitude des adultes envers la sexualité des jeunes.* Bruxelles: CRIES.

Davidson, M. (1962). *The World, the Flesh and Myself.* Washington: Guild Press.

Davidson, M. (1971). *Some Boys.* London: Bruce & Watson.

Dover, K. J. (1978). *Greek Homosexuality.* London: Duckworth.

Edward, A. (1983). *Kit.* Amsterdam: Coltsfoot.

Fisch, M. (1971). *Unzucht mit Kindern.* Frankfurt am Main: Gemini.

Föster, M. (1984). *Jürgen Bartsch.* Essen: Torso.

Foucault, M. (1984). *Histoire de la sexualité. Tome 2. L'usage des plaisirs.* Paris: Gallimard.

Freund, K. (1981). Assessment of Pedophilia. In Cook, M., and Howells, K., (Eds.), *Adult Sexual Interest in Children.* London: Academic Press.

Gagnon, J. H., and Simon, W. (1970). *Sexual Encounters between Adults and Children.* New York: SIECUS.

Gebhard, P. H., Gagnon, J. H., Pomeroy, W. B., and Christenson, C. V. (1965). *Sex Offenders.* New York: Harper & Row.

Gieser, R. L. (1979). *Hidden Victims.* Boston: Deacon Press.

Gerbener, H. (1966). *Die Kriminalität der Kinderschändung im Landgerichtsbezirk Duisburg in den Jahren 1950–1954.* Bonn: Universität.

Giese, H. (1964). *Der homosexuelle Mann in der Welt.* Zweite Auflage. Stuttgart: Enke.

Giese, H., and Schmidt, G. (1968). *Studenten-Sexualität.* Reinbek: Rowohlt.

Gordon, R. (1978). Paedophilia: Normal and Abnormal. In Kraemer, W. (Ed.), *The Forbidden Love.* London: Sheldon Press.

Groth, A. N. (1978). Patterns of Sexual Assault Against Children and Adolescents. In Burgess, A. W., Groth, A. N., Holmstrom, L. L. and Sgroi, S. M., *Sexual Assault of Children and Adolescents.* Lexington: Lexington Books.

Gurwell, J. K. (1974). *Mass Murder in Houston.* Houston: Cordovan.

Haeberle, E. J. (1978). *The Sex Atlas.* New York: Seabury.

Hanry, P. (1977). *Les enfants, le sexe et nous.* Toulouse: Privat.

Hart de Ruyter, Th., and Zijl, L. B. M. van der (Eds.). (1976). *De seksuele ontwikkeling van kind tot volwassene.* Leiden: Stafleu.

Hass, A. (1979). *Teenage Sexuality.* New York: Macmillan.

Hennig, J. L. (1979). Thomas, 30 ans; Bruno, 15 ans; le nouveau couple zig-zag. *Recherches* 37:137–166.

Herdt, G. H. (1981). *Guardians of the Flutes.* New York: McGraw-Hill.

Herdt, G. H. (Ed.). (1982). *Rituals of Manhood.* Berkeley: University of California Press.

Herek, G. M. (1984). Attitudes toward Lesbians and Gay Men: A Factor-Analytic Study. *Journal of Homosexuality,* 10 (1/2): 39–51.

Holland, I. (1972). *The Man without a Face.* New York: Bantam.

Howells, K. (1980). Social Reactions to Sexual Deviance. In West, D. J. (Ed.), *Sex Offenders in the Criminal Justice System.* Cambridge: Institute of Criminology.

Ingram, M. (1977). "Filthy"—Reaction to Paedophilic Acts. *Libertarian Education,* 21, 4–5.

Ingram, M. (1979). The Participating Victim: A Study of Sexual Offenses against Pre-pubertal Boys. In Cook, M., and Wilson, G. D. (Eds.), *Love and Attraction.* Oxford: Pergamon.

Jersild, J. (1964). *De paedoftle.* København: Nyt Nordisk Forlag.

Kentler, H. (1970). *Sexualerziehung.* Reinbek: Rowohlt.

Kerscher, I. (Ed.). (1977). *Konfliktfeld Sexualität.* Neuwied: Luchterhand.

Kerscher, I. (1978). Sexuelle Handlungen zwischen Kindern und Erwachsenen. In Pacharzina, K., and Albrecht-Désirat, K., *Konfliktfeld Kindersexualität.* Frankfurt am Main: Päd.extra.

Krist, G. (1976). *Pedofilie.* Leuven: Katholieke Universiteit.

Landis, J. T. (1956). Experiences of 500 Children With Adult Sexual Deviation. *Psychiatric Quarterly Suppl.* 30, 91–109.

Lane, E. (1978). *Game-Texts.* San Francisco: Gay Sunshine.

Last J. (1966). *Mijn vriend André Gide.* Amsterdam: van Ditmar.

Lempp, R. (1968). Seelische Schadigung von Kindern als Opfer von gewaltlosen Sittlichkeitsdelikten. *Neue Juristische Wochenschrift* 21 (49), 2265–2268.

Lessing, T. (1925). *Haarmann.* Berlin: Schmiede.

Levine, M. P. (1980). The Sociology of Male Homosexuality and Lesbianism. *Journal of Homosexuality,* 5 (3), 249–275.

Matzneff, G. (1974). *Les moins de seize ans.* Paris: Julliard.

McCaghy, C. H. (1967). Child Molesters. In Clinard, M. B. and Quinny, R. (Eds.), *Criminal Behavior Systems.* New York: Holt, Rinehart & Winston.

McCaghy, C. H. (1971). Child Molesting. *Sexual Behavior,* 1 (5), 16–31.

Mohr, J. W., and Turner, R. E. (1967). Sexual Deviations. Part 4: Pedophilia. *Applied Therapeutics,* 9 (4), 362–365.

Möller, M. (1983). *Pedofiele relaties.* Deventer: van Loghum Slaterus.

Murdoch, I. (1976). *Henry and Cato.* London: Chatto & Windus.

Newton, D. E. (1978). Homosexual Behavior and Child Molestation. *Adolescence,* 13 (49), 29–43.

O'Carroll, T. (1980). *Paedophilia—The Radical Case.* London: Owen.

Olsen, J. (1974). *The Man with the Candy.* New York: Pocket Books.

Oskamp, A. (1980). *Man en macht.* Amsterdam: van Gennep.

Patzer, H. (1982). *Die griechische Knabenliebe.* Wiesbaden: Steiner.

Peters, F. (1951). *The World at Twilight (Finisterre).* New York: Lancer.

PIE (1976). *Survey of Members.* London: Paedophile Information Exchange.

Pieterse, M. (1982). *Pedofielen over pedofilie.* Zeist: NISSO.

Pietropinto, A., and Simenauer, J. (1979). *Gonado.* Katwijk aan Zee: Servire. (Dutch translation of *Beyond the Male Myth,* 1977, New York: Times Books).

Potrykus, D., and Wöbcke, M. (1974). *Sexualität zwischen Kindern und Erwachsenen.* München: Goldmann.

Prigny, J. M. (1959). *Marc.* Paris: Table Ronde.

Reiss, A. J. (1967). Sex Offenses: the Marginal Status of the Adolescent. Is Gagnon, J. H., and Simon, W. (Eds.), *Sexual Deviance.* New York: Harper & Row.

Rennert, H. (1965). Untersuchungen zur Gefährdung der Jugend und zur Dunkelziffer bei sexuellen Straftaten. *Psychiatrie, Neurologie und Medizinische Psychologie,* 17 (10), 361–367.

Righton, P. (1981). The Adult. In Taylor, B. (Ed.), *Perspectives on Paedophilia.* London: Batsford.

Rochefort, C. (1969). *Printemps au parking.* Paris: Grasset.

Rossman, P. (1976). *Sexual Experience between Men and Boys.* New York: Association Press.

Rouweler-Wuts, L. (1976). *Pedofielen in contact of conflict met de samenleving?* Deventer: van Loghum Slaterus.

Ryan, J. (1986). A Boy Prostitute's Perspective. *Gay Community News,* 20–26 July.

Sables, L. des (1976/77). Résultats d'une enquête auprés d'un groupe de pedérastes. *Arcadie,* 276, 650–657; 277, 35–45.

Sandfort, T. (1979). *Pedoseksuele kontakien en pedofiele relaties.* Zeist: NISSO.

Sandfort, T. (1980). Pedofilie en pedoseksuele contacten. In Frenken (Ed.), *Seksuologie.* Deventer: van Loghum Slaterus.

Sandfort, T. (1982). *The Sexual Aspect of Paedophile Relations.* Amsterdam: Pan/Spartacus.

Sandfort, T. (1984). *Om het ftjne gevoel.* Baarn: In den Toren.

Schérer, R., and Hocquenghem, G. (1976). Co-ire. *Recheches,* 22.

Schillemans, A. (1983). Vrouwen tegen pedofilie. *Jeugd en Samenleving,* 13 (2), 133–139.

Schlegel, W. S. (1966). *Sexualinstinkte des Menschen.* München: Rütten and Loening.

Schorsch, E. (1973). Häufige Merkmalskombinationen bei Sexualstraftätern. *Monatschrift für Kriminologie und Strafrechtsreform,* 56 (4), 141–150.

Schult, P. (182). *Gefallene Engel.* Berlin: Gmünder.

Sengers, W. J. (1970). Pedofilie. In Zeldenrust, D., de Koning, P. P. J., Sengers, W. J., Schaik, C. T. van, Kwast, S. van der, and Mulder, W. G., *Gewoon bizonder.* Amsterdam: Humanitas.

Socrides, C. W. (1954). Meaning and Content of a Pedophiliac Perversion. *Journal of the American Psychoanalytic Association,* 7, 84–94.

Sonenschein, D. (1983). *What is Pedophilia Anyway?* Private publication.

Sorensen, R. C. (1973). *Adolescent Sexuality in Contemporary America.* New York: World Publishing.

Stekel, W. (1922). *Psychosexueller Infantilismus.* Berlin: Urban & Schwarzenberg.

Stewart A. (1968). *Sandel.* London: Panther Books.

Swanson, D. W. (1968). Adult Sexual Abuse of Children. *Diseases of the Nervous System,* 29 (10), 677–683.

Taylor, B. (Ed.). (1981). *Perspectives on Paedophilia.* London: Batsford.

Tesch, G. (1956). *Never the Same Again.* New York: Pyramid Books.

Thorstad, D. (1980). Loving Boys. Discussion with G. Hocquenghem. *Semniotext(e) Special,* 1, 18–35.

Tripp, C. A. (1975). *The Homosexual Matrix.* New York: New American Library.

Tuohy, F., and Murphy, M. (1976). *Down under the Plum Trees.* Waiura (New Zealand): Alister Taylor.

Verlaine, P. (1868). *Oeuvres libres.* Segovia: de Herlagnez.

West, D. J. (1977). *Homosexuality Re-examined.* London: Duckworth.

West, D. J. (1980). Treatment in Theory and Practice; Points from the Discussion. In West, D. J. (Ed.), *Sex Offenders in the Criminal Justice System.* Cambridge: Institute of Criminology.

Wheeler, S. (1967). Sex Offenses: a Sociological Critique. In Gagnon, J. H., and Simon, W. (Eds.), *Sexual Deviance.* New York: Harper & Row.

Wilson, P. (1982). *The Man They Called a Monster.* North Ryde: Cassell Australia.

Wolters, W. H. G. (Ed.). *Seksueel misbruik van kinderen en jonge adolescenten.* Nijkerk: Intro.

Wyss, R. (1967). *Unzucht mit Kindern.* Berlin: Springer.

Yaffé, M. (1981). The Assessment and Treatment of Paedophilia. In Taylor, B.(Ed.). *Perspectives on Paedophilia.* London: Batsford.

Zeegers, M. (1977). *Psychiatrie.* Utrecht: Bohn, Scheltema & Holkema.

Reprinted from: Edward Brongersma, "Boy-Lovers and Their Influence on Boys: Distorted Research and Anecdotal Observations." In *Journal of Homosexualtiy,* 20(1–2), pp. 145–173. Copyright © 1991 by Haworth Press, Inc., Binghamton, NY. Reprinted by permission. ✦

Part III

Medicalized Forms of Deviance

One of the most popular ways to look at deviance in the last thirty years has been through a medical perspective. This approach to deviance emphasizes the idea that deviant behaviors either be explained by reference to medical "causes" or that some physical or medical conditions can be viewed as a form of deviance. The readings in this section look at both of these approaches. The main theme is that any kind of "difference," even medical conditions, can be seen as deviant.

Equating difference with deviance is significant because of the effects this view can have on the person who is labeled. Something that is different can only become deviant when others label the difference as bad, less valuable, dangerous, wrong, or simply deviant.

The articles in this section demonstrate that individuals who are labeled deviant have a strong desire to hide or justify their differences. As you will see in the readings about people who are overweight, who are infertile, who stutter, or who are homosexual, individuals may go to great lengths to "cover" or "explain" their differences. Accounting for difference is a critically important way to avoid being labeled deviant. When individuals can point to medical "causes" for their difference, they may be able to minimize the effects of being seen as different and thus avoid a deviant label altogether.

In the first article in this section, Elizabeth Hottle gives us an insider's view of the experiences of an individual identified as different and labeled as deviant. She discusses her personal experiences growing up as a person who stutters. As she explains, once she was known as a "stutterer," this label became the primary way she was known by others. This tells us that when individuals are known for something different, the "difference" may become the main factor influencing how people think about them. Or, in sociological terms, deviance can become a "master status." For deviants, this means that they are likely to be known for only one thing. However, this one thing—the master status—is likely to be something they really do not want as their main identity.

Whether the problem is stuttering, being overweight, or some other characteristic, the deviant label, especially when the condition is something beyond one's control, can be extremely uncomfortable. It may make individuals feel as if they must explain themselves to others. In the second article in this section, Cliff English examines the ways that some overweight people try to explain their size to others. As he points out, most overweight people cannot avoid detection, so they may feel an overwhelming need to explain or justify their weight. In this case, medical explanations can help a lot.

The third article of this section, which looks at the medical treatment of intersexed infants, shifts the focus from the deviant person to how people look at those who have medical conditions that make them different. Suzanne J. Kessler considers infants born with genitals that cannot be distinguished as either male or female. As she notes, doctors and parents find this situation to be a highly stressful, one that must be "fixed." We thus see a reliance on medical technology to fix deviant attributes in infants who are healthy and "normal" in all other respects. This article clearly shows how the presence of a deviant attribute is stressful to others, even when they and the deviant individual have no control over the condition. The need to "do something," and what that "something" should be, becomes a priority for those associated with the deviant. Medicine can be a way to destigmatize deviance, but Kessler demonstrates to us how medicine can be used to correct and control deviance.

In the fourth article in this section, on involuntary childlessness, Charlene Miall considers medicalized deviance from a different perspective. She explores the ways that infertile women (and women married to infertile men) conceal the fact that they are unable to have children. In an interesting contrast to the justifications provided by some overweight people who rely on medical accounts, Miall finds that involuntarily childless women work to avoid medical explanations. Miall finds that women think that public knowledge of their infertility could lead to beliefs that they are flawed or in some way inferior. Therefore, because infertile women's "difference" is not readily visible, they work to construct accounts that emphasize other, nonmedical factors to explain their childlessness.

The articles in this section emphasize how medicine can be used to identify, construct, and treat deviance and how medically different individuals use or avoid medical explanations to account for their "deviance." The final article in the section, by Susan E. Kelly, examines the debate within the gay and lesbian community over whether genetic explanations for homosexuality should be used to overcome deviant labels and achieve equal rights. Interestingly, Kelly points out that gays and lesbians have only recently overcome previous medical definitions as mentally ill and deviant. Although there are benefits to embracing genetic explanations, Kelly notes that some in the gay and lesbian community warn against doing so.

Throughout these five articles, we see that deviants are pressured to provide explanations for their differences. Typically, the explanations people give to account for their differences focus on shifting responsibility away from themselves. Whether the individual labeled as deviant can be readily identified or the difference can be hidden is something that influences the way people construct and present their accounts. This process applies to deviants who hold some degree of responsibility for their differences, as well as to those (such as intersexed newborns) who have no control over their differences. And, it applies to those who are responsible for caring for those who are "different."

As you read the articles in this section, think about the role that social institutions such as medicine play in defining, justifying, and "curing" deviance. Medicine is an especially powerful institution—one that few people are willing to challenge, particularly when they are personally labeled as "deviant." What is the impact on an individual when she or he is labeled medically deviant? What would make one individual (say an overweight person) draw on medical explanations for deviance and another (such as an infertile woman) avoid such accounts? Why are doctors and parents so eager to repair the "deviance" of intersexed infants? And finally, what danger—if any—is there in embracing medical explanations for difference. ✦

10

Making Myself Understood: The Labeling Theory of Deviance Applied to Stuttering

Elizabeth Hottle

This article presents the experiences of a young woman who stutters. Hottle describes her struggles to overcome her speech impediment and how being a stutterer came to be the primary way she was identified. Regarding deviance, this article shows us that when there is something "different" about an individual, that one point of difference (or deviance) may become the only factor on which others focus. As a result, people defined as deviant may be seen as nothing but deviants. This may result in individuals feeling as if they have no good qualities and defining themselves as deviant or worthless.

Since childhood, I have had a stutter that makes a regular appearance in my oral interactions and, at one time or another, has affected nearly all facets of my life. My frustrated parents and I tried in vain to locate a solution, they hoping that years of speech therapy would pay off, me dreaming for a miracle cure that could instantly remove this painfully humiliating trait. Sadly, neither happened; my stutter has, however, gradually abated over the past few years, and I still retain hopes that it will eventually fade away

completely. I have come to believe that my improvement, and at least partial acceptance of the fact that I will probably have some semblance of a speech impediment for the rest of my life, have come about not *because* of the efforts of my parents and therapists, but in spite of them. My purpose is to use labeling theory to explain how years of therapy and encouragement not to stutter actually contributed to the problem.

Labeling theory, as explained by Nancy Waxler (1974) and Edwin Schur (1971), examines how a person is conceptualized and treated by others after symptoms of "deviance" appear. It is not the original behavior and its cause that is important, but rather the societal response and processes activated by the behavior. . . .

Thus, labeling theorists explain the emergence of deviant behavior as a function of the way in which certain people are seen and treated by others. Accordingly, one cannot be considered a "deviant" unless one has been labeled as such by others or oneself. Behaviors exist which may be deviant in one situation or society but perfectly acceptable in another, as well as those which either begin or cease to be considered deviant as a society's perspectives change over time.

In providing a cause for the origin and continuation of deviance, the labeling school suggests that a society's identification of individuals as "deviant" may, in effect, lock them into that role. . . . and rewarded for responding in an appropriate manner, they find it easier simply to play the parts assigned to them. Nancy Waxler's application of this theory to mental illness can also explain stuttering. Just as the response of others to initial symptoms of mental illness greatly influence its eventual outcome, the responses of parents and teachers to the hesitant, repetitive speech of the young child largely determine whether this behavior will pass or become a chronic affliction. . . .

Wendell Johnson (1946:446) termed stuttering a "diagnosogenic" affliction, discovering that actual stuttering only began in children after their normal speech patterns had been labeled as such, and therefore that the "diagnosis. . .is one of the causes of the disorder." He then continued to define stuttering not as dysfluency, which can be found in the speech of even "non-stutterers," but as the attempt to avoid this dysfluency.

Gunther Bergmann and Joseph Forgas (1985:231) also suggest that parents, in the attempt to help a child whom they have labeled a stutterer, may actually make speaking even more difficult for the child. They assert that "high expectations of a child by ambitious parents, upward social mobility, and great emphasis on communicative competence are paradoxically some of the family characteristics that may play a role in the etiology of stuttering in childhood." These factors may not actually cause stuttering, but if a child raised in this sort of family shows any signs of "abnormal" speech, the child may instantly be branded as a deviant in need of fixing. The parents' negative evaluation of the child's early speech, which is often a direct attempt to please them, can lead to feelings of failure and worthlessness and a strong aversion to any dysfluency.

I experienced such negative reactions myself, and at an age when one's parents' opinions are still of some importance, the realization that you have disappointed them can be crushing. On January 2, 1987, at the age of 12, I wrote in my diary: "Mother is trying so hard to get me to work on you-know-what. It's terrible to watch her sigh, look at Daddy, then at me. . . I love my Mother, and yet I'm causing her to suffer. How could I?"

The child, then, learns that proper speech is fluent, and the anxiety created by her attempt to maintain fluency at all times in turn causes nervousness and embarrassment when faced with a dysfluency or potential dysfluency. In the attempt to avoid dysfluency, the child exhibits behaviors considered to be characteristic of stutterers, such as exaggerated pauses, shallow breathing, repetition of sounds or entire words, avoidance of "hard" words or insertion of sounds such as "ah" and "um" (Johnson 1946:452).

For most childhood stutterers, myself included, the first formal indication that they talk "wrong" comes in the form of speech therapy. I remember attending speech therapy in school as early as the second grade. It was always an ordeal. Those of us with this "problem" were openly removed from the classroom at scheduled times and taken to a separate room where the therapist attempted to "teach" us how to speak correctly. This physical separation, coupled with the obvious message from the therapist that my speech was "abnormal," contributed greatly to my feelings of failure and "differentness."

One incident in particular stands out in my mind. At the end of the school year, some of the other children in my therapy group received certificates of accomplishment. When I questioned the therapist as to why I didn't get one, she explained that, unlike me, the other children had achieved the goal of fluency and were therefore being rewarded. Most likely she used this as a means of encouraging those of us who "failed" to try harder to succeed the next year, but to me this seemed to be a direct indication that my stutter was *my* fault and that I was a less than adequate person because of it.

Johnson (1946:459) would agree that the methods of most therapists strengthen the stutterer's view of dysfluency as abnormal or wrong. "What the so-called speech correctionist says, in effect, is this: 'Don't stutter. Whatever you do, don't stutter. You can even talk in this strange manner that I am suggesting, but don't stutter.'" My own therapist tried to train me to speak fluently. The goal of speech programs generally is to eliminate stuttering completely, for any dysfluency is seen as a mistake or failure.

My most distinctive encounter with speech therapy came in the form of the Precision Fluency Shaping Program (PFSP), an intensive fluency course in which I worked with a specially trained therapist three hours a day for three days a week during two months of my fifth grade year. The program helps stutterers to speak fluently through the use of "targets," such as the Gentle Onset, which re-train the individual as to the proper method of speaking. The Introduction to the program manual describes its goal: "The emphasis in this program is placed upon the systematic reconstruction of movements and forces in the speech responses of stutterers" (Webster, 1982:1). The individual is seen as having complete control over his or her own speech, and it is assumed that all have the ability to speak "normally," that is, fluently.

The Introduction (Webster, 1982:2) continues, stating:

> It should be made clear to both therapists and stutterers that in no way is it initially to be inferred or assumed that the stutterer is "at fault" because he stutters . . . it is assumed that the stutterer must eventually become totally responsible for *how* he speaks . . . the stutterer gradually becomes responsible for producing certain types of behaviors learned while moving through the program.

Logic, however, would seem to dictate that responsibility for one's fluency is accompanied by responsibility for one's dysfluency. This program implies to persons seeking help that they *are*, in fact, "at fault," that they stutter simply because they cannot or will not speak correctly. It clearly separates "stutterers" from "normal" speakers and suggests that the "stutterers" are the defective ones.

On June 17, 1986, at the age of 11, I wrote in my diary: "You know what my speech problem is? I don't try. I try to try but I don't try hard enough so I don't try." At this point, about one and one half years after I had completed the PFSP, I obviously had totally internalized the notion that I was, indeed, responsible for my stutter and had taken to berating myself quite frequently for it. Almost one year later, on May 1, 1987, at the age of 12, I wrote: "I'm in a state of shock. I just taped myself talking and listened t o it. God, I had no idea how *bad* I sound! I'm so embarrassed. Now I know how much work I have to do on it."

Therapy functioned as a very effective method of permanently labeling me a stutterer. As a form of organizational processing, speech therapy sent to me the clear message that my behavior was unacceptable and in need of correction. Applying Johnson's ideas, this constant insistence that I was abnormal served only to heighten my anxiety about my speech problem. Certainly, when one is being told repeatedly that stuttering is bad and that one should attempt to eliminate it, any instance of dysfluency will contribute to the individual's sense of despair and hopelessness.

In *Labeling Deviant Behavior*, Edwin Schur (1971:69) proposes the concept of role engulfment, in which deviants are "'caught up' in the deviant role." They become not persons whose behavior is considered deviant, but deviant persons. Their "behavior is increasingly organized around the role;" the stigmatized behavior has become their identity. As seen by Schur, the two most important factors for individuals becoming engulfed in their roles are how they are seen by others and how they see themselves. People can respond two ways to the attempts of others to identify them as their deviance; they can become engulfed in the role but still not believe it, or they can accept the views of others and begin to see themselves as others do.

For a person who stutters, role engulfment is a very real possibility. The PFSP manual refers to the person being treated as the "stutterer." In this program, stuttering is not seen as a condition, it is seen as a fundamental identity. The wording of the manual subtly expresses the belief that a person cannot stutter and be normal. The two categories are mutually exclusive. The methods of speech therapy which I encountered necessarily, as a function of their basic philosophy, constantly reminded me of my label. The PFSP, "intended for use only in an intensive manner" (Webster 1982:4), forces the "stutterer" to think constantly about the fact that he or she *is* a stutterer by utilizing the concept that, ideally, one works to transfer the skills learned in therapy sessions to all facets of life. I attended therapy sessions three days a week and was given practice exercises to do everyday, and, therefore, during this period my speech became even more prevalent in my thoughts. . . .

These messages came not only from therapists and other, formal agents of control, but from the people I interacted with on a daily basis. A stutter is an extremely difficult condition to hide as a result of our society's emphasis on oral communication. Little things that others took for granted, such as reading aloud in class or making a telephone call, made my speech the focus of other's attention—or, at least, this is how I perceived it. Bergmann and Forgas (1985:246) explain, "Stutterers exhibit quite unrealistic expectations concerning the reactions of their interaction partners." I assumed that every time I spoke, everyone was listening to me and to my stutter specifically. Although I was rarely mocked to my face, I was convinced that everyone talked about and belittled me behind my back. I expected certain responses from others and tended to perceive and react to them, whether they occurred or not. This sense of degradation in the eyes of others is expressed in my diary entry from July 7, 1987, when I was 12. One of my sister's friends had written a story, for a contest, about a girl who stuttered. She brought it to my house and showed it to my mother, who showed it to me. I read it and told her I liked it, but then, completely horrified by her totally inaccurate portrayal of a child with a stutter, I wrote: "It only hurts when people tease you! [A statement made by the story's main character to a curious friend.] Ha! And like people would ask questions about it! They don't. But the look on their faces, in their naive little eyes—makes you want to cry, scream, hit them—die. God, what if Mother does put me in therapy at school? That would be the final straw. I just couldn't take it." She did. I found school therapy an extremely painful experience, not so much because of what went on in the sessions, but because it was a definite symbol of my differentness. Throughout middle and high schools, in fact, when I was pulled from class to see the therapist, I never once told anyone where I was going.

One interesting incident that happened to me in the beginning of seventh grade confirms Schur's notion that role engulfment may even affect individuals whose deviance is unknown. When I first met someone, he or she would not instantly label me as a stutterer; I was normal until I spoke, or until I spoke disfluently in a way that was obviously different from a "non-stutterer's" dysfluency. Until that occurred, I was what Goffman (1963:42) calls "discreditable"—a condition in which "differentness is not immediately apparent, and not known beforehand." Even before a person had come to perceive me as anything but normal, I was a discreet deviant; a person who, according to Schur (1971:71), "may well find his self-concept and behavior affected by his knowledge that he could be so labeled and by his awareness of others' views

of people 'like' himself." On this particular occasion, I was in the special class I attended once a week as part of the Talented and Gifted program into which I had been placed. As It was the beginning of the year and we did not all know each other, the teacher had us do an activity designed to "break the ice." (I live in dread of these "games," because they usually involve repeating the names of everyone in the group and my instant "discrediting.") We each received a card on which to write certain information about ourselves, then taped it to our shirts so we could wander the room, learning things about each other. One thing we were told to write was "something that makes you sad"—and one boy whose card I read proclaimed that he was saddened by "people who stutter." This student was very involved in drama, which probably explained his pity for those who cannot express themselves orally. What this was to me was an open confirmation of what I had known all along: that I was pitied—and surely also ridiculed—by people, even if their opinions were never expressed directly to me.

One who has never been through this experience might assume that the intensive therapy and very negative evaluations I gave to myself as well as perceived from others would be strong encouragement and motivation to speak fluently. However, the definitive labels I received from myself and others only served to more deeply ingrain me in the role of a "stutterer." This, I believe, resulted in "secondary deviance," a concept first proposed by Edwin Lemert (1972:63) which "refers to a special class of socially defined responses which people make to problems created by the societal reaction to their deviance." The individual becomes "a person whose life and identity are organized around the facts of deviance." Once a person has been labeled as deviant, he may be expected or even encouraged to accept the role; at the very least, others will assume the fact of his deviance and, even if he makes massive efforts to eradicate it from his character, will still view the person in terms of the stigma.

In the face of these colored expectations, individuals may find it easier and more advantageous to fulfill the roles imputed to them. In his essay on secondary deviation,

Schur (1974:15) notes that "the concept of *validation* of status and identity is central to an understanding of secondary deviation." In order to receive the vital identity-confirming responses, individuals are pressured to accept openly the identities imposed upon them. I had been labeled as a "stutterer" by all those with whom I came in frequent contact—they expected my speech to be dysfluent, and if by chance it was not, it was seen as chance. Lemert (1972:84–85) asserts that "once deviance becomes a way of life, the personal issue often becomes the costs of making a change rather than the higher status to be gained through rehabilitation;" and, as I was confronted with what I took to be the only way to overcome my stutter—the training I received in therapy—I resigned myself to always being a "stutterer." Most likely, even if my impediment had disappeared, my label would not have; I would still be seen as a stutterer, eventually my role might have changed to the "girl who *used* to talk funny."

We may never learn what factors, biological or environmental, interfere in the development of speech in children to produce original dysfluencies. From the research I have conducted, and, more importantly, from my own personal experience, it seems clear that the way in which originally stuttering is conceptualized and treated plays a major part in the duration of this condition. To those who encounter a stuttering child, I would strongly suggest that his or her dysfluency be treated as what it most likely is: a passing stage in the evolution of language. Speech therapists need to concentrate on making children feel comfortable with their speech, however fluent or dysfluent it may be. I have learned firsthand what a powerful and debilitating label "stutterer" can be, and I now realize how unnecessary my frustration and pain were; had my parents and teachers known what I now know, my stutter might have been but a passing annoyance. Instead, it became what I believe I can rightly

call an "affliction," setting me apart from others and leading to a damaged sense of self which I have only recently been able to escape. On June 30, 1986, an eleven-year-old girl, overcome with despair and self-loathing, wrote a diary entry that ended with: "Please, Lord, help me overcome this. It's ruining my life." I realize now that this can only happen if I *allow* my stutter to take over, to consume my entire being—and I believe that, as I now enter adulthood, I finally have the strength and maturity to put my impediment aside, to separate myself from my speech and truly come to understand I am not "a stutterer," I am a person.

References

Bergmann, Gunther and Joseph P. Forgas. 1985. Situational Variation in Speech Dysfluencies in Interpersonal Communications. Pp. 229–252 in *Language and Social Situations*. Joseph P. Forgas (ed.). New York: Spring-Verlag.

Goffman, Erving. 1963. *Stigma: Notes on the Management of Spoiled Identity*. New York: Simon and Schuster.

Johnson, Wendell. 1946. *People in Quandaries: The Semantics of Personal Adjustment*. New York: Harper and Brothers.

Lemert, Edwin N. 1972. 2d ed. *Human Deviance, Social Problems, and Social Control*. Englewood Cliffs, NJ: Prentice-Hall.

Schur, Edwin. 1971. *Labeling Deviant Behavior*. New York: Harper and Row.

Waxler, Nancy E. 1974. Culture and Mental Illness: A Social Labeling Perspective. *The Journal of Nervous and Mental Disease* 159, 6 (December):379-395.

Webster, Ronald L. 1982. *The Precision Fluency Shaping Program: Speech Reconstruction for Stutterers, Vol. 1*. Roanoke, VA: The Hollins Communications Research Institute.

11

Food Is My Best Friend: Self-Justifications and Weight Loss Efforts

Cliff English

English looks at the justifications that overweight people use to explain their physical size to others. Because they can be easily identified, they are not able to hide their deviance. As a result, English argues, they develop ways of accounting for their deviance, and these accounts often attempt to limit individual responsibility. English notes that overweight people often embrace medical explanations for their condition.

We live in a culture where body weight and appearance are major concerns for most Americans. A 1965 study reported that close to ten million Americans were on diets and another 42 million were concerned about their waist lines (Wyden, 1965; Wyden et al. 1968). . . . As a people, we are told that up to one-third of us are overweight and that being obese is hazardous to our health (Jeffrey et al., 1977; Stuart, 1978). At the same time, most Americans seem obsessed with the pursuit of food and drink. The average American family spends one-third of its income on food, and dining out is considered one of the most popular American pastimes. In fact, a major opinion poll in 1982 reported that eating was the favorite leisure activity for adult men and women. And while fattening, rich and expensive foods are constantly sought

out, Americans, especially American women (Hall et al., 1981), are continually concerned with dieting and losing weight. We overeat, overdrink, diet, fast, exercise, put on and take off weight on a regular basis and with an unparalleled intensity. These contradictory behaviors and thoughts are exemplified by the different and contradictory meanings of the word "fat." *Webster's New World Dictionary* (1971) defines "fat" as: (1) containing or full of fat; oily; greasy; (2) fleshy; obese; plump; (3) thick; broad; (4) fertile; productive; as fat land; (5) profitable; lucrative; as a fat job; (6) prosperous; (7) plentiful; ample; (8) stupid; dull. These contradictions are further complicated when looking at the consumption of food with its multiple meanings and functions. In many social situations eating is a central recreational activity. We seem to consume food for a variety of reasons that have little to do with satisfying physiological hunger (Rodin, 1978; 1977). Some of us eat in response to negative feelings such as depression, anxiety, or sadness. For others, eating provides an alternative behavior to facing boredom and loneliness. One respondent poignantly expressed her excessive dependence on eating food when she commented, "Food is my best friend. It is always there, it never lets you down and it tastes good. . . . " Finally, most of us associate eating fine foods with the celebration of a special event, such as a birthday or wedding anniversary.

Given our cultural and social emphasis on food and food consumption and our lack of exercise, it is not surprising that weight problems plague so many of us. In fact, one could ask why more Americans do not have a weight problem. It seems that the counterbalance to our overemphasis on food and eating is our current cultural definition of physical attractiveness as svelte, thin and sylphlike. Clearly fat people are viewed as physically unattractive and socially unacceptable (Tobias et al., 1980). In addition, they tend to be described in pejorative terms as lazy, dull, unclean, and stupid. These views are further reinforced by the Judeo-Christian ethic with the moralistic view that gluttony is sinful (Lyman, 1978). In fact, some researchers have indicated that fat people are constantly subjected to stigmatization (Goffman, 1963; Cahnman, 1968; Allon, 1973; Millman, 1980). The consequences of stigmatization have far-reaching implications for both overweight individuals and clinicians dealing with the issues surrounding weight loss. This problem is the central focus of this paper.

Methods

The data for this ethnographic study were gathered primarily through participant observation of weight loss therapy groups. Eight different groups were observed over a one-year period of time. Each group was composed of 15 females whose average weight was 270 pounds. Therefore, the results of the study are based primarily on groups of adult obese/overweight women. The program was based in a university-sponsored medical clinic, which was referred to by insiders as "the bad habits clinic." Weight-loss was only one of a number of problem areas that the clinic addressed; others included sexual dysfunction, smoking, other drug and alcohol related problems. All eight of the weight loss groups were conducted by the same therapist, a Ph.D. clinical psychologist. Data gathering consisted of the researcher directly observing the group interaction, which took place around a table similar to that of a college seminar. The researcher situated himself off to one side so as to draw as little [attention] to his presence as possible. Each group was conducted in the same format by the therapist.

Initially the study was exploratory, in that no formal hypotheses were developed, and no formal research questions were constructed. Data collection consisted of note taking by the observer and comparison of observations with the therapist after each session. The sessions started with each member briefly engaging in private consultation with the therapist; this took anywhere from 20 to 30 minutes. During this period the rest of the participants would engage in informal conversations. In the early stages of the program this consisted of exchanging biographical information, but as the study progressed the observer was able to steer these conversations into specific research questions and conduct formal/informal interviews.

Researchers who have conducted studies of fat people report conflicting experiences in terms of cooperation. One researcher (Cahnman, 1968) found such a high incidence of guilt and shame that communication was very difficult to maintain. A more recent study (Millman, 1980) reported respondents open and eager to cooperate; it was this latter response that characterized this research. In fact, once the observer revealed to heavy individuals that he was doing research on fat people, he was overwhelmed with potential respondents. Data gathering then extended beyond the therapy groups to include formal/informal interviews in bars, on airplanes, in restaurants, and at parties. A constant theme among these respondents was that no one could understand what it was like to be fat unless they had actually had the experience. Consequently they felt that there was a tremendous misunderstanding of fat people. Terms such as: "I am going to tell it like it is" or "To set the record straight" were not unusual. A similar phenomenon occurred in group sessions, particularly when a member had revealed what she/he perceived as a particularly sensitive and/or significant event. In these instances they would on occasion turn to the observer and say, "Are you sure you're getting all of this down because it is important?" This willingness to cooperate among respondents allowed the scope of the study to go beyond the members of the therapy groups.

Treatment Philosophy and Brief Program Description

The weight reduction program was a conservative approach to weight loss using behavioral self-control principles and nutritionally sound dietary practices. Alterations in life-styles, eating habits, and activity patterns were encouraged as well as the application of general self-control strategies. Participants were informed at the outset that the rate of weight loss would be moderate and behavior changes would be gradual. Females were advised to expect a loss of one to two pounds a week. In addition, participants were told that they would learn techniques and strategies that would enable them to continue weight loss and weight control for the rest of their lives. Participants selected a 1000 to 1200 calorie diet of their choice in consultation with a licensed nutritionist.

The treatment consisted of 12 sessions scheduled on a weekly basis and four follow-up sessions scheduled on a monthly basis. The total length of the program, including follow-up, was seven months. Treatment sessions were approximately two hours in length, with the first 20 to 30 minutes devoted to private weigh-ins. At this time each client's progress and problems were briefly discussed and, if needed, additional individual sessions were scheduled.

Each treatment session was organized around a self-control or eating-behavior control theme. In addition, clients were provided with a behaviorally-oriented weight reduction text and self-control reading materials to facilitate group discussions, as well as self-monitoring forms to highlight weight loss progress and increase awareness of daily eating patterns.

The program fee was $180.00, payable in advance. Prior to admission, prospective clients were required to: (1) sign a treatment contract, (2) obtain written consent to participate from their physician, (3) complete the Minnesota Multiphasic Personality Inventory (MMPI), and (4) undergo a clinical interview. If these admission requirements were satisfied, clients were asked to make an attendance deposit of $30.00. This money was returned to each client at the end of the program if the client attended at least 14 of the 16 scheduled sessions.

It is interesting to note that all but two of the 120 participants completed the program and three made goal weight.

Stigmatization: A Re-examination

Fat people are constantly being singled out for special attention solely on the basis of their weight. Job discrimination, higher life insurance premiums, taunts and ridicule of children are only a few examples of discrimination and stigmatization. Weight loss is a major concern of heavy people, and our respondents reported how they continually go on and off diets, often experiencing substan-

tial weight loss. As one put it, "Hell, I've probably lost 5,000 pounds in my life so far." Or as another stated the problem: "It's been like a yo-yo effect for most of my life. Every time I lose weight, I put it back on, and the most discouraging part is I keep putting on more each time."

This weight loss-weight gain experience is difficult for both thin and fat people to understand. Some of the confusion can be traced to the fact that there may be different types of obesity. For example, many Americans have had the experience of being overweight at various times in their lives. For a substantial number, weight gain has been a reaction to a specific life situation that produced depression, tension, loneliness, and other emotional problems. Once the situation resolves itself, weight loss frequently occurs, as the following demonstrates: "I only lose weight when I am single. As long as I am not married I have no weight problem at all. The trouble is I have been married three times and each time I have gotten fatter." This type of weight problem has been referred to as reactive obesity (Haber, 1980) and the condition frequently is not long-term in nature.

For other heavy people their weight problems frequently go as far back as childhood. These individuals have the history of weight gain, weight loss and subsequent weight gain. "When I was a child it was always 'Big Fat Annie'; I just don't think I'll ever be thin. It seems like all my life I have been trying to lose weight and I never seem to get anywhere. Sometimes I ask myself, 'Is it really worth it?'" It is the individual with a chronic weight problem who poses the most complex problems. These individuals present case histories that consist of a constant losing battle with weight loss. It is to this group and their particular set of problems that we now turn our attention.

The stigmatization fat people are subjected to is critical in understanding how they view and attempt to manage their weight problems. In some respects the nature of their stigmatization is unique when compared to other stigmatized groups. Goffman has argued that the "fully and visibly" stigmatized are different from other deviant groups, because they cannot utilize "passing or covering" as impression management strategies (Goffman, 1963); at the same time they are not viewed as completely responsible for their deviance. Thus while the cripple, the blind, and the ugly are stigmatized and this status creates difficulties, their stigmatization is mitigated to a certain extent because they are not considered fully responsible for their condition. On the other hand, the criminal, the alcoholic and the prostitute, while viewed as being responsible for their identities, can engage in "covering and passing" as a means of managing their deviant identities. The extent of stigmatization a group is subjected to can be conceptualized in the following manner:

Stigmatization Model		
	High visibility	Low visibility
High Responsibility	+	-
	+	+
Low Responsibility	+	-
	-	

It follows then that fat people are one of the few groups in our society who fall into the first cell. Their excessive weight makes "passing and covering" impossible, and their excessive eating behavior results in others viewing them as personally responsible. It is this unique set of conditions that contributes significantly to their reliance on accounts as a means of managing their stigma. We should point out that this is only true for the chronically overweight individual. We would argue that the mildly overweight adult male can conceal his weight by the careful selection of clothing and further mitigate his heaviness by indicating, "It's really all muscle" or "It's just a beer gut." This type of passing and covering and the offering of an account results in low visibility and places him in the fourth cell of our stigmatization paradigm.

Accounts

Previous research has indicated that fat people internalize the judgments others make about their condition (Alton, 1973; Cahnman, 1968). Given the unique nature of their stigmatization, fat people are frequently forced to offer explanations about their con-

dition, and these explanations can be categorized as accounts. Accounts, as conceptualized by Scott and Lyman (1968) and subsequently elaborated on by Goffman (1971), consist of "statements by social actors to relieve themselves of culpability for untoward or unanticipated acts." Scott and Lyman identify two types of accounts: excuses and justifications. Goffman introduces a third, apology.

Excuses. The most common mode of excuse fat people utilize is what has been termed defeasibility. This involves the malfunctioning of intent in the sense that the actor at the time of the activity was not acting with complete knowledge, voluntariness, or total consciousness. One of the charges fat people continually face is their lack of "willpower" in terms of food consumption. In response to this accusation, our respondents offered the explanation that indeed they do lack willpower in this regard, but it is a consequence of a tragic flaw in their character. In other words, they are not like "normal people" because they are flawed. This flaw is a consequence of forces beyond their control; common statements are:

- "If I only had more willpower I wouldn't be in this fix."
- "I am my own worst enemy."
- "It all breaks down to mind over matter."
- "It takes an awful lot of self-discipline, which I don't have much of."

A second form of defeasibility is one that traces weight problems to early childhood socialization. This explanation places the blame on transmitted parental attitudes towards food and eating patterns. It takes the following forms:

- "My mother has always encouraged me to eat. She has never wanted me to lose weight. She thinks to be heavy is to be healthy, and I am the only one of six children who is healthy in her eyes."
- "My family saw giving you food as giving you love. They would compliment me on eating so much by saying things like 'Guess what? Betty ate a whole chicken for dinner last night!'"

- "I was force-fed as a child, had to eat everything on my plate."

Observer: "What if you didn't, what would they do?"

"Slap me! We were poor, and when we had money my father would go out and stock up on food. To this day I can't stand not to have the cupboards full, and I still feel guilty if I leave food on my plate."

Explanations involving a tragic flaw represent an effort to reduce personal responsibility while still remaining consistent with a societal view of the problem.

Justification. Another type of account developed by Scott and Lyman is justification. This explanation involves the admission on the actor's part that the behavior is wrong but the uniqueness of the situation makes it appropriate. Justification took the following forms among our respondents:

- "I might as well start eating again. That fool Reagan is messing everything up so bad I might as well go out with a full stomach."

- "A few weeks ago I was driving from my sister's house. She had fixed me a nice lunch and dinner to eat on the trip. Out on the turnpike there was an accident and I was stuck there for almost an hour. You know what it is like to be stuck in traffic? It is enough to drive you crazy. By the time the traffic got moving I had eaten both the lunch and the dinner."

As Scott and Lyman point out, justification can take the form of the "sad tale" in which the actor reconstructs a biography that justifies the behavior:

- "Just last week I was denied adoption of a young child by an agency after waiting three years. No wonder I overeat when none of my needs are being met. It's enough to make me eat two pound cakes."

Apologies. Erving Goffman has argued that apologies contribute a third type of account. Apology has several elements as conceptualized by Goffman; a central feature involves "a gesture through which an individual splits himself into two parts, the part that

is guilty of an offense and the part that dissociates itself from the delict and affirms a belief in the offended rule" (Goffman, 1971:113). Two features of apology that are central to fat people are the "vilification" of self and "performance of penance." It should be pointed out that fat people go to great lengths to conceal their excessive eating. This is related to the unique stigmatization they experience since excessive eating in public would constitute primary deviance. Research has demonstrated that fat people do not engage in deviant eating patterns in public (Kissileff et al., 1978; Stunkard et al., 1980). In fact our respondents reported how they took great care to maintain this hidden deviance.

- "I used to carry M&Ms on the way to work and I would eat a big package on the way to work and another on the way home. But the worst was Oreo cookies. My face was always black from them. Two or three packages a day . . . I was always washing the black off my face, so that no one could notice."

- "I never drink at cocktail parties. I wait for everyone else to get smashed to the point that they don't notice me. Then I really hit the finger sandwiches, peanuts, and whatever else is around."

- "My problem is when I am alone. I would be so ashamed if people saw me eating like this. Before I went to a hypnotist I had jars of peanut butter hidden all over the house. I didn't touch the jar in the cabinet, but I was constantly dipping my fingers in the other jars. Some days I would eat two or three jars of peanut butter."

Explanations about binge eating provide excellent examples of how overweight people use both vilification of self and the performance of penance to account for their excessive eating. Briefly, binge eating is a relatively short duration, solitary activity that most frequently occurs at home during the early or late evening. It is usually precipitated by interpersonal conflict or negative feeling states, i.e., boredom, depression, or anger, and is followed by negative, derogatory self-statements (Loro, 1980). The present study indicates that fat people account for binge eating episodes through apologies. This apology process occurs in the following way. First, the person engages in vilification of self through self-abusive and self-critical statements. For example:

- "After I binge, I really feel awful and disgusted. I mean how can a responsible, mature adult do such repulsive and revolting things? I mean I ate a dozen donuts and they didn't even taste good. You know, sometimes I think I'm an animal, yeah, a hungry hyena."

The final part of the apology consists of the performance of penance, usually by committing the "sin" of binge eating. For example:

- "After I have binged, I feel huge for the next couple of days. I feel so fat and guilty. I really crucify myself . . . Sometimes after a binge I take off all my clothes to look at my disgusting body in the mirror."

This penance may take other forms, such as extreme dieting, fasting or starvation, extreme exercising or substance abuse. This latter form of penance involves purging the body with laxatives, diuretics, and emetics (Russell, 1979; White et al., 1981). Typically, the remorseful person is trying to assuage intense guilt induced by excessive eating or binge eating, usually while trying to reduce his or her weight or diet.

Discussion

These findings indicate that fat people engage extensively in the use of accounts to explain their eating behaviors and weight problems. This reliance on accounts can be viewed as a reaction against the stigmatization to which they are subjected. While it is the case that fat people can hide their deviant eating patterns, they cannot hide their highly visible weight problems. Furthermore, in contrast to other stigmatized groups, they are held completely responsible for their condition. These two factors contribute significantly to their need for accounts to explain their excessive weight. At the same time, the use of accounts serves other purposes. On one level, these accounts represent an acceptance of the societal view of their weight problem; namely, it is their own fault or re-

sponsibility. On another level, while the account represents an admission of responsibility, it also serves as a means of reducing responsibility by introducing additional information in the form of apologies, excuses, and justifications. These accounts serve to mitigate personal responsibility in a socially acceptable fashion. Because of their high visibility, fat people encounter many situations where they feel compelled to offer explanations for their condition.

This analysis does not exhaust the total range of accounts used by fat people. Surprisingly, none of our respondents involved the excuse of "biological drives" (Scott and Lyman, 1968), particularly since there is a growing body of literature that suggests a relationship between physiological/biochemical processes and weight control difficulties (Allon, 1973; Deluise et al., 1980; Wolley et al., 1979). Since all the respondents were highly motivated clients who had joined a behaviorally-oriented weight reduction group, we speculate that they had given up using biological drives or organic explanations for their weight problems. It may be, however, that different populations of fat people, i.e., adult-onset obese males and childhood-onset obese females, use different types of accounts to explain their weight control difficulties. Future research on obesity and weight reduction will examine further the role of accounts in facilitating or impairing weight control. Such research could have far-reaching implications for clinicians who treat the obese as well as for stigmatized fat people in general.

References

Allon, Natalie. 1973. "Group Dieting Rituals." *Society*, 10 (January-February), 36–42.

Allon, Natalie. 1973. "The Stigma of Overweight in Everyday Life." In Bray, C. A., ed: *Obesity in Perspective*. Vol. 2, Part 2. Washington, D.C., United States Government Printing Office: 83–102

Berland, Theodore. 1974. *Rating the Diets*. Skokie, Illinois: Publications International.

Bray, George A. 1978. "Definition, Measurement and Classification of the Syndromes of Obesity." *International Journal of Obesity*, 2:99–112.

Cahnman, Wemer J. 1968. "The Stigma of Obesity." *Sociological Quarterly,* 9(Summer):283–299.

Deluise, Mario, Blackburn, George L., and Flier, Jeffrey S. 1980. "Reduced Activity of the Red-Cell Sodium-Potassium Pump in Human Obesity." *The New England Journal of Medicine,* 303:1017–1022.

Goffman, Erving. 1963. *Stigma.* Englewood Cliffs, NJ: Prentice Hall.

Goffman, Erving. 1971. *Relations In Public.* New York: Basic Books.

Haber, Sandra. 1980. "Obesity: Towards an Integration of Theoretical Perspectives." Unpublished paper.

Hall, Sharon Martinelli, and Havassy, Barbara. 1981. "The Obese Woman; Causes, Correlates, and Treatment." *Professional Psychology,* 12:163–170.

Hanna, Charles F., Loro, Jr., Albert D., and Power, D. Dolan. 1981. "Differences in the Degree of Overweight: A Note on Its Importance." *Addictive Behaviors,* 6:61–62.

Jeffrey, D. Balfour, and Katz, C. Roger. 1977. *Take It Off and Keep It Off.* Englewood Cliffs, NJ:Prentice Hall.

Kissileff, K. S., Jordan, H. A., and Levitz, L. S. 1978. "Eating Habits of Obese and Normal Weight Humans." *International Journal of Obesity,* 2:379.

Lyman, Sanford M. 1978. *The Seven Deadly Sins.* New York: St. Martin.

Millman, Marcia. 1980. *Such A Pretty Face.* New York: W. W. Norton.

Orbach, Susie. 1978. *Fat is a Feminist Issue.* London: Paddington Press.

Rodin, J. 1977. "Research on Eating Behavior and Obesity; Where Does it Fit in Personality and Social Psychology?" *Personality and Social Psychology Bulletin,* 3:333–355.

Rodin, J. 1978. "Environmental Factors in Obesity." *Psychiatric Clinics of North America,* 1:581–592.

Russell, George F. M. 1979. "Bulimia Nervosa: An Ominous Variant of Anorexia Nervosa." *Psychological Medicine,* 9:429–448.

Scott, M. B., and Lyman, S. M. 1968. "Accounts." *American Sociological Review,* 33:46–62.

Seltzer, Carl, and Mayer, Jean. 1965. "A Simple Criterion of Obesity." *Post-Graduate Medicine,* 38:101–107.

Stunkard, Albert, Coll, Milton, Lundquist, Sara, and Mayer, Jean. 1980. "Obesity and Eating Style." *Archives General Psychiatry,* 37:1127–1129.

Tobias, Alice L., and Gordon, Judith Bograd. 1980. "Social Consequences of Obesity." *Journal of the American Dietetic Association,* 76:338–342.

White, William C., and Boskind-White, Marlene. 1981. "An Experimental-Behavioral Approach to the Treatment of Bulimarixia." *Psychotherapy: Theory, Research and Practice,*18.

Wolley, S. C., Wolley, O. W., and Dyrenforth, S. R. 1979. "Theoretical, Practical and Social Issues in Behavioral Treatment of Obesity." *Journal of Applied Behavior Analysis,* 12:3–25.

Wyden, P. 1965. *The Overweight Society.* New York: William Morrow.

Wyden, Peter, and Wyden, Barbara. 1968. *How the Doctors Diet.* New York: Trident Press.

12

The Medical Construction of Gender: Case Management of Intersexed Infants

Suzanne J. Kessler

This article explores the medical treatment of infants born with ambiguous genitals. In such cases, doctors are faced with decisions about what sex to "make" the child. Because the child cannot be categorized as either a boy or a girl, it is defined as flawed, or deviant. In almost all instances, then, doctors believe it necessary to "do something" to make the child "normal." In this respect, we see that the presence of a deviant person, even when the deviant is a newborn baby, creates a great degree of discomfort and confusion for others. As a result, whenever possible, authorities who have the ability to erase the evidence of deviance typically feel a responsibility for using their skills to "correct" the deviance.

The birth of intersexed infants, babies born with genitals that are neither clearly male nor clearly female, has been documented throughout recorded time (Bullough 1976; Ellis 1942; Fiedler 1978; Foucault 1980). In the late twentieth century, medical technology has advanced to allow scientists to determine chromosomal and hormonal gender, which is typically taken to be the real, natural, biological gender, usually referred to as "sex" (Kessler and McKenna 1985). Nevertheless, physicians who handle the cases of intersexed infants consider several factors

beside biological ones in determining, assigning, and announcing the gender of a particular infant. Indeed, biological factors are often preempted in their deliberations by such cultural factors as the "correct" length of the penis and capacity of the vagina.

In the literature of intersexuality, issues such as announcing a baby's gender at the time of delivery, postdelivery discussions with the parents, and consultations with patients in adolescence are considered only peripherally to the central medical issues—etiology, diagnosis, and surgical procedures (Bolkenius et al. 1984; Glassberg 1980; Lee et al. 1980). Yet members of medical teams have standard practices for managing intersexuality that rely ultimately on cultural understandings of gender. The process and guidelines by which decisions about gender (re)construction are made reveal the model for the social construction of gender generally. Moreover, in the face of apparently incontrovertible evidence—infants born with some combination of "female" and "male" reproductive and sexual features—physicians hold an incorrigible belief in and insistence upon female and male as the only "natural" options. This paradox highlights and calls into question the idea that female and male are biological givens compelling a culture of two genders.

Ideally, to undertake an extensive study of intersexed infant case management, I would like to have had direct access to particular events, for example, the deliveries of intersexed infants and the initial discussions among physicians, between physicians and parents, between parents, and among parents and family and friends of intersexed infants. The rarity with which intersexuality occurs, however, made this unfeasible.[1] Alternatively, physicians who have had considerable experience in dealing with this condition were interviewed. I do not assume that their "talk" about how they manage such cases mirrors their "talk" in the situation, but their words do reveal that they have certain assumptions about gender and that they impose those assumptions via their medical decisions on the patients they treat.

Interviews were conducted with six medical experts (three women and three men) in the field of pediatric intersexuality: one clinical geneticist, three endocrinologists (two of them pediatric specialists), one psychoendocrinologist, and one urologist. All of them have had extensive clinical experience with various intersexed syndromes, and some are internationally known researchers in the field of intersexuality. They were selected on the basis of their prominence in the field and their representation of four different medical centers in New York City. Although they know one another, they do not collaborate on research and are not part of the same management team. All were interviewed in the spring of 1985, in their offices, and interviews lasted between forty-five minutes and one hour. Unless further referenced, all quotations in this article are from these interviews.

The Theory of Intersexuality Management

The sophistication of today's medical technology has led to an extensive compilation of various intersex categories based on the various causes of malformed genitals. The "true intersexed" condition, where both ovarian and testicular tissue are present in either the same gonad or in opposite gonads, accounts for fewer than 5 percent of all cases of ambiguous genital (Castro-Magana, Angulo, and Collipp 1984). More commonly, the infant has either ovaries or testes, but the genitals are ambiguous. If the infant has two ovaries, the condition is referred to as female pseudohermaphroditism. If the infant has two testes, the condition is referred to as male pseudohermaphroditism. There are numerous causes of both forms of pseudohermaphroditism, and although there are life-threatening aspects to some of these conditions, having ambiguous genitals per se is not harmful to the infant's health.[2] Although most cases of ambiguous genitals do not represent true intersex, in keeping with the contemporary literature, I will refer to all such cases as intersexed.

Current attitudes toward the intersex condition are primarily influenced by three factors. First are the extraordinary advancements in surgical techniques and endocrinology in the last decade. For example, female

genitals can now be constructed to be indistinguishable in appearance from normal natural ones. Some abnormally small penises can be enlarged with the exogenous application of hormones, although surgical skills are not sufficiently advanced to construct a normal-looking and functioning penis out of other tissue.[3] Second, in the contemporary United States the influence of the feminist movement has called into question the valuation of women according to strictly reproductive functions, and the presence or absence of functional gonads is no longer the only or the definitive criterion for gender assignment. Third, contemporary psychological theorists have begun to focus on "gender identity" (one's sense of oneself as belonging to the female or male category) as distinct from "gender role" (cultural expectations of one's behavior as "appropriate" for a female or male).[4] The relevance of this new gender identity theory for rethinking cases of ambiguous genitals is that gender must be assigned as early as possible in order for gender identity to develop successfully. As a result of these three factors, intersexuality is now considered a treatable condition of the genitals, one that needs to be resolved expeditiously.

According to all of the specialists interviewed, management of intersexed cases is based upon the theory of gender proposed first by John Money, J. C. Hampson, and J. L. Hampson in 1955 and developed in 1972 by Money and Anke A. Ehrhardt, which argues that gender identity is changeable until approximately eighteen months of age.[5] "To use the Pygmalion allegory, one may begin with the same clay and fashion a god or a goddess" (Money and Ehrhardt 1972:152). The theory rests on satisfying several conditions: the experts must insure that the parents have no doubt about whether their child is male or female; the genitals must be made to match the assigned gender as soon as possible; gender-appropriate hormones must be administered at puberty; and intersexed children must be kept informed about their situation with age-appropriate explanations. If these conditions are met, the theory proposes, the intersexed child will develop a gender identity in accordance with the gender assignment (regardless of the chromosomal gender) and will not question her or his assignment and request reassignment at a later age.

Supportive evidence for Money and Ehrhardt's theory is based on only a handful of repeatedly cited cases, but it has been accepted because of the prestige of the theoreticians and its resonance with contemporary ideas about gender, children, psychology, and medicine. Gender and children are malleable; psychology and medicine are the tools used to transform them. This theory is so strongly endorsed that it has taken on the character of gospel. "I think we [physicians] have been raised in the Money theory," one endocrinologist said. Another claimed, "We always approach the problem in a similar way and it's been dictated, to a large extent, by the work of John Money and Anke Ehrhardt because they are the only people who have published, at least in medical literature, any data, any guidelines." It is provocative that this physician immediately followed this assertion with: "And I don't know how effective it really is." Contradictory data are rarely cited in reviews of the literature, were not mentioned by any of the physicians interviewed, and have not diminished these physicians' belief in the theory's validity (but see Diamond 1982).

The doctors interviewed concur with the argument that gender be assigned immediately, decisively, and irreversibly, and that professional opinions be presented in a clear and unambiguous way. The psychoendocrinologist said that when doctors make a statement about the infant, they should "stick to it." The urologist said, "If you make a statement that later has to be disclaimed or discredited, you've weakened your credibility." A gender assignment made decisively, unambiguously, and irrevocably contributes, I believe, to the general impression that the infant's true, natural "sex" has been discovered, and that something that was there all along has been found. It also serves to maintain the credibility of the medical profession, reassure the parents, and reflexively substantiate Money and Ehrhardt's theory.

Also according to the theory, if operative correction is necessary, it should take place as soon as possible. If the infant is assigned the male gender, the initial stage of penis re-

pair is usually undertaken in the first year, and further surgery is completed before the child enters school. If the infant is assigned the female gender, vulva repair (including clitoral reduction) is usually begun by three months of age. Money suggests that if reduction of phallic tissue were delayed beyond the neonatal period, the infant would have traumatic memories of having been castrated (Money 1974). Vaginoplasty, in those females having an adequate internal structure (e.g., the vaginal canal is near its expected location), is done between the ages of one and four years. Girls who require more complicated surgical procedures might not be surgically corrected until preadolescence (Castro-Magana et al. 1984.) The complete vaginal canal is typically constructed only when the body is fully grown, following pubertal feminization with estrogen, although more recently some specialists have claimed surgical success with vaginal construction in the early childhood years (Braren et al, 1980). Although physicians speculate about the possible trauma of an early childhood "castration" memory, there is no corresponding concern that vaginal reconstructive surgery delayed beyond the neonatal period is traumatic.

Even though gender identity theory places the critical age limit for gender reassignment between eighteen months and two years, the physicians acknowledge that diagnosis, gender assignment, and genital reconstruction cannot be delayed for as long as two years, since a clear gender assignment and correctly formed genitals will determine the kind of interactions parents will have with the child (Rubin, Provenzano, and Luria 1974). The geneticist argued that when parents "change a diaper and see genitalia that don't mean much in terms of gender assignment, I think it prolongs the negative response to the baby. . . . If you have clitoral enlargement that is so extraordinary that the parents can't distinguish between male and female, it is sometimes helpful to reduce that somewhat so that the parent views the child as female." Another physician concurred: parents "need to go home and do their job as child rearers with it very clear whether it's a boy or a girl."

Diagnosis

A premature gender announcement by an obstetrician, prior to a close examination of an infant's genitals, can be problematic. Money and his colleagues claim that the primary complications in case management of intersexed infants can be traced to mishandling by medical personnel untrained in sexology (Money 1974; 1975; 1983; Money et al. 1955; 1969; 1972; 1981). According to one of the pediatric sexologists interviewed, obstetricians improperly educated about intersexed conditions "don't examine the babies closely enough at birth and say things just by looking, before separating legs and looking at everything, and jump to conclusions, because 99 percent of the time it's correct. . . . People get upset, physicians I mean. And they say things that are inappropriate." For example, he said that an inexperienced obstetrician might blurt out, "I think you have a boy, or no, maybe you have a girl." Other inappropriate remarks a doctor might make in postdelivery consultation with the parents include, "You have a little boy, but he'll never function as a little boy, so you better raise him as a little girl." As a result, said the pediatric endocrinologist, "the family comes away with the idea that they have a little boy, and that's what they wanted, and that's what they're going to get." In such cases parents sometimes insist that the child be raised male despite the physician's instructions to the contrary. "People have in mind certain things they've heard, that this is a boy, and they're not likely to forget that, or they're not likely to let it go easily." The urologist agreed that the first gender attribution is critical: "Once it's been announced, you've got a big problem on your hands." "One of the worst things is to allow [the parents] to go ahead and give a name and tell everyone, and it turns out the child has to be raised in the opposite sex."[6]

Physicians feel that the mismanagement of such cases requires careful remedying. The psychoendocrinologist asserted, "When I'm involved, I spend hours with the parents to explain to them what has happened and how a mistake like that could be made, *or not really a mistake but a different decision*" (my emphasis). One pediatric endocrinologist said, "[I] try to dissuade them from previous misconceptions, and say, 'Well, I know what they meant, but the way they said it confused you. This is, I think, a better way to think about it.'" These statements reveal physicians' efforts not only to protect parents from concluding that their child is neither male nor female but also to protect other physicians' decision-making processes. Case management involves perpetuating the notion that good medical decisions are based on interpretations of the infant's real "sex" rather than on cultural understandings of gender.

"Mismanagements" are less likely to occur in communities with major medical centers, where specialists are prepared to deal with intersexuality and a medical team (perhaps drawing physicians from more than one teaching hospital) is quickly assembled. The team typically consists of the original referring doctor (obstetrician or pediatrician), a pediatric endocrinologist, a pediatric surgeon (urologist or gynecologist), and a geneticist. In addition, a psychologist, psychiatrist, or psychoendocrinologist might play a role. If an infant is born with ambiguous genitals in a small community hospital, without the relevant specialists on staff, she or he is likely to be transferred to a hospital where diagnosis and treatment are available. Intersexed infants born in poor rural areas where there is less medical intervention might never be referred for genital reconstruction. Many of these children, like those born in earlier historical periods, will grow up and live through adulthood with the condition of genital ambiguity—somehow managing.

The diagnosis of intersexed conditions includes assessing the chromosomal sex and the syndrome that produced the genital ambiguity, and may include medical procedures such as cytologic screening; chromosomal analysis; assessing serum electrolytes; hormone, gonadotropin, and steroids evaluation; digital examination; and radiographic genitography (Castro-Magana et al. 1984). In any intersexed condition, if the infant is determined to be a genetic female (having an XX chromosome makeup), then the treatment—genital surgery to reduce the phallus size—can proceed relatively quickly, satisfying what the doctors believe are psychological and cultural demands. For example, 21-hydroxylase deficiency, a form of female pseudohermaphroditism and one of the most common conditions, can be determined by a blood test within the first few days.

If, on the other hand, the infant is determined to have at least one Y chromosome, then surgery may be considerably delayed. A decision must be made whether to test the ability of the phallic tissue to respond to (HCG) androgen treatment, which is intended to enlarge the microphallus enough to be a penis. The endocrinologist explained, "You do HCG testing and you find out if the male can make testosterone. . . . You can get those results back probably within three weeks. . . . You're sure the male is making testosterone—but can he respond to it? It can take three months of waiting to see whether the phallus responds." If the Y-chromosome infant cannot make testosterone or cannot respond to the testosterone it makes, the phallus will not develop, and the Y-chromosome infant is not considered to be a male after all.

Should the infant's phallus respond to the local application of testosterone or a brief course of intramuscular injections of low-potency androgen, the gender assignment problem is resolved, but possibly at some later cost, since the penis will not grow again at puberty when the rest of the body develops (Money 1974). Money's case management philosophy assumes that while it may be difficult for an adult male to have a much smaller than average penis, it is very detrimental to the morale of the young boy to have a micropenis (Lee et al. 1980). In the former case the male's manliness might be at stake, but in the latter case his essential maleness might be. Although the psychological consequences of these experiences have not been empirically documented, Money and his colleagues suggest that it is wise to avoid the problems of both the micropenis in childhood and the still undersized penis postpuberty by reassigning many of these infants to the female gender.[7] This approach suggests that for Money and his colleagues, chromosomes are less relevant in determining gender than penis size, and that, by implication,

"male" is defined not by the genetic condition of having one Y and one X chromosome or by the production of sperm but by the aesthetic condition of having an appropriately sized penis.

The tests and procedures required for diagnosis (and, consequently, for gender assignment) can take several months (Hecker 1984). Although physicians are anxious not to make a premature gender assignment, their language suggests that it is difficult for them to take a completely neutral position and think and speak only of phallic tissue that belongs to an infant whose gender has not yet been determined or decided. Comments such as "seeing whether the male can respond to testosterone" imply at least a tentative male gender assignment of an XY infant. The psychoendocrinologist's explanation to parents of their infant's treatment program also illustrates this implicit male gender assignment "Clearly this baby has an underdeveloped phallus. But if the phallus responds to this treatment we are fairly confident that surgical techniques and hormonal techniques will help this child to look like a boy. But we want to make absolutely sure and use some hormone treatments and see whether the tissue reacts." The mere fact that this doctor refers to the genitals as an "underdeveloped" phallus rather than an overdeveloped clitoris suggests that the infant has been judged to be, at least provisionally, a male. In the case of the undersized phallus, what is ambiguous is not whether this is a penis, but whether it is "good enough" to remain one. If at the end of the treatment period the phallic tissue has not responded, what had been a potential penis (referred to in the medical literature as a "clitoropenis") is now considered an enlarged clitoris (or "penoclitoris"), and reconstructive surgery is planned as for the genetic female.

The time-consuming nature of intersex diagnosis and the assumption, based on gender identity theory, that gender should be assigned as soon as possible thus present physicians with difficult dilemmas. Medical personnel are committed to discovering the etiology of the condition in order to determine the best course of treatment, which takes time. Yet they feel an urgent need to provide an immediate assignment and genitals that look and function appropriately. An immediate assignment that will need to be retracted is more problematic than a delayed assignment, since reassignment carries with it an additional set of social complications. The endocrinologist interviewed commented: "We've come very far in that we can diagnose eventually, many of the conditions. But we haven't come far enough. . . . We can't do it early enough . . . Very frequently a decision is made before all this information is available, simply because it takes so long to make the correct diagnosis. And you cannot let a child go indefinitely, not in this society you can't. . . . There's pressure on parents [for a decision] and the parents transmit that pressure onto physicians." A pediatric endocrinologist agreed: "At times you may need to operate before a diagnosis can be made. . . . In one case parents were told to wait on the announcement while the infant was treated to see if the phallus would grow when treated with androgens. After the first month passed and there was some growth, the parents said they gave it a boy's name. They could only wait a month."

Deliberating out loud on the judiciousness of making parents wait for assignment decisions, the endocrinologist asked rhetorically, "Why do we do all these tests if in the end we're going to make the decision simply on the basis of the appearance of the genitalia?" This question suggests that the principles underlying physicians' decisions are cultural rather than biological, based on parental reaction and the medical team's perception of the infant's societal adjustment prospects given the way her/his genitals look or could be made to look. Moreover, as long as the decision rests largely on the criterion of genital appearance, and male is defined as having a "good-sized" penis, more infants will be assigned to the female gender than to the male.

The Waiting Period: Dealing With Ambiguity

During the period of ambiguity between birth and assignment, physicians not only must evaluate the infant's prospects to be a good male but also must manage parents' un-

certainty about a genderless child. Physicians advise that parents postpone announcing the gender of the infant until a gender has been explicitly assigned. They believe that parents should not feel compelled to tell other people. The clinical geneticist interviewed said that physicians "basically encourage [parents] to treat [the infant] as neuter." One of the pediatric endocrinologists reported that in France parents confronted with this dilemma sometimes give the infant a neuter name, such as Claude or Jean. The psychoendocrinologist concurred: "If you have a truly borderline situation, and you want to make it dependent on the hormone treatment . . . then the parents are . . . told, 'Try not to make a decision. Refer to the baby as "baby." Don't think in terms of boy or girl.'" Yet, when asked whether this is a reasonable request to make of parents in our society, the physician answered: "I don't think so. I think parents can't do it."

New York State requires that a birth certificate be filled out within forty-eight hours of delivery, but the certificate need not be filed with the state for thirty days. The geneticist tells parents to insert "child of" instead of a name. In one case, parents filled out two birth registration forms, one for each gender, and they refused to sign either until a final gender assignment had been made (Bing and Rudikoff 1970). One of the pediatric endocrinologists claimed, "I heard a story; I don't know if it's true or not. There were parents of a hermaphroditic infant who told everyone they had twins, one of each gender. When the gender was determined, they said the other had died."

The geneticist explained that when directly asked by parents what to tell others about the gender of the infant, she says, "Why don't you just tell them that the baby is having problems and as soon as the problems are resolved we'll get back to you." A pediatric endocrinologist echoes this suggestion in advising parents to say, "Until the problem is solved [we] would really prefer not to discuss any of the details." According to the urologist, "If [the gender] isn't announced people may mutter about it and may grumble about it, but they haven't got anything to get their teeth into and make trouble over for the child, or the parents, or whatever." In short, parents are asked to sidestep the infant's gender rather than admit that the gender is unknown, thereby collaborating in a web of white lies, ellipses, and mystifications.[8]

Even while physicians teach the parents how to deal with others who will not find the infant's condition comprehensible or acceptable, physicians must also make the condition comprehensible and acceptable to the parents, normalizing the intersexed condition for them. In doing so they help the parents consider the infant's condition in the most positive way. There are four key aspects to this "normalizing" process.

First, physicians teach parents normal fetal development and explain that all fetuses have the potential to be male or female. One of the endocrinologists explains, "In the absence of maleness you have femaleness. . . . It's really the basic design. The other [intersex] is really a variation on a theme." This explanation presents the intersex condition as a natural phase of every fetal development. Another endocrinologist "like[s] to show picture[s] to them and explain that at a certain point in development males and females look alike and then diverge for such and such reason." The professional literature suggests that doctors use diagrams that illustrate "nature's principle of using the same anlagen to produce the external genital parts of the male and female" (Mazur 1983; Money 1974:218).

Second, physicians stress the normalcy of the infant in other aspects. For example, the geneticist tells parents, "The baby is healthy, but there was a problem in the way the baby was developing." The endocrinologist says the infant has "a mild defect, just like anything [else] could be considered a birth defect, a mole or a hemangioma." This language not only eases the blow to the parents but also redirects their attention. Terms like "hermaphrodite" or "abnormal" are not used. The urologist said that he advised parents "about the generalization of sticking to the good things and not confusing people with something that is unnecessary."

Third, physicians (at least initially) imply that it is not the gender of the child that is ambiguous but the genitals. They talk about "undeveloped," "maldeveloped,"' or "unfinished" organs. From a number of the physicians interviewed came the following explanations: "At a point in time the development proceeded in a different way, and sometimes the development isn't complete and we may have some trouble . . . in determining what the *actual* sex is. And so we have to do a blood test to help us" (my emphasis). "The baby may be a female, which you would know after the buccal smear, but you cannot prove it yet. If so, then it's a normal female with a different appearance. This can be surgically corrected"; "The gender of your child isn't apparent to us at the moment"; "While this looks like a small penis, it's actually a large clitoris. And what we're going to do is put it back in its proper position and reduce the size of the tip of it enough so it doesn't look funny, so it looks right." Money and his colleagues report a case in which parents were advised to tell their friends that the reason their infant's gender was reannounced from male to female is that "the baby was . . . 'closed up down there' . . . when the closed skin was divided, the female organs were revealed, and the baby discovered to be, *in fact*, a girl" (emphasis mine). It was mistakenly assumed to be a male at first because "there was an excess of skin on the clitoris" (Money et al. 1969:211).

The message in these examples is that the trouble lies in the doctor's ability to determine the gender, not in the baby's gender per se. The real gender will presumably be determined/proven by testing, and the "bad" genitals (which are confusing the situation for everyone) will be "repaired." The emphasis is not on the doctors creating gender but in their completing the genitals. Physicians say that they "reconstruct" the genitals rather than "construct" them. The surgeons reconstitute from remaining parts what should have been there all along. The fact that gender in an infant is "reannounced" rather than "reassigned" suggests that the first announcement was a mistake because the announcer was confused by the genitals. The gender always was what it is now seen to be.

Finally, physicians tell parents that social factors are more important in gender development than biological ones, even though they are searching for biological causes. In essence the physicians teach the parents Money and Ehrhardt's theory of gender development.[9] In doing so, they shift the emphasis from the discovery of biological factors that are a sign of the "real" gender to providing the appropriate social conditions to produce the "real" gender. What remains unsaid is the apparent contradiction in the notion that a "real" or "natural" gender can be, or needs to be, produced artificially. The physician/parent discussions make it clear to family members that gender is not a biological given (even though, of course, their own procedures for diagnosis assume that it is), and that gender is fluid. The psychoendocrinologist paraphrased an explanation to parents thus: "It will depend, ultimately, on how everybody treats your child and how your child is looking as a person. . . . I can with confidence tell them that generally gender [identity] clearly agrees with the assignment." Similarly, a pediatric endocrinologist explained: "[I] try to impress upon them that there's an enormous amount of clinical data to support the fact that if you sex-reverse an infant . . . the majority of the time the alternative gender identity is commensurate with the socialization, the way that they're raised, and how people view them, and that seems to be the most critical."

The implication of these comments is that gender identity (of all children, not just those born with ambiguous genitals) is determined primarily by social factors, that the parents and community always construct the child's gender. In the case of intersexed infants, the physicians merely provide the right genitals to go along with the socialization. Of course, at normal births, when the infant's genitals are unambiguous, the parents are not told that the child's gender is ultimately up to socialization. In those cases, doctors do treat gender as a biological given.

Social Factors in Decision Making

Most of the physicians interviewed claimed that personal convictions of doctors ought to play no role in the decision-making process. The psychoendocrinologist explained: "I think the most critical factors [are] what is the possibility that this child will grow up with genitals which look like that of the assigned gender and which will ultimately function according to gender . . . That's why it's so important that it's a well-established team, because [personal convictions] can't really enter into it. It has to be what is surgically and endocrinologically possible for that baby to be able to make it . . . It's really much more within medical criteria. I don't think many social factors enter into it." While this doctor eschews the importance of social factors in gender assignment, she argues forcefully that social factors are extremely important in the development of gender identity. Indeed, she implies that social factors primarily enter the picture once the infant leaves the hospital.

In fact, doctors make decisions about gender on the basis of shared cultural values that are unstated, perhaps even unconscious, and therefore considered objective rather than subjective. Money states the fundamental rule for gender assignment: "Never assign a baby to be reared, and to surgical and hormonal therapy, as a boy, unless the phallic structure, hypospadiac or otherwise, is neonatally of at least the same caliber as that of same-aged males with small-average penises" (Money, 1975:610). Elsewhere, he and his colleagues provide specific measurements for what qualifies as a micropenis: "A penis is, by convention, designated as a micropenis when at birth its dimensions are three or more standard deviations below the mean. . . . When it is correspondingly reduced in diameter with corpora that are vestigial . . . it unquestionably qualifies as a micropenis" (Money et al, 1981:18). A pediatric endocrinologist claimed that although "the [size of the] phallus is not the deciding factor . . . if the phallus is less than 2 centimeters long at birth and won't respond to androgen treatments, then it's made into a female."

These guidelines are clear, but they focus on only one physical feature, one that is distinctly imbued with cultural meaning. This becomes especially apparent in the case of an XX infant with normal female reproductive gonads and a perfect penis. Would the size and shape of the penis, in this case, be the deciding factor in assigning the infant "male" or would the perfect penis be surgically destroyed and female genitals created? Money notes that this dilemma would be complicated by the anticipated reaction of the parents to seeing "their apparent son lose his penis" (money 1968). Other researchers concur that parents are likely to want to raise a child with a normal-shaped penis (regardless of size) as "male," particularly if the scrotal area looks normal and if the parents have had no experience with intersexuality (Besheshti et al. 1983). Elsewhere Money (1974:216) argues in favor of not neonatally amputating the penis of XX infants, since fetal masculinization of brain structures would predispose them "almost invariably [to] develop behaviorally as tomboys, even when reared as girls" Money 1974:216). This reasoning implies, first, that tomboyish behavior in girls is bad and should be avoided; and, second, that it is preferable to remove the internal female organs, implant prosthetic testes, and regulate the "boy's" hormones for his entire life than to overlook or disregard the perfection of the penis.[10]

The ultimate proof to these physicians that they intervened appropriately and gave the intersexed infant the correct gender assignment is that the reconstructed genitals look normal and function normally once the patient reaches adulthood. The vulva, labia, and clitoris should appear ordinary to the woman and her partner(s), and the vagina should be able to receive a normal-sized penis. Similarly, the man and his partner(s) should feel that his penis (even if somewhat smaller than the norm) looks and functions in an unremarkable way. Although there is no reported data on how much emphasis the intersexed person, him- or herself, places upon genital appearance and functioning, the physicians are absolutely clear about what they believe is important. The clinical geneticist said, "If you have a seventeen-year-old young lady who has gotten hormone therapy and has breast development and pubic hair and no vaginal opening, I can't even entertain the notion that this young lady wouldn't want to have corrective surgery." The urologist summarized his criteria: "Happiness is the biggest factor. Anatomy is part of happiness." Money (1974:217) states, "The primary deficit [of not having a sufficient penis]—and de-

stroyer of morale—lies in being unable to satisfy the partner." Another team of clinicians reveals their phallocentrism, arguing that the most serious mistake in gender assignment is to create "an individual unable to engage in genital [heterosexual] sex" (Castro-Magana et al. 1984:180)

The equation of gender with genitals could only have emerged in an age when medical science can create credible-appearing and functioning genitals, and an emphasis on the good phallus above all else could only have emerged in a culture that has rigid aesthetic and performance criteria for what constitutes maleness. The formulation "good penis equals male; absence of good penis equals female" is treated in the literature and by the physicians interviewed as an objective criterion, operative in all cases. There is a striking lack of attention to the size and shape requirements of the female genitals, other than that the vagina be able to receive a penis.

In the late nineteenth century when women's reproductive function was culturally designated as their essential characteristic, the presence or absence of ovaries (whether or not they were fertile) was held to be the ultimate criterion of gender assignment for hermaphrodites. The urologist interviewed recalled a case as late as the 1950s of a male child reassigned to "female" at the age of four or five because ovaries had been discovered. Nevertheless, doctors today, schooled in the etiology and treatment of the various intersex syndromes, view decisions based primarily on gonads as wrong, although, they complain, the conviction that the gonads are the ultimate criterion "still dictates the decisions of the uneducated and uninformed" (Money 1974:215). Presumably, the educated and informed now know that decisions based primarily on phallic size, shape, and sexual capacity are right.

While the prospect of constructing good genitals is the primary consideration in physicians' gender assignments, another, extra-medical factor was repeatedly cited by the six physicians interviewed—the specialty of the attending physician. Although generally intersexed infants are treated by teams of specialists, only the person who coordinates the team is actually responsible for the case. This person, acknowledged by the other physicians as having chief responsibility, acts as spokesperson to the parents. Although all of the physicians claimed that these medical teams work smoothly with few discrepancies of opinion, several of them mentioned decision-making orientations that are grounded in particular medical specializations. One endocrinologist stated, "The easiest route to take, where there is ever any question . . . is to raise the child as female. . . . In this country that is usual if the infant falls into the hands of a pediatric endocrinologist. . . . If the decision is made by the urologists, who are mostly males,. . . they're always opting, because they do the surgery, they're always feeling they can correct anything." Another endocrinologist concurred: "[Most urologists] don't think in terms of dynamic processes. They're, interested in fixing pipes and lengthening pipes, and not dealing with hormonal, and certainly not psychological issues. . . .'What can I do with what I've got.'" Urologists were defended by the clinical geneticist: "Surgeons here, now I can't speak for elsewhere, they don't get into a situation where the child is a year old and they can't make anything." Whether or not urologists "like to make boys, as one endocrinologist claimed, the following example from a urologist who was interviewed explicitly links a cultural interpretation of masculinity to the medical treatment plan. The case involved an adolescent who had been assigned the female gender at birth but was developing some male pubertal signs and wanted to be a boy. "He was ill-equipped," said the urologist, "yet we made a very respectable male out of him. He now owns a huge construction business—those big cranes that put stuff up on the building."

Postinfancy Case Management

After the infant's gender has been assigned, parents generally latch onto the assignment as the solution to the problem—and it is. The physician as detective has collected the evidence, as lawyer has presented the case, and as judge has rendered a verdict. Although most of the interviewees claimed that the parents are equal participants in the

whole process, they gave no instances of parental participation prior to the gender assignment. After the physicians assign the infant's gender, the parents are encouraged to establish the credibility of that gender publicly by, for example, giving a detailed medical explanation to a leader in their community, such as a physician or a pastor, who will explain the situation to curious casual acquaintances. Money argues that "medical terminology has a special layman's magic in such a context; it is final and authoritative and closes the issue." He also recommends that eventually the mother "settle [the] argument once and for all among her women friends by allowing some of them to see the baby's reconstructed genitalia" (Money 1975:613). Apparently, the powerful influence of normal-looking genitals helps overcome a history of ambiguous gender.

Some of the same issues that arise in assigning gender recur some years later when, at adolescence, the child may be referred to a physician for counseling. The physician then tells the adolescent many of the same things his or her parents had been told years before, with the same language. Terms like "abnormal," "disorder," "disease," and "hermaphroditism" are avoided; the condition is normalized, and the child's gender is treated as unproblematic. One clinician explains to his patients that sex organs are different in appearance for each person, not just those who are intersexed. Furthermore, he tells the girls "that while most women menstruate, not all do . . . that conception is only one of a number of ways to become a parent; [and] that today some individuals are choosing not to become parents." The clinical geneticist tells a typical female patient: "You are female. Female is not determined by your genes. Lots of other things determine being a woman. And you are a woman but you won't be able to have babies."

A case reported by one of the pediatric endocrinologists involving an adolescent female with androgen insensitivity provides an intriguing insight into the postinfancy gender-management process. She was told at the age of fourteen "that her ovaries weren't normal and had been removed. That's why she needed pills to look normal . . . I wanted to convince her of her femininity. Then I told her she could marry and have normal sexual relations . . . [her] uterus won't develop but [she] could adopt children." The urologist interviewed was asked to comment on this handling of the counseling. "It sounds like a very good solution to it. He's stating the truth and if you don't state the truth . . . then you're in trouble later." This is a strange version of "the truth," however, since the adolescent was chromosomally XY and was born with normal testes that produced normal quantities of androgen. There were no existing ovaries or uterus to be abnormal. Another pediatric endocrinologist, in commenting on the management of this case, hedged the issue by saying that he would have used a generic term like "the gonads." A third endocrinologist said she would say that the uterus had never formed.

Technically these physicians are lying when, for example, they explain to an adolescent XY female with an intersexed history that her "ovaries . . . had to be removed because they were unhealthy or were producing 'the wrong balance of hormones'" (Dewhurst and Grant 1984:1193). We can presume that these lies are told in the service of what the physicians consider a greater good—keeping individual/concrete genders as clear and uncontaminated as the notions of female and male are in the abstract. The clinician suggests that with some female patients it eventually may be possible to talk to them "about their gonads having some structures and features that are testicular like" (Mazur 1983:422). This call for honesty might be based at least partly on the possibility of the child's discovering his or her chromosomal sex inadvertently from a buccal smear taken in a high school biology class. Today's litigious climate is possibly another encouragement.

In sum, the adolescent is typically told that certain internal organs did not form because of an endocrinological defect, not because those organs could never have developed in someone with her or his sex chromosomes. The topic of chromosomes is skirted. There are no published studies on how these adolescents experience their condition and their treatment by doctors. An endocrinologist interviewed mentioned that her adolescent patients rarely ask specifically what is wrong with them, suggesting that they are accomplices in this evasion. In spite of the "truth" having been evaded, the clinician's impression is that "their gender identities and general senses of well-being and self-esteem appear not to have suffered" (Mazur 1983:422).

Conclusion

Physicians conduct careful examinations of intersexed infants' genitals and perform intricate laboratory procedures. They are interpreters of the body, trained and committed to uncovering the "actual" gender obscured by ambiguous genitals. Yet they also have considerable leeway in assigning gender, and their decisions are influenced by cultural as well as medical factors. What is the relationship between the physician as discoverer and the physician as determiner of gender? Where is the relative emphasis placed in discussions with parents and adolescents and in the consciousness of physicians? It is misleading to characterize the doctors whose words are provided here as presenting themselves publicly to the parents as discoverers of the infant's real gender but privately acknowledging that the infant has no real gender other than the one being determined or constructed by the medical professionals. They are not hypocritical. It is also misleading to claim that physicians' focus shifts from discovery to determination over the course of treatment: first the doctors regard the infant's gender as an unknown but discoverable reality; then the doctors relinquish their attempts to find the real gender and treat the infant's gender as something they must construct. They are not medically incompetent or deficient. Instead, I am arguing that the peculiar balance of discovery and determination throughout treatment permits physicians to handle very problematic cases of gender in the most unproblematic of ways.

This balance relies fundamentally on a particular conception of the "natural" (see Smith 1979). Although the deformity of intersexed genitals would be immutable were it not for medical interference, physicians do not consider it natural. Instead they think of, and speak of, the surgical/hormonal altera-tion of such deformities as natural because such intervention returns the body to what it "ought to have been" if events had taken their typical course. The nonnormative is con-verted into the normative, and the normative state is considered natural. The genital ambi-guity is remedied to conform to a "natural," that is, culturally indisputable, gender di-chotomy. Sherry Ortner's claim that the cul-ture/nature distinction is itself a construc-tion—product of culture—is relevant here. Language and imagery help create and main-tain a specific view of what is natural about the two genders and, I would argue, about the very idea of gender—that it consists of two exclusive types: female and male (Orthner 1974). The belief that gender consists of two exclusive types is maintained and perpetu-ated by the medical community in the face of incontrovertible physical evidence that this is not mandated by biology.

The lay conception of human anatomy and physiology assumes a concordance among clearly dimorphic gender markers—chromo-somes, genitals, gonads, hormones—but physicians understand that concordance and dimorphism do not always exist. Their understanding of biology's complexity, how-ever, does not inform their understanding of gender's complexity. In order for intersexual-ity to be managed differently than it currently is, physicians would have to take seriously Money's (1975) assertion that it is a misrep-resentation of epistemology to consider any cell in the body authentically male or female. If authenticity for gender resides not in a dis-coverable nature but in someone's proclama-tion, then the power to proclaim something else is available. If physicians recognized that implicit in their management of gender is the notion that finally, and always, people con-struct gender as well as the social systems that are grounded in gender-based concepts, the possibilities for real societal transforma-tions would be unlimited. Unfortunately, nei-ther in their representations to the families of the intersexed nor among themselves do the physicians interviewed for this study draw such far-reaching implications from their work. Their "understanding" that par-ticular genders are medically (re)constructed

in these cases does not lead them to see that gender is always constructed. Accepting genital ambiguity as a natural option would require that physicians also acknowledge that genital ambiguity is "corrected" not be-cause it is threatening to the infant's life but because it is threatening to the infant's cul-ture.

Rather than admit to their role in perpetu-ating gender, physicians "psychologize" the issue by talking about the parents' anxiety and humiliation in being confronted with an anomalous infant. The physicians talk as though they have no choice but to respond to the parents' pressure for a resolution of psy-chological discomfort, and as though they have no choice but to use medical technology in the service of a two-gender culture. Neither the psychology nor the technology is doubted, since both shield physicians from responsibility. Indeed, for the most part, nei-ther physicians nor parents emerge from the experience of intersex case management with a greater understanding of the social con-struction of gender. Society's accountability, like their own, is masked by the assumption that gender is a given. Thus, cases of in-tersexuality, instead of illustrating nature's failure to ordain gender in these isolated "un-fortunate" instances, illustrate physicians' and Western society's failure of imagina-tion—the failure to imagine that each of these management decisions is a moment when a specific instance of biological "sex" is transformed into a culturally constructed gender.

References

Besheshti, Mojtaba, et al. 1983. "Gender Assign-ment in Male Pseudohermaphrodite Chil-dren." *Urology* (December):604–607.

Bing, Elizabeth and Esselyn Rudikoff. 1970. "Di-vergent Ways of Parental Coping with Her-maphrodite Children." *Medical Aspects of Human Sexuality* (December):73–88.

Bleier, Ruth. 1984. Science and Gender: *A Cri-tique of Biology and Its Theories on Women.* New York: Pergamon.

Bolkenius, M., R. Daum, and E. Heinrich. 1984. "Pediatric Surgical Principles in the Manage-ment of Children with Intersex." *Progressive Pediatric Surgery*, 17:33–38.

Braren, Victor, et al. 1980. "True Hermaphroditism: A Rational Approach to Diagnosis and Treatment." *Urology* 15 (June):569–574.

Bullough, Vern. 1976. *Sexual Variance in Society and History.* New York: Wiley.

Castro-Magana, Mariano, Moris Angulo, and Platon J. Collipp. 1984. "Management of the Child with Ambiguous Genitalia." *Medical Aspects of Human Sexuality,* 18 (April):172–188.

Dewhurst, J. and D.B. Grant. 1984. "Intersex Problems." *Archives of Disease in Childhood,* 59 (July-December):1191–1194.

Diamond, Milton. 1982. "Sexual Identity, Monozygotic Twins Reared in Discordant Sex Roles and a BBC Follow-up." *Archives of Sexual Behavior,* 11(2):181–186.

Diamond, Milton. 1976. "Human Sexual Development: Biological Foundations for Social Development." In Frank A. Beach (Ed.), *Human Sexuality in Four Perspectives,* (pp. 22–61). Baltimore: Johns Hopkins University Press.

Ellis, Havelock. 1942. *Studies in the Psychology of Sex.* New York: Random House.

Fiedler, Leslie. 1978. *Freaks: Myths and Images of the Second Self.* New York: Simon & Schuster.

Foucault, Michel. 1980. *History of Sexuality.* New York: Pantheon.

Freud, Sigmund. [1925] 1976. "Some Psychical Consequences of the Anatomical Distinctions between the Sexes." In J. Strachey (Ed. and translator) *The Complete Psychological Works,* Vol. 18. New York: Norton.

Glassberg, Kenneth I. 1980. "Gender Assignment in Newborn Male Pseudohermaphrodites." *Urologic Clinics of North America,* 7 (June):409–421.

Kessler, Suzanne J. and Wendy McKenna. 1985. *Gender: An Ethnomethodological Approach.* Chicago: University of Chicago Press.

Lee, Peter A., et al. 1980. "Micropenis. I. Criteria, Etiologies and Classification." *Johns Hopkins Medical Journal,* 146:156–163.

Lev-Ran, Arye. 1978. "Sex Reversal as Related to Clinical Syndromes in Human Beings." In John Money and H. Musaph (Eds.), *Handbook of Sexology 11: Genetics, Hormones and Behavior,* (pp. 157–73). New York: Elsevier.

Mazur, Tom. 1983. "Ambiguous Genitalia: Detection and Counseling." *Pediatric Nursing,* 9 (November/December):417–431).

Money, John. 1974. "Psychologic Consideration of Sex Assignment in Intersexuality." *Clinics in Plastic Surgery* 1 (April): 215–22.

Money, John. 1975. "Psychological Counseling: Hermaphroditism." In L.I. Gardner (Ed). *Endocrine and Genetic Diseases of Childhood and Adolescence,* (pp. 609–618). Philadelphia: Saunders.

Money, John. 1983. "Birth Defect of the Sex Organs: Telling the Parents and the Patient." *British Journal of Sexual Medicine* 10 (March):14

Money, John et al. 1981. "Micropenis, Family Mental Health, and Neonatal Management: A Report on Fourteen Patients Reared as Girls," *Journal of Preventive Psychiatry* 1,(1): 17–27.

Money, John and Anke A. Ehrhardt. 1972. *Man and Woman, Boy and Girl.* Baltimore: Johns Hopkins University Press, 1972.

Money, John, J. G. Hampson, and J. L. Hampson. 1955. "Hermaphroditism: Recommendations Concerning Assignment of Sex, Change of Sex, and Psychologic Management." *Bulletin of the Johns Hopkins Hospital,* 97:284–300.

Money, John, Reynolds Potter, and Clarice S. Stoll. 1969. "Sex Reannouncement in Hereditary Sex Deformity: Psychology and Sociology of Habilitation." *Social Science and Medicine,* 3: 207–16.

Ortner, Sherry B. 1974. "Is Female to Male as Nature Is to Culture?" In Michelle Zimbalist Rosaldo and Louise Lamphere (Eds.), *Woman, Culture, and Society,* (pp. 67–87). Stanford, CA: Stanford University Press.

Rubin, Jeffrey, F.J. Provenzano, and Z. Luria. 1974. "The Eye of the Beholder: Parents' Views on Sex of Newborns." *American Journal of Orthopsychiatry* 44(4):512–519.

Smith, Richard W. 1979. "What Kind of Sex is Natural?" In Vern Bullough (Ed.) *The Frontiers of Sex Research* (pp. 103–111). Buffalo: Prometheus.

Stoller, Robert J. 1968. *Sex and Gender.* New York: Aronson.

Endnotes

1. It is impossible to get accurate statistics on the frequency of intersexuality. Chromosomal abnormalities (like XOXX or XXXY) are registered, but those conditions do not always imply ambiguous genitals, and most cases of ambiguous genitals do not involve chromosomal abnormalities. None of the physicians interviewed for this study would venture a guess on frequency rates, but all agreed that intersexuality is rare. One physician suggested that the average obstetrician may see only two cases in twenty years. Another estimated that a specialist may see only one a year, or possibly as many as five a year.

2. For example, infants whose intersexuality is caused by congenital adrenal hyperplasia can develop severe electrolyte disturbances un-

less the condition is controlled by cortisone treatments. Intersexed infants whose condition is caused by androgen insensitivity are in danger of malignant degeneration of the testes unless they are removed. For a complete catalog of clinical syndromes related to the intersexed condition, see Lev-Ran (1978).

3. Much of the surgical experimentation in this area has been accomplished by urologists who are trying to create penises for female-to-male transsexuals. Although there have been some advancements in recent years in the ability to create a "reasonable-looking" penis from tissue taken elsewhere on the body, the complicated requirements of the organ (both urinary and sexual functioning) have posed surgical problems. It may be, however, that the concerns of the urologists are not identical to the concerns of the patients. While data are not yet available from the intersexed, we know that female-to-male transsexuals place greater emphasis on the "public" requirements of the penis (e.g., being able to look normal while standing at the urinal or wearing a bathing suit) than on its functional requirements (e.g., being able to carry urine or achieve an erection) (Kessler and McKenna, 1985:128–32). As surgical techniques improve, female-to-male transsexuals (and intersexed males) might increase their demands for organs that look and function better.

4. Historically, psychology has tended to blur the distinction between the two by equating a person's acceptance of her or his genitals with gender role and ignoring gender identity. For example, Freudian theory posited that if one had a penis and accepted its reality, then masculine gender role behavior would naturally follow (Sigmund Freud, [1925] 1976).

5. Almost all of the published literature on intersexed infant case management has been written or co-written by one researcher, John Money, professor of medical psychology and professor of pediatrics, emeritus, at the Johns Hopkins University and Hospital, where he is director of the Psychohormonal Research Unit. Even the publications that are produced independently of Money reference him and reiterate his management philosophy. Although only one of the physicians interviewed publishes with Money, all of them essentially concur with his views and give the impression of a consensus that is rarely encountered in science. The one physician who raised some questions about Money's philosophy and the gender theory on which it is

based has extensive experience with intersexuality in a non-industrialized culture where the infant is managed differently with no apparent harm to gender development. Even though psychologists fiercely argue issues of gender identity and gender role development, doctors who treat intersexed infants seem untouched by these debates. There are no renegade voices either from within the medical establishment or, thus far, from outside. Why Money has been so single-handedly influential in promoting his ideas about gender is a question worthy of a separate substantial analysis. (See Money, 1974; 1975; 1983; Money et al, 1981; Money and Ehrhardt, 1972; Money, Hampson and Hampson, 1955; Money, Potter, and Stoll, 1969).

6. There is evidence from other kinds of sources that once a gender attribution is made, all further information buttresses that attribution, and only the most contradictory new information will cause the original gender attribution to be questioned (Kessler and McKenna, 1985).

7. A different view is argued by another leading gender identity theorist: "When a little boy (with an imperfect penis) knows he is a male, he creates a penis that functions symbolically the same as those of boys with normal penises" (Stoller, 1968).

8. These evasions must have many ramifications in everyday social interactions between parents and family and friends. How people "fill in" the uncertainty so that interactions remain relatively normal is an interesting issue that warrants further study. Indeed, the whole issue of parental reaction is worthy of analysis. One of the pediatric endocrinologists interviewed acknowledged that the published literature discusses intersex management only from the physicians' point of view. He asks, "How [do parents] experience what they're told; and what [do] they remember. . . and carry with them?" One published exception to this neglect of the parents' perspective is a case study comparing two couples' different coping strategies. The first couple, although initially distressed, handled the traumatic event by regarding the abnormality as an act of God. The second couple, more educated and less religious, put their faith in medical science and expressed a need to fully understand the biochemistry of the defect (Bing and Rudikoff, 1970).

9. Although Money and Ehrhardt's socialization theory is uncontested by the physicians who treat intersexuality, and [this theory] is presented to parents as a matter of fact, there is actually much debate among psychologists about the effect of prenatal hormones on brain structure and ultimately on gender role behavior and even on gender identity. The physicians interviewed agreed that the animal evidence for prenatal brain organization is compelling but that there is no evidence in humans that prenatal hormones have an inviolate or unilateral effect. If there is any effect of prenatal exposure to androgen, they believe it can easily be overcome and modified by psychosocial factors. It is this latter position that is communicated to the parents, not the controversy in the field. (For an argument favoring prenatally organized gender differences in the brain, see Diamond, 1976; for a critique of that position, see Bleier, 1984).

10. Weighing the probability of achieving a perfect penis against the probable trauma such procedures might involve is another social factor in decision making. According to an endocrinologist interviewed, if it seemed that an XY infant with an inadequate penis would require as many as ten genital operations over a six-year period in order to have an adequate penis, the infant would be assigned the female gender. In this case, the endocrinologist's practical and compassionate concern would override purely genital criteria.

Reprinted from: Suzanne J. Kessler, " The Medical Construction of Gender: Case Management of Intersexed Infants." In *Signs: Journal of Woman in Culture and Society*, 16(1), pp. 3–26. Copyright © 1990 by The University of Chicago Press. Reprinted by permission. ✦

13

The Stigma of Involuntary Childlessness

Charlene E. Miall

Miall explores the experiences and beliefs of married women who, although they may want them, do not have children. Infertile women, and women married to infertile men, often believe they will be seen by others as physically disabled and inferior. Therefore, they expect others to stigmatize them. In order to manage their situations, these women develop ways to explain their childlessness and avoid being defined as deviant. By concealing their medical conditions and attributing their childlessness to other factors, these women believe they can avoid being defined as inferior.

. . . Two traditional fertility norms continue to be widely accepted in North America: (1) all married couples should reproduce and (2) all married couples should *want* to reproduce (Veevers, 1980:3, emphasis added). It is within this context that Veevers (1972) conceptualizes childlessness—whether voluntary or involuntary—as a form of deviant behavior in marriage, a violation of prevailing norms of acceptable conduct. When cultural norms and values encourage reproduction and celebrate parenthood, childlessness becomes a potentially stigmatizing status which can adversely affect the identities and interpersonal relationships of married persons. . . .

Involuntary Childlessness: Analytic Distinctions

Estimates indicate that from one in five (Burgwyn, 1981; Kraft et al., 1980) to one in ten couples (Mosher, 1982) may be involuntarily childless—that is, infertility affects their relationship. Within western nations infertility is usually estimated to occur in 10 to 15 percent of the population (Benet, 1976; Menning, 1975; National Center for Health Statistics, 1985). Generally, medical researchers distinguish between *primary* infertility and *secondary* infertility. Couples are considered to have primary infertility if they fail to conceive after one year of regular intercourse without contraception and if conception has never occurred before. Couples are considered to have secondary infertility if they fail to conceive following one or more births, or, following conception, fail to carry a pregnancy to term (McFalls, 1979).

Involuntary childlessness can be conceptualized as a form of physical disability. It is a chronic condition that meets biopsychological, social role, and legal criteria for disability. Most cases of involuntary childlessness are medically diagnosed as the consequence of some form of physical impairment—for example, there may be disease-related or genetic malformations of the male or female reproductive organs. Certain forms of involuntary childlessness may be related to psychological factors, although the numbers so afflicted appear small (Weinstein, 1962). Involuntary childlessness also meets a social role definition of disability (Nagi, 1966) in that couples are prevented from reproducing, a social role expectation that has great relevance in western society. Finally, involuntary childlessness is treated legally as a form of disability. For example, many adoption agencies in the United States and Canada require documented proof of infertility in a relationship before they will accept adoption applications for infants. . . .

Pronatalism and Social Definitions of Childlessness

Involuntary childlessness can be a devastating blow to some individuals (Kraft et al.,

1980; Menning 1977; Pfeffer and Woollett, 1983; Zimmerman, 1982). The negative impact of involuntary childlessness is undoubtedly related to the pronatalistic views of marriage that pervade western society. Indeed, contemporary endorsement of the fertility norms of having and wanting children transcends sex, age, race, religion, ethnic, and social class divisions in North America (Pohlman, 1969, 1974; Russo, 1976; Veevers, 1980, 1983). This commitment to parenthood in western society has been attributed to the Judaeo-Christian tradition which sees children as blessings from heaven and barrenness as a curse or punishment (Burgwyn, 1981; McFalls, 1979; Pohlman, 1970). Like leprosy and epilepsy, infertility bears an ancient social stigma.

Women in particular may be seriously affected by childlessness (Russo, 1976; Veevers, 1972). Our social and cultural institutions continue to emphasize the importance of motherhood for the female role (Broverman et al., 1972; Fox et al., 1982; Russo, 1976; Veevers, 1980). In the clinical literature, women's sexual and psychological adjustment is tied to childbearing (Pohlman, 1970; Rossi, 1977). . . .

Individuals usually learn that they are infertile or involuntarily childless later in life, after they are married with presumably well-established adult identities. Given pronatalistic attitudes, a significant part of this identity for men and women probably revolves around the expectation of conceiving, bearing, and rearing children. The awareness that one is infertile therefore, may have profound consequences for the social identity and behavior of the actor.

Although the social context strongly suggests that involuntarily childless individuals, and particularly women, are subject to stigmatization, there has been no empirical research on this issue. Therefore, in this paper, I explore the perceptions of involuntarily childless women to determine if they view infertility as a stigmatizing or discreditable attribute. . . . In addition, I examine the ways in which involuntarily childless women handle this attribute in interaction with others.

In addition, I examine fertile women who are married to husbands with documented infertility. I consider these women to be involuntarily childless because they desire to bear children but are unable, in present circumstances, to do so. However, if these women share the stigma of infertility, it is in the sense of possessing a courtesy stigma (Birenbaum, 1975:348; Goffman, 1963)— that is, their stigma is based on their association with someone who has a stigmatizing attribute, and not on their own personal attributes. I am particularly interested in whether there are discernible differences in perceptions of infertility and use of information management strategies between the physically infertile, and the physically fertile who are childless. . . .

Method

. . . I conducted a pre-tested, standardized, open-ended interview (Patton, 1980) with 30 involuntarily childless women. In addition, 41 involuntarily childless women completed a questionnaire identical to the interview schedule. . . . Twelve respondents were fertile themselves but married to infertile men— that is, they shared a courtesy stigma.

Perceptions of Involuntary Childlessness

The Stigma Potential of Infertility

. . . Nearly all the respondents categorized infertility as something negative, as representing some sort of failure, or an inability to work normally. In addition, women experiencing or sharing infertility regarded it as a discreditable attribute—that is, most were concerned that an awareness of problems with fertility would cause others to view them in a new and damaging light (see Miall 1985). One woman summed it up for most respondents:

> We expected things to work out. We led the golden lives until this happened to us. It's the worst thing that ever happened to us. My husband and I are high achievers. We work together and it works out. Therefore, it's even harder for us to accept this because we don't have control over something that's so easy for other people.

These respondents often became aware of possible infertility before they consulted a physician. For example, many women became suspicious when they failed to conceive after six months or a year without birth control. The majority of these women secretly arranged to visit a doctor or a fertility clinic to avoid public awareness of difficulty. Some respondents found it difficult to "express a reason for their secretive behavior. Often the statements "It's a private matter," or "It's nobody's business" were offered as rationales. . . .

On the other hand, most respondents expressed the sentiment that the admission of possible problems with infertility was in some way an admission of failure, which in turn might have serious consequences for the person doing the disclosing. One woman felt that admitting to possible problems with reproduction was

> an admission that you're not a whole person . . . either sexually or anatomically or both. That there's something wrong and I guess reproduction, the ability to reproduce strikes at the very essence of one's being. . . .

In fact, nearly all the respondents in the study experienced feelings of anxiety, isolation, and conflict as they explored the possibility of personal infertility. Most were concerned that an awareness of their infertility problems would cause others to view them in a new and damaging light. As one respondent put it:

> I do believe it lessens you in some people's eyes, makes you different and possibly even morally suspect like God is punishing you or something. Somehow infertility lessens your accomplishments for some people.

When respondents did tell others of their decision to seek help, the people they told were usually medical personnel, had experienced reproductive problems themselves, or already knew either of the decision to start a family or of difficulties with previously announced, but ultimately unsuccessful, pregnancies. However, most of the respondents did not inform others of problems they were having.

In order to explore the implications of "courtesy stigma" for fertile women with infertile husbands, I compared their perceptions and initial responses to the possibility of personal infertility to those of the other women. No discernible differences emerged, either in their definitions of infertility or in their initial responses to the realization of possible infertility. In all cases, these women defined infertility as a discreditable or negative attribute, were the first to approach a doctor or clinic for help, and told no one of their decision to do so. This observation supports the contention that failure to conceive is perceived, at least initially, as the woman's problem.

Initial Disclosure Patterns

Following a diagnosis of possible reproductive problems, nearly half the physically infertile women found it difficult to disclose to their families and friends that they were having problems. These respondents linked the difficulty in telling others to personal feelings of inadequacy and shame. Indeed, all the infertile respondents spoke of a personal sense of failure associated with their involuntary childlessness, a perception reflected in the observations contained in self-help and anecdotal literature on infertility (Menning, 1977; Pfeffer and Woollett, 1983). As one infertile woman observed:

> You have to admit failure to some extent. . . . It's the business of having to admit some problem or abnormality; this business of feeling like some sort of freak.

However, several respondents also indicated that they had difficulty in revealing their infertility to their families because they anticipated serious consequences for the persons being told. . . .

Many respondents revealed infertility problems only at the time they applied for adoption. In fact, disclosure of the intention to adopt amounted to an admission of infertility and was often accompanied by a desire for secrecy.

In three interviews, respondents claimed that they had never discussed their infertility with anyone but their doctors and their social worker at the adoption agency. One woman, who learned of her infertility through a previous marriage, expressed the fear she felt about disclosing it to her new husband prior to their marriage:

> I went through agony when we were going out because I was afraid to tell my husband about my infertility. When he did ask me to marry him, I went through a long period when I wouldn't tell him. I'd just say we can't get married and so on. I did my years in hell.

Overall, more than half the infertile respondents indicated that they hesitated in telling others. Two-thirds engaged in some sort of information management—that is, they admitted that they did not always reveal the exact details of their condition—and nearly one-third admitted giving inaccurate answers to questions about their childlessness.

The responses of women with infertile husbands indicate that they were particularly likely to find it difficult to tell family and friends that they were having fertility problems in their relationship. In addition, they were more likely to give inaccurate answers to others' questions about their childlessness. However, as expected, they were less likely to feel as personally stigmatized as did the infertile respondents.

In view of these findings, it could be argued that women with a courtesy stigma find it more difficult to tell family and friends of their problem precisely because of the nature of the infertility. Women with reproductive disorders for example, may have miscarriages or other obvious signs of reproductive difficulty. A general awareness of this difficulty may preclude the need to announce formally and irrevocably their problems with the reproductive process. Women whose husbands have low or non-existent sperm counts (the most probable cause of male infertility) are not likely to conceive. This lack of observable reproductive difficulty may make it easier in the short term for these women to avoid the appearance of having fertility problems, but harder in the long term to disclose the difficulty.

It could also be argued that women with a courtesy stigma have more difficulty telling others because of the greater perceived stigma associated with male infertility. I found that nearly two-thirds of the infertile respondents and over half the courtesy stigma respondents felt that male infertility is viewed more negatively than female infertility. These respondents considered male infertility more discrediting to masculinity than female infertility to femininity, and associated male infertility with impotence or a lack of virility. As one courtesy stigma respondent put it:

> Somehow it's just a medical problem for her but a real assault on his masculinity to the man. It's often wrongly thought to be associated with impotence.

Whereas infertile women may have difficulty telling others of their childlessness because of personal feelings of shame or stigma, women with an infertile husband may have difficulty because of the perceived need to protect their partner from the even greater stigma associated with male sexual dysfunction. . . .

While nearly two-thirds of the infertile women expressed feelings of openness, warmth, and understanding toward other infertile individuals, only 17 percent of the women with a courtesy stigma felt this kind of rapport. As I expected, the women with a courtesy stigma were much less likely to identify themselves with other infertile individuals. Indeed, they strongly distinguished themselves from women with "real" fertility problems. As one woman put it:

> I'm one of those couples where it's the husband who has the infertility problem. Mostly I've met women who have fertility problems. Thank God I'm not one of them. When I see what they've been through; when I hear the stories. I don't know if eventually one gets reconciled but thank God I missed all that.

Thus courtesy stigma respondents seemed less concerned about their own personal "inadequacy" as childless and more concerned with the difficulty of managing information about their husbands' infertility.

The possibility of conceiving children may also have lessened feelings of stigmatization. Presumably, courtesy stigma women could make use of artificial insemination or leave an infertile marriage if they chose to bear a child, an option not available to infertile women. . . .

Involuntary Childlessness and Information Management

Nearly two-thirds of all respondents indicated that they engaged in some form of information control about their childlessness. To isolate patterns of behavior surrounding involuntary childlessness, I asked respondents about their patterns of disclosure and about the techniques they used to handle situations and persons likely to make them feel uncomfortable. Although variations emerged, the strategies used by these women to handle information about infertility closely resembled those observed by Schneider and Conrad (1980) in their study of epilepsy. These strategies included: (1) selective concealment; (2) therapeutic disclosure; and (3) preventive disclosure. In addition, I found evidence of deviance avowal, and a strategy of practiced deception.

Infertility and Selective Concealment

. . . [R]espondents displayed patterns of selective concealment even in those instances when secrecy was the major strategy for handling the discovery of infertility in the relationship. For example, respondents who told no one of their decision to seek help, or of their status as involuntarily childless, nevertheless conveyed concern about the infertility in the relationship to medical personnel and, later, to adoption workers. Apart from these disclosures to professionals, nearly all the respondents decided whether to conceal or disclose their infertility based on their perception of others as genuine or trustworthy. They learned to judge or recognize people who might make them feel uncomfortable about their childlessness and to avoid them. . . .

When it was not possible to avoid contacts with such people, respondents used the strategy of concealment in conversation by avoiding or changing sensitive subjects. For instance, one respondent described her efforts to "pass" as normal as follows:

On occasion at parties, I've tried to avoid the topic. Even though no one has done anything that might upset me, I believe in being prepared for the possibility of it happening. My whole approach is to be as low key as possible, not to get excited, to show we are normal.

However, respondents often made selective disclosures to others to test their reactions. These reactions contributed to the evolution of other strategies or to the continued use of selective disclosure or secrecy in the face of negative responses (see Schneider and Conrad, 1980:39). Thus the discovery of infertility in the relationship was initially marked by a desire for secrecy which lessened over time and was replaced by some form of disclosure for therapeutic or preventive reasons.

Therapeutic Disclosure

Therapeutic disclosure can be defined as the selective disclosure of the discreditable attribute to others in order to enhance self-esteem or to renegotiate personal perceptions of stigma. Infertile respondents used therapeutic disclosure more often than courtesy stigma respondents. Typically, such disclosures were made to family, close friends, or other infertile people. As one woman revealed, disclosure to her family was cathartic:

Initially I felt uncomfortable until I sat down and talked about it with my husband and my family, about how I felt I was failing. Then I felt better for having gotten it all out.

Therapeutic disclosure also allowed for renegotiation of the negative meanings attached to infertility. One woman who had experienced several miscarriages observed that talking with her friends allowed her to put her own infertility in perspective:

One thing I always tell people to do is to talk to their women friends if they are having trouble conceiving or miscarrying because I learned something I didn't know; that almost every woman I knew had at least one miscarriage and it was very supportive having friends say, "Look I lost a kid too" because it's not the kind of thing that people tell you.

Generally, infertile women perceived the disclosure of infertility as most therapeutic when done with other infertile couples. However, disclosure to nonsupportive audiences was also considered therapeutic by some respondents:

There was a lot of stammering going on and they just didn't know how to react and maybe it was a little unfair on our part. In a couple of situations we just blurted it out and I don't think we did it very well. And yet every time we talked about it we felt better. Sometimes we imposed on people by telling them.

. . . To sum up, infertile women used therapeutic disclosure as a strategy to relieve anxiety, to restore self-esteem, and to renegotiate personal perceptions of infertility as discreditable. Indeed, several respondents observed that the ability to reveal infertility at all was suggestive of the beginning of adjustment to the possession of a stigmatizing attribute.

Preventive Disclosure

Preventive disclosure can be defined as the selective disclosure to others of the discreditable attribute, with a view to influencing others' actions or ideas about oneself, or about infertility in general (see Schneider and Conrad, 1980:40). Respondents using this strategy anticipated that their childlessness would become known at some future date to the people with whom they were interacting. In order to influence others' perceptions of them, respondents used such devices as the medical disclaimer (Hewitt and Stokes, 1978), deviance avowal, and practiced deception.

The use of a *medical disclaimer* involves the presentation of a "blameless, beyond-my-control medical interpretation . . . to reduce the risk that more morally disreputable interpretations might be applied by naive others" who become aware of a discreditable attribute (Schneider and Conrad, 1980:41). Several infertile women revealed their infertility by using the medical analysis of their condition to avoid greater perceived negative consequences. As one woman observed:

Because of the nature of our infertility problem, it was a medically open and shut

case. . . . There was an anatomical deficit in that I'd had my tubes taken out. . . . So when people would say to me, "Well maybe there's artificial insemination," I would say, "There's no medical way." If the reason is not an anatomical reason or a reason for which they can't find a reason, I think people will chime in with "Well maybe you're not doing it right" and you don't want to leave yourself open to that.

In addition, respondents who were able to do so would reveal their infertility as an uncontrollable side effect of another medical condition, such as diabetes or kidney disease, so that reproductive disorder was not the main issue. This use of medical disclaimers indicates that medical definitions are widely accepted as legitimate accounts for a potentially stigmatizing problem. . . .

In adopting the strategy of *deviance avowal*, individuals actively seek or acquiesce to a deviant label. I found evidence of two forms of deviance avowal among these women. First, women with a courtesy stigma took responsibility for the infertility of their husbands; and, second, women revealed their infertility to avoid the negative perceptions associated with being childless by choice.

All the courtesy stigma respondents admitted to accepting readily others' perceptions of them as responsible for the couple's infertility. This deviance avowal differentiated the courtesy stigma women from the other respondents who attempted, for the most part, to avoid designations of infertility or to renegotiate infertility as a discreditable attribute. . . .

The willingness to accept perceived responsibility for the infertility appeared to be aimed at avoiding the more negative implications of male infertility. As one courtesy stigma respondent humorously noted:

When I tell them we can't have children, I generally try to leave the impression that it's me. I may mutter "Tubes you know" or "Faulty plumbing." I think it's easier for me to go with that than to deal with the idea that maybe my husband "can't get it up."

Several respondents in this study also revealed their infertility to avoid the more negative connotations of being falsely accused of voluntary childlessness. For example, women who were reluctant to tell others of their infertility problems were hurt and frustrated when others assumed that they did not want children.

> I know at one point I overheard someone saying, "Oh, they're too selfish, they're too interested in going on fancy holidays. Material things, that's why they're not having children." It was so untrue and it hurt.

. . . The involuntarily childless women in this study appeared to regard voluntary childlessness as more stigmatizing given their own efforts to renegotiate their childlessness from deliberate to involuntary—a strategy also employed by voluntarily childless individuals (Veevers, 1980).

Practiced deception differs from concealment in that respondents readily admit to being infertile. However, they distort or alter the circumstances contributing to their childlessness. Practiced deception can also be distinguished from deviance avowal. In practiced deception, *both* members of the infertile dyad accept responsibility for the infertility—whether it's true or not—while deviance avowal involves one member who accepts sole responsibility for infertility caused by the other member of the dyad.

Practiced deception in revealing infertility was apparently used to enhance self-esteem. Most respondents who employed this strategy *rehearsed* it beforehand. . . . As one woman solely responsible for the couple's infertility revealed:

> My husband and I actually discussed how we would respond to others after we got the classic question from the first person we told [his mother], "Whose fault is it?" We agreed to present it as a joint problem of trifling proportions individually but enough to ensure that we as a couple would not be able to have our own children. We left them with the suspicion that with someone else we could. Love keeps us together see?

Most other respondents who provided inaccurate answers presented their infertility as a joint problem:

> We fudge the issues and pretend that it's both of us. Usually by fudging the issue you never give a clear answer. I don't think that it's any of their business.

Indeed, the practiced deception by performance teams (Goffman 1959:91) extended, on occasion, to self-help group meetings wherein participants avoided revealing whose condition was contributing to the infertility. In addition to enhancing self-esteem, preventive disclosure may also have been a way of testing acquaintances who had the potential to become good friends, or a way of preventing a loss of self-esteem if the infertility was discovered by these acquaintances later.

In many instances, couples progressed from one strategy to another as they managed information. Specifically, respondents appeared to move from a strategy of early selective concealment to disclosure for therapeutic or preventive reasons. Respondents appeared to link this progression to increased adjustment to childlessness. As one respondent put it:

> I don't think at first that there is much that can be done other than to listen if people want to talk. Often I find though that people only want to talk about it when they are, so to speak, on the mend. They are coming to terms with their infertility. . . . Until you start to accept it, you may avoid that kind of thing [talking] like the plague.

. . . Although progression appears linked to increased adjustment, it may also reflect audience responses to the revelation of infertility. As others' reactions were tested through selective disclosures, these reactions prompted the use of other strategies or continued secrecy in the face of negative responses.

Discussion and Conclusions

. . . My results offer new insight into the various strategies that people use to manage potentially stigmatizing information. Although the strategies employed by these women were similar to those observed by Schneider and Conrad (1980) in their study of epilepsy, some important differences were evident. First, respondents perceived therapeutic disclosure to be beneficial even when the audience was unsupportive. Second, I explicitly conceptualized and documented the use of deviance avowal as a device for preventive disclosure. . . . Finally, I found that respondents used practiced deception as a strategy to enhance self-esteem and to influence others' perceptions of them, a process not noted in Schneider and Conrad's work.

The personal possession or secret sharing of infertility has profound consequences for the social identity and behavior of actors. For example, respondents generally engaged in self-diagnosis of a potential problem with the reproductive process. Most of them remained secretive as they explored the possibility that they or their spouses might be infertile. In the majority of cases, initial visits to a doctor or a fertility clinic were arranged in such a way as to avoid public awareness of difficulty. Given this kind of secretive behavior, it is reasonable to conclude that the women expected some negative or devaluing response, at the very least, if their difficulty became known (Goode, 1981). Indeed, most respondents linked their secretive behavior to a fear that awareness of a problem with fertility would cause others to view them in a new and damaging light.

In addition, respondents themselves categorized infertility as discreditable, as something negative, as representing some sort of failure. Most discussed experiences of anxiety, isolation, and conflict as they privately explored the possibility of personal infertility. Indeed, to avoid feelings of personal inadequacy, many of the respondents excluded themselves from gatherings such as baby showers or avoided their pregnant friends *prior* to the revelation of involuntary childlessness. . . .

My findings strongly suggest that a complete appreciation of the evolution of a deviant identity must include an analysis of the intricate interplay between self-labeling and the perceived disapproval and rejection by social audiences. Indeed, the apparent existence of a self-labeled, discreditable identity in the absence of visible deviant behavior offers additional support for the concept of deviance as an inner essence which can exist independent of behavior (Katz, 1972;

Petrunik and Shearing, 1983). In addition, this study clearly demonstrates the interpretive nature of the interactional sequence. Specifically, my evidence indicates that the emergence of a discreditable identity involves actors' use of generalized normative perspectives to interpret their attribute. In addition, actors' interpretations of encounters with others and their evaluations of social audiences affect the strategies they employ to negotiate more positive labels. . . .

References

Benet, Margaret. 1976. *The Character of Adoption.* London: Cox and Wyman.

Birenbaum, Arnold. 1975. "On managing a courtesy stigma." Pp. 347–57 in Frank Scarpitti and Paul McFarland (eds.), Deviance: Action, Reaction, Interaction. Reading, MA: Addison-Wesley.

Broverman, Inge, Susan Vogel, Donald Broverman, Frank Clarkson and Paul Rosenkrantz. 1972. "Sex role stereotypes: a current appraisal." Journal of Social Issues 28:59–78.

Burgwyn, Diana. 1981. Marriage Without Children. New York: Harper and Row.

Fox, Greer, Bruce Fox and Katherine Frohardt-Lane. 1982. "Fertility socialization: the development of fertility attitudes and behavior." Pp. 19–49 in Greer Fox (ed.), The Childbearing Decision: Fertility Attitudes and Behavior. Beverly Hills, CA: Sage.

Goffman, Erving. 1959. The Presentation of Self in Everyday Life. New York: Doubleday.

_____. 1963. Stigma. Englewood Cliffs, NJ: Prentice-Hall.

Goode, Erich. 1981. "Deviance, norms, and social reaction." Deviant Behavior, 3:47–53.

Hewitt, John and Randall Stokes. 1978. "Disclaimers." Pp. 308–19 in Jerome Manis and Bernard Meltzer (eds.), Symbolic Interactionism, 3rd edition. Boston: Allyn and Bacon.

Katz, Jack. 1972. "Deviance, charisma, and rule-defined Behavior." Social Problems 20:186–202.

Kraft, Adrienne, Joseph Palombo, Dorena Mitchell, Catherine Dean, Steven Meyers and Anne Wright-Schmidt. 1980. "The psychological dimensions of infertility." American Journal of Orthopsychiatry 50:618–28.

McFalls, Joseph. 1979. *Psychopathology and Sub-Fecundity.* New York: Academic Press.

Menning, Barbara. 1975. "The infertile couple:a plea for advocacy." Child Welfare 54:454–60.

_____. 1977. *Infertility: A Guide for the Childless Couple.* Englewood Cliffs, NJ: Prentice-Hall.

Miall, Charlene. 1985. "Perceptions of informal sanctioning and the stigma of involuntary childlessness." Deviant Behavior 6:383–403.

Mosher, William. 1982. "Infertility trends among U.S. couples: 1965–1976." Family Planning Perspectives 14:22–27.

Nagi, S. 1966. "Some conceptual issues in disability and rehabilitation." Pp. 100–13 in Marvin Sussman (ed.), Sociology and Rehabilitation. Washington, DC: American Sociological Association.

National Center for Health Statistics. 1985. "Fecundity and infertility in the United States, 1965–82." Advance Data From Vital and Health Statistics. No. 104. DHHS Pub. No. (PHS) 85–1250. Public Health Service. Hyattsville, MD, February 11, 1985.

Patton, Michael. 1980. Qualitative Evaluation Methods. Beverly Hills, CA: Sage.

Peck, Ellen and Judith Senderowitz (eds.). 1974. Pronatalism: The Myth of Mom and Apple Pie. New York: Thomas Y. Crowell.

Petrunik, Michael and Clifford Shearing. 1983. "Fragile facades: stuttering and the strategic manipulation of awareness." Social Problems 31:125–38.

Pfeffer, Naomi and Anne Woollett. 1983. The Experience of Infertility. London: Virago.

Plummer, Kenneth. 1979. "Misunderstanding labeling perspectives." Pp. 85–121 in David Downes and Paul Roch (eds.), Deviant Interpretations. Oxford: Martin Robertson and Company.

Pohlman, Edward. 1969. The Psychology of Birth Planning Cambridge, MA: Schenkman.

_____.1970 "Childlessness: intentional and unintentional." Journal of Nervous and Mental Disease 151:2–12.

_____. 1974. "Motivations in wanting conceptions." Pp. 159–90 in Ellen Peck and Judith Senderowitz (eds.), Pronatalism: The Myth of Mom and Apple Pie. New York: Thomas Y. Crowell.

Rossi, Alice. 1977. "A biosocial perspective on parenting." Dedaelus 106:1–31.

Russo, Nancy. 1976. "The motherhood mandate." Journal of Social Issues 32:143–79.

Schneider, Joseph and Peter Conrad. 1980. "In the closet with illness: epilepsy, stigma potential and information control." Social Problems 28:32–44.

Veevers, Jean.1972. "The violation of fertility mores: voluntary childlessness as deviant behaviour." Pp. 571–92 in Craig Boydell, Carl Grindstaff and Paul Whitehead (eds.), Deviant Behaviour and Societal Reaction. Toronto: Holt, Rinehart and Winston.

_____. 1979. "Voluntary childlessness: a review of issues and evidence." Marriage and Family Review 2:1–26.

_____. 1980. Childless by Choice. Toronto: Butterworth.

_____. 1983. "Researching voluntary childlessness: a critical assessment of current strategies and findings." Pp. 75–96 in Eleanor Macklin and Roger Rubin (eds.), Contemporary Families and Alternative Lifestyles. Beverly Hills, CA: Sage.

Weinstein, Eugene. 1962. "Adoption and infertility." American Sociological Review 27:408–12.

Zimmerman, Shirley. 1982. "Alternatives in human reproduction for involuntary childless couples." Family Relations 31:233–41.

14

Genetic Essentialism and Social Deviance: Intersections of Genetic Science and Collective Identity Movements

Susan E. Kelly

Kelly examines the increasing tendency of medicine to rely on genetic markers of deviance and normalcy. She explains the medical research in support of a "gay gene" and relates it to the efforts of gay men and lesbians to achieve civil rights and equality. Interestingly, gays and lesbians have only recently escaped medical definitions of deviance, yet many are eager to embrace medical explanations for homosexuality. Still, within the gay and lesbian community, there are those who warn against such a tactic. This article reveals the costs and benefits inherent in embracing a deviant label, particularly when one's difference is identified and explained by an institution as powerful as the medical establishment.

Introduction

"Were you born that way? Personality, temperament, even life choices. New studies show it's mostly in your genes." (*Life*, April 1998).

Accompanying this headline are striking images of a double helix and individuals posed to represent a variety of social stereotypes—overweight women, misbehaving children, a thrill seeker with his clothes aflame. The images and text are telling indicators of the cultural power the "new" genetic science has come to possess. While most behavioral geneticists would disagree with the extent of genetic determinism claimed by this headline, the message that genes control the most essential aspects of ourselves—our personality, our proclivities, even our choice of mates—has quickly made its way into the realm of popular discourse. Researchers recently have claimed a genetic basis for "deviant" behaviors ranging from criminality to homosexuality, as well as "normal" personality characteristics such as shyness and aggression. Some of these studies raise considerable controversy, depending on the meaning and significance of the behavior under study. Research into sexual orientation, especially findings that appear to support the notion of relatively simple links between genes and same sex attraction, is an example of research that provokes intense debate.

Genetic explanations for behaviors considered deviant—such as homosexuality, mental illness, or criminality—appear to provide compelling evidence that at least some forms of social deviance are inherent and essential aspects of those who display them. The scientific and cultural emphasis on deterministic explanations for human behavior has a sordid and troubling history, one in which genetic explanations have served to reproduce social biases rather than biological realities. Because of this history, and because human behavioral genetic research is so closely tied to explication of variations from "normal" behavior, genetic research is increasingly important to the social meanings of deviance and normality. Genetic essentialist or determinist interpretations of the origins of deviance are frequently hailed as rational, scientific advancements over Freudian/post-Freudian or social constructionist explanations. While much attention is paid to the discriminatory and stigmatizing potential of genetic findings, particularly in employment and insurance decisions, less emphasis has been given to the responses of deviant communities themselves to what might be called genetic labeling. I will explore the relationship between the rising social credibility of genetic science to explain differences in human behavior, and the collective identity processes and strategies of groups whose deviance has been the subject of behavioral genetic research. I focus on the high profile research into the genetics of sexual orientation and responses of gay and lesbian identity movements, in which deviant identity is both deployed strategically and contested internally.

Given the historical entanglement of human genetics with repressive and conservative social and political ideologies, it might be expected that social movements that are organized around "deviant" identities will resist genetic explanations as dangerous labeling. However, responses to genetic claims concerning deviant behavior from collectivities already labeled deviant, including gay and lesbian identity movements and advocacy organizations for the mentally ill, are proving to be dynamic, varied, and contingent. Rather than assuming resistance, the thesis developed in this essay is that genetic explanations for deviance may become the object of reflexive consideration and negotiation by movements actively engaged in collective identity construction. Because they touch upon elements of identity that have social and political consequences, genetic explanations may enter into ongoing processes through which oppressed identity groups locate themselves relative to systems of dominance. Potentially labeled groups may respond to genetic findings according to how they define and negotiate the "identity stakes"—the political, social, and individual consequences perceived to follow from particular identity strategies.

In this essay, I assume that behavioral genetic claims are social, rather than merely raw scientific facts. Genetic explanations of deviant behavior possess symbolic value and may be viewed within collective identity groups as tools (Swidler 1986) or cultural resources (Williams 1995) to be mobilized toward the pursuit of movement goals. Cultural resources can be understood in many of the same ways as are conventional resources such as money and organization. They shape and are shaped by a movement's interests and actions; they have both internal and external uses in pursuit of expressive and strategic social movement dimensions. Their effectiveness depends not only on how they are framed and used by social movements but on their "consumption and interpretation by others . . . Symbols that have only internal meaning for a movement will have little impact on the political [or social or cultural] arena" (ibid: 127).

Genetic claims, because they are fraught with social, cultural, and political implications, have potential for deployment as cultural resources by social movements for which identity construction is central. Genetic causation theories concerning traits or behaviors defined as deviant, such as same sex attraction, address identity issues with potential social and political consequences, including whether deviance is ascribed (inherent and constitutive of a person or group) or socially acquired or constructed in specific social contexts. Such claims are likely to articulate with internal frames (Benford 1993) about collective identity and its deployment as a movement strategy. Genetic claims concerning deviance are themselves open to interpretation, they carry significant historical baggage, and are the subject of intense public interest and controversy. The focus of this analysis, therefore, is on how genetic claims and their implications are negotiated, disputed, embraced, or managed by members of collective identity groups.

The New Genetics: A Troubled Revolution

Human behavioral genetics currently raises social anxieties that reflect negative political and ideological associations genetics gained earlier in this century. Human genetics as a research enterprise began with the eugenic (literally meaning "good in birth") idea that the physical, mental, and behavioral qualities of the human race could be improved by programs to manage and manipulate heredity (Kevles 1985). Eugenic movements flourished in the United States and across Europe at the turn of the century. In the United States, eugenic ideas and programs were favored by many members of the political and intellectual elite, and by both social conservatives and social reformers. But in the early human genetic sciences, social prejudice frequently masqueraded as scientific judgment. Social distinctions of race, ethnicity, and class were commonly attributed to biology, and held to be manifestations of a natural hierarchy of human character. American eugenicists influenced immigration restriction and miscegenation laws with the goal of improving and protecting the genetic purity of "desirable" members of the population. The reinforcement of existing social stratification by biological deterministic thinking became the basis for public health programs, adopted in many states, for sterilization of the genetically "unfit." By 1931, 30 states had passed compulsory sterilization laws applying to individuals categorized as feebleminded, alcoholic, epileptic, sexually deviant, or mentally ill. When eugenic sterilization laws were challenged in the 1927 *Buck v. Bell* case, the U.S. Supreme Court ruled the practice constitutional (Kevles 1985).

Internationally, social and cultural variations in factors including religion, scientific tradition, and degree of racial mixing were reflected in eugenic programs with different emphases and biases. In France and Brazil, for example, sterilization and other coercive measures were rejected (Paul 1995). In some countries, however, eugenics took on a much darker cast. The eugenic science and programs of the United States were adopted and expanded to fit ideological programs of racial hygiene during the German Nazi era, and eventually became the justification for massive racially-based extermination campaigns. American and European biologists strove to distance themselves and genetic science from the horrors committed under Nazi eugenics programs, yet the association is one that continues to linger.

The "new" genetics is represented in the United States by the Human Genome Project, a multimillion dollar research effort established in the late 1980s to identify and map the entire human genome. The genome project is science performed on an enormous scale and with dazzling sophistication. Political and public support for the project has been bolstered by scientists' promises of revolutionary changes in medicine and of dramatic biotechnological advances in pharmaceuticals and gene-based therapies. However, many observers remain apprehensive about the potential misuse of genetic information, information that has been described as "the key to what makes us human, what defines our possibilities and limits as members of the species *Homo sapiens*" (Kevles and Hood 1992:vii). A primary fear is that genetic knowledge may lead to new forms of discrimination and stigmatization based on human difference—on deviance—in guises perhaps more subtle than that of eugenics. This apprehension, which has sparked heated controversy among academics and scientists including within the American Psychological Association (Tobach and Proshansky 1976), was expressed in vivid terms by Peter Breggin, director of the Center for Psychiatry in Bethesda, Maryland, during a controversial conference on genetic aspects of violence. "Behavioral genetics is the same old stuff in new clothes. . . It's another way for a violent, racist society to say people's problems are their own fault, because they carry 'bad' genes" (quoted in Mann 1994 at 1686). Such critiques also enter popular discourse, as exemplified in the title of an article on biological explanations for violence in a recent issue of *Discover* magazine—"Scapegoat Biology" (Kevles and Kevles 1997: 58).

Genetic scientists and their critics continue to struggle over the meaning that genes, and the claims being made for them, are coming to hold not only in the way we think about disease, but in how we are coming to think about normality, human nature, and even free will. As the quote from *Life* indicates, genetic science is quickly emerging (or re-emerging) as a compelling organizing framework for understanding human phenomena. Critics argue that the gene is not only a biological structure, it is a potent cultural symbol (Nelkin and Lindee 1995), an icon of modernity, scientific achievement, and the desire to control human destiny. Despite the actual complexity and indeterminacy of genetic information, genetic claims have entered powerfully into our cultural repertoire. "Having a gene for" predisposition to disease or to a behavioral trait is becoming in and of itself a condition of identity. It is the power of genetic labels to construct identities, as well as to support certain views of society, that make their current implications for studies of deviance and stigma so compelling.

Social Consequences of Genetic Information

A gene is a biochemical structure that "codes" for the composition of specific proteins that are the building blocks of living cells and tissues. Distinct, identifiable traits that are linked to a single gene and passed through generations in predictable patterns are called Mendelian traits (after Gregor Mendel, the Polish monk who discovered the laws of inheritance in the mid-1800s). Human eye color was discovered to be a Mendelian trait in 1907. But the "simple" idea of the inheritance of traits has proven to be extremely complex when applied to the range of attributes, from diseases to behaviors, that constitute the human condition. A few diseases that involve the human neurosystem have been attributed to a single disabled gene, Huntington's Disease being perhaps the best known example. However, the genetic components of the vast majority of complex human behaviors are believed to lie in multiple-gene and gene-environment systems that are extremely difficult to characterize precisely. Debates about the relative contributions of genes and environment (broadly defined to include material and social elements) to human behaviors—the old nature versus nurture dilemma—have given way in the scientific community to explorations of complex and over-lapping interactions between genetic and environmental factors.

Nonetheless, the cultural image of human behavioral genetics continues to involve reductionist and binary propositions, usually expressed in terms of determinist or constructivist origins. Genes are frequently thought of as the over-riding determinants of human biological and psychological destinies. Popular rhetoric supposes that a gene represents an immutable and irreducible unit of the human self. The correlation between a potentially active gene and a behavior pattern is assumed to indicate cause and effect.

Biological determinist arguments have been forwarded as explanations of deviance and social problems as well as of the social order: if human behavior is the result of individual genetic inheritance, then bad genes must be the cause of deviant behaviors such as criminality and violence. Where past eugenic programs were concerned primarily with the biological and moral degeneration of races or populations, the current interest in genetic explanations for human behavior provides a basis for an ideology of the individuation of deviance; the location of the causes of deviant behavior in an individual body (although that body may share biological pre-destiny with other, similarly deviant bodies). Critics of the search for genetic components of human behavior argue that biological or genetic determinist models of social deviance support simplistic models of cause and effect, and societal approaches to social problems that focus on individual bodies: discrimination, discipline, medical treatment, and perhaps in the future, genetic manipulation. Social models of deviance—models that point to structural inequality, processes of labeling, the social creation and enforcement of deviance categories—risk being collapsed into the ambiguous category of "environment." The fact that behavioral geneticists themselves must come to some concrete, precise definition of a behavior such as homosexuality in order to study it leads many critics to fear that the search for genetic components to human behavior continues to be science in the service of social norms, social prejudices, and social hierarchies. Further, the very choice of behavioral areas for study—for example, aggression-related criminality rather than white collar crime—reflects and reinforces social biases.

Genetic science, focusing both on pathological and "normal" differences among humans, has great potential to blur boundaries between deviance as a social problem and deviant behavior as disease. Past uses of genetic science support these fears, and the rhetoric surrounding the current genome effort provides contemporary evidence. Discussions of behavioral genetics frequently slip between attributions of genetic influence on traits such as "emotional stability" that exhibit "normal variation" and traits such as depression that "fall within the pathological range" (Sherman 1997:581).

At this time, the most powerful mechanisms for controlling genetic deviance in individual and social bodies occur in the arena of reproduction, and specifically in the routine clinical practices of prenatal genetic testing and selective abortion. Prenatal screening and testing procedures are currently the most widespread applications of genetic technology to humans (Lippman 1991). Prenatal diagnosis of conditions such as Down Syndrome, and relatively common diseases such as cystic fibrosis, is routinely offered to pregnant women who are at "high risk" of bearing an affected child. As scientific knowledge of genetic components of disease and other conditions expands, so does the potential definition of genetic deviance. The questions of what is a disease, which conditions fall outside the normal range, and what is a desirable or undesirable life—is life as a deaf or gay person better avoided?—are rapidly becoming part of the social institutions of reproduction and parenting (Marteau, Michie, Drake and Bobrow 1995). Some critics have pointed to prenatal diagnostic practices as a "backdoor to eugenics" (Duster 1990), through which individual decisions, albeit subject to social pressure, are the mechanism whereby standards of normality and health are enforced. Which human traits are classified as "normal," and which deviant, how these definitions emerge, and with what broader social and cultural meaning,

are questions of paramount importance in the genetic era.

Genetically defined or interpreted deviance intersects with norms concerning health (individual and public), prevention, and responsibility. Genetic labeling thus bears social consequences that flow beyond the boundaries of the scientific or medical. A genetic explanation for a form of deviant behavior may serve to relieve an individual or group of the moral stigma of their condition, because it provides "proof" that the condition is not the result of sinfulness or weak character but of factors beyond their control. The identification of a biological reason for deviance may be greeted with relief by individuals grappling with identity and seeking to minimize stigma or imputations of immorality. Claims of the genetic causation of a trait may provide justification for protection against discrimination on the basis of a "natural" and immutable status. If homosexuality is a product of a particular gene or genes, for example, it would tend to validate the position of those who claim same sex orientation to be a natural category of sexuality and not a lifestyle choice. However, a genetic explanation for a trait may serve to transform deviance into a disease. Homosexuality has only recently begun to lose its association with mental illness. Finally, a genetic explanation may place an additional burden on deviant individuals to take whatever steps are necessary to prevent, alleviate, or cure their condition. These pressures appear currently to be most acute with regard to reproductive decisions, but may extend to an individual's efforts to correct or normalize an existing genetic condition. Some advocates for the disabled fear the creation and stigmatization of the category of "elective disability" for individuals who choose not to avail themselves of means to correct or normalize their condition (for example, deaf persons who refuse cochlear ear implants) (Tucker 1998). Similarly, the label of elective deviance might come to signify individuals who choose not to normalize their behavior through available medical means, means that may at some point include behaviorally directed gene therapies.

Genes and Collective Identity

Collective identity construction—defined here as both "an individual pronouncement of affiliation" (Friedman and McAdam 1992: 157) and self-conscious delineation of a distinct, strategic definition of self supportive of collective action—has recently emerged as an important and problematic activity of social movements and as an object of social movement research. In contemporary identity-based political movements, the self-conscious construction of a collective identity may be a major movement goal (for example, the creation of politicized lesbian-feminist identity communities (Taylor and Whittier 1992)). Collective identity formation is an important political and cultural strategy, where, as in gay and lesbian rights movements, it may enable mobilization and action and serve as the basis for civil rights and individual empowerment goals. Identity constructs are reflexive, dynamic, and subject to negotiation as symbols and actions for challenging existing systems of domination. Identity constructs are shaped from without as well as from within, as they are in continual interaction with external social and political landscapes (including counter-movements).

The medical, political, and cultural ascendency of genetics as an explanatory framework for human behavior raises issues that are relevant to the self-conscious construction of individual and group identities. Behavioral genetic science offers interpretations of elements of identity that are central to social movement strategies, ranging from gay and lesbian rights to advocates for the severely mentally ill. These elements—the determined, essential, and immutable, or socially constructed and contingent nature of human traits and conditions—are directly relevant to movement processes of boundary construction (establishing difference), developing consciousness (embracing or resisting "natural" deviant status), and the ongoing deployment of identity toward movement goals (e.g., the reduction of stigma for the mentally ill and their families, or claims to civil rights status based on sexual orientation). The remainder of this essay will examine the interplay between recent scientific announcements concerning the biology of sexual orientation and the deployment of these claims as cultural resources and in collective identity negotiation processes within gay and lesbian communities. The analysis focuses on discussions of "gay biology" published in major news outlets, scientific journals, and the gay press from 1991 to 1996. Reliance on public sources has limitations for analysis of some aspects of social movements (see for specific discussion of this point Williams 1995); however, here the focus is on the negotiation and deployment of genetic claims as cultural resources—publicly available and reflexively constructed.

Genetic findings concerning socially controversial issues receive nearly immediate media coverage through established rituals of science reporting. Recent scientific studies purporting to substantiate biological explanations for sexual orientation received widespread media coverage that largely supported their cultural absorption as scientific confirmation that homosexual orientation should be understood as innate and essential. The interpretation of scientific findings in media reports is frequently provided by the scientists themselves. In the case of these studies, several of the researchers forwarded the interpretation that their findings, and the motivations behind their studies, was "pro-gay"—that is, conducted toward goals including facilitating the acceptance of gay men and lesbians by the general public.

I posit three modes through which genetic claims were enlisted, resisted, or negotiated as cultural resources: 1) Specific movement goals (e.g., civil rights protection), 2) Political identity construction processes (instrumental and cultural movement functions); and 3) Individual identity construction (expressive movement functions).

Recent Science of Sexual Orientation

Of recent claims of major breakthroughs in the search for biological causes of homosexuality in humans, three studies have garnered the greatest attention—one from neuroanatomy and two from behavioral genetics. A study by Simon LeVay (1991) that suggested differences in brain structure between homosexual and heterosexual men launched the current avid scientific and media interest. The part of the brain identified by LeVay as varying by male sexual orientation, the hypothalamus, had previously been experimentally associated with direct control over sexual behavior in rats. LeVay examined post-mortum samples from the brains of forty-one subjects—thirty-five men and six women. Subjects were classified as homosexual or heterosexual based upon evidence in the medical records, including whether the subject had died of AIDS. While acknowledging methodological and interpretive limits to the study, LeVay forwarded the notion that biological and probably genetic correlates to the designations homosexual and heterosexual will eventually be found. "'If there are environmental influences . . . they operate very early in life, at the fetal or early-infancy stage, when the brain is still putting itself together. I'm very much skeptical of the idea that sexual orientation is a cultural thing'" (Gelman, Foote, Barrett and Talbot quoted in Halley 1994:503).

Genetic evidence has emerged from studies using the behavioral genetic methodologies of "twin studies" and pedigree and linkage analysis. In a twin study, researchers look for evidence of a genetic component to a behavior or trait by examining whether it appears in identical twins, non-identical (fraternal) twins, and non-twin siblings in proportions greater or less than one would expect from the distribution of the trait in the population at large. Related methods are segregation or adoption studies using twins or siblings reared apart. Differences in behavior are measured as a function of the closeness of genetic relationship and the degree of difference in environments. In 1991, J. Michael Bailey and Richard Pillard published what was at the time the largest and most carefully designed twin study of male sexual orientation, using twins and adopted brothers (Bailey and Pillard 1991). It was regarded as providing the strongest evidence to date that any biological differences between gay and straight men may cause, rather than result from, differences in sexual orientation (an ambiguity not resolved through LeVay's anatomical study). Two years later, Dean Hamer and colleagues (Hamer et al. 1993) published

results of a pedigree (family tree) and linkage analysis study with an even bolder genetic claim—a linkage between DNA markers on the X chromosome and male homosexuality. Hamer's research team observed higher rates of homosexuality in maternal rather than paternal relatives of gay men, suggesting that homosexuality might be genetically transmitted through the mother (X chromosome). In 1995, Hamer published the results of additional research that supported this finding. The latter study addressed some methodological critiques leveled against the previous research. Hamer's team also analyzed pairs of lesbian siblings but found no genetic link (Hu 1995).

Movement Goals: Civil Rights Protection Stakes and Shifting Counter-Movement Strategies

A core area of debate within and across gay and lesbian identity movements concerns the "cause" of same sex attraction and its expression—whether homosexuality is essential (inherent, immutable, and constitutive of the individual) or constructed, the manifestation of historically and societally contingent beliefs about sexuality, gender, and desire. Essentialist/constructivist debates have significant correlates to gay and lesbian identity politics and are perceived to have large political implications for how those who engage in homosexuality are treated in the larger society—whether they should be criminally prosecuted, medically treated, or legally protected as a minority. Over the period of time under study, media representation of responses from gay and lesbian communities encompassed two arguments: on the one hand, if homosexuality is innate or due to biological factors, it should be tolerated as a natural variation, thus supporting civil rights claims based on sexual orientation as a "natural" and immutable category. According to an opposing logic, the localization of a "gay gene" or genes poses the potential for heightened forms of surveillance, discrimination, and possible eugenic policies or practices directed against homosexuals. The specific implications of genetic claims were complicated by changes and diversity in movement goals over time, and by conflicting identity requirements/emphases involved in different movement goals. They were shaped in part by how the claims were interpreted and responded to by counter-movements (anti-homosexual rights organizations). The scientific reports were not relevant to or supportive of all aspects of a diverse movement. That is, the more heterogeneous or diverse the movement's goals, the more problematic the response over time to genetic claims regarding deviant identity.

Scientific claims that sexual orientation is biologically determined made more plausible legal arguments that lesbians and gay men comprise a minority population warranting meaningful constitutional protection. According to this argument, homosexuals constitute a suspect class under the Equal Protection Clause of the Constitution in part because the characteristic that differentiates them, and that constitutes the basis of discrimination against them, is innate and immutable. These arguments have been directed against a Supreme Court decision in 1986 (Bowers v. Hardwick), and subsequent lower court decisions, in which it has been held that what the Supreme Court referred to as "homosexual sodomy" is not protected from criminalization. Under the current legal climate, the definition of homosexuality (and heterosexuality) has been assumed by the state or courts (Halley 1993). Hinging on the logic through which homosexuals are identified (through behavior, self identification, or some other mechanism) are a number of civil rights issues, including U.S. military policies on gay service members. Claims that sexual orientation is genetic were perceived by some as providing a potentially effective counter to dominant powers (such as the government) that possess and wield the prerogative to define the boundaries of homosexual identity. That is, genetic causation theories, with the validation of scientific backing, were seen by some as obviating or trumping the power of governments to define and identify sexual deviance.

As scientist Simon LeVay himself noted:

Is homosexuality immutable or a chosen lifestyle? The last time the Supreme Court ruled on this matter, it was argued that it was biological, but nobody believed it.

This work may show that sexual orientation is genetically determined like skin color, and may therefore have implications for the civil rights of gays and lesbians (quoted in Halley 1994:504).

The claim that biological causation supports the goals of equal protection and equal rights for gays and lesbians received wide exposure. Richard Green, a psychiatrist who conducts research on sexual orientation development in children, was quoted in a 1993 article in the *New York Times* as arguing that "(i)f sexual orientation were demonstrated to be essentially in-born . . . most laws that discriminate against gays and lesbians, including sodomy laws, housing and employment discrimination laws, all would fall" (Angier 1993:24). Similarly representative of how pro-civil rights arguments were represented in media, an article in the *Wall Street Journal* (Jefferson 1993) declared that "the discovery of a definitive biological cause of homosexuality could go a long way toward advancing the gay-rights cause. If homosexuality were found to be an immutable trait, like skin color, then laws criminalizing homosexual sex might be overturned. A Hawaii supreme court judge recently noted that a biological basis for homosexuality could tip the scales toward legalization of same-sex marriages. Job protection for homosexuals—the law in eight states—might be extended throughout the country. Moreover, a biological link could do much to dispel the belief that people choose to be homosexual. Recent polls indicate that Americans who think homosexuality isn't chosen are far more likely to favor gay rights than those who believe otherwise."

Genetic and other biological studies were presented as good evidence against anti-homosexual claims that homosexuality is "spread" by "recruitment"—an argument that has been employed to bar gay men and lesbians from teaching positions in schools, and that underlies (by some interpretations) the military's policies regarding homosexual service members. A *US News and World Report* article declared: "Outside the scientific world, it seems homosexuals have much to gain from proof that their sexuality is determined by their genes. A born-that-way explanation would disprove those who say homosexuality is a perversion and encourage gays to seek counseling to change their ways. It would explode the logic of denying gay men positions as teachers, since it would make silly the fear that they could recruit to homosexuality anyone not born that way. And it would give parents a guilt-free answer to the Freudians who claim the sons turned out that way because they played with dolls or got the wrong love from Mom and Dad" (Watson, Shapiro and Streisand 1995:94).

In 1993, the persuasive force of genetic and other biologically determinist arguments regarding same sex orientation was publicly put to test during constitutional challenges to Colorado's Amendment 2 prohibiting the extension of equal protection to gays and lesbians. Opponents of Amendment 2 employed expert scientific witnesses who testified, with a variety of scientific evidence, that homosexuality is genetically or biologically determined. Proponents of Amendment 2 countered with refutations of the scientific experts and evidence, declaring that arguments for the innateness of homosexuality are flawed, politically motivated, or contradicted by other studies (Pankratz 1993; Boot 1992). Opponents of the amendment failed to convince the judge of the fundamental point of genetic arguments: rather than removing sexual orientation from debate with anti-homosexual political opponents, the debates were simply transferred to the arena of scientific research and refutation. Those who approved of the research because they thought it might lead to greater acceptance of homosexuality have probably found that "(H)omophobia, like other forms of bigotry, does not need a reason . . . What it needs is a rationalization, and that may be premised on any . . . theory that happens to be convenient at the moment" (Byrne quoted in McKenzie 1998:1J.).

By 1995, more conservative responses concerning genetic causation were emerging among members of gay and lesbian rights movements, as anti-homosexual movements shifted arguments to cope with possible biological evidence, the discriminatory potential of genetic testing was more widely discussed, and as a variety of civil rights goals appeared to require different identity strategies. Paul Wysocki, a gay community activist in San Jose, California was quoted as saying that "This is a blessing and a curse at the same time. . . . We have to talk about the ethics of this now, rather than wait for the research to be farther advanced. Ten years from now it may be too late" (Legon 1995). The Washington D.C.-based Pro-Life Alliance of Gays and Lesbians warned of the possibility of gay fetuses being aborted, and sought backing for introduction of a federal law outlawing abortions based on the fetus' gender or possible sexual orientation (Legon 1995). Philip Arcidi (1995:101), the President of the Alliance, wrote that:

> As scientists become more adept at deciphering the DNA codes, they will be able to predict with increasing accuracy whether an unborn child is predisposed to grow up lesbian and gay. As this knowledge becomes more readily available, prospective parents will have to ask themselves if they are willing to assume the challenge of raising a potential gay son or lesbian daughter, or whether they should abort and retry.

Genetic causation theories initially appeared to subvert psychoanalytic arguments concerning the etiology of homosexuality that provide the basis for both secular and religiously-motivated claims that homosexuality can be cured. A New York analyst who was described as a principal architect of the homosexual conversion belief, was quoted in *The Detroit News* as saying, "Homosexuality is a pattern designed to avoid deeper anxieties. . . . The patient chooses a substitute because the road to sexual relations with the opposite sex is blocked by anxiety. We relieve that anxiety and open up the road to him so that he can make conscious choices. You see . . . the irony and tragedy of male homosexuality . . . is that the homosexual is vainly trying to find his lost masculinity in the body and genitals of the other partner" (quoted in *The Detroit News* 1993). Conversion "therapy" has more recently been revitalized as an anti-homosexual strategy of the conservative Christian political right, in spite of high failure rates (Silverstein 1991). The genetic claims and their interpretations appeared, however, only to bolster the "disease" and "treatment" arguments propounded. Anti-homosexual rhetoric shifted accordingly: the issue was not the mechanism behind the "disease" of homosexuality, but that it [homosexuality] remained identified a sickness for which some form of treatment, biochemical if not psychoanalytic, could be employed.

Genetic causation theories of homosexual identity were not supportive of, or directly relevant to, other emerging elements of gay and lesbian movement social and political agendas, in particular the issue of gay and lesbian parenting and adoption. Pursuit of acceptance for gay and lesbian parenting and parental rights has involved rhetorical strategies that minimize, rather than emphasize, differences between homosexual and heterosexual individuals and unions. An identity-defining emphasis on sexuality is far less relevant to these goals. Gay men and lesbians fighting for acceptance as parents were more likely to pursue strategies to turn the public focus away from homosexuality as an essential and defining characteristic and specifically to allay the notion that homosexual parents would reproduce—by genetics or parenting—same sex orientation in their children.

Collective Identity Construction and Internal Frame Disputes

Scientific reports concerning genetic causes for homosexuality intersected with internal and external movement debates concerning alternative framings of sexuality as identity constructs (cf. Warner 1993). Changes in sexual identity politics over the past decade, most notably the emergence of queer, transgendered and bisexual identities, have complicated gay and lesbian communities and the significance or strategic usefulness of gay biology. Many from these communities (as well as some gay men and lesbians) reject the view that they constitute a minority distinguished by a stable, natural identity, a view that runs counter to the strategic deployment of genetic claims to a distinguishable homosexual type/body.

The successful articulation of a public collective identity has played a strong role in the organization and strategies of gay and lesbian movements. The strategy of building a collective identity around same sex orientation has given to gay and lesbian social movements a "quasi-ethnicity" (Gamson 1995:391) "complete with its own political and cultural institutions, festivals, neighborhoods, even its own flag." A quasi-ethnic identity—an identity that would put gays and lesbians on the same civil rights footing as Afro-Americans, Hispanics, and women—is based on a fixed, natural, essential category of person, a person with same sex desires.

Over the past decade, however, gay and lesbian identity movements have been experiencing internal controversy over the definition, inclusiveness, and political efficacy of the binary and monolithic categories of hetero and homosexuality. At the same time that biological evidence for at least male homosexuality gained public attention, advocates of alternative sexualities began to challenge the notion of a stable, natural homosexual identity. Debates have centered on the content of collective identity (whose definition of gay counts?) and over the viability and political usefulness of various sexual identities (do such discrete categories as gay, lesbian, man, woman even exist, and do such distinctions forward or interfere with political struggles?) (Gamson 1995). "Queer" and bisexual identities are elements of an alternative vision of the goals of sexuality-based politics, one that argues that subordinated communities should not endorse the identities through which dominant groups suppress them. Influenced by academic constructivist theory, and defining itself against conventional lesbian and gay politics, the goals of queer activism include disassembling the notion of stable sexual identities and boundaries. This alternative strategy holds that sexual identities are social and historical products, not natural and intra-psychic ones; that culture, not nature, gives people their sexual orientations (cf. essays in Warner 1993). Queer, bi- and transsexual identity politics are anti-assimilationist, anti-essentialist, and anti-determinist.

Scientific claims for a genetic basis for sexual orientation have been perceived as either not relevant to the political and cultural goals of "queer" identity activism, or as supportive of oppressive identity categorizations. Further, the academic trends from which queer identity activisms draw theoretical sustenance contain broader constructivist themes concerning scientific activity and knowledge itself. According to constructivist perspectives on science, the "reality" of scientific claims regarding sexual orientation are no less problematic than are other forms of historically contingent, locally produced knowledge.

Genetic causation claims have therefore entered into ongoing negotiations and divisions within sexuality-based identity movements concerning not only political strategies such as civil rights status, but more fundamental cultural and political debates over the nature of sexuality, sexual categories, and identity.

Individual Identity Narratives

As represented through a media theme of individual identity narratives, some homosexuals—primarily gay men—received objective validation of their subjective beliefs about their homosexual orientation through either hearing about, or in some cases participating in, genetic scientific research. Genetic causation claims for sexual orientation were represented as powerful, scientific tools for individual identity organization in the face of social stigma and familial rejection or guilt. These narratives were connected to several of the researchers themselves, who provided compelling accounts of their own identity interests in discovering innate reasons for same sex orientation. For example:

LeVay's own life became unglued when his lover of 21 years, Richard Hersey, got AIDS in the late 1980s. After burying Hersey, the openly gay Salk Institute researcher tumbled into a deep depression and had to be hospitalized for two weeks. Upon his release, LeVay found that returning to his old work—the influence of environment on development—seemed pointless" (*The Detroit News* April 26, 1993).

Genetic explanations, and the sometimes exaggerated estimations of genetic causality claimed in the media, are represented as providing a key to own and familial acceptance of the homosexual, a compelling and acceptable "reason" for deviant identity. The role of genetic explanations as counter-logic to personal responsibility beliefs held both by gay men and their families is represented as powerful, affirming, liberating, and exculpating. Genetic claims can be employed to counter a range of sexual deviance causation theories—from toxic parenting to sexual disenchantment—with one stroke of compelling reasoning.

Conclusion

Human behavioral genetics is, and is likely to remain, inextricably linked with broader societal perceptions of what is normal, desirable, heritable, and mutable in human nature. Genetics is further likely to contribute to ongoing social and political debates about social deviance and appropriate societal responses to deviance. In the past, biological determinist ideologies have meshed with—influencing and being influenced by—dominant ideological beliefs about the social order, social inequality, and human rights. This chapter has taken up the question of human genetics and deviance within the contemporary setting, focusing specifically on responses of social movement communities organized around the formation of collective, deviant identities. Collective identity formation and negotiation has been identified as a central dynamic of new social movements whose members are concerned with protecting and improving their social, political, legal, and experiential standing, and that are actively engaged in re-defining the terms through which they are considered deviant. I have suggested that genetic claims concerning the causes of deviant identity attributes may be used as cultural resources by social movements, as symbolic as well as scientific artifacts that bolster, support, or counter the logic of movement, or counter-movement, strategies.

Genetic claims enter the public arena in dramatic and widely accessible ways that permit their alternative interpretation, assimilation, or resistance as symbolic tools and as framing devices. They are "social level constructions" (Williams 1995:127) that depend for their usefulness on their public, "external" as well as internal interpretation. Media reports of research purporting to identify evidence of a genetic basis for male homosexuality were responded to quickly by gay and lesbian movements, according to their fitness, relevance, and efficacy as cultural resources for deployment toward movement goals. Genetic claims operated on several different levels as symbolic tools; they related in different ways to extant and dynamic movement logics, both instrumental and expressive. Genetic causation claims concerning elements of deviant identity were put into play in the socio-political environment; such claims ran counter to internal movement cross-currents concerning the fundamental nature of identity construction. Finally, genetic claims became part of individual identity narratives for some homosexuals, providing a rationale for interpersonal reconciliation and re-interpretation of self and deviance.

The framework presented here allows us to think of genetic information, or more broadly, genetic explanations for what is different about an individual or group, as more than scientific products, but as cultural constructs that can be resisted, negotiated, and strategically deployed. Political and social uses and implications of identity are not unique to gay and lesbian identity movements, but are salient to other collectivities organized around deviant—and potentially genetically labeled—identities. As the impacts of genetic science on society and individuals continue to unfold, how scientific claims intersect with the societal organization of deviance will have significant implications for stigma, discrimination, and the range of possible responses to human variation.

References

Angier, Natalie. 1993. "Study of Sex Orientation Doesn't Neatly Fit Mold." *New York Times* (July 18, 1993): 24.

Arcidi, Philip. 1995. "Roe v. Wade: Death Warrant for Homosexuals." *Human Life Review*. Winter: 101–102.

Bailey, J. Michael and Richard C. Pillard. 1991. "A Genetics Study of Male Sexual Orientation." Archives of *General Psychiatry* 48:1089.

Benford, Robert D. 1993. "Frame Disputes Within the Nuclear Disarmament Movement." *Social Forces*. 71:677–701.

Boot, Michael. 1992. "Controversial Researcher Focus of Rights Debate." *The Denver Post* (September 27, 1992):6A.

Duster, Troy. 1990. *Backdoor to Eugenics*. New York: Routledge.

Friedman, Debra and Doug McAdam. 1992. "Collective Identity and Activism." In Aldon Morris and Carol McClurg Meuller (eds.), *Frontiers in Social Movement Theory*. New Haven: Yale University Press: 156–173.

Gamson, Joshua. 1995. "Must Identity Movements Self-Destruct? A Queer Dilemma." *Social Problems* 42(3):390–407.

Halley, Janet. 1993. "The Construction of Heterosexuality." In Michael Warner (ed.) *Fear of a Queer Planet: Queer Politics and Social Theory*. Minneapolis: University of Minnesota Press: 82–102.

Halley, Janet. 1994. "Sexual orientation and the politics of biology: A critique of the argument from immutability." *Stanford Law Review* 46 Rev. 503.

Hamer, Dean H., Stella Hu, Victoria L. Magnuson, Nan Hu, and Angela M.L. Pattatucci. 1993. "A linkage between DNA markers on the X chromosome and male sexual orientation." *Science* 261:321.

Hu, S., A.M. Pattatucci, C. Patterson, L. Li, D.W. Fulker, S.S. Cherny, L. Kruglyak, and D.H. Hamer. 1995. "Linkage Between Sexual Orientation and Chromosome Xq28 in Males but Not in Females." *Nature Genetics* 11(3):248–256.

Jefferson, David J. 1993. "Science Besieged: Studying the Biology of Sexual Orientation has Political Fallout." *Wall Street Journal* (August 12, 1993):A1.

Kevles, BettyAnn H. and Daniel J. Kevles. 1997. "Scapegoat Biology." *Discover (The World of Science)*. Disney copyright:58–62.

Kevles, Daniel J. 1985. *In the Name of Eugenics: Genetics and the Uses of Human Heredity*. Cambridge: Harvard University Press.

Kevles, Daniel J. and LeRoy Hood. 1992. *The Code of Codes: Scientific and Social Issues in the Human Genome Project*. Cambridge: Harvard University Press.

Legon, Jeordan. 1995. "Gay Genes" finding opens ethical debate. *San Jose Mercury News* (November 4, 1995):FIX.

LeVay, Simon. 1991. "A Difference in Hypothalamic Structure Between Heterosexual and Homosexual Men." *Science* 253:1034.

Lippman, Abby. 1991. "Prenatal Genetic Testing and Screening: Constructing Needs and Reinforcing Inequalities." *American Journal of Law and Medicine* 17:15–50.

Mann, Charles C. 1994. "Behavioral genetics in transition." *Science* 264:1686–1689.

Marteau, Theresa, Susan Michie, Harriet Drake, and Martin Bobrow. 1995. "Public Attitudes Towards the Selection of Desirable Characteristics in Children. *Journal of Medicine Genetics* 32:796–798.

McKenzie, Aline. 1998. "The Science of Sexual Orientation: Is it Your DNA, Your Environment or Just Your Choice? Biological Studies Fail to Settle Cultural Debate About Gays, Lesbians." *Dallas Morning News* (May 31):1J.

Nelkin, Dorothy and Susan M. Lindee. 1995. *The DNA Mystique: The Gene as Cultural Icon.* New York: W.H. Freeman.

Pankratz, Howard. 1993. "Sexual Orientation 'Gene Linked': Professor's Testimony Supports Claim of Gay Community." *The Denver Post* (October 14, 1993):1B.

Paul, Diane. 1995. *Controlling Human Heredity: 1856 to the Present.* New Jersey: Humanities Press.

Sherman, Stephanie L., et al. 1997. Behavioral Genetics 97: ASHG Statement. "Recent Developments in Human Behavioral Genetics: Past Accomplishments and Future Directions." *American Journal of Human Genetics* 60:1265–1275.

Silverstein, Charles. 1991. "Psychological and Medical Treatments of Homosexuality." In J.C. Gonsiorek and J.D. Weinrich (eds.), *Homosexuality: Research Implications for Public Policy.* Sage: Newbury Park, CA: 101–114.

Swidler, Ann. 1986. "Culture in Action: Symbols and Strategies." *American Sociological Review* 51:273–286.

Taylor, Verta and Nancy Whittier. 1992. "Collective Identity in Social Movement Communities." In Aldon Morris and Carol McClurg Meuller (eds.) *Frontiers in Social Movement Theory.* New Haven: Yale University Press: 104–129.

Tobach, Ethel and Harold M. Proshansky (eds.). 1976. *Genetic Destiny: Race as a Scientific and Social Controversy.* New York: AMS Press.

Tucker, Bonnie Poitras. 1998. "Deaf Culture, Cochlear Ear Implants, and Elective Disability." *Hastings Center Report* 28(4):6–14.

Warner, Michael (ed.) 1993. *Fear of a Queer Planet: Queer Politics and Social Theory.* Minneapolis: University of Minnesota Press

Watson, Traci, Joseph P. Shapiro, and Betsy Streisand. 1995. "Is there a 'gay gene'?" *US News and World Report* (November 13, 1995):93–96.

Williams, Rhys H. 1995. "Constructing the Public Good: Social Movements and Cultural Resources." *Social Problems* 42(1):124–144.

Part IV

Intimate Forms of Violence

In previous sections, we've seen that deviance is practically everywhere in society. In fact, what is considered "normal" is often defined by comparing it to deviant behavior. Another area where this occurs is in ways of thinking about and defining violence.

Most people assume they are most likely to be safe in their homes and are more likely to become victims of violence in public places. But as the articles in this section suggest, these assumptions are far from the truth. The fact is that people are more likely to be assaulted by someone they know, often in their own homes, than they are to be attacked by a stranger. Furthermore, people's perceptions and definitions of violence are strongly influenced by their relationship to the person by whom they are attacked, as well as by where the assault occurs.

On a conceptual level, the articles in this section all focus on how people define their experiences with violence. The authors emphasize that the way we think about actions and actors determines whether they are labeled deviant. As we shall see, behaviors that may be clearly violent and abusive to one person may be defined differently by another. Drawing from the studies presented in this section, you should better understand what sociologists mean when they say that deviance is socially constructed.

Recognizing that people's definitions may differ greatly, we can begin to understand how society's responses to violence—or indeed any form of deviant behavior—also vary widely. The way people define acts as deviant or not deviant sets up expectations in our minds. These expectations affect how we act toward victims and perpetrators of violence, including whether we provide resources to victims or punish offenders. In this manner, definitions result in real experiences.

In her article, "How Women Define Their Experiences of Violence," Liz Kelly explores the way that women name and define their experiences with violence and sexual assault. Drawing on interviews with women who have been victims of violence, she shows how women's perceptions and definitions vary, depending on the duration of the abuse, how well they knew the perpetrator, their preconceived ideas about acceptable levels of violence, and their definitions of violence, rape, and sexual assault. Until people define an assault as violent, deviant, or wrong, they may live with a deep sense of having been abused, but they are likely to blame themselves, rather than the perpetrator. In addition, they are not likely to demand that society punish those who have assaulted them.

Just as victims' definitions affect the way society responds to violence, stereotypes about where violence is likely to occur and beliefs about who is an appropriate victim also affect people's reactions. In his examination of the abuse of women in rural areas, Neil Websdale debunks the myth that wife abuse is a problem rooted in urban poverty.

He shows how the isolation of rural life is only one of the barriers that entraps women in violent relationships. The women Websdale interviewed also confronted mainstream beliefs—held by friends, neighbors, relatives, and authorities—about the proper role of women in families. They had to contend with a belief system holding that men have an obligation to control their families, that women are naturally subservient to men, and that women who are beaten must deserve or enjoy it. Like the women in Kelly's study, they had to overcome internalized beliefs that it is a wife's duty to provide sexual services to her husband, whether she wants to or not. Defining physical and sexual assault in the home as deviant was difficult enough for the women in Websdale's study; convincing others was even harder.

As Websdale's article demonstrates, the culture in which people live and the cultural values and beliefs into which they have been socialized have strong influences on how they interpret acts of deviance, including forms of violence. Georgia Anetzberger and her colleagues suggest just how strong these factors can be in their examination of the perceptions and definitions of elder mistreatment among four ethnic groups. Clearly, the way individuals are socialized to think of something as deviant or not deviant has a major impact on how they experience their lives.

Like Websdale's research, Becky Marrujo and Mary Kreger's study of lesbian violence shows how preconceived notions about domestic violence can distort perceptions about who is likely to be a victim and who is a perpetrator. The context of violence within same-sex relationships may lead victims to fail to define their partners' behavior as abuse and may make outsiders reluctant to intervene.

Just as people are likely to misperceive violence in lesbian or gay relationships, Jane Gilgun shows how the roles played by men and women in their sexual abuse of children may lead people to overlook violence that is occurring almost right in front of them. In addition to providing the perspectives and definitions of perpetrators, Gilgun demonstrates how such individuals are often able to conceal their behavior by establishing relationships with children that fall within the normative range. Most people tend to believe that they know which adults their children are safe with and that they would know a sexual predator if they saw one. These are misperceptions that child sexual abusers use to their own advantage by establishing relationships and social contexts in which their interactions with children appear "normal" and harmless.

Finally, Robert Hale provides insight into convicted rapists' definitions of the rapes they have committed. Drawing on interviews with incarcerated rapists, Hale reveals to us that men have specific motives in mind when they plan and carry out a sexual assault. Writing from the perspective of the deviant, Hale provides a rare look into the thought processes, motives, and rationales of men who have committed rape. By doing so, he expands on sociologists' commonly held assumption that rape is a violent act used to control or punish women. Hale does find that some of the men in his sample committed rape for this reason, but he reports on a number of other definitions of the situation. The information provided by taking the perspective of the deviant is important for understanding why rape occurs and for designing programs to prevent this crime. It also provides an unusual insight into the way that deviants can rationalize and define their behavior as normal.

All of the articles in this section have two important things in common. First, they show how intimate relationships can be violent. Second, and more important for our understanding of deviance, they show that the ways deviants (and others) define their actions and experiences are critical factors in whether, and to what degree, particular actions and behaviors are interpreted as deviant. Deviance, then, is clearly not something that exists in its own right. Rather, it is a "social construct"—something that exists only when individuals (whether perpetrators, recipients/victims, or social control authorities) apply definitions to actions that "create" the deviance aspect of the action.

These articles all strongly suggest that a holistic look at the context in which deviance occurs is an essential component of a complete understanding of deviance and deviants. As you read them, think about how definitions are determined and applied. What are the factors that perpetrators and victims focus on when defining acts as deviant? How do earlier life experiences influence people's processes of definition and interpretation? What are the consequences of defining and interpreting actions as nondeviant when other people do perceive them as deviant? Are individuals better off if they fail to realize they have been victims of deviance? ◆

15

How Women Define Their Experiences of Violence

Liz Kelly

Kelly *describes how women explain and define their violent victimization in different ways. These differences are evident in their vocabulary, their reliance on stereotypes to explain what happened to them, and how their responses to victimization are influenced by their definitions of what happened. Regarding deviance, this article shows that even though people may have similar experiences, they may have very different ways of thinking about them and constructing their experiences in their minds.*

In order to define something, a word has to exist with which to name it. . . . The name, once known, must be applicable to one's own experience. Although this seems self-evident, neglecting this factor has significant implications for research design, analysis, and conclusions in the domain of woman abuse. Access to a name is the first step in defining experiences of sexual violence. [T]he term *sexual violence* is used to refer to all forms of violence women and girls experience from men and boys. One central theme of the research project on which this chapter is based has been to explore the similarities and differences among a range of forms of violence. Distinctions between "sexual" and "physical" assaults are considered false and/or arbitrary, both from the perspective of feminist theory (MacKinnon, 1979; 1982) and in terms of

how women experience violence and abuse (Kelly, 1988). . . .

In feminist writing on the patriarchal structure and content of language (see, for example, Daly, 1979; Spender, 1980), writers stress that women's experience is silenced and made invisible by the lack of words with which to name it. A major contribution of feminist social action around sexual violence has been to provide and create new words with which to describe and name our experience. For example, the terms *battered woman and sexual harassment* did not exist [30] years ago. Even if a name exists and is known, the way it is understood can vary greatly. For example, feminists have challenged the limited traditional definitions of forms of sexual violence by expanding the definition of *rape* to include unwanted and/or forced intercourse between husband and wife and by including psychological abuse and coercive sex in the definition of domestic violence. Limited definitions tend to draw on stereotypes of forms of sexual violence, stressing particular features and ignoring others.

This [article] explores the themes of naming, defining, and redefining sexual violence, using data from an in-depth study of how women experience and cope with sexual violence. After examination of current definitions of sexual violence, the feminist perspective underlying the methodology and analysis is presented. After detailed discussion of the factors affecting how women defined their experiences of sexual violence, implications for research design, intervention, and feminist research and practice are summarized.

The Importance of Definitions

In our culture, the meaning of words such as *rape, battering* or *incest* are often taken for granted. These terms are often employed uncritically in social science research as analytic categories defined before the research is begun. The reports of women who have been victimized are then recorded with these predetermined categories. This often results in the distortion and even exclusion of instances of sexual violence, as it fails to take account of the complexity of how women define and understand their own experience(s).

Several researchers has recently acknowledged the importance and complexity of this issue, and have begun to change the kinds of questions they ask women. For example, in the past, researchers would ask, "Have you ever been raped?" This question assumed that the woman and the researcher shared a common definition of what counts as rape. However, many women did not define an experience as "rape," although it may be so defined by an outside observer (Finkelhor and Yllö, 1983; Russell, 1982). Now, more open-ended terms are used, such as "have you ever been forced to have sex?" How questions are posed influences the kinds of incidence figures obtained by research. . . .

Although many researchers are aware of this fundamental problem, there is still little research to date that examines whether women define certain experiences as violence of a particular sort and/or that explores the definitional parameters by which women label incidents as sexual violence. For example, although there have been a considerable number of investigations of attitudes toward rape (see Pugh, 1983), only a minority of studies explicitly examine the underlying implicit question—how rape is defined (Schepple and Bart, 1983; Zellman, Goodchilds, Johnson, and Giarusso, 1981). There are almost no studies to date that explore women's definitions of battering, incest, or sexual harassment. . . .

How Women Define Sexual Violence: An Empirical Study

The goals of my research were: (1) to document the range of sexual violence women experience in their lives, (2) to explore the links between different forms of sexual violence, and (3) to study the long-term impact of rape, incest, and domestic violence. My interest in the process of defining and naming sexual violence developed while analyzing the interview data.

Sample

In-depth interviews were conducted with 60 women, 48 of whom also took part in follow-up interviews. In order to reach a wider spectrum of women than is commonly studied (usually women who report to official or voluntary agencies), women were contacted by a number of methods including articles and letters in newspapers and magazines, and solicitation through radio announcements, talks, and discussions at a range of community women's groups. Thirty women volunteered because they had experienced rape, incest or battering (10 in each category). Another 30 women were interviewed who did not necessarily identify themselves as survivors of any form of sexual or physical abuse. The predominantly white sample was characterized by women ranging in age, social class, marital status, occupation, and sexual orientation.

Methodology

. . . The interview guide was carefully developed so that women could report events they experienced as abusive but had not named as a particular form of sexual violence. Interview questions about various forms of sexual violence were organized chronologically, moving through childhood and adolescence to adulthood. Early questions used open-ended terms. Women were asked if they had ever felt pressured to have sex, had ever had a negative sexual experience in childhood or adolescence, or had ever experienced violence in intimate relationships. Later questions referred explicitly to rape, incest, and domestic violence. It was therefore possible to explore factors that affected how women defined their own experiences over time. In data analysis, women's own definitions were respected and terms such as pressurized sex and coercive sex have been used to reflect this. . . .

Results

The results will be summarized according to major content areas: (1) how women defined events when they first occurred and whether these definitions changed over time; (2) stereotypes; (3) the coping strategies of forgetting and minimizing; and (4) the process of redefinition.

Defining Sexual Violence

Certain of the detailed questions on rape, incest, and domestic violence referred to how women defined the events when they first occurred and whether these definitions had changed over time. Over 60% of the women did not initially define their experiences as a form of sexual violence. However, 50% of the incidents of physical abuse by a partner were defined as "violence" as the abuse continued. About 70% of the women changed their definitions of their experiences over time, almost always in the direction of relabeling an incident as abuse. Even though women experienced similar acts of assaults against them by men, they often defined these experiences in very different ways. This, coupled with the fact that women were often not sure how to define or label particular events, confirms the importance of the issues of naming and defining.

> I didn't really understand what he was doing. I knew that it was wrong, but I didn't understand—I didn't know what sex was so I couldn't call it sex.
>
> I called it not being very nice (laughs). I knew there was something wrong with it, I knew I didn't like it but I don't think I had a name for it. The older I got, the more I came to see it as abusive. It's only very recently, the last year say, that I see it as incest.

Some of the names that have been applied to domestic violence caused problems for some women. *Wife beating* implies that violence only happens to married women. The terms *beating* and *battering* tended to be understood in terms of severe, frequent physical violence.

> What he did wasn't exactly battering but it was the *threat*. I remember one night I spent the whole night in a state of terror, nothing less than terror *all night*. . . . And that was *worse* to me than getting whacked. . . . That waiting without confrontation is just so frightening.

> Quite a lot of time he wasn't physically violent but there was just *threat all the time* you see. . . . It was mental cruelty, as there was always the threat of physical violence.

> Mental violence is something you can't pinpoint. I suppose physical violence is there . . . but you can't define mental torture. It comes in very funny ways.

In some situations, women, as girls or as adults, felt abused but were unable to name their experience at the time. Even when a name is known, however, women may not apply it to their own experience.

Certain forms of sexual violence are closer to acceptable "normal" behavior than others. Acts that were extensions of typical male behavior, and so further away from stereotypic definitions of sexual violence, were often difficult for women to define as abuse. For example, many men make assumptions of intimacy with women working in certain jobs, such as bar work or waitressing. It is difficult for women to name behaviors as "sexual harassment" when this same behavior is accepted and expected by customers, employers, and occasionally, female coworkers.

Many instances of sexual abuse and early incidents of incestuous abuse were extensions of affection considered appropriate between adults and children. Women remembered the confusion they felt in such circumstances, not understanding why being kissed or hugged by a male relative or friend made them feel so uncomfortable.

> He'd say, "Let's do a jigsaw" and when I went to sit down his hand would be there. I just thought it was ridiculous always having to sit on his hand.

For this woman, and for most of the incest survivors interviewed, the pattern of incestuous abuse changed. For one woman, however, her father's behavior remained an extension of accepted affectionate behavior. It took her much longer than the other incest survivors to define his behavior as abusive.

The way women distinguished between pressurized sex, coercive sex (assaults women described as being "like rape"), and rape clearly highlights the ambiguity of many situations for women. Over 80% of the women interviewed had felt pressured to have sex, often on a number of occasions by different men. Responding to the question about pressure to have sex, many women qualified their answer by saying there was no physical force. Women were often unsure how to define their experience when physical force was not used and when there were no obvious injuries. Moreover, the "seriousness" of the abuse was questioned, often despite the woman's own feelings and reactions. Being coerced to have sex or being raped by men with whom women had previously had consensual sex were extensions of the more common pressure. Knowing the man and the previous nature of the relationship made defining the event as rape more difficult.

In many instances of forced or coerced sex, women submitted because of the perceived threat of violence. They were not physically hurt nor did they resist throughout. Both of these factors influenced how they defined the event afterwards.

> I don't know whether to regard it as an assault or not. Last summer I was hitching to the coast. This man who gave me a lift was chatting and I said I was unemployed and poor and he said, "Well, I know one way you can earn some money quickly." He said if I gave him a blow job, he'd pay me five pounds. I didn't want to, but he became very insistent and said, "I'll give you ten." took it out of his wallet while steering erratically across the road. His manner frightened me *very much*. I didn't know what would happen if I kept insisting no. I thought the best thing to do was to accept this arrangement, as it might prevent me from being raped or physically hurt—so that's what I did.

She added during the follow-up interview:

> I think it was an assault because I was definitely coerced. . . . My feelings about it are contradictory—on the one hand, I feel that I perhaps had some choice in submitting to it and on the other I was forced.

Stereotypes

Every person has his or her own common sense definition of what constitutes different forms of sexual violence, which are often linked to explanations of why sexual violence happens, who commits it, and which women experience it. Definitions can be limited or broad in their scope. Many of the more limited, "common sense" definitions of forms of sexual violence draw on stereotypes. Stereotypes are highly simplified descriptions that exclude certain factors while stressing others. For many women, accepting these lim-

ited definitions and stereotypes results in a disjunction between the reality of their experience and how they are encouraged by society to interpret it.

Stereotypic representations of sexual violence suggest that violence is relatively infrequent, takes place in particular circumstances, and is directed at certain types of women by certain types of men. Such stereotypes imply that it is relatively easy to distinguish between what is and what is not sexual violence. But many of the experiences documented in the interviews did not fit the stereotypic definitions, and so the women were often unlikely to name an experience as a particular form of sexual violence at the time. For example, rape is stereotypically defined as sexual assault by a stranger who uses high levels of physical force against a woman he doesn't know (Chandler and Tomey, 1981; Holmstrom and Burgess, 1978). The woman is expected to resist throughout. This stereotype prevented a number of women from defining their experience of forced sex as rape at the time of the assault:

> For a while, I didn't even think it was rape since I had let him into the house and I knew him. I had this idea that rape was something that happened to you in an alley.

> Well, I suppose I thought that rape was something that happens to you on the street, like with a complete stranger. [ironic laugh]

> It wasn't classic textbook—as I then thought rape was.

This limited definition of rape also affected whether women defined sexual assaults by family members as rape:

> I thought rape was a violent act and the woman got hurt, physically hurt. . . . When I look back now I feel, yes, I must have been raped. But not in the way most people mean rape—the public view of rape. I feel I've been raped but it's an acceptable rape.

> In a way I suppose what happened with my father was almost always rape, wasn't it? It was always against my wishes—yeah, I've never thought of it like that before.

Because rape is stereotypically defined as a rare experience between a woman and an anonymous assailant, many women who were forced to have sex repeatedly within intimate relationships, or who had been forced to have sex by a number of men, did not define these experiences as "rape." Often, women who had been repeatedly coerced to have sex defined one incident "rape" and the others "forced sex." This linguistic device protected women from acknowledging that they had been raped more than once. The incident labeled rape was usually the one where the man used the most physical force, where the woman resisted throughout, or where the relationship between the woman and the man was least close, such as forced sex by an acquaintance or friend rather than a partner. Part of the difficulty in defining assaults by friends, partners, or relatives as rape may be that the rapist is someone for whom the woman has, or once had, positive feelings. The stereotypes of rapists and child molesters seldom fit women's friends, lovers, husbands, or fathers, even when they had committed acts of sexual assault.

In contrast, the "common sense" stereotypes of domestic violence focus on other social and psychological characteristics. "Battered wives" are portrayed as poor, weak, and downtrodden and as nagging women who "deserve" to be hit. Stereotypes of batterers often focus on aggressive personalities or alcohol abuse. Battering is defined as frequent, life threatening violence. These stereotypes seldom fit women's experiences. One woman helped establish a refuge for battered women in her town. Although her husband was beating her at the time, she did not make the conscious connection between her situation and that of the women she was helping:

> I just thought that the incidents of violence that I—in order to be a battered woman you had to be really battered. I mean OK, I had a couple of bad incidents, but mostly it was pretty minor, in inverted commas, "violence." I didn't see myself in that category, as a battered woman at all.

Another woman stated:

> I feel now that the sort of image of the battered woman being basically ill-educated, inarticulate and poor is totally misconceived. Not nearly enough is written and talked about women who are not beaten up by drunken husbands every week, but who were in my situation.

Coping Strategies: Forgetting and Minimizing

Anyone who has worked with abused women or done research on sexual violence will have noticed that many women forget experiences of abuse, have vague and sketchy memories of the actual incidents of abuse and may use phrases like, "It wasn't that bad, really." Rather than interpret these responses, as some in the mental health community tend to, as evidence of deception, resistance, or manipulation, they must be understood as the result of two common adaptive coping strategies to experiences of victimization: forgetting and minimizing.

Forgetting. It is obvious that in order to define an event one must know that it has happened. Initially, I was surprised when women told me they had forgotten abusive experiences for long periods of time. I stopped being surprised as more and more women discussed this and as I myself remembered previously forgotten personal experiences during the research. We forget experiences in order to cope with an event that we do not understand, cannot name, or that places acute stress on our emotional resources. McCombie (1976) is one of a number of researchers to note that an immediate response of a substantial number of women to rape is to want to forget the experience. Forgetting is one of a range of coping strategies women use in relation to sexual violence.

Forgetting can take several different forms. When we have no words with which to name and understand experiences, memories are likely to be suppressed. The memory can become conscious only when we have the knowledge that enables us to make rational sense of the event(s) and of our reactions. This form of forgetting was particularly common to the women interviewed who reported childhood sexual abuse or rape. Almost 60% of the women who had been raped and 62% of the women who had been incestuously abused forgot their experience for a period of time. Women who had been battered were likely to suppress details of the assaults, but not the whole experience:

I think half of me having a bad memory is because I don't want—I choose not to remember.

Remembering, for these women, almost always involved some sort of trigger: a book or article, a television program, dreams, giving birth, experiencing another assault, or talking to other women.

For a long time I didn't think about it [incest]. It hadn't happened. It didn't exist. If I saw him, it would come into my mind for a split second. It wasn't until . . . I can remember the exact day—I was in a group and women were talking about what had happened to them. I was wondering what I could do because I hadn't any experiences like that and suddenly I thought, "Oh yes you have."

I didn't really want to think of it [incest]. It was just part of life that I forgot.

I told you events, like the miscarriage, but there was other stuff as well. I had been raped by him [her husband] and it came out in a group session. It just came into my head and I started crying and suddenly it all came out.

Many memories were triggered for the women by the interview and/or by reading their transcript. The fact that a number of women had not recalled certain events but remembered them later points to how prevalent the adaptive coping strategy of forgetting is and to the impossibility of accurately assessing incidence through single questions in survey questionnaires.

For some women, another factor contributing to forgetting was not wanting to be defined by self or by others as "victims." The shame and self-blame that many women recall following assaults may contribute to this, as does the stigma and blame that women expected from others. It is interesting that a number of the triggers prompting women to remember involved hearing or reading comments that blamed abused women:

I *had* to make him understand. It was really important to me and to make him stop

talking. Like an idiot, I suddenly said, "Well this is what happened to me," and I totally freaked out. I suddenly thought, "Oh my God, this *is* what happened to me!"

Women often forgot incidents that they did not define as "serious" and/or that happened frequently. For example, when discussing street harassment, many women commented on the fact that it was a common experience but they could not remember specific incidents.

Forgetting was helpful for some women, giving them time to gather strength before coping with the experience and its effects. For other women, however, forgetting had serious consequences. The abusive experience had affected their feelings, behavior, and attitudes toward themselves and others, but they had no way of understanding how. The most extreme example of this was a woman who had been sexually abused by a number of family friends in childhood. She had only begun to remember the abuse when we first met. Since 18, she had been convinced she was "mad," and had tried to injure herself and commit suicide numerous times, resulting in 13 hospitalizations with drug and electroconvulsive therapy. She attributed the recent improvement in her mental health to knowing that her behavior was the result of abuse. She was extremely angry that no one involved in her treatment had attempted to discover the cause of her distress.

Minimizing. The term minimizing refers to the process whereby women tried to limit the importance and impact of incidents that they defined as abusive to some degree. They either minimized the seriousness of the assault in order to minimize its effects or they minimized the effects in order to minimize the assault. In both cases, this required the control and suppression of women's feelings and reactions at the time and over time. For example, if women believed others would not define their experiences as serious, they described and/or publicly responded to the events in ways that were often at odds with their emotional reactions. On the other hand, many women minimized the effects on them in order to cope with ongoing abuse. These must again be seen as adaptive coping strategies. . . .

J. Radford (1987) notes the frequency with which women respondents in a community incidence study prefaced accounts of street harassment and assault with remarks such as "nothing really happened" or "I was lucky really." She suggests that comparing one's experience to something "worse," such as rape, is a coping strategy that makes one's own experience seem less serious and enables women to continue with their daily lives. By minimizing the event, the fear and threat of possible future assaults is also minimized. Minimizing requires women to deny the reality of their experience at the time, and to define as "not serious" consequences that may, in reality, be lasting and severe.

> Looking back, it wasn't that bad, but for me it was the most awful thing that ever happened.

> It was very confusing to know what to make of it at the time. I had a clash of attitudes—sort of not wanting to make a fuss because, in fact, I had got away quite light, but actually feeling quite damaged.

Getting "away quite light" in this case meant not being raped. This woman had, however, been terrified at the time and recalled experiencing many of the reactions of women immediately after a rape.

Women experiencing physical abuse in intimate relationships also minimized its severity. Very few of the women who had experienced physical violence by their partners only once or infrequently defined these events as domestic violence. Frequency of violence was, in fact, the most important factor influencing how soon a woman defined a man's behavior as abusive. When there were long gaps between incidents, women minimized the violence by focusing on the nonabusive times, and hoping that it would not occur in the future.

> It was really cyclical actually, really incredible. And the odd thing was that in the good periods I could hardly remember the bad times. It was almost as if I was leading two different lives.
>
> There are long gaps sometimes . . . if it had been continuous battering then I'd

have just gone. There were always times of hope.

Taking the severity of the violence seriously, specifically its life threatening nature, prompted many women to leave violent men. For a number of women, it was only in retrospect, after they had left, that they could acknowledge the severity of the violence and its effects on them.

The Process of Redefinition

Definitions of sexual violence are usually perceived as fixed in time. But names and definitions are not static. Women's understandings of what happened to them often change over time. Many factors contribute to this, including the creation of terms (such as "battering" or "marital rape") that allow women to name experiences previously silenced, the personal development of the woman over time, and the availability of a supportive and accepting social network. This process of redefinition is most evident when women have been battered or have suffered incest as children. As women begin to redefine incidents as sexual violence, they often may make connections with other experiences, which are also named as sexual violence. . . .

Over time, women often remember more details of what happened to them, and so redefine events in new ways. At the same time, redefining what they have experienced often enables them to remember more of the abuse. This process can be extremely distressing and painful. But through the process of redefinition, women began to focus on and validate their own feelings and reactions—a crucial aspect of working through the experience of sexual violence. A quote from one incest survivor who began redefining her sexual abuse during our interviews illustrates this process.

> The things that I was unsure about were basically the things that I came out with about the incest thing. I hadn't worked that out at all and it just all came out. It was really revelatory to me because I'd never . . . I'd always accepted it, that there was something wrong between me and my father, something indistinguishably

wrong about our relationship, but I never verbalized it ever, but it really came out with your questions. It was only through reading it over that I realized what I'd said and seeing how hard certain questions were for me to answer and therefore recognizing there were big blocks about certain things. I now know that my father had sexual feelings towards me . . . that the way he was with me, even the violence, was a way of communicating with me sexually . . . but to say that it's incest, I think incest is too much of a decision right now.

It was clear from the interviews that, through the process of redefinition, women were focusing on their own feelings and reactions rather than on stereotypes or limited definitions or the perceptions of others. They were no longer minimizing the severity of the assault(s) or the effects on them. Remembering and redefining are empowering for women in a number of ways. In acknowledging abuse, women are able to look at and find ways of coping with its effects. They are also likely to develop precautionary strategies in order to prevent further abuse. These strategies involve taking more control over their lives and choices. For example, many women placed a positive value on developing a strong belief in their right to say "no" to sex when they didn't want it. The process often involved women shifting blame from themselves to the abusive man, which enabled them to express anger. This anger, and the determination to keep control of one's life, were linked to politicization for several women, who felt that their sympathy for feminism was a result of understanding their own experience.

Conclusions

For women, naming and defining experiences of sexual violence is not a simple process. It may not take place until many years after an abusive experience has occurred. This process, regardless of its timing, is a crucial and empowering one involving claiming one's experiences, coping with its effects. . . .

This research also points to possible directions for preventive action. Many children experience sexual violence before they have

words to encode what happened to them, or they lack the vocabulary to describe to others what has occurred. The development of sex education programs that provide children with a proper vocabulary can significantly address this problem. For example, in the United States, prevention programs are being developed that emphasize children's right to control who touches them and how.

But the first step is to develop names and definitions of sexual violence that accurately reflect women's experiences from their own frames of reference. Feminists have made great progress in extending current definitions and providing new names for sexual violence. Much energy has been directed toward legal reform, establishing codes of conduct, and changing professional practice. We need to focus more on reaching women with our analyses. The way we name and understand our experiences is not a static process. It is changing and dynamic. It may be a never-ending process as we understand more about the many subtle ways sexual violence can be experienced. It is essential that we develop a language, names, and definitions, that reflect our growing understanding. Feminist research can make a major contribution in this area.

References

Chandler, S. and M. Tomey. 1981. The Decisions and Processing of the Rape Victim Through the Criminal Justice System." *California Sociologist,* 4(2), 156–169.

Daly, M. 1979. *Gyn/Ecology.* London: Women's Press.

Finkelhor, D. and K. Yllö. 1983. Rape in Marriage: A Sociological View. In D. Finkelhor, R. Gelles, G. Hotaling, and M. Straus (Eds.), *The Dark Side of Families.* Newbury Park, CA: Sage.

Holmstrom, L. and A. Burgess. 1978. *The Victims of Rape: Institutional Reaction.* New York: John Wiley.

Kelly, L. 1988. *Surviving Sexual Violence.* Cambridge: Polity Press.

MacKinnon, C. 1979. *Sexual Harassment of Women.* New Haven: Yale University Press.

McCombie, S. 1976. Characteristics of Rape Victims As Seen in Crisis Intervention. *Smith College Studies in Social Work,* 46:137–158.

Pugh, M.D. 1983. Contributory Fault and Rape Convictions: Loglinear Models for Blaming the Victim. *Social Psychology Quarterly,* 46(3), 233–242.

Radford, J. 1987. Policing Male Violence—Policing Women. In J. Hanmer and N. Maynard (Eds.), *Women, Violence and Social Control.* London: Macmillan.

Radford, L. 1987. Legalising Woman Abuse. In J. Hanmer and M. Maynard (Eds.), *Women, Violence and Social Control.* London: Macmillan.

Russell, D. 1982. *Marital Rape.* New York: MacMillan

Scheppie, K. and P. Bart. 1983. Through Women's Eyes: Defining Danger in the Wake of Sexual Assault. *Journal of Social Issues,* 39(2):63–80.

Spender, D. 1980. *Man-Made Language.* London: Routledge and Kegan Paul.

Stanko, E. 1985. *Intimate Intrusions.* London: Routledge & Kegan Paul.

Zellman, G. J. Goodchilds, P. Johnson, and R. Giarusso. 1981. *Teenagers' Application of the Label "Rape" to Nonconcensual Sex Between Acquaintances.* Unpublished paper.

16

Rural Woman Abuse: The Voices of Kentucky Women

Neil Websdale

Websdale explores the violence and abuse that women in rural communities experience in their homes. Most people associate domestic violence with urban poor people, but Websdale points out that women in rural communities suffer a great degree of abuse as well. Websdale points out the inaccuracies of common assumptions and stereotypes about where violence and deviance are likely to be found. Moreover, he discusses how rural beliefs about violence and deviance affect women's perceptions of themselves as battered, as well their friends' and family's tendency to believe that they have been beaten.

According to the extant research literature, rural areas are far less likely to witness violent crime than urban areas. However, this does not mean there are not highly significant forms of violent crime in rural communities. In this exploratory article, I use ethnographic data to provide rich empirical evidence about one such form of violent crime: woman abuse. The magnitude and seriousness of woman abuse have been well documented in the research literature (see Dobash and Dobash, 1979; Finkelhor and Yllo, 1985; Hanmer and Saunders, 1984; Pagelow, 1981; Radford and Russell, 1992). This literature focuses almost exclusively on urban areas. Rural woman abuse has therefore been much neglected in the burgeoning research on domestic violence. I employ the term *woman abuse* instead of terms such as *domestic violence* or *family violence*, because the latter terms fail to convey the fact that offensive violence between adults in families is largely perpetrated by men against women. . . .

Rural and Urban Social Life

According to the U.S. Census Bureau, a community is rural if it has a population of less than 2,500 inhabitants. While heeding Bachman's (1992: 547) reservations about labeling a unit as large as a state as rural, it is nevertheless possible to describe some states as "primarily rural" or "more rural" than others. Using the U.S. Census definition, Kentucky ranks eighth out of the 50 states and the District of Columbia, with 48.2% of its population being rural. Among those states with a higher percentage of rural dwellers than Kentucky (Vermont, West Virginia, Maine, Mississippi, South Dakota, North Carolina, and New Hampshire), only North Carolina has a larger rural population. From these figures, it seems reasonable to present Kentucky as a state that, at least in terms of population, typifies those most rural states in the country. . . .

Rural communities continue to define the roles of men and women more narrowly than urban communities. In the latter, women have moved into paid employment in larger numbers and into a greater range of occupations. Rural women receive lower pay than women receive in urban areas (Gorham, 1992). In rural areas, the division of labor between men and women is more stereotypically gendered (Fassinger and Schwarzweller, 1984; Gagné, 1992). This includes rural women being more rigidly tied to housework and child care (Bushy, 1993; Gagné, 1992). For example, Patricia Gagné's (1992) ethnographic study of Raven Ridge, a small, rural, central Appalachian community, revealed a strong gendering in family life. She notes, "When men worked, they tended to commute shorter distances and rarely traveled with children. Few prepared meals, did housework, or took care of children after work" (p. 394).

Images of rural women's place are also intimately tied up with religious culture. The stronger influence of fundamentalist religion in rural areas bolsters this ideology of separate spheres of social action for men and women. . . .

Geographical isolation in rural areas often amplifies the subordination and loneliness of many women in the home. Such isolation sometimes provides opportunities for batterers to attempt to control women in ways that either would not be possible in cities or would not be as effective. Duncan and Lamborghini (1994) found similar isolation in their analysis of a chronically poor, coal-dependent, Appalachian community. Likewise, rural women will be more cut off from the potentially beneficial services of the state, such as better health care and social services, public transportation, independent housing, educational opportunities, and licensed child care.

The greater homogeneity of rural areas and the allegedly greater strength of the rural collective conscience have led to stereotypical assumptions that rural areas were and are less criminogenic and much less prone to violence than their urban counterparts. While this logic may be borne out by current research evidence on public-sphere violence, it is not supported by what little we know about private-sphere rural violence. . . .

Accessing Rural Woman Abuse: The Ethnographic Method

. . . Ethnographic methodologies are a well-established research tradition in sociology. They include methods such as overt and covert observation of social life, overt and covert participant observation, and various forms of interviewing. . . . The desire of ethnographers to "tell it like it is" means that understanding social life turns on whether or not the sociologist can access the attitudes and meanings of social actors themselves through the research medium. . . . More than anything [else], my ethnographic approach is designed to present rural woman abuse through the eyes and words of the women who have experienced it. . . .

As a college professor, I lived and worked in a small town in eastern Kentucky for a period of 2 years. I made contact with the director of the local spouse-abuse shelter and the leaders of the Kentucky Domestic Violence Association (KDVA) and informed them of my desire to study rural woman abuse. . . . In short, the KDVA and seven individual shelters opened their doors to me and allowed me to interview resident battered women. . . .

Although these interviews with battered women formed the centerpiece of the ethnography, I engaged in a number of other activities in order to immerse myself in local culture and make some sense of rural woman abuse. In addition to interviewing women, I conducted focused interviews with police officers, social workers, judges, spouse abuse shelter workers, and attorneys. In total, I interviewed 85 people as part of the project. These interviews were conducted over a 3-year period from 1991 through 1994. During this time, I also served on the advisory board of one of the spouse-abuse shelters, attended fund-raisers, rode with police officers to observe their performance at "domestics," observed domestic abuse court cases, acted as an external evaluator of a Homeless Job Training Initiative grant at the seven spouse-abuse shelters where I conducted my interviewing, and acted as a source of research information for the KDVA. Perhaps most important, I lived and worked in the community for 2 years, albeit in some ways as an outsider. These other experiences augmented my interview findings.

Woman Abuse in Rural Regions: The Missing Words of Battered Women

In fiscal year 1991-1992, the KDVA housed 2,300 battered women for varying periods of time. The rural outreach programs from each of the 16 shelters in the state reveal that many rural battered women cannot or will not use the services of shelters. This suggests there is a potentially large number of rural battered women whose plight is either not known or not officially documented.

State police officer Davis, who patrols several remote rural counties in Eastern Kentucky, reported that fully half of his assault calls involved domestics: "I'd say 50% of them are assaults associated with domestics." Municipal police officer Rudy also pointed to the central place of domestic disorder in the small town of Lovelace in rural Eastern Kentucky:

> Websdale: Is domestic violence a thing that you deal with very often?
> Rudy: Yes. I'd say that probably it rates real high as one of our complaints goes. We have quite a few of those.

Municipal officer Hogan notes that "domestic violence" is a deeply ingrained feature of social life in rural communities in Kentucky. He opines: "The urban and the rural settings are altogether different. And you've got things that we encounter that's almost an accepted way of life. I mean, you're combattin' something that's been goin' on in this part of the country for years and years and years."

Circuit Judge Fonda reported a very high level of domestic violence in the two rural counties over which she presides. Most of this abuse was directed at women who, she perceived, reported the abuse accurately to her. . . .

It is not my argument that acts of woman abuse differ greatly in rural areas. My impression (pending more quantitative research) is that rural woman abuse is at least as prevalent as urban woman abuse. This is the impression of most of my interviewees, be they battered women or those working professionally in the field. . . .

The lifestyles of rural women may make it especially difficult to escape from their batterers or to use the services of spouse abuse shelters. A number of the women I interviewed did not have access to a car or did not have a license to drive. At times, abusive partners controlled their physical movements by recording the mileage reading on any vehicle that was left at home. Other abusers disabled the vehicle in some way. Some of the households in rural areas did not have phones. In some cases where phones were present, the abuser was known to take the phone receiver out with him when he left the house. Some battered women who live up what is locally called a "hollow" (a secluded dirt road cul-de-sac with a small number of houses on it) seem

to live extraordinarily isolated lives. Several of these women reported not having had any friends for years. With no public transportation and large distances between houses, they reported that it was often physically difficult to engage in community life.

The isolation of some rural settings appears to put battered women at a considerable disadvantage. Some women reported it was simply too difficult to leave a hollow or other isolated setting. Penny. . .was typical of many of the rural women I interviewed. With four young children and a violent husband, who she felt kept her pregnant to keep her out of the reach of other men, Penny was isolated both socially and geographically. Her nuclear family lived "on top of a mountain" about 8 miles from the nearest small town. Penny's house was separated from others by several acres of woodland. Her husband, Billy, through a variety of controlling tactics, played an active part in maintaining her isolation.

> Websdale: Tell me a little bit about your involvement with the community. Were you involved with social groups, church groups, or stuff like that at all?
> Penny: No. Not really. It's mostly like farm land. I didn't really get involved in the groups. Billy really didn't let me get involved. He was the type that wanted you to stay home, didn't want you to associate, be anywhere around men. . . . Nobody was allowed up there on the hill.

As in Penny's case, the limiting effects of isolation were compounded if women had children to care for. In cases where the abuser's parents lived next door or in the same house, it was especially difficult to get away. I make these points because the women who were the victims of this abuse did plan their escape. They did devise strategies to resist the abuse of their partners. It is not the finding of these interviews that battered women in rural areas are backward or suffer from what some psychologists call learned helplessness. On the contrary, there are very real geographical, economic, and social constraints that amplify the controls exerted by the terrorist-like tactics of their partners.

Physical Abuse

In this article, physical abuse refers to assaults, such as kicking, punching, slapping, choking, shooting, knifing, hair pulling, biting, and burning. Like a number of other interviewees who had resided in rural communities for a long period, Sally knew of other women who reported experiencing woman abuse. She lived in the small rural community of Sale.

> Websdale: What do you mean, it [woman abuse] goes on a lot?
> Sally: There are a lot of people, my friends, that got married and I know their husbands beat them. And the law does nothin'.
> Websdale: How do you know this? Through informal conversations?
> Sally: Yeah, with them.

With Sally, we sense an underbelly to rural social life characterized by systemic violence against women in families. This underbelly is something well-known to at least some women.

Barbara, who endured physical abuse for 4 years at the hands of her violent husband, recalled the first time she was physically abused:

> Barbara: We had a house. He'd come in, was drinkin', and I was at the kitchen stove cookin'. The next thing I knew he came in there and just kicked me right between the legs. I turned around and I said, 'What's wrong with you?" And he just started slappin' me and kickin' me, and that's when he twisted my arm and broke it. I kept coverin' my face, and he just kept kickin' it and kickin' and kickin'. He grabbed me by the hair and the head, and he threw me in the living room. Then he just went on to the bed. All like it wasn't nothin'. Like he didn't do anything.

Barbara's words echo those of a number of other interviewees, who talked of the way their abusers seemed to see their abusive behavior as culturally sanctioned or as insignificant. Again, such sentiments point to the existence of a subculture of acquiescence or tolerance on the part of some rural men when it comes to woman abuse.

Intimate violence against women cannot be divorced from the broader rural sociocultural setting, which includes a long-established tradition of gun ownership. A gun can be used to threaten or shoot people. Although rates of gun ownership are higher in rural areas, research indicates that people in rural regions are more likely to use their guns for hunting and not crime (Bordua and Lizotte, 1979; Bureau of Justice Statistics, 1990; Weisheit et al. 1994). . . . In rural areas, perpetrators of woman abuse may not use their guns to rob strangers on the street, but from my ethnographic data, it is clear that many of them think nothing of using guns to intimidate their wives or partners. It could be that rural isolation aggravates the tendency to use handguns against intimate others for purposes of intimidation.

To her detriment, June found that a gun can also be used as a bludgeoning instrument. June described how she was pistol whipped by her abuser in a particularly gruesome ceremony of subordination:

> June: He got drunk. He laid down and went to sleep, but I walked down the road and visited my neighbor. Me and her has been friends for a long time. When I come back he was sittin' in the dark in his bedroom. He was sittin' on the bed. Had this 357 Magnum. He said, "June, you get down on this floor right now. You crawl to me." And when I got to his feet, he took that pistol and hit me right alongside of the head. I thought I was gonna die. I still got the knot from it. He said, "If you even act like you're gonna run, I'll blow your brains all over this wall." I couldn't help it. I took off anyhow. And I run all the way up the road just screamin' and hollerin' cause there was blood all over me, my shoes, my clothes. It was runnin' down the side of my face. And I got to this neighbor's house and they didn't believe nothin' I was tellin' 'em. They just wasn't believin' me. But she did get a washrag and wash some of the blood off of me.

In this excerpt, we witness two important and paradoxical themes about the social context within which physical violence against rural women is embedded. First, June is not entirely isolated; she returns to her abuser from visiting a neighbor she had known for a long time. Second, other neighbors, even when presented with the spectacle of her injuries, did not believe that she had been abused. June's description of events is not unique. Her isolation was relative. She did have a female friend nearby. Yet the response of unknown neighbors was one of disbelief.

Karen talked of being threatened with a gun by her abuser:

> Websdale: Has he ever pulled a gun on you?
>
> Karen: One night about 2 months ago he did. He said, "If you leave, I'll blow your head off." And he had the gun right by the bed.

Her abuser intimidated her with guns in other ways that may be more common in rural settings, where gun use is more widely accepted for hunting:

> Karen: He'd shoot somethin'. He'd say, "That could be your head, you know."
>
> Websdale: So he'd shoot something in the house?
>
> Karen: No. Not in the house. We'd be out walkin' around and bein' normal, you know. And he'd shoot a bottle or can and say, "that could be your head."

Bernice, who lived in the small town of Graperise in the heart of rural eastern Kentucky, endured what she described as continuous threats against her life. Many women, like Bernice, reported a multitude of different forms of physical abuse:

> Websdale: Can you describe the forms of physical abuse?
>
> Bernice: He had slapped me, kicked me, choked me, pulled my hair, threw things at me. Hit me with a 2 by 4, put a gun to my head, put a knife to my throat.

Similarly, Toni reported an extensive history of physical victimization at the hands of her sadistic husband: "He would hit me with belts, and he would say, 'don't you like that?' and I would be cryin' and he would tell me to stop cryin' and quit bein' a baby."

Bernice and Toni's interviews reveal something of the range of physical abuse directed at rural women. . . . Of particular importance here are women's reports of lack of transportation, geographical isolation that renders escape difficult, absence of effective social services intervention, and a cultural climate that fosters a view of women as subordinate. All of these factors tend to limit resistance and exacerbate abuse.

Sexual Abuse

. . . Russell (1990) argues for seeing wife rape as one pole on a continuum of sexual relations within marriage, with "voluntary, mutually desired, and satisfying sex at the other end" (p. xxvii). In between these two extremes, she situates what she calls "coercive sex" (without physical force or the threat of physical force) and "unwanted sex.". . . . Most women I interviewed reported having had "unwanted sex" or sex "to keep him quiet." This is not to say there is not a clear connection between marital rape and wife battering. Finkelhor and Yllo (1985) found that 50% of wife rape victims had also been battered. In addition, they note that battered women were roughly twice as likely to be the victims of multiple marital rapes.

Roughly half of the women I interviewed reported being forcibly raped by their abusers. June was one woman who reported a variety of forms of sexual violence:

> June: One time he made me leave with this one guy. He said, "Take her out and fuck her, I can't do nothin' for her." And that guy did. He took him up on it.
>
> Websdale: So he felt like you were his property or something?
>
> June: A piece of meat, I reckon.
>
> Websdale: Were there any other forced forms of sexual activity?
>
> June: Well, yeah, he did force me to do him blow jobs.

Connie is a typical example of a rural battered woman who engaged in nonconsensual sex with her abuser. Her participation kept him from "getting mad" and fulfilled his expectation that wives should service their husbands sexually.

Websdale: Were there any times in the 5 years that you were with him that he forced you to have sex or that you had sex against your will?

Connie: Not really forced. There was a lot of times that I really didn't want to, and he thought a woman should. And that was real uncomfortable.

Websdale: So you just felt that it was something you should do because you are a wife or something?

Connie: I didn't want to make him mad.

Websdale: Did that happen very often?

Connie: Quite often. I got to the point where I could live my whole life without it.

Toni talks about being assaulted while having sex. On occasion, her abuser held a knife to her throat in the full knowledge that she had been sexually molested at knifepoint as a child.

Toni: When we went to bed. He put a knife to my throat.

Websdale: He held a knife to your throat? When you say he held a knife to your throat, was he forcing you to have sex with him or was he just doing that to be cruel, or what was the reason?

Toni: He wasn't forcin' me to have sex with him. But he just liked that. . . . I don't think he would have brought a knife or anything like that to bed if I hadn't told him about my being sexually abused as a child. . . . He knew how I sat and cried over it and how it hurt.

In common with at least half of the interviewees, Katie reported that she had been forced to provide sexual services she explicitly told her abuser she did not want to provide.

Websdale: And when you say the sexual abuse was constant, what do you mean?

Katie: Um, he would force me. This is gross, but I'm going to say it. He would force me to give him head. He would force me to do things that I didn't want to do. That I was totally against.

These case illustrations do not tell us anything about sexual abuse that has not already been reported from urban areas. However, the sexual abuse of battered women in rural areas is not addressed by the extant research literature on either domestic violence or rural social life in general. The empirical evidence from my interviews shows that the rural family in Kentucky is not the idyllic and tranquil locus of social activity that the statistics on violent crime may suggest.

Emotional Abuse

Every woman I interviewed reported experiencing emotional abuse. Most reported this form of abuse in tandem with physical and/or sexual abuse. The effectiveness of emotional abuse as a means of controlling women is often enhanced by the rural geocultural milieu. Within this milieu many battered women live extremely isolated lives. Those women who reported living in physical isolation talked of the way that isolation amplified their abuser's ability to control them. Women who lived in smaller communities or within earshot of neighbors told how rural sociocultural mores dictated a certain place for women vis-à-vis men. Whether battered women's isolation is geographical, sociocultural, or both, many women find themselves without the emotional support of friends, neighbors, social services, and family. This lack of support makes it more difficult for victims of abuse to summon their psychological resources against the controlling behaviors of their abusers.

Just as the rural geocultural context provides men ample opportunities to control women, we must also remember that the individual control maneuvers of abusers may, in and of themselves, be the root of women's sociocultural and geographical isolation. Some women reported that abusers sought housing in isolated places to keep them away from the community and especially other men. Others noted that abusers, to varying degrees, discouraged the women from having close relationships with their family and friends. Still others noted that abusers had a generalized hostility toward agents of the state, be they social workers, police, health professionals, or others, and that this too made women more reluctant to seek professional help.

The emotional abuse of rural women, especially that designed to limit their physical and social mobility, forms a central part of an overall strategy of social control, even though it does not necessarily break the law. . . .

Typical examples of this emotional abuse include: continuous attacks on women's self-esteem, angry verbal outbursts, withholding of money, extreme jealousy, false accusations of infidelity, control over women's physical movement, isolation from friends and family, and threats of violence and other adverse consequences. Some women reported that the emotional abuse was worse than the physical or sexual abuse, insofar as it left deep-seated psychological scars. Others expressed confusion about the disjuncture between woman abuse and the ideals of harmonious family life. These ideals of harmonious family life may be more powerful in rural areas.

Ariel told of how her husband controlled her presentation of self and her bodily movement:

Ariel: I'm not allowed to go anywhere. I'm not allowed to cut my hair. I'm not allowed to wear makeup.

Websdale: So when you say not go anywhere, you mean like go to the mailbox or go to the store or . . .?

Ariel: Out. Like one day this past week there's nothin' there to eat. There's no refrigerator. So I told him, "I'm hungry and I want to go to town and get me somethin' to eat." I had $20. He put $20 in my purse. I'm gonna go to town and get somethin' to eat. He said, "OK." He said, 'Well, I'm going. I'll see you this evenin' about 5:00." And this is like 6:00 in the mornin'. Well, he got up and he went and turned my car ignition on. So it run my battery down. When I went out there at 11:00 to start it up to go get somethin' to eat, my battery was dead. There are little things that he would do to make sure that he knew where I was at. I wasn't allowed to go to my friends unless he went. Or to the store unless he went.

Ariel's case typified those in which the movement of rural women is seriously compromised by their abusers' tactics. The impact of being immobilized was all the greater in a rural area because of the lack of public transportation and the large distance separating her residence from those of others who might provide support or alternative accommodation.

Control of movement means much more, however, than abusers' disabling motor vehicles. As noted above, battered women were also cut off from their families. Margaret informed me that her husband restricted her access to her own family:

Margaret: He didn't want me to go around my family. He didn't give any reason. He just told me as long as I lived in his house, under his roof, I'd do what he said.

Websdale: How did you feel about that?

Margaret: Well I lived there. I didn't have any other choice. He lived there before I did.

Nancy's abuser had a generalized contempt for anything that reminded him of her relationships with other people: "He tore up my high school graduation pictures and destroyed anything that related to other people outside of the home."

Some women reported that abusers checked their movements by asking their children. Carla is a case in point. Again, it is not that such surveillance never occurs in urban areas. Rather, the surveillance of rural women has not been well-documented, and its impact as a social control mechanism may be greater because of their isolation.

Websdale: Did he ever try to control your movements? Tell you where you could go?

Carla: Yeah, he always did that. He'd come back home and accuse me and started askin' our little 3-year-old, "Who was here to see Mommie today? Who was with Mommie today? What was their names?" Start questionin' that little 3-year-old. And a 3-year-old ain't gonna know what to say. But he always said, "I bet you ran around with somebody, I bet you done this, I bet you done that with someone." I was always accused of stuff.

Another form of emotional abuse reported by women was the abuser's attempts to control the temperature of the family home, even if the abuser was not present in the home. Some men did this by disabling the thermostat, and others refused to provide money to heat the house. Serena talked of her husband's behavior with regard to heating their home: "He would follow me and turn the heat down. He refused to give me money for the gas.". . . .

Battered women who had reentered the education system found that abusers often derided their efforts and/or destroyed their curricular materials. Such emotional abuse was more likely to take place if the abuser was of a lower educational standing than his partner. This finding concurs with O'Brien (1971), who found that men were more likely to use violence against women if they did not have clear educational superiority over them.

Carly, who was in college at the time of the interview, reported that her husband was threatened by her educational advancement. In this excerpt, her husband abusively and without foundation implies that Carly's educational journey was moving her toward a different sexual orientation: "He calls me an educated bitch and resents my education. He overheard me talking to my friend about a film on homosexuality I had seen in a sociology class. He accused me of being homosexual."

In a manner consistent with reports of urban woman abuse, Jenny informed me that her husband emotionally hurt her by violating things that were dear to her: "He attacked my dogs and ripped pages out of my Bible."

Typifying the nature of emotional abuse in both rural and urban areas, Mona's abuser increased his controlling tactics as the relationship wore on:

> Mona: At first he wanted to pick on my friends. Then he said I did not need to see my family. Then he began to check the mileage on my car and wait for me while I was at work. He would follow me when I got off work. He continually accused me of seeing someone else.

. . . [R]ural women did not passively accept this abuse. They developed strategies about how to change it, to leave the relationship, protect themselves and their children, and sometimes how to exact revenge. At the time of the interviews, the women were living in spouse-abuse shelters in an active attempt to avoid being victimized. The excerpts that follow report women's resistance and are included as a corrective in case readers are left with the impression that rural battered women somehow acquiesced in their own victimization.

Roxy was especially angry about her husband's propensity for spending large amounts of their income on cocaine. She reported how she had worked out a way to shoot her husband if he hurt her again:

> Roxy: I'm gonna tell you what I did. I didn't actually do it, I just thought about it. He had came home, he was with a friend of his named Steven. And they were doin' cocaine. And I just got really mad. I was sittin' there watchin' TV, I didn't say anything. It was on a Saturday and he had his little ol' pistol, just a .25. I guess that could kill somebody. And he was tellin' me he just went and spent $100 for some cocaine. Well, I got mad. I couldn't take it. So he started cussin' me and stuff. So he left with his friend, Steven. I was sittin' there and I thought to myself I should go in, get this little pistol, and if he comes in and even acts like he's gonna put his hands on me, I'm gonna blow his leg off. I would never shoot to kill, but I'd hurt him.

Bonita schemed to escape from her abuser while he was away hunting. Notice the use of language in this excerpt, as she asked his permission to go over to her mother's while he is away. On one level, Bonita recognized her subordinate position, but she was still able to use it to her advantage. Her escape was planned in conjunction with her mother and social service workers. Without this support, Bonita may well have not managed to get away.

> Bonita: Well, my father-in-law's a coon hunter and my husband went with him the other night and I told him, "Can I go stay with Mom, can I visit with Mom while you go huntin'?" And he said, "Yeah." So my sister-in-law took me over there. When he come to get me I was gone.

Angela decided to leave her abusive husband after the nature of his abuse changed. Her husband wanted to start having sex with her daughter-in-law and also to force her daughter-in-law to have sex with other men.

> Angela: My daughter-in-law told me, "He is gonna have me too, he was gonna force me to go to bed with another man." I said, "No, no way" I said, "I'm out of here," . . . I packed my suitcase, put it in the back of the car and I left.

Brenda was threatened with a butcher's knife by her violent husband. She broke free, called the police and went to the shelter with her children.

> Brenda: We had got into it because he was messing around with [old] ladies and stuff like that. And so I called him. I told him he had to move out. He refused to move out, and he took a butcher knife and was gonna stab me in my side. But I broke loose from him. I ran out the door. I went to my neighbor's house and I called police. . . . The police brought me here and we've stayed here maybe 2 weeks. . . .

Future Directions: Some Theoretical and Policy Implications Suggested by the Empirical Evidence

The main contribution of this article is to offer empirical data about the much ignored social phenomenon of woman abuse in rural communities. . . . As noted, in spite of the multiple barriers faced by rural women, these women did engage in many acts of resistance and developed strategies to avoid being vulnerable to victimization. Such resistance attests to the agency of battered women in extremely adverse social situations. Although this issue is not the immediate focus of the article, it is also clear that battered women are often distanced from social service providers, schooling, health care, public transportation, and support from the criminal justice system. In short, there is a disjuncture between the everyday lives of rural battered women and the potentially supportive apparatus of the state (see Websdale, 1995).

Problems with service providers stem in part from the geographical isolation of rural areas, which makes it more difficult to travel to doctors' offices, regional hospitals, other social service providers, and schools. However, there are also characteristics of rural communities themselves that seem to work against the interests of battered women. This is especially the case with local law enforcement providers, whose support of battered women is sometimes compromised by their personal relationships with abusive men. This does not mean that there is a conspiracy among men in rural areas to keep battered women in a subordinate social position. Rather, it means that at times male police officers (by far the majority in rural Kentucky) will not enforce the law against abusive men who, because of their violent behavior toward their spouses, should be arrested. A number of women alluded to the poor support and what they perceived as a "compromised" response on the part of rural police. Interviewees made a qualitative distinction between the performance of state police and local rural police (sheriffs and municipal officers), with the former providing much more support for women. This support was reflected in a much greater willingness to make arrests, remove men from the home as opposed to removing women from the home, and inform battered women of their rights under the law.

Cynthia, a rural battered woman, was rather typical of women who did not call the police. She commented, "I was too scared to call because the officers knew my husband, I knew they wouldn't do anything." This intimacy between officer and abuser also worked against Janice calling the local sheriff's department during domestic altercations: "He was good buddies with the brother of my abuser. And that's the same way with the Sheriff's Department. That's the main reason why they didn't respond."

The case of Donna from Graperise illustrates the greater level of confidence that battered women have in the ability of the state police to intervene against their abusers: "Graperise Police Department does not bother him. The sheriff's department doesn't bother him. The only people that would like to see him go to jail and pay for the things that he's done is the Kentucky State Police."

Part of the reason rural battered women are more confident the state police will assist them is that the state police are detached from local politics. Sheriffs are elected and are sometimes reluctant to arrest abusers who offer them political support. In addition, some sheriffs have been involved in corrupt activities such as illegal drug running, turning a blind eye to illegal marijuana production (especially so in eastern Kentucky), bootlegging, and illegal gambling (see Davis and Potter, 1991). . . .

The rural compromise means something different when it comes to battered women seeking health care or social services. Leaving aside the difficulties of transportation from remote rural areas to the small towns that may offer these services, some battered women expressed concerns about the lack of privacy involved in going to an agency where they knew the personnel offering the services. Acknowledging they had been battered was one thing, but presenting injuries to local health providers who might gossip about them was also threatening to women. Similarly, seeking assistance from social service providers to obtain financial support to attempt to break away from an abusive relationship or to seek help around abuse issues also went against the grain of rural cultural mores. In some cases, these mores dictated that women should weather the storm in their abusive relationships and not break ranks by confiding in outsiders, such as social service providers. . . .

My interview data suggest that social and geographical isolation (and the attendant privatization of domestic relations) are central to the social condition of many rural battered women. In order to better contextualize rural woman abuse, we must integrate data on intimate violence against rural women with the extant literature on at least the following issues: the higher rates of marriage in rural areas; the greater disparities between men's and women's earnings in rural areas; the more limited involvement of rural women in public sphere activities, such as paid work and formal politics; the discourse on women's rights, which has tended to be concentrated in urban centers; the stronger and more patriarchal influence of religion in ru-

ral areas; and, in a related vein, the differences between rural and urban patriarchal ideology in general. The possibility that patriarchal ideology may be stronger in rural areas is particularly significant. As Michael Smith (1990) found, women who report their husbands espousing a patriarchal ideology in the domestic context are more likely than those who do not report such expression to recount being assaulted by those husbands.

My brief theoretical focus on private and public patriarchy, rural and urban patriarchy and some of the possible idiosyncrasies of rural patriarchy have certain implications for social policy. Urban areas have seen women move into the public sphere in larger numbers both in the paid workplace and institutional politics. In general, these areas have been more accommodating of women's rights. Differences between rural and urban gender relations beg the important questions: Can we apply those urban policies that appear to have some chance of reducing the victimization of women to the rural cultural milieu? If shelters have served women in urban areas, can we assume their impact has been and will be the same in rural areas? If the barriers (physical, cultural, economic) to women and children leaving violent homes are more substantial in rural areas, how should we take account of such a fact in creating viable social policies? This may mean that funding for shelters in rural areas needs to be more substantial than in cities. It may also mean that structural changes need to be introduced into law enforcement in rural areas to deal with what I have called the rural compromise. At still another level, the provision of social and health services may have to be more cognizant of the need for privacy and confidentiality, especially when working with battered women and their families. Finally, the infrastructure of rural areas and the social condition of women in those areas must change in tandem with the other changes, in order to see any appreciable inroads into the social problem of rural woman abuse. This means more than improving public transportation and includes the provision of more educational and employment opportunities for women in conjunction with supports such as more extensive child care to enable women to take advantage of such opportunities.

References

Bachman, R. (1992). Crime in nonmetropolitan America: A national accounting of trends, incidence rates, and idiosyncratic vulnerabilities. *Rural Sociology, 57,* 546–560

Bordua, D. J., and Lizotte, A. J. (1979). Patterns of illegal firearms ownership. *Law and Policy Quarterly,* 1, 147–175.

Bureau of Justice Statistics. (1990). *Handgun crime victims* (Special Report). Washington, DC: U.S. Department of Justice.

Bushy, A. (1993). Rural women: Lifestyle and health status. *Rural Nursing,* 28, 187–197.

Davis, R. S., and Potter, G.W. (1991). Bootlegging and rural entrepreneurship. *Journal of Crime and Justice,* 14, 145–159.

Dobash, R. E., and Dobash, R. (1979). *Violence against wives.* New York. Free Press.

Duncan, C. M., and Lamborghini, N. (1994). Poverty and social context in remote rural communities. *Rural Sociology,* 59, 437–461.

Fassinger, R. A., and Schwarzweller, H. K. (1984). The work of farm women: A midwestern study. In H. K. Schwartzweller (Ed.), *Research in rural sociology and development* (pp. 37–60). Greenwich, CT: JAI.

Finkelhor, D., and Yllo, K. (1985). *License to rape. Sexual abuse of wives.* New York: Holt, Rinehart & Winston.

Friedland, W. H. (1982). The end of rural society and the future of rural sociology. *Rural Sociology,* 47, 589–608.

Gagné, P. L. (1992). Appalachian women: Violence and social control. *Journal of Contemporary Ethnography,* 20:387–415.

Gorham, L. (1992). The growing problem of low earnings in rural areas. In C. Duncan (Ed.), *Rural poverty in America* (pp. 21–39). New York: Auburn House.

Hanmer, J., and Saunders, S. (1984). *Well-founded fear: A community study of violence to women.* London: Hutchinson.

Hartmann, H. (1981). The family as the locus of gender, class, and political struggle: The example of housework. *Signs,* 6, 366–394.

O'Brien, J. E. (1971). Violence in divorce-prone families. *Journal of Marriage and the Family,* 33, 692–698.

Pagelow, M. (1981). *Woman battering.* Newbury Park, CA: Sage.

Radford, J., and Russell, D. (Eds.). (1992). *Femicide.* New York: Twayne.

Russell, D. E. H. (1990). *Rape in marriage.* Bloomington: Indiana University Press.

Smith, M. D. (1990). Patriarchal ideology and wife beating: A test of a feminist hypothesis. *Violence and Victims,* 5, 257–273.

Websdale, N. (1995). An ethnographic assessment of the policing of domestic violence in rural eastern kentucky. *Social Justice* 22, 102–122.

Weisheit, R., Falcone, D., and Wells, E. (1994). *Rural crime and rural policing.* Washington, DC: National Institute of Justice, Research in Action, U.S. Government Printing Office.

17

Defining Elder Mistreatment in Four Ethnic Groups Across Two Generations

Georgia J. Anetzberger
Jill E. Korbin
Susan K. Tomita

In this article, the authors examine the way that members of four ethnic groups define abuse and exploitation of elderly family members. By identifying differences in how family members view a variety of physical, emotional, and financial types of treatment, the authors show how deviance differs by type of social culture. This article shows that what is considered deviant in one culture or context can and does vary widely. When definitions of events vary, so too will reactions to them.

Introduction

The Problem of Elder Mistreatment

Elder mistreatment is recognized as a problem affecting large numbers of older Americans (US House Select Committee on Aging 1990). Estimates suggest that two million instances are reportable under state laws each year (Tatara 1992). Research on elder mistreatment began in the late 1970s with initial focus on the general nature and scope of the problem (e.g., Lau and Kosberg 1979; Block and Sinnott 1979). . . .

This investigation builds upon pioneer research in the area of group variation in elder mistreatment. It examines perceptions of elder mistreatment across four ethnic groups (European-American, African-American, Puerto Rican, and Japanese-American) and two generations (elder and 'baby boom' caregiver).

Differences by Generation

While the potential importance of ethnic group identity and generation in the study of elder mistreatment has been noted (Bookin and Dunkle 1985; Fulmer and O'Malley 1987; Sourcebook of Criminal Justice Statistics 1982), there has been little systematic research concerning the influence of either on the definitions of the problem, and the proposed interventions associated with those definitions. In one of the few investigations considering generational differences, Hudson (1994) compared the meaning of elder abuse among middle-aged and older adults to that derived from a nationwide panel of elder mistreatment experts. . . . Their perceptions showed some variation by age, gender, and race. Similarly, in a Middletown study on public perceptions about elder mistreatment, Blakely and Morris (1992) found younger adults and caregivers more likely to consider elder abuse a serious problem and to report it.

Differences by Ethnic Group

The literature indicates that the prevalence and perception of elder mistreatment may differ by ethnic group (Galbraith and Zdorkowski 1986; Sourcebook of Criminal Justice Statistics 1982). However, there has been limited inquiry into elder mistreatment and ethnic group (Stein 1991). At least two reasons exist for this knowledge gap. First, most elder mistreatment research has involved exclusively or predominantly white samples (Giordano and Giordano 1984; Wolf, Godkin and Pillemer 1982; Pillemer 1986; Steinmetz 1988). Second, ethnic group identity has not typically been regarded as a variable of significance in elder abuse research (Chen, Bell, Dolinsky, Doyle and Dunn 1982; Greenberg, McKibben and Raymond 1990). . . . While Pillemer and Finkelhor (1988) found no ethnic differences in rates of self-reported elder mistreatment, some literature suggests a greater incidence of elder mistreatment among whites of European descent (Block and Sinnot 1979; Chen et. al. 1982; Gioglio and Blakemore 1983; Giordano and Giordano 1984; Greenberg et al. 1990). Nonetheless, there is little basis at present to suggest mistreatment propensity by ethnic group itself. However, similarity in incidence of elder mistreatment across ethnic groups does not preclude differences in perception of the problem which may have important implications in responding to it.

The available literature on elder mistreatment cross-culturally indicates substantial variability in the treatment of elders (Glascock and Feinman 1981; Myerhoff 1978). Cross-cultural research has indicated that cultural stereotypes about veneration of elders do not necessarily prevent mistreatment or exploitation (Goldstein, Schuler and Ross 1983; Goldstein, Ku and Ikels 1990; Ikels 1990). Moon and Williams (1993) compared the perceptions of elder mistreatment and help-seeking patterns among African-American, Caucasian American, and Korean American elderly women by presenting them with 13 scenarios of mistreatment. The Korean-Americans were less likely to perceive the scenarios as abusive while the African-Americans were more likely to perceive them as mistreatment. The African-Americans also were more likely to use emergency response, law enforcement and legal systems while Korean-Americans were more likely to use informal assistance. These help-seeking patterns varied depending on the scenario. One possible explanation for the low incidence of labeling a situation as mistreatment or seeking help among Korean-Americans is the Korean culture's emphasis on family harmony over individual needs, and suffering and enduring as an expectation (Moon and Williams 1993).

Native Americans. The literature on elder mistreatment among Native Americans indicates awareness of the problem (DeBruyn, Hymbaugh and Valdez 1988; Great Lakes Inter-Tribal Council 1988, Yakima Indian Nation 1989). Krassen, Maxwell and Maxwell (1992) examined elder mistreatment from a social-structural perspective among two geographically different reservations of Plains Indians, the Lone Mountain and the Abundant Lands Reservations. Elder mistreatment in the form of physical abuse and neglect was more common at Lone Mountain, and on a community level was associated with high unemployment, little income potential from the land, and significant substance abuse. In contrast, the Abundant Lands Reservation residents had a housing improvement program and varied sources of income from agriculture, town-based employment, tourism, crafts, and fire fighting. The. differences in the treatment of the elderly were attributed to variations in economic opportunities for the younger residents. Brown's (1989) study of the Oljato Chapter of the Navahos found evidence of various forms of mistreatment, with a predominance of neglect. The Navaho viewed neglect among themselves as more serious than for other ethnic groups because of its greater lack of cultural acceptance among Navaho people.

Japanese. Tomita (1994), considering the Japanese, echoed Brown's focus on cultural factors that contribute to variability in the definition of elder mistreatment. For example, despite the overt absence of conflict within Japanese families, silence and avoidance, while subtle, may be used as extreme forms of punishment, and may be as emotionally devastating as physical abuse. Preliminary work by Chinook and Amata (1990) on the bullying of mothers-in-law by their daughters-in-law in Japan suggests that the most common manifestations of mistreatment were no conversation, saying disagreeable things, and ignoring the other person.

Hispanics., Research on elder mistreatment among Hispanics has been rare, perhaps because of the emphasis on family solidarity (Arias and Handly 1990; Sanchez-Ayendez 1988). In Texas, Hall (1986) studied a stratified sample of 126 minority elderly from a larger sample of mistreated elderly. A comparison of minority with non-minority victims produced no clear profile of differences, but the minority elders constituted a greater proportion of the victim sample than their numbers in the population would suggest. Hall and Andrew (1984) included a subsample of Hispanics (N = 45) in their analysis of elder mistreatment reports to the Texas Department of Human Services, and found that Hispanic victims were more likely to be female, poor, isolated, and without medical care than a comparable sample of Anglo and African-American victims.

African-Americans. Cazenave (1983), Crystal (1987), and Griffin and Williams (1992) note that the research on elder mistreatment among African-Americans is sparse, and largely the result of analysis of larger samples, which often lack sufficient numbers of African-American elderly and do not explore the qualitative details of African-American life or the Black elderly. Cazenave (1983) and Griffin and Williams (1992) have suggested various risk factors for elder mistreatment among African-American families, including low income, poor health, and inverse generational family support. The importance, of these factors is supported most recently by Griffin's (1994) exploratory study that examined ideas about mistreatment among African-Americans in rural North Carolina. Griffin (1994) found through interviews of ten victims and six of their perpetrators that financial exploitation was the most prevalent type of mistreatment. Physically abusing elders was unacceptable among rural African-Americans; poverty was pervasive in the mistreatment situations; and African-American perpetrators of elder mistreatment were involved in dependent, mutually beneficial relationships with elders. Similar to Moon and Williams' (1993) results mentioned earlier, Korbin, Anetzberger, Thomasson and Austin (1991) in a small, case study sample found that African-American elders were more likely to seek legal recourse against their abusive adult off-spring than were Caucasians. Comparing victims reported under Wisconsin state law, Longres, Raymond and Kimmel (1991) found that African-American victims were more likely than non-African-American victims to be younger, experiencing a life-threatening form of mistreatment, and willing to use services offered, with alleged perpetrators more likely to be female and daughters of the victims.

Methodology

Building upon previous research in defining elder mistreatment, this study examined the perception of elder mistreatment across ethnic groups and generations. Data were gathered in eight focus group sessions composed of four ethnic groups and two age groups. The four ethnic groups included in the study were: European-Americans, African-Americans, Puerto Ricans, and Japanese-Americans. An elder and a caregiver group were conducted for each ethnic group. The elder age group consisted of persons 60 years and older. The caregiver age group was composed of caregiver adults in the 'baby boom' generation, that is, born between 1946 and 1964. . . .

Participants for each focus group were recommended by staff members of agencies serving elders and their adult offspring caregivers. It addition to meeting the criteria of age, and caregiver-elder relationship, participants were sought who self-identified with the ethnic groups of interest to the study. Participants also were perceived by agency representatives as able and willing to express opinions in group settings. Sixty-two individuals were included in the study, as indicated in Table 17.1.

Table 17.1

Study participants by ethnic group and age group

| | Age group | | |
Ethnic group	Elders	Caregivers	Total
European-Americans	9	9	18
African-Americans	8	8	16
Puerto Ricans	7	5	12
Japanese-Americans	9	7	16
Total	33	29	62

Results

Best Things and Good Treatment

In answer to the questions about 'best things that family can do for an elderly person', 51 respondents emphasized providing emotional support. . . . This was the top choice for all ethnic groups and both generations. Respondents expressed this choice variously. Typical answers included 'love them', 'be supportive' and 'show respect'.

Japanese-Americans evidenced the greatest preference for providing emotional support, with every respondent from this ethnic group listing it among the top three best things. In contrast, the greatest variability of answers to this question was found among African-Americans, who also emphasized providing emotional support less than did the other ethnic groups. African-Americans were almost as likely to suggest protecting rights/interests or to give multiple responses as they were to suggest providing emotional support.

The second choice among respondents for 'best things that family can do for an elderly person' fell to either assisting with personal care (i.e., activities of daily living) or protecting rights/interests. Again, this was true across ethnic groups and generations. Illustrations of personal care were frequently given, with an emphasis on bathing and feeding. With respect to protecting rights/interests, primary emphasis was placed on helping the elder to remain independent as long as possible.

The top choices for 'very good treatment of an elderly person by a family member' were comparable to those listed for 'best things'. The only notable difference rested with a highlighting of activity (e.g., listening, visiting, keeping in touch) under good treatment and a highlighting of emotions (e.g., love, respect, understanding) under best things.

Worst Things and Bad Treatment

There was difference among the ethnic groups with regard to what they considered the 'worst things that a family member can do to an elderly person'. . . . Psychological neglect was the top choice for worst things among European-Americans and Puerto Ricans (along with psychological abuse in the latter regard), psychological abuse among Japanese-Americans and African-Americans (along with unmet expectations in the latter regard). Psychological neglect included such behaviors directed at the elder as not communicating, excluding from activities, and

isolating. Psychological abuse was illustrated by mocking, scolding, and yelling at the elder. Examples of unmet expectations given by respondents included not being there when needed, no gifts, and disregarding wishes or opinions.

Among all ethnic groups, Japanese-Americans placed the greatest emphasis on psychological abuse as the worst thing. Four-fifths of Japanese-American respondents considered it among the worst things compared to one-half of African-Americans and European-Americans and just one-third of Puerto Ricans. Only African-Americans listed exploitation among the worst things, with one-third of respondents from this ethnic group reporting it. The second ranked worst thing also varied by ethnic group, with nearly every ethnic group naming different items. European-Americans and Puerto Ricans mentioned psychological abuse; Japanese-Americans physical abuse, psychological neglect, and unmet expectations; and African-Americans physical and psychological neglect.

The two generations offered comparable responses, with both identifying psychological neglect and psychological abuse as the first and second worst things that a family member can do to an elderly person. . . . Beyond this, however, caregivers placed more emphasis on unmet expectations and physical abuse, while elders emphasized physical neglect. . . .

Response to Mistreatment

When asked what they would do if they 'thought an elderly person was being mistreated by a family member', the most common response given across all ethnic groups was talk to the proper authorities. . . . This was the first ranked response for Puerto Ricans and the second ranked response for the other ethnic groups. European-Americans and African-Americans preferred contacting agencies which serve elders and Japanese-Americans preferred talking to family or friends about the incident.

There were notable differences between generations and genders in responding to elder mistreatment. . . . Caregivers were twice as likely to contact service agencies as were elders (54.5 vs 24.0%); male respondents were four times more likely to call the police than were female respondents (63.6 vs 16.7%).

Hypothetical Situations

Seven hypothetical situations involving the interactions of adult children with elder parents were described to the focus groups for their assessment as to whether or not the interactions represented elder mistreatment. . . .

A number of patterns emerged. . . . In general, the focus groups did not regard as mistreatment acts done to promote caregiving, even when elders were resistive to them. For instance, none of the focus groups considered caregivers forcing incontinent elders to wear disposable underwear against their will . . . as mistreatment. Likewise, focus group participants were reluctant to label as mistreatment making elders with heart conditions take prescribed medications . . . and cajoling elders out of money . . . In contrast, the focus groups tended to label deliberate acts of aggression outside of the caregiving context as mistreatment. For example, all responding groups found taking the money of elders without their permission . . . or striking elders . . . to be mistreatment. Yelling at elders was seen in the same light nearly as often. . . .

Among the ethnic groups, Puerto-Ricans were most likely to regard the aforementioned hypothetical situations as elder mistreatment. They also were the most unequivocal in their assessments. Puerto Ricans considered the hypothetical situations as mistreatment 73% of the time, and every situation was classified as mistreatment or not. No situation was qualified based on circumstances, intent, or some other factor. At the other end of the spectrum, European-Americans and Japanese-Americans were the least likely to label a situation as elder mistreatment, and Japanese-Americans were the least unequivocal in their assessments.

European-Americans and Japanese-Americans regarded the hypothetical situations as elder mistreatment only 55% of the time, and Japanese-Americans qualified their assessments 29% of the time.

Among the generations, elders were more likely to identify a hypothetical situation as mistreatment than were caregivers. Two-thirds of the situations were regarded is mistreatment by elders, only half by caregivers.

Finally, in examining the congruence between generations by ethnic group, the greatest similarity was found among Puerto Ricans and Japanese-Americans. Elders and caregivers in both groups agreed with each other in their assessment of the hypothetical situations for which they provided responses. This was not true for African-Americans or European-Americans. African-American elders and caregivers were in agreement two-thirds of the time, European-American elders and caregivers just one-half of the time.

Focus Group Profiles

Below are the summarized responses made by members of each focus group to the research questions and vignettes. Specific quotes (identified by the respondent's initials) are offered to clarify general observations. The profiles provide an overview of how family care and elder mistreatment are perceived by focus group; they do not indicate the variation in perception that may be present among individual group members.

European-American elders. Family was regarded as the major source of help and support for older people by European-American elders. Yet, they also felt that family should be careful not to provide so much assistance that elders become dependent. By the same token, elders must never be too demanding of their families.

Caregiving required a series of compromises, especially for elders needing assistance. For example, forcing elders to wear disposable underwear against their will was not regarded as mistreatment. . . . Rather, caregivers were seen as simply trying to control the problem of incontinence. Respondents were resentful of those elders who either refused the disposable underwear or removed them once on. Similarly, restraining an elder in a chair was viewed as acceptable if the elder would otherwise fall or wander. Respondents commenting on the use of restraints were less concerned about the feelings of restrained elders than about the manageability of caregiving.

When the demands of family caregiving became too great, according to respondents, it was important for caregivers to seek outside assistance. Among options mentioned were adult day care, support groups, respite, and nursing home placement. When elders found themselves becoming too demanding of family members, the respondents felt that the elders should change their behavior. For example, DF told how she resented her daughters-in-law, because she saw them as keeping her sons from helping her as much as she wanted. Eventually she realized that she was being overly demanding of her sons. Relations with her daughters-in-law improved once she became more independent and did more things herself.

European-American elders tended to regard only extreme forms of behavior as mistreatment. Beating and hitting with an object illustrated physical abuse, stealing money was exploitation, and no contact with the elder represented psychological neglect. More subtle forms of behavior tended to be labeled 'inappropriate', 'unacceptable', or 'immature'. . . .

European-American caregivers. Taking care of an older person was very difficult, according to European-American caregivers. For the caregiver it was hard to know how much or what help to offer, and for the elder it was hard to accept the help offered. It was also difficult for caregivers to watch elders decline and for elders to experience decline.

However, placement of elders in nursing homes was seen as problematic. In the opinion of respondents, not visiting residents represented neglect and mixing mentally impaired residents with those having only physical limitations constituted abuse. Respondents felt that elder mistreatment was greater in institutional than domestic settings, because once placed 'people are forgotten'.

This group was more likely to define exploitive-type situations as mistreatment than other potential forms of elder abuse. For example, respondents considered it exploitive for an adult child to withdraw money from the parent's account without the latter's

knowledge . . . and exploitive for an adult son to cajole his mother out of money. . . . In contrast forced use of medications or restraints could merely represent facets of aging and necessary aspects of care.

African-American elders. African-American elders felt that the most important thing that family offered elderly members was love. Conversely, the worst was to withhold love. Love was realized through the extension of respect and assistance. Love was considered withheld when elders were ignored or subjected to harsh or profane language. In the opinion of EG, 'Love keeps you living. People thrive on love'.

Respondents agreed that whether or not an act represented mistreatment often depended upon the particular circumstances involved. Therefore, the meaning of an act was derived from its context. HM suggested, 'There are so many factors involved. Unless you know all the details, it's hard to say anything'. By way of illustration, an elderly parent might be forced to take medication against her will . . . if she was mentally impaired. Without a mental impairment, however, the act was abusive.

The importance of context even applied to acts which under ordinary circumstances clearly indicated abusive behavior to the respondents. An illustration of this was the use of profanity. HM elaborated, 'The use of profanity depends on the family, because some families 'let it all hang out' and use profanity regularly, so the use of profanity may be all right (in these families)'. Two other group members gave examples of the acceptability of profanity in specific families.

African-American caregivers. African-American caregivers stressed the responsibility of the oldest daughter to provide care for elderly relatives, both her own parents and her parents' siblings. DT, for example, not only was the primary caregiver for her mother, she also did the banking and service arrangements for her mother's brother. Although this uncle had seven children of his own, DT was asked to take him into her home when he began calling 911 . . . repeatedly and could no longer live alone.

Although caregiving was often viewed as a difficult arrangement, elder mistreatment was unacceptable. It was understandable in some forms, but it was never considered the respectable thing to do. For instance, most respondents regarded yelling at an elder as something that occasionally happened. 'Yelling may be the only way to express yourself', according to JK. It crossed a threshold and became mistreatment when cursing or other offensive language was involved. Likewise, ignoring an elderly relative was understandable when that person was demanding and dependent. Nonetheless, it still represented mistreatment. KC reflected, 'I know a lot of caretakers who are on the edge and resentful'.

Puerto Rican elders. The best things that family could do for elderly members were to help and love them, according to the Puerto Rican elders. Of these two things, love was more important, because it provided the basis for other positive aspects of interaction. Family showed love when they made sacrifices, tried to understand, and responded as needed. To PV, 'They show they love me when I call saying, "I am sick" and they are right there in five minutes'.

These respondents felt that sometimes children failed to show love, because they did not receive love from their parents while they were growing up. Nonetheless, elders felt that they should be respected simply because they were elders and brought the children into the world. FG stated, 'The people who brought those children into the world must be loved no matter what they say. The children must respect them, be considerate with them, and love them forever'. Added LM, 'People have to care and love the elders, because we older people are not as young people. Sometimes our words go wrong and we don't know what to say. So our children must have mercy and try to help us more'.

Puerto Rican caregiver. According to Puerto Rican caregivers, there was an emotional connection that was taught and maintained between the generations. As a result, adult children never separate entirely from their parents or from their own children. In Hispanic tradition elders should be treated with respect and provided adequate care. Conversely, elders should set good examples, role modeling appropriate behavior for younger generations.

Among the generations, elders have more latitude in their actions. For example, if an elder parent hits an adult child, it would never be acceptable for the adult child to hit in return.

TM explained, 'You're never too old to get a spanking, but the child can't strike back'. Likewise, if an elder gives unsolicited advice to an adult child about parenting, . . . the adult child should simply listen to the elder's views, and recognize the importance to the elder of contributing in a meaningful way to how the family functions. Getting angry and yelling were regarded by Puerto Rican caregivers as neither respectful nor useful.

Japanese-American elders. Japanese-American elders identified 'rough treatment' as the worst thing that the family can do to elderly members. Rough treatment included both physical and psychological abuse, although the former was considered worse. According to the elders, once an adult child hits an elder, it is never forgotten; it is an irreversible act. In contrast, if an adult child spoke roughly to an elder, the child still could be corrected by the elder.

An important form of bad treatment recognized by Japanese-American elders was psychological neglect. Being avoided, isolated, or excluded was dreaded by these elders. Similarly, an adult child regarding the elder as a burden was evidence of bad treatment. In the face of bad treatment, the elder assumed the role of passive recipient, suffering invisibly,

In general, acts of omission were regarded as bad treatment, and acts of commission as elder mistreatment. Because the former were culturally and historically familiar, elders usually responded with resignation, 'It cannot be helped'. In contrast, elder mistreatment was a foreign concept to the respondents. Overall strong cultural norms against any form of physical aggression were expressed.

Japanese-American elders talked about the importance of avoiding conflict. This was done by feigning ignorance or not interfering in a situation. According to TI, 'We are all very nervous . . . one should speak with caution'. Faced with bad treatment, Japanese-American elders said that they would try to endure the situation and not say anything. Faced with elder mistreatment, they would seek the assistance of outside authorities.

Japanese-American elders also considered the context of situations before labeling them as bad treatment or elder mistreatment. An adult son repeatedly asking his mother for money until she feels guilty and gives it to him . . . might be regarded as acceptable behavior on the part of the son if he was impaired and unable to ask others for financial help. Trickery, too, was preferred over force in invoking elder compliance. For instance, if an elder refused to take needed medication, it was better to mix the medication with juice or cajole the elder than force its use.

Japanese-American caregivers. Japanese-American caregivers ranked the worst things that family could do for elderly members according to the severity, irreversibility and duration of the acts. On this basis, physical abuse was generally considered the worst, because it was 'such a direct . . . aggressive act . . . undeniable . . . a breach . . . a sense of violation of your personhood'. Psychological abuse ranked second, followed by physical neglect. However, being hit once was preferred over constant verbal assault. Likewise, being hit once was preferred over purposefully and repeatedly ignoring an elder. In addition, some of the caregivers, imagining themselves as elderly, preferred being hit to enduring drawn-out periods of silence. A verbal or physical confrontation would increase the chance of resolving the problem at hand, while being treated with silence for long periods was considered hurtful and torturous. In other instances, silence was seen as acceptable in order to avoid conflict or the escalation of emotions that would result in serious conflict.

In contrast, the best things that family could do for elderly members related to providing necessary assistance and offering companionship. These acts were most positively regarded when performed without request from elders and when completed without compromising the elder's self-determination.

The caregivers recognized special circumstances under which acts of elder mistreatment might be regarded as understandable. For example, an adult son repeatedly asking his mother for money until she feels guilty and gives it to him . . . was more acceptable when the mother was wealthy or the son had no savings or assets.

Discussion

The results of this study lend support to those from other investigations into ethnic group identity and elder abuse. As with the Korean-Americans in Moon and Williams' (1993) sample, the Japanese-Americans here chose informal assistance for responding to elder mistreatment situations. Japanese culture, too, emphasizes family over self, the (collective man) over the individual (Roland 1988). To these groups, therefore, preferred sources of assistance are found in the family and community and not among outsiders, such as police and helping professionals (Tomita 1994). Also, these results support the work of Kaneko and Yamada (1990) in that manifestations of bad treatment in the opinion of Japanese-American respondents included avoiding or excluding elders.

With regard to Hispanics, the Puerto Ricans in this study voiced the same strong family orientation evident in the writings of Sanchez-Ayendez (1988) and Farias and Handly (1990). According to focus group participants, elderly members were so important to family tradition and functioning that actions directed against elders other than the most positive ones of love and respect had a tendency to be regarded as unacceptable at best and abusive at worst.

. . . African-Americans in this study placed more emphasis on psychological abuse than on physical abuse as unacceptable behavior by family members. Also, like Hudson's (1994) investigation on the meaning of elder abuse among middle-aged and older adults, African-Americans in this study put considerable emphasis into elder rights. Finally, similar to findings from Longres, Raymond and Kimmel (1991), there was a willingness among African-Americans here to contact agencies which serve elders in response to mistreatment. The findings further suggested that the most likely perpetrators of mistreatment were the daughters of victims (especially the oldest), by virtue of having the primary caregiving role in the family,

The ethnic groups and generations in this study showed both similarities and differences in their response to questions and reactions to hypothetical situations. Greatest similarity was found in the emphasis on family provision of emotional support to elders as a 'best thing'. Greatest difference was found in the top choices for 'worst things' and preferred responses to elder mistreatment. This suggests agreement on what constitutes desired family dynamics, and disagreement on what constitutes the antithesis, that is, elder mistreatment and how to address it. . . .

Also, this study explored some theoretical propositions which may explain the ethnic group differences with respect to elder mistreatment. One proposition suggests what the culture promotes or condemns determines how elder mistreatment is played out. For example, perhaps a strong norm of veneration of the elderly, as among Japanese-Americans (Osako 1979), contributes to subtle and hidden forms of mistreatment. Likewise a cultural emphasis on family harmony and not on individuality (Yee 1990) may promote subordination by elders with accompanying dread of mistreatment, because they know that outside intervention is highly unlikely. Another possibility is that in cultures which promote interdependent, mutually beneficial relationships, where two-way generational support is taken for granted, such as among Africa-Americans (Taylor 1985), financial exploitation may be committed more frequently. Finally, the elder's degree, of 'culture-boundness' may determine the likelihood of asking for outside help; that is, elders who are not culture bound, who for whatever reasons do not adhere to family 'we-ness' or to intergenerational support, such as non-first generation European-Americans (Luppen and Becerra 1987), may be more likely to ask for outside or agency help.

Finally, generational and gender differences which emerged from this study remain areas for further research as well. For example, it is uncertain why caregivers were more

likely to contact service agencies than elders, or why men were more likely to call the police than women. In the former regard, partial explanation might be found in the usual greater willingness of younger generations to use community services than elders (Biegel, Farkas and Wadsworth 1993). In the latter regard, calling the police might reflect the typical reluctance of men to use other forms of assistance, such as community services or informal support (Stone 1986). . . .

References

Biegel D.E., Farkas, K. J. and Wadsworth, N. (1993). Social service programs for older adults and their families: Service use and barriers. In P. K. H. Kim (ed.), *Services to the aging and aged: Public policies and programs* (pp. 141–178). New York: Garland.

Blakely B.E. and Morris, D. C. (1992). Public perceptions of and responses to elder mistreatment in middletown, *Journal of Elder Abuse & Neglect* 4: 19–37.

Block M. and Sinnott, J. (1979). *The battered elder syndrome: An exploratory study*. College Park, MD: Center on Aging, University of Maryland.

Bookin D. and Dunkle, R. (1985). Elder abuse: Issues for the practitioner. *Social Casework* (Jan):3–12.

Brown A.S. (1989). A survey on elder abuse in one native american tribe. *Journal of Elder Abuse & Neglect* 1:17–37.

Cazenave N. 1983. Elder abuse and black americans: Incidence, correlates, treatment, and prevention. In J.I. Kosberg (ed.), *Abuse and maltreatment of the elderly: Causes and interventions* (pp. 187–203). Boston: John Wright.

Chen P., S.L. Bell, Dolinsky, D. L., Doyle, J., and Dunn, M. (1981). Elderly abuse in domestic settings: A pilot study. *Journal of Gerontological Social Work* 4:3–17.

Crystal S. (1987). Elder abuse: The latest 'crisis'. *The Public Interest* 88:56–66.

DeBruyn L.M, Hymbaugh, K., and Valdez, N. (1988). Helping communities address suicide and violence: The special initiatives team of the Indian Health Service. *American Indian and Alaska Native Mental Health Research* 1:55–65.

Farias L. and Handly, J. (1990). Protective service issues and Hispanic clients: Mexican Americans as an example. In J. Boyajian (ed.), *Adult protective services practice guide* (pp. 5–11). St. Paul, MN: Minnesota Department of Human Services.

Fulmer T.T. and O'Malley, T.A. (1987). *Inadequate care of the elderly: A health care perspective on abuse and neglect.* NY: Springer Verlag.

Galbraith M. and Zdorkowski, R. (1986). Systemizing the elder abuse literature. In M. Galbraith (ed.), *Elder abuse: Perspectives on an emerging crisis* (pp. 168–176). Kansas City, KA: Mid-America Congress on Aging.

Gioglio G. R. and Blakemore. R. (1983). *Elder abuse in New Jersey: The knowledge and experience of abuse among older New Jerseyans.* Trenton, NJ: New Jersey Department of Human Resources.

Giordano N. H. and Giordano, J. A. (1984). Individual and family correlates of elder abuse. Unpublished manuscript.

Glascock, A. and Feinman, S. (1981). Social assessment of burden: Treatment of the aged in non industrial societies. In C. Fry (Ed.) *Dimensions: Aging, culture and health* (pp. 13–31). New York: Praeger.

Goldstein M., Schuler, S., and Ross, J. (1983). Social and economic forces affecting intergenerational relations in extended families in a Third World country: A cautionary tale from south asia. *Journal of Gerontology* 38:716–724.

Goldstein, M., Ku, Y., and Ikels, C. (1990). Household composition of the elderly in two rural villages in the Peoples's Republic of China. *Journal of Cross-Cultural Gerontology* 5:119–130.

Great Lakes Inter-Tribal Council. (1988). Effective public awareness efforts in tribal communities. Paper prepared for Administration on Aging, DHHS.

Greenberg, J., McKibben, M., and Raymond, J. A., (1990). Dependent adult children and elder abuse. *Journal of Elder Abuse & Neglect* 2:73–86.

Griffin, L. W. (1994). Elder mistreatment among rural African-Americans. *Journal of Elder Abuse & Neglect* 6:1–27.

Griffin, L. W. and Williams, O. J., (1992). Abuse among African-American Elderly. *Journal of Family Violence* 7:19–35.

Hall, P. A. (1986). Minority elder maltreatment: Ethnicity, gender, age, and poverty. *Journal of Gerontological Social Work* 9:53–72.

Hall, P. and Andrew, S. (1984). Minority elder maltreatment: Ethnicity, gender age, and poverty. Unpublished manuscript.

Hudson, M. (1994). Elder abuse: Its meaning to middle-aged and older adults, Part II: Pilot results. *Journal of Elder Abuse & Neglect* 6:55–81.

Ikels, C. (1990). The resolution of intergenerational conflict: perspectives of elders and their family members. *Modern China* 16:379–406.

Kaneko Y. and Yamada, Y. (1990). Wives and mothers-in-law: Potential for family conflict in post-war Japan. *Journal of Elder Abuse & Neglect* 2:87–99.

Korbin J., Anetzberger, G., Thomasson, R., and Austin, C. (1991). Abused elders who seek legal recourse against their adult offspring: Findings from an exploratory study. *Journal of Elder Abuse & Neglect* 3:1–18.

Krassen, Maxwell E. and Maxwell, R. J., (1992). Insults to the body civil: Mistreatment of elderly in two plain Indian tribes. *Journal of Cross-Cultural Gerontology* 7:3–23.

Lau, E. and Kosberg, J. (1979). Abuse of the elderly by informal care providers. *Aging* 299–300: 10–15.

Longres J., Raymond, J., and Kimmel, K. (1991). Black and white clients in an elder abuse system. Unpublished manuscript.

Moon, A. and Williams, O. (1993). Perceptions of elder abuse in help-seeking patterns among African-American, Caucasian American, and Korean-American elderly women. *The Gerontologist* 33:386–395.

Myerhoff, B. (1978). Aging and the aged in other cultures: An anthropological perspective. In E. Brauwens (ed.), *The anthropology of health* (pp. 151–166). St. Louis, MO: Mosby.

Osako, M. M. (1979). Aging and family among Japanese Americans: The role of ethnic tradition in the adjustment to old age. *The Gerontologist* 19:448–455.

Pillemer K .A. (1986). *Elder abuse and neglect: Research recommendations from the research conference on elder abuse and nNeglect.* Durham, NC: Family Research Laboratory.

Pillemer, K. A. and Finkelhor, D. (1988). The prevalence of elder abuse: A random sample survey. *The Gerontologist* 28:51–57.

Roland, A. (1988). *In search of self in India and Japan: Toward a cross-cultural psychology.* Princeton, NJ: Princeton University Press.

Sanchez-Ayendez, M. (1988). The Puerto Rican family. In D.H. Mindel, R.W. Habenstein and R. Wright, Jr. (eds.), *Ethnic families in America: Patterns and variations*, 3d ed. (pp. 173–195). New York: Elsevier.

Stein, K. F. (1991). *Working with abused and neglected elders in minority populations: A synthesis of research.* Washington, DC: National Aging Resource Center on Elder Abuse.

Steinmetz, S. K. (1988). *Duty bound: Elder abuse and family Care.* Newbury Park, CA: Sage.

Stone, R. (1986). Aging in the eighties, age 65 and over: Use of community services, *National Center for Health Statistics Advance Data* 124:1–5.

Tatara, T. (1992). *Elder abuse: Questions and answers*. Washington, DC: National Aging Resource Center on Elder Abuse.

Taylor, R. J. (1985). The extended family as a source of support to elderly blacks. *The Gerontologist* 25:488–495.

Tomita, S. K. (1994). The consideration of cultural factors in the research of elder mistreatment with an in-depth look at the Japanese. *Journal of Cross-Cultural Gerontology* 9:39–52.

US House Select Committee on Aging. 1990. Elder abuse: A decade of shame and inaction. Washington, DC: US Government Printing Office.

Wolf, R., Godkin, M. A., and Pillemer, K. A. (1984). *Elder abuse and neglect: Final report from three model projects*. Worcester, MA: Center on Aging. University of Massachusetts Medical Center/ Center of Aging.

Yakima Indian Nation. (1987). Don't wound my spirit: Guide to protecting elders from abuse, neglect and exploitation. Unpublished manuscript.

Yee, B. W. K. (1990). Gender and family issues in minority groups, *Generations* 14:39–42.

18

Definition of Roles in Abusive Lesbian Relationships

Becky Marrujo
Mary Kreger

This article challenges traditional views of violent relationships by suggesting that there are not just two roles—perpetrator and victim. By looking exclusively at lesbian women, the authors suggest that some women are co-participants in violence and that even when one woman is victimized by another, she may fail to recognize the behavior as abuse because it is perpetrated by a woman. Rather than looking at violent people, then, we are forced to consider the ways that stereotypes and preconceived notions can distort our perceptions of what is actually happening.

Discussion of the Concepts

During the past two decades of academic, professional, and grassroots interest in domestic violence, the focus has been on exploration and explanation of heterosexual domestic violence. Much has been written and debated from the perspectives of two roles, that of the perpetrator and the victim. Topics explored have included the severity, type, and frequency of violent acts; the psychological characteristics of the perpetrator and victim; the effects of the violence on the victim; violence in the family histories of both victim and perpetrator; and many others. Given the adequacy of research findings on the above topics, few persons would disagree that most

heterosexual violence is directed toward the female by a male perpetrator and that females sustain the most severe injuries. Within this heterosexual model of victim and perpetrator, the roles become gender specific. Whenever either of these persons comes into contact with a helping system or the criminal justice system their roles are defined by gender.

However, when researchers, professionals, and others attempt to apply this model to female-to-female intimate violence (lesbian battering), problems of definition become apparent. One cannot rely on gender to define the roles, especially when both women report using violence to resolve conflict in the relationship. In these cases, one needs a more precise and definitive explanation of the roles and dynamics of the lesbian battering relationship. As one searches the literature for more adequate definitions of the phenomena, one encounters the concept of "mutual battering," originally applied to heterosexual women, who use physical aggression against male perpetrators. This concept has been strenuously debated since its introduction. Essentially, the concept (as applied to heterosexual couples) promotes the notion that both males and females use physical and emotional aggression to resolve conflict in relationships. The use of the violence does not have to occur at the same time, and the roles of victim and perpetrator are blurred, non-existent, or fluid.

To support the notion of mutual battering, incidence studies which show that women use violence against men have been cited (Steinmetz, 1977–78; Straus, 1980; Straus, Gelles, and Steinmetz, 1980). To refute the notion, others concentrated on omissions in incidence studies, such as identification of which partner sustained the most severe injuries, which partner initiated the physical aggression, and the motive for the physically aggressive act. These writers noted that women most frequently sustain the most severe injuries, do not initiate the violence, and only use physical aggression in self-defense. Thus, two terms have been used to define women who use violence in relationships: that of a "mutual combatant" and that of a "self-defending victim." The mutual combatant has been defined as the woman who fights back and may at times initiate the violence, whereas the self-defending woman may use physical aggression to prevent further injury.

In discussion of the terms as they apply to heterosexual victims, Saunders (1988) raised the question of whether "fighting back" and "self-defense" were mutually exclusive terms. He acknowledged that many survivors reported a retaliatory anger at the time of the self-defensive act of physical aggression. He proposed that the terms were not mutually exclusive and that many women did not distinguish between self-defense and fighting back. His conclusions appear to support the viewpoint that abused women who use physical violence are "self-defending victims" rather than "mutual combatants." Renzetti (1992) stressed that not all violent acts are the same; that there is a difference between initiating the act of violence and using self-defense or retaliation; and that both severity of injuries and determining who used the violence in self-defense are important. Yet, in her study, she reported that 78% of her sample (n = 100) of lesbians reported that they had either defended themselves or fought back against an abusive partner. Of these, 18% described behavior that could be termed fighting back or "trading blow for blow or insult for insult" (Renzetti, 1992: 110). Lie et al. (1991), in a study of lesbians who reported being both victims and perpetrators of violence, reported that 30.3% perceived their aggression as self-defensive and 39.4% viewed it as mutual aggression.

Conceptually, both terms need further refinement and definition. Researchers and others do not address such critical factors as the motive of the abused woman (both heterosexual and lesbian), whether the woman's use of physical aggression is a pattern of behavior rather than an isolated incident, and the sequence of events leading to the act of either mutual combat or self-defense. Definition and measurement of the woman's motive for the use of physical aggression could address issues related to retaliatory anger, the intent to "get even," to inflict injury, and to escalate the violent incident. If the woman uses the physical aggression to retaliate ("get even," inflict injury, or to escalate the violent incident), is she defined as a self-defending victim or as a mutual combatant? Further, if the woman has established a pattern of repeated use of physical aggression, can she be considered a self-defending victim or a mutual combatant? Finally, does the sequence of events, specifically the initiation of the violent incident, define her as a mutual combatant or a self-defending victim?

These factors have not been adequately addressed for heterosexual or lesbian women. Critical differences between the two populations also need further exploration, especially in light of observations such as "the only difference in interpersonal dynamics and perpetration of violence in battering in lesbian couples is that lesbian women report physically fighting back more often than women who are battered by men" (Walker, 1986: 76).

Discussion of the Clinical Population and the Clinical Process

The authors will present clinical observations on a total of 62 lesbians who identified themselves as either victims or perpetrators of physical and emotional aggression toward their partners. The majority of the women sought intervention on a voluntary basis, and a minority (11%) were court-ordered into treatment. The court-ordered population was required to complete 36 weeks of state-certified treatment on the dynamics of domestic violence. Other women were referred from a variety of agencies, including battered women's shelters, private practitioners, and criminal justice agencies.

The women, including the court-ordered women, represent a cross section of the population in terms of employment, education, religious affiliation, and social class. Of the 62 women, 76% were white and 24% were women of color (7 were African-American, 6 were Hispanic-American, and 2 were Native-American). They ranged in age from 20 to 51 years. Of the total, 34 women were living with their partners when they completed treatment. These women were seen in individual, couples, and/or group sessions.

Because of the authors' previous experience with primarily heterosexual battered women, they sought to address the issues presented by the women in the present sample from the perspectives of the roles of victim and perpetrator. The authors solicited intake information from these two perspectives. The initial interview and intake topics were developed with questions specific to either the victim's or perpetrator's experience. The authors accepted their self-reports and developed a treatment plan based upon commonly accepted models of support and safety intervention for the victim and confrontation and containment of the perpetrator's anger. A few weeks into the treatment, a percentage of the women who had self-reported as victims began to describe a pattern of fighting back during the violent episodes. After repeated reports of patterns of fighting back in the relationships, the authors revised their intake and initial interview questionnaires. The revised material asked more open-ended questions about the abusive relationship, the episode leading to intervention (voluntary and involuntary), and the pattern of violence for the couple.

The revised questionnaire asked the women to tell whether there had ever been either physical or emotional abuse in the relationship. Further questions asked the women to respond to the range of either physical or emotional abuse experienced (from pushing/grabbing to the use of weapons and screaming/yelling). The women were asked both if they had ever inflicted an injury on their partner (either emotional or physical) and if they had ever sustained an injury from their partner. The women were also asked to describe the last violent incident (the one leading to intervention) and to identify who initiated the aggressive act. In addition, they were asked to give their understanding of causation of the violent incident. Other questions were related to whether the police were called and the women's opinions as to whether this domestic violence incident required police intervention. Finally, each woman was asked if she thought she was in an abusive relationship; if there had been other violent incidents in this relationship; if her style of "fighting" had changed over time

and how her style of "fighting" had changed; if medical treatment was ever needed for either partner after an abusive incident; and a description of other abusive relationships (if this was not the first abusive relationship).

The information gathered from the first interview was then used as a foundation to begin exploration of the abusive relationship. Other information gathered included clinical observations within the individual and/or group setting.

Discussion of Clinical Observations and Interviews

Based on responses to the initial questionnaires, and information from individual and/or group sessions with their lesbian clients in abusive relationships, the authors found that a substantial percentage (34%) reported a pattern of fighting back. The term "fighting back" as used by the authors means a repeated pattern of physical and/or emotional aggression in response to the partner's aggressive act. It is to be distinguished from self-defense because it became an established pattern of response and is not confined to an isolated violent incident. Further, the self-reported intent of the fighting back during the violent incident is to hurt, injure, or get even with the partner.

The authors also found that 27% of their lesbian clients had many of the psychological characteristics commonly used to describe male heterosexual perpetrators. Similarly, 39% of their clients exhibited psychological characteristics most often ascribed to heterosexual victims. To clarify the various roles, the authors defined three separate roles for the lesbians involved in abusive relationships. The roles of *primary aggressor* (similar to heterosexual perpetrators), *primary victim* (similar to heterosexual victims), and *participant* (one who self-reports an established pattern of fighting back) were the terms used to clarify the roles assumed by their clients.

The definition of the three roles (primary aggressor, participant, and primary victim) allowed the authors more flexibility in the treatment and exploration of the dynamics of the abusive relationship. . . .

The lesbians whom the authors identified as primary aggressors exhibited many of the same psychological characteristics of perpetrators. They were pathologically jealous, controlling in the relationship, highly intrusive into their partners' activities, avoided responsibility for the violent incident(s), had a sense of personal entitlement in most areas, and were focused on their own needs rather than their partners' needs. They also tended to experience problems with anger containment outside of the home environment (e.g., at work or with other friends and family). They felt more than adequate in the relationship, blamed their partners for various shortcomings, and were male-privilege identified.

On the other hand, primary victims were generally depressed and felt inadequate in the relationship. They generally were not jealous, controlling, or intrusive, but they were overly responsible for others, and focused on their partners' needs rather than their own. They generally fostered an illusion of having control in the relationship and often manipulated the environment or situation to maintain their personal safety. Occasionally, primary victims reported "fighting back." However, further exploration of the incidents revealed that their intent was to get away from the primary aggressor or to attain personal safety. Typically, they had no established pattern of fighting back and no intent to hurt their partners.

Participants, as defined by these authors, exhibited some jealousy, but were not necessarily pathologically jealous. They were controlling in some areas of the relationship, but not overly intrusive and controlling. Often they experienced minor problems with anger management outside the home. They generally accepted responsibility for "fighting back" during the violent incident. In both group and individual sessions, they expressed a high degree of retaliatory anger and often rage toward their partners. They used language that was descriptive of their anger level and their intent, such as "I wasn't going to let her get away with it [the violence] this time." They also reported fighting back as an established pattern in the abusive relationship. In other areas, discussed previously, their adaptations were more fluid. Often-

times, they had more characteristics of the victim than the perpetrator. But while they were experiencing "retaliatory anger," their language and behavior were more like that of a primary aggressor.

Usually, the primary aggressor initiated the physical and/or emotional violence; the participant did not initiate the violence, but had an established pattern of "fighting back"; and the primary victim neither initiated the violence nor had a pattern of "fighting back." The primary victim rarely fought back and, on those occasions when she did, it was only to secure her personal safety.

These differences were related to how each woman responded to and handled the conflictual situation leading to the violent incident. On the one hand, the primary aggressor was interested in escalating the conflict and its resultant violence and was fully engaged in the fight. In contrast, the participant, once the conflict had been initiated, fought back for the duration of the violent incident and was not interested in disengaging from the conflict. The primary victim was interested in disengaging from the conflict, de-escalating the violent incident, and securing her personal safety. Further, the primary aggressor and the participant often reported feeling "victimized" by the fight, whereas the primary victim reported being "confused." Both the primary aggressor and the participant expressed much clarity about the actual violent incident(s), whereas the primary victim expressed confusion. However, the clarity expressed by the former was related to the motive for the violence, rather than the details of it. The primary aggressor often expressed victimization; for example, "She [her partner] did x to me," whereas the participant expressed retaliatory anger, such as "I wasn't going to let her get away with it." In contrast, the primary victim expressed clarity about the actual sequence and details of the violent incident, but not the perpetrator's motive.

Finally, the authors found that the roles of primary victim and primary aggressor were more defined and rigid than the role of participant. Often lesbians who were classified as participants described themselves as primary victims in previous abusive relationships.

Implications of Clinical Observations and Proposed Roles

The proposed roles of primary aggressor, primary victim, and participant have been offered as an invitation to researchers and others to develop a more adequate and precise definition of possible roles assumed by lesbians involved in abusive relationships. The role of participant has been offered by the authors to explain the behavior of lesbians who repeatedly fought back with the intent to hurt their partners. The authors rejected the use of "mutual combatant" to describe these women because of the inadequacy of the term. Also, the term mutual combatant denotes equality in terms of infliction of injuries and responsibility for initiating the act of physical and/or emotional abuse. The lesbian defined as a participant did not initiate the violent incident(s) and did not consistently inflict the same level of injuries on her partner that she sustained herself.

Given the present paucity of information on lesbians who fight back and the roles assumed by those involved in abusive relationships, the proposed roles could facilitate adequate intervention. Use of the proposed terms would enable clinicians and others to more accurately define treatment goals and methods. However, like other summaries of clinical observations, the roles proposed by these authors will need to be validated through further empirical research.

References

Lie, G., Schilt, R., Bush, J., Montagne, M., and Reyes, L. (1991). Lesbians in currently aggressive relationships: How frequently do they report aggressive past relationships? *Violence and Victims*, 6, 121–135.

Renzetti, C. M. (1992). *Violent betrayal: Partner abuse in lesbian relationships*. Newbury Park, CA: Sage Publications.

Saunders, D. G. (1988). Wife abuse, husband abuse, or mutual combat? A feminist perspective on the empirical findings. In K. Yllo and M. Bograd (Eds.), *Feminist perspectives on wife abuse* (pp. 90–113). Newbury Park, CA: Sage Publications.

Steinmetz, S. K. (1977–1978). The battered husband syndrome. *Victimology: An International Journal*, 2, 499–509.

Straus, M. A. (1980). Victims and aggressors in marital violence. *American Behavioral Scientist*, 23, 681–704.

Straus, M. A., Gelles. R. J., and Steinmetz, S. K. (1980). *Behind closed doors: Violence in the American family*. New York: Doubleday/Anchor.

Walker, L. (1986). Battered women's shelters and work With battered lesbians. In K. Lobel (Ed.), *Naming the violence* (pp. 73–76). Seattle, WA: Seal Press.

19

Avengers, Conquerors, Playmates, and Lovers: Roles Played by Child Sexual Abuse Perpetrators

Jane F. Gilgun

Gilgun examines the way adults who sexually abuse children define their relationship with their victims and how they use those definitions to make their access to children easier. She shows that definitions of the situation are important for how victims interpret their experiences and that the way in which other adults in the child's life define or interpret a relationship between an abusive adult and a child can affect whether the sexual abuse is detected.

Effective practice with persons who have been sexually abused in childhood requires an understanding of child victims' relationships with perpetrators. The importance of children's points of view is self-evident. Children, however, speak from their own perspectives and cannot speak for perpetrators. In addition, they may have neither language nor the experience to understand what takes place in sexually abusive relationships (Gilgun, 1986) and may fail to disclose significant details of their abuse (Steward, Bussey, Goodman, and Saywitz, 1993). Therefore, perpetrators' accounts of their sexual rela-

tionships with children can be of enormous help in understanding victims' experiences.

This article presents a continuum of victim-perpetrator relationships from the point of view of perpetrators. Developed from intensive, open ended interviews, the continuum demonstrates in perpetrators' own words a range of ways perpetrators view their relationship with child victims. Adult abusers' perspectives on abuse are seldom taken into account in our understanding of child sexual abuse. In addition to having immediate clinical applications, such information can enhance public policy and prevention programs.

The research on which this article is based has features that distinguish it from other research on child sexual abuse. The research method is phenomenological, an approach that seeks to understand insider perspectives of informants (Bogdan and Biklen, 1992; Morse 1992; Patton, 1990). Research on child sexual abuse depends largely on surveys, case records, reviews, large samples, and quantitative data analysis. The perspectives considered are rarely those of the subjects themselves, but those of researchers, which, though important, need to be supplemented by the perspectives of the research subjects themselves.

The goal of this research was to develop knowledge that would empower victims and contribute to the prevention of child sexual abuse. It was intended to be emancipatory in both its goals and its processes, that is, to seek social change and to empower oppressed groups (Lather, 1991). The persons victimized by perpetrators were conceptualized as being oppressed, and their emancipation was sought.

Emancipatory research involves informants in the development of research findings. During the research process, researchers share their interpretations with informants to determine whether their understanding of the informants' point of view is accurate. The research process also provides informants with opportunities to reflect upon their own situations, perhaps view their situations in a new light, undergo personal transformation, and become empowered to work for social change. Although transformation of informants was not a goal of the present research, it was a hoped-for consequence. Few examples of this type of research are evident in social work literature.

Definition of Child Sexual Abuse

Child sexual abuse constitutes an abuse of power, whereby an older or more powerful person takes advantage of a child for the purpose of sexual gratification (Finkelhor 1984; Gilgun and Connor, 1989; Hartman and Burgess, 1989). The age and size of perpetrators translate into superior knowledge, authority, and ability to manipulate and intimidate children. Child victims readily perceive the size and authority of adults and usually comply with adult requests because they believe they have no choice. Victims have vague and sometimes explicit fears about what perpetrators might do if they do not comply (Gilgun 1986).

The anticipation of sexual gratification appears to impel perpetrators to transgress against children in ways that clearly threaten children's development. For perpetrators, child sexual abuse is an intense, highly erotic, highly gratifying sexual pleasure (Gilgun and Connor, 1989; Finkelhor, 1984; Hartman and Burgess, 1989). Children, on the other hand, are intimidated and confused by the sexual behavior and may experience short- and long-term trauma (Briere, 1992; Browne and Finkelhor, 1986; Burgess, 1992). They frequently do not understand the inappropriateness of adult-child sexual contact and are unable to interpret the meanings of the sexual behaviors (Gilgun, 1986). When children experience physical pleasure, they often find it extremely difficult to integrate such pleasure with other aspects of the abusive experience (Bass and Davis, 1988; Finkelhor, 1979).

Child sexual abuse may be, at least partially, a distortion of the intense and sometimes sensual connections between children and parents and others who may love children. More than 30 years ago, Pauncz (1951) coined the term "Lear complex" as the adult counterpart to the Oedipal complex. The term is taken from the name of the title character in Shakespeare's *King Lear*, who loved his daughter Cordelia intensely. Mothers sometimes experience sensual pleasure while nursing their infants and most adults, upon reflection, can recall instances of joyful connection with children not related to sexual gratification but which were highly pleasurable, such as sharing a funny story or showing a child a newborn litter of kittens. Perpetrators, however, turn a mutually beneficial, natural process into sexual gratification taken at the expense of children.

Abusive behaviors undermine responsible and responsive caregiving. Responsible care providers are sensitive to and responsive to the "ever-changing demands of the maturing, individuating child" (Erickson, Sroufe, and Egeland, 1985, p. 164). They initiate age-appropriate activities and tasks, respect and encourage the development of children's autonomy, and gradually relinquish their control over their children by encouraging them to develop attachments to their peers (Ainsworth, 1992; Baumrind, 1989). Clearly, perpetrators of child sexual abuse violate these basic norms of sensitive, responsible child rearing.

Typologies

Child-sexual-abuse perpetrators are heterogeneous (Quinsey, 1986; Williams and Finkelhor, 1992). In attempting to characterize the subjective states of child molesters and to account for how they gained access to children, Groth and Birnbaum (1979) described anger, power, and sadistic assaulters who used either psychological pressure or physical force to gain compliance. For these researchers, physical force referred to child rape, and psychological pressure took the form of manipulation. Some perpetrators take out their anger at someone else on the child. Power rapists enjoy controlling children, and sadistic assaulters enjoy hurting them physically.

On the basis of Freudian theory, Groth (1983) suggested two other types of perpetrators: the fixated and the regressed child sexual abuser. Fixated persons' psychosexual development is arrested, and they are attracted primarily to children. Regressed perpetrators, on the other hand, have a primary sexual interest in age peers, and their sexual abuse of children represents a departure from their usual sexual interest.

Like Groth, other researchers have used abstract, psychological language to categorize adolescent and adult male and female perpetrators. O'Brien (1984) classified the types of adolescent male perpetrators with whom he worked in clinical practice as naive experimenters, undersocialized child exploiters, sexual aggressives, sexual compulsives, disturbed impulsives, and peer-group influenced. Knight and Prentky (1990) categorized adult male child molesters along the dimensions of degree of fixation and amount of contact with children and subdivided these two categories by descriptors such as social competence, meaning of contact, degree of injury, sadism, and narcissism.

Matthews, Matthews, and Speltz (1991) classified adult female perpetrators into three groups: teacher/lover, intergenerationally predisposed, and male coerced. Using exclusively abstract language, Williams and Finkelhor (1992) categorized incestuous fathers into five types: sexually preoccupied, adolescent regressives, instrumental sexual gratifiers, emotionally dependent, and angry retaliators.

These typologies show great variety among types of offenders as well as among classification schemes. For the most part, however, the language used in these typologies is abstract and provides little insight into how perpetrators view their own behavior with children. In other words, the perspectives are those of the researchers, "outsiders" to the processes they describe. How, for example, an "instrumental sexual gratifier" may interpret his or her own behavior cannot be deduced from the terminology. Similarly, terms such as control and power do not specify the behaviors that they attempt to describe. How these abstractions translate into specific thoughts and actions on the part of perpetrators remains unknown. In addition, it is not clear how such language may help practitioners conduct assessments and devise treatment plans or how these typologies may enhance policy and prevention programs.

These typologies have an additional limitation; they cannot accommodate the multiple facets of individual perpetrators' personalities and how perpetrators may change their behaviors. For example, a perpetrator conceivably can be both narcissistic and sadistic, or he may be a disturbed impulsive and sexually compulsive. A perpetrator may be very angry and express this anger as control one time and sadism another time. Typologies, then, are difficult to apply concretely because perpetrators rarely represent any single type.

A continuum constructed from the accounts of perpetrators can help overcome the limitations of typologies. The categories of the continuum presented here are not mutually exclusive; perpetrators accounts' showed fluidity across categories; that is, perpetrators' perceptions of their relationships with children sometimes shifted. In addition, the categories are based on the accounts of perpetrators; therefore, the pictures of perpetrators that they convey are crisp and focused and can help practitioners view perpetrators from insiders' perspectives. Insiders' perspectives use the language of everyday life. In this report, the categories of the continuum are described in detail so that they might be useful in clinical practice. Finally, the categories are placed within the larger context of previous research and theory as well as cultural themes. Typologies generally are not linked to previous research and theory and larger cultural themes; when such links are established, implications of findings for policy and programs become more clear.

Method

The study consisted of multiple, intensive interviews with 20 men and 3 women who had committed child sexual abuse. They were recruited on a volunteer basis from maximum and medium security prisons, community-based treatment programs, and voluntary support groups. They ranged in age from 21 to 56 years, with a modal age of 32. The sample was drawn predominantly from a white working and middle-class population; educational levels of subjects ranged from eighth grade to master's degree. Most of the perpetrators were married at the time of the interview. Informants abused both boys and girls within and outside their family, but in most cases perpetrators were parents of or parental figures to their victims.

Researchers widely acknowledge that random samples are not possible in child-sexual-abuse research because most sexual abuse is not detected and most perpetrators, therefore, are not known. The sample in the study described here consists of known perpetrators who volunteered to participate in the research, who may differ from unknown perpetrators and those who do not volunteer. Although concerns about the nature of the sample must be addressed, phenomenological research focuses on understanding how subjects experience events under study (Bogdan and Biklen, 1992). Commonly, individual accounts, research literature, and themes from within the culture are studied in an effort to develop a "thick description" (Geertz, 1973) of phenomena, that is, a multilayered description of perspectives of multiple informants in sociocultural context.

Phenomenological research produces patterns of behaviors and meanings, not numbers and probabilities, and does not presume to exhaust all the possible patterns and meanings that may characterize phenomena (Bogdan and Biklen, 1992; Morse, 1992; Patton, 1990). However, phenomenological researchers assume that the patterns discovered in their research will illuminate and foster understanding of similar situations and problems.

The research process was structured by an interview guide that investigated subjects' demographics, history of friendships, family history, history of exposure to violence and abuse, and other forms of violence. The timing and wording of questions were individualized on the basis of researcher-informant interaction. The researcher frequently clarified her understanding and interpretation of informants' perspectives with phrases such as "Did I get it right if I say that you were thinking about what you wanted and not what the child wanted?" The purpose of the interviews was to engage informants in the construction of accounts that were as close to informants' perspectives as possible.

The number of interviews varied from one three-hour interview with one informant to approximately 40 interviews over a one-year period with three informants. Other interviews ranged in number from 6 to 13 per perpetrator, with an average of 9. The average number of interview hours was 12. Detailed descriptions of abuse and accurate constructions of perpetrators' perspectives were sought throughout the interviews.

Interviews were tape recorded, transcribed verbatim, and coded. The author served as the sole interviewer. In addition, field notes were taken during and after the interviews; these data are part of the analysis on which this report is based. Coding was conducted according to protocols in Strauss and Corbin (1990) and Gilgun (1992). Subjects signed an informed consent form and were encouraged not to answer any question they did not want to answer. They were told that they could withdraw from the research at any time without negative repercussions.

Results

The perpetrators of child sexual abuse interviewed for this research had a wide variety of relationships with their child victims. As discussed earlier, these relationships were placed along a continuum. The concept of closeness to the child was used to anchor the continuum; it emerged as an organizing concept in the analysis. No sense of closeness characterized the categories at one end of the continuum and a deep sense of closeness characterized the other end. "Avenger" was the extreme category at the "no sense of closeness" end of the continuum and "soulmate" was at the other end. Between these categories lay the following self-descriptions: taker, controller, conqueror, playmate, and lover. Each of these types of relationships represented intense sexual pleasure for perpetrators. These characterizations are not exhaustive; future research may show additional ways in which perpetrators viewed themselves in their relationship with victims (see Figure 19.1). Also, perpetrators' relationships with victims can shift over the course of an abusive incident, and perpetrators may have different types of relationships with different victims.

Figure 19.1

A Continuum of Victim-Perpetrator Relationships from the Point of View of Perpetrators

Avengers	Takers	Controllers	Conquerers	Playmates	Lovers	Soulmates
inflict pain on sexual body parts or inflict emotional pain	take what they want	bargain for what they want	use seduction, pretence	perceive self as age peer, sex as fun	view child as equal partner and self as loving person	have identity confusion between self and child

No sense of closeness————————————————————————————Deep sense of closeness

Note: Perpetrators can have a variety of types of relationships with the same victim; perpetrators can have different types of relationships with different victims.

Avengers

The objective of perpetrators who viewed themselves as avengers was to harm the child or someone who loved the child. Sometimes this meant inflicting pain on the child's sexual body parts. At other times, this meant having sexual contact with the child while taking pleasure in the knowledge that this behavior would hurt the persons who loved the child.

The following account illustrated how some perpetrators justify their vengeance.

> "I wanted to hurt her [physically]. She wouldn't be running her mouth off anymore about being a virgin. To me, she was just a prick teaser."

> When she cried as he was about to rape her, he said, "You ain't gonna take no cherry home." Then he said, "I shoved it in, tearing her vagina." He also said, "I get the best ejaculation when I'm inflicting pain."

This victim was nine years old, the daughter of a man for whom the perpetrator worked. He said he overheard the little girl talking to her friends about "still having her cherry." Whether she said this is not verifiable, and if she did say this, what it meant in context might be different from how the perpetrator interpreted it. When she sat in a chair or bent down to pick something up and he was able to see her underpants, he interpreted her behavior as sexual teasing. He felt justified taking vengeance upon her because she

was a "prick teaser" and prick teasers "get you all worked up and then they go jump on someone else." He felt the child "asked for it" and gave him an "invitation." He said about her, "I'll show your little ass." "Showing," he explained, meant he would "slap them down, jump on them, and talk about it later." That's what he did.

Another man said that at least part of the reason he abused his 11-year-old stepdaughter was to "get back at" his mother-in-law. He said he was to angry and felt inadequate about the "verbal abuse" his mother-in-law gave him, which reminded him of how his own mother treated him.

> There's been two women in my whole life that treated me this way [verbally abusive] and that I loved and wanted to love me, but didn't. That was my mother and my mother-in-law. . . . I got to the point where I would do anything to hurt her [mother-in-law]. And I did.

He sexually abused the girl whom he perceived as his mother-in-law's favorite grandchild. When he abused the child, he imagined how much this would hurt his mother-in-law if she knew.

For these two men, acting on motives resulted in sadistic behavior, they enjoyed inflicting pain. Vengeance arises from the perception of being insulted, becoming angry, and seeking redress for the perceived insult (Sabini and Silver, 1992). The typologies of Groth and Birnbaum (1979) and Knight and

Prentky (1990) also note the existence of sadistic behaviors among some child molesters. In addition, Groth and Birnbaum classified some child molesters as being motivated primarily by anger, and Williams and Finkelhor (1992) identified an angry retaliator type. None of these researchers, however, tied both anger and sadism to revenge motives.

Other research and theory support these interpretations. Revenge is a motive for some rapists (Scully, 1990). In revenge rapes, rapists target (1) persons who are members of groups that rapists believe deserve to be terrorized, such as females who are members of enemy groups in war, (2) individuals who are attached to persons whom the rapists want to hurt, such as husbands or boyfriends, or (3) particular persons whom rapists seek to punish.

Both men quoted here justified their behaviors using cultural themes that view women in negative ways. Some persons believe that women who are "prick teasers" are fair game and get what they deserve. Herman (1990) pointed out, "A number of large-scale surveys conducted primarily with high school and college students indicate that a majority of students consider the use of force acceptable . . . if 'a woman gets a man sexually excited'" (p. 179). Also, mothers-in-law are often portrayed in our culture as interfering harpies, which for highly disturbed individuals may justify cruel behavior toward them or, by extension, toward persons the mother-in-law loves.

Takers

Some perpetrators approached their child victims as if the children were a commodity to be used and then discarded. In other words, they simply took what they wanted. They did not think about, or care about, or seem to be connected to what victims wanted, nor were they concerned about the possible consequences of their behavior for the children.

Takers could be fathers, stepfathers, acquaintances, or strangers to the children. A father who assaulted both his son and daughter from the time they were three or four years old presented himself as having some

consideration for the physical comfort of his daughter. He described his behavior during sodomy:

> I was concerned enough that I didn't want to physically hurt her, but at the same time, you know, I was after more of what I wanted for me, rather than anything for her. [If she said it hurt] what I would do is I would say, "OK. We'll wait a minute and we'll try again." And just continue like that until I got what I wanted. Kind of getting her used to it at the same time. It was somewhat considerate of her feeling. I wasn't just gonna boom, you know, ram her all at once.

This man obviously missed the cruel irony of his words and behavior because all he could focus on was what he wanted.

Another father visited his young adolescent daughter whenever he wanted an orgasm, usually after he had an upsetting encounter in his professional or personal life. He said that sometimes he "only needed three or four minutes of her masturbating me and . . . bang, and it's done. And I was gone. . . . That's what I needed at the time." He expressed no concern about his daughter.

A stepfather who abused his stepdaughter for approximately seven years, from the time she was 4 until she was 11, also raped his wife. He said,

> There was no saying no [to sex]. I raped my wife forcefully many times. . . . It was the same with the sexual abuse of my stepdaughter. There was no stopping once I started. No turning back. Why stop? I enjoyed it.

His insight into the effects of his behavior appeared fragmented. At one point he said, "I didn't think of other people's feelings." At another time he said about his stepdaughter, "I knew I was hurting her the whole time I was doing it." He didn't stop because "it was convenient" and "I enjoyed it."

Perpetrators who abused children outside their families also took what they wanted. A man who assaulted children younger than age four said, "I just wanted to sexualize them." By sexualize he meant "getting your rocks off in a different way." A woman who sexually abused children when she was an adolescent also displayed "taker" behaviors:

> I . . . sexually abused kids I babysat. This really gave me some clues to what happened to me when I was that young . . . they were like babies, young kids I would manipulate their vaginal area, and I would masturbate around them.

Takers simply took from children what they wanted with no concern as to how their actions affected the children. The behavior of takers corresponds to some extent to Groth and Birnbaum's (1979) definition of force in child sexual abuse, which they define as child rape. These two researchers, however, provide a cursory and abstract discussion of force. The perpetrators' descriptions are much more powerful and provide insight into how children may experience sexual abuse by perpetrators who simply take sex from them.

Feminists discuss male privilege as pertaining to men with superior physical or social power who believe they are entitled to take what they want from others without regard for the consequences to the victim (Armstrong 1978; Sanday 1990; Scully 1990). Access to sex may even be considered a male "right." About half the states in the United States do not have laws against marital rape, and most of the states with such laws passed them in the past decade. A sense of privilege is more frequently associated with males than with females. Yet, as this discussion indicates, women also can take sexual advantage of children.

Moral behavior is based on "the necessity of acting sometimes with especial and conscious regard for oneself" (Dewey, 1980: 158), while being "responsible . . . accountable, [and] responsive to the needs and claims of others" (p. 170). Takers distort this basic moral principle. In Dewey's moral framework, they isolate their behaviors from the consequences of those behaviors.

Controllers

Takers sometimes controlled the activities of their victims by bargaining for sexual favors. Two men required their stepdaughters to masturbate them before they would give them permission to do ordinary things, such

as go outside to play. One man recalled what he said to his stepdaughter:

> Do this [masturbate me] or you're not going out again. I always got my way. She'd say no a day or a couple of days, but she'd give in. I liked . . . the actual sex. . . . Then the controlling, being in control of her life completely, was a thrill for me. I thought about it more than I thought about my wife.

The man discussed previously, who used his stepdaughter to get back at his mother-in-law, said that he and his stepdaughter worked out a series of hand signs indicating how many strokes on his penis she would give in exchange for permission to do various ordinary things, such as visit her grandmother. One finger meant one stroke, two fingers meant two strokes, and so forth. When her mother and stepfather were in the same room, the stepdaughter would position herself so her mother could not see her and give hand signals to gain permission for an activity.

The control theme parallels Groth and Birnbaum's (1979) discussion of control among child molesters, although these researchers did not discuss in detail how molesters exert control over child victims. Control of women is a prominent issue in feminist literature. Sexual harassment in the workplace, whereby promotions and benefits are traded for sexual favors, parallels the perpetrator-as-controller theme.

Conquerors

Perpetrators who approached their victims as conquerors used various ploys to get the children to become sexually involved with them. In general, the methods they used were "appropriate" to the ages of children. For example, they might pose as buddies, playmates, or lovers. One man pretended he was in love with his son's 13-year-old girl friend:

> Here I am with this pretty girl. That was one of the thoughts that went through my mind. This is going to be my conquest. . . . I was setting her up to be a person the way I wanted her to be for my gratification and my needs.

He seduced her and took pictures of her in the nude. He said he felt quite disconnected from her and did not love her but wanted her to fall in love with him so that she would be available to him for sex. He actively courted this adolescent by buying her clothes and jewelry, taking her to dinner, and flattering her with attention.

Perpetrators may court young men by posing as "buddies" or "friends." One man described his attempted seduction of a 16-year-old boy from his church:

> I had him over and bought him some wine to drink and was trying to get him to where I could break down his defenses. We were in bed together, were going to sleep, and I started wrestling with him, which is one of the ways I used to try to make physical contact and, you know, accidentally on purpose touch him on the crotch area and so on.

Breaking down defenses is a common pressure tactic in acquaintance rape (Sanday, 1990). This perpetrator used such tactics on most of his boy victims, usually including smoking marijuana and watching videos as part of the seduction. When he was in graduate school, he used his status as "college guy living in an apartment" to impress adolescent males. Later, he used his status as a social worker in group homes to persuade boys to have sex with him. He gave the boys "anything that would've worked" to get them to engage in sexual activities with him. He had intense feelings for some of his victims, but was blind to the ways in which he abused his power.

Another man, who acted as if he were a playmate of his victims, abused several girls between the ages of 11 and 14. He took the girls roller skating and to the movies and had "wienie" roasts at his farm. He said that he considered one girl "a teen prostitute—there for the taking." This man posed as a playmate of the nine-year-old girl whose sadistic rape was discussed earlier. She said she wanted to go pigeon hunting and he said he would take her. Instead, he took her to an isolated part of the woods, although he "knew damn well there ain't no pigeons there."

These perpetrators' methods correspond to Groth and Birnbaum's (1979) child mo-

lesters who manipulate their victims. They seduce their victims by giving them what they want and by saying what they want to hear. In her work on fraternity gang rape, Sanday (1990) described seduction tactics whereby men spent time with a woman, bought her drinks, and danced with her in an effort to "work a yes out" (p. 113). Such ploys are a cynical means of using others for sexual gratification. Herman (1990) pointed out that coercive methods of gaining sexual access may represent a crude exaggeration of prevailing norms. The socialization of men to be sexually aggressive encourages them to use others as sexual objects. Some perpetrators applied this cultural script to children.

Playmates

Some perpetrators viewed themselves as peers of their child victims. Sex was only one of the "fun" things they did with their victims. A father described his fondling of his daughter:

> It was like playing, a lot of laughter. It was like being a kid again. . . . It was like my whole mind just went way, way, regressed way back.

Another man said,

> I had a Boy Scout troop. I felt like a kid with the Boy Scouts, camping, playing baseball. In fact, I wouldn't have known any difference except they called me Mr. Pete.

This same man molested a group of girls:

> I knew they were kids. I didn't think of myself as an adult. Then I had friends. I had seven. I'd go right back to damned loneliness after the weekend was over, even with my wife there and [the rest of my family]. With kids around, the loneliness went away—building the fire, getting the wienie roast ready. Just like Cinderella. Poof, I'd turn into a kid, where I'm 10 years old again.

These perpetrators illustrate how some child molesters regress (Howells, 1981; Groth and Birnbaum, 1979). These men were married and had children; they also claimed that they had frequent sexual intercourse with their wives. However, in their regressive states, they became emotionally starved children and adolescents. Their emotional deprivation was exacerbated by their refusal to tell anyone that they needed to be comforted, reassured, and accepted. They interpreted their emotional pain as a sign of weakness and evidence that they were not masculine enough. Disclosing personal loss and sadness threatened their identity as men. They believed common cultural injunctions such as "big boys don't cry" and "don't be a sissy" and were unable to work through their intense feelings of emotional deprivation.

Lovers

In describing their relationships with child victims, some perpetrators appeared to be infatuated or in love with their victims. One man described how he felt the first time he saw a particular boy:

> I remember thinking, "That's a kid that I want to have sex with." It's sort of like seeing a beautiful model. From then on I was, like, infatuated with that kid. . . . It was more a feeling of excitement and arousal and infatuation.

Using the language of female-male courtship, he elaborated on his experiences with several other boys:

> All of a sudden, you see someone across the room that you're attracted to, and then if you're able to somehow fulfill that fantasy, go meet the person. Ask her out for a date, she accepts, and you go.

Another man expressed a deep sense of closeness and tenderness for his stepson, whom he abused when the boy was between the ages of 11 to 14:

> I guess the most important part would be when we first started touching. It's kind of new and close. I guess the fact that my touching could give him an erection meant a lot to me, and it also meant a lot to me when he touched me.

They masturbated and performed oral sex with each other. He said, "The relationship had came [sic] to mean something to me." He felt the boy was the only person who loved him. Thus, for this man, who had sex with his stepson in the shed in back of their trailer, his sexual relationship with his stepson, who was 35 years younger than he, was his most meaningful personal relationship. Confident that their relationship was mutual, he was hurt and confused when his stepson testified against him in court.

Some perpetrators said they were in love. Two men had long-term relationships with their stepdaughters—one lasted 12 years and the other 7 years. Both men dreamed about running away with their victims. One man wanted to take his stepdaughter to a desert island, and the other man wanted to make a model out of his stepdaughter.

Some perpetrators perceived themselves as being the same emotional age as their victims. Others saw their victims as being older than they actually were. The stepfather who abused his stepdaughter for 12 years had a sudden insight while at the beach with her and other members of his family: "She was a skinny little 10-year-old in a bathing suit." But his insight was momentary, and he continued his sexual activity with her for six more years. Another man bought his daughter jewelry and seductive women's clothing, took her to expensive restaurants, and had candlelight dinners with her. He was in his late thirties and she was 13. In prison for this molestation as well as another, he said "Other people must've thought I looked ridiculous, an old fool acting like a teenager in love with a pubertal girl dressed up like a woman."

One of the female perpetrators described her regressive, lover-type relationship. A youth director at her church, she had a "committed" four-year relationship with a girl who was 14 years younger than she and who was 14 years old when they met.

> I was really, and all the way along had been, very committed to this. I would not have gotten involved if I was not committed. The sexual thing came along with the expression just in our relationships. It wasn't so much a sexual issue as a whole relationship issue for us. It seemed right in the context. . . . It was like I became that age again. She helped me with a lot of things . . . that's really good, so now I can do that stuff more.

Besides regressing into adolescence, this woman reversed roles with her victim. The adolescent girl helped her shop for clothes.

The perpetrator viewed the relationship as being mutually helpful, whereby they helped each other with abandonment and dependency issues.

Infatuation, love, and emotional closeness are teacher/lover themes elaborated by Matthews et al. (1991) in their discussion of women perpetrators. The women in their sample acted as mentors who taught younger people about sex. Pauncz (1951) suggests that perpetrators who fall in love or become infatuated are examples of the "Lear complex" gone awry. Finkelhor (1984) pointed out that in our culture, men are socialized to seek sexual partners who are smaller and younger and that they may find it difficult to "distinguish between sexual and nonsexual forms of affection" (p. 12)—a phenomenon evident in perpetrators who love children sexually. Extreme emotional deprivation may also play a part. Men do not receive permission to admit such deprivation, although in the example described above, the woman perpetrator was also unable to work through major emotional blocks in her own early life.

Soulmates

Adult perpetrators who perceive themselves as soulmates of their victims confuse themselves with children. They are drawn to and see themselves in their child victims.

One man who abused approximately 40 children identified with the pain he perceived in some children:

> The pain I felt growing up was like having a vise get tighter and tighter around my gut. I could see pain in children. I wanted to comfort them.

His way of comforting was to be sexual with them.

Another man identified with and sexualized the loneliness he saw in boys:

> The boys I'm attracted to are 12 to 13. They look like me and they look lonely the way I was lonely at that age. I would become sexually aroused. I did all I could to get those boys to be sexual with me.

He said that he had always "yearned for a brother or sister" and had a distant relationship with his father. He saw himself as giving that kid something I didn't have, and

secondly, to get something I didn't have. So it was to fulfill my need and the kid's need for closeness.

With some perpetrators, identification with the victim occurred but it remained unclear whether such identification was linked to sexual arousal. For example, the man who sadistically raped a nine-year-old girl saw her as a "prick teaser," yet at other times identified with her when other children made fun of her. He said, "[She] was like me. The other kids made fun of her because she was such a little snob." He said that when he was a child, kids made fun of him because he wore dirty, smelly clothes to school. Thus, abuse of her seemed motivated by self-hatred.

Knight and Prentky (1990) and Howells (1981) discuss narcissism in certain types of child molesters. Within a narcissistic framework, perpetrators' child love objects are actually projected aspects of themselves. Perpetrators who view themselves as soulmates project parts of themselves onto their victims. In identifying with children, they may believe that they are comforting the children while comforting themselves. Such behaviors may be exacerbated by cultural stereotypes that inhibit boys and some girls from expressing their vulnerability through verbal expression and prosocial behaviors.

Combinations of Themes

For most perpetrators, multiple themes were evident in their relationships with their child victims. Other than the man who viewed his son's 13-year-old girl friend as a conquest, typically two or more themes were at work in the relationships. Lovers, for example, sometimes viewed their victims as soulmates; they could also be takers. The man who raped his wife also raped his stepdaughter at times (taker), felt he was in love with her at other times (lover), and controlled her by bargaining for sexual "favors" (controller). A man who played the role of avenger at times experienced his victim as a soulmate; at other times he was a conquerer playing the role of playmate.

Some perpetrators had different types of relationships with different victims. One man, for example, had been in love with a child victim for more than 10 years; with other victims, he acted as an avenger, a taker, a playmate, and a soulmate. One female perpetrator was a taker in her relationships with the children whom she babysat, but was both a taker and a nurturer (lover) with her two younger brothers.

Fifty years ago, Apfelberg, Sugra, and Pfeffer (1944) noted schizoid qualities in perpetrators, and Weiner (1962) pointed out their splitting tendencies. Perpetrators' self-described tendency to switch from one type of relationship to another in thematic terms supports this conceptualization of perpetrators. Perpetrators are also noted for their self-centered disregard for the well-being of their child victims (Apfelberg et al., 1944; Gebhard, Gagnon, Pomeroy, and Christenson, 1965; Gilgun, 1988; Groth and Birnbaum, 1979; Peters, 1976; Weiner, 1962). In this study, perpetrators' disregard for the children was evident regardless of their relationship with the children. Although takers describe a particular type of relationship, in the final analysis, all perpetrators are takers.

Discussion

Descriptions of how perpetrators see themselves in relation to child victims can be painful to read and to imagine. Yet these children need the support of professionals, parents, and others to help them articulate their experiences and to work through the effects of such experiences. With increasing evidence that children often do not disclose significant details of their own abuse (Steward et al. 1993), we need to ask ourselves whether children are picking up cues from professionals and others, who are signaling their own pain about these details. Misinterpreting or not knowing how to interpret these signals, children may respond by cutting their own accounts short. As responsive and responsible adults, we must work through our own reluctance to confront these issues so that we can read subtle cues indicating abuse and provide support to these children.

"Starting where clients are" remains a rule of thumb for practice. In instances of child sexual abuse, a first step may be for us to imagine what it would be like to be used as an object of vengeance, control, conquest,

play, love, or identification. When perpetrators can switch from one mode to another for no discernible reason, as is true in most cases, imagine the confusion children experience and their struggles to interpret these behaviors. Putting ourselves in children's shoes can be difficult and may require a lot of processing time in individual and group supervision.

Practitioners should enter case situations with a variety of hypotheses and, in the flow of assessment and intervention, test these hypotheses for their fit. Theoretical frameworks should never be imposed on clients; rather practitioners need to listen to clients and, as appropriate, probe to draw clients out. These practice principles also apply in work with persons sexually abused in childhood. The themes of the continuum can be used as hypotheses; when the timing is appropriate, practitioners may probe for signs that the children may have experienced one or more of these types of relationships. The continuum can be used in similar ways with perpetrators.

These findings also can be used in educational contexts, within a treatment setting, or in a more formal educational setting such as workshops for victims, perpetrators, and their families and training for professionals. In clinical work with children, adolescents, or adults maltreated in childhood, practitioners may sense that clients can benefit from a brief explanation of the various types of relationships that perpetrators perceive themselves as having with child victims. As in all clinical work, timing is critical in work with sexual abuse victims and perpetrators. Families of victims and perpetrators and professionals participating in workshops and other educational programs are likely to develop a deeper understanding of victimization experiences through exposure to the continuum presented here.

These findings, however, should not be used to excuse the behavior of perpetrators. Emotional starvation and socialization practices may be factors leading to perpetration. Nevertheless, perpetrators are responsible for their own behavior and nothing justifies harming another person. Feeling sympathy for the difficult histories of some perpetrators cannot be used to encourage victims to minimize the injustices that have been inflicted on them. Child sexual abuse is a clear instance of a serious transgression against children.

Clinicians generally approach child molestation on individual, psychodynamic, and interpersonal levels. Policy and programming, especially prevention and education programs, focus on social change and on preventing the development of molesting behavior in the first place. Challenging models of male conduct—such as the unmanliness of feeling hurt and lonely and the manliness of being sexually aggressive and exploitative—by proposing policies and programs that promote other more humanitarian alternatives will support prevention efforts.

References

Ainsworth, M. D. (1992). A consideration of social referencing in the context of attachment theory and research. In S. Feinman (Ed.), *Social referencing and the social construction of reality in infancy* (pp. 349–367). New York: Plenum.

Apfelberg, B.,Sugra, C., and Pfeffer, A. (1944). A psychiatric study of 250 sex offenders. *American Journal of Psychiatry*, 100, 762–770.

Armstrong, L. (1978). *Kiss Daddy good night*. New York: Hawthorne.

Bass, E., and Davis, L. (1988). *The courage to heal*. New York: Harper & Row.

Baumrind, D. (1989). Rearing competent children. In W. Damon (Ed.), *Child development today and tomorrow* (pp. 349–378). San Francisco: Jossey-Bass.

Bogdan, R. and Biklen, S. K. (1992). *Qualitative research for education* (2nd ed.). Boston: Allyn Bacon.

Briere, J. N. (1992). *Child abuse trauma*. Newbury Park, CA: Sage Publications.

Browne, A. and Finkelhor, D. (1986). Impact of child sexual abuse: A review of the research. *Psychological Bulletin*, 99, 66–77.

Burgess, A. W. (Ed.). (1992). *Child rrauma: Issues and research*. New York: Garland.

Dewey, J. (1908/1980). *Theory of the moral life*. New York: Irvington.

Erickson, M. F., Smufe, L. A., and Egeland, B. (1985). The relationship between quality of attachment and behavior problems in preschool in a high-risk sample. In I. Bretherton and E. Waters (Eds.), *Growing points of attachment theory and research (pp. 147–166). Monographs of the Society for Research in Child Development*, 50 (1–2, Serial No. 209).

Finkelhor, D. (1979). *Sexually victimized children*. New York: Free Press.

Finkelhor, D. (1984). *Child sexual abuse: New theory and research*. New York: Free Press.

Gebhard, P. H.,Gagnon, J. H.,Pomeroy, W. B., and Christenson, C.V. (1965). *Sex offenders: An analysis of types*. New York: Harper and Row.

Geertz, C. (1973). *The interpretation of cultures*. New York: Basic Books.

Gilgun, J. F (1986). Sexually abused girls' knowledge of sexual abuse and sexuality. *Journal of Interpersonal Violence*, 1: 309–325.

Gilgun, J. F. (1988). Self-centeredness and the adult male perpetrator of child sexual abuse. *Contemporary Family Therapy*, 10, 216–234.

Gilgun, J. F (1992). Definitions, methods, and methodologies in qualitative family research. In J. F. Gilgun, K. Daly, and G. Handel (Eds.), *Qualitative methods in family research* (pp. 22–39). Newbury Park, CA: Sage Publications.

Gilgun J. F. and Connor, T. (1989). How perpetrators view child sexual abuse. *Social Work*, 34, 249–251.

Groth, A. N. (1983). The incest offender. In S. M. Sgroi (Ed.), *Handbook of clinical intervention in child sexual abuse* (pp. 215–239). Lexington, MA: Lexington Books.

Groth, A. N., and Birnbaum, J. (1979). *Men who rape: The psychology of the fffender*. New York: Plenum.

Hartman, C. R., and Burgess, A. W. (1989). Sexual abuse of children: causes and consequences. In D. Cicchetti and V Carlson (Eds.), *Child maltreatment: Theory and research on the causes and consequences of child abuse and neglect* (pp. 95–128). New York: Cambridge University Press.

Herman, J. L. (1990). Sex offenders: A feminist perspective. In W. L. Marshall, D. R. Laws, and H. E. Barbaree (Eds.), *Handbook of sexual assault* (pp. 177–193). New York: Plenum.

Howells, K. (1981). Adult sexual interest in children: Considerations relevant to theories of aetiology. In M. Cook and K. Howells (Eds.), *Adult sexual interest in children* (pp. 55–94). London: Academic Press.

Knight, R. A. and Prentky, R. A. (Eds.). (1990). *Handbook of sexual assault: Issues, forms, and treatment of the offender* (pp. 23–52). New York: Plenum.

Lather, P. (1991). Getting smart: Feminist research and pedagogy with/in the postmodern. New York: Routledge.

Matthews, R., Matthews, J. K., and Speltz, K. (1991). Female sexual offenders: A typology. In

M. Q. Patton (Ed.), *Family sexual abuse: Frontline research and evaluation* (pp. 199–219). Newbury Park, CA: Sage Publications.

Morse, J. M. (1992). *Qualitative health research.* Newbury Park, CA: Sage Publications.

O'Brien, M (1984). *Adolescent sexual offenders: An outpatient program's perspective on research directions: An outpatient program's perspective on research directions.* Paper presented at the 13th annual Child Abuse and Neglect Symposium, (May 23), Keystone, CO.

Patton, M.Q. (1990). *Qualitative evaluation and research methods* (2nd ed.). Newbury Park, CA: Sage Publications.

Pauncz, I. (1951). The concept of adult libido and lear complex. *American Journal of Psychotherapy,* 5: 187–195.

Peters, J. J. (1976). Children who are victims of sexual assault and the psychology of offenders. *American Journal of Psychotherapy,* 30, 398–421.

Quinsey, V. L. (1986). Men who have sex with children. In D. N. Weisstub (Ed.), *Law and mental health: International perspectives,* 2, (pp. 140–172). New York: Pergamon.

Sabini, J., and Silver, M. (1992). The moral dimension in social psychology. In D. N. Robinson (Ed.), *Social discourse and moral judgment* (pp. 75–86). New York: Academic Press.

Sanday, P. R. (1990). *Fraternity gang rape: Sex, brotherhood, and privilege on campus.* New York: New York University Press.

Scully, D. (1990). *Understanding sexual violence.* Boston: Unwin Hyman.

Steward, M.S., Bussey, K., Goodman, G. S., and Saywitz, K. J., (1993). "Implications of developmental research for interviewing children. *Child Abuse and Neglect,* 17, 25–37.

Strauss, A. and Corbin, J. (1990). *Basics of qualitative research.* Newbury Park, CA: Sage Publications.

Weiner, I. B. (1962). Father-daughter incest: A clinical report. *Psychiatric Quarterly,* 36, 607–632.

Williams, L. M. and Finkelhor, D. (1992). *The characteristics of incest fathers.* Report submitted to the National Center on Child Abuse and Neglect (July 31). University of New Hampshire, Durham, NH.

20

Motives of Reward Among Men Who Rape

Robert Hale

This article explores the ways that men think about their crimes and what they see as the goal of rape. By looking at the various ways that men think about rape, we see that rapists do have specific goals in mind when they select victims and sexually assault them. This suggests to us that men who rape do actively consider both the rewards and possibility of being caught and punished for their actions. Violence is a part of all rapes, and many rapists consciously consider the effect that their violence will have on the emotional, physical, and psychological states of their victims. Concerns about being caught are taken into consideration, but are typically outweighed by the desire to hurt a victim.

Rape and those who commit rape have been the focus of a range of studies since the mid-1970s. The statistical and demographic characteristics of rape have been analyzed in an attempt to better understand the circumstances of this crime. The background characteristics of men who commit rape also have been explored in an attempt to develop a composite or profile. In addition, the motivations of men who commit rape have been examined to better understand what compels the rapist. . . .

Deterrence of criminal behavior is achieved as the individual balances beliefs of potential punishment against the anticipated risk of the criminal act. . . .

While studies of rape have a long history, Scully (1990) and Scully and Marolla (1984; 1985; 1995) have produced a progression of highly regarded works exploring the motives of reward among men who commit rape. In addition, Decker, Wright, and Logie (1992) have produced a model study of perceptual deterrence. They encourage future research that attempts to cross-validate perceptual deterrence across different types of offenses and offenders. This study will merge the ideas of rape and perceptual deterrence to a sample of men convicted for rape in an attempt to identify the anticipated gains (rewards) that motivate these men. . . .

Explanations of Rape

. . . .Traditionally, the rapist is seen as compelled to rape, driven by either "uncontrollable urges" (Edwards, 1983) or a "disordered personality" (Scully and Marolla, 1984). Attributing rape to an uncontrollable impulse implies that normal restraints of self-control are reduced or erased by an innate sex drive. The major thesis is that sexual deprivation causes predisposed individuals to lose control of their behavior and force a victim into unwanted sexual relations (Symons, 1979).

The "disordered personality" approach tends to attribute rape to a mental illness or disease. Rape is thought to be a symptom of some deeply rooted abnormality, either cognitive or organic. Lanyon (1986) believes that all sexual offenders, not just rapists, are acting from the same sickness, although the sickness is not identified. Ellis and Hoffman (1990) state that a "mutant gene" may be the cause, but they do not rule out other genetic or hormonal influences. Scully and Marolla (1985, p. 298) point out that the "belief that rapists are or must be sick is amazingly persistent," and Lanyon (1986, p. 176) asserts that this belief "tends to be the view held by the judicial system, by social service agencies, and the general public." The further implication of either of these approaches is that thinking is not a part of the process of rape; this holds particular consequences for the etiology of the crime and rehabilitation of men who commit rape.

However, an abundance of research shows that thinking and choice are a part of the rapist's construction of the crime, and the learning approach is a common theme in the literature on rape. From this perspective a number of typologies of men who rape have been created (Burgess, 1991; Holmes, 1991; Knight and Prentky, 1987; Scully and Marolla, 1985, 1995). Scully (1990) and Weiner, et al. (1990) identify three categories of rape; Holmes identifies five categories of rape, the same number given by Knight and Prentky; while the Scully and Marolla study (1985) describes six categories of motive for rape. Although there is some overlap between the descriptions in these studies, there are also some mutually exclusive categories. From the studies noted above and other sources, eight categories of reward for rape can be identified.

The first category originates in the work of Black (1983) and is expanded by Scully and Marolla (1985). The rapist commits his crime but views his act as a legitimate form of revenge. This view is referred to as "The Punishment Model" by Felson and Krohn (1990). In these rapes, men are seeking to hold accountable and punish a female for some action that the rapist subjectively perceives as an insult. The action may have been committed directly by the victim, or she may be a victim of "collective liability," in which the victim is a representative of a larger class of individuals (Black, 1983; Scully and Marolla, 1984).

The revenge motive is common when the victim is the primary source of frustration, whereas punishment is often the goal when the victim is held accountable for collective liability. In these rapes, the rapist views his action as an attempt to subordinate women for an attempt to challenge male dominance. This perception comes from the rapist's belief that he has the right to discipline and punish.

The second category reflects an anger within the rapist, often emerging from his perception that a woman is interested in having sex with him but later refuses to fulfill his desire. This category would be comparable to the "deniers" found by Scully (1990). When seeking this type of reward, the rape becomes a means to a specific end, which is sexual satiation. The rapist believes he can seize what he desires, reflecting his belief that even if a woman declines sexual advances, rape is a suitable means to what is desired (Groth and Birnbaum, 1979; Holmes, 1991).

The third category reflects the desire of the rapist that the sex act be performed totally for his satisfaction, without regard for the feelings or emotions of the victim. Thus, the rapist can avoid feelings of intimacy and caring while having his desires fulfilled. This approach would be applicable in some respects to the impersonal, anonymous sex that often occurs in casual "one-night stands" and between prostitutes and their customers (Felson and Krohn, 1990; Russell, 1988, 1995; Scully and Marolla, 1995).

The fourth category of reward includes rapists who commit their crimes for the excitement they receive. The sex is secondary to the rush of emotion that goes along with the act. Sexual deviants do not emerge at the most severe levels of deviance or illegality: Evidence abounds that chronic sexual deviants have a long history of involvement with "nuisance" sex behaviors before progressing into such crimes as rape (Holmes, 1991; Rosenfield, 1985). Some rapists have reported feelings of an intense "high" as they anticipate and then complete the rape (Knopp, 1984; Warren et al., 1991). Rapists who report this goal as a reward are seen as pushing the limits of excitement and personal enjoyment to the ultimate illegal extreme.

The fifth category includes those who rape for the adventure or challenge the act affords them. The gang rapist is typical of those included in this category. The challenges of forcing the victim to complete a sex act and of being able to perform sexually in front of other male participants and the danger inherent in attempting a rape are often cited as reasons for rape by those included in this category (Holmes, 1991). This category is similar to the proving of "masculinity" observed by Russell (1989), Kimmel (1996), and Messner (1989). The danger of the act seems to be the motivating factor for these men: The danger lies either in the risk of identification and capture or in the potential inability to perform in the situation. The thrill lies in the promotion of loyalty and brotherhood among those associated with the commission of the rape.

The sixth category reflects the notion that the underlying motivation for rape is domination of the victim, rather than the sex that accompanies the rape. The goal of this type of rapist is to ensure that women are frightened and intimidated sufficiently to not challenge the power and superiority of males (Deming and Eppy, 1981; Herman, 1995).

The seventh category has its basis in the evolutionary theory of rape, which proposes that rape originates from pressures of natural selection that require men to be more aware of sexual opportunities, to have sexual relations with a wide variety of sexual partners, and to use force when necessary to fulfill their sexual desires (Quinsey, 1984; Shields and Shields, 1983; Symons, 1979; Thornhill and Thornhill, 1983, 1987).

The final category was proposed by Abel and Blanchard (1974) and is detailed by Prentky and Burgess (1991). The reward for the rapist in this category is the physical fulfillment of a fantasy. The role of fantasy has been documented as a precursor to a number of violent crimes, including serial rape (MacCullough et al., 1983; Warren et al., 1991). The consensus is that the fantasy-world beliefs of many sadistic offenders become overt behavior when the offender feels compelled to live out his fantasy.

This study will measure the motives of reward among a sample of men incarcerated for committing rape; the men will be asked to rank order their motives for committing their crime. Then, based on the motive, the men will be asked whether a low or high likelihood of arrest would deter their committing the crime. From these results, the type of men who rape that would be deterred by the risk of incarceration should be apparent.

Data and Methods

The subjects in this study were a sample of the population of men incarcerated for rape within two maximum-security state penitentiaries in the Deep South. . . .

Data were collected at two different times. First, subjects were briefed about the purpose of the study and then were asked to complete a questionnaire. This questionnaire gathered demographic information before presenting the eight categories of reward for committing rape. The men also consented to

an interview, which was conducted at another time. During the interview, subjects were asked to provide details behind their motives. . . .Subjects were selected at random to provide the follow-up interviews. The questionnaire and interviews were administered during counseling sessions and were conducted by either the leader of the counseling session or the author. Men in this study were surveyed over a three-year period that ended in 1996.

. . . .Only those convicted of rape against an adult female were included in the study. While definitions of what constitutes rape can vary, men in this study had been found guilty under statutes that required "forcible sexual intercourse" achieved "against her (the victim's) will." Those convicted of other sex offenses, such as nuisance sex offenses, sexual assault or molestation, offenses involving pornography, or pedophilia, were excluded from the analysis. Subjects must have been convicted of the charge of rape in order to be included in the final sample. This stipulation created a sample of 132 subjects. Two potential problems could arise from using this sample. One is that subjects might provide answers for which they would anticipate being rewarded in some way, perhaps with preference for early release. To bypass this issue of validity, subjects were informed that all answers would be anonymous and that prison counselors would not know who did or did not respond to the survey. It was also stressed that no inmate would receive preferential treatment for completing the survey, just as no respondent would be deprived of benefits for refusing to participate.

A second flaw is that the entire model could be seen as speculative since all subjects are incarcerated at the time of the survey and thus cannot fully answer concerning their motivation as if they were truly free to act on their perceptions of risk and reward. Surveying men who were not incarcerated might provide the better measure of cost and benefit, rather than posing artificial situations to men who are not free to act. . . .

The group of 132 rapists had an average age of 32.6, with a range from 17 to 67 years of age. The mean educational level of the sample was 12.5 years, with a range from seventh grade to post-college graduate education. At the time of their offenses, 72% had been or were married and another 13% had been living with a woman. The majority (57% were employed in skilled or unskilled labor positions.

The group had a lengthy involvement of sex offenses. On average, they began their sex offenses (e.g., voyeurism, exhibitionism, and scatophilia) in their early teens (mean = 13.4), and they committed their first rape at age 17.4. Of the sample, 85% had a prior conviction for a sexual offense, and 52% had a prior rape conviction. Most reported being heterosexual (82%), 7% reported being homosexual, 5% reported being bisexual, and 8 of the men chose not to answer this question.

. . . .The goal of this study is to examine how men incarcerated for rape view the rewards of their actions. Subjects in this study were asked to remember a rape they had committed or had thought about committing. Each respondent was then asked to fill in details describing the crime, such as the time of day and characteristics of the setting and of the victim; the goal was to make the crime situation as real as possible to the respondent. Subjects were then presented with eight categories of potential reward and were asked to select which reward would compel them to commit the rape.

Subjects were asked to rank order the eight categories of reward that would influence them to commit rape. . . .After the men had ordered their perceptions of the reward they anticipated, they were asked to consider how the risk of apprehension would affect the likelihood of committing rape. . . .The men were asked whether they would attempt to commit the rape they had visualized earlier within the context of the amount of reward anticipated and the risk of apprehension. Four responses were possible: (1) No; (2) Not Likely; (3) Likely; (4) Yes.

Results

Table 20.1 provides four types of information. The second column (Number) details how often each category was selected as the primary goal for committing rape by the 132 respondents; the third column (Percent) lists what percentage of the men are reflected by the number in column two.

Twenty-eight men (21%) answered they would rape for the reward of "Revenge and Punishment." Twenty-three of the men (17%) committed rape "To exert control or power" while 19 (14%) committed rape to release "Anger."

The cumulative points given to each category were then calculated; these scores are derived from the addition of the scores given to each category by each of the 132 respondents. The highest possible score for any category in this column is 1,056, assuming each of the men gave that particular category the highest score of eight; as shown, "Anger" is the motive receiving the highest cumulative score, followed by those whose motive was "To fulfill or experience a fantasy" and those raping for "Revenge and Punishment."

Although the reward of "Revenge and Punishment" is the single highest category, the

Table 20.1

Frequency of Selection as Primary Goal for Committing Rape

Category	Number	Percent	Cumulative Points	Average Score
Revenge/Punishment	28	21	963	7.3
Anger	19	14	1003	7.6
Impersonal Sex	9	6	726	5.5
To Feel Good	4	3	950	7.2
Adventure/Danger	18	13	831	6.3
Control/Power	23	17	752	5.7
Masculinity	14	10	946	7.2
Fulfill A Fantasy	17	12	990	7.5

cumulative totals reveal that more men were raping out of "Anger" or "To fulfill or experience a fantasy." The category of "Anger" as a reward received a cumulative number of 1003 points, while the category "Fulfill A Fantasy" received a cumulative total of 990 points. The category of "Revenge and Punishment" received 963 points and was the third highest category in terms of cumulative points. . . .

When the rapist is seeking a reward of personal satisfaction and enjoyment, he is more likely to defy a "High Risk" of apprehension in order to commit the rape. Follow-up interviews with rapists in this category affirmed the hypothesis that the high risk of apprehension added to the satisfaction derived from the rape. According to "Vance," an inmate who fits into this category:

> The idea that she might later figure out who I was added to the thrill, at the time. . . .I had seen her around, and I'm sure that she had seen me. Plus, the place where I got her (in a car parked outside a shopping center) was pretty open, too. I guess I picked that spot because I knew there was more chance of getting caught. But I never figured it was going to happen.

For men in this category, the attempt to commit rape in spite of a high risk of apprehension added to the pleasure of completing the act. Their satisfaction was actually the result of two separate situations.

In only two other categories of reward were the men willing to chance a high risk of apprehension, . . . when the reward was either the danger or challenge of the rape or to fulfill a fantasy. Research points out that these rapes are often committed in front of an audience, such as instances of gang rape (Holmes, 1991; Scully and Marolla, 1984; Scully, 1990). When witnesses are present, whether or not they are active participants in the rape, the risk of apprehension increases. It is assumed that those who are willing to commit rape in front of witnesses are aware of the increased risk of apprehension. As "Larry" pointed out:

> The guys that were with me that night, we had known each other forever, we had grown up together. They had stuff on me,

and I had stuff on them. I knew they would not talk, 'cause I could turn on them, and they knew it.

Thus, the rapist who is seeking an adventure in spite of a high risk of apprehension appears to believe that his accomplices will not corroborate the crime.

Those who rape in order to experience a fantasy also appear to be unconcerned when the risk of apprehension is high. Fantasy is an integral part of not only "normal" sexual relations but also of deviant and criminal sexual acts (Burgess et al., 1986; Holmes, 1991; Prentky and Burgess, 1991). . . . Fantasy is defined as a series of thoughts that preoccupy the individual into the rehearsal of the script. As the fantasy evolves, it may include feelings, emotion, and dialogue (Burgess, 1991). . . .

[T]he fantasy of rape provides a secondary motive for rape for many men in this study. Research has asserted that fantasies of violence are often a precursor to violent behaviors (Cohen et al., 1971; MacCullough et al., 1983; Prentky et al., 1985; Warren et al., 1991). These fantasies are thought to be linked to the rapist's feelings of anger, of revenge, or of danger and adventure. The rapist is motivated by these emotions and has fantasized a script that allows for their resolution. This assumption was borne out through follow-up interviews with men who fit this classification. Typical of those who raped out of a motive of revenge was "Ken," who stated:

> I had a dream of getting even to her for the divorce. Then she remarried and I lost track of her. Even though I didn't have no interest in finding her, I still hated her for what she had done. I wished of getting back at her, but the only thing I could do was to hurt somebody like her, who reminded me of her. It still wasn't enough, but I felt better after I did it (rape).

The revenge expressed by "Travis" had a longer history:

> I never felt like my own mother ever cared for me. She was always off doing her own thing, she never seemed to have time for me. Never seemed to care. The only women I ever got involved with were those I could treat however I wanted. And it was

never good. I used to sit around and think of ways of getting even, when I had the chance. I figure now it goes back to my mother. I probably knew it then, but I couldn't help myself. And I'll probably do the same if I ever get out of here.

While some who raped from a motive of revenge had over time put some thought into their actions, the anger-rapist was more impulsive. His act of rape stemmed from an immediate situation that, in the perception of the rapist, was an affront that demanded a response. For "Dan," the affront was the discovery his wife was having an affair:

When I heard this, I just lost my cool. You know, how they say a heat of passion thing, or something like that? Everything just turned red and black in my head, like something went off. . . .I looked at her, and thought, "If you are giving it to someone else, then I'll take it any way I want to." I saw it as having sex, although I was forcing her to, and I knew she didn't want to. At least, not the way I was making her do it. . . .They called it rape later, but I didn't see it that way. . . .I'm not sure I see it that way even now.

Sometimes the anger-rape has nothing to do with an affront by another person. For "Doug," it was simply a combination of events, none of which were directly related to a female:

That night I was really pissed off about a lot of things. I mean, not really a lot of things, but some thing were really eating at me. I had been looking for a job, and that was not going well. Money was tight, and I was getting hassled over the bills. I was just mad at everything in general, nothing seemed to be going my way. And then, out in the bar, I saw this girl who seemed to have it all together, who seemed to have a lot. I decided right then I was going to show her before the night was over what it was like to lose something. . . what it felt like to hurt.

Discussion

This study provides support for the idea that rape can occur for a variety of motives. Among these motives, violence is certainly an issue to consider. While definitions of vio-

lence vary, emotions of danger, hatred, and revenge, along with beliefs of punishment and privilege, are repeatedly used as descriptions. In this study, violence emerges as a leading factor in rape. More men rape out of revenge, or to punish the victim, than for any other single motive, while anger is a latent motive for many men who commit rape.

Given the amount of research detailing rape as a crime of violence, these findings are not surprising. The data add support to the contention that violence is an integral part of the link between men and rape. . . .Evidently men who rape from a motive of revenge or anger are not considering, or affected by, the danger of committing the act. As mentioned earlier, many of the men whose primary motive was the element of danger were involved in gang rapes or were seeking personal satisfaction; revenge and anger were not part of the incident. Similarly, men who raped with the motives of anger or revenge were not concerned with the danger, but were more concerned with correcting a perceived "Wrong" (Katz, 1988). . . .

The link between power, anger, and revenge as factors in rape has long been noted, but this study fails to provide support for it. They key variable seems to be "power," as anger and revenge have been discussed as important within this study. It is plausible that men in this study did not want to admit (either to themselves or the researcher) that they were seeking power, given that power rapists tend toward insecurity with doubts about their masculinity (Holmes, 1991; Maletzky, 1991; Scully and Marolla, 1995). It may also be that the anger and revenge felt by these men simply overshadowed the need for power, although all three sensations were present.

While the analyses in this study show that violence is a factor influencing many men to commit rape, violence is present in every case. Certainly rape is a violent act, and the control of a victim often requires that violence be used by the perpetrator. However, there are motives for rape that do not include violence. When men are committing rape "to feel good," to experience a new "adventure," or to "fulfill a fantasy," violence does not have to be a part of the script. It is entirely possible that "Larry" and "Vance" committed their crimes without intending to use violence. Of course, this explanation is certainly open to debate, depending on the definition of violence and the definition of the situation; however, from the perspective of the perpetrator, there are instances when rape does occur without violence.

Responses in this study imply that the majority of rapists are not suffering from psychoses or other serious psychiatric disorders, as those from the "disordered personality" perspective would believe. Certainly, these men have a distorted perception of the role of sex and of females. This is not, however, a full sign of mental illness or other cognitive impairment. It is more a reflection of poor judgment, which is more typical of faulty social or learning skills. . . .

References

Abel, G.G., and Blanchard, E. B. (1974). "The role of fantasy in the treatment of sexual deviation." *Archives of General Psychiatry*, 30, 467–475.

Black, D. (1983). "Crime as social control." *American Sociological Review*, 48, 34–45.

Burgess, A.W. (Ed.) 1991. *Rape and sexual assault: A research handbook*. New York: Garland.

Burgess, A.W., Hartman, C. R., Ressler, R. K., Douglas, J., and McCormack, A. (1986). "Sexual homicide: A motivational model." *Journal of Interpersonal Violence*, 1:251–272.

Decker, S., Wright, R., and Logie, R. (1992). "Perceptual deterrence among active residential burglars: A research note." *Criminology*, 31: 135–147.

Deming, M.B. and Eppy, A. (1981). "The sociology of rape." *Sociology and Social Research*, 64:357–380.

Edwards, S. (1983). "Sexuality, sexual offenses, and conception of victims in the criminal justice process." *Victimology: An International Journal*, 8:113–128.

Ellis, L. and Hoffman, H. (Eds.). (1990). *Crime in biological, social, and moral contexts*. New York: Praeger.

Felson, R.B. and Krohn, M. (1990). "Motives for rape." *Journal of Research in Crime and Delinquency*, 27(3):222–242.

Groth, A.N. and Birnbaum, J. (1979). *Men who rape*. New York: Plenum Press.

Herman, J.L. (1995). "Considering sex offenders: A model of addiction. In P. Searles and R. Berger (Eds.), *Rape and society* (pp. 74–98). Boulder, CO: Westview Press.

Holmes, R. (1991). *Sex crimes*. Newbury Park, CA: Sage Publications.

Holmes, R. DeBurger, J. and Holmes, S. T. (1988). "Inside the mind of the serial murderer." *American Journal of Criminal Justice*, 13(1), 1–9.

Katz, J. (1988). *Seductions of crime*. New York: Basic Books.

Kimmel, M. (1996). *Manhood in America: A cultural history*. New York: Free Press.

Knight, R.A. and Prentky, R. A. (1987). "The developmental antecedents and adult adaptations of rapist subtypes." *Criminal Justice and Behavior*, 14(4), 403–426.

Knopp, F. (1984). *Retraining adult sex offenders: Methods and models*. Syracuse, NY: Safe Society Press.

Lanyon, R. I. (1986). "Theory and treatment in child molestation." *Journal of Consulting and Clinical Psychology*, 54, 176–182.

MacCullough, M., Snowden, P., Wood, J, and Mills, H. (1983). "Sadistic fantasy, sadistic behavior, and offending." *British Journal of Psychiatry*, 143:20–29.

Maletzky, B. (1991). *Treating the sexual offender*. Newbury Park, CA: Sage Publications.

Messner, M. (1989). "When bodies are weapons: Masculinity and violence in sport." *International Review of the Sociology of Sport*, 25(3), 203–220.

Prentky, R. A. and Burgess, A. W. (1991). "Hypothetical biological substrates of a fantasy-based drive mechanism for repetitive sexual aggression." In A. W. Burgess (Ed.), *Rape and Sexual Assault* (pp. 235–256). New York: Garland.

Prentky, R. A., Cohen, M. L., and Seghorn, T. K. (1985). "Development of a rational taxonomy for the classification of sexual offenders: Rapists. *Bulletin of the American Academy of Psychiatry and the Law*, 13, 39–70.

Quinsey, V. L. (1984). "Sexual aggression: Studies of offenders against women." In D. Weisstub (Ed.), *Law and mental health: International perspectives*, (Vol. 1, pp. 84–121). New York: Pergamon.

Rosenfield, A. (1985, April). "Sex offenders: Men who molest, treating the deviant." *Psychology Today*, 8–10.

Russell, D. E. H. (1988). Pornography and rape: A causal model. *Political Psychology*, 9, 41–73.

Russell, D. E. H. (1989). "Sexism, violence, and the nuclear mentality." *Exposing nuclear phallocies* (pp. 63–74). New York: Pergamon.

Russell, D. E. H. (1995). "White man wants a black piece." In P. Searles and R. Berger (Eds.), *Rape and society* (pp. 129–138). Boulder, CO: Westview Press.

Scully, D. (1984). "Convicted rapists' vocabulary of motives: Excuses and justifications." *Social Problems*, 31(5), 530–544.

Scully, D. (1990). *Understanding sexual violence: A study of convicted rapists*. Boston: Unwin Hyman.

Scully, D. and Marolla, J. (1985). "Riding the bull at Gilley's: Convicted rapists describe the rewards of rape." *Social Problems*, 32(3), 251–263.

Scully, D. and Marolla, J. (1995). "Riding the bull at Gilley's: convicted rapists describe the rewards of rape." In P. Searles and R. Berger (Eds.), *Rape and Society* (pp. 58–73). Boulder, CO: Westview Press.

Shields, W.M. and Shields, L. M. (1983). "Forcible rape: An evolutionary perspective." *Ethology and Sociobiology*, 4, 115–136.

Symons, D. 1979. *The evolution of human sexuality*. New York: Oxford University Press.

Thornhill, R. and Thornhill, N. W. (1983). "Human rape: An evolutionary analysis." *Ethology and Sociobiology*, 4, 137–173.

Warren, J. I., Hazelwood, R. R, and Reboussin, R. (1991). "Serial rape: The offender and his rape career." In A. Burgess (Ed.), *Rape and Sexual Assault* (pp. 275–311). New York: Garland.

Weiner, N. A., Zahn, M. A., and Sagi, R. J. (1990). *Violence: Patterns, causes, and public policy*. New York: Harcourt Brace Jovanovich.

Part V

Deviant Sports

Scholars who study deviance often overlook the world of sports, but the articles in this section show that in fact a lot of deviance occurs in sports, and it comes in a variety of forms. Some people consider certain sports deviant because they involve activities they think are "too extreme" or inhumane. Similarly, some sports involve excessive violence. When athletes go to extremes to hurt each other, observers may label the sport deviant. But labeling does not always hold across the board. Sometimes people label sports deviant only when certain individuals participate in them. And even among sports that are considered normal, athletes sometimes engage in deviant behavior off the field. Whether it is the sport itself (as in cockfighting or the extreme violence of rugby), the people who engage in the activity (as with women hockey players), or postgame activities that include violence against women, these articles demonstrate that sports is a world filled with deviance.

The first two articles in this section, concerning female hockey players and male rugby players, focus on sports as a gendered institution. Although both can be violent, most people do not consider ice hockey or rugby to be deviant sports. Still, in the first article, Nancy Theberge draws on her research with women hockey players to show how a "normal" sport may be considered deviant when the athletes are female. Her article shows that when a woman suits up and plays ice hockey, some people are likely to think she is stepping outside of appropriate feminine gender roles. Most people in Western culture do not expect women to be aggressive and tough. When they are, they are likely to be thought of as deviant. Interestingly, women who play ice hockey realize this, so they develop ways to insulate themselves from the negative consequences of deviant labels. Women hockey players draw together in a close community very different from male athletes.

Theberge's article is a nice complement to Steven P. Schacht's examination of the way gender is used to establish community and "normalcy" in the sport of rugby. The women in Theberge's study did not rely on stereotypes or "put downs" of men to feel good about themselves as athletes or as women. But, for the men in Schacht's study, sexism and insulting remarks about women and gay men played an important role in uniting them as a team and making them feel good about themselves as athletes. Rugby is a violent game that involves a great deal of competition about masculinity. As a result, sex and sexuality become central features of the game, and many rugby players engage in "extreme" displays of heterosexuality and masculinity. Schacht describes how rugby players engage in behavior most people would consider deviant to show that they are "normal" (masculine, heterosexual) men.

Theberge and Schacht look at deviance in normal sports, but Steven Worden and Donna Darden look at a sport many people think is deviant. Cockfighting is illegal in most states. Many people think the unnecessary cruelty to the animals involved makes the sport deviant. A cockfight typically ends when one bird kills the other or when one of them is so exhausted it just quits fighting. Worden and Darden reveal that, even within a deviant world, some people are considered normal and others deviant, helping us understand that deviance and normalcy are culturally defined. Even in a deviant world, social norms exist to structure and guide behavior. When participants violate these rules, they are deviant both to the outside world and within the subculture.

The final article in this section looks at how deviance related to the world of sports occurs off the playing field. Todd W. Crosset and his colleagues explore male athletes' involvement in violent acts against women. Drawing directly on the ideas presented in the other three articles, Crosset describes how deviance can be found within a sport and how displays and tests of masculinity can influence athletes' behavior, even away from the actual sport. Most people would not think of male student athletes as deviant, but Crosset provides convincing data to show that they are more likely than nonathletes to physically and sexually assault women. This suggests that acts and attitudes considered normal and desirable in one area of life—the sexism and violence that occur in sports—can easily lead to deviance in other areas. Values and behaviors that can make one a hero on the sports field can easily make one a deviant (in fact, a criminal) away from the sports arena.

All in all, these four articles show us how deviance can be found in all areas of our lives. Just as individual activities or intimate relationships can be permeated by deviance, so too can recreational activities. Sports is an important institution in American culture. However, these articles should lead us to question what is it about sports that we value and how the context in which a behavior occurs can shape whether we think of it as normal or deviant. ✦

21

Gender, Sport, and the Construction of Community: A Case Study From Women's Ice Hockey

Nancy Theberge

Theberge looks at how a women's hockey team constructs a sense of community and how individual players use the support of other team members to avoid being labeled as deviant. Hockey has traditionally been defined as a men's sport because of the speed and aggression required. Women players redefine the game and do so in a way that emphasizes skills (such as finesse) brought to the game, even though traditional ideas about hockey still emphasize the sport as masculine. Therefore, women players must find ways of maintaining a feminine identity, which is accomplished largely through drawing support from other women players.

One of the most significant features of sport participation involves the experience of team membership. This point has received particular emphasis in discussions of men's sports. Gruneau and Whitson (1993) argue that being part of the team is one of the defining features of the work life of male professional hockey players. Particularly important is the bonding that grows from the ca-

maraderie and time spent having fun collectively; time, as one retired player has put it, "to act stupid together" (Gruneau and Whitson, 1993, p. 118).

The significance of men's sports teams is deeper than the enjoyment of shared experiences. The subculture of men's sport is also one of the most important bases for the reproduction of masculine hegemony. One of the clearest documentations of this process is Curry's (1991) analysis of fraternal bonding on men's university teams in the United States. Curry's research explores how the subculture of the locker room is a setting for the celebration of masculinity and men's physical prowess. Essential elements of this project are the degradation of women and gay men and the association of sport with hypermasculinity. Curry (1991, p. 133) suggests that "sexism in locker rooms is best understood as a part of the larger project that supports male supremacy."

Women athletes spend extensive time together in pursuit of a common goal and have ample opportunity to experience the camaraderie and togetherness that men on teams enjoy. And yet the problematic relationship of gender and sport provides a very different context for the experience of community in women's sport. In contrast to male athletes, who receive widespread attention and support, women athletes often compete in obscurity and with little public support. . . .

The analysis of the dynamics of women's athletic teams offers promise for extending our understanding of the connections between sport and gender. As a contribution to this effort, this paper examines social relations on a women's ice hockey team. The analysis considers the experiences that unite the team and the shared interests and concerns that define the team as a community. Particular attention is paid to the significance of team members' commitment and identity as hockey players and to the place of gender and sexuality in the construction of community. The conclusion contrasts the results of this research with related work on the subculture of men's sport.

The Setting and Methodology

The analysis is based upon research I conducted over a 2-year period with the "Blades," a club team playing in a league located in a large Canadian metropolitan area. The Blades compete at the highest level of women's hockey in Canada. . . .

The research reported here is based on fieldwork and interviews conducted between November 1992 and July 1994. The analysis draws primarily on fieldwork that began in November 1992 and continued through the completion of that season in April 1993 and for the entire 1993–94 season, from October until April. . . .

Gender Relations

One of the major issues in women's sport concerns relationships with men and the male-dominated sport structure. As may be expected, this issue is highly significant in ice hockey, a sport long dominated by men and a "flag carrier of masculinity" (Bryson, 1990). As is the case elsewhere in sport, men are well represented at all levels of the organization and administration of women's ice hockey. . . . [T]he Blades coaches and general manager are men.

Another important component of the Blades organization is the supporters who regularly attend games and in some cases practices. These supporters for the most part are parents and partners of the players. Attendance at Blades games is sparse; on a given evening there may be 50 people, and typically all of them have personal connections to a player on one of the teams. Blades supporters, many of whom wear team jackets as visible markers of their association with the team, generally are the majority of spectators. A core group of 20 or so parents and partners come to most games and some practices. Many of these also make the trip to out-of-town tournaments. During games they sit together, share comments on the team's and individual players' performances, and yell encouragement to the players and complaints to the officials.

. . .While other teams in the league have experienced coaching turnover, the Blades coach has been with the team for nearly a decade. John [the team's head coach] is one of the most highly qualified coaches in women's hockey in Canada. He is an intense man who imposes high expectations on the players. Because of this, they have mixed feelings about him. Collectively and individually players periodically tire of his intensity and criticisms. At the same time, they acknowledge and appreciate his contribution to their development as a team and individually. Most indicated that without him the Blades would not be the team it is and they would not be the players they are.

The general manager, Stephen, is also central to the team identity. One of his contributions is to counter John's intensity and demands. Stephen is a friendly and approachable man who often jokes with the players and inquires about their needs and concerns. Stephen's responsibility for the team's financial affairs includes securing sponsorships and organizing fund-raising activities. Along with John, Stephen also oversees ice rental for practices and games, a particularly important task, since securing ice time is a frequent concern in women's hockey. . . .

Perhaps the most frequently used descriptor of the Blades organization is the term *professional*. This refers to the commitment and dedication of players, coaches, and management. The team's identity is grounded in its sense of professionalism and pride in its accomplishments. These accomplishments are generally credited to the contributions of the general manager and coaches, in addition to those of the players. The central role of men in the management of the Blades organization is thus a significant aspect of the social organization of the team.

The Change Room as a Setting for Team Dynamics

The majority of team members are heterosexual, white, and Anglo Canadian. The team also includes several lesbians, a woman of color, a Jew (whose absence from team events on religious holidays is a visible marker of her cultural identity), and a Francophone. Two players are married, and the partners of several of the lesbian and heterosexual players regularly come to games and are part of the Blades' "community.". . . . Amidst this diversity, they share an identity that is grounded in being hockey players and members of the Blades. The most important setting for the shaping of these concerns and interests is the change room, where the players assemble before and after games and practices. . . .

While the change room is generally the preserve of the team, there are some exceptions that occur under clearly defined circumstances. The coaches and Stephen regularly visit before and after games. When they do so, the men tap on the door, wait for an indication that their entry is OK, and then enter. In a typical pregame scenario, the players spend 20 minutes or so dressing and chatting, and shortly before they are to go on the ice, the coaches enter and review the game plan. Stephen sometimes comes in to hear this discussion. After games, the coaches and Stephen often come to the change room to remark on the play and talk about team activities. Generally, they do this immediately after the game and then leave so the players can change in privacy. While a few players dress and leave quickly, most linger for a period of up to half an hour. The only other person (apart from myself) who has access to the change room is a male trainer. The trainer's access is less restricted than the coaches' and general manager's, as he frequently ministers to players while the others dress. When this occurs, the trainer turns his back to the rest of the team in an obvious effort to minimize his view of players as they change.

The change room in the team's home arena is a small area, perhaps 15 feet square, in which there barely is room for players and their large equipment bags. Facilities in other arenas where the Blades practice and play are generally like this or somewhat bigger, allowing players to spread out a bit more comfortably. Despite some variation in the space available, when they are together in the change room, players typically are in cramped quarters. Within these quarters they chat in small groups or collectively. While there are no formal seating assignments, there is predictability to the arrangements in

that several of the older and more senior players always sit in the back, where they face others who come in. This same group of players dominates discussion to some extent, although the cramped quarters virtually ensure the inclusion of everyone in the room.

. . While players occasionally discuss their work, in general the absence of work-related talk is striking. One exception is "shop talk" that sometimes occurs among four players who are teachers. As well, one player is a dentist and her profession occasionally is the target of humor. Two women who also play together on their university team sometimes dress together and discuss their school lives and the university team's activities. To a considerable extent, however, when the players come together they leave their jobs and student lives behind.

Team Dynamics and the Focus on Hockey

The topic that constitutes the constant thread of conversation is hockey. "Hockey talk" covers several fronts. One focus is equipment. Regular game preparation includes taping sticks, tending to skates, and adjusting helmets, pads, and various parts of players' uniforms. Players trade tape, implements to sharpen and clean their skates, and occasionally screwdrivers to adjust helmets and a saw to cut off sticks. Discussions about equipment—what people are using, what is new, what is comfortable, what is working, where one can get a particular model of something—provide the stuff of daily chatter and a focus for group identification.

One of the simplest pieces of equipment was at times a particular focus. Over the course of a season, hockey players use great amounts of tape. They wind tape around their sticks to improve puck control and they use another type of tape to secure their stockings in place. Some players on the Blades (as likely on all hockey teams) seem never to have their own tape. These players receive regular teasing for being chronic "borrowers." A memorable instance of this involves C., who is generally acknowledged to be the worst of the chronic borrowers. In the team's Christmas gift exchange one year, C. received several rolls of tape, including one that matched the team uniform color (in distinction to the ordinary clear or black tape that was regularly used). For several games and practices afterward, teammates went out of their way to compliment C. on her "special" colored tape and to request—and take—some of it. After one practice, in a group show of gratitude for her contribution, players collected the used tape and returned it to C. in a ball. While C. exhibited some chagrin at this teasing, she also managed to muster some humor to join in the group's laughter and enjoyment.

Tape was also a focus of team interest in more serious times. The generally light and relaxed tone of the change room is transformed some before major games, most notably in tournaments. On these occasions, talk is reduced and tends to be more focused on hockey. In addition, team dynamics in tournaments tend to take on a life of their own, in which particular developments or themes provide a thread for that weekend. During one of the most important tournaments the team played, one such theme was tape. Players lent and borrowed tape freely, joked about doing so, and in general spent an unusual amount of time in talk around this most ordinary piece of equipment. On this particular weekend, it seemed that talk about tape served as a means for the team to connect and focus and in this way deal with the stress of the competition.

Another aspect of the focus on hockey concerns team activities. . . . At other times, talk focuses on travel arrangements to games and practices, tournament travel and lodging arrangements, plans for the team Christmas party and gift exchange, and fund-raising activities. Hockey talk also includes reports of league games involving other teams and pregame discussions of the opposition for that evening.

The main focus of hockey talk is the Blades' on-ice activities. These discussions occur most frequently after games, when the overall play and particular events occupy the team's interest. Commentary on the play might concern the opposing team's performance (described as lackluster, or as "sticky"), the officiating (usually criticized,

though occasionally complimented), and the Blades' own play (uninspired, or "clicking" and "together"). The performance of individuals also comes in for comment; opposing players are criticized and occasionally ridiculed. When the team discusses the play of its own members, this is usually in a teasing vein. In these group settings, individual players on the Blades are never singled out for criticism.

Following games in which the play is especially intense, hockey talk in the change room is particularly animated. As the team files into the room, there is a notable air of excitement. While some begin the regular ritual of undressing, others delay while focusing on the reconstruction of events. Individuals involved in particular plays report and often demonstrate what has occurred and contrast this with the officials' calls. The team carries on in this manner, alternately collectively and in smaller groups. It was on occasions such as these that I was most struck by the group's shared identity and connections as athletes and hockey players in particular: The scene was a group of women, drenched in sweat and with their skates and other equipment physically imposing, united in their exhilaration and pleasure in the retelling of the action they had just experienced together.

Gender, Sexuality, and Team Dynamics

As indicated, a significant feature of the Blades is the involvement of men in management and coaching. In this respect, the Blades organization, in distinction to the team (of players), is clearly an instance of the broader pattern of men's domination in positions of power and authority in women's sport. Within the confines of the team itself, gender has a different presence.

One aspect of gender concerns the degree and manner in which men are a focus of the routine chatting and joking that occupy the team's time together. This occurs in several ways. One is as part of the ongoing discussions of players' daily lives. During the period I was with the team one player became engaged and began to take marriage preparation courses. Others became involved with boyfriends. Discussions about these events are examples of such routine talk. A good part of these exchanges involves quizzing and teasing players about their relationships with men. When it became known that one player had a new boyfriend, another asked her when he was going to come to a game so they could "check him out.". . . Another target of teasing was a player who briefly dated a prominent player on one of the local professional teams.

Married players and those in long-term relationships with men also are the focus of some of this banter. The husbands of the two married players regularly attend games and practices. One of these men usually carries his wife's equipment bag and drops it at the door to the change room. One evening the team was assigned to a different room than usual and, not knowing this, he brought the bag to the wrong room. His wife spoke to him with some exasperation, "Dave, it's room 2!" When the team assembled, another player who had witnessed this exchange repeated and mimicked it with exaggeration, affecting the tone of a bullying wife.

Another instance of regular involvement of men concerns the taping of sticks, noted previously. Often this is done for the players while they dress, by husbands, boyfriends, fathers, coaches, and trainers (and thus, always by men). On one occasion, a player left the change room while the group was dressing and returned with sticks that had been taped by one player's husband and another's father and which she had been asked to deliver. It is notable that the player who delivered the sticks is lesbian, while the players to whom she delivered them are heterosexual. When she delivered the sticks, the first player said, "I need to get a man." While offered in a joking fashion, this statement was also a public acknowledgment and commentary on the differences among players in their relations with men.

Another theme of change room discussions is sex. These discussions usually begin as, or become, humorous. A player's mention of her boyfriend's allergies to shellfish prompted a question about the symptoms. She replied that "he gets swollen." A third person said, "You do that to him," and the player responded, "only in the crotch." A dis-

cussion about training routines led to a player's commenting on working muscles in the pelvic region. This led to jokes about movement when making love. Another discussion followed from a player saying she had a cold sore in her mouth. A second player said, in a serious vein, "Don't have oral sex." This then led to jokes about what people, including the players themselves, do in bed. An event that was the subject of discussion for an extended period involved one of the married players who sustained an injury in the genital area during a game. The injury took some weeks to heal, during which she was forced to miss a game and practice and then to play with discomfort. During this period inquiries about her injury provided the context for remarks about her sex life and how both she and her husband were coping with her condition.

Several features of the humor around discussions of sex are notable. One is that these discussions include both lesbian and heterosexual players. The involvement of lesbians in discussions of sex is demarcated. Most often they take part in general discussions of "people's" rather than their own sexual activities and in the teasing of heterosexual players about their relationships with men. There are exceptions to this demarcation. The talk about working muscles in the pelvic region that led to discussion of love-making practices involved lesbian and heterosexual players. The advice to avoid oral sex when she had a cold sore came from a heterosexual to a lesbian player, and the follow-up banter about their sex lives included these and other players.

Another important feature of discussions about sex is that to a considerable extent, men are absent or their presence is incidental, as in the story about a boyfriend's allergies. Most often, the target of humor is a generalized female other or the players themselves. Again, there are exceptions, in the form of occasional jokes about men's sexual performance. These jokes are, however, rare and are always generalized, rather than being about or directed toward the actual men in the players' lives.

Relations Between Lesbian and Heterosexual Players

All of the lesbians on the team are in relationships and are out to the team; to varying degrees all of the lesbian partners are members of the community of team supporters. In the players' talk about their daily lives, references to lesbian partners are common. Another context in which conversations include references to partners is discussions of travel plans to out-of-town tournaments. Lesbian as well as heterosexual players are asked if their partners are coming. In addition, the network of friendships on the team crosses boundaries of sexuality, and there are several instances of lesbian and heterosexual players who are close friends and socialize together. In that lesbian players and their partners are fully members of the team community, sexuality seems to be irrelevant to the dynamics of team relations. In the players' discussions of their social lives, the lesbian players are guarded, although they are not completely closeted. Examples of this involve occasions when some went to a lesbian social event after a game or practice. One such occasion occurred after a game at an out-of-town tournament, when a heterosexual player, speaking to the group and no one in particular, asked what people were doing for the evening. A lesbian player responded that she was going to a club. The first player asked if she could go and knowing looks were then exchanged among several lesbian and heterosexual players. One of the heterosexual players volunteered that she would be comfortable going to a "women's club" but her male partner, who was with her at the tournament, would not. In the end, the group who went to the club was comprised only of lesbian players and their partners.

. . . An exchange between a lesbian and a heterosexual player, in which their sexualities were the focus, was the occasion for one of the most memorable moments of humor that occurred in the time I was with the Blades. The incident began with talk of a newspaper article on women and sport that several players had read. The article discussed a tendency among women athletes to emphasize their femininity in order to counteract the stereotype of women athletes as "butch." The players picked up this theme and S., a lesbian, reminisced about her childhood when girls played with Barbie dolls. A heterosexual player responded, "No, S., you played with Barbie dolls but I played with Ken dolls." S., the most talkative player on the team, was rendered speechless but grinning while a roar of laughter and delight enveloped the room.

Challenges to Camaraderie: Competition Among Team Members

The camaraderie of the change room is one aspect of the social organization of the team. Other aspects of team dynamics offer some contrast to the bonding that occurs in this setting. Over the course of my first season with the team, in his pregame talks John sometimes admonished players to avoid what he called the "I thing" and not to "get on each other" on the bench. On first hearing these remarks, I was unclear what he was referring to. In informal discussions and interviews with players, I learned in greater detail of a perception of rivalry among some players for ice time. A factor that some players thought contributed to this tension was that in this particular year, the team was large, with a "long bench." This intensified the competition for playing time. One player described this situation:

> We had a frustrating year because we had too many players. That was really the whole problem. We had six defense, ten forwards. That's a big bench for the talent we have out there. With thirty minute games, ten minute periods, to have six defense and ten forwards is outrageous. It's crazy because half of us didn't even, in some games you wouldn't even break a sweat. You're in such good physical condition and you're used to double shifting a lot, to go and do a shift and then come back and sit three, three and a half minutes before your next shift out is crazy. So I think there was a lot of frustration that way. And that would get on everybody's back, or the odd one that didn't get the ice time would get really frustrated and start little smart remarks. But that's just, that's human nature.

Another player offered an example of conflict over playing time:

> On the ice [players] probably had the words, you know if one person took too long, like ten seconds over their shift or something like that, yeah 'get off the ice' and things like that. But you know you're going to have that.

This player, however, disagreed with her teammate, quoted above, on the available ice time:

> There's enough ice time. They [players who complain about ice time] just got to get it out of their heads that they have to be out there all the time. Because we wouldn't win if they were. We win with three lines. And they do know, deep down they know. It's just that during the season they just want to get more. That's just the way it is. You would have that on all teams, I think.

This player also discussed the team's tendency to leave these tensions outside the change room. "Once you get in the change room, it's hard to confront that person face to face. Like when everyone's around, I mean that's pretty bad.". . .

Discussion and Conclusion

The research reported here contributes to a small but growing literature on women's sport experiences. Among important contributions in this regard are Birrell and Richter's (1987) examination of recreational softball and Wheatley's (1994) analysis of rugby. These earlier studies show how women challenge masculine hegemony in sport through the adoption of alternative values and sporting forms. The present study turns attention to the processes and activities that enable women to construct a community in the male-dominated and masculine preserve of hockey. Like other analyses in team sport settings, this research shows how women claim a space and create an alternative to the dominant values and practices in men's sport.

The analysis has examined the experiences of women athletes who compete in a particular social context. The Blades are an elite team playing at the highest level of women's hockey. Players and management take pride in their common dedication to their sport and to their team. Team dynamics are on occasion marked by tension between players and the coach and among players. Within this context, players construct a community marked by several features.

One feature is the focus on hockey. The team's shared interest in hockey ranges widely, from men's professional and Olympic sports to league and team affairs, equipment, and anticipatory talk about upcoming games and tournaments. Within this broad spectrum, the hockey talk that engages the team most powerfully concerns the *practice* of the sport. Following games that were particularly physical or otherwise exciting, the dressing room was a loud and raucous place where players shared stories, punctuated with demonstrations and commentary, about their on-ice challenges and accomplishments. These occasions are defining moments in the construction of the team as a community.

A second aspect of team dynamics concerns the place of gender and sexuality in the construction of community. Within an organizational context in which men play important roles in both the management of team affairs and the circle of team supporters, the Blades' dressing room provides a space where the players come together as hockey players and women. The bonding and group identification that occur in this space show important contrasts to the misogyny and homophobia that Curry (1991), Kane and Disch (1993), and Messner (1994) have documented in men's locker rooms. Where the work of these authors has shown how men's athletic subcultures are grounded in an oppositional project that objectifies and degrades women and gay men, men have a quite different place in the humor and teasing that occur in the women's locker room studied here. In that men play a prominent role in the lives of many of the players, they are present in the stories and jokes the women tell about themselves and their lives. This presence is for the most part incidental to the narratives. In addition, men are rarely the target of derision, ridicule, or objectification.

The place of sex in the subculture of the change room also shows important contrasts to practices documented in men's sport subcultures. With few exceptions, such as advice from one player to another to avoid oral sex when she has a cold sore, these discussions of sex are humorous and sometimes racy in their graphic references to sexual practices. Again, however, while sexual practices often are the subject of discussion and humor, this talk is rarely directed at others. In contrast to the targeting and degradation of women that occurs in men's locker rooms, men figure rarely or incidentally in most of the humor around sex in the women's locker room under examination here.

Contrasts are also evident in the place of sexuality in men's and women's locker rooms. With the Blades, differences in players' sexual orientation are acknowledged although rarely discussed. My experience with the team suggests that in the private space of the change room, these differences are in an important sense irrelevant. The camaraderie, friendships among team members, recognition of female as well as male partners, and an instance of humor that pointed to players' sexuality all give evidence to the inclusiveness of the team in regard to sexuality.

It would of course be naive to believe that the homophobia that pervades sport is absent or irrelevant to the experience of women's hockey or to a particular team. What is sometimes referred to as the "image thing" in women's sport—referring to the stereotype of women athletes as lesbians—is an important but rarely discussed concern in women's hockey as the sport struggles to gain greater public acceptance. With the Blades, this is evident in the team's dress code, which prohibits players from wearing jeans or track suits to practices, games, and other team functions, and in a general expectation that the players will comport themselves with "class" when representing the team. Players on the Blades understand and on occasion are annoyed by stereotypes of women athletes and the attendant pressures they experience to counteract these stereotypes. In contrast, they see themselves, and wish to be seen, as hockey players. Their experience in the sport and more specifically on the Blades offers regular and powerful confirmation of their status as athletes. Perhaps the most significant aspect of team membership is that it offers a context in which women hockey players collectively affirm their skills, commitment, and passion for their sport. The analysis presented here suggests that the construction of community on a women's sport team is grounded fundamentally in this shared identity and passion and experienced in a way that unites women from diverse backgrounds and social locations.

References

Birrell, S. and Richter, D. (1987). Is a diamond forever? Feminist transformations of sport. *Women's Studies International Forum*, 10, 395–409.

Bryson, L. (1990). Challenges to male hegemony in sport. In M. Messner and D. Sabo (Eds.), *Sport, men, and the gender order: Critical feminist perspectives* (pp. 173–184). Champaign, IL: Human Kinetics.

Curry, T. J. (1991). Fraternal bonding in the locker room: A profeminist analysis of talk about competition and women. *Sociology of Sport Journal*, 8, 119–135.

Gruneau, R. and Whitson, D. (1993). *Hockey night in Canada*. Toronto: Garamond.

Kane, M. J., and Disch, L. J. (1993). Sexual violence and the reproduction of male power in the locker room: The Lisa Olson incident. *Sociology of Sport Journal*, 10, 331–352.

Messner, M. A. (1994). Women in the men's locker room? In M. Messner and D. Sabo (Eds.), *Sex, violence & power in sport* (pp. 42–52). Freedom, CA: Crossing Press.

Wheatley. L. (1984). Subcultural subversions: Comparing discourses on sexuality in men's and women's rugby songs. In S. Birrell and C. Cole (Eds.), *Women, sport, and culture* (pp. 193–211). Champaign, IL: Human Kinetics.

22

Misogyny On and Off the 'Pitch': The Gendered World of Male Rugby Players

Steven P. Schacht

Schacht examines how gender is central to men's interactions on a rugby team. Rugby teams are all-male, but athletes use definitions of masculinity and femininity to interpret the actions of players, both on and off the field. This article demonstrates that those who are defined as breaking the informal rules about the game and personal interactions are viewed more negatively than those who break the written rules of the game. In terms of deviance, then, the official rules of a group are less important than the informal norms of interaction.

The values traditionally associated with most sports are nearly synonymous with that of being a "man." Competitiveness, strength, aggressiveness, instrumentality, and often violence not only are values central to sports but also are qualities strongly associated with contemporary notions of masculinity (Bryson, 1987; Graydon, 1983; Sabo and Runfola, 1980; Theberge, 1981). Furthermore, sport often is viewed as femininity's antithesis. The way almost all sports are practiced not only differentiates men from women but also demonstrates that males are physically superior to women. As Judith Lorber (1994, 41) states, "Sports illustrate the ways bodies are gendered by social practices

and how the female body is socially constructed to be inferior." As such, the glorified institutional and individual worship of sporting rituals not only strengthens male solidarity but also directly supports and maintains male cultural hegemony (Bennett et al., 1987; Bryson, 1987; Theberge, 1987), the socially constructed "natural" supremacy of males over females in society (Kane and Snyder, 1989, 77). . . .

While an endless array of sporting events have in their creation and practice been demonstrated to support masculine hegemony (Bryson, 1987; Fine, 1987; Graydon, 1983; Hargreaves, 1986; Kidd, 1987; Kimmel, 1990; Messner, 1989; 1990a; Sabo and Panepinto, 1990; Theberge, 1981), rugby football would have to be considered a quintessential example of these types of sporting practices. From the interaction that occurs on the playing field, "the pitch," to the equally important after-game (match) social activities, rugby is a historically grounded sporting ritual firmly entrenched in a masculine world (Donnelly and Young, 1985; Dunning, 1986; Sheard and Dunning, 1973).

There are many excellent analyses of how men use sports such as rugby to construct different, sometimes competing, images of masculinity. Unfortunately, many of these same studies have failed to explicitly explore the importance of images of femininity and of women that are simultaneously and relationally constructed in settings where men do masculinity. At best, many of these studies on masculinity treat images of femininity as secondary factors, while in even more extreme cases, men are analyzed in terms that marginalize women to the point that they are rendered almost invisible. . . .

Thus, while this study specifically investigates how male rugby players construct and interactionally live up to shared images of masculinity in this setting, it also explicitly explores how these same men continually and simultaneously construct. . . misogynistic images of femininity.

Setting and Methods

The observations in this article are based on two different university rugby clubs. The first set of observations was made from the fall of 1990 to the summer of 1991 at a medium-sized university in Utah. The next set of observations was made at a rugby club at a second medium-sized university in Missouri from the fall of 1991 to the spring of 1992. At the first setting, I was initially approached by the coach and asked to be an academic adviser for the club. Before agreeing to this responsibility, several of the players further asked me to come watch them play in a match. I only had to attend one match and witness the rigorous, violent play to decide that this would be a fascinating research setting. I agreed to be the adviser for the club. . . .

Realizing that my actual participation in this setting was the only way it could be adequately explored (Styles, 1979), I enlarged my role from just "academic adviser" to also that of "player." This broader role entailed not only going to many of the practices but also playing in several matches. I fully believe if I had not participated in practices and played in actual matches, I would have never gained the respect of the participants or access to the information that enabled me to understand the activity from their perspective (Stoddart, 1986).

Entrance to the second setting was similar. There my sponsorship came from a rookie player, and I was only invited to assume the role of player. As a result, I felt that I was never fully accepted into the second setting as I was in the first. The different levels of acceptance are not that surprising. First-year players are usually not treated as full members of the setting. More important, in the first setting my sponsorship was from a coach and several established players, and this, combined with the official role of club adviser, meant more respect. . . .

Rugby as a Masculine Ritual

In exploring the rugby ritual, three themes are most salient: "survival of the fittest," "no pain, no gain," and "relational rejection of the feminine." Since many of the observations could simultaneously fit into two or all of the themes, these categories were not conceived as mutually exclusive but merely serve as a loose framework to explore the gendered world of rugby players. . . .

Survival of the Fittest

The coaches' role in most organized sports is significantly distinct from that of the players. Although in an interactive sense both coaches and players may participate together at practices, during games, players take the field while coaches are relegated to the sidelines where they direct the activities taking place. Thus, in most sports there is not only clearly prescribed roles for those involved in the activity but also a recognized hierarchical structure to which the participants are expected to adhere.

To a certain extent, the opposite was true for both of the clubs I observed. Although the coaches did hold leadership roles on the teams, they also played. . . . In the two settings I participated, coaches were experienced players. Further, these players often were willing to use physical force to protect their coaching positions. Usually this is a moot issue since coaches (unofficial and official) tended to be some of the largest or most athletic members of the club. Occasionally, however, I witnessed players questioning the authority of the coaches. In one instance the coach, after being "cheap-shotted" (an illegal low tackle from behind) several times by the same player during a full-tackle practice (this player was also doing this to other teammates), responded in the following manner, "Fuck off, Todd! Come on! You think you're so tough? Want a piece of me, or what?" This verbal admonishment was accompanied by the coach physically knocking Todd onto the ground with a more than apparent willingness to back up his actions with more force.

At another practice with the other club, just the opposite occurred—the coach was cheap-shotting his teammates, but the resultant outcome was nearly identical. In this case, one of the coaches was hacking and tripping teammates during a game of bump (two-handed touch rugby). Considering that hacking is illegal during matches and even more inappropriate against one's own teammates, the players' complaints would seem quite justified. After the coach had hacked one particular rookie player several times (who was quite good and respected but not a team leader), the player stood up after being tripped and threw the ball at the coach. The following exchange ensued:

> Tripped player: Fuck off! What the hell do you think you're doing? You. . . asshole.

> Coach and perpetrator: Fuck you, you pussy. Just shut the fuck up, or I'll bend you over [and] fuck ya like a bitch. This is my team, I've played for the past four years. Put my money and blood into it. If you don't like the way I play, you can get the fuck out of here.

Although this interaction was a breach of what is expected during practice and both players eventually cooled off (partially because the coach stopped hacking), it demonstrates the existing social hierarchy, how it is sometimes contested, and the potential for violence that ensures its continuance in this setting. Further, the coach's statement invoked a gendered image whereby the recipient of his wrath was relationally conceptualized as situationally being on the same level as a woman. In other words, for the coach to demonstrate his apparent masculine superiority, he threatened to treat the other player in a manner that he thought appropriate to someone having a woman's subordinate status.

Although coach-player hierarchies in rugby typically do not involve actual violence, these examples demonstrate that the threat of violence is ever present. Such a normative order highlights the centrality of violence in rugby. More important, it reinforces what being a "man" is all about in this setting. That is, experienced coaches instruct new initiates about the ritual and the appropriate values and behaviors associated with rugby. Here, the key underlying value is the "survival of the fittest." Those who are the biggest, the strongest, the most experienced, and willing to threaten to use physical violence—the most masculine—are the leaders. Situationally doing order-by-violence, combined with differing skill levels, creates a stereotypically masculine hierarchy: coaches at the top, then other experienced players, rookie players, nonplayers, and finally images of women at the bottom. This hierarchy becomes even more apparent in the discussion of the other rituals in the next two sections.

No Pain, No Gain

With many players adorning their cars with bumper stickers that read, "Give Blood, Play Rugby," one does not need to look far to discover the centrality of pain to rugby. As observers of this male ritual have concluded, rugby is "an extremely rough game—the 'ruck' provide(s) the opportunity for kicking [hacking] and racking players who are lying on the ground [while] the scrum [a play in which the teams bind together into two evenly balanced packs that are physically opposing each other to determine possession of the ball] offers opportunities for. . . punching, eye-gouging, and biting" (Donnelly and Young, 1985: 21). Assuredly, one can easily see that such practices not only involve the infliction but also the experience of pain.

Of course inflicting and taking pain are central to the ritual in other sports (Curry, 1991; Messner, 1990b; Sabo, 1989; Sabo and Panepinto, 1990), but this seems even more true in rugby, where one is not allowed to wear any form of outer protection. For instance, in similar physical contact sports such as American football or hockey, which unequivocally are violent and result in many injuries, one is still afforded shoulder pads, helmets, elbow pads, and other exterior forms of protection. Although rugby is just as violent, the only equipment one wears on the pitch is a kit (a pair of shorts, a rugby shirt, and matching socks) and boots (cleats that can be used to hack and rack other players to inflict pain); only a few players wore a mouthpiece during practices and games. No protective cup was worn during practice or matches. Because of this, at the very least, the opportunity for inflicting and experiencing pain definitely is increased.

Perhaps the best and only reasonable way of measuring pain and its importance to this setting is through observed and experienced injuries. In all the matches I witnessed and participated in, there was always at least one injury and, typically, numerous injuries. Many of the injuries were fairly minor, such as bruised shins, blackened eyes, broken and sprained fingers, and numerous other abrasions. With these minor types of injuries, the following exchange after a player broke his finger was fairly typical:

> (Coach) Are you all right? (Player) No. I think I broke my finger. (Coach) Let me see. (The finger is bent at a ninety degree angle in a direction of another finger). Pop it back in, we'll check it after the game.

. . . Not surprisingly, injured players who try to conceal any pain they might be experiencing and who do not complain are held in high regard and respected. This is even more true if the player is severely hurt and continues to play. Players are not supposed to make a big deal about an injury when it occurs; this is to be done after the game by other players, if done at all.

An extreme example of this was when a team leader apparently broke his collarbone during a match. Not only did he continue to play for a short period, but he went to the party after the match and was in practice the following week without an overt complaint. When he finally did come out of the match, I asked him why he continued to play. He responded,

> It takes balls to play. Can't be a fucking pussy. If you want to kick some ass, you're going get your fucking ass kicked sometimes. [gesturing to the other team] Just don't let them fucking bastards know they hurt ya.

. . . The definition of masculinity is so rigid in many male sporting events that if a player becomes injured and refuses to play or simply cannot, his status as a group member is in jeopardy and can be quickly lost (Curry, 1991, 126–27). Conversely, injured players who continue to play are seen as exemplifying masculinity—they are "a man's man."

Although "taking it" is an important part of the game, inflicting real pain (to be differentiated from imagined pain, which is discussed next) seems to be less important. When a player from an adversary team was injured by the actions of a member of one's own club, it was typically explained in terms of the perpetrator reacting to the bad play of the other team or a good play that resulted in an accident. Either way, an injured player from another team seldom warranted more than a remark or two; for example, "He had it coming" or "It was an accident. I just meant to tackle him, not hurt him."

Imagined pain to be inflicted, on the other hand, often did play a vital role in this setting. More specifically, a great deal of discussion before matches was in terms of "kicking some ass" of the upcoming opponents. Sometimes these discussions were in terms of individual experiences of teammates who have previously been injured in a match against an upcoming opponent with hopes of getting retribution on the team or an individual. . . .

The role of pain for rugby players thus appears to be more in terms of being, "man enough to take it" and not in administering it. Quite literally, it appears to be far more important to talk about individual battle scars from play than opponents scarred from one's actions. Injuries are, in a sense, medals that attest to one's masculinity to be proudly discussed and embellished on in the future (over time, injuries often become more severe than they initially were). Even the blood from cuts and abrasions often were proudly smeared across the front of one's jersey for all to see (I have even witnessed some players smear teammates blood on themselves). . . .

In total, injuries often allow more experienced players to differentiate themselves from initiates and nonplayers, in general; nonplayers, of course, are feminine males who are perceived as not tough enough or lacking the courage to play, and women. As such, pain further reinforces relational conceptions of hierarchy and male superiority.

Relational Rejection of the Feminine

Rugby players use numerous techniques to relationally distance themselves from the feminine; ultimately, these practices are interactionally based and often quite misogynistic. While most of these practices are applied to women, they also are used in a homophobic fashion on males who do not measure up to rugby players' images of being a "man." Such actions enable the players to relationally define what masculinity is and, perhaps more important, what it is not.

In the setting of team practices, only players are expected to attend. Nonplayers, especially women who show up, are ignored; if she is one of the player's girlfriends, he often can expect to be given a hard time about her presence. This is further reinforced by the custom of sexually harassing attractive women who walk by the practice pitch. For instance, when an attractive woman passes by during a practice, all of the players are expected to stop whatever they are doing and clap and whistle at her. . . .

Regardless, such comments almost always elicited the expected response from the woman, who becomes overtly nervous and walks more quickly to escape the sexual harassment. Quite simply, the players' use of "harassment is a way of ensuring that women will not feel at ease, that they will remember their role as sexual beings available to men and not to consider themselves equal citizens participating in public life" (Bernard and Schlaffer, 1989: 387). These remarks serve as reminders to both the players and the women who pass by of the gender hierarchy being constructed in this setting: men at the center (the top), with women relationally being chased off and not even allowed on the sidelines.

Practices also involved the use of derogatory comments made almost exclusively by more experienced players directed at less experienced players' performances. One of the most typical comments made when newer players were seen as making mistakes was, "Come on girls/ladies" or, for lack of aggressiveness, "What is wrong with you? Are you a faggot [sometimes 'pussy' instead of faggot was used] or what?" In Missouri, an Ultimate Frisbee team practiced at the same time on an adjacent field, and they were continually used as an example of not measuring up to being true men. For instance, sometimes when a younger player made a mistake, he was told to go join the "pussies" or "faggots" who were playing frisbee, something he might be able to handle.

Such a relational normative order is consistent with a larger culture that defines superiority in contrast to what is seen as deviant and an infraction rather than enactment. That is, the world seems more defined in terms of the "thou shalt not" or the "thou shalt not be," in this case, than by the endless array of acceptable possibilities (Rubington and Weinberg, 1973: 1–10; Schacht and Turner, 1995). The sexist, sometimes homophobic comments expressed by rugby players served a nearly identical function. When such comments were made about outside members, it did not matter if the targets were actually homosexual or feminine. The real meaning and intent of such comments, in combination with those directed at group members was to relationally establish boundaries of what masculinity was not—women and the feminine—and to continually remind the participants of the setting of this "fact."

Similar rituals also were used during matches. For instance, at the beginning of a match, or at the half, the ruggers who were playing would often get in a circle and then shout out, "Girls" or "No fat chicks." This was directed to the sidelines with the apparent intention, in the first case, that "girls" was being used to relationally reinforce the notion that the "men" were on the pitch. The second one, "no fat chicks" enabled the players to cognitively and relationally distance themselves from the feminine and, through its apparent inverse image, "attractive chicks" also specified who were desirable subordinates/cheerleaders on the sidelines.

The culmination of the activities at practices and matches is the rugby party, sponsored by the home club after the game. Here, combined with nearly unlimited quantities of alcohol (almost always beer), is where masculinity is most fully celebrated and femininity most forcefully and relationally put in a subordinate position. At parties, unlike practices where women are not allowed or at games where they are relegated to the role of supporting spectators, women are expected to attend and play an active role in their own denigration (women who attend parties are often called rugger-huggers, rugby hags, and rugby whores).

While most of the discussion at parties revolves around the match(es) and getting some "pussy" that night, all of the activities culminate in the singing of rugby songs. Although I heard numerous songs at these parties, I will discuss only the two that I heard most frequently. Due to regional variations, these songs may not always be sung using the same verses; however, their themes are overwhelmingly consistent.

The first song directly plays on the "no pain, no gain" theme. It is titled "The S and M Man" and is sung to the popular tune "The Candy Man." This song also served as the basis of a drinking game in which new verses were created continuously. Those who participated and messed up were forced to drink a full beer, sometimes from the dirtiest cleat that could be found (called shoot the boot), before the song continued. While the chorus is always sung, each verse is improvised as the song progresses. The following two verses are ones I was able to completely recall; however, other verses sung in this song are strikingly similar.

The S and M Man

The S and M man

The S and M man

(Chorus) The S and M man

Cause he covers it with love

and makes the hurtin' feel good

who can take a baby, throw it on a bed,

and fuck it in the soft spot of its head

(CHORUS)

Who can take your grandmother,

cut a hole in her back,

and fuck her in this bloody crack

(CHORUS)

Masculinity is defined in this song in terms of real men, S and M men, sexually harming women and, in some instances, children. Moreover, the pain experienced by the one being subordinated is seen as an inevitable, desirable outcome of this process. With full beer cups in hand, rugby players celebrate the subordination of others through a physical and social process whereby their actions forcibly feminize that which is not seen as masculine. . . .

The second song involves the active participation of at least one female who is solicited—often coerced—under the false pretense that the players want to serenade her as their "rugby queen" with a "nice" song. She is either placed on a player's shoulders or on a chair with several players directly in front of her. In both cases, she is situated in a manner that forcibly ensures her participation for the entire song—on a player's shoulders or trapped on top of a chair where she cannot get down until she is allowed to. This accomplished, the song "Alouette" is sung to the tune "Alouette."

Alouette

CHORUS: Alouette, gentille Alouette.

Alouette, gentille plumerai.

(Start with chorus first and insert it [chorus] between each verse.)

Leader: Does she have the scraggly hair?

Group: Yes, she has the scraggly hair.

Leader: Scraggly hair.

Group: Scraggly hair.

Leader: Alouette.

Group: Alouette.

(Chorus)

Leader: Does she have the furrowed brow?

Group: Yes, she has the furrowed brow.

Leader: Furrowed brow.

Group: Furrowed brow.

Leader: Scraggly hair.

Group: Scraggly hair.

Leader: Alouette.

Group: Alouette.

(Chorus)

(Continue in this fashion, adding the current descriptive phrase and then repeating all previous descriptive phrases.)

Two glass eyes?

Broken nose?

Two capped teeth?

Double chin?

Swinging tits?

Pot belly?

Clammy thighs?

Furry thing?

Note should be made that I frequently heard the "swinging tits" verse sung as "saggy tits," which often led to the subsequent group chant of "show us your tits." If this was chanted loud and long enough, and the targeted woman had consumed enough alcohol, the coercion sometimes resulted in the "rugby queen" displaying her breasts.

Due to the coercion and force used and that some women cry and become visibly upset, this ritual is a psychological, almost physical, form of gang rape. For the moment, through the rugby queen's "compliance" in showing her breasts or becoming upset, masculinity appears relationally omnipotent. No one present would dare question its authority and apparent superiority. On the contrary, drunken, jovial players celebrate masculinity's construction and existence. That the price of its meaning is directly purchased at a woman's expense seems to make it that much more valuable, and, perhaps without it, masculinity would have no basis or significance in this context.

When I asked the players why they sang this song, especially when women became upset, all perceived such a practice as innocuous; that is, in their own words, "It's just a joke," "It's not suppose to hurt anyone," "It doesn't mean anything," "It's just good fun," and "C'mon, she likes it. Otherwise she wouldn't agree to do it." These comments are strikingly similar to those reported by Lyman (1987) in his discussion of a penis-envy joke carried out by fraternity men in the presence of sorority women. The men in Lyman's case study also saw nothing wrong with their actions; it was just a joke, with no harm intended, and nothing more than "fun." Lyman (1987, 158) also found that these fraternity men further defended this joke with the as-

sertion that jokes are really play and "necessary in order to create a special male bond."

Rugby players's singing of "Alouette" is, without question, also seen as play. But like many games men play, it is also serious business. Through the "playful" singing of this song, the players use their rugby queen as a conspicuous medium to relationally create a "special" male bond of superiority. In other words, women and images of the feminine, like in many larger societal settings, provide both the basis and the parameters for doing masculinity. . . .

Discussion

College campuses throughout the United States provide numerous settings for men and women to do gender. Since for some young men school itself often is viewed as potentially emasculating (Messerschmidt 1993, 92–6), many seek out and partake in extracurricular activities such as sports to shore up conceptions of masculinity. Rugby provides an "excellent" outlet for some White, middle-class men to physically demonstrate their masculine superiority. . . .

Rugby players situationally do masculinity by reproducing rigid hierarchical images of what a "real man" is in terms of who is strongest, who can withstand the most pain, and who relationally distances himself from all aspects of femininity through forms of misogynistic denigration.

This is not to say these real or imagined conceptions of femininity and women are framed as passive or never resisting their subordination. On the contrary, in rugby, since the whole practice is based on the image of a worthy foe, a powerful image of femininity often is present. Or, as Simone de Beauvoir (1953, 216) elegantly stated,

> The man who likes danger and sports is not displeased to see [a] woman turn into an amazon if he retains the hope of subjugating her. . . [for] the greater his pride the more dangerous he likes his adventures to be: it is much more splendid to conquer Penthesilea than it is to marry a yielding Cinderella.

. . . .Rugby, like other sporting events, is literally a practice field where the actors learn how to use force to ensure a dominate position relative to women, feminine men, and the planet itself. . . .

References

Adler, Patti A. and Peter Adler. 1987. *Membership roles in field research.* Newbury Park, CA: Sage.

Andrews, P. 1990. Rugby on America's Pacific Coast. Presented at the 10th Annual Las Vegas Invitational Steinlager Rugby Challenge Program, December 1–2, Las Vegs, NV.

Banks, Leo. 1990. One heap of trouble: "Rugby is the sport of gentlemen" yea, right. Presented at the 10th Annual Las Vegas Invitational Steinlager Rugby Challenge Program, December 1–2, Las Vegas, NV.

Bartky, Sandra Lee. 1990. *Femininity and domination: Studies in the phenomenology of oppression.* New York: Routledge and Kegan Paul.

de Beauvoir, Simone. 1953. *The second sex.* Middlesex, England: Penguin.

Bennett, Roberta S., Gail Whitaker, Nina Jo Woolley Smith, and Anne Sablove. 1987. Changing the rules of the game: Reflections towards a feminist analysis of sport. *Women's Studies InternationalForum* 10:369–79.

Bernard, Cheryl, and Edit Schlaffer. 1989. "The man in the street": Why he harasses. In *Feminist frontiers II: Rethinking sex, gender, and society,* edited by Laurel Richardson and Verta Taylor 384–87. New York: Random House.

Bryson, Lois. 1987. Sport and the maintenance of masculine hegemony. *Women's Studies International Forum* 10:349–60.

Connell, R. W. 1995. *Masculinities.* Berkeley: University of California Press.

Cook. Judith A., and Mary Margeret Fonow. 1986. Knowledge and women's interest: Issues of epistemology and methodology in feminist sociological research. *Sociological Inquiry* 54:2–29.

Curry, Timothy Jon. 1991. Fraternal bonding in the locker room: A profeminist analysis of talk about competition and women. *Sociology of Sport Journal* 8:119–35.

Denzin, Norman K. 1989. *Interpretive interactionism.* Newbury Park, CA: Sage.

Donnelly, Peter, and Kevin M. Young. 1985. The reproduction and transformation of cultural forms in sport: A contextual analysis of rugby. *International Review for Sociology of Sport* 20:19–37

Dunning, Eric. 1986. Sport as a male preserve: Notes on the social sources of masculine identity and its transformation. *Theory, Culture, & Society* 3:79–90.

Dunning, Eric, and Kenneth Sheard. 1979. *Barbarians, gentlemen and players: A sociological study of the development of rugby football.* Oxford, UK: Martin Robertson.

Eichler, Margrit. 1988. *Nonsexist research methods: A practical guide.* Boston: Unwin Hyman.

Elias, Norbert and Eric Dunning. 1986. Folk football in medieval and early modern Britain. In *Quest for excitement: Sport and leisure in the civilizing process,* edited by Norbert Elias and Eric Dunning, 175–90. New York: Basil Blackwell.

Fine, Gary Allan. 1987. *Wth the boys: Little league baseball and preadolescent culture.* Chicago: University of Chicago Press.

Gardner, Carol Brooks. 1980. Passing by: Street remarks, address rights, and the urban female. *Sociological Inquiry* 50:328–56.

Graydon, Jan. 1983. "But it's more than a game. It's an institution": Feminist perspectives o n sport. *Feminist Review* 13:5–16.

Hargreaves, Jennifer A. 1986. Where's the virtue? Where's the grace? A discussion of the social production of gender relations in and through sport. *Theory, Culture, & Society* 3:109–21.

Kane, Mary Jo, and Eldon Snyder. 1989. Sport typing: The social "containment" of women in sport. *Arena Review* 13:77–96.

Kidd, Bruce. 1987. Sports and masculinity. In *Beyond patriarchy: Essays by men on pleasure, power, and change,* edited by Michael Kaufman, 250–65. Toronto, Canada: Oxford University Presss.

Kimmel, Michael S. 1990. Baseball and the reconstitution of American masculinity, 1880–1920. In *Sport, men and the gender order: Critical feminist perspectives,* edited by Michael A. Messner and Donald R. Sabo, 55–65. Champaign, IL: Human Kinetics.

Lorber, Judith. 1994. *Paradoxes of gender.* New Haven, CT: Yale University Press.

Lyman, Peter. 1987. The fraternal bond as a joking relationship: A case study of the role of sexist jokes in male group bonding. In *Changing men: New directions in research on men and masculinity* by Michael S. Kimmel, 148–64. Newbury Park, CA: Sage.

MacKinnon, Catherine A. 1987. *Feminism unmodified: Discourses on life and law.* Cambridge, MA: Harvard University Press.

Marcus, George, and Michael Fischer. 1986. *Anthropology as cultural critique.* Chicago:University of Chicago Press.

Messerschmidt, James W. 1993. *Masculinities and crime: Critique and reconceptualization of theory.* Lanham MD: Rowman & Littlefield.

Messner, Michael A. 1989. Masculinities and athletic careers. *Gender & Society* 3:71–98.

Messner, Michael A. 1990a. Boyhood, organized sports, and the construction of masculinities. *Journal of Contemporary Ethnography* 18:416–44.

Messner, Michael A. 1990b. When bodies are weapons: Masculinity and violence in sport. *International Review for the Sociology of Sport* 25:203–18.

Riesman, David, and Ruel Denney. 1951. Football in America: A study in culture diffusion. *American Quarterly* 3:309–25.

Rubington, Earl and Martin S. Weinberg. 1973. *Deviance*. 2d ed. New York: Macmillan.

Sabo, Donald. 1989. Pigskin, patriarchy and pain. In *Men's lives*, edited by Michael S. Kimmel and Michael A. Messsner, 184–86. New York: Macmillan.

Sabo, Donald F. and Joe Panepinto. 1990. Football ritual and the social reproduction of masculinity. In *Sport, men, and the gender orde: Critical feminist perspectives,* edited Michael A. Messner and Donald F. Sabo, 115–26. Charnpaign, IL: Human Kinetics.

Sabo, Donald F. and Ross Runfola. 1980. *Jock: Sports and male identity*. Englewood Cliffs, NJ: Prentice Hall.

Schacht, Steven P. 1996. Feminist fieldwork in the misogynist setting of the rugby pitch: Becoming a sylph to survive and personally grow. Unpublished manuscript, Gonzaga University, Spohm, WA.

Schacht, Steven P. and Ronny E. Turner. 1995. The iron grapplers of the squared circle: Stigma and the moral careers of professional wrestlers. *The Journal of Culture and Society* 95:1–26.

Sheard, Kenneth and Eric Dunning. 1973. The rugby football club as a male preserve. *International Review of Sport Sociology* 3/4:5–21.

Stanley, Liz and Sue Wise. 1979. Feminist Research, feminist consciousness and experiences of sexism. *Women's Studies International Quarterly* 2:359–74.

Stoddart, Kenneth. 1986. The presentation of everyday life: Some textual strategies for "adequate ethnography." *Urban Life* 15:103–21.

Stoltenberg, John. 1996. How power makes men: The grammar of gender identity. Unpublished manuscript.

Styles, Joseph. 1979. Outsider/Insider: Researching gay baths. *Urban Life:* 8:135–52.

Theberge, Nancy. 1981. A critique of critiques: Radical and feminist writings on sport. *Social Forces* 60:341–53.

Theberge, Nancy. 1987. Sport and women's empowerment. *Women's Studies International Forum* 10:387–93.

West, Candace and Don H. Zimmerman. 1987. Doing gender. *Gender & Society* 1:125–51.

23

Knives and Gaffs: Definitions in the Deviant World of Cockfighting

Steve Worden
Donna Darden

This article looks at how men involved in cockfighting construct definitions of what is normal, deviant, and fair within the rules of their sport. While those involved in this sport understand that mainstream society sees them as deviant, they largely reject such labels. Still, based on the types of weapons an individual cockfighter uses with a bird, those inside the sport have clear definitions of deviance. Worden and Darden provide an important insight into how deviant behavior can exist on multiple levels, both within and outside the deviant world.

It was about 10:00 on a Sunday morning, and Bobby had borrowed his parents' big late-model Buick to go to the fight because it had air-conditioning. In the back seat six roosters peered excitedly out of the windows of their varnished wooden cases. In the front seat, the three of us were squeezed in together, arguing over who had to sit in the middle. About ten miles out of town, Bobby realized that he had forgotten to bring the tarpaper.

At the next town, we pulled into a lumberyard and paid for a roll of tarpaper. As we drove across the lumberyard to pick up the roll, several employees watched us. The roosters sensed the excitement and began crowing for all they were worth. As they hit full cry, the workers pointedly stared at us, snickering and shaking their heads.

We looked at each other sheepishly and Bobby shook his head, "You can just tell what they're thinking: nothin' sorrier than a bunch of rooster fighters goin' to a chicken fight on a Sunday morning!" We just looked at each other and laughed.

. . . Although supporters argue that cockfighting is the oldest and most universal sport in the world, the study of it as a complex and diffuse social world seems to have been somewhat neglected. Of the workers who have looked at cockfighting (or "cocking" as many participants prefer to call it), many have analyzed it as a "pariah group" encountering society's disapproval and harassment (Bryant, 1982; Hawley, 1989; McCaghy and Neal, 1974; Ritzer and Walczak, 1986). . . . We will explore the complex internal dynamics of this unique social world, bracketing external issues of legitimacy and morality. Following traditional symbolic interactionist theory, we believe it more useful to study cocking by examining the social objects used within the subculture rather than by dwelling on the controversy surrounding the violation of the norms of the larger society. . . .

The basic object of a cockfight is to pit two roosters against each other in a fight to the finish, which usually means the death of one- or both-of the birds. Gambling is usually a very important component of the activity; depending on the setting, as explained below, very large sums of money may exchange hands. Bird owners and spectators bet. Most often, the birds are specially bred and raised strains of cocks. Although some cockers fight their roosters with their natural or "naked" heels, most cockers arm their roosters with some type of metal spur, or "heel," that adds to the violence and bloodshed for which the sport is generally disvalued by outsiders.

Therefore, we will begin by examining the meanings associated with these metal spurs. Heels, sometimes called "steels," strongly differentiate and divide the social world of cocking. When cockers meet, the first question they ask each other is, "What kind of chickens do you have?" This question qualifies or disqualifies one as a member of the "fraternity of cockers." If a person seems to be a member, the second question might be, "What kind of heels do you fight in?" As we shall see, the answer to this second question is crucial because it reveals the expectations and assumptions that people use in acting toward one another in specific situations.

Setting and Methods

This paper is based upon ongoing research that began in the spring of 1989. The data were obtained through participant observation, intensive interviewing, and analysis of secondary materials. The naturalistic study took place along the border region of eastern Oklahoma and western Arkansas. Worden did the primary research and observation, with Darden's role limited to locating respondents and secondary research. This is not a world in which the principal figures would easily accept a middle-class female college professor as an interviewer-participant.

Observation took place at 12 formal cockfights or "derbies" and six informal cockfights or "hack fights." Settings varied from relatively posh legal "major circuit" private clubs to small rural game clubs and to apparently illegal "brush pits" in a corner of a farmer's barn. Numbers of participants at these events ranged from 400 to 500 for a major circuit club, 25 to 30 for a small derby at a brush pit, and 2 or 3 for an informal brush fight. Interviews with main informants and informal conversations with many different participants were carried out over a period of 19 months. The number of informants is limited by the illegal nature of cocking in the states in which the interviews occurred. A purposive sample was deliberately undertaken to enable casual interviewing of a cross section of rooster breeders, handlers, gamblers, pit owners, referees, sew-up girls, and other ancillary personnel. Furthermore, for the purposes of interviewing participants in a clearly illegal activity, information from those living in "illegal" states was emphasized.

As a check on the validity of the interview responses and observations, we carefully studied 24 issues of one national cocking publication, *The Gamecock*. We also looked at issues of other national magazines such as *Feathered Warrior* and *Grit and Steel* for negative cases. Finally, an informant read and commented on this paper and corroborated its major conclusions as well as our interpretations of supporting data.

The participant phase of this research involved feeding, working with, and transporting game fowl for a period of 23 months. In keeping with Blumer's (1969) insistence on getting a close familiarity with the empirical world, Worden helped take care of chickens, attached wing bands to stags and cocks, and helped "dub" or trim roosters' combs. Ongoing discussions of gamecock and cockfighting accompanied these activities. Discussions with informants or a group of informants lasted anywhere from 15 minutes to 5 hours. Worden engaged in almost weekly discussions or activities having to do with the raising and fighting of game fowl with cockfighters.

A particular problem for this study involved gaining access to the social world. Participants in cocking refer to themselves as members of the "fraternity of cocking." Entry into the brotherhood proceeds by degrees and is particularly difficult because cockfighting is illegal in 44 states and controversial in the others.

At first, the interviews and observations were only partially successful in entering into the cockfighting network. During an attempt at an interview with one taciturn informant, for example, Worden was cut off abruptly. "Talkin' doesn't have much to do with fightin' roosters. You do it, you don't talk about it," the cocker told him. It was only after his active involvement by transporting roosters and helping prepare for a gamecock fight that Worden could even pass as a semipartisan.

Many cockfighters still refuse to discuss cocking in any detail with anyone who does not own and actively fight roosters in the arenas or "pits." Until then, the researcher may be suspected, especially by older cockers, of being "an agent for the humane society." As one older cocker commented, "Until he raises and fights some of his own roosters, I'm not going to talk to him."

However, several informants felt that it was a good thing that "finally someone would tell our side of the story." Most cockers whom we studied approved of our research because it focused on the interpretive and subjective experiences of cockers. . . .

Despite the vagaries associated with studying a controversial, defensive, and generally illegal sport, we have found that the social world is naturally divided up into distinct orientations based on the use of some social objects. We explore these ideas more fully below.

Heels as Social Objects

One of the first choices a cocker has to make is the kind of heel (artificial spur) in which he fights his roosters. To underestimate the importance of the type of spurs a person uses on his roosters is to disregard the importance of a central object. The heel is probably the fundamental indicator of the meanings of cocking for a participant. The following discussion shows some of the practical as well as symbolic aspects of using one type of heel: the gaff.

Fighting the Gaff

The gaff is a 1- to 2 1/2-inch-long, slightly curved steel spur, perfectly round and tapering to an extremely sharp point. Gaffs come in different shapes such as "bayonets," "jaggers," and "regulation" and may be pointed at various angles termed as "full-drop," "high," or "medium" points. Cockers may pay as much as $130 a pair, although most gaffs cost around $75 a pair. Generally gaffs are made out of extremely light, tempered, high carbon/tungsten steel and may be nickel-chromium or even gold plated. A cocker often carries his entire set of gaffs in a polished walnut case lined with velvet, which seldom leaves his side in a cockfight.

Heeling the Gaff

The gaff is affixed to a socket embedded in soft calfskin that is designed to fit over the rooster's spur. The rooster's leg and the natural heel are carefully padded with moleskin to cushion the gaff as it is fitted onto the rooster's leg. The person tying on the gaffs, the heeler, wraps the leather carefully around the rooster's leg so that the gaff fits down solidly over the trimmed-off natural spur.

In the act of heeling some of the "recipe knowledge" associated with the gaff is evident. Esoteric ritual usually surrounds this secretive act, which often takes place in seclusion behind a closed door, behind a barn, or out in the brush. . . .

A heeler may stand a certain way or use special kinds of waxed strings. It often takes a yard or more of string to tie a gaff securely to the leg of a rooster. Other heelers show some disregard for the ceremony: "I just use dental floss, I just tie the gaffs on good and tight, but not too tight, and that's it," one heeler commented.

At one fight a heeler working with a rooster happened to say in an offhand way, "You know, I have never seen one of these actually come off. I guess I make too big of a deal of it. But, I sure don't want to have one come off, either." Onlooking heelers agreed.

Part of the mystery of the ritual may stem from the necessity for two people to complete the heeling. Two people stand facing each other; one holds the bird and places its feet on the heeler's chest. The heeler, the one with the bird's feet on his chest, can feel the feet contract or relax as he ties the gaffs. Thus, he can judge the proper fit of the heels when he feels the muscles or toes of the bird tightening. Heeling must be done very carefully to ensure that the toes and muscles of the bird have full flexibility and circulation. The heeler then pops the knuckles of the bird to loosen up its toes.

In another style of heeling, one person holds a rooster tightly against himself and holds out one leg for heeling. Then the rooster is turned around for the fitting of the gaff on the other leg.

A properly fitted and tied set of gaffs will enable the bird to fly up into the air, hold its legs out in front of itself, and repeatedly strike its opponent in the head or body. The cocker hopes the gaffs have been properly tied so they will not come loose or break. Either possibility would almost certainly mean the death of the rooster and loss of the fight.

Fighting in the Gaff

Specific rules governing cockfights vary from somewhat arbitrary house rules to the standardized Wortham's rules (Wortham,

1965). Particularly in brush pits, with a volunteer referee, there may not be any final authority on the rules, since many people may be uncertain about the details. Often spectators are asked to referee, and there may not be much consistency. As one older cocker said, "That's why when I referee, I always carry a copy of Wortham's rules in my back pocket. I can just pull it out at any time and show people what it says in black and white."

Usually a fight begins when the referee tells the handlers holding the roosters to "flirt them" or "bill them." In this process, the two handlers stand side by side, next to each other, holding the gamecocks so that they can peck at each other.

When the roosters become angry at each other they begin to show their aggressiveness and energy. It is at this point that the handlers and the people in the crowd make wagers on their favorites. The wagering may stop after the roosters begin to fight or, depending on the rules, spectators can continue to make wagers as the fight progresses, and the odds change as the audience revalues the merits of the roosters and their handlers.

After the billing, the referee says, "Fly 'em," and the two handlers stand facing each other and hold their roosters, by the legs, out in front of them. As the roosters lunge at each other and flap their wings, their hackle feathers generally stand out from their necks, indicating readiness to fight. If, however, in the billing a rooster refuses to peck at another or refuses to demonstrate willingness to fight when flown, it will not be fought.

At the last stage of the preparation for battle, the referee tells the handlers to go to the score lines approximately 8 feet apart in the dirt. The handlers get ready by putting the roosters on the line. At the verbal command "Pitt" the roosters are released.

When the roosters see each other they run toward each other and either begin to attack or to calculate through feints and dodges the other's moves. Then, when they meet, it is usually as Geertz (p. 8, 1972) described it: "the cocks fly almost immediately at one another in a wing-beating, head thrusting, leg-kicking explosion of animal fury so pure, so absolute, and in its own way so beautiful as to be almost abstract, a Platonic concept of hate."

Handling in the Gaff Fight

When the roosters become entangled with each other or "hung" with spurs tangled up in each other, as they generally do in the gaff fight, the referee calls "handle," and each rooster's handler runs to disentangle his gamecock. But they do not run too fast to help them because the birds may become disentangled and attack the handler. A combination of speed and discretion is required. An inviolate rule stipulates that the handler whose rooster has been hurt by a gaff pulls out the gaff: "You always remove the gaff from your own bird. Otherwise, the other handler may twist it around and make the injury worse."

In removing a gaff from your own bird, you use one open hand to hold your opponent's rooster in place while you wait for the other handler. Although it is considered very unfair, if the referee is not looking, a person can press down too hard on the other bird, "mashing" it and thereby injuring it further. If a person is caught mashing another bird, he may be required to forfeit the match. Beyond that, as one person said, "It is just bad sportsmanship. It is cheating like that which gives the sport a bad name because it appears that the only important thing is winning money."

After untangling the birds, each handler retreats to his end of the pit with his bird and begins to try to minister to its injuries. Depending on the injury, the handler will stroke its back to warm up the spinal cord, breathe on its neck to warm it, and even put its beak in his mouth to try to pull up material that may be clogging the bird's throat. Onlookers and supporters in the audience will call advice to the handler as to how to care for the rooster. Generally, if the bird is in pretty good shape, it needs only to walk around in order to "adjust itself." This requires that the handler stand between his bird and the opposing rooster so that they cannot see each other as they rest for 20 seconds.

Several handlers insisted that you can tell by the feel of the rooster when it will or will not fight. "It is as if there is a current of electricity running through his body. You can feel it in your hands and when you feel that, all you do is just be as gentle as possible in handling the bird and he will feel your confidence in him and he will win for you." Another handler agreed: "It must be the tension in their muscles or something but when you feel that, you know that no matter how badly hurt, he will continue to fight. On the other hand, I had one rooster that wasn't really hurt at all, but when I put him down, he didn't have that electricity and he just sat there and wished that he was somewhere else."

'Draggin' the Roosters

Roosters fighting with gaffs may batter at each other for anywhere from a few minutes to an hour or longer. As one cocker put it, "There's a lot of noise from the wing flappin' but if they are not cutting, it's all show. They may not be doing any damage to one another at all. But the crowd gets all excited at the noise and action." Some cockers say that they get bored if the roosters are not aggressively fighting. If the roosters simply settle down and wrestle with each other's beaks, onlookers will begin to yell at the rooster, "Hit him, don't kiss him" or "Now you've got him, finish him off!"

Although cockers regard the better birds as those that are able to finish off their opponents in the first few minutes of the fight, at the first buckle (when the birds first engage), many times the winner will not be decided until the birds are exhausted. As the fighting slows, the referee may decide that the fight is slowing down the momentum of the cockpit and order the handlers to "drag 'em."

On this command, the two birds are moved out of the main pit to a smaller pit called the "drag pit." The fight in the drag pit can last as long as 2 hours or more until a winner is decided. In the smaller pit, the bird that is able to peck last at its opponent wins. This rule is to ensure that the bird with the most determination or strength, or "gameness," wins. No bird that refuses to fight can win the match.

An observer looking for gruesomeness in the gaff fight would most likely find it in the drag pit, where the fowl are fighting injured or exhausted. However, gamecocks rarely make a noise of complaint about their injuries and rarely try to get away from their opponents. It is this refusal to run and the fowl's constant effort to try to kill its opponent that cockers who fight in the gaff value most highly. They call it gameness, and gaff-fighting cockers say that it is only by fighting in the gaff fight that true gameness can be measured.

Gaffs and Gameness

This willingness of gamecocks to fight regardless of their chances of victory is probably the most prized element in the social world of cocking. A great rooster can "break high" and hold its head back with its feet out in front of its body. A great rooster is also a "good cutter," a bird that carefully points its spurs and hits deeply and rapidly in the vulnerable areas of the opponent, and it is smart and uses judgment in feinting and timing blows.

However, the most admired roosters are the ones that defiantly try with their last dying gasps to reach and kill their opponents. Such a cock is then awarded the highest compliment: it is "deep" game, "bitterly" game, or "dead" game. As one person described it, "I guess I really like the courage, or what we think of as courage, of the gamecock." The main point, argue cockers, is that gameness can be measured only in the longer gaff fight.

A rooster's gameness is tested by his willingness to attack his opponent repeatedly in a fight that may last from 5 minutes to several hours. A rooster may be exhausted and almost unable to move, but, owing to the relative simplicity of its biology and its rapid metabolism, it often will recover, regain its strength, and come back from almost impossible odds to win the fight.

According to the majority of gaff fighters, "true" cockers fight with only gaffs and disdain the knife (explained below), calling the knife the "slasher." As one gaff-fighting cocker related:

> You will never see me attending a slasher fight as a spectator or a participant. I will never knowingly sell fowl that are to be used in the slasher; if the day comes that only slashers are the weapons of combat, that is the day I will leave the sport.

Fighting the Knife

The knife is a 1- to 3-inch-long, razor-sharp steel blade, carefully affixed to one leg of the rooster. Since cockers consider chickens to be "left-legged," they attach the knife to the left leg. Although much ritual surrounds heeling the gaff, cockers deem heeling the knife to be a particularly arcane art because of the versatility of the knife. They discuss and debate the placing and pointing of the blade. Heelers learn from other heelers how to accomplish this task, although some video training tapes are available. The crucial role of heeling is such that often in recording in a magazine the winner of a particular match, the owner, the handler, and the heeler of the particular entry all get credit.

Knives can be either fork knives or socket knives. Socket knives are generally just fitted over the rooster's trimmed-down natural spur and tied; fork knives can be fitted on the leg of the rooster with a fork of steel straddling the spur. Thus the fork knife can be adjusted or aimed with great flexibility according to the capabilities of the bird. It is crucial when heeling a knife to keep a scabbard on the knife at all times because of the likelihood of serious injury if the rooster becomes excited and decides to attack its handler or become a "man-fighter."

Handling in the Knife Fight

Although it is not uncommon for a handler in a gaff fight to receive several puncture wounds in his hands or arms or even a gaff run through his hand, a rooster with a knife can be more dangerous. Many handlers carry long scars, and we heard one anecdote:

> One handler was attacked by his own rooster and received a gash in a main artery near his groin area. He bled to death in the pit before anyone could help him.

Because of the knife's extraordinary sharpness and deadliness, matches between fowl with these weapons may be over in a matter of seconds. The two birds' handlers "flirt 'em" and "fly 'em" just as in the gaff fights. Then they remove the scabbards. In the knife fight, when the birds attack, often one bird climbs higher in the air or "breaks higher" than its opponent. If one bird is above the other, it can slash and kill its opponent with one quick swipe. As one cocker put it, "This one will break higher and cross over the other one. When he does that, he kills the other one with one quick slash across the throat. That's why I call him Cut-throat."

Because of the nature of the blades and their destructiveness, the birds do not often become entangled with each other as they do in gaff fights. When the birds do become "hung" and the referee signals the handlers to untangle their charges, they do it very carefully. Drag pits are unnecessary in knife fighting because of the lethality of the fight. Fights typically do not even slow down because the birds rarely become exhausted. One usually kills the other in a matter of a few minutes, if not seconds. . . .

Cockers' Definition of the Gaff Versus the Knife

Although using the knife or the gaff has considerable implications for equipment, handling, heeling, and the length of the cockfight, it is clear that the choice of heels has a central role in indicating a major division within the social world of cocking.

Cockers who use gaffs often regard the knife as extremely detrimental to the sport for three reasons. First is the high mortality rate of the roosters in the knife fight, even those that win. As one said, "It's simply a waste of good chickens." Another said, "In the knife, even the winner usually dies or is so injured as to be only good for brood stock." Not only do many breeders not want to see 2 years of breeding and feeding lost in a matter of seconds, but also the quick death and high mortality have implications for whether this is still a sport for the "little guy."

Second, because of the high rate of attrition, it takes many fowl for a cocker to enter knife fights consistently. Some breeders simply do not have enough chickens to be able to fight in knife fights. "You may need several hundred chickens in your yard just to have enough cocks and stags to fight one season. Only the biggest breeders can have that many chickens. It's not for the little guy," a veteran cocker explained.

. . . Third, other cockers argue that knife fights are a threat to the core values of cocking. Because of the importance of one bird's breaking higher than another, it may be that luck and accident determine the winner. The most sacred of all qualities, "gameness," does not enter as a factor. It is no longer a sport of courage. . . .

Supporters of knife fighting disagree. They contend that "In a short knife (less than 1 inch long) fight, a fight may last 30 to 45 minutes and a bird will have to prove that he is game in order to win." Even supporters of the knife concede that luck has a lot to do with which bird wins, compared to the situation in gaff fighting. Many knife fighters appeal to other values in favoring their fights. One knife fighter believed that Southerners especially like to fight the knife: "I guess it's just because us Southern boys don't have the patience of the Yankees, we want to get it over in a hurry. Maybe it is the hot weather or something."

The popularity of knife fighting is growing, and there are several reasons. The knife season lasts longer; during warm weather, roosters molt and may be too sore or too stressed for a long fight but may still be able to fight the shorter knife fight. The shortness of the bouts is one of the main reasons for the growing popularity of knife fights. The knife fight may take only seconds or at the most a few moments, so that the wagering that accompanies the match can take place rapidly and the spectacle can be more exciting for the audience. In the knife fight, the victor can be decided in a few seconds, compared to the longer time in the drag pit at the gaff fight.

The difference between knife and gaff fights can be felt tangibly in the different arenas. A medium-sized club in which gaff fights are fought has the leisurely feel of a livestock barn at a county fair. For $6, spectators sit on wooden bleachers, with the smell of animals and fresh dirt in the air. Women, children, and old men in the crowd visit with each other and drink soft drinks. The excitement is low-key, and entries are frequently late in arriving. The greatest excitement in the gaff derby centers on the last fight, in which the winner of the overall prize money is determined.

In contrast, in an arena where knife fights are held, the admission is usually $20 and middle-aged and older men predominate. With the faster pace of fighting and with beer sold on the premises, an atmosphere of a western bar prevails. As one cocker said about knife fighting, "The gamers like it more. It keeps the action moving faster."

Because of the speed of the fights and perhaps because of the larger size of the wagers, different "feeling rules" (Hochschild, 1979) seem to apply at knife fights: there is more shouting, more clustering of groups, and more agitation. An interviewee agreed, "It's real excitin'. Little groups of men are hustlin' back and forth from the ring to the cockhouses, takin' birds in and carryin' 'em out. Everyone seems like they will bet on anythin' just for the excitement of it."

The type of wagering that accompanies the knife fight represents a difference in the styles of cockfighting, too. In a gaff fight, one person may lay a personal wager with a person standing next to him just as a person may make an informal bet with a person sitting next to him on a barstool watching a basketball game in a tavern. The wager in cocking may be informed by knowledge about the particular handler, his age, his skill, and the type of rooster he is fighting. Gaff fighting in particular demands more skill in caring for and handling a rooster over a longer period of fighting.

In contrast to the gaff fights, in a knife fight the breed, the handler, and the skill in handling the bird count less because of the increased importance of luck. One cocker said:

> I can take an ol' Leghorn out of the barnyard and put a knife on him and he may-kill a good rooster just because of his luck in getting off the ground first. But he would not be game enough to fight for more than a few seconds.

Many gamblers may be less concerned with backing a particular handler or a particular strain of rooster and more concerned with just "getting some action.". . .

This conspicuous disdain for the traditions of the breeding and raising of game-fowl, in addition to the inability of many smaller cockers to raise enough roosters to fight in the knife arenas, feeds the controversy within the social world of cocking. As one cocker complained, "The knife is the gambler's tool." He urged other cockers not to fight with the knife, pleading, "Don't let the sport go to gamblers, dope dealers, and 'money men'."

Other cockers argue that knife fighting is ruining the sport as they know it: "We seem to be losing the family atmosphere and drifting into a high-rolling, semi-pro type sport. My feelings are that the big money events are being played up too much. Big money attracts an element we don't need or want."

One informant did not like raising roosters to fight in the knife. "I've taken care of these roosters, fed 'em and doctored 'em, for over two years. And then I am supposed to let them get killed in a matter of seconds just because of luck?" However, that particular breeder's "backer," a physician in Chicago who helped finance the breeder's operation and put up money for entries, insisted that they enter their fowl in knife fights. The informant reluctantly complied, but he said that he still hated it. He finally concluded:

This is going to be illegal everywhere in ten years and it's because of the knife. It attracts the dopers, the big money gambles, and the wrong type of people. Because of that it attracts bad publicity, too, from TV.

Supporters of the knife argue that gaff fights are more painful for roosters than knife fights and that fighting in the knife is more humane. They insist that the "humaniacs" were after the sport long before there was widespread fighting in the knife. They note that public disapproval of the sport does not distinguish between the types of heels used. However, other cockers agree that as the larger and more conspicuous knifefighting clubs attract more attention and alarm from the average person, as well as the "animal rights fanatics," it is likely that stiffer laws against cocking will be passed and enforced. Ironically, some people see such an outcome as positive for the sport: it could cause the sport to go back to the informal low stakes of the brush pit fighting conducted for the conviviality of the sport rather than the money.

Summary

. . . The various meanings of the tools, participants, and different settings serve to illustrate that cocking is a complex, multilayered process, with different orientations and intentions among the various participants. Involved in the carrying out of this form of joint action are rooster merchants, gamblers, breeders and feeders, handlers, heelers, pit owners, and proponents and opponents of styles of fighting. Crucial distinctions clarifying segments of this social order revolve around the use of the knife or the gaff. On the one hand we have the typification of the "good ol' boy" with his traditional populist values and the old-time country sportsmanship; on the other, we see the typification of commercialized breeding operations, greedy chicken peddlers, big money gamblers, and a fast lifestyle.

People use these typifications to fit together lines of action in which they are continually taking into account other people and situations and reacting to them. With the increased interest being paid to cocking because of the growing publicity that the more conspicuous pits attract, it seems reasonable to anticipate increased hostility to cocking, which will drive it further underground. . . .

References

Blumer, Herbert. 1969. *Symbolic Interactionism.* Englewood Cliffs, NJ: Prentice-Hall.

Bryant, Clifton D. 1982, "Cockfighting in Socio-Historical Context: Some Sociological Observations on a Socially Disvalued Sport." *The Gamecock,* 45:80–85.

Geertz, Clifford. 1972. "Deep Play: Notes on the Balinese Cockfight." *Daedalus,* 101:1–27.

Hawley, F. Frederick. 1989. "Cockfight in the Cotton: A Moral Crusade in Microcosm." *Contemporary Crises,* 13:129–44.

Hochschild, Arlie R. 1979. "Emotion Work, Feeling Rules, and Social Structure." *American Journal of Sociology,* 85:551–75.

McCaghy, Charles, and Arthur G. Neal. 1974. "The Fraternity of Cockfighters: Ethical Embellishments of an Illegal Sport." *Journal of Popular Culture,* 8:557–69.

Ritzer, George, and David Walczak. 1986. *Working: Conflict and Change* (3rd ed.). Englewood Cliffs, NJ: Prentice-Hall.

Wortham, D. Henry. 1965. *Wortham's Rules*. Hartford, AR: Marburger Publishers.

24

Male Student-Athletes and Violence Against Women: A Survey of Campus Judicial Affairs Offices

Todd W. Crosset
James Ptacek
Mark A. McDonald
Jeffrey R. Benedict

The authors examine the relationship between participation in intercollegiate athletics and men's violence against women. They find that male student-athletes are overrepresented in incidents of sexual and physical assault against women. This suggests that certain qualities that are highly valued in some arenas (e.g., aggression, taking control) may be defined as deviant when acted out in other settings. Definitions of deviance do not necessarily carry over into all aspects of an individual's life. Just because a man is considered a deviant or criminal in his social relationships does not mean that he cannot be viewed as a hero in other settings, such as the sports arena.

In recent years, an ongoing public debate has developed regarding the propensity of male athletes to commit assaults against women. A succession of publicized battering and rape cases in the 1990s involving high-profile athletes has led to increased media coverage of violence against women and sports (for a review of cases see, Nack and Munson, 1995; Nelson, 1994). Some members of the media have suggested that athletes are more prone to commit acts of violence against women. This claim is disputed by those who believe that athletes are scrutinized more intensely because of their notoriety (Dershowitz, 1994). They contend that thousands of assaults against women go unmentioned in news reports each year, yet seldom does a case involving an athlete or any other celebrity go unpublicized. This practice, they argue, creates a distorted perception regarding the proportion of athletes who commit assaults against women and fails to account for the large number of athletes who do not commit violent acts.

Astonishingly, the relationship between athletes and sexual assault has only recently been studied by social scientists. This research has produced evidence to support both assertions (Crosset, Benedict, and McDonald, 1995; Koss and Gaines, 1993). The press has overstated the extent of the problem of athletes and violence against women, but evidence nonetheless suggests an association between athletic involvement and violence against women. The purpose of this study is to further explore the association between reported incidents of violence toward women and athletic affiliation. More specifically, we examine the association between collegiate athletic affiliation and reports to camps judicial affairs offices of battering and sexual assault.

Literature Review

Definitional Issues

In feminist theory and research, battering and the sexual abuse of women are seen as interrelated and frequently simultaneous crimes. The concept of "violence against women" seeks to locate these two types of assaults along a continuum of abuse that women routinely suffer in interactions with men. This approach criticizes the narrowness and even artificiality of legal definitions of violence. For instance, Catherine MacKinnon (1982) contends that battering is a sexualized type of violence against women, as it frequently takes place in the bedroom, is often precipitated by sexual jealousy, and is eroticized in popular culture. Offering support for this argument, Liz Kelly reports that in her qualitative study of 60 women, "All but one of the women who experienced domestic violence in this study defined aspects of the abuse as sexual. . . . Many gave in to men's demands for sex because of fear of further abuse" (1988: 133). In her study of wife rape, Diana Russell (1990) found that in most of the marriages where women reported wife rape, they also reported battering.

At the level of women's experience, "physical" and "sexual" dimensions of violence generally overlap. Battering and sexual abuse, then, are aspects of a continuum of men's violence against women (Kelly, 1988). Because most campus rapes take place during dates (Koss, cited in Warshaw, 1988), battering and sexual assaults on college campuses are perhaps best viewed as overlapping kinds of crimes. Each type of assault draws its power to frighten and terrorize from the commonness of violence against women, and from women's knowledge that the state (Walby, 1990) and the academy (Stein, 1995) have been reluctant to intervene.

Because we see battering and sexual assault as interrelated crimes, data on reported battering and sexual assault by athletes are presented together. However, due to methodological limitations and the confidentiality of college records, we do not know if any of the male student-athletes charged with battering were also charged with sexual assault. For statistical accuracy, then, we treat the two data sets as distinct.

Social Milieu and Violence Against Women

A number of researchers concerned with violence against women have adopted a multi-causal approach to explain the phenomenon of rape and domestic violence (Baron and Straus, 1989; Malamuth, Stockloskie, Koss, and Tanaka, 1991; Thorne-Finch, 1992). The approaches argue that aggression against women results from a complex combination of structural and social-psychological factors. . . .

Malamuth et al. (1991) note that "proximate" social factors, such as peer group environment and masculine hostility toward women, have far more influence as predictors of sexual aggression than more remote factors, such as violence experienced as a child. In a study of dating violence on college campuses in Canada, DeKeseredy and Kelly (1995) found that peer support of abuse and social ties with abusive peers are predictors of violence against women. Further, there is support for the notion that training for violent occupations such as the military "slips over" into personal lives (Haskell and Yablonsky, 1983; Shwed and Straus, 1979). Additionally, there is evidence that men's proficiency at criminal violence on the streets may slip over into their private lives (Isaac, Corcoran, Brown, and Adams, 1994). . . .

Malamuth et al. (1991) conclude that future research should focus on the following social factors: (a) factors that contribute to the practice and acceptance of coercion and hostility; (b) factors that promote aggression against targets perceived as weaker or as out groups (e.g., sex segregation), and (c) factors that promote sexism and violence against women (e.g., eroticism of domination). To this list, Baron and Straus (1989) would likely add the contribution of social dislocation (e.g., poverty, unemployment, divorce) to violence against women.

Athletes and Violence Against Women

Beginning in the late 1970s, academics and social critics began discussing the connections between the culture of sport and violence against women (Sabo and Runfola, 1980). In many regards, men's sport resembles a rape culture. Athletics is highly sex segregated. By design, dominant forms of sport promote hostile attitudes toward rivals and gaining at the expense of another team or person (Kidd, 1990; Messner, 1992; Messner and Sabo, 1994). Male athletic teams often garner high status for physically dominating others (Sabo, 1980). Further, organized competitive sports for men have been described as supporting male dominance and sexist practices (Bryson, 1987; Kidd, 1990; MacKinnon, 1987; Messner, 1992; Whitson, 1990). Tim Curry (1991), in his study of conversation fragments from a male locker room, found statements that were consistent with what might be found in a rape culture and supported hypermasculine ideology. . . .

Despite journalistic accounts of athletes' violence against women and the above sociological speculations, social scientists have been conducting empirical research on the relationship between athletic participation and violence against women for a relatively short period of time. To date, most academic references to athletes as sexual aggressors involve gang rapes (Ehrhart and Sandler, 1992; O'Sullivan, 1991). There is little doubt that men in sex-segregated groups (sports teams, fraternities, the military) are more likely to commit acts of group sexual assault (Ehrhart and Sandler, 1992; Koss and Gaines, 1993; O'Sullivan, 1991; Sanday, 1981; 1990). However, less is known about the impact of sporting subcultures and other forms of violence against women like battering and simple sexual assault (single perpetrator).

Koss and Gaines (1993) attempted to ascertain the influence of athletic affiliation on sexual aggression using stepwise multiple regression analysis of 13 variables. The dataset was compiled from self-reports on one Division I college campus. Four variables—nicotine use, drinking intensity, hostility toward women, and athletic affiliation—were positively correlated with sexual aggression ($p \leq$ .05). Of these four variables, nicotine use and drinking to get drunk were stronger predictors of sexual aggression than were athletic involvement and hostility toward women.

Crosset et al. (1995) followed up Koss and Gaines's (1993) study with an investigation of official reports of sexual assaults on 30 college campuses. This study examined campus police records and judicial affairs records. Researchers found that varsity athletes were over-represented as reported perpetrators of simple sexual assault in judicial affairs records ($p \leq$ .05). They found no significant difference in campus police records. Some of these findings are discussed in the present article.

Less is known about battering and athletic participation. The objective of the present study is to examine the relationship between membership on men's varsity sports teams in NCAA Division I universities and officially reported incidents of woman battering. The study compares the rates of reported cases of battering for varsity athletes versus the rest of the male student population. Of the 10 Division I universities providing data for this study, recorded incidents of battering were obtained from 9 of them over 3-year period. The study uses statistical analyses to test the purported relationship between membership on a varsity sports team and officially reported cases of battering. These findings will then be discussed in relation to earlier findings regarding athletes and sexual assault drawn from the same dataset.

Method

. . . This study examines institutional dimensions of men's violence against women through an analysis of officially reported incidents of violence against women. In general, there are three locations on a college campus where a survivor can officially report a violent assault: campus police, judicial affairs, or a rape crisis/counseling center. Of these, the first two keep records on the perpetrator. Most campus police records do not distinguish between simple assault and domestic assault. Only at judicial affairs offices did we find a consistent record of battering. However, at nearly all institutions, judicial affairs offices did not indicate whether an alleged perpetrator is a student-athlete. Institutions participating in our study were asked to provide the total number of male students enrolled, student-athlete enrolled, sexual assaults reported, and sexual assaults reported that involved a student-athlete by cross-referencing the names of accused perpetrators with the names on official athletic rosters. The figures were calculated at each institution to protect privacy rights.

We purposely selected Division I institutions. We assumed that these institutions were most likely to support insulated athletic subworlds and systems of affiliation among athletes that, according to the literature (Curry, 1991; Messner, 1992; Messner and Sabo 1994; Sabo, 1980) might lead to problematic behavior. . . .

Findings

. . . For the combined 3 years, male student-athletes comprised 3.0% of the total male population, yet represented 35% of the perpetrators reported (n = 20). Based on the findings of earlier research (Crosset et al., 1995; Koss and Gaines, 1993), we hypothesized from the outset the direction of the difference between the student-athletes and the rest of the male student population. Therefore, a one-tailed t test was conducted on these data to compare the battering perpetrator rate of male student-athletes with that of the rest of the male student population.

We tested the appropriateness of combining the 3 years of data for further analysis. Because we found no significant difference between the years, we were able to combine the 3 years to create a larger sample for analysis. . . .

The t test performed on the combined judicial affairs data (1991–1993) reveals statistically significant differences between male student-athletes and other male students (t = -1.77, p ≤ .05). For the combined 3 years, male student-athletes comprised 3.0% of the total male population, yet represented 35% of the reported perpetrators (n = 20). This result indicates an association between collegiate athletic membership and reports of battering to judicial affairs offices.

Summary of Previously Reported Sexual Assault Findings

Using data collected from the same sample, we previously reported on the association between athletes and reported sexual assaults (Crosset et al., 1995). In this initial examination of the data, we tested the findings for significance with a two-tailed test. The t test performed on the combined judicial affairs data (1991–1993) revealed statistically significant differences between male student-athletes and other male students (t = -2.47, p ≤ .05). For the combined 3 years, male student-athletes were 3.3% of the total male population, but were 19% of the reported perpetrators (n = 69). This result indicates an association between collegiate athletic membership and reports of sexual assault to judicial affairs offices.

Limitations

Given the prevalence of violence against women, the number of incidents examined in the current sample (sexual assault, 69; battering, 21) is small. Caution must be employed when dealing with such a small sample.

The data only include those assaults officially reported to judicial affairs. Whereas the conditions under which women will report sexual assault and battering are not fully understood, we can assume that reports are not random. Any sample based on official reports, therefore, is not a representative sample of the violence against women that takes place on college campuses. The benefit of working with official reports is the generally high reliability of the claims.

We sought to construct a survey that would be completed and returned. Therefore, we did not seek information beyond that which could be ascertained from judicial affairs records and athletic rosters. Our study does not include an analysis of other factors associated with men's aggression toward women; we have no information on the circumstances under which actual cases of assault occurred. We only know whether the reported perpetrator was a member of an intercollegiate sport team.

Given the nature and scope of this research, conclusions based on the data are necessarily limited. We can only report on the statistical relationship between membership on men's intercollegiate spot teams in Division I universities and official reports of violence against women at those universities. To draw conclusions as to the frequency of sexual assault or battering committed by collegiate athletes would be a misapplication of these findings. We only examined if athletes were over-represented in reported cases of violence against women. Given these limitations we believe these findings should be viewed in conjunction with other research— as a piece of a larger body of research (Muehlenhard and Linton, 1987).

Conclusion

The findings indicate that male college student-athletes, compared to the rest of the male student population, account for more than their share of the reported battering and sexual assault complaints to judicial affairs offices on the campuses of 10 Division I institutions. However, it needs to be emphasized that it is not clear if the association between athletic affiliation and violence against women is causal or the result of behavior only indirectly related to sport (e.g., hostile attitudes toward women, binge drinking, sex-segregated living arrangements, or peer group support for violence). Further, the study does not address what effect judicial affairs offices have on a woman's willingness to report athletes.

These findings lend support to other research that links athletic participation and acts of violence against women (Curry, 1991; Koss and Gaines, 1993; O'Sullivan, 1991) in two ways. First, because it relies on official reports, we can assume that the data are fairly reliable. Research based on official reports can be used to counter those who might dismiss the findings based on data from self-reports. Second, because we sampled a number of Division I institutions, this research strengthens previous works on athletes and violence against women that focus on single institutions.

Implications

Clearly, caution must be employed when discussing the implications of our findings. The popular press has overstated the problem in the past, in part by misrepresenting scientific research (Crosset et al., 1995). But the contention that athletes' violence against women only appears to be a problem because athletes are being targeted by the media is not supported by the findings. The findings of this research indicate the existence of a problem. College varsity athletes are over-represented in reports of battering and sexual assault in our sample of Division I judicial affairs records. The implication of these findings is that university athletic departments, judicial affairs offices, and university officials need to counter potential contributing factors that may be encouraging varsity athletes to be violent toward women.

Further Research

The lack of rigorous research in this area points to one obvious avenue of study: replication. From the current research we are unable to explain the association between varsity athletic membership and violence against women. It is possible that the association we found has little to do with athletic participation, but rather is associated with some o their behavior indirectly related to athletics. Despite the association between intercollegiate athletic membership and reports of sexual assaults and battering, far stronger associations have been found between alcohol use and sexual assault, and between nicotine use and sexual assault (Koss and Gaines, 1993). Those who attempt replication, then, will want to test more variables.

Beyond a focus on athletes, what is needed is a thorough examination of the relationship between athletics and violence against women. Such an investigation, we believe, should situate the problem in its historical, institutional, and interactional contexts (Dobash and Dobash, 1983). Historically, sport has been a resource for men to display masculinity. But this isolated and secretive male world has only recently come under the scrutiny of historians and social scientists. By and large, masculinity in sport has been defined in contrast with, if not wholly separate from, women and womanhood. But the meaning of sport as it relates to masculinity is contested and changes over time (Gorn and Goldstein, 1993; Oriard, 1993). As the meaning of manhood in sport changes, so do the relations between men, and between men and authority, pain, and violence. How these transformations in the meaning of manhood affect men's violence against women has yet to be explored. . . .

In the existing social scientific literature, the institutional tolerance of men's violence is often neglected (Fine, 1989). We need to examine the collegiate athletics industry. This industry, with its income production and status enhancement functions, has links to professional sports, alumni, the entertainment/news industry, sports equipment corporations and local economies. To what extent does this industry silence women who have been abused by college athletes while it protects and exploits male student-athletes?

In pursuing this research at the interactional level, it will be important to investigate the consequences and meanings of abuse in the violent incidents between women and male student-athletes. To what extent does a male student's participation in contact sports such as football, basketball, and hockey intensify the power of his violent threats against a woman? What role does a man's intimate domination of women play in group interactions with fellow athletes? Such investigations should go beyond the abstract distinctions made by the criminal justice system (and the campus justice system) between "physical" and "sexual" assaults, and address the continuum of violent behaviors identified in feminist research (Kelly, 1988).

Finally, if sexual aggression is a form of behavior that is influenced by social and group cultural factors (Brownmiller, 1975; Russell, 1975; Sanday, 1981; 1990), subject to control and change, intervention and education may reduce the frequency of sexually aggressive behaviors among men, including athletes. Recently, social activists and educators have developed sexual assault prevention programs specifically designed to reach athletes (Katz, 1995; Parrot, Cummings, Marchell, and Hofer, 1994). Social researchers must go beyond describing the problem; they must investigate the effect of these programs and make recommendations for more effective interventions.

References

Baron, L., and M. Straus. 1989. *Four Theories of Rape.* New Haven, CT: Yale University Press.

Brownmiller, S. 1975. *Against Our Will.* New York: Simon and Schuster.

Bryson, L. 1987. "Sport and Maintenance of Masculine Hegemony." *Women's Studies International Forum,* 10:349–360.

Crosset, T., J. Benedict, and M.A. McDonald. 1995. "Male Student-Athletes Reported for Sexual Assault: Survey of Campus Police Departments and Judicial Affairs." *Journal of Sport and Social Issues,* 19:126–140.

Curry, T. 1991. "Fraternal Bonding in the Locker Room: A Profeminist Analysis of Talk About Competition and Women." *Sociology of Sport Journal,* 8:119–135.

Dekeseredy, W. and K. Kelly. 1995. "Sexual Abuse in Canadian University and College Dating Relationships: The Contribution of Male Peer Support." *Journal of Family Violence,* 10:41–53.

Dershowitz, A. 1994. "When Women Cry Rape—Falsely." *Boston Herald* (August 6):13.

Dobash, R. P. and R.E. Dobash. 1983. "The Context-Specific Approach." In D. Finkelhor, R.J. Gelles, G.T. Hotaling, and M.A. Straus (Eds.), *The Dark Side of Families: Current Family Violence Research* (pp. 261–276). Beverly Hills, CA: Sage.

Ehrhart, J. and D. Sandler. 1992. *Campus Gang Rape: Party Games?* Washington, DC: Center for Women Policy Studies.

Fine, M. 1989. "The Politics of Research and Activism: Violence Against Women." *Gender & Society,* 3:549–558.

Gorn, E. And W. Goldstein. 1993. *A Brief History of American Sport.* New York: Hill and Wang.

Haskell, M.R. and L. Yablonsky. 1983. *Criminology: Crime and Criminality.* Boston: Houghton Mifflin.

Isaac, N.E., D. Corcoran, M.E. Brown, and S.L. Adams. 1994. "Men Who Batter: Profile from a Restraining Order Data Base." *Archives of Family Medicine,* 3:50–54.

Katz, J. 1995. "Mentors in Violence Prevention." *Harvard Educational Review,* 65:163–174.

Kelly, L. 1988. *Surviving Sexual Violence.* Minneapolis: University of Minnesota Press.

Kidd, B. 1990. "The Men's Cultural Center: Sports and the Dynamic of Women's Oppression/Men's Repression." In M. Messner and D. Sabo (Eds.), *Sport, Men and the Gender Order: Critical Feminist Perspectives,* (pp. 31–42). Champaign, IL: Human Kinetics.

Koss, M. and J. Gaines. 1993. "The Prediction of Sexual Aggression by Alcohol Use, Athletic Participation and Fraternity Affiliation." *Journal of Interpersonal Violence,* 8:94–108.

Malamuth, N. R. Stockloskie, P. Koss, and T. Tanaka. 1991. "Characteristics of Aggressors Against Women: Testing a Model Using a National Sample of College Students." *Journal of Consulting and Clinical Psychology,* 59:670–681.

MacKinnon, C. 1982. "Violence Against Women: A Perspective." *Aegis,* (Winter):51–57.

MacKinnon, C. 1987. *Feminism Unmodified: Discourses on Life and Law.* Boston: Harvard University Press.

Messner, M. 1992. *Power at Play: Sports and the Problems of Masculinity.* Boston: Beacon.

Messner, M. and D. Sabo. 1994. *Sex, Violence, and Power in Sports: Rethinking Masculinity.* Freedom, CA: Crossing.

Muehlenhard, C. and M. Linton. 1987. "Date Rape and Sexual Aggression in Dating Situations: Incidence and Risk Factors." *Journal of Counseling Psychology*, 34:186–196.

Nack, W. and L. Munson. 1995. "Sports' Dirty Secret." *Sports Illustrated*, (July 31):62–74.

Nelson, M.B. 1994. *The Stronger Women Get, The More Men Love Football: Sexism and the American Culture of Sports*. New York: Harcourt Brace.

Oriard, M. 1993. *Reading Football: How the Popular Press Created an American Spectacle*. Chapel Hill, NC: University of North Carolina Press.

O'Sullivan, C. 1991. "Acquaintance Gang Rape on Campus." In A. Parrot and L. Bechhofer (Eds.), *Acquaintance Rape: The Hidden Crime*, (pp. 120–156). New York: John Wiley.

Parrot, A., N. Cummings, T.C. Marchell, and J. Hofer. 1994. "A Rape Awareness and Prevention Model for Male Athletes." *Journal of American College Health*, 42:179–184.

Russell, D. 1975. *The Politics of Rape: The Victim's Perspective*. New York: Stein and Day.

Russell, D. 1990. *Rape in Marriage*. Bloomington, IN: Indiana University Press.

Sabo, D. and R. Runfola (Eds.). 1980. *Jock: Sports and Male Identity*. Englewood Cliffs, NJ: Prentice-Hall.

Sanday, P. 1981. "The Socio-Cultural Context of Rape: A Cross-Cultural Study. *Journal of Social Issues*, 37:5–27.

Shwed, J.A. and M.A. Straus. 1979. *The Military Environment and Child Abuse*. Unpublished manuscript, Family Violence Research Program, University of New Hampshire.

Stein, N. 1995. "Sexual Harassment in School: The Public Performance of Gendered Violence." *Harvard Educational Review*, 65:145–162.

Thorne-Finch, R. 1992. *Ending the Silence: The Origins and Treatment of Male Violence Against Women*. University of Toronto Press.

Walby, S. 1990. *Theorizing Patriarchy*. Oxford: Basil Blackwell.

Warshaw, R. 1988. *I Never Called It Rape*. New York: Harper and Row.

Whitson, D. 1990. "Sport and the Social Construction of Masculinity." In M. Messner and D. Sabo (Eds.), *Sport, Men and the Gender Order: Critical Feminist Perspectives*, (pp. 19–30). Champaign, IL: Human Kinetics.

Reprinted from: Todd W. Crosset, James Ptacek, Mark A. McDonald, and Jeffrey R. Benedict, "Male Student-Athletes and Violence Against Women: A Survey of Campus Judicial Affairs Offices." In *Violence Against Women*, 2(2), pp. 163–179. Copyright © 1996 by Sage Publications, Inc. Reprinted by permission. ✦

Part VI

Deviance in Occupations

Most people think deviance involves only strange people and unusual activities that occur out on the margins of society. But deviant behavior really exists in all aspects of life, even among people we think of as "normal." Many people are deviant in their relationships, recreational activities, and work, but they manage to keep most others from knowing about it or from thinking of them as deviant or criminal. In this section, we look at deviance in occupational activities and how workers manage deviance that is part of their job.

The five articles in this section indicate that deviance can be found in a wide variety of work situations. It might involve "deviant" occupations, such as prostitution or drug dealing. When it does, sociologists are interested in how workers get involved in and learn to do the job, how they manage a deviant identity, and how they come to think of their work as normal. Deviance can also be quite common in highly respected professions. In these cases, sociologists are interested in learning how professionals engage in deviant acts yet think of their behavior as normal. In short, researchers who study occupational deviance are mainly interested in five issues: how workers get socialized into deviant jobs, how those in nondeviant occupations redefine workplace norms so that deviance becomes normal, how the structure of the job encourages or allows for deviance,

how workers rationalize their deviant behavior, and how they manage their public image.

The first two articles in this section look at deviant occupations. In the first article, Colin Clark and Trevor Pinch study a fraudulent auction, in which people are deceived into thinking they are getting high-quality goods when, in reality, they are paying high prices for junk. Clark and Pinch give us an in-depth look at how fraudulent sellers use teamwork to convince skeptical customers that they are legitimate salespeople. The second article, by Thomas C. Calhoun, looks at the participation of young men in male prostitution. Like Clark and Pinch, Calhoun describes how these young men manage their public image to potential clients. Moreover, Calhoun explains how teenage boys get socialized into male prostitution and how they rationalize their participation in behaviors they consider deviant. As Calhoun shows, these young men do not think of themselves as gay, nor do they consider their interactions with clients as real sex.

The remaining articles in this section focus on legitimate occupations in which deviant behavior occurs. In his examination of hospital nurses' theft of supplies and medicines, Dean Dabney focuses on how nurses define illegal behaviors as nondeviant. Dabney demonstrates that the nurses know that they are not permitted to take and use drugs while on the job, but the norms inside their work group are different from the official rules. Because of these informal workplace norms, nurses may break hospital rules by taking drugs or supplies, but as long as they stay within the standards set by other nurses, they do not consider what they are doing as wrong or deviant. The nurses do not ignore the rules; instead, through informal interactions with each other over time, they redefine the norms and definitions of deviance. Only when a nurse "goes too far" and breaks informal workplace norms are other nurses likely to label her or him as deviant. Interestingly, nurses are more likely to be sanctioned if they violate informal norms than if they break official hospital rules.

The final two articles in this section look at deviance in the academic world, on the part of college students and professors. We usually think of university life as one of hard work and high ethical standards, but these two articles reveal that this is not always the case. Donald McCabe studied the cheating behavior of thousands of students at more than thirty schools and reports that a majority of students have cheated on exams or papers at least once. Students know that cheating is wrong, but as McCabe points out, they think they have good reasons for cheating that outweigh the rules against it. Moreover, students emphasize the importance of good grades, using the "ends" (grades) to justify the "means" (cheating). By describing how students rationalize their own deviant behavior, McCabe shows how deviance is redefined, at least in the minds of the deviants themselves.

Finally, John W. Heeren and David Shichor examine deviance among university faculty. The authors explain that the rewards that professors get for their work are often small and arrive long after the work is completed. On top of that, the pressures to "publish or perish" are great. So, some professors think it is okay to bend or even break the rules

to get ahead. Heeren and Shichor explain that one of the most important rewards a professor can achieve is prestige based on scholarly work. But such work can take years in a highly competitive occupation. Moreover, failure not only means less prestige but can also mean getting fired. Like students who cheat, some professors think the ends justify the means.

It is interesting, as we end this section, to remember that many people think that deviant behavior is something done by strange or odd people who freely choose to do deviant—even illegal—things. But the articles by McCabe and by Heeren and Shichor remind us that social pressures can compel people to cross the line between normative and deviant behavior.

To summarize, deviance in occupations is defined by norms established and held by members of an occupation. Official rules help to define deviance, but workers themselves play an important role in redefining the rules. This suggests that deviance exists on several levels. While some behaviors may be forms of official deviance, they may not be defined as deviant by those persons who actually work in the occupation. Moreover, social norms define deviance as well. But occupational norms can also motivate some professionals to engage in deviance. This is an issue that raises some interesting questions for sociologists: Do the rules and expectations, or the way the workplace is structured, actually make some people become deviant? What level of norms (the official rules or the informal, day-to-day expectations) have more influence on people's behaviors? What are the result and importance of sanctions placed on people who violate the official rules of their jobs, but not the informal norms? Is it really deviance to violate an occupational norm if doing so helps achieve the overall goal of one's job? ✦

25

The Anatomy of a Deception: Fraud and Finesse in the Mock Auction Sales 'Con'

Collin Clark
Trevor Pinch

Clark and Pinch describe a "mock auction"—one in which buyers are deceived into thinking they are getting high-quality goods for low prices when, in fact, they are purchasing items of little value. This article demonstrates that even among individuals whose "job" is based on deviant activities, carefully defined norms and procedures guide their actions. Deviance in some jobs may be an occasional and spontaneous event, but in other occupations, such as running a mock auction, deviant actions are carefully planned and orchestrated. Clark and Pinch show that planning and teamwork can be important to carrying out deviant activities.

The Mock Auction is a form of confidence trick where money is obtained by a salesperson lulling a crowd of shoppers into buying goods at prices that are much higher than what they had been led to expect. The con consists of a preliminary phase and a main sale. In the preliminary phase a variety of items are given away or offered at exceptionally cheap prices. Some of these items are only offered to those members of the auction audience who indicate a willingness to pay the stipulated 'bid-price,' and these bidders usually do not have full knowledge of what the goods they are bidding for actually are or precisely how much they will cost to buy. Successful bidders are allowed to participate in the main sale and are rewarded with treats—substantial reductions or extra goods provided free of charge. As the auction progresses and more expensive goods are offered, the requisite bid-price rises and greater discounts are given. In the final and most expensive sale, however, the bidders, who have prepaid for their goods in the expectation of receiving even greater 'cash and kind' remunerations, are given no cash discounts and obtain treats that, invariably, turn out to be only cheap goods.

In many confidence tricks some form of swindle is perpetrated by means of confidence building, false representation, an appeal to greed and betrayal of trust. Whilst there are clear similarities between the Mock Auction and other situations where professional con-artists attempt systematically to obtain money from their victims by deception, the Mock Auction differs from other 'cons' in three important ways. First, the deception is undertaken on a group of prospective victims, en masse, at any one time. Second, the Mock Auction does not succeed by virtue of the perpetrator masking the fact that conning is the interactional project being conducted. Victims of traditional cons usually realize that they have been deceived only when the swindle is over and the perpetrators are well out of harm's way. Throughout the Mock Auction, though, the seller will often hint at (and sometimes even flaunt) the possibility that wrongdoing and deception may be on the agenda. Moreover, these deceivers usually do not endeavor to hurry away from their victims or the scene of the con. They are more likely, instead, to commence the next sale with another group of prospective victims. Third, and perhaps most surprisingly given the previous points, this type of sale is usually conducted in an orderly and non-hostile manner; few of the victims complain directly to the seller, seek immediate redress over having been deceived or have to be 'cooled out' (Goffman, 1959a) by the seller after the sale has finished.

Given that the cost to the victims of the Mock Auction can be significant, in terms of financial loss, humiliation and peer-ridicule, two issues of considerable interest arise. First, how does the seller/deceiver persuade members of the auction audience, who usually have no a prior interest in being deceived or making a purchase, to part with substantial sums of money in what are highly unusual and thus undoubtedly suspicious circumstances? Second, how is the deception managed such that the maintenance of orderly economic transactions is the rule rather than the exception?. . .

Background to the Mock Auction

Mock auctions have a long history in the United Kingdom. Mayhew (1987) notes the existence of a very similar sales tactic in Victorian London. Allingham (1976) refers to such routines being used in England during the early 1930s. These sales were originally worked at fayres, street markets, galas and other places where crowds were to be found (such as horse race meetings and outside factory gates). Nowadays, largely due to the effect of the Mock Auction Act of 1961, which makes this type of sale a criminal offense, it is to be found in less high-profile environments such as at coastal resorts during the summer holiday season, and in one-day sales in church and village halls. Nevertheless, it is still not uncommon for Mock Auctions to be held in vacant high street stores and on street markets on a one-off ('here today, gone tomorrow') basis.

The Mock Auction is usually conducted from a raised platform and the seller is separated from the audience by a long and high sales counter. A variety of sale items (known as 'flash') are displayed on this counter and around the walls of the sales site to create a retailing atmosphere. The sale is staffed by a crew which consists of i) the Mock Auctioneer (The 'Top-Man'—who, without exception, is male) who conducts the sales; ii) someone whose task is to attract an audience (or 'edge') at the start of the routine (an 'Edge Puller'); and iii) a number of assistants ('Floor Workers'), who either work behind the sales counter or reside between this counter and the front of the audience, moving in and out

of the audience collecting money and distributing goods during the routine.

Research Method and Data Base

Our study is based primarily upon an examination of 5 audio and/or video recordings of real-life Mock Auctions collected in Britain. This data-base was supplemented with observations of other routines (both covert and official), and a small number of informal interviews with Mock Auction workers (both active and retired), victims, and other related personnel (such as Trading Standards Officers and journalists). Our findings comprise a synthesis of our analysis of these recordings with the 'insider understandings' provided by the Top-Man and their aides and the 'outsider understandings' provided by the accounts and explanations of the victims and officials.

The typical routine can be split into the following five stages:

STAGE 1: 'Pulling a Pitch' (Attracting a crowd to the sale)

STAGE 2: 'Steaming Up the Edge' (Getting the crowd excited and in the frame of mind to buy)

STAGE 3: 'The Nailer' (The first mass sale)

STAGE 4: 'The Ram' (The main sale)

STAGE 5: 'End Games' (Where bonus sales are made)

We will now examine each of these stages and the sub-routines within them.

First Phase: 'Pulling a Pitch'

The routine begins with the Edge-Puller attempting to attract the largest possible crowd to the sales site. The reason for doing this is not simply because the larger audience the greater is the likelihood that mass sales will be obtained—the Mock Auction is not solely a numbers game. Its success also crucially relies on the positive inferences and opinions which audience members draw from each other, and these are more easily facilitated with the help of a large and compacted crowd.

In 'one-off' sales—say for a single evening in a village hall—local householders will be leafleted with handbills publicizing the sale. At seasonal or static sales sites (such as at coastal resorts) the Edge-Puller has to attract passers-by into the shop with talk. Such casual prospects generally appear to have no interest in attending such a sale; they are, for example, often reluctant to move from the pavement into the shop to listen to the seller's patter. From the start they are suspicious of such explicit sales tactics and remain 'on their guard'.

For both types of sales the method of attracting an audience is essentially the same—prospective victims are lured to the sales site by the promise of exceptional bargains. The bargains are exceptional in the sense that these goods are offered for sale at around 10%–20% of their normal retail sales price. This contrasts sharply with the 10%–50% reductions that characterize sales in high street stores. A series of contrasts are announced between the claimed worth or usual selling price of the various goods that are offered, and the much lower price that will actually be charged. . . .

In non-advertised sales the Edge-Puller announces a series of extremely low prices for the goods offered for sale. . . . These bargain offers are repeated until enough passers-by have been attracted. Supportive explanations such as "I've lost the boxes for these goods" are provided to explain away and account for the lower than normal (and thereby potentially troublesome) selling price of the goods (Pinch and Clark 1986). To further offset the reservations of those passers-by who have stopped at the sale, a number of guarantees about the authenticity of the sales offer and how fairly the sale will be conducted are also usually announced.

> EP: There's no point in me standing up 'ere this evening, telling you good people that that's a fiver (i.e. a 'ghetto-blaster')—just a minute—that that's a fiver, if ah'm gonna charge you twenty pounds for it. Obviously, you'll just turn round an' say "Well you told me it was a fiver", and you wouldn't buy it, and you'd be quite right in order not to do so. Nobody will force anybody to buy anything they don't want. What I'm trying to say to you is this ladies an' gentlemen. It's as simple as this: You're

under no obligation whatsoever in this shop. When I start this sale in a moment's time, if all you wish to purchase is an electric toaster at a pound, then you wish to go on your way, then you're quite welcome to do so. Nobody will force anybody to buy anything they don't want.

The reason that the goods can be offered at such cheap prices and that such 'guarantees' can be expressed is quite simple: the sale items announced as a means of attracting a crowd are, as we shall see, never actually sold and the obligations associated with the guarantees have never, therefore, to be met.

Second Phase: 'Steaming Up' the Edge

The Edge-Puller hands over the running of the sale to the Top-Man who then attempts to build an even larger audience and to foster a sales atmosphere of unparalleled generosity. This is managed through a series of mini-sales where goods are either given away free or are sold at cheap or token prices. There are three basic elements in this phases of the sale: 1: 'Plundering'; 2: The 'Hintern and Smother'; and 3: 'Taking the gamble'.

Plundering the Edge

The Top-Man begins by distributing items such as pencils, combs and packs of playing cards (known as 'plunder') to members of the audience, often free of charge and, ostensibly, to foster audience responsiveness (e.g., "To wake you all up a little bit"):

> TM: Right, to make start. 'Ere, these're nice. They came out of Woolworths last night. At half past twelve.
>
> As: [Small laughs]
>
> TM: Nobody knows they've gone missing yet!
>
> As: [Small laughs]
>
> TM: What they are, they're odd packs of playing cards. There's 52 in a pack, an' two jokers, rather like me an' him down here [i.e. FW]. My price. I think you'll like. FORGET about 40 [pence], 30 or 20, the first half dozen of you with your arms up in the air, anywhere in the shop, very

quickly [BANG] ah'll take FIFTEEN, who wants a pack?

As: [Practically everyone in the audience raises a hand]

TM: Quickly. You do, you do. You do. You do, you do, you do. Who else wants one? They're nothing! Quickly. Gentleman there, one over there. Can you close in off my doorway. Either close in, or carry on walking. DON'T BLOCK UP MY BACK PASSAGE!

These goods are thrown fiercely into the crowd, loosely in the direction of those people who have raised their hands. Often they are aimed at the heads of these audience members, especially those who are situated toward the middle and front of the sales counter. To protect themselves, many of the audience raise their arms and otherwise attempt to dodge these 'missiles' before scrambling for the items on the ground. By throwing the goods toward the front of the crowd the Top-Man is able to entice the audience nearer to him. By virtue of the highly audible and visible commotion that ensures he is also able to attract additional passers-by to the sales site. With the active though unwitting participation of the crowd the Top-Man can thus build an even larger audience—an 'execution pitch'—that is, an audience of a size that would turn up for public executions in medieval times.

The Hintern and Smother

To accentuate this commotion, larger (and vastly more expensive) collections of goods are then offered for sale at extremely low prices, but only to those people who respond first. These goods typically are the same item of stock that had been announced by the Edge-Puller to attract passers-by to the sale, or were advertised as special sale lots in the hand bills. . . .

Only one of these goods are actually sold. The Hintern is so-called because the sale essentially is fictitious—it is only hinted at; the audience member that the Top-Man appears to address and sell the goods to does not exist. Only the cheap items—ashtrays and playing cards—were handed out; the most expensive items are returned (surreptitiously by the floor workers) and hidden behind the counter (known as 'scheisted'). The audience usually remain oblivious to what is happening. In fact, the items which are sold (goods which are knows as 'ream') are handed over to the audience solely for the purpose of deflecting attention away from (i.e., smothering) a 'hintern' lot as it is being replaced under the counter by a floor worker.

For this sub-routine to work successfully, the 'smother lots' have to provide a sufficient distraction for the audience. To achieve this, gaudy items (i.e., cheap but visually expensive looking goods such as glass or even vases which are cut to give the appearance of being crystal) are used and are sold at markedly contrasting cheaper prices to the goods which have been hinted.

A rapid-fire series of hintern and smother sales [is] usually carried out. The audience jostle and compete with each other for the opportunity to purchase the goods that apparently are being sold. As one victim recalled:

At first me and my mother both stood there, and she kept saying to me "Get your hand up. Go on and get your hand up." And I was embarrassed, because what I was feeling was that everybody was gonna think "look at her, putting her hand up for everything," you know? "She's bloody greedy." But everyone was doing it. And in the end I moved further to the front, away from my mother. I moved to the side and sort of like squeezed in between people. I was thinking that if I was closer he might notice me a little bit more. I was stood on my tip-toes—I mean, I'm tall anyway—I was stood nearer shorter people so that I could stand on my tip-toes and he could notice me more.

This excitement and commotion also seem to prevent the audience from recognizing that many of the goods are not being handed over. Few would-be buyers dare look away from the Top-Man to monitor who the fortunate recipient of the (hinted) goods is for fear of not catching the Top-Man's eye and thereby missing their own opportunity to receive the next (fictitious) line that will soon be offered.

That the hinted goods are never going to be handed out to the audience is felicitous for the task in which the Top-Man is engaged. It enables him to fulfill the Edge-Puller's obligation to sell the previously announced range of goods cheaply, without incurring any financial or stock losses, or receiving accusations of breaking promises and deceiving the audience. With this procedure the Top-Man also is able indiscriminately to choose any item of stock and apparently sell those goods at an extremely cheap price. This accentuates the bargain nature of the selling price. The audience have now been presented with what they typically deem to be sufficient proof that the sale is being conducted by someone who appears to be not in the least bit worried about making a loss.

Taking the Gamble

The final element in this stage of the sale consists of the Top-Man engineering 'bids' for goods at a particular price, and also rewarding the first person to make a bid for reacting quickly and taking a gamble. This lucky member of the audience not only wins the 'auction' and thereby receives the goods, s/he also receives a massive reduction in cash or kind. In this type of sequence, as is typical, the goods are, again, not handed over as this bidder is also fictitious. The floor men often collude in these conspiracies by nodding and pointing in the same direction to where the nonexistent bidder chosen by the Top-Man would be standing. To enhance the plausibility of the deception, the Top-Man may have a (make-believe) conversation with the chosen bidder. It seems that the audience 'hear' the nonexistent bidder's responses by virtue of the Top-Man talking as a recipient—i.e. responding as if the fictitious individual in the audience had actually said something positive about the goods (e.g. "What's that you said?" "You like that?" "Fantastic." "That's what I like to hear.")

At this stage of the routine the basic principles that are being instilled into the audience are that the selling process is unorthodox; it is a series of sales of unparalleled generosity; and that only a few fortunate, quick responding individuals will be lucky enough to receive the goods that are being auctioned.

Furthermore, these procedures begin to constitute the selling as being a business where risk-taking pays off for the fortunate (though so far fictitious) individuals who have had the courage to take a gamble and have responded quickly to the sales offers.

Third Phase: The Nailer

This stage—the first mass sale—officially precedes and unofficially prefaces the upcoming main ('Ram') sale. A 'nailer' is an item of stock which is offered to the audience 'blind' (such as a necklace in a box). Members of the audience are asked to (and do) purchase these unseen goods and part with their cash . . . before having full knowledge of what, if anything, the boxes contain. The official incentive for the audience participating in such a sale is that the opportunity to participate in the main sale (and to thereby receive even more generous bargains) is provisional on them buying one of these sale lots.

The deployment of nailers is designed unofficially to serve four purposes: i) to locate suitable individuals ('mug punters') for the subsequent and main part of the sale (the Ram); ii) to begin the process of separating these individuals from non-buyers and sceptics who may have a disruptive effect when the Mock Auction reaches its climax; and iii) to ensure that these prospective victims stay at the sales site and, more specifically, do not walk away prior to the main sale; and iv) to further affirm the unorthodox, risk-taking, bargain receiving nature of the selling process.

In the nailer phase, a number of sub-routines occur in the following order: 1) obtaining individual purchasing responsiveness; 2) obtaining mass purchasing responsiveness; 3) the discrepancy; and 4) separating the 'buyers from the spyers'.

Obtaining Individual Purchasing Responsiveness

Rather than attempting immediately to accomplish the undoubtedly difficult task of obtaining a mass of purchases of unseen and unspecified goods, the process of nailing is managed incrementally (see also Clark and Pinch, 1988). First of all, members of the audience are asked to express only an 'interest' in the goods rather than an explicit intent to purchase them. The Top-Man does not reveal what is inside the box and will often state that it may, in fact, be empty. An individual who had indicated an interest in the goods is then selected from the crowd. Once this person has confirmed his/her 'bid' for the possibly empty box, the item in the box is revealed and s/he is offered these goods with a vast reduction in price for having 'taken a gamble'.

The bidder then hands over money and receives the goods. The audience [has] now seen someone take a gamble which has paid off in the form of the bidder receiving a very large price reduction.

Obtaining Mass Purchasing Responsiveness

Another member of the audience is then asked to bid for unseen goods, usually in a different and larger box. But now the risk this bidder takes is, in two ways, much greater. First, the bid price is higher. Second, the bidder is asked to hand over his/her cash prior to receiving (and seeing) the goods to demonstrate that the bid is genuine. Whilst the Top-Man holds on to the goods, the bidder's cash is returned, the price of the unseen goods is reduced, and this 'treat' is then offered to the rest of the audience at the same reduced price.

By initially selling to only one or two willing buyers, skeptical members of the audience have been provided with a more credible reference point—one from within their own rank—as to both the desirability of making a purchase, and the trustworthiness of the seller. In selecting such 'opinion formers' the Top-Man will endeavor to choose only those individuals whom he judges are likely to be malleable to his suggestions but who will, at the same time, be treated by the rest of the audience as credible sources of information. This selection process is more generally called 'Clocking the "Divvie"' (i.e., recognizing a fool from whom you can obtain a dividend). Fortuitously, the first party with his/her hand up in the air is also likely to be the most enthusiastic and malleable.

With these preliminary sales the Top-Man is also able to accentuate his seemingly flagrant disregard for sensible sales practice: He sells goods at prices lower than he could have obtained, and he returns money to audience members that he could have kept.

The Discrepancy

After the money for these goods has been collected the Top-Man will mention a discrepancy that has arisen between the greater number of bidders' hands that have been raised compared to the actual amount of money than he has received. The Top-Man speaks of there being people who have attempted to outwit him and obtain the goods for free ('cheating buggers'). This discrepancy is fictitious. The unofficial objective of this play is to instill consternation and competitiveness in the audience. The possibility that genuine bidders are being outdone by others of a more deviant inclination also creates additional pressure on would-be buyers to respond early. The discrepancy, as we shall see, also serves a purpose later in the routine as well as in the main Ram phase of the sale.

Separating the 'Buyers from the Spyers'

The final stage of nailing consists of the Top-Man separating those members of the audience (and their friends and family) who have purchased a nailer, from those in the audience who have not.

Precisely how the non-buyers are separated from those who have made a purchase depends on whether or not the sale is being conducted in an open or closed setting (e.g., in an outdoor market, or a lock-up store/hall respectively). Open sales situations, where passers-by cannot easily be prevented from entering or leaving the audience, make this type of separation difficult. At these venues the Top-Man will send non-buyers to the back of the sales site and will turn off his microphone or speak less loudly so that only those people who have purchased a nailer will be able fully to hear what he is saying. If the routine is being conducted in a lock-up shop then the non- buyers (known as "spyers" or "monkeys") will be told to leave, the doors being closed behind them. Again, supportive explanations are provided for undertaking this unusual course of action. For example, one Top-Man proposed that the non-buyers should be excluded from the sales site for reasons of safety—as soon as they heard the bargain offers that were to come, they would storm to the front of the stall and crush the other buyers. Those individuals who are asked to leave usually do so. It is also very rare to see any nailer purchasers leave at this stage of the sale or to express any sympathy for those individuals who have been asked to leave.

The audience members who remain now have the shared identity of being purchasers (or being 'with' purchasers such as family and friends). Consequently, the potentially negative effect of having non-buyers, sceptics, or onlookers who may openly revel in the downfall of others during the upcoming sale is significantly reduced.

The 'nailer' items are not immediately handed over to those individuals who have paid for them. A rationale for this is provided by the Top-Man referring, once more, to the previous discrepancy and to the possibility of there still being one or two cheats in the audience. Of course, in allowing the friends and family of those individuals who have bought a nailer to stay at the sales site, the Top-Man can always be certain that the audience will perceive that there are more individuals present than actual purchasers.

One can now begin to see the finesse of the nailer stage as a preliminary to the main sale. The price of the nailer goods is designed to be low enough to create a large response to an unusual sales offer, yet they [the goods] are priced high enough to 'nail' the feet of these purchasers to the sales site until they do receive the goods. This action thus ensures that a large number of audience members, who all share a common bond with the Top-Man (a 'punting history') remain for the main sale.

Fourth Phase: The Ram

The Ram is the central and, for the Top-Man, the most profitable phase of the Mock Auction. All the previous auctions that have been conducted during the preliminary sales by the Top-Man are designed to bear fruition here. This part of the sale progresses in a strict sequential fashion, as follows: 1) the

higher risk; 2) describing the goods; 3) resolving the risk; 4) working on the first Ram bidder; 5) obtaining mass bids; 6) the miscount; 7) the Ram itself; and 8) delivering the treat or 'topments'.

The Higher Risk

As in the nailer phase (and for the same reasons), the Top-Man starts another sale by working on specific individuals in the audience. Now, both the risk as well as the potential rewards that may accrue for those who bid for the goods are greater. The type of goods offered in these sales are usually similar to the expensive hintern lots 'sold' previously. However, instead of asking for a bid of say £1–£5 the Top-Man will usually ask for £15–£25, adding the proviso that the actual amount that will have to be paid will be "much less." Moreover, individuals may, again, be asked to bid on unseen goods, or something even more vague such as "what's on my mind," or "what's in my other hand" (that is, the hand that the Top-Man has placed inside the front pocket of his trousers).

This creation of a higher risk at a higher price is used to preface the higher risk and the higher price that will be required from those audience members who bid for the items in the imminent Ram sale. It is also used to get the audience to display the more substantial sum of money needed, . . . a procedure that is a small but significant step along the road to getting them to actually part with it.

This type of sale is not resolved immediately. Before taking any money off the bidders the Top-Man temporarily moves on to describe the goods that will be offered in the main sale. At this point all the audience have at stake is the money most of them have given for the nailer (which they have not yet received), and a couple of individuals have also given up substantially larger sums of money for items in the above type of sale.

Describing the Goods

A selection of goods are offered in the main sale (such as watches, jewelry, car stereos, clock radios, rings, china, crystal glassware, cutlery and carving sets). Offering a choice enhances sales as it increases the possibility that more audience members will bid for (and be seen by other audience members to bid for) at least one of those items. The Top-Man formulates these goods as bargains largely by using standard rhetorical devices such as contrasts, descriptive lists, etc. (Atkinson, 1984; Pinch and Clark, 1986). Only after having done this are the previous bidders dealt with.

Resolving the Risk

All of the money which had been handed from the previous bidders is now returned. These bidders receive plunder items and, given that they are handed over free of charge, the bidders accept them with exceptional enthusiasm. Along with the rest of the audience, these bidders seems willing to dismiss the point that their bids originally were for other items of stock.

The delay in dealing with these risk-takers serves to play upon any remaining fears of the audience that their trust in the seller may be misplaced. By now the audience should be thinking along the lines of "is this higher risk not going to pay off as did the previous risks that were taken?" (i.e. in the hintern and smother phase). By suspending the handing back of the risk-takers' money, these suspicions are accentuated—a process which makes their eventual subversion even more dramatic and trust enhancing. The audience are given more proof that is designed to get them to believe that they can trust the Top-Man after all. This makes it somewhat easier for the Top-Man to obtain mass purchases; others in the audience are now even more likely to take such a gamble themselves. Yet the gamble which they are about to take will not pay off in the way they are likely to have anticipated.

Working on the First Ram Bidder

The Top-Man now moves back to describing the selection of goods on offer, and asks for bids on these goods. But rather than asking these bidders immediately to pay for those goods, the Top-Man again addresses only one of the bidders (another presumed 'Divvie') and asks, first, if the bid was "genuine"; second, if the bidder "could pay"; and

finally, what items the bidder has "chosen." The item of stock that is named is then placed on the sales counter. The Top-Man then states that this bidder will be treated further. But one important caveat is added by the Top-Man: He asks the bidder to state whether or not s/he will be happy if s/he handed over cash for the goods and there was nothing else added to them, no additional discount given. In our corpus, and without exception, the bidder at this point stated that s/he would be happy. But the Top-Man then states that *he* would *not* be happy if this were to occur; rather, the Top-Man then reiterates that he will "treat" the bidder "further." The cash that this bidder had handed over to demonstrate that the bid is genuine is then returned.

The phrase to "treat further," coupled with the handing back of the bidder's cash, is built to suggest strongly that the bid-price (or at least a substantial portion of it) will be handed back to the bidders for having taken such a gamble. Given the previous sales that have occurred, as the risk has now been increased (price-wise) the rewards may also be anticipated to be greater.

Obtaining Mass Bids

The other members of the audience who have expressed an "interest" in the goods and have made a bid by raising their hands are now individually asked the same three questions. No mention is made of having to pay for these goods. In each case the Top-Man states that he will treat the bidder further.

The Miscount

As a pretext for getting those audience members who have expressed an interest in the goods to *display their bid money*, another discrepancy is raised, now between the number of goods that have been set aside and the larger number of audience members who have bid for the goods. This discrepancy is produced by the Top-Man over-counting the number of hands that have been raised in the audience (either by counting some hands twice or inventing fictitious hands). The bidders are asked to show their money to prove that they are genuine. Thus, whilst money was originally asked about only to show that bidders *could* pay (not, as implied, that they will *have* to pay) now, because of the fictitious discrepancy, the public display of money serves as proof that the bids are genuine.

To get these bidders to *part with their cash* the Top-Man claims that his sales staff have become confused. Another basis for the Top-Man offering a selection of goods for sale thus becomes apparent. Although the goods apparently are ready to be handed over to the audience members, the floor worker states that he has not been paying attention and does not know which particular individuals in the audience are supposed to receive which particular goods. In response, the Top-Man requests the audience members who had previously expressed an interest in the goods to, again, show their money to indicate that they are genuine bidders. Whilst each bidder is being addressed individually (with "If I treat you further will you say thank you?") the floor worker goes around collecting their money. This is done for all the bidders.

The Ram

In comparison to the elaborate build-up to this sale, the Ram itself is a model of simplicity. At first, little else happens other than the ram goods being handed over and the Top-Man reiterating that "if he had promised nothing then he owes nothing."

Only after the ram goods have been handed over are the nailer items finally given out. If a very proficient Top-Man is working the sale, the handing over of the nailer is undertaken in such a way as to create suspicion amongst audience members that this item may in fact be the only treat that they will receive. . . .

Delivering the Treat or 'Topments'

The nailer item does not transpire to be the only treat in store for people who have purchased the Ram goods. The treat is eventually added though turns out not to be a massive reduction in price but, rather, the addition of extra goods free of charge on top of what has been bought ('Topments'). Like the nailer items, these goods are wrapped in order to conceal their identity and, in particular, their cheapness. As a means of claiming the goods are high-value the Top-Man will allude to the possibility that they have been obtained illegally (e.g. "Put it in your pocket and don't show anyone what it is. If a man in a blue uniform (i.e. a policeman) asks you where you got that, you've found it, you didn't get it from me.")

Fifth Phase: 'End Games'

An the optional part of the mock auction, used after the Ram sales have successfully been conducted and when some of the victims of the previous sales have remained at the sales site to see if any further bargains will be offered, is for the Top-Man to sell goods to members of the audience on a one-to-one basis. Here, individual victims will be 'bled dry'—that is, taken for all the money they have got or (if they have credit cards in their possession) are willing to part with. One such sale is the 'M.O.T.' ('Money on Top') where the victims buy goods and also receive their bid money back from the Top-Man, but they still make a loss on the sale. Here is a short account of such an exchange between a seller and victim recalled by a retired Top-Man (and working with 1960's prices). The Top-Man is recounting what he would say to an individual who has already bid 10 pounds for a canteen of cutlery:

> "You've bid me 10 pounds. I'll tell you what I'll do, gimme your 10 pound note." You take her 10 pound note, you open the canteen, you put the 10 pounds in and shut the lid with the 10 pounds hanging out. You say, "Madam, your 10 pounds in cash, and the canteen is 27 pounds worth, how much is that?" She says "37 pounds." You say, "Right, you've got 37 pounds of commercial value there, including the money, bid me 20 pounds for the lot, money as well." She says "I'll have it." You're selling her own tenna back but you're copping 20 pounds.

In this type of case the victims effectively buy their own money back. The success of the con rests on the speed at which the sale is conducted and the buyers not realizing (at least until well after the goods have been purchased) they have created the exceptional bargain that is offered by contributing their own money.

Discussion and Conclusion

One way of developing an understanding of why the Mock Auction con is so successful would be to study the victims for traits that would explain their participation in this type of sale and also their tendency to not complain after having been deceived. We might find that they have an abnormal penchant for taking risks; that they possess more money than they have sense; that they have an abnormally greedy or unusually gullible nature; or that their lack of confidence or physical stature renders them incapable of pursuing redress over the economic injustices that are perpetrated against them. But in searching only for these types of factors we would surely fail to appreciate how fully this con essentially is managed and the grounds upon which the success of this routine primarily is based. Our study of the Mock Auction indicates that it is fundamentally a rhetorical and interactional accomplishment, and that the Top-Men—who seem to work from the premise that all outsiders are prospective suckers—above all else, are patter-merchants. The talk of these salespeople is by no means cheap, especially for those who are deceived. . . .

Victims of cons usually do not wish to acknowledge publicly that they have been deceived. They are generally treated unsympathetically by their peers, and their misfortune is often quietly held by others to be indicative of socially embarrassing personal deficiencies such as greed and gullibility. To complain would be to reveal publicly that they are a victim, or are gullible, or are a 'bad sport' to others in the audience, especially to their friends and family who may also have attended (and participated in the sale). These victims tend therefore to rationalize their predicament and, in an attempt to maintain or restore their face (Goffman, 1955) will privatize the event, treating it as something which, although somewhat unfortunate, can nevertheless be shrugged off and their losses 'put down to experience'.

In essence, at the Mock Auction the victims effectively get what they have paid for. But what they buy is not only the goods that have been offered for sale. They treat their active (perhaps shameful) participation and unwitting collusion in this sales con as having an interactional cost which, like the goods they have bought, can be paid off with an economic currency. For the vast majority of these victims the money that they hand over to the Top-Man seems but a small price to pay for the maintenance of social order and the silence which allows them privately to preserve their own personal esteem.

References

Allingham, P. (1973). *Cheapjack*. London: George Allen and Unwin.

Atkinson, J. M. (1984). *Our Masters' Voices: The Language and Body Language of Politics*. London: Methuen.

Clark, C., Pinch, T. (1988). "Selling by Social Control." In N. Fielding (Ed.) *Actions and Structures* pp. 119–141. London: Sage.

Goffman, E. (1955). "On Face-Work: An Analysis of Ritual Elements in Social Interaction." *Psychiatry*, 18, pp. 213–231.

——. (1959a). "On Cooling the Mark Out." Psychiatry, 15, pp. 461–463.

Mayhew, H. (1987). *Mayhew's London Underworld*. P. Quennell (Ed). London: Century.

Pinch, T. and Clark, C. (1986). "The Hard Sell: 'Patter-Merchanting' and the Strategic (Re) Production and Local Management of Economic Reasoning in the Sales Routines of Market Pitchers." *Sociology*, 20, 2, pp. 169–191

26

Male Street Hustling: Introduction Processes and Stigma Containment

Thomas C. Calhoun

Calhoun explains how young men are socialized into prostitution and how they rationalize participating in sexual activities they consider deviant. Hustlers believe that same-sex sexual activities are deviant but do not consider their sexual activities to be "real" sex. Instead, to control the stigma that will result from others knowing about their activities, hustlers avoid identifying themselves as gay men and carefully control who knows about their activities. These individuals see their deviant actions as a means to an end. They know they are engaging in deviant behavior, but they work to avoid a reputation as someone who has sex with men for money.

. . . . The male street hustler is the most visible of prostitutes because he often operates on street corners, out of bus terminals, or in hotel lobbies (Butts 1947; Reiss 1961; Weisberg 1984). Unlike the *call boy*, who either operates alone by advertising in an underground newspaper or works with a pimp, the street hustler neither advertises (excluding the signs conveyed by dress or physical demeanor) nor works for anyone else (Caukins and Coombs 1976). It is difficult to gather data on *kept boys* because they generally have relationships with only one other individual who meets most of their needs. Since street hustlers operate in the open, they are more accessible to the researcher.

Given society's negative views toward those who engage in homosexual activity, a hustler usually prevents others from learning of his participation. Should his homosexual activities become known, the hustler risks others important to him redefining him negatively. He may face social and familial ostracism. . . .

This article discusses the process used by male street hustlers as they attempt to negotiate a sexual transaction with their customers. The focus is on the nuances and subtleties in the interaction between hustler and would-be-customer, which are designed to prevent others from learning about their discrediting behavior. (This article does not address "covering" and "passing" strategies with significant others such as family members or peers.). . .

The research literature provides limited reference to the process whereby street hustlers and their tricks arrive at a decision to engage in sex. Six pickup methods commonly identified in the literature for initiating contact are: got a light (Butt 1947; Jersild 1956; Raven 1963); got a cigarette or time (Butt 1947; Jersild 1956; Reiss 1961); eye contact (Butts 1947; Reiss 1961); cruise (Bell and Weinberg 1978; Coombs 1974; Humphreys 1970; Leznoff and Westley 1956; Rechy 1977; Reiss 1961); smile or nod of head (Coombs 1974; Reiss 1961); and hitchhiking (Reiss 1961). These methods relate to initial contact; they do not explain systematically what happens after initial contact is made. Prus and Irini (1980) discuss other steps in the process; however, their research is directed toward female prostitutes. Although much has been written recently about male prostitution (Bour, Young and Henningsen 1984; Boyer 1989; Coleman 1989; Earls and David 1989; Humphreys 1970; Lowman 1987; Mathews 1988; Sullivan 1988), only one scholarly article provides a detailed discussion of the entire interaction that transpires between male customer and the male street hustler (Luckenbill 1984). Luckenbill identifies seven stages: making contact; assessing suitability; agreeing to a sale; coming to terms; moving to a suitable setting; making the exchange; and terminating the sale. The stages identified here parallel those identified by Luckenbill (1984).

Methods and Sample

The data were obtained from interviews with 18 young male prostitutes over the course of 3 months in 1984; all subjects were from a southern community with a population of just more than 200,000. In addition to the formal interviews, information was also obtained from other hustlers through informal conversations and by systematic observations.

The subjects were between the ages of 13 and 22 years. The average age is 17.6 years and the modal age is also 17. Of the 18 subjects, 15 are white and the remaining three are black. . . . The overall education level of the street hustlers in this sample is low. Half of the 18 subjects were currently not attending school, 7 of these dropped out before obtaining a high school diploma, and the other 2 subjects completed high school. . . . Sixteen of the 18 subjects were single and living at home with a parent or adult guardian. The remaining 2 subjects were married and had established independent households.

In this community, only one part of town was used by male prostitutes to arrange for sexual encounters with other males—the downtown area behind a gay bar. Female street walkers operated in another section of town, approximately five blocks away.

Entrance into the "subculture" of male prostitution is difficult because many young male prostitutes are mistrustful and suspicious of outsiders, especially those seeking information about street prostitution and their involvement in it. Meeting the principal informant occurred quite by accident. While observing informally one evening, Tony approached me as I sat in the parking lot directly across from a popular pickup spot. Because Tony was interested in "turning a trick," I could only identify myself as a researcher and state my purpose.

Each time following our first encounter, when Tony would come on "the block," he would come over and talk with me. As time passed, a mutual trust developed between us. After we became friends, he helped introduce me to other hustlers. The recorded interviews took place at locations convenient to both the hustler and myself; some lasted only 30 minutes, whereas others lasted more than 2 hours.

Entry

Before we can appreciate the intricacies of hustlers' defense processes, we need to focus first on (1) how they learn about street hustling; (2) what instructions, if any, they are provided; and (3) then move to the process used by hustlers to negotiate a sexual transaction.

The data indicate two major pathways leading young males to street prostitution: peer introduction, including friends, siblings, and/or relatives; and situational discovery, including those situations in which a young person learns about male prostitution without conscious effort.

The data indicate that the majority of these hustlers learn about street hustling from their friends who are participants. From these interactions the new recruit is given (in varying degrees) instructions, motives, and techniques for carrying out this deviant activity (Sutherland and Cressey 1978). In rare instances some hustlers stumble on this activity and subsequently become participants, lending credence to Matza's (1964) notion of "drift."

Peer Introduction

Research on teenage male prostitution has demonstrated that the majority of juveniles are introduced to street prostitution through their associations and interactions with significant others (Allen 1980; Butts 1947; Ginsburg 1967; James 1982; Jersild 1956; Raven 1968; Reiss 1961; Ross 1959; Weisberg 1984). Most of the subjects in this study confirm this finding. Fourteen of the 18 respondents indicated that they were introduced to street hustling by a friend. In discussing how he became involved in male prostitution, Mike "C" said:

> This dude told me about it. I went with him behind 'The Bar' and he kept talking about it. It seemed like he didn't want to tell me. He just wanted me to be there and watch or something. I was standing there just freaking out on all of it. He went across the street and talked to somebody. He said 'Mike, this dude will give you 50 dollars to do so and so. . . .' I said, "no," cause I was freaking out.

Perhaps Mike "C"'s friend was intentionally vague because he did not know how Mike "C" would react to the knowledge that he was a street hustler. Yet another plausible explanation for his friend's vagueness is that it would make it easier for Mike "C" to reject the chance to participate in this kind of sexual activity.

In some situations a friend takes an active part in exposing the minor to street hustling. James related the following story about how he learned about hustling from his friend:

> One night we was sitting down there on 'The Wall'–we was just sitting there. Cause I didn't know nothing about it. This guy comes up and says, 'Let's go up to my apartment for awhile.' He says 'I ain't into it tonight. I'm trying to break my friend into it. He ain't never been out.'

The presence of an experienced hustler can serve two functions: it may reduce the anxiety the new recruit feels about participating in homosexual encounters; and, secondly, having an experienced street hustler with the novice can help him learn the necessary skills.

Some juveniles who have friends that are prostitutes will indicate a need for money, and the friends may then offer a way to eliminate the financial hardship (Allen 1980; Butts 1947; Caukins and Coombs 1976; Raven 1968; Reiss 1961). Bill said:

> I know this friend. I said 'Damn, I need some money.' He said, 'I know how to git it.' He showed me the tricks so that I would know what to do. So I tried it and the guy gave me the money.

Although friends constitute the largest group of people who introduce others to prostitution, siblings and/or other relatives are also influential (Reiss, 1961). Of the 14 subjects who were introduced to hustling by another person, 2 were introduced by a sibling or other relative. Boo said:

> I followed my brothers down there. I said, 'What are y'all doing there?' They said 'hustling.' I said, 'What do you do?' They said 'Just go up to one of these cars and just make sure it ain't no cop—ask if they're a cop first. Then you can name your price.'

In this case the young person was introduced and given instructions about hustling by his older brothers. Other juveniles learn about street prostitution from a relative, other than a sibling, who recognizes the financial benefits. Henry, a black teenager, related the following:

> I first found out about hustling from my cousin. He said 'do you want to make some money?' I said, 'What are you talking about?' He said, 'down to the gay bar.' I'd never really thought about it. So one night he asked me about it again and I said, 'Yeah, I'll go down there with you.' I had made up my mind to hustle myself because I wanted to see what it was all about.

An offer to earn money was extended; however, it was not initially accepted. Money may be the primary inducing factor, but Henry's response suggests that other factors may also be important.

Situational Discovery

Although 14 teenagers were introduced to street hustling by a significant other (i.e., family member or friend), the remaining 4 subjects learned about street prostitution by chance. In the literature about street male prostitutes there is limited reference to this method of introduction (Allen 1980; Butts 1947; Caukins and Coombs 1976; Craft 1966; Ginsburg 1967; MacNamara 1965). Kenny stated:

> I was out riding around on my bike, and I seen a man sitting. I stopped and talked to him for a while and I said, 'What are you doing down here?' He says, 'I'm making money.' I said, 'How?' He said 'Letting these queers suck my dick.' I said, 'What

do you mean?' He says, 'Fags, you know what fags are, don't you?' I said, 'Yeah, I've heard of them.' 'Well, I'm letting them suck my dick.' I said, 'Is that how you're making money?' He said, 'Yeah you should try it.' So that night, that same night that he told me about it, I took my bike and I hid it. I came back down here. I was scared 'cause it was the first time I had ever done something like that. And I went out with this dude. He gave me 30 dollars to go out with him. Me and him went out, and he sucked my dick. Ever since then I've been down there.

The male prostitute Kenny spoke with provided him incentives for participating in this activity—money and sex—and, by implication, conveyed a dislike for homosexuals. During their conversation, participation in prostitution was portrayed as "no big deal." Also the tone of the conversation implies that one can participate in hustling and maintain a sense of masculinity. The usage of terms such as "fags" and "queers" suggest that men who buy sexual services from other males are not "normal." In this sense, the prostitute is able to separate his sense of self from his perception of homosexuals (Goffman 1963; Warren 1972).

Peer Socialization

The literature on male prostitution does not give specific information concerning what young males are told by their introducer as they begin hustling. In his now classic study, Reiss (1961) identifies norms that govern the interactions between hustlers and their tricks, such as: the interaction must be for monetary gains and sexual gratification must not be sought; the sexual encounter must be restricted to mouth-genital fellation; the participants must remain effectively neutral during the sexual encounter; and violence can only be used when the shared expectations between the participants is violated. . . .

Each subject was asked what instructions, if any, were provided by the person who introduced them to street prostitution. The most common instruction given the soon-to-be hustlers by their mentors were: the location of the prostitution area; which acts a

hustler should perform and an idea of the cost for performing these acts; assessment of the potential customer as a law enforcement agent; and something about customer behavior. Ron reported the greatest number of instructions during the interview. He said he was told:

> . . . Let them give me head $20 and nothing else. Be careful about some of the mother fuckers. . . not to let 'em fuck you in the ass, not to give them no head. . . be careful about the police, they'll stop and ask you a bunch of shit.

The hustling instructions given to Ron contain at least three themes: (1) he was told what sex acts were acceptable; (2) he was given some idea about how much to charge for the specific type of sex; and (3) he was warned about law enforcement.

Although some hustlers reported receiving extensive instructions, others were given few. They had to learn on their own. David said:

> He didn't know how it was going on or anything but he did tell me one thing, 'Make sure that you'd ask if they was a cop.' Other than that he really didn't tell me a whole lot about it.

Some young people were given no instructions whatsoever and they, too, had to learn for themselves. Mink stated, "I learnt it on my own. Really, I learnt it the hard way."

The Negotiation Process

During informal conversations, interviews, and observations with street hustlers, the following sequence appears as the typical order in which sexual interaction occurs; however, not all interactions pass through each stage as presented. Some stages may be skipped. The stages to be discussed are: initial contact; confirmation; negotiation of the sexual act and fees; and negotiation of location. For analytical purposes, the initial contact stage, the confirmation stage, and the negotiation of location stage are used to illustrate how these hustlers manage the threat of stigma (i.e., arrest and subsequent labeling as a homosexual prostitute). The negotiation of [the] acts/fees stage of the process is used primarily in managing an identity as nonhomosexual.

Initial Contact

For the trick and hustler to reach a mutually acceptable agreement about the buying and/or selling of sexual favors they must be able to talk with each other. Although the hustler and potential customer may occupy the same physical space, there is no guarantee their copresence indicates desire or availability for sex. Hustlers must develop strategies for identifying potential tricks and strategies for making the initial contact once a potential trick has been identified.

One method of identifying a potential trick is cruising. Mink, a 20-year-old hustler, with typical views about the subtleties and intricacies of this process, stated:

> They circle around the block, and they'd look at you, and they'd circle the block again. They'd pull over and stop. And so you are thinking to yourself, in your mind, 'This guy is wanting me. I'm gonna go up and see what he wants.'

In this case, the hustler is aware of the fact that perhaps the individual who is cruising the block might be a potential customer; however, he does not commit himself initially to being recognizable as a male prostitute.

Once a potential customer has been identified, the hustler may "nod his head or wave" at the trick. This gesture can signal a willingness by the hustler to enter into conversation with the potential trick, which may result in a sexual transaction. As the customer is cruising the block trying to determine if the young male is a hustler, he generally uses gestures to communicate his interest. One respondent told me:

> When somebody's trying to pick you up, they're staring at you. They wave at you, they nod their head for you to walk on down the street so they can talk to you.

Although an initial gesture has been offered, neither the sender of the message nor the hustler is sure that the other is the kind of person he seeks. The hustler may not respond to the gestures for a number of reasons, such as prior knowledge about the trick; the hustler may be waiting for a specific individual; he may have to be home early; or he may be just "hanging out" and is not interested in pursuing a sexual encounter. Assuming the hustler has identified a potential trick, additional efforts may be made to further verify the assessment.

The hustler initially does not commit himself, and his message may be vague and structured so as to force the potential trick to state his purpose. One respondent said after he makes contact with the potential customer: "I'm gonna ask him for a cigarette or I'm going to ask him for a light, and then you tell him, 'Hey man, look you doing anything tonight.'" In other situations, the hustler disguises his purpose from the customer by making reference to a need for employment. One hustler said:

> I go up and say, 'Hey man do you know where I can get a job?' He'll say, 'I might.' Then I say, 'Where? Do you care if I get in and sit down a minute.' He says, 'O.K.' And I get in there and sit down, and they drive, and then we start talking about it.

Structuring the interaction in this manner, the hustler is using disidentifiers by not linking himself initially to prostitution. He only tries to verify if the individual is a potential trick. Before the interaction proceeds any further, the hustler needs to know that the person to whom he is talking is not someone (i.e., the police) who could officially sanction his behavior by arresting him and attaching the label "deviant" to him.

Confirmation

If the hustler is satisfied with his assessment of the potential trick, then he will generally ask if the potential trick is a policeman before discussing negotiating sexual favors. Bill said:

> I talk to him, I say, 'Hi, my name is Bill, how are you doing.' Then I ask them if they are the police or anything to do with the police. And sometimes, if they got an antenna or two on the car, I don't get in. Then I ask them what they looking for tonight.

Hustlers believe that if a potential trick is a police officer he must say so, for failure to do so constitutes entrapment. According to

Mitch, "It's a law that requires that he cannot say he is not a policeman if he is." James, in discussing an encounter he had with a potential trick and how he deals with them if he thinks they are the police, said:

'Are you a cop?' That's the first question I ask and if they say yes—you run like hell. If they are a cop, they have to tell you; if they don't they can't arrest you.

Asking the potential trick if he is a cop then serves two functions. First, hustlers believe if the potential customer does not answer the question truthfully the court case will be dismissed should he be arrested for prostitution. Second, if a policeman informs the hustler of his identity, the hustler can terminate the conversation without telling the policeman he is a prostitute. . . .

The hustlers' understanding of this law is incorrect; however, whether or not hustlers are correct in their interpretation, they make a concerted effort to avoid arrest in an attempt to prevent significant others from learning about their involvement in this type of deviant behavior.

Negotiation of Sexual Act

If the hustler finds the potential trick acceptable, the conversation moves to a more intimate level—sexual negotiation. These negotiations first center around the specific act to be performed followed by a negotiation of the fee.

Negotiating the Act. The potential trick may tell the hustler the sexual activity he desires. At this point the hustler and trick attempt to reach an agreement. If an agreement cannot be reached, the interaction ceases. As one hustler stated: "If I don't like it, I don't go. If he asks me to suck his dick, I say no I don't do that.' If the initial offer is rejected, the hustler may make a counter offer. Bill, when discussing the negotiation process stated: "There is a couple of things that I don't do. I tell them, and if they still want to do something then they tell me. If it's alright with me then we do it." In some situations the hustler can be rather adamant about which sexual acts he will perform. Mink illustrated this when he said:

I always told them that all I wanted was to get sucked off, and that was it. If they'd ask me, do you do more than that, I'd tell them, 'No that's all I do.' You give me head, that's it.

A trick may want the hustler to provide other sexual services, but the hustler generally holds his ground about what he is willing to do. If the trick accepts the counter offer, the conversation continues; if it is rejected, the trick or hustler may make another offer or terminate the conversation.

. . . . The negotiations between the trick and hustler are complex. The hustler generally enjoys a dominant position in these encounters because he has the option of deciding whether or not he will engage in the requested sexual activity. Male prostitutes, as a category, will not perform any and all sexual acts.

Negotiating the Fee. When the hustler and trick have agreed on the act or acts to be performed, the hustler must decide how much to charge, and the trick must decide if he will pay the price. Many factors influence the cost: the nature of the act being requested; the perception of the trick; and other situational factors, such as a need to be home early or an inability to get picked up.

Nature of Act

The number of acts requested are diverse, but the acts hustlers say they are willing to provide is limited. David best reflects the importance of the act when he stated:

If they just want to suck my dick that's fine. He'll suck you off. Suck each other off for a reasonable price. But after that I'd ask for more. If somebody's going to fuck me they have to look decently—really appealing to me. I don't let anybody that don't look appealing fuck me or vice versa. But even if he was appealing there's going to be a jacked up price, about $60.

At least three themes are evident in this quote: (1) David is aware that tricks may request a number of sex acts; (2) the sexual act requested influences the cost (e.g., anal sex more than oral sex); and (3) participation in some acts (i.e., anal sex) is influenced by his perception of the customer. Generally, the more atypical the act requested the more the hustler will charge.

Perception of Trick

If the hustler suspects the trick is under the influence of alcohol or drugs, he will try to extract more money. Asking Mitch why he charged one customer $15 and the other $75 to perform the same act, he said: "Well, the one that I would be charging $75, he would be tore up on drugs, and I would be taking advantage of the situation." Aside from attempting to take advantage of the trick's condition, one respondent said that "if I think he is rich I charge him high." Believing a trick is rich is based on dress, the presence of jewelry, or the automobile driven.

Other Constraints

Most hustlers in this study live at home, and their parents expect them home by a certain time. If the hustler is pressed for time, the price he normally would charge may be lowered. Reflecting on time restrictions, Glenn stated he lowered his price "lots of times on nights when I had to be home early and couldn't make a trick." Two conditions are operating in Glenn's case: (1) time and (2) the difficulty in getting picked up. This young male, like other hustlers, may have difficulty in being picked up for several reasons: the number of available tricks may be limited; tricks may be available but they may not want this hustler for a variety of reasons; and the number of hustlers on the street may exceed the number of available tricks. These conditions may force the hustler to lower his price.

Negotiation of Location

If the hustler and trick have agreed to the act(s) to be performed and the price, one final decision must be made: where to consummate the deal. The 18 hustlers in this study reported having sex with tricks in three locations: 16 in apartment/houses; 11 in cars in parking lots; and 8 in motels or hotels.

The trick is given some latitude in choosing where the sexual transaction is to take place; however, a major concern of the hustler is how best to protect his privacy. Although information was obtained only from hustlers, it is also reasonable to assume that privacy is also a concern of the customer,

since arrest could lead to loss of family, friends, and perhaps his job. One hustler said:

> Sometimes you might go to a hotel that they have already rented or you might go to their houses, you might even stay in the car, but you would go away from society. You would go where you wouldn't have any attention.

Despite the variety of locations, it is not clear from the data if hustlers have a preference as to where the sexual encounter should take place. Again, privacy is a common concern. Performing these acts in public increases the probability of detection by law enforcement, and to be caught in the act is the easiest way for one's cover to be blown (Goffman 1963).

The sexual act can influence the location, since some activities cannot easily be accomplished in a car (i.e., anal intercourse). Some activities require the trick to either take the hustler to his house, with an attendant risk of discovery should a family member come home unexpectedly, or to rent a room in a motel where the risk of discovery is minimal. The latter, however, would require additional expenditures, therefore, the sexual desires of the trick must also be balanced with practical considerations.

Once the act is completed, the trick will return the hustler to the downtown area or take him to another location. Most hustlers in this study did not return to the prostitution site but were dropped off at other locations— a strategy used to avoid detection. If the hustler has been successful in negotiating and completing the sexual transaction, he can continue to engage in this discrediting behavior without being publicly labeled and identified as a discredited person.

Discussion

The majority of these hustlers became involved in male prostitution as a result of peer introduction. Their friends provided them with the necessary instructions, motives, and techniques for carrying out this deviant activity. As presented here, one of the key instructions given these hustlers by their introducers was the type of sexual acts they should engage in with their tricks. Other instructions included the location of the prostitution area, how to minimize police detection, and ideas about customer behavior.

. . . . In the negotiation process between hustlers and customers, several techniques were highlighted that help these hustlers avoid arrest and the subsequent label of homosexual prostitute. Particular emphasis is placed on three stages of the negotiation process: initial contact, confirmation, and location of the sexual act. In each of these stages, hustlers made every attempt to prevent others, particularly those with official sanctioning powers, from learning about their involvement in street prostitution. Of those strategies identified, making sure the individual who is cruising is a would-be customer; ascertaining if the customer is connected with law enforcement; and carrying out the sexual transaction out of the public's view are all designed to avoid arrest.

This research suggests that the interactions between a street hustler and a trick are a complex process requiring each party to "read" the other. The hustler must be skilled in these negotiations, for failure to do so could result in arrest and subsequent stigmatization. . . .

References

Allen, Donald M. 1980. "Young Male Prostitutes: Psychosocial Study." *Archives of Sexual Behavior,* 9:399–425.

Bell, Alan P. and Martin S. Weinberg. 1978. *Homosexualities: A Study of Diversity among Men and Women.* New York: Simon & Schuster.

Bour, Daria, Jeanne P. Young and Rodney Henningsen. 1984. "A Comparison of Delinquent Prostitutes and Non-Prostitutes on Self Concept." In Sol Chaneles (Ed.) *Gender Issues, Sex Offenses, and Criminal Justice,* (pp. 89–102). New York: The Haworth Press,

Boyer, Debra. 1989. "Male Prostitution and Homosexual Identity." *Journal of Homosexuality,* 17:1–2:151–184.

Butts, William Marlin. 1947 "Boy Prostitutes of the Metropolis." *Journal of Clinical Psychopathy,* 8:673–681.

Caukins, Sivan E. and Neil R. Coombs. 1976. "The Psychodynamics of Male Prostitution." *American Journal of Psychotherapy,* 30:441–451.

Churchill, Wainwright. 1967. *Homosexual Behavior Among Males.* New York: Hawthorn Books.

Coleman, Eli. 1989. "The Development of Male Prostitution Activity Among Gay and Bisexual Adolescents." *Journal of Homosexuality,* 17:1–2, 131–149.

Coombs, Neil K. 1974. "Male Prostitution: A Psychosocial View of Behavior." *American Journal of Orthopsychiatry,* 44:782–789.

Earls, Christopher M. and Helen David. 1989. "A Psychosocial Study of Male Prostitution." *Archives of Sexual Behavior,* 18:5, 401–419.

Ginsburg, Kenneth N. 1967. "The 'Meat Rack': A Study of the Male Homosexual Prostitute." *American Journal of Psychotherapy,* 21:170–184.

Goffman, Erving. 1963. *Stigma.* Englewood Cliffs, NJ: Prentice-Hall.

Humphreys, Laud. 1970. *Tearoom Trade: Impersonal Sex in Public Places.* Chicago: Aldine Press.

James, Jennifer. 1982. "Entrance into Juvenile Male Prostitution." *Final Report.* Washington, DC: Department of Health and Human Services.

Jersild, Jens. 1956. *Boy Prostitution.* Copenhagen: G.E.C. Gad.

Lenoff, M. and W. A. Wesley. 1956. "The Homosexual Community." *Social Problems,* 3:256–263.

Lowman, J. 1987. "Taking Young Prostitutes Seriously." *The Canadian Review of Sociology and Anthropology,* 24:99–116.

Luckenbill, David F. 1984. "The Dynamics of the Deviant Sale." *Deviant Behavior,* 5:337–353.

MacNamara, Donald E. J. 1965. "Male Prostitution in American Cities: A Socio-economic or Pathological Phenomenon?" *American Journal of Orthopsychiatry,* 35:204.

Mathews, Paul W. 1988. "On 'Being a Prostitute.'" *Journal of Homosexuality,* 15:3–4, 119–35.

Matza, David. 1964. *Delinquency and Drift.* New York: John Wiley.

Prus, Robert and Styllianoss Irini. 1980. *Hookers, Rounders, and Desk Clerks: The Social Organization of the Hotel Community.* Salem, WI: Sheffield.

Raven, Simon. 1963. "Boys Will Be Boys: The Male Prostitute in London." In Hendrik M. Ruitenbeek (Ed.) *The Problem of Homosexuality in Modern Society,* (pp. 279–290). New York: E. P. Dutton & Company.

Rechy, John. 1977. *The Sexual Outlaw: A Documentary.* New York: Grove Press.

Reiss, Albert, J., Jr. 1961. "The Social Integration of Queers and Peers." *Social Problems,* 9:102–120.

Ross, H. Laurence. 1959. "The 'Hustler' in Chicago." *Journal of Student Research*, 1:13–19.

Sullivan, Terrace. 1987. "Juvenile Prostitution: A Critical Perspective." *Journal of Marriage and Family Review*, 12:113–134.

Sutherland, Edwin H. and Donald R. Cressey. 1978. *Criminology* (10th ed). Philadelphia: Lippincott.

Warren, Carole A. B. 1972. *Identity and Community in the Gay World*. New York: Wiley.

Weisberg, D. Kelly. 1984. *Children of the Night: A Study of Adolescent Prostitution*. Lexington, MA: Lexington Books.

27

Neutralization and Deviance in the Workplace: Theft of Supplies and Medicines by Hospital Nurses

Dean Dabney

This article provides a look at theft and drug use among hospital nurses. Drawing on interviews, Dabney first demonstrates that nurses freely admit to stealing supplies and drugs. Even more interesting is that they don't see anything wrong with their theft, except under some limited circumstances. Nurses judge their deviance against the norms they have established among themselves, not according to official hospital rules, which forbid theft. Dabney shows that deviants do not disregard the rules altogether; rather, they operate within a set of norms that they establish for themselves.

The nursing profession is not without its share of employee deviance. This deviance takes many forms. Some of the most prevalent and potentially destructive examples of nursing deviance are the theft of drugs or supplies. A nationwide study of drug theft in hospitals (McCormick et al., 1986) found that nurses were implicated in 70% of the drug losses (more that 112,000 dosage units over a 1-year period). Moreover, a large-scale survey of nurses' on-the-job substance abuse behaviors conducted by the American Nurses Association (ANA, 1984) estimated that 8–

10% of the nation's 1.7 million nurses are dependent on drugs or alcohol. A similar large-scale study conducted by the Michigan Nurses Association (MNA, 1986) estimated that nurses are five times more likely to abuse substances than are members of the general public. The Michigan study went on to estimate that one in seven nurses will abuse substances during their careers. With these figures in mind, the research reported here attempts to provide contextuality to nurses' involvements in organizational deviance, using existing criminological theory. Specifically, this analysis draws on components of differential association, social learning theory, and techniques of neutralization to explain the aforementioned forms of nursing deviance. The goal is to identify both the positive and the negative normative definitions associated with nurses' deviant behavior and to illustrate how the nursing work group supplies its members with a series of neutralizing rationalizations that are then used to modify these definitions.

Theoretical Orientation

The learning process that leads to deviant behavior has long fascinated criminologists. Sutherland's (Sutherland, 1949; Sutherland and Cressey, 1970) differential association theory was the first to suggest that the learning process behind criminal behavior is the same as that behind non-criminal behavior. At the center of Sutherland's theory is the concept of "definitions." According to Sutherland, these definitions serve as the normative attitudes and beliefs toward behavior. When an individual has the knowledge of how to commit an act and t he opportunity presents itself, that individual's behavior will hinge on his or her normative perception of the act. An excess of definitions favorable to an act increases the likelihood of its occurrence, and an excess of negative definitions decreases the likelihood of its occurrence.

Social learning theory (Akers, 1985) expands on Sutherland's (Sutherland, 1949; Sutherland and Cressey, 1970) concept of definitions. According to social learning theory, normative definitions are the result not only of association, but [also] of imitation and differential reinforcement. More important, social learning theory asserts that definitions favorable to deviant acts can take on one of two forms: They can simply define the act as morally correct or they can redefine a morally incorrect act in a favorable light. In the latter case, a set of excuses, justifications, or rationalizations serve as vocal or internal discriminative stimuli for the deviant act. . . .

Social learning theory incorporates the notion of neutralization from Sykes and Matza's (1957) "techniques of neutralization" theory. Sykes and Matza formulated five distinct typologies of justifications or rationalizations: *denial of responsibility, denial of injury, denial of victim, condemnation of condemner, and the appeal to higher loyalties.* . . .

Building on the concept of normative definitions, I attempt, in this analysis to identity neutralizing definitions that manifest themselves within the nursing work group and thus facilitate various forms of organizational deviance. Interview data are used to demonstrate that the nursing work group creates and maintains its own system of work group norms. For the most part, these definitions correspond with the accepted norms of the hospital and even those of the larger society. However, in some cases, the established organizational norms of the hospital conflict with work group norms. In this case, the work group either provides the individual nurses with a set of rationalizations for violating the hospital's organizational and legal rules or institutes procedural shortcuts or innovative adaptations to circumvent existing hospital policy.

I argue that incoming nurses are aware of the formal organizational definitions against taking supplies and medicines for personal or unauthorized use. Nevertheless, observations in hospitals reveal that nurses readily engage in taking such properties. The contention here is that such behaviors are facilitated by nurses learning a series of justifications and rationalizations that portray theft as not really deviant when committed under certain conditions. Consistent with social learning theory, I argue that these rationalizations are the direct result of reinforcement from other nurses. As nurses are socialized into a particular work group, they tend to change their general normative definition to conform to that held by the work group. These norms do not compel or require deviations from the hospital or legal regulations. Nor do they portray such deviations as something a "good" nurse should do. Rather, they simply excuse the acts as not really wrong when committed under some circumstances. . . .

Deviance and Neutralizations in the Workplace

Several past research efforts have approached the use of employee deviance from a similar theoretical perspective. For example, in studying what he called "blue-collar theft" among workers at an electronics factory, Horning (1970) found evidence that employees constructed their own definitions of what did and did not constitute "real" theft within the organization. These definitions depend on the property involved. The respondents classified property into three categories: company property, personal property, and property of uncertain origin. The misappropriation of personal property or company property was seen as theft. However, a similar definition was not applied to property of uncertain origin. In this case, the workers felt justified in taking the property. . . .

In this research, I applied the neutralization concept to a sample of nurses. Specifically, I hypothesized that certain types of hospital property, such as supplies and some forms of medicines, would be afforded uncertain ownership status. At the same time, "harder" drugs such as narcotics should clearly be defined as hospital property and should not be taken. Thus, one would expect that, in addition to offering individual nurses the motives and techniques needed to steal drugs and supplies from the hospital, the nursing work group will also offer the individual an arsenal of justifications that can be sued to make these behaviors acceptable in the light of societal or administrative norms.

Method

I used a snowball sampling technique (Babbie, 1989; Berg, 1989) to find nurses to participate in this research. The sample began with three informants who served as the interviews participants as well as the core of the snowball. Once each informant was interviewed, I asked them to refer me to other nurses they knew who might hold views on or have first-hand information regarding deviance among nurses. . . . This process was continued until a sample of 25 registered nurses was located and interviewed.

Interviews were arranged at the informants' convenience, in their homes, in a neutral location, or in a lounge at their work site. I conducted all of the interviews during the summer of 1991. Each interview was structured as a conversation and lasted approximately 60–90 minutes. The interview conversations focused on several topics, including employee theft among nurses. . . .

Sample Characteristics

The sample had the following demographic characteristics. Subjects ranged in age from 22 to 53 years, with a mean age of 33.25 years. Twenty-one of the 25 nurses were female and 4 were male. All 25 respondents were Caucasian. Twenty-two of these nurses described themselves during the interview as middle class. The remaining 3 respondents described themselves as working class. Regarding marital status, 9 states they were single and 16 said they were married. The religious composition of the sample was rather diverse. Thirteen individuals identified themselves as Catholic, 3 as Lutherans, 3 as Protestants, and 3 and Presbyterians, and 2 respondents claimed to be nondenominational. Similarly, there was a great deal of variation in the types of nursing credentials held by the respondents. Eleven nurses [had] received educational credentials from a diploma school before completing their registered nurse examination. Six of the nurses had received an associate's degree in nursing. The 8 remaining nurses in the sample [had] received their bachelor's degree in nursing.

All of the nurses involved in this study were working in some sort of critical care nursing position. . . . These nursing positions were held in three different hospitals located in a single major metropolitan area in the northeastern part of the United States. Each of the hospitals was a non-profit teaching hospital with more than 500 beds. In terms of the nursing experience of the sample, the respondents' nursing careers varied from 9 months to 30 years. The average career length for the sample was 8.88 years.

Results

Theft of General Supplies

All of the nurses claimed to have seen other nurses stealing supplies from hospital stock, and 23 admitted to personal involvements in these activities. In fact, most of the nurses laughed when asked if they had ever seen nurses stealing supplies. When discussing the topic of supply theft, it was customary for nurses to offer a long and diverse list of popular theft items.

All of the nurses implied that supply theft was accepted behavior among the nursing work group. This is evidenced by the fact that most nurses estimate that 100% of the nursing staff reported involvements in supply theft. Only 4 nurses estimated that fewer than 50% of the nursing staff were involved in supply theft.

The nurses often made statements that clearly illustrated the group acceptance of supply theft. This can be seen in the following exchange that took place between the interviewer and a 37-year-old intensive care unit nurse:

"Do they try to hide it [supply theft] from colleagues?"

"No, not at all."

"So it is accepted behavior?"

"Yes, it kind of bothers me, but. . . ”

Despite this group acceptance of supply theft, the nurses were very cognizant of the fact that their behaviors were against the law as well as the norms established by hospital policy. For example, one 28-year-old nurse offered the following normative definition of supply theft: "Probably if you get deep down to it, it is probably morally wrong because it is not yours. But it doesn't bother me in the least. Not in the least! Isn't that awful?" Another nurse, this one a 26-year-old ICU nurse had this to say about the normative definition of supply theft:

> I steal scrubs. I have a million pairs at home. Cut them off and make shorts. I realize it is a debt but you don't think about it. You think that they won't miss it but you know they do. I mean the scrub loss is $11,000 a month. They take a beating.

. . . The most common rationalization justified supply theft as a fringe benefit that goes along with the job. For example, a 47-year-old ICU step-down (an intermediate care unit) nurse claimed that her supply theft was "a way of supplementing one's income." In full, 88% of the nurses justified their own, and their observed, theft of general supplies in this manner. This trend is obvious in the statement made by another 28-year-old ICU nurse. When asked if she saw supply theft as a fringe benefit, she said, "Yeah, it's kind of a compensation. . . I really don't think about it. You just take it. It is no big deal."

It is interesting to note that the scope of this neutralization of supply theft was tempered by work group limitations. Not all forms of supply theft were positively defined by the work group. Only theft in moderation was rationalized. This is obvious in the quote offered by a 33-year-old ICU step-down unit nurse. She said, "If they were taking garbage bags full, people would be upset, but everyone takes something once in a while. It is a kind of fringe benefit for us."

Theft of Over-the-Counter Medicines

A similar trend emerged regarding the theft of over-the-counter medicines. Twenty-one of the nurses admitted that they had themselves stolen certain medicines, usually Tylenol, from hospital stock. Once again, the theft appeared to be quite extensive. For example, when asked to clarify her claim that someone steals Tylenol every day on her unit, a 26-year-old ICU nurse said, "Yeah, if you have a headache, you go take one [Tylenol] out of the drawer." . . .

As was the case with supply theft, the theft of over-the-counter drugs was rationalized by work group definitions. This point is illustrated in the following exchange, which occurred with a 25-year-old ICU step-down nurse:

"Is drug theft looked down on by nurses?"

"Probably drugs but not things like Tylenol."

"Have you ever taken over-the-counter meds?"

"Oh yeah, things like Tylenol or Motrin."

"How did you get them?"

"I just walk up to the drawer and take them."

"So people see you and they don't say anything?"

"That's right."

Once again, nurses had to justify the theft of over-the-counter drugs as it was known to be against hospital regulations. These rationalizations were also usually based on the fringe benefit rationalization and were tempered by the amount taken and the frequency with which it occurred.

Theft of Non-Narcotic Medicines

A slightly different pattern arose, however, concerning the theft of medicines other than simple pain and headache remedies. In this case, non-narcotic drugs such as Darvoset N100, a mild analgesic, or tranquilizers such as Xanax or Ativan were frequently mentioned. Although these drugs do require a doctor's prescription, they are dispensed in the same way as other non-narcotic medicines, through the unit dose system. Under this system, each patient is given his or her daily allotment of these medicines, and they are kept in each patient's room. A nurse must chart the administration of these medicines, but a key is not required to gain access to them. The majority of the nurses explained that there is often an excess of these types of medicines left on the unit. This is sometimes due to over-prescribing by physicians or because the intended patient dies or is transferred before the medication is dispensed. . . .

In all, 15 nurses described eyewitness accounts in which nurses took advantage of these stockpiled non-narcotic drugs by taking them. For example, a 26-year-old clinical coordinator of an ICU stated, "Today one of the nurses had a sore leg so she took some Darvoset out of her patient's drawer."

The misappropriation of these stockpiled non-narcotic drugs appeared to be accepted behavior among the nurses. For example, one 23-year-old ICU step-down nurse said, "At 6:00 anything that is left in the drawers is free game because it should have been given throughout the day."

Evidence of nurses comparing the theft of these mild analgesics to over-the-counter drugs was offered by a 25-year-old nurse working in an ICU step-down unit. When asked if she had ever seen another nurse take medicines from the hospital, she replied, "Yes, stuff like Valium, Tylenol, Motrin, or even Xanax." Further questioning of this nurse showed that she made no distinction between the severity of these thefts. . . .

The general acceptance of non-narcotic drug theft is underscored by the finding that, although 22 nurses reported having witnessed theft and/or use of controlled substances, none reported these situations to superiors. . . . Few of the nurses who had seen other nurses take drugs could offer what they felt were completely accurate estimates of how many different times they had seen such behavior. For instance, one female, 28-year-old step-down unit nurse explained, "Yes, nurses do it for their own uses but they only take the stuff that isn't locked up. If it isn't locked up it is fair game. I don't know how many times I have seen it happen." . . .

All of the nurses explained that pharmacy policy disapproved of stockpiling non-narcotic medicines. Theses nurses also understood that hospital regulations did not allow them to misappropriate or ingest these drugs. Still, they rationalized doing so. These rationalizations usually resembled Horning's (1970) notion of property of uncertain ownership. He found that over time, the factory workers in his study had come to collectively redefine some forms of company property as having an uncertain ownership status and thus normatively accepted the removal of these materials for personal use. The idea was that the material were no longer "really" the property of the company. In the present cases of the stockpiled drugs, the nurses engaged in a similar process. In short, because there was no direct controls on these accumulated drugs, the work group saw them as fair game.

Theft of Narcotic Medicines

Each of the 25 nurses made a clear distinction between the theft of unit doses drugs, which are all controlled substances, and the narcotic drugs that are kept under constant lock and key. Although nurses routinely used terminology such as "no big deal" to describe the use or theft of medicines such as Darvoset N100, no such definition was afforded to the locked-down narcotics. Here the work group norms were clearly in line with the societal and administrative definitions. When asked about narcotic drug theft, one 33-year-old ICU step-down nurse replied, "I think it is terrible. Narcotics you mean? Yeah, I think it is terrible. They are highly addictive and it ends up being a problem. It turns into a vicious circle and something bad happens." . . .

A negative work group definition of narcotic drug theft translated into minimal reported incidents of theft. Only one nurse admitted to stealing narcotics, and this was an isolated case that occurred many years earlier. Furthermore, there were only four eyewitness reports of narcotics theft.

Although these nurses brushed off the other forms of theft discussed earlier, they claimed that they would report nurses who stole narcotics. This once again illustrates the strong work group controls placed on employee theft among nurses. For example, one 27-year-old oncology nurse said, "It depends on what they are taking. If it is something minor then okay, but if it is something like a narc, I would report them."

A 48-year-old ICU nurse amplified this point about the theft of narcotics. He said, "I don't put up with that. If I saw it, I would have no problem busting them and turning them in." . . .

Discussion

There are clearly two types of normative definitions functioning in the nurses' work environment: formally states hospital policies and informal work group mores. Both of these forces serve as guides for nurses' behavior. However, these two sets of definitions are sometimes at odds with one another. For example, in the case of supply theft, or non-narcotic drug theft, nurses are presented with two very different definitions of acceptable behavior. The administrative policies establish these behaviors as theft that is not permitted. At the same time, the work group socializes its members to tolerate and even condone such behavior as non-theft. Faced with this predicament, nurses appear more inclined to choose the latter alternative. It appears that the strength and persistence of these work group norms increase the probability that nurses will engage in these forms of behavior. This is evidenced by the fact that, for each of the above-mentioned forms of deviance (i.e., supply theft, over-the-counter drug theft, and non-narcotic drug theft), nurses reported substantial knowledge of an involvement in these activities.

Nurses neutralize the administrative definitions and redefine the theft in a way that lessens inhibitions against the behaviors. These donations favorable to theft take many forms. They are often determined by the nature and extent of the improprieties. The one commonality shared by all of these neutralizations is the fact that they originate from within the work group and are disseminated to the nurses through an informal socialization process. As a consequence, violations are widespread. This process is directly in line with the theoretical propositions of differential association and social learning theory. . . .

The findings presented in this article lend support to the facilitating role that neutralizing definitions play in differential association and social learning theory. The accounts given by the nurses in this study portray on-the-job deviance. As expected theoretically, normative definitions appear to originate from various sources and are often in conflict with one another. Those definitions that receive strong work group support were more apt to prevail. When these informal work group norms allow nurses to justify theft on the job, it is likely to occur. These justifications may originally have developed following the commission of various forms of employee theft to change the normative perception of the behavior in question. However, once they become part of the work subculture, they seem to be incorporated into the occupational socialization process. Thus, new nurses appear to learn them before committing theft. This temporal ordering issue is also evidenced by the fact that nurses indicated that they will continue engaging in these various forms of employee deviance. This suggests that these normative definitions are being used as discriminant stimuli that serve to shape future behaviors.

The sources of normative conflict between the nursing work group's and the hospital administration's definitions of proper behavior may well be traced to the overarching way in which nurses conceive of their work objective. As Hollinger and Clark (1983) observed in a study of hospital employees, nurses tend to see themselves as caregivers whose job is to help their patients at any cost. Within this self-conception, nurses are able to justify certain behaviors such as taking supplies, as the patient is not harmed. Instead, it is the hospital, who they claim does not appreciate them, that incurs the loss. Similarly, when nurses condone over-the-counter or non-narcotic drug theft, it is done under the premise that taking the drugs is done to improve the nurses' disposition. The thinking is that this allows them to better treat the patients (e.g., How can I treat a patient if I am stressed out or have a headache?). From this perspective, nurses' impairment actually enhances patient care. At the same time, taking narcotics does not fit into this paradigm, as these drugs are thought to have an adverse effect on patient care. This pattern of nurses' behavior leads one to agree with Hollinger and Clark's notion that although many hospital employees enjoy their jobs from a care-giving perspective, they dislike the hospitals in which they must deliver this care. As such, the neutralizations used to justify and even condone nurses' deviance against the hospital would seem to make a great deal of sense as they are done to benefit the patients. . . .

References

Akers, Ronald L. 1985. *Deviant Behavior: A Social Learning Approach*. Belmont, CA: Wadsworth.

American Nurses Association. 1984. *ANA Cabinet on Nursing Practice: Statement on the Scope for Addiction Nursing Practice*. Kansas City, MO: Author.

Babbie, Earl. 1989. *The Practice of Social Research*, 5th Ed. Belmont, CA: Wadsworth.

Berg, Bruce L. 1989. *Qualitative Research Methods for the Social Sciences*. Needham Heights, MA: Allyn and Bacon.

Hollinger, Richard C. and John P. Clark. 1983. *Theft by Employees*. Lexington, MA: Lexington Books.

Horning, Donald. 1970. "Blue Collar Theft: Conceptions of Property, Attitudes Toward Pilfering, and Work Group Norms in a Modern Industrial Plant." In. E.O. Smigel and H.L. Ross (Eds.) *Crimes Against Bureaucracy* (pp. 46–64). New York: Van Nostrand Reinhold.

McCormick, William C., Ronald C. Hoover, and Joseph B. Murphy. 1986. "Drug Diversion From Hospitals Analyzed." *Security Management,* 30:41–8.

Michigan Nurses Association. 1986. *Fact Sheet: Chemical Dependency of Nurses*. East Lansing, MI: Author.

Sutherland, Edwin H. 1949. *White Collar Crime*. New York: Dryden.

Sutherland, Edwin H. and Donald R. Cressey. 1970. *Criminology*, 8th Ed. Philadelphia: J.B. Lippincott.

Sykes, Gresham M. and David Matza. 1957. "Techniques of Neutralization: A Theory of Delinquency." *American Sociological Review,* 22:664–70.

28

The Influence of Situational Ethics on Cheating Among College Students

Donald L. McCabe

McCabe examines the ways in which college students at thirty-one schools justify cheating on tests and assignments. Most students admit that they have cheated at least once during their college careers, even though they know that cheating is wrong. But they rationalize their behavior by blaming the situation or other people, or by focusing on the value of a respected goal—good grades. The article suggests that cheating in college is common but, that, more importantly, most people think they have good reasons for breaking the rules.

Numerous studies have demonstrated the pervasive nature of cheating among college students (Baird 1980; Haines, Diekhoff, La-Beff, and Clark 1986; Michaels and Miethe 1989; Davis et al. 1992). This research has examined a variety of factors that help explain cheating behavior, but the strength of the relationships between individual factors and cheating has varied considerably from study to study (Tittle and Rowe 1973; Baird 1980; Eisenberger and Shank 1985; Haines, et al. 1986; Ward 1986; Michaels and Miethe 1989; Perry, Kane, Bernesser, and Spicker 1990; Ward and Beck 1990).

Although the factors examined in these studies (for example, personal work ethic, gender, self-esteem, rational choice, social

learning, deterrence) are clearly important, the work of LaBeff, Clark, Haines, and Diekhoff (1990) suggests that the concept of situational ethics may be particularly helpful in understanding student rationalizations for cheating. . . .

LaBeff et al. believe a utilitarian calculus of "the ends justifies the means" underlies this reasoning process and "what is wrong in most situations might be considered right or acceptable if the end is defined as appropriate" (1990, p. 191). As argued by Edwards (1967), the situation determines what is right or wrong in this decision-making calculus and also dictates the appropriate principles to be used in guiding and judging behavior.

Sykes and Matza (1957) hypothesize that such rationalizations, that is, "justifications for deviance that are seen as valid by the delinquent but not by the legal system or society at large" (p. 666), are common. However, they challenge conventional wisdom that such rationalizations typically follow deviant behavior as a means of protecting "the individual from self-blame and the blame of others after the act". . . .

Using a sample of 380 undergraduate students at a small southwestern university, La-Beff et al. (1990) attempted to classify techniques employed by students in the neutralization of cheating behavior into the five categories of neutralization proposed by Sykes and Matza (1957): (1) denial of responsibility, (2) condemnation of condemners, (3) appeal to higher loyalties, (4) denial of victim, and (5) denial of injury. Although student responses could easily be classified into three of these techniques, denial of responsibility, appeal to higher loyalties, and condemnation of condemners, LaBeff et al. conclude that "it is unlikely that students will either deny injury or deny the victim since there are no real targets in cheating" (1990, p. 196).

The research described here responds to LaBeff et al. in two ways; first, it answers their call to "test the salience of neutralization . . . in more diverse university environments" (p. 197) and second, it challenges their dismissal of denial of injury and denial of victim as neutralization techniques employed by students in their justification of cheating behavior.

Methodology

The data discussed here were gathered as part of a study of college cheating conducted during the 1990–1991 academic year. A seventy-two item questionnaire concerning cheating behavior was administered to students at thirty-one highly selective colleges across the country. Surveys were mailed to a minimum of five hundred students at each school and a total of 6,096 completed surveys were returned (38.3 percent response rate). Eighty-eight percent of the respondents were seniors, nine percent were juniors, and the remaining three percent could not be classified. Survey administration emphasized voluntary participation and assurances of anonymity to help combat issues of non-response bias and the need to accept responses without the chance to question or contest them.

The final sample included 61.2 percent females (which reflects the inclusion of five all female schools in the sample and a slightly higher return rate among female students) and 95.4 percent U.S. citizens. The sample paralleled the ethnic diversity of the participating schools (85.5 percent Anglo, 7.2 percent Asian, 2.6 percent African American, 2.2 percent Hispanic and 2.5 percent other); their religious diversity (including a large percentage of students who claimed no religious preference, 27.1 percent); and their mix of undergraduate majors (36.0 percent humanities, 28.8 percent social sciences, 26.8 percent natural sciences and engineering, 4.5 percent business, and 3.9 percent other).

Results

Of the 6,096 students participating in this research, over two-thirds (67.4 percent) indicated that they had cheated on a test or major assignment at least once while an undergraduate. This cheating took a variety of different forms, but among the most popular (listed in decreasing order of mention) were: (1) a failure to footnote sources in written work, (2) collaboration on assignments when the instructor specifically asked for individual work, (3) copying from students on tests and examinations, (4) fabrication of bibliographies, helping someone else cheat on a test,

and (6) using unfair methods to learn the content of a test ahead of time. Almost one in five students (19.1 percent) could be classified as active cheaters (five or more self-reported incidents of cheating). This is double the rate reported by LaBeff et al. (1990), but they asked students to report only cheating incidents that had taken place in the last six months. Students in this research were asked to report all cheating in which they had engaged while an undergraduate—a period of three years for most respondents at the time of this survey.

Students admitting to any cheating activity were asked to rate the importance of several specific factors that might have influenced their decisions to cheat. These data establish the importance of denial of responsibility and condemnation of condemners as neutralization techniques. For example, 52.4 percent of the respondents who admitted to cheating rated the pressure to get good grades as an important influence in their decision to cheat with parental pressures and competition to gain admission into professional schools singled out as the primary grade pressures. Forty-six percent of those who had engaged in cheating cited excessive workloads and an inability to keep up with assignments as important factors in their decisions to cheat.

In addition to rating the importance of such preselected factors, 426 respondents (11.0 percent of the admitted cheaters) offered their own justifications for cheating in response to an open-ended question on motivations for cheating. These responses confirm the importance of denial of responsibility and condemnation of condemners as neutralization techniques. They also support LaBeff et al's (1990) claim that [an] appeal to higher loyalties is an important neutralization technique. However, these responses also suggest that LaBeff et al.'s dismissal of denial of injury as a justification for cheating is arguable.

. . . Denial of responsibility was the technique most frequently cited (216 responses, 61.0 percent of the total) in the 354 responses classified into one of Sykes and Matza's five categories of neutralization. The most common responses in this category were mind block, no understanding of the material, a fear of failing, and unclear explanations of assignments. . . .Condemnation of condemners was the second most popular neutralization technique observed (99 responses, 28.0 percent) and included such explanations as pointless assignments, lack of respect for individual professors, unfair tests, parents' expectations, and unfair professors. Twenty-four respondents (6.8 percent) appealed to higher loyalties to explain their behavior. In particular, helping a friend and responding to peer pressures were influences some students could not ignore. Finally, fifteen students (4.2 percent) provided responses that clearly fit into the category of denial of injury. These students dismissed their cheating as harmless since it did not hurt anyone or they felt cheating did not matter in some cases (for example, where an assignment counted for a small percentage of the total course grade).

Detailed examination of selected student responses provides additional insight into the neutralization strategies they employ.

Denial of Responsibility

Denial of responsibility invokes the claim that the act was "due to forces outside of the individual and beyond his control such as unloving parents" (Sykes and Matza 1957: 667). For example, many students cite an unreasonable workload and the difficulty of keeping up as ample justification for cheating.

> Here at. . . . you must cheat to stay alive. There's so much work and the quality of materials from which to learn, books, professors, is so bad that there's no other choice.

> It's the only way to keep up.

> I couldn't do the work myself.

The following descriptions of student cheating confirm fear of failure is also an important form of denial of responsibility:

> . . . a take-home exam in a class I was failing.

> . . . was near failing.

Some justified their cheating by citing the behavior of peers:

> Everyone has test files in fraternities, etc. If you don't, you're at a great disadvantage.

> When most of the class is cheating on a difficult exam and they will ruin the curve, it influences you to cheat so your grade won't be affected.

All of these responses contain the essence of denial of responsibility: the cheater has deflected blame to others or to a specific situational context.

Denial of Injury

. . . A key element in denial of injury is whether one feels "anyone has clearly been hurt by (the) deviance." In invoking this defense, a cheater would argue "that his behavior does not really cause any great harm despite the fact that it runs counter to the law" (Sykes and Matza 1957: 667–668). For example, a number of students argued that the assignment or test on which they cheated was so trivial that no one was really hurt by their cheating.

> These grades aren't worth much therefore my copying doesn't mean very much. I am ashamed, but I'd probably do it the same way again.

> If I extend the time on a take home it is because I feel everyone does and the teacher kind of expects it. No one gets hurt.

As suggested earlier, these responses suggest the conclusion of LaBeff et al. that "(I)t is unlikely that students will. . . deny injury" (1990: 196) must be re-evaluated.

The Denial of the Victim

LaBeff et al. failed to find any evidence of denial of the victim in their student accounts. . . . At least four students (0.1% of the self-admitted cheaters in this study) provided comments elsewhere on the survey instrument which involved denial of the victim. The common element in these responses was a victim deserving of the consequences of the cheating behavior and cheating was viewed as "a form of rightful retaliation or punishment (Sykes and Matza 1957: 668).

This feeling was extreme in one case, as suggested by the following student who felt her cheating was justified by the

realization that this school is a manifestation of the bureaucratic capitalist system that systematically keeps the lower classes down, and that adhering to their rules was simply perpetuating the institution.

This 'we' versus 'they' mentality was raised by many students, but typically in comments about the policing of academic honesty rather than as justification for one's own cheating behavior. When used to justify cheating, the target was almost always an individual teacher rather than the institution and could be more accurately classified as a strategy of condemnation of condemners rather than denial of the victim.

The Condemnation of Condemners

Sykes and Matza describe the condemnation of condemners as an attempt to shift "the focus of attention from [one's] own deviant acts to the motives and behavior of those who disapprove of [the] violations. [B]y attacking others, the wrongfulness of [one's] own behavior is more easily repressed or lost to view" (1957: 668). The logic of this strategy for student cheaters focused on issues of favoritism and fairness. Students invoking this rationale describe "uncaring, unprofessional instructors with negative attitudes who were negligent in their behavior" (LaBeff et al., 1990: 195). For example:

In one instance, nothing was done by a professor because the student was a hockey player. . . .

I would guess that 90% of the students here have seen athletes and/or fraternity members cheating on an exam or papers. If you turn in one of these culprits, and I have, the penalty is a five-minute lecture from a coach and/or administrator. All these add up to a 'who cares, they'll never do anything to you anyway' attitude here about cheating.

Concerns about the larger society were an important issue for some students:

When community frowns upon dishonesty, then people will change.

If our leaders can commit heinous acts and then lie before Senate committees about their total ignorance and innocence, then why can't I cheat a little?

In today's world you do anything to be above the competition.

In general, students found ready targets on which to blame their behavior and condemnation of the condemners was a popular neutralization strategy.

Appeal to Higher Loyalties

The appeal to higher loyalties involves neutralizing "internal and external controls. . . by sacrificing the demands of the larger society for the demands of the smaller social groups to which the [offender] belongs. [D]eviation from certain norms may occur not because the norms are rejected but because other norms, held to be more pressing or involving a higher loyalty, are accorded precedence" (Sykes and Matza 1957: 669). For example, a difficult conflict for some students is balancing the desire to help a friend against the institution's rules on cheating. The student may not challenge the rules, but rather views the need to help a friend, fellow fraternity/sorority member, or roommate to be a greater obligation which justifies the cheating behavior.

Fraternities and sororities were singled out as a network where such behavior occurs with some frequency. For example, a female student at a small university in New England observed:

There's a lot of cheating within the Greek system. Of all the cheating I've seen, it's been men and women in fraternities and sororities who exchange information or cheat.

The appeal to higher loyalties was particularly evident in student reactions concerning the reporting of cheating violations. Although fourteen of the thirty-one schools participating in this research had explicit honor codes that generally require students to report cheating violations they observe, less than one-third (32.3 percent) indicated that they were likely to do so. When asked if they would report a friend, only four percent said they would and students felt that they should not be expected to do so.

For others, the decision would depend on the severity of the violations they observed and many would not report what they considered to be minor violations, even those explicitly covered by the school's honor code or policies on academic honesty. Explicit examination or test cheating was one of the few violations where students exhibited any consensus concerning the need to report violations. Yet even in this case many students felt other factors must be considered. For example, a senior at a woman's college in the northeast commented:

> It would depend on the circumstances. If someone was hurt, *very likely*. If there was no single victim in the case, if the victim was [the] institution. . . , then *very unlikely*.

Additional evidence of the strength of the appeal to higher loyalties as a neutralization technique is found in the fact that almost one in five respondents (17.8 percent) reported that they had helped someone cheat on an examination or major test. The percentage who have helped others cheat on papers and other assignments is likely much higher. Twenty-six percent of those students who helped someone else cheat on a test reported that they had never cheated on a test themselves, adding support to the argument that pressure to help friends is quite strong.

Conclusions

From this research it is clear that college students use a variety of neutralization techniques to rationalize their cheating behavior, deflecting blame to others and/or the situational context, and the framework of Sykes and Matza (1957) seems well supported when student explanations of cheating behavior are analyzed. Unlike prior research (LaBeff et al., 1990), however, the present findings suggest that students employ all of the techniques described by Sykes and Matza, including denial of injury and denial of victim. Although there was very limited evidence of the use of denial of victim, denial of injury was not uncommon. Many students

felt that some forms of cheating were victimless crimes, particularly on assignments that accounted for a small percent of the total course grade. . . .

References

Baird, John S. 1980. "Current Trends in College Cheating." *Psychology in Schools,* 17:512–522.

Davis, Stephen F., Cathy A. Grover, Angela H. Becker, and Loretta N. McGregor. 1992. "Academic Dishonesty: Prevalence, Determinants, Techniques, and Punishments." *Teaching of Psychology,* In press.

Edwards, Paul. 1967. *The Encyclopedia Of Philosophy,* No. 3, Paul Edwards (Ed.). New York: Macmillan Company and Free Press.

Eisenberger, Robert, and Dolores M. Shank. 1985. "Personal Work Ethic and Effort Training Affect Cheating." *Journal of Personality and Social Psychology,* 49:520–528.

Haines, Valerie J., George Diekhoff, Emily LaBeff, and Robert Clark. 1986. "College Cheating: Immaturity, Lack of Commitment, and the Neutralizing Attitude." *Research in Higher Education,* 25:342–354.

LaBeff, Emily E., Robert E. Clark, Valerie J. Haines and George M. Diekhoff. 1990. "Situational Ethics And College Student Cheating." *Sociological Inquiry,* 60:190–198.

Michaels, James W., and Terrance Miethe. 1989. "Applying Theories of Deviance to Academic Cheating." *Social Science Quarterly,* 70:870–885.

Perry, Anthony R., Kevin M. Kane, Kevin J. Bernesser, and Paul T. Spicker. 1990. "Type A Behavior, Competitive Achievement-Striving, and Cheating Among College Students." *Psychological Reports,* 66:459–465.

Sykes, Gresham M., and David Matza. 1957. "Techniques of Neutralization: A Theory of Delinquency." *American Sociological Review,* 22:664–670.

Tittle, Charles, and Alan Rowe. 1973. "Moral Appeal, Sanction Threat, and Deviance: An Experimental Test." *Social Problems,* 20:488–498.

Ward, David. 1986. "Self-Esteem and Dishonest Behavior Revisited." *Journal of Social Psychology,* 123:709–713.

Ward, David, and Wendy L. Beck. 1990. "Gender and Dishonesty." *The Journal Of Social Psychology,* 130:333–339.

29

Faculty Malfeasance: Understanding Academic Deviance

John W. Heeren
David Shichor

Heeren and Shichor identify and describe deviant behavior among university professors. Most people think that university professors are honest, ethical people. But this article shows that deviance can be found in almost any occupation. The fact that deviance is common even among people who would rarely be suspected of wrongdoing indicates that deviance is a cultural universal. In fact, we can expect to find deviance in almost any segment of society.

If deviance is considered to be "any behavior or attribute for which an individual is regarded as objectionable in a particular social system" (Glaser, 1971: 1), then every organization and every occupational context provides opportunities for legal and/or ethical deviance. Yet, only limited attention has been paid to deviance in the academy. Some analysts (Johnson and Douglas, 1978: 227) have suggested this reflects an inclination of social scientists to "protect their own kind," that is, professors. . . .

Academic Organization and Roles

Professors work in institutions of higher education. These institutions developed out of medieval European universities, which were autonomous intellectual communities of scholars and students in larger urban settlements with external support mainly from the endowments of benefactors (Ben-David, 1971). This situation has changed. Instead of existing as an intellectual community in which all of the participants are partners, universities and colleges have become employers and professors have become employees. This change has been accompanied by an increasing portion of governance being taken over by full-time administrators, who act as agents of the employer in managing the institution.

Professors teach, research, and participate in the governance of their academic university (Clark, 1987) whether they are at a major research university or a community college. This does not deny that institutions vary in the emphasis placed on these responsibilities and that professors may carry out one of these tasks to the exclusion of the others. For example, the more prestigious a university, the more likely faculty performance will be evaluated on the basis of publications and the ability of the faculty member to obtain research grants, rather than on the basis of teaching performance.

Some organizational analysts have argued that there is very little integration among the diverse activities that comprise the academic profession (Light, 1974). Other analysts identify common threads and de-emphasize the apparent fragmentation (Clark, 1983; Ruscio, 1987). One scheme that has been used to portray the commonality among the disciplines is Merton's (1973) formulation of the "ethos," or normative, requirements of science, a scheme which Clark (1983: 93) and Braxton (1991) view as comprising the ethos of the academic profession. These four norms are (1) universalism, the truth of statements should be separated from the person who makes them; (2) "communism," knowledge should be freely shared with others; (3) disinterestedness, research should be guided by the wish to extend knowledge, rather than for personal motives; and (4) organized skepticism, the commitment to mutual critical review of scholarly work. . . .

One additional consideration involves the adaptation of faculty roles within the academic system. A widely accepted distinction is that between cosmopolitans and locals (Gouldner, 1957; Loether, 1974). Cosmopolitans are faculty members who are highly committed to their professional role and skills, have a moderate level of loyalty to their institutions, and have a reference group comprised of scholars in the discipline. Locals are marginally committed to their professional role but are loyal to their institution. They typically serve on numerous committees, are active in campus politics, and have an inner reference group of other university colleagues, most of whom are also locals. The more prestigious the university, the greater is the likelihood that the faculty will have a cosmopolitan orientation. In less prestigious universities, the local orientation tends to be more prevalent. . . .

Typology of Academic Deviance

There are various types of deviant behavior in which faculty members may be involved, and two dimensions of activities are useful to describe the nature of academic deviance. First, there is the distinction between occupational and professional types of deviant behavior. The former refers to violations of the general moral and ethical codes prevailing in a society. This type of deviance represents the "normal crimes of normal people in the normal circumstances of their work" (Mars, 1982: 1). Professional deviance, on the other hand, involves breaches of the professional norms associated with occupations, and is considered unacceptable by members of the profession. . . .

The second distinction involves academic deviance being directed against property or against persons. Many acts of deviance have both property and interpersonal effects, thus leading to some overlap in the categories. Nevertheless, the intersection of these two dimensions yields four basic categories of academic deviance (see Figure 29.1). The first two involve occupational misbehavior which either (1) victimizes persons or (2) misuses resources that do not belong to the perpetrator. The other two categories pertain

to professional malfeasance. Again, this can be either (3) interpersonal, resulting in harm to others in academia or (4) fraudulent use of intellectual property. The following discussion analyzes these categories of academic deviance.

Figure 29.1

Dimensions and Types of Academic Deviance

Norms Violated

Focus of Deviation		Occupational	Professional
	Property	Theft or misuse of funds or resources	Plagiary or falsification of data
	Interpersonal	Sexual harassment or exploitation	Misevaluation of others as referee for grants, jobs, articles, etc.

Occupational Deviance

The forms of occupational deviance among academics do not differ greatly from those in other occupations. Just as white collar workers or laborers may pilfer property belonging to the organization which employs them, so also may professors. Another more dramatic example is university misuse of research overhead funds. Recently, fifteen universities have been accused of overbilling the federal government for collateral expenses on research grants (Jackson, 1991). Professors were not directly involved in the decisions to misuse these funds, but some professors were beneficiaries of this type of deviance.

Another example of occupational deviance which has property implications involves conflicts between the professional and the personal interests of academics. Drug-related research might be biased by the researchers' financial interest in the funding provided by pharmaceutical companies (Wheeler, 1990). Similarly, faculty members receive consulting fees or even small grants for applied research from students in their graduate or professional programs who are also employed by funding agencies.

Occupational deviance with interpersonal implications includes such behavior as sexual harassment of students or fellow employees. Employees are clearly protected by statute, while students are most often covered by university regulations regarding harassment (Elgart and Schanfield, 1991). Specific behaviors that constitute harassment, such as assault or demand for sexual favors, are easily identified while others are much more subtle and difficult to delineate in abstract legal or ethical terms. Courts are likely to require that the harassment be "unwelcome" and that it cause sufficient harm "to create an abusive working environment" (Elgart and Schanfield, 1991: 27). University regulations are much less uniform in their definitions of harassment, with some very restrictive and others quite broad in line with local campus traditions. . . .

Professional Deviance

Professional deviance is complex since it reflects the distinctive features of university and disciplinary organizations, including their constitutive roles, opportunity structures, and systems of social control. Moreover, the likelihood of any specific deviations will reflect the perpetrator's involvement in one or more of the three main academic roles as well as the cosmopolitan or local adaptation the person has developed.

Professional deviance, such as property offenses, takes the form of misappropriating intellectual property. Two forms of this type of deviance are plagiary and the fabrication or misrepresentation of research findings. Since publication of research findings is modeled after the system of private property, plagiary is equivalent to theft. . . . This kind of deviance is directly related to the reward system of scholarship which positively sanctions achievement with public recognition for the individual most directly responsible for the contribution. Collateral forms of deviance include failing to properly reference the works of others, appropriating the ideas

of others, and taking credit for the research of graduate students.

While exploitation of students is unacceptable (Cahn, 1986), it is probably widespread among cosmopolitans in major research universities (Hagstrom, 1965). As Ben-Yehuda (1986: 11) succinctly states:

> Whatever the circumstances may be, if one's name appears as the first (or only) author on a scientific work she/he did not conduct, one is getting credit for something she/he did not do. This is a fraudulent, deviant act which very much contradicts the expressed ethos of science.

This issue is relevant mainly in the case of cosmopolitans, since locals seldom have graduate students conducting publishable research. ·

Underrepresenting one's contribution rather than the more typical overrepresentation of authorship has been explored by Zuckerman (1968). Specifically, Zuckerman found that scientists whose accomplishments and reputation were already outstanding and secure, such as Nobel laureates, placed their names last on co-authored publications or, in extreme cases, omitted their names for fear of overshadowing their co-authors. . . . Since the harm is perceived as minimal and mostly accrues to those who are competitors of the junior associate of the famous senior scholar, this type of deviance is unlikely to be punished if it is recognized. This form of deviance by its nature is most likely to be characteristic of cosmopolitans.

In addition to these major types of professional property deviation, there is also a wide range of violations that fit into this category. Perhaps the most common violations are the various attempts to stretch the value of academic work by, for example, publishing the same or similar papers in different journals, overfunding a research project by various agencies so that expenses or salary are doubly compensated, padding a curriculum vita, or using a favorable letter written by a journal editor as if it represented a final acceptance of an article for publication. With respect to teaching, a typical offense is the failure of a professor to update course materials to reflect current work in the discipline. While these kinds of activities are probably quite common, they are considered to be mildly deviant and easily detectable with proper oversight in most cases.

Professional deviance that is interpersonal in its object is more subtle. We should begin by noting that a good deal of the work done by academics necessarily involves evaluations of the work of other academics in their roles as scholars, teachers, and colleagues. This is evident in the process of refereeing journal articles and grant proposals, as well as faculty evaluation of colleagues who are candidates for promotion or tenure. Similar kinds of evaluations of junior colleagues take the form of letters of recommendation.

Most published books and articles go through a refereeing system that "involves the systematic use of judges to assess the acceptability of manuscripts submitted for publication" (Zuckerman and Merton, 1971: 66). Grant applications go through a similar evaluation process. Since the major attribution of status in academia occurs on the basis of grants and publications, the referee process represents the most significant gatekeeping practice in academia. A faculty member's publication record may affect not only academic status but also material success in the form of tenure and promotion, job offers, book contracts, consultation, and fellowships. Frequently a junior faculty member's tenure may be contingent on favorable decisions in refereeing. The expectation regarding refereeing is that evaluators are to be impartial (Cahn, 1986). Anonymous reviewing is most frequently used as a device to implement this ideal.

Deviance in refereeing involves breaches of impartiality. For example, a reviewer may recognize the author of a manuscript and either give the paper a more favorable review than it deserves or urge its rejection based on personal rather than professional criteria. This kind of partiality can help or cause harm to an individual, a whole school within a discipline, or a particular academic perspective. . . .

First, in many disciplines there appears to be a fundamental ambiguity as to what precisely constitutes a genuine contribution to the corpus of the discipline, allowing subjective factors to play a role in the editorial decision (Bakanic, McPhail, and Simon, 1987; Hargens, 1988; Berardo, 1989). As noted by Cole, Cole, and Simon (1981), criteria are vague in the reviewing process for federal research grants, indicating that chance and disagreement among reviewers is as important as quality in explaining funding decisions.

A second factor is the general lack of accountability of reviewers. Not only are referees trusted to disqualify themselves if they recognize the author of a paper, in many instances their judgments are also covered by anonymity. Thus, unwarranted criticisms and praises are allowed to pass without any negative consequences for the reviewers.

Third, some part of the problem may be due to the criteria crisis in academia (Singer, 1989). Because of the proliferation of professional journals and the number of papers submitted for publication, there is an increased demand for qualified reviewers. Because of the shortage of expert reviewers, people with limited knowledge and experience may determine what will be published. The readiness to judge a paper, without having a certain level of expertise about the specific topic, can be construed as a form of academic deviance.

Letters of recommendation also provide opportunities for deviance. Academicians are often asked to write these letters for colleagues or students. Professional ethics would seem to require a completely honest opinion by the recommender, based solely on the abilities of the person being recommended. Like refereeing, these evaluations play a crucial role in one's advancement on the career ladder, for example, by securing a position or gaining an award or fellowship. Cahn (1986: 49) emphasizes the importance and the problematic nature of this issue:

> The wrong approach is to provide a deceitful letter that exaggerates positive traits while disregarding negative ones. Those who engage in such dishonesty may view themselves as merely doing someone a favor with an innocuous fib. . . . As a result of the deception, other applicants may lose out on a vital opportunity. All are victims not of a harmless joke, but of outright

dishonesty, the betrayal of a scholar's trust.

If deception is in the opposite direction, that is, writing an inaccurate or negative recommendation, it can be seen as a malicious attempt to block the professional opportunities of a person who placed trust in the goodwill and objectivity of the academician.

Evaluation also occurs in teaching and the relations of students and professors. While undervaluation of students' work may occur based on a personal dislike of a student, a more recent and common deviation appears to be in the direction of overvaluing the work of students. The basis of this evaluation may be individual traits such as physical attractiveness or importance to the athletic program, thus reflecting the intrusion of particularistic criteria into the grading of academic performance.

Perhaps a more widespread instance of such overevaluation of students is known as grade inflation. Whether grade inflation is meant to attract or retain students in an increasingly competitive environment of enrollment-driven budgets or to improve student evaluations of a faculty member for promotional purposes, it represents deviance insofar as standards are lowered and ulterior reasons are in force (Eckert, 1988). One national survey of college faculty (*Orange County Register*, 1989) found that sixty-two percent of the faculty considered grade inflation to be a problem at their institution. Since teaching is likely to be a more important activity for locals than for cosmopolitans, and the pressure to recruit and retain students is stronger at less prestigious universities, this kind of deviance is more likely to occur at teaching institutions.

Another issue relevant to the category of professional and interpersonal deviance is the handling of potential harm to human subjects in research. This issue has been especially important in the biomedical and social sciences. In the former area experimentation with new drugs is involved, while in the latter, concern has been expressed about the possible effects on human subjects of participating in experiments, surveys, or ethnographic studies. The major ethical issues concerning the use of human subjects are (1) the securing of informed consent from the participants and (2) the presentation of the risk-benefit ratio to the participants (Barber, 1990). Researchers are required to make themselves accessible to scrutiny by outsiders. Academicians do not always follow these ethical prescriptions, however. In the past, for example, the full risk of drug experiments was not always disclosed; participants in psychological experiments were misled about the purposes of the project, and coercive settings (for example, prisons) were used. . . .

Sources of Academic Deviance

A final objective is to account for the occurrence of the various forms of academic deviance detailed above. Though the importance of the attractions of deviance has recently been reemphasized (Katz, 1989), it appears inadequate to merely look at the motives or attractions that deviance holds for potential participants. . . . It is also necessary to look at the opportunity structure, systems of social control and other enabling processes which exist in the situation of deviance.

It would appear that the attractions of the occupational types of offenses described above are not particularly strong for those who pursue an academic career. If it is accurate to state that academics make career choices in terms of the teaching and learning which are the inherent components of the academic role (Bowen and Schuster, 1986), then such activities as theft of material property or interpersonal violence would seem to be relatively remote from the typical academic life style.

The apparent infrequency with which occupational deviance is observed among academics may, however, have more to do with the norms and controls, as well as the opportunities available. Like other professionals, academics have considerable autonomy in their work. Moreover, those who might observe, be victimized by, or report occupational deviance are likely to have a lower status than the alleged offender. At the same time, potential complainants are usually involved in at least the margins of the academic social world (such as janitors, campus police, students, secretaries) and are expected to respect the scholars who are its leaders. . . .

Finally, the academic world is somewhat insulated from the remainder of society and is likely to evince a boundary-maintaining response to the reporting of evidence of the occurrence of deviance. Many department chairs and university administrators would prefer to minimize any publicity associated with such reported deviations. This reaction seems to be consistent with other observations of the importance of adverse publicity in controlling white collar offenses (Braithwaite, 1985).

With regard to professional deviance, the situation is far more complex. The rewards or attractions of these kinds of deviation are more consistent with the values that are central to academic life. Given that academic stratification is based on recognition conducted through a system of peer evaluation (Merton, 1973), it is reasonable to expect that deviations involving intellectual property (for example, manipulating facts or plagiarizing) or the misuse of authority or prestige for allies or against opponents could easily be seen as accessible avenues to scholarly position. As with the occupational deviation noted above, the controls on academics are not especially stringent. One of the most widely held values in the academy is academic freedom (Bowen and Schuster, 1986: 53–54). The effect of this freedom is to grant scholars autonomy in their professional roles. . . . Beyond the academic freedom to teach, research, and write on virtually any topic, there are other expressions of the trust granted to faculty members. For example, reviews of grant applications and articles for publication are anonymous. Also, letters of recommendation and committee decisions on tenure and promotion operate with a layer of anonymity, justified by the notion of academic freedom (Weeks, 1990) that protects potential deviants. In sum, many of the most crucial and potentially deviant academic decisions are invisible to outsiders and to those most affected by the deviation.

This analysis neglects one important dimension of the academic world, its temporal aspect. In the vast majority of cases, while the immediate rewards of academic success and recognition are relatively meager, the most important rewards are associated with a more long-term and distinguished connection to scholarship. To establish a significant professional reputation, it is necessary to associate one's name over a series of research projects and publications. The concept of a career of scholarly output is particularly crucial to understanding academic success. Single acts of plagiarism or fudging findings are not likely to provide significant reward. It could only do so if such deviations in are extended in a career-long pattern. Furthermore, if deviations are extensive or if publication and discovery are so spectacular as to provide immediate recognition, they would receive careful scrutiny and would be compared to other findings. Accordingly, the odds of being discovered increase sharply. . . .

Moreover, instances of discoveries that are really fabrications will be discredited by later replications. just as legal decisions can be reversed and medical diagnoses can be revised, the academic profession has self-correcting mechanisms based on the collective knowledge of its disciplines. As Cole and Cole (1973: 257) write,

> Falsifying data is highly unlikely to bring eminence. If the falsified study is unimportant, it will be just as ignored as an unimportant honest study. If the falsified study is important, it will soon be replicated and the "incorrect" results pointed out to the embarrassment and possible discreditation of its publisher.

Three qualifications can be added to this analysis. First, disciplinary knowledge is most effective in operating as a corrective or control mechanism only in the long run. One example is the many decades it took to discover the research errors of Cyril Burt on the contribution of heredity to intelligence. Second, replication as a corrective may be most likely in situations where the fraudulent contribution is considered to be highly significant to the discipline (Zuckerman, 1977). Thus, the situation may be very different at nonelite universities where locals seek not breakthroughs and eminence, but the few publications required for tenure. As Singer

(1989) has suggested, the rapid expansion of academic publications has led to a criterial crisis in which the actual quality of publications is only infrequently judged. Finally, there are problems with the widespread utilization of replication. Most importantly, scientists are encouraged to make new discoveries and replication studies are not considered prestigious or interesting (Ben-Yehuda, 1985).

Conclusion

In this study we have attempted to provide a framework for explaining the kinds of academic deviance that exist in the modern university setting. By looking at two dimensions, types of norms violated (occupational vs. professional) and focus of deviation (property vs. interpersonal), the major ethical problems of the professoriate are delineated and a basis for understanding the relations among these kinds of deviance is established. Although the model does not provide an exhaustive assessment of the causes of academic deviance, it is useful in indicating the motives for or rewards which might accrue to academic deviants and the organizational characteristics that allow deviance to occur or hamper its control by professional groups, faculty, or members of society.

The analysis of academic deviance in this study has several implications. First, it has theoretical significance in providing a single framework within which deviance and control in universities and professional associations can be understood. This framework not only clarifies academic deviance, but also brings out some features shared with deviance among other professionals. Thus, fraud, conflict of interest, shoddy work, violations of public trust, exploitation of others based on professional authority, and a reluctance to have outside oversight of professional behavior are phenomena seen among professions generally. However, there are differences as well. Outside their professional associations, for example, doctors and lawyers as opposed to academics are more likely to organize as profit-making entities. As a result, they are exposed to two sets of expectations, one based on their professional standing, the other based on their commercial involvement. This commercial orientation seems to be the major factor leading to such deviance as frivolous lawsuits, unnecessary surgery, and overprescription of medications (Coleman, 1989: 112–118). In the case of academics, universities and disciplinary organizations do not present such discrepant expectations. Therefore, academic deviance parallel to that found in profit-making professions is much more limited in extent.

Second, it appears that university and government controls typically have been focused on occupational deviance in academia. For example, overhead in government contracts, sexual harassment, and affirmative action have been prominently publicized. Lately, more attention is being devoted to professional deviance with an emphasis on maintaining academic standards and scrutinizing research practices and results. Since occupational deviance tends to be more visible, control efforts are likely to be more effective in this area.

Moreover, since publicity is a most effective means of controlling professional deviance, one interesting aspect of such control involves the role of those who make the public aware of this deviance. Contrary to most other institutional settings where they are scorned, these whistleblowers are likely to be respected in academic circles as a consequence of the dominant values which emphasize freedom of inquiry and skepticism. It is even possible to base one's professional reputation on the debunking of the work of earlier researchers. However, it must be understood that academic freedom cuts both ways. At the same time as it facilitates internal control of professional deviance, it tends to constrain external control by government. This is because virtually any attempt at governmental control of professional deviance is likely to be perceived by the academic community as an infringement on the basic value of freedom in academia. . . .

References

Bakanic, Von, Clark McPhail, and Rita J. Simon. 1987. "The Manuscript Review and Decision Making Process." *American Sociological Review,* 52:631–642.

Barber, Bernard. 1990. *Social Studies of Science*. New Brunswick, NJ: Transaction.

Ben-David, Joseph. 1971. *The Scientist's Role in Society*. Englewood Cliffs, NJ: Prentice-Hall.

Ben-Yehuda, Nachman. 1983. *Deviance and Moral Boundaries*. Chicago: University of Chicago Press.

Ben-Yehuda, Nachman. 1986. "Deviance in Science: Towards the Criminology of Science." *British Journal of Criminology*, 26:1–27.

Berardo, Felix M. 1989. "Scientific Norms and Research Publication Issues and Professional Ethics." *Sociological Inquiry*, 59:249–256.

Bowen, Howard R., and Jack H. Schuster. 1986. *American Professors: A National Resource Imperiled*. New York: Oxford University Press.

Braithwaite, John. 1985. "White Collar Crime." *Annual Review of Sociology*, 11:1–25.

Braxton, John M. 1991. "The Influence of Graduate Department Training on the Sanctioning of Scientific Misconduct." *Journal of Higher Education*, 62:87–108.

Cahn, Steven M. 1986. *Saints and Scamps: Ethics in Academia*. Totowa, NJ: Rowman & Littlefield.

Clark, Burton R. 1983. *The Higher Education Sytem: Academic Organization in Cross-National Perspective*. Berkeley: University of California Press.

Clark, Burton R. 1987. *The Academic Life: Small Worlds, Different Worlds*. Princeton, NJ: Carnegie Foundation.

Cnudde, Charles, and Betty A. Nesvold. 1985. "Administrative Risk and Sexual Harassment: Legal and Ethical Responsibilities on Campus." *PS*, 18:780–789.

Cole, Jonathan R., and Stephen Cole. 1973. *Social Stratification in Science*. Chicago: University of Chicago Press.

Cole, Stephen, Jonathan R. Cole, and Gary A. Simon. 1981. "Chance and Consensus in Peer Review." *Science*, 214:881–886.

Coleman, James William. 1989. *The Criminal Elite: The Sociology of While Collar Crime*. New York: St. Martin's Press.

Durkheim, Emile. [1893] 1957. *The Division of Labor in Society*. New York: Free Press.

Eckert, Edward K. 1988. "The Day I Realized the Game Was Over." *Chronicle of Higher Education*, (June 1): 48.

Elgart, Lloyd D., and Lillian Schanfield. 1991. "Sexual Harassment of Students." *Thought and Action*, 7:21–42.

Glaser, Daniel, 1971 *Social Deviance*. Chicago: Markham.

Glaser, Robert D., and Joseph S. Thorpe. 1986. "Unethical Intimacy: A Survey of Sexual Contact and Advances Between Psychology Educators and Female Graduate Students." *American Psychologist*, 41:43–51.

Glazer, Myron Peretz, and Penina Migdal Glazer. 1989. *The Whistle-Blowers: Exposing Corruptionin Government and Industry*. New York: Basic Books.

Gouldner, Alvin. 1957. "Cosmopolitans and Locals: Toward an Analysis of Latent Social Roles." *Administrative Science Quarterly*, 2:281–306.

Hagstrom, Warren. 1965. *The Scientific Community*. Carbondale: Southern Illinois University Press.

Hargens, Lowell L. 1988. "Scholarly Consensus and Journal Rejection Rates." *American Sociological Review*, 53:139–151.

Jackson, Robert L. 1991. "Audit Ties 15 Universities to Government Overcharges." *Los Angeles Times* (May 10): A4.

Johnson, John, and Jack Douglas. 1978. *Crime at the Top*. New York: Lippincott.

Katz, Jack. 1989. *Seductions of Crime: Moral and Sensual Attractions in Doing Evil*. New York: Basic Books.

Light, Donald. 1974. "The Structure of the Academic Professions." *Sociology of Education*, 47:2–28.

Lipset, Seymour Martin. 1969. "Socialism and Sociology." In Irving Louis Horowitz (Ed.) *Sociological Self-Images* (pp. 143–175). Beverly Hills, CA: Sage.

Little, Craig B. 1989. *Deviance and Control*. Itasca, IL: Peacock.

Loether, Herman. 1974. "Organizational Stress and the Role Orientations of College Professors." In Phyllis Stewart and Muriel Cantor (Eds.) *Varieties of Work*. Chicago: Markham.

Mars, Gerald. 1982. *Cheats at Work*. London: Unwin.

Merton, Robert K. 1973. *The Sociology of Science*. Chicago: The University of Chicago Press.

Mulkay, Michael. 1976. "Norms and Ideology in Science." *Social Science Information*, 15:637–656.

Newsweek. 1990. "Taking Offense." (December 24): 48–54.

Orange County Register. 1989. "Professors Satisfied with Jobs." (November 6): A5.

Ruscio, Kenneth P. 1987. "Many Sectors, Many Professions." In Burton Clark (Ed.) *The Academic Profession*. Berkeley, CA: University of California Press.

Schur, Edwin M. 1965. *Crimes Without Victims: Deviant Beltavior and Public Policy.* Englewood Cliffs, NJ: Prentice-Hall.

Shils, Edward. 1983. *The Academic Ethic.* Chicago: University of Chicago Press.

Singer, Benjamin D. 1989. "The Criterial Crisis of the Academic World." *Sociological Inquiry,* 59:127–143.

Weeks, Kent M. 1990. "The Peer Review Process." *Journal of Higher Education,* 61:198–219.

Wheeler, David L. 1990. "Two Academic Organizations Offer Their Own Sets of Guidelines to Help Research Units Answer Conflict-of-Interest Questions." *Chronicle of Higher Education,.* (March 7): A21.

Zuckerman, Harriet. 1968. "Patterns of Name-ordering Among Authors of Scientific Papers." *American Journal of Sociology,* 74:276–291.

Zuckerman, Harriet.1977. "Deviant Behavior and Social Control in Science." In Edward Sagarin (Ed.) *Deviance and Social Change* (pp. 87–138). Beverly Hills, CA: Sage.

Zuckerman, Harriet, and Robert K. Merton. 1971. "Patterns of Evaluation in Science." *Minerva,* 9:66–100.

Reprinted from: John W. Heeren and David Shichor, "Faculty Malfeasance: Understanding Academic Deviance." In *Sociological Inquiry,* 63(1), pp. 47–63. Copyright © 1993 by University of Texas Press. Reprinted by permission. ✦

Part VII

Deviant Subcultures

One way to think about deviant people is to examine those who look alike and who gather in groups to do things that many others find odd or different. In short, they form a subculture. Deviant people do get together in groups and engage in deviant behavior. But, this is a superficial way to think about deviant subcultures.

Subcultures play a number of roles in deviant behavior. For some people, deviant subcultures reinforce beliefs they already hold. For others, exposure to a subculture may cause them to question their mainstream beliefs. And for many, finding other deviant people in subcultural settings is a way to form important relationships with others like themselves—to find support for an alternative identity and day-to-day deviant behaviors.

No matter what role a deviant subculture plays for an individual, the fact is that when a person is recognized as a member of a deviant subculture, society will view him or her differently. When a group is labeled, people assume that those associated with it all deserve the same label. But there is variety among seemingly similar subcultures, and members of a deviant subculture are as diverse as members of other social groups.

This diversity is clearly evident in the first article in this section, by Columbus Hopper and Johnny Moore. Their article on women in outlaw motorcycle gangs offers a scarcely seen view of the diversity within this subculture. Hopper and Moore show that some of the commonly held stereotypes are true: Within the gang, women are sexual objects, servants, and moneymakers who are generally looked down on by sexist and misogynist men. But life is not all bad. Hopper and Moore note that mothers are treated respectfully, that children are treated with kindness, and that many outlaw motorcycle women also live nondeviant lives in mainstream society, where they hold jobs, keep house, and raise children. Although they are part of a deviant subculture, these women lead lives that are clearly more complex than the stereotype would lead us to expect.

This complexity and diversity is also evident in Kevin Young and Laura Craig's article on nonracist Canadian skinheads. According to these authors, assumptions that all skinheads are violent, racist, sexist, homophobic, and anti-establishment are wrong. Some skinhead groups do hold these beliefs, but the tendency to think of all skinheads as the same—or to wrongly label them—leads people to treat them on the basis of a deviant label rather than on the bases of beliefs they do hold. Interestingly, people interpret clothing, hair style, and other accouterments as symbols of attitudes and behaviors that the person may not even have.

Members of mainstream society are not the only ones to hold negative views of deviant subcultures. As Mark Fenster indicates in his study of "queer punks," members of one deviant subculture may stigmatize and marginalize individuals whose deviance goes beyond what is acceptable to that group. According to Fenster, both those who are gay or lesbian (or "queer") and those who identify as "punks" find that one or the other of these two aspects of identity comes into conflict with the two subcultural groups to which they could potentially belong. Punks stigmatize "queers," and gays and lesbians marginalize punks. To find acceptance, individuals need to create an alternative deviant subculture in which both components of identity overlap. Finding a "queer punk" community through magazines that cater to such individuals is an important aspect of identity validation. In this instance, interaction is limited to the media. The queer punk community, which is geographically dispersed, is sustained through the sharing of common beliefs and interests via "fanzines." Queer punks use this medium to find the community and identity validation lacking in the gay/lesbian and punk subcultures.

Rick Houlberg explains how the magazine of a sadomasochistic club provides members with a common framework for understanding themselves and developing a sense of community. He demonstrates the importance of having a way to communicate with others who participate in a particular form of deviance, even if the interaction is indirect. Through the magazine, sadomasochistic enthusiasts gain a better understanding of themselves, find a community of similar others that supports and legitimates deviant behavior and identity, and help members find suitable outlets for their interests.

Finally, Karen A. Joe and Meda Chesney-Lind describe the importance of community and belonging in the subcultural context of a youth gang. Contrary to beliefs that juveniles join gangs to engage in crime, Joe and Chesney-Lind found that young people join gangs as a way of coping with the pressures of stressful and violent home life, chaotic and crime-ridden neighborhoods, poor educational opportunities, and a lack of social outlets. Joining a gang relieves boredom and provides a sense of belonging. The gang is an alternative family—a place where teens are accepted and understood despite their prob-

lems—that protects members from outsiders. Although gang members engage in deviant behavior—using drugs, fighting, stealing—the gang is a haven for coping with the many problems members face in communities that are marginalized and poor. Joe and Chesney-Lind argue that when studying gangs, or other types of deviance, it is important to look at the social context in which they exist.

The articles in this section indicate that many societal assumptions about deviant subcultures are clearly false. For instance, some members of deviant subcultures, such as Canadian skinheads and biker women, espouse mainstream, nondeviant values and beliefs, and their behaviors reflect these ideologies. In other cases, such as gangs, a subculture may form so members can acquire mainstream goals, such as the desire for family and stability. Finally, in other subcultural groups, such as queer punks, subcultures may ostracize certain members as "deviant deviants" and compel them to seek community in yet another subculture.

Individual involvement in deviant subcultures can range from a small, minor part of life to an overwhelming, dominant aspect of day-to-day living. Regardless of the prominence of the subculture in their lives, belonging to such a group is a high priority for most members. Providing contact with similar others and a space to develop a sense of community are among the most important things subcultural groups provide for deviants.

The relationship between deviant identity and community is an interesting paradox for social scientists. If deviant identity is bolstered by a deviant subcultural community, how does that identity emerge in the absence of such communities? And why do some members of society reject mainstream values and behaviors in favor of membership in a deviant subculture? Moreover, why does membership in a subculture that has been labeled as deviant lead to outsider assumptions of deviant attitudes and activities, even when such beliefs and behaviors are absent? If members of deviant groups accept mainstream values, albeit in amplified versions, why are they labeled deviant, as opposed to simply overzealous? And, if a subculture fulfills the functions of mainstream social in- stitutions, why is it, and its members, likely to be labeled deviant?

As you read the articles in this section, ask yourself how the roles of women and the attitudes of men in outlaw motorcycle gangs similar to those of mainstream society. Think about why Canadian skinheads, whose behavior is similar to that of most working class youth, are labeled deviant. Consider why queer punks are marginalized both in the gay and lesbian community and in the punk scene. Ask yourself what sadomasochists gain from reading a magazine that caters to their sexual fantasies. And, finally, think about why some juveniles join gangs and how a youth gang is similar to or different from an extended family. ✦

30

Women in Outlaw Motorcycle Gangs

Columbus B. Hopper
Johnny Moore

Hopper and Moore look at the way a deviant subculture is structured and how marginal or deviant members within the group are valued and integrated into the subculture. By focusing on the role of women in a heavily male-dominated subculture, they show that systems of social stratification marginalize subcultures in mainstream society but also establish hierarchies within the group. The values of society as a whole are not necessarily rejected by a subculture; instead, they are reshaped to further the overall values of the subculture. This suggests that male gang members draw on and exaggerate the marginal place of women in society to define women's roles within the gang.

This article is about the place of women in gangs in general and in outlaw motorcycle gangs in particular. . . . The first gangs were of two types: those motivated primarily as fighters and those seeking financial gain. Women were represented in both types and they shared a remarkably similar reputation with street gang women more than 100 years later (Hanson, 1964). They were considered "sex objects" and they were blamed for instigating gang wars through manipulating gang boys. The girls in the first gangs were also seen as undependable, not as loyal to the gang, and they played inferior roles compared to the boys.

The first thorough investigation of youth gangs in the United States was carried out by Thrasher (1927) in Chicago. Thrasher de-

voted very little attention to gang girls but he stated that there were about half a dozen female gangs out of 1,313 groups he surveyed. He also said that participation by young women in male gangs was limited to auxiliary units for social and sexual activities.

Short (1968) rarely mentioned female gang members in his studies, which were also carried out in Chicago, but he suggested that young women became gang associates because they were less attractive and less socially adequate compared to girls who did not affiliate with gangs.

According to Rice (1963), girls were limited to lower status in New York street gangs because there was no avenue for them to achieve power or prestige in the groups. If they fought, the boys thought them unfeminine; if they opted for a passive role, they were used only for sexual purposes.

Ackley and Fliegel (1960) studied gangs in Boston in which girls played both tough roles and feminine roles. They concluded that preadolescent girls were more likely to engage in fighting and other typically masculine gang actions while older girls in the gangs played more traditionally feminine roles.

Miller (1973; 1975) found that half of the male gangs in New York had female auxiliaries but he concluded that the participation of young women in the gangs did not differ from that which existed in the past. Miller also pointed out that girls who formed gangs or who were associates of male gangs were lower-class girls who had never been exposed to the women's movement. After studying black gangs in Los Angeles, Klein (1971) believed that, rather than being instigators of gang violence, gang girls were more likely to inhibit fighting.

The most intensive studies of female gang members thus far were done by Campbell (1984; 1986; 1987) on Hispanic gangs in New York City. Although one of the three gangs she studied considered itself a motorcycle gang, it had only one working motorcycle in the total group. Therefore, all of the gangs she discussed should be thought of as belonging to the street gang tradition. . . .

As Campbell reported, girl gang members shared typical teenage concerns about proper makeup and wearing the right brands of designer jeans and other clothing. Contrary to popular opinion, they were also concerned about being thought of as whores or bad mothers, and they tried to reject the Latin ideal that women should be totally subordinate to men. The basic picture that came out of Campbell's work was that gang girls had identity problems arising from conflicting values. They wanted to be aggressive and tough, and yet they wished to be thought of as virtuous, respectable mothers.

Horowitz (1983; 1986; 1987) found girls in Chicano gangs to be similar in basic respects to those that Campbell described. The gang members, both male and female, tried to reconcile Latin cultural values of honor and violence with patterns of behavior acceptable to their families and to the communities in which they existed.

The foregoing and other studies showed that girls have participated in street gangs as auxiliaries, as independent groups, and as members in mixed-gender organizations. While gangs have varied in age and ethnicity, girls have had little success in gaining status in the gang world. . . .

Unlike street gangs that go back for many years, motorcycle gangs are relatively new. They first came to public attention in 1947 when the Booze Fighters, Galloping Gooses, and other groups raided Hollister, California (Morgan, 1978). This incident, often mistakenly attributed to the Hell's Angels, made headlines across the country and established the motorcycle gangs' image. It also inspired *The Wild Ones*, the first of the biker movies released in 1953, starring Marlon Brando and Lee Marvin.

Everything written on outlaw motorcycle gangs has focused on the men in the groups. Many of the major accounts (Eisen, 1970; Harris, 1985; Montegomery, 1976; Reynolds, 1967; Saxon, 1972; Thompson, 1967; Watson, 1980; Wilde, 1977; Willis, 1978; Wolfe, 1968) included a few tantalizing tidbits of information about women in biker culture but in none were there more than a few paragraphs, which underscored the masculine style of motorcycle gangs and their chauvinistic attitudes toward women.

Although the published works on outlaw cyclists revealed the fact that gang members enjoyed active sex lives and had wild parties with women, the women have been faceless; they have not been given specific attention as functional participants in outlaw culture. Indeed, the studies have been so one-sided that it has been difficult to think of biker organizations in anything other than a masculine light. We have learned that the men were accompanied by women but we have not been told anything about the women's backgrounds, their motivations for getting into the groups or their interpretations of their experiences as biker women.

From the standpoint of the extant literature, biker women have simply existed; they have not had personalities or voices. They have been described only in the contemptuous terms of male bikers as "cunts," "sluts," "whores," and "bitches." Readers have been given the impression that women were necessary nuisances for outlaw motorcyclists. . . .

In this article, we do four things. First, we provide more details on the place of women in arcane biker subculture, we describe the rituals they engage in, and we illustrate their roles as moneymakers. Second, we give examples of the motivations and backgrounds of women affiliated with outlaws. Third, we compare the gang participation of motorcycle women to that of street gang girls. Fourth, we show how the place of biker women has changed over the years of our study and we suggest a reason for the change. We conclude by noting the impact of sex role socialization on biker women.

Methods

The data we present were gathered through participant observation and interviews with outlaw bikers and their female associates over the course of 17 years. Although most of the research was done in Mississippi, Tennessee, Louisiana, and Arkansas, we have occasionally interviewed bikers throughout the nation, including Hawaii. The trends and patterns we present, however, came from our study in the four states listed.

During the course of our research, we have attended biker parties, weddings, funerals, and other functions in which outlaw clubs were involved. In addition, we have visited in gang clubhouses, gone on "runs" and enjoyed cookouts with several outlaw organizations. . . .

The main reason we were able to make contacts with bikers was the background of Johnny Moore, who was once a biker himself. During the 1960s, "Big John" was president of Satan's Dead, an outlaw club on the Mississippi Gulf Coast. He participated in the rituals we describe, and his own experience and observations provided the details of initiation ceremonies that we relate. As a former club president, Moore was able to get permission for us to visit biker clubhouses, a rare privilege for outsiders. . . .

At some parties, such as the "Big Blowout" each spring in Gulfport, there were a variety of nonmembers present to observe the motorcycle shows and "old lady" contests as well as to enjoy the party atmosphere. These occasions were especially helpful in our study because bikers were "loose" and easier to approach while partying. We spent more time with three particular "clubs," as outlaw gangs refer to themselves, because of their proximity.

In addition to studying outlaw bikers themselves, we obtained police reports, copies of Congressional hearings that deal with motorcycle gangs, and indictments that were brought against prominent outlaw cyclists. Our attempt was to study biker women and men in as many ways as possible. We were honest in explaining the purpose of our research to our respondents. They were told that our goal was only to learn more about outlaw motorcycle clubs as social organizations.

Dilemmas of Biker Research

Studying bikers was a conflicted experience for us. It was almost impossible to keep from admiring their commitment, freedom, boldness, and fearlessness; at the same time, we saw things that caused us discomfort and consternation because bikers' actions were sometimes bizarre. We saw bikers do things completely foreign to our personal values. Although we did not condone these activities, we did not express our objections for two reasons. First, we would not have been able

to continue our study. Second, it was too dangerous to take issue with outlaws on their own turf.

Studying bikers was a risky undertaking for us, even without criticizing them. At times when we were not expecting any problems, conditions became hazardous. In Jackson, Tennessee, for example, one morning in 1985 we walked into an area where bikers had camped out all night. Half asleep and hung over, several of them jumped up and pulled guns on us because they thought we might be members of a rival gang that had killed five of their "brothers" several years earlier. If Grubby, a biker who recognized us from previous encounters, had not interceded in our behalf, we could have been killed or seriously injured. . . .

It was hard to fathom the chasm between bikers and the rest of us. Outlaw cyclists have no constraints except those their club mandates. When a biker spoke of something being "legal," he was referring to the bylaws of his club rather than to the laws of a state or nation. A biker's "legal" name was his club name that was usually inscribed on his jacket or "colors." Club names were typically one word, and this was how other members and female associates referred to a biker. Such descriptive names as Trench Mouth, Grimy, Animal, Spooky, and Red sufficed for most bikers we studied. As we knew them, bikers lived virtually a tribal life-style with few restraints. The freedom they enjoyed was not simply being "in the wind"; it was also emotional. Whereas conventional people fear going to prison, the bikers were confident that they had many brothers who would look out for them inside the walls. Consequently, the threat of confinement had little influence on a biker's behavior, as far as we could tell.

Perhaps because society gave them so little respect, the bikers we studied insisted on being treated with deference. They gave few invitations to nonmembers or "citizens" and they were affronted when something they offered was refused. Our respondents loved to party and they did not understand anyone who did not. Once we were invited to a club party by a man named Cottonmouth. The party was to begin at 9:00 p.m. on a Sunday night. When we told Cottonmouth that we had to leave at seven in the evening to get back home, we lost his good will and respect entirely. He could not comprehend how we could let anything take precedence over a "righteous" club party.

Bikers were suspicious of all conversations with us and with other citizens; they were not given to much discussion even among themselves. They followed a slogan we saw posted in several clubhouses: "One good fist is worth a thousand words." Studying outlaw cyclists became more difficult rather than easier over the course of our study. They grew increasingly concerned about being investigated by undercover agents. . . . At times, over the last years of our study, respondents whom we had known for months would suddenly accuse us of being undercover "pigs" when we seemed overly curious about their activities.

Our study required much commitment to research goals. We believed it was important to study biker women and we did so in the only way open to us—on the terms of the bikers themselves. We were field observers rather than critics or reformers, even when witnessing things that caused us anguish.

Problems in Studying Biker Women

Although it was difficult to do research on outlaw motorcycle gangs generally, it was even harder to study the women in them. In many gangs, the women were reluctant to speak to outsiders when the men were present. We did not hear male bikers tell the women to refrain from talking to us. Rather, we often had a man point to a woman and say, "Ask her," when we posed a question that concerned female associates. Usually, the woman's answer was, "I don't know." Consequently, it took longer to establish rapport with female bikers than it did with the men.

Surprisingly, male bikers did not object to our being alone with the women. Occasionally, we talked to a female biker by ourselves and this is when we were able to get most of our information and quotations from them. In one interview with a biker and his woman in their home, the woman would not express an opinion about anything. When her man left to help a fellow biker whose motorcycle had broken down on the road, the woman turned into an articulate and intelligent individual. Upon the return of the man, however, she resumed the role of a person without opinions.

The Place of Women in Outlaw Motorcycle Gangs

. . . To the casual observer, all motorcycle gang women might have appeared the same. There were, however, two important categories of women in the biker world: "mamas" and "old ladies." A mama belonged to the entire gang. She had to be available for sex with any member and she was subject to the authority of any brother. Mamas wore jackets that showed they were the "property" of the club as a whole.

An old lady belonged to an individual man; the jacket she wore indicated whose woman she was. Her colors said, for example, "Property of Frog." Such a woman was commonly referred to as a "patched old lady." In general terms, old ladies were regarded as wives. Some were in fact married to the members whose patches they wore. In most instances, a male biker and his old lady were married only in the eyes of the club. Consequently, a man could terminate his relationship with an old lady at any time he chose, and some men had more than one old lady.

A man could require his old lady to prostitute herself for him. He could also order her to have sex with anyone he designated. Under no circumstances, however, could an old lady have sex with anyone else unless she had her old man's permission.

If he wished to, a biker could sell his old lady to the highest bidder, and we saw this happen. When a woman was auctioned off, it was usually because a biker needed money in a hurry, such as when he wanted a part for his motorcycle or because his old lady had disappointed him. The buyer in such transactions was usually another outlaw.

Rituals Involving Women

Outlaw motorcycle gangs, as we perceived them, formed a subculture that involved rituals and symbols. Although each group varied in its specific ceremonies, all of the clubs we studied had several. There were rites among bikers that had nothing to do with women and sex but a surprising number involved both.

The first ritual many outlaws were exposed to, and one they understandably never forgot, was the initiation into a club. Along with other requirements, in some gangs, the initiate had to bring a "sheep" when he was presented for membership. A sheep was a woman who had sex with each member of the gang during an initiation. In effect, the sheep was the new man's gift to the old members.

Group sex, known as "pulling a train," also occurred at other times. Although some mamas or other biker groupies (sometimes called "sweetbuffs") occasionally volunteered to pull a train, most instances of train pulling were punitive in nature. Typically, women were being penalized for some breach of biker conduct when they pulled a train.

An old lady could be forced to pull a train if she did not do something her old man told her to do, or if she embarrassed him by talking back to him in front of another member. We never observed anyone pulling a train but we were shown clubhouse rooms that were designated "train rooms." And two women told us they had been punished in this manner.

One of the old ladies who admitted having pulled a train said her offense was failing to keep her man's motorcycle clean. The other had not noticed that her biker was holding an empty bottle at a party. (A good old lady watched her man as he drank beer and got him another one when he needed it without having to be told to do so.) We learned that trains were pulled in vaginal, oral, or anal sex. The last was considered to be the harshest punishment.

Another biker ritual involving women was the earning of "wings," a patch similar to the emblem a pilot wears. There were different types of wings that showed that the wearer had performed oral sex on a woman in front of his club. Although the practice did not exist widely, several members of some groups we studied wore wings.

A biker's wings demonstrated unlimited commitment to his club. One man told us he earned his wings by having oral sex with a woman immediately after she had pulled a train; he indicated that the brothers were impressed with his abandon and indifference to hygiene. Bikers honored a member who laughed at danger by doing shocking things.

The sex rituals were important in many biker groups because they served at least one function other than status striving among members. The acts ensured that it was difficult for law enforcement officials, male or female, to infiltrate a gang.

Biker Women as Moneymakers

Among most of the groups we studied, biker women were expected to be engaged in economic pursuits for their individual men and sometimes for the entire club. Many of the old ladies and mamas were employed in nightclubs as topless and nude dancers. . . .

Motorcycle women who danced in the nightclubs we observed remained under the close scrutiny of the biker men. The men watched over them for two reasons. First, they wanted to make sure that the women were not keeping money on the side; second, the cyclists did not want their women to be exploited by the bar owners. Some bikers in one gang we knew beat up a nightclub owner because they thought he was "ripping off" the dancers. The man was beaten so severely with axe handles that he had to be hospitalized for several months.

While some of the biker women limited their nightclub activities to dancing, a number of them also let the customers whose tables they danced on know they were available for "personal" sessions in a private place. As long as they were making good money regularly, the bikers let the old ladies choose their own level of nightclub participation. Thus some women danced nude only on stage; others performed on stage and did table dances as well. A smaller number did both types of dances and also served as prostitutes.

Not all of the moneymaking-biker women we encountered were employed in such "sleazy" occupations. A few had "square" jobs as secretaries, factory workers, and sales persons. One biker woman had a job in a bank. A friend and fellow biker lady described her as follows: "Karen is a chameleon. When she goes to work, she is a fashion plate; when she is at home, she looks like a whore. She is every man's dream!" Like the others employed in less prestigious labor, however, Karen turned her salary over to her old man on payday.

A few individuals toiled only intermittently when their bikers wanted a new motorcycle or something else that required more money than they usually needed. The majority of motorcycle women we studied, however, were regularly engaged in work of some sort.

Motivations and Backgrounds of Biker Women

In view of the ill treatment the women received from outlaws, it was surprising that so many women wanted to be with them. Bikers told us there was never a shortage of women who wanted to join them and we observed this to be true. Although it was unwise for men to draw conclusions about the reasons mamas and old ladies chose their life-styles, we surmised three interrelated factors from conversations with them.

First, some women, like the male bikers, truly loved and were excited by motorcycles. Cathy was an old lady who exhibited this trait. "Motorcycles have always turned me on," she said. "There's nothing like feeling the wind on your titties. Nothing's as exciting as riding a motorcycle. You feel as free as the wind."

Cathy did not love motorcycles indiscriminately, however. She was imbued with the outlaw's love for the Harley Davidson. "If you don't ride a Hog," she stated, "you don't ride nothing. I wouldn't be seen dead on a rice burner" (Japanese model). Actually, she loved only a customized bike or "chopper." Anything else she called a "garbage wagon."

When we asked her why she wanted to be part of a gang if she simply loved motorcycles, Cathy answered:

There's always someone there. You don't agree with society so you find someone you like who agrees with you. The true meaning for me is to express my individuality as part of a group.

Cathy started "puffing" (riding a motorcycle) when she was 15 years old and she dropped out of school shortly thereafter. Even with a limited education, she gave the impression that she was a person who thought seriously. She had a butterfly tattoo that she said was an emblem of the freedom she felt on a bike When we talked to her, she was 26 and had a daughter. She had ridden with several gangs but she was proud that she had always been an old lady rather than a mama.

The love for motorcycles had not dimmed for Cathy over the years. She still found excitement in riding and even in polishing a chopper. "I don't feel like I'm being used. I'm having fun," she insisted. She told us that she would like to change some things if she had her life to live over, but not biking. "I feel sorry for other people; I'm doing exactly what I want to do," she concluded.

A mama named Pamela said motorcycles thrilled her more than anything else she had encountered in life. Although she had been involved with four biker clubs in different sections of the country, she was originally from Mississippi and she was with a Mississippi gang when we talked to her. Pamela said she graduated from high school only because the teachers wanted to get rid of her. "I tried not to give any trouble, but my mind just wasn't on school."

She was 24 when we saw her. Her family background was a lot like most of the women we knew. "I got beat a lot," she remarked. "My daddy and my mom both drank and ran around on each other. They split up for good my last year in school. I ain't seen either of them for a long time."

Cathy described her feelings about motorcycles as follows:

I can't remember when I first saw one. It seems like I dreamed about them even when I was a kid. It's hard to describe why I like bikes. But I know this for sure. The sound a motorcycle makes is really exciting—it turns me on, no joke. I mean really! I feel great when I'm on one. There's no past, no future, no trouble. I wish I could ride one and never get off.

The second thing we thought drew women to motorcycle gangs was a preference for macho men. "All real men ride Harleys," a mama explained to us. Generally, biker women had contempt for men who wore suits and ties. We believed it was the disarming boldness of bikers that attracted many women.

Barbara, who was a biker woman for several years, was employed as a secretary in a university when we talked to her 1988. Although Barbara gradually withdrew from biker life because she had a daughter she wanted reared in a more conventional way, she thought the university men she associated with were wimps. She said:

> Compared to bikers, the guys around here (her university) have no balls at all. They hem and haw, they whine and complain. They try to impress you with their intelligence and sensitivity. They are game players. Bikers come at you head on. If they want to fuck you, they just say so. They don't care what you think of them. I'm attracted to strong men who know what they want. Bikers are authentic. With them, what you see is what you get.

Barbara was an unusual biker lady who came from an affluent family. She was the daughter of a highly successful man who owned a manufacturing and distributing company. Barbara was 39 when we interviewed her. She had gotten into a motorcycle gang at the age of 23. She described her early years to us:

> I was rebellious as long as I can remember. It's not that I hated my folks. Maybe it was the times (1960s) or something. But I just never could be the way I was expected to be. I dated "greasers," I made bad grades; I never applied myself. I've always liked my men rough. I don't mean I like to be beat up, but a real man. Bikers are like cowboys; I classify them together. Freedom and strength I guess are what it takes for me.

Barbara did not have anything bad to say about bikers. She still kept in touch with a few of her friends in her old club. "It was like a family to me," she said. "You could always depend on somebody if anything happened. I still trust bikers more than any other people I know." She also had become somewhat reconciled with her parents, largely because of her daughter. "I don't want anything my par-

ents have personally, but my daughter is another person. I don't want to make her be just like me if she doesn't want to," she concluded.

A third factor that we thought made women associate with biker gangs was low self-esteem. Many we studied believed they deserved to be treated as people of little worth. Their family backgrounds had prepared them for subservience.

Jeanette, an Arkansas biker woman, related her experience as follows:

> My mother spanked me frequently. My father beat me. There was no sexual abuse but a lot of violence. My parents were both alcoholics. They really hated me. I never got a kind word from either of them. They told me a thousand times I was nothing but a pain in the ass.

Jeanette began hanging out with bikers when she left home at the age of 15. She was 25 when we talked to her in 1985. Although he was dominating and abusive, her old man represented security and stability for Jeanette. She said he had broken her jaw with a punch. "He straightened me out that time," she said. "I started to talk back to him but I didn't get three words out of my mouth." Her old man's name was tattooed over her heart.

In Jeanette's opinion, she had a duty to obey and honor her man. They had been married by another biker who was a Universal Life minister. "The Bible tells me to be obedient to my husband," she seriously remarked to us. Jeanette also told us she hated lesbians. "I go in lesbian bars and kick ass," she said. She admitted she had performed lesbian acts but she said she did so only when her old man made her do them. The time her man broke her jaw was when she objected to being ordered to sleep with a woman who was dirty. Jeanette believed her biker had really grown to love her. "I can express my opinion once and then he decides what I am going to do," she concluded.

In the opinions of the women we talked to, a strong man kept a woman in line. Most old ladies had the lowly task of cleaning and polishing a motorcycle every day. They did so without thanks and they did not expect or want any praise. To them, consideration for others was a sign of weakness in a man. They wanted a man to let them know who was boss.

Motorcycle Women Versus Street Gang Girls

The motorcycle women in our study were similar to the street gang girls described by Campbell and Horowitz because their lives were built around deviant social organizations that were controlled by members of the opposite sex. There were, however, important differences that resulted from the varying natures of the two subcultures.

As our terminology suggests, female associates of motorcycle gangs were women as opposed to the teenage girls typically found in street gangs. The biker women who would tell us their age averaged 26 years, and the great majority appeared to be in their mid-20s. While some biker women told us they began associating with outlaws when they were teenagers, we did not observe any young girls in the clubs other than the children of members. . . .

All of the biker women we studied were white, whereas street gang girls in previous studies were predominantly from minority groups. We were aware of one black motorcycle gang in Memphis but we were unable to make contact with it. Biker women were not homogeneous in their backgrounds. While street gangs were composed of "home boys" and "home girls" who usually grew up and remained in the areas in which their gangs operated, the outlaw women had often traveled widely. Since bikers were mobile, it was rare for us to find a woman who had not moved around a lot. Most of the biker women we saw were also high school graduates. Two had attended college although neither had earned a degree.

While Campbell found girls in street gangs to be interested in brand name clothes and fashions, we did not notice this among motorcycle women. In fact, it was our impression that biker ladies were hostile toward such interests. Perhaps because so many were dancers, they were proud of their bodies but they did not try to fit into popular feminine dress styles. As teenagers they may have been clothes-conscious, but as adults biker women did not want to follow the lead of society's trend setters.

Biker women were much like street gang girls when it came to patriotism. They were proud to be Americans. Like biker men, they had conservative political beliefs and would not even consider riding a motorcycle made in another country.

As another consequence of the age difference, biker women were not torn between their families and the gang. Almost all of the old ladies and mamas were happy to be rid of their past lives. They had made a clean break and they did not try to live in two worlds. The motorcycle gang was their focal point without rival. Whereas street gang girls often left their children with their mothers or grandparents, biker women did not, but they wanted to be good mothers just the same. The children of biker women were more integrated into the gang. Children went with their mothers on camping trips and on brief motorcycle excursions or "runs." When it was necessary to leave the children at home, two or three old ladies alternately remained behind and looked after all of the children in the gang.

The biker men were also concerned about the children and handled them with tenderness. A biker club considered the offspring of members as belonging to the entire group, and each person felt a duty to protect them. Both male and female bikers also gave special treatment to pregnant women. A veteran biker woman related her experience to us as follows:

> Kids are sacred in a motorcycle club. When I was pregnant, I was treated great. Biker kids are tough but they are obedient and get lots of love. I've never seen a biker's kid who was abused.

As mentioned, the average biker woman was expected to be economically productive, a trait not emphasized for female street gang members or auxiliaries. It appeared to us that the women in motorcycle gangs were more thoroughly under the domination of their male associates than were girls described in street gang studies.

The Changing Role of Biker Women

During the 17 years of our study, we noticed a change in the position of women in motorcycle gangs. In the groups we observed in the 1960s, the female participants were more spontaneous in their sexual encounters and they interacted more completely in club activities of all kinds. To be sure, female associates of outlaw motorcycle gangs have never been on a par with the men. Biker women have worn "property" jackets for a long time, but in the outlaw scene of 1989, the label had almost literally become fact.

Bikers have traditionally been notoriously active sexually with the women in the clubs. When we began hanging out with bikers, however, the men and the women were more nearly equal in their search for gratification. Sex was initiated as much by the women as it was by the men. By the end of our study, the men had taken total control of sexual behavior, as far as we could observe, at parties and outings. As the male bikers gained control of sex, it became more ceremonial.

While the biker men we studied in the late 1980s did not have much understanding of sex rituals, their erotic activities seemed to be a means to an end rather than an end in themselves, as they were in the early years of our study. That is to say, biker sex became more concerned with achieving status and brotherhood than with "fun" and physical gratification. We used to hear biker women telling jokes about sex but even this had stopped. . . .

Early motorcycle gangs were organized for excitement and adventure; moneymaking was not important. Their illegal experiences were limited to individual members rather than to the gang as a whole. In the original gangs, most male participants had regular jobs, and the gang was a part-time organization that met about once a week. At the weekly gatherings, the, emphasis was on swilling beer, soaking each other in suds, and having sex with the willing female associates who were enthusiastic revelers themselves. The only money the old bikers wanted was just enough to keep the beer flowing. They did not regard biker women as sources of income; they thought of them simply as fellow hedonists.

Most of the gangs we studied in the 1980s required practically all of the members' time. They were led by intelligent presidents who had organizational ability. One gang president had been a military officer for several years. He worked out in a gym regularly and did not smoke or drink excessively. In his presence, we got the impression that he was in control, that he led a disciplined life. In contrast, when we began our study, the bikers, including the leaders, always seemed on the verge of personal disaster.

A few motorcycle gangs we encountered were prosperous. They owned land and businesses that had to be managed. In the biker transition from hedonistic to economic interests, women became defined as moneymakers rather than companions. Whereas bikers used to like for their women to be tattooed, many we met in 1988 and 1989 did not want their old ladies to have tattoos because they reduced their market value as nude dancers and prostitutes. We also heard a lot of talk about biker women not being allowed to use drugs for the same reason. Even for the men, some said drug usage was not good because a person hooked on drugs would be loyal to the drugs not to the gang.

When we asked bikers if women had lost status in the clubs over the years, their answers were usually negative. "How can you lose something you never had?" a Florida biker replied when we queried him. The fact is, however, that most bikers in 1989 did not know much about the gangs of 20 years earlier. Furthermore, the change was not so much in treatment as it was in power. It was a sociological change rather than a physical one. In some respects, women were treated better physically after the transition than they were in the old days. The new breed did not want to damage the "merchandise."

An old lady's status in a gang of the 1960s was an individual thing, depending on her relationship with her man. If her old man wanted to, he could share his position to a limited extent with his woman. Thus the place of women within a gang was variable. While all women were considered inferior to all men, individual females often gained access to some power, or at least they knew details of what was happening.

By 1989, the position of women had solidified. A woman's position was no longer influenced by idiosyncratic factors. Women had been formally defined as inferior. In many biker club weddings, for example, the following became part of the ceremony:

You are an inferior woman being married to a superior man. Neither you nor any of your female children can ever hold membership in this club or own any of its property.

Although the bikers would not admit that their attitudes toward women had shifted over the years, we noticed the change. Biker women were completely dominated and controlled as our study moved into the late 1980s. When we were talking to a biker after a club funeral in North Carolina in 1988, he turned to his woman and said, "Bitch, if you don't take my dick out, I'm going to piss in my pants." Without hesitation, the woman unzipped his trousers and helped him relieve himself. To us, this symbolized the lowly place of women in the modern motorcycle gang. . . .

References

Ackley, E. and B. Fliegel.1960. "A Social Work Approach to Street-Corner Girls." *Social Problems*, 5: 29–31.

Campbell, A. 1984. *The Girls in the Gang* New York: Basil Blackwell.

Campbell, A. 1986. "Self Report of Fighting by Females." *British Journal of Criminology*, 26: 28–46.

Campbell, A. 1987. "Self-Definition by Rejection: The Case of Gang Girls." *Social Problems*, 34: 451–466.

Eisen, J. 1970. *Altamont.* New York: Avon Books.

Hanson, K. 1964. *Rebels in the Streets.* Englewood Cliffs, NJ: Prentice-Hall.

Harris, M. 1985. *Bikers.* London: Faber & Faber.

Horowitz, R. 1983. *Honor and the American Dream.* New Brunswick, NJ: Rutgers Univ. Press.

Horowitz, R. 1986. "Remaining an Outsider: Membership as a Threat to Research Rapport." *Urban Life*, 14: 238–251.

Horowitz, R. 1987. "Community Tolerance of Gang Violence." *Social Problems*, 34: 437–450.

Klein, M. 1971. *Street Gangs and Street Workers.* Englewood Cliffs, NJ: Prentice-Hall.

Miller, W. 1973. "Race, Sex and Gangs." *Society*, 11: 32–35.

Miller, W. 1975. *Violence by Youth Gangs and Youth Groups as a Crime Problem in Major American Cities.* Washington, DC: Government Printing Office.

Montegomery, R. 1976. "The Outlaw Motorcycle Subculture." *Canadian Journal of Criminology and Corrections*, 18: 332–342.

Morgan, R. 1978. *The Angels Do Not Forget.* San Diego: Law and Justice.

Reynolds, F. 1967. *Freewheeling Frank.* New York: Grove Press.

Rice, R. 1963. "A Reporter at Large: The Persian Queens." *New Yorker*, 39: 153.

Saxon, K. 1972. *Wheels of Rage.* (privately published)

Short, J. 1968. *Gang Delinquency and Delinquent Subcultures.* Chicago: University of Chicago Press.

Thompson, H. 1967. *Hell's Angels.* New York: Random House.

Thrasher, F. 1927. *The Gang: A Study of 1 313 Gangs in Chicago.* Chicago: University of Chicago Press.

Watson, J. 1980. "Outlaw Motorcyclists as an Outgrowth of Lower Class Values." *Deviant Behavior*, 4: 31–48.

Wilde, S. 1977. *Barbarians on Wheels.* Secaucus, NJ: Chartwell Books.

Willis, P. 1978. *Profane Culture.* London: Routledge & Kegan Paul.

Wolfe, T. 1968. *The Electric Kool-Aid Acid Test.* New York: Farrar, Straus & Giroux.

Reprinted from: Columbus B. Hopper and Johnny Moore, "Women in Outlaw Motorcycle Gangs." In *Journal of Contemporary Ethnography*, 18(4), pp. 363–387. Copyright © 1990 by Sage Publications, Inc. Reprinted by permission. ✦

31

Beyond White Pride: Identity, Meaning, and Contradiction in the Canadian Skinhead Subculture

Kevin Young
Laura Craig

This article examines the range of meanings, activities, and beliefs among groups of skinheads. Although skinheads are commonly seen as racist, political, and violent, this article shows that this picture is not always an accurate one. According to Young and Craig, skinheads hold differing values and beliefs, and some groups of skinheads hold beliefs that directly contradict those of other skinhead groups. This indicates that the labels society places on groups are not always accurate and, in fact, may mistakenly suggest that a large subculture exists when instead there are several distinct groups.

Unlike other flamboyant post-war youth subcultures, . . . for a variety of people and generations throughout the world the label "skinhead" conjures an immediate, if often stereotypical, sense of what the group represents. Much of what is known of the skinhead movement. . . stems from the aggressive behavior of the first generation of British skin-

heads in the late 1960s and the 1970s, or from the more organized and xenophobic practices of the present generation of ultraright skinhead gangs that are active across Europe. The current moral panic associated with skinheads largely derives from the fact that countries such as the United Kingdom, Germany, the Netherlands, Belgium and France are known to have experienced an increase in white-supremacist skinhead attacks on refugees, immigrants and gays (Maclean's, Nov. 23, 1992; Bjorgo and Wilte, 1993).

Of course, the deviant reputation of skinheads stems not only from their behavior but also from the very menacing image they project or, in other words, their style. According to Brake, style is made up of three main ingredients: image, which includes costume and accessories; demeanor, which includes gait, posture and practice; and argot, or the use of a distinct vocabulary (1985:12). . . . Since the first generation of British skinheads, surprisingly little research into the various manifestations of the subculture has been conducted. Exceptions to this are Walker's (1980) study of second generation London skinheads, Burr's (1984) analysis of London skinheads' drug-related lifestyles, and Moore's (1990) study of the relationship between alcohol consumption patterns and ethnic identification among Australian skinheads. Notably, none of these studies looked at North American skinheads.

North American youth subcultures have arguably not enjoyed the same flamboyant history as their British counterparts. Early American sociologists have consistently, if unpersuasively, argued that working-class American youths find membership in a gang a more viable option than membership in a youth subculture (A. Cohen, 1955; Miller, 1958; Cloward and Ohlin, 1960). . . .

Skinheads began to appear in the United States and Canada in the late 1970s. Coplon (1988:65) argues that, initially at least, North American skinheads spanned numerous socioeconomic groups and races. Nazi skinheads became visible for the first time in the Haight-Ashbury district of San Francisco in 1985 (Coplon, 1988:65). In Canada, skinhead groups have sprung up in numerous urban settings including Montreal's east end, Vancouver's Granville St. Mall and Robson St., Edmonton's Jasper Avenue, and Calgary's and Toronto's downtown areas. . . .

Hamm (1993) has speculated that the rise in popularity of the American neo-Nazi skinhead movement parallels the popularity of late 20th-century conservative politics, policies and cultures (of, for instance, the Reagan and Bush administrations). Social programmes reconstituted or simply withdrawn during the 1980s in the U.S. and Canada have, he argues, amplified the gap between the rich and poor (48). In such a period of socioeconomic retrenchment, Hamm suggests, the climate was favorable to the resurgence of forms of intolerance. At this time, so the argument runs, right-wing groups scapegoated immigrants for their alleged role in contributing to high unemployment and the inequitable distribution of social resources. The skinhead subculture, with its emphasis on territoriality, xenophobia and jingoism, appealed to youths experiencing disillusionment with their economic plight and with the political climate. . . .

Most of what is written on skinheads in the United States and Canada concerns neo-Nazi members of the subculture. Much of this surprisingly slim literature has been compiled by "watchdog" groups such as Klanwatch, the Centre for Democratic Renewal (CDR) and the Jewish organization B'nai Brith, which monitor the activities of right-wing organizations. Hamm's (1993) criminological study of American neo-Nazi skinheads, Finsella's (1994) analysis of far-right activities in Canada, and Baron's (1994) study of roughly 140 street kids in Edmonton, some of whom labeled themselves as skinheads, are notable exceptions. Organized neo-Nazi skinheads—these were in the Chicago area—first came to the attention of the New York-based Anti-Defamation League (ADL) in 1984 (Suall and Lowe, 1988:141). Agencies monitoring right-wing behavior speculate that the population of neo-Nazi skinheads in the United States is rising, and that their violence poses an increasingly serious threat to social order (Suall and Halpern, 1993:1). . . .

Locally, nationally and internationally, skinheads have participated in anti-Semitic vandalism such as the desecration of ceme-

teries and synagogues (in November 1989, three extremist Calgary skinheads spray painted Celtic crosses, swastikas and the slogan "6 million is not enough" on what they mistakenly thought was a synagogue). North American skinheads have also been known to victimize gays or persons thought to be gay. For example, in Montreal in December 1992, a 51-year- old man was beaten to death by six teenage skinheads (*Calgary Herald*, Dec. 5, 1992:A10). All of the offenders were charged with first-degree murder. . . .

In an era of neo-conservatism, and as attitudes to youth crime . . . become more punitive, skinheads are increasingly featured in media reports and the control culture. Indeed, the term "skinhead" has become synonymous with violence, intolerance, and hate. Public perceptions, however, are replete with ambiguities and misunderstanding. A "new" brand of young white supremacists, referred to as "skinheads" by the media, does not conform to traditional skinhead style; members frequently resemble average, middle-class teens. Despite their conventional appearance, these extremist youths are involved in aggressive political behavior that promotes domination by the "white race."

The Center for Democratic Renewal, an American organization that monitors hate groups, was using the term "skinhead" to refer to "violence-prone, Nazi-like groupings and individuals" (CDR, 1986:1). According to its definition, skinheads do not necessarily have shaved heads or adopt the typical skinhead style. The common public reaction is to view all skinheads as racist although there are skinheads who conform to the typical style of dress while claiming to have no racist sentiments.

What is missing from popular representations, then, is the fact that, like other flamboyant subcultures or social movements, skinheads are not entirely homogeneous in their values, goals and practices. While exact membership information remains sketchy, we know that skinhead culture extends beyond the limited borders of neo-Nazi involvement. For example, one group of skinheads claims that its major purpose is to directly counter white-supremacist values and to discourage disaffected youth from being absorbed into right-wing activities. This is the group Skinheads Against Racial Prejudice, or SHARP. Literature produced by SHARP contends that this organization began in New York City in 1987 and that it now has chapters in major cities throughout the United States, Canada and Europe. . . .

Theoretical Underpinnings

Beginning with the early work of Albert Cohen (1955), youth subcultures have been seen in delinquency research as providing "solutions" to unrewarding, alienating or otherwise problematic social conditions. As seminal as his early contributions were to North American work in this area, Cohen's argument that subcultural norms and values tend to directly oppose those of the dominant culture has consistently been called into question in subsequent deviancy/youth literature. Cloward and Ohlin (1960), for example, used delinquency to show that youthful rebellion assumes not one homogeneous adaptive pattern but, in fact, numerous forms. Cultural studies approaches appearing in the 1970s and 1980s in Britain expanded on these early theoretical notions by exploring the possibility of the simultaneously transformative and reproductive capabilities of subcultures. In that and other work, it has been suggested that the majority of adolescents hold values similar to those of the parent culture and do not exhaustively— behaviorally, stylistically or otherwise—rebel at all. . . . Further, even in cases of subcultures whose members strategically use "bricolage" to self-identify, to shock and to elicit a deviant status (this would include very graphic youth subcultures such as skinheads and punk rockers), the potency of any resistance implied by the group's image is considerably mediated by its often rather conservative value system and what seems to be its inevitable co-option into mainstream society. . . .

Despite the interest in skinheads shown by the media and control culture, we know of no in-depth studies of Canadian skinheads. Indeed, while there is a growing literature on Canadian youth crime, and particularly on the controversial Young Offenders Act, the bulk of Canadian work on youth culture is actually quite recent (see Friesen, 1990; Baron, 1989; Tanner, 1992; Baron, 1994; Creechan and Silverman, 1995; Gordon, 1995; O'Bireck, 1996; Tanner, 1996), and one could argue that more research, especially of an ethnographic nature, is needed. As Tanner (1992:224) has explained:

> Crime and delinquency have been studied more thoroughly in Canada than. . . types of deviant youth culture. . . . This country has not had extensive experience with the extreme forms of youth subcultural deviance which invite both moral panic and sociological analysis.

This study thus not only fills a void regarding what is known of the skinhead movement in Canada, but also contributes to ethnographic research on North American youth subcultures in general.

Method

In order to gain an understanding of the meanings associated with membership for participants in a self-described "non-political" branch of the Canadian skinhead subculture, participant observation and semi-structured interviews were carried out with skinheads living in a Western Canadian city. Skinheads generally organize themselves into groups or "crews," often distinguished on the basis of their political orientation (i.e., racist, anti-racist, "non-political"). The Oi! skinhead crew in this study was identified by its members as being of the "non-political" variety. Fifteen skinheads considered themselves part of the crew at the time of the study. All except one were male. Subjects ranged in age from 15 to 26, with most being in their late teens. The length of time that they had considered themselves skinheads ranged from eight months to five years.

. . . The participant observation portion of the study involved meeting with subjects weekly at their local "hang-outs," which included food courts, coffee shops and pubs. In meetings with the crew, our role was closest to what Gold might call "observer as participant" (1958:220–21), although "just being around" and group discussion (Willis, 1980) proved to be equally valuable methods. Subjects were aware that ours was a "field" relationship, and we made no pretense of being actual members or wanting to join the group. Data from the field consisted of notes, which were written up directly following each visit in the field. In all, 75 hours of participation were logged over a four-month period.

In order to tap information regarding the values and practices of the skinhead subculture, semi-structured interviews were conducted using snowball sampling techniques (Berg, 1989:60). Fifteen semi-structured interviews were taped and subsequently transcribed. Thirteen interviews took place with single subjects, one with two subjects present, and another with three. There were 18 subjects in all, including two females and one male who were associated with the group, not members per se. . . .

Identity, Meaning, and Contradiction in the Canadian Skinhead Subculture

Introduction to the Crew

Without exception, the skinheads in this study had been members of other youth subcultures including punks, skaters and White Power skinheads before becoming "non-political" Oi! skinheads. Although the specific focus of their interests may have been different, the general reasons for joining these groups were unsurprising. These were articulated as a sense of belonging and security, winning "instant" friends, and being able to share similar values and experiences. One feature of their backgrounds seemed to have consistently predisposed them to join a non-political skinhead group—their involvement in, or desire to distance themselves from, White Power skinhead groups. As we discuss below, all subjects actively refuted any ongoing connection with the organization or ideology of far-right skinheads.

Becoming Oi! skinheads provided our respondents with a status more accurately described as deviant than criminal. Membership allowed them to enjoy, as they described it, the rebelliousness and symbolic intimidation of the skinhead uniform, while at the same time maintaining regular work and feeling positive about their role as contributing members of the community. . . .

We learned early on in the fieldwork that membership really meant being a weekend deviant. As K—— explained: "Being a non-political skinhead is about going out, working all day, and then being able to . . . go out to the pubs on the weekend, play darts and pool, and hang out as a group together." In other words, membership entailed a certain amount of mobility between the subculture and the mainstream, or what one subject called "normal life." This was clearly demonstrated in the case of the much-discussed work ethic. Since it is subculturally meaningful to be employed in conventional jobs, temporary modification of many of the traditional accouterments of the subculture while pursuing work (wearing shoes other than the intimidating Doc Marten boots, concealing tattooed body parts, allowing the requisite cropped hair to grow out) is condoned behavior.

The crew met collectively once or twice a month. Most meetings occurred at a downtown drinking establishment in a pedestrian mall. The frequency of meetings seemed to be dictated by the current disposable income of the members. When most of the members were working, they socialized more regularly because money to be spent on alcohol could be pooled. The general attitude was that there was no point in getting together unless copious amounts of beer could be consumed. For cultural and economic reasons, beer, perceived as an inexpensive "working man's drink," was by far the alcoholic beverage of choice.

The crew had been meeting at one particular pub for over a year for three reasons: it attracted a range of similarly disreputable "outsiders"(street people, dipsomaniacs, bikers); it provided leisure activities viewed as appropriate by members (pool tables and darts); and its proprietors rewarded skinheads' frequent attendance by providing drink discounts and by occasionally playing skinhead music. In fact, the crew's options for alternative drinking establishments had been severely limited by its prior involvement in violent encounters in other pubs and bars in the downtown area.

Besides meeting once or twice a month as a whole, groups of two to six members of the crew would meet for coffee or beer at least once a week. Common meeting places included a particular area of a food court in a downtown mall, coffee shops, a crew member's house (usually their parents') or apartment, and local nightclubs. Driven by a disdain for what was viewed as middle-class pretension, the skinheads preferred locations perceived as disreputable, such as coffee shops and restaurants with paneled walls, mirrors, "mini"-jukeboxes at the tables, vinyl booths and large smoking sections.

Judging from the occupational and educational backgrounds of their parents, the subjects represented two quite distinct class backgrounds. Using Veltmeyer's (1986) class typology, one-third of the skinheads and ex-skinheads came from middle-class homes, and two-thirds came from working-class backgrounds. Despite the presence of middle-class participants, all subjects expressed pride in being "working-class."

Comparison of the respondents across educational and employment levels also revealed disparate backgrounds. Three of the practicing skinheads had some university or college education, and three had completed Grade 12, while five had not completed high school. The working skinheads were employed in a variety of service and manual labor jobs. None of the subjects aspired to professional or managerial positions, or work otherwise defined as white-collar. Occupational ambitions were vague; some expressed interest in going back to school to learn a trade. All stated that they desired a comfortable and "traditional" style of life, including a house and a family. . . .

'Shaved for Battle': Oi! Style

While vestiges of the original English skinhead look of the late 1960s can still be found today, Canadian skinhead style has not been adopted wholesale from Britain. In fact, skinhead style has been subject to modification since its first appearance in Britain, in conjunction with changing political and cultural circumstances. Despite some variation, however, there are obvious similarities between the style of 1990s Canadian skinheads and the early English skinheads. Much of the clothing worn by the current subjects was a conscious replication of original skinhead attire. For example, R—— acknowledged the appeal of the prototypical skinhead style:

> I've always dressed like a skinhead, just without the suspenders and the boots. I was always wearing tight jeans and flannel shirts, and I've always had short hair. The braces, I think they look neat, and they're just part of the style. They don't really hold up my pants or nothing because most of my pants fit me but I think they look cool.

Although braces served no functional purpose, they were worn because members considered them to be both an integral part of the skinhead "uniform" and a giveaway clue as to subcultural membership.

The style adopted by the participants in the current study included cropped hair, suspenders, black or cherry red boots that were usually steel-toed and mid-calf in length, and jeans rolled up to reveal the intimidating boots. Tops included pressed white or pinstriped dress shirts, white t-shirts, and t-shirts with Canadian insignia. Several members customized t-shirts by taking skinhead album covers to clothing stores where images are transferred onto clothing. Participants accorded special status to such unique t-shirts as well as to hard-to-acquire brands and items such as "Ben Sherman" and "Fred Perry" shirts—both part of the original skinhead attire. Often, the crew would spend many hours discussing stores that were rumored to keep such items in stock, or the possibility of saving money to mail-order them from England. . . .

In Canada, the meaning of colors chosen for boot laces and suspenders has often been region-specific. According to the respondents, for example, wearing red laces in Vancouver in the mid-1980s meant that the skinhead was a communist or "Red Skin," whereas in Calgary it meant that s/he was a neo-Nazi Skin. In some regions wearing yellow laces meant that the skinhead was a member of the National Front, while in others it meant that s/he had assaulted a police officer or was a member of SHARP. All of the respondents insisted that color coding had become so confusing that it had lost its initial meaning in their city, although in other settings (Germany, England and elsewhere in Canada) it maintains significance. . . .

Rather than the "Crombie" overcoats worn by the original skinheads (Brake, 1974; Marshall, 1991), two-thirds of the respondents owned black or green "flight jackets," often purchased at army surplus stores. As one of many examples of bricolage, these jackets, originally standard issue of the United States Air Force, have been appropriated by skinheads from many countries, including Britain (Marshall, 1991:161) the United States (Coplon, 1988:60) and Canada, to signify national pride and political orientation. Flight jackets tended to be decorated with emblems of the skinhead's country of origin. Since flight jackets have become increasingly popular with many young people in Western Canada, several subjects remarked that one could distinguish a jacket owned by a skinhead by the presence of patches displaying Canadian emblems. . . .

'I Hate the Commie Scum': Skinheads, Social Class and the Protestant Work Ethic

As previously noted, since the publication of Albert Cohen's *Delinquent Boys* (1955), youth subcultures have been viewed as collective solutions to problems in the social, political or economic structure. Subsequent American and British work has interpreted such collective solutions in relation to unique class experiences (Cloward and Ohlin, 1960; Coleman, 1961; Downes, 1966; P. Cohen, 1972; Clarke et al., 1976). Brake, for example, argues that the values of subcultures tend to intersect with the class context in which they emerge: "Membership of a subculture necessarily involves membership of a class culture and a subculture may be an extension of, or in opposition to, the class culture" (1985:6). However, subcultural membership as a response to collective problems linked to class position does not seem to explain all that clearly the existence of subcultures, such as the skinhead subculture, in Canada. . . .

In a classic attempt at role-taking, all respondents in the current study expressed pride in being working-class, although only two-thirds actually came from such backgrounds. To participants, being working-class meant that one either had work or was actively seeking employment rather than embracing joblessness or welfare as a lifestyle.

It was imperative for all members to be seen as being independent. For example, those who lived with their parents were quick to emphasize that they paid room and board. Many defined themselves as working-class: they claimed not to have professional or managerial aspirations and were satisfied with a modest, rather than extravagant, style of life. As T——, a veteran member, reported:

> To me, "working class" means you basically work for a living. You're not rich, you're not on the edge of poverty. You're just in between. . . . You work. You have to work your whole life just to get by.

To all respondents, in fact, being working-class implied employment, making enough money to subsist, and being independent of financial assistance from the state or one's family. However, not all of the respondents were gainfully employed; almost half of them were networking at the time of the study. Despite being unemployed, these subjects claimed to be looking for full-time work. The skinhead version of involuntary joblessness stood in contrast to their perceptions of unemployed punks, for example, for whom unemployment and welfare were viewed as a voluntary lifestyle choice.

By claiming to be working-class, skinheads were able to differentiate themselves from members of other youth subcultures. One subject went so far as to argue that in this respect the skinhead subculture was "classier than most subcultures. . . ." All subjects perceived themselves to be "clean-cut" and aggressively chastised those they thought were not. For example, it was not uncommon for them to verbally harass males wearing long hair and what they saw as ambiguously gendered styles of dress. Generally viewed as feminine, long hair was also associated with "hippies" who, confusingly, were defined by crew members as "long-haired male university students. . . lazy and left-wing."

. . . Further, subjects claimed not to use or sell drugs because, as they explained, drugs inevitably led to the destruction of one's own life and that of others. Drug use was viewed as being a left-wing "hippie kind of activity." Paradoxically, skinheads, while harboring few reservations about using violence to articulate subcultural commitment, condemned passive violence to oneself through drug use. Being unkempt, on welfare, and "doing drugs" were perceived as characteristics of punks and hippies—both of which were broadly viewed as parasites living off the state. . . .

'This Land is Ours': Ambiguous Positions on Race

While none of the subjects in the study professed to be far-right or neo-Nazi, obvious ambiguities and contradictions emerged in their positions on race and ethnicity. Broadly speaking, crew members articulated superficial understandings of the genesis of the skinhead movement. As such, most of the crew referred to themselves as "non-political" on the grounds that they professed to be as open to multiracial membership and influences within the subculture as the early English skins, who were attracted to West Indian music and rhythms. . . .

While some members were not openly racist, and appeared guarded in—even uncertain of—their views on race, others discussed their beliefs about such things as immigration and the meaning of being Canadian in quite cavalier ways. A typical case was M——who, having professed commitment to the present "non-political" skinhead group, went on to confess:

> I'm a racist. I don't make my way of life about it or anything. Like, I can say "nigger" and not feel guilty about it, you know what I mean? But I don't say "well there's a nigger, let's go beat him up, I hate his guts, he deserves to die," you know. I mean, it's not his fault.

Rather simplistically, M—— argued that the difference between neo-Nazi skinheads and so-called "non-political" skinheads was that neo-Nazis were openly hostile toward non-whites, whereas those who were nonpolitical kept any controversial views they might harbor strictly between members.

Further evidence of skinheads' contradictory position on race could be seen in their musical tastes. Generally, subjects did not view their "non-political" stance as being incongruous with listening to traditional skinhead music, much of which has clear White Power tones and incentives. In fact, more than half of the crew members identified this as the music they listened to most often. White Power, a genre of music favored by neo-Nazi skinheads, is also a term that refers to the possibility of world domination by the "white race." J——, who had been a skinhead for roughly a year and a half, explained that White Power music was his favorite because "[i]t gets my blood going. It makes me feel mean. . . . I don't go and beat somebody up after listening to it; it's just a rush for me. Some people do drugs and I listen to my music." All of the respondents reported they were attracted to the beat of White Power music, that it made them feel "aggro" (aggressive), and many said that they achieved an "adrenaline rush" by listening to it. Most denied that the (often explicitly racist) lyrical content was an important dimension of the music.

While all respondents displayed a liking for White Power music, two-thirds demonstrated a strong antipathy toward rap. . . . The skinheads took particular offence at black performers endorsing violence against whites in their music. For example, one subject explained the details of "The Shot," a song by Ice Cube that simulates a doctor telling a patient named "Mr. White," who is visiting the doctor for a "shot," to "turn your head and brace yourself." The next sound heard is that of a loud gunshot. B—— used this example to illustrate that White Power music is treated unfairly by the media in receiving unfavorable coverage and being labeled "racist," while black artists are able to achieve mainstream recognition with similarly controversial material.

In response to the question "Are race or ethnicity factors important in determining who can be a skinhead?" all of the respondents denied that there were restraints to Oi! skinhead membership. To support their claim, most subjects referred to skinheads they knew who were of such diverse ethnic backgrounds as Jewish, Lebanese, Korean and Aboriginal Canadian. Although the idea of skinheads of non-white heritage seemed to be unproblematic to the respondents, it was evident that members from different ethnic groups must demonstrate that they consider themselves first and foremost Canadian, and not expect any "special treatment" because of their ethnicity. A——, a third-generation Canadian skinhead of Lebanese-Scottish descent, was often cited by crew members as an exemplar of the relative meaninglessness of ethnicity in becoming a part of their group. A—— considered himself "truly Canadian" but went on to undermine his own case for personal tolerance by expressing concern that new immigrants were not "fitting in these days" because of cultural and political differences with other "true Canadians.". . .

Finally, subjects went to great pains to distinguish between personal beliefs and formal politics. While their ideologies could clearly be placed as right-of-centre on the political spectrum, subjects did not consider their participation in the political environment as significant. Because they believed that they were not actively attempting to alter the racial composition of communities, Oi! skinhead members defined their personal beliefs as "non-political." Neo-Nazi skinheads on the other hand, were viewed as explicitly political as a result of their notorious public expressions of hostility aimed at immigrants, non-whites and gays.

'Kings of the Jungle': Skinheads and the Gender Order

The conventional rules of skinhead behavior in many ways represent an attempt by members to conform to traditional versions of working-class masculinity or "masculinism. . . ." This involves displays of force and aggression and implies derogatory attitudes toward women and gays, as well as displays of crudity and excess. . . .

The skinhead uniform itself and the symbols and rituals adopted by group members combine to achieve obvious hyperaggressive and hypermasculine effects. However, as Marshall observed in his study of the skinhead movement, one does not have to be physically large to experience the empowering potential of skinhead membership:

> Anyone who has ever had a crop and pulled on a pair of boots can tell you story after story about why being a skinhead made them feel ten feet tall when they were five foot nothing (1991:3).

The desire of skinheads to behave in aggressive ways and to be viewed as manly indicates their acceptance of a gender ideology built on notions of dominance and force. In our forays into the subculture, we observed that many physically unimposing young men are attracted to the subculture because it provides a chance, in B——'s words, to feel "more powerful." As small-framed S—— explained, an appeal of the subculture was "the intimidation, like when people walk by and say, 'Oh my God, there's a skinhead,' you know. I really like that feeling." S—— noted that he had always thought that skinheads looked "tough" and "cool," and that he wanted to become a member because of the shock, even fear, that the skinhead style elicits in certain people. Of course, being young, working-class, relatively unskilled and/or unemployed, many of the respondents enjoyed only marginal social positions. In this respect, being physically intimidating and confrontational provided many of them with a sense of self-esteem, or what D—— described as "a total ego boost."

. . . For the skinheads, manliness was measured in a number of ways, such as hair length and actual practices per se. For example, if a member allowed his hair to grow out longer than roughly half an inch, crew members would heckle him for, in C——s words, "looking like a hippie"—a particularly undesirable state since hippies were perceived rather stereotypically as unclean, sexually ambiguous and pacifist. Hostility to longer hair was mediated only when hair was grown for the purpose of seeking employment. Compliance with a strong work ethic, a central tenet of the skinhead subculture, meant that exchanging the deliberately intimidating crop for a slightly more respectable look was acceptable. However, even in these cases, hair would never be grown longer than three-quarters of an inch. To test subcultural integrity, crew members constantly monitored. . . whose hair had been grown out.

. . . S——, one of the youngest crew members, who had never been in a fistfight, was frequently tagged a "pussy." Curiously, his avoidance of crew-related violence had led to the careful scrutiny of his sexuality by more veteran members. As with physical bravery, sexual prowess was perceived as one way of proving one's manliness. S——'s case was made doubly suspicious as a result of his shyness around women. On several occasions, members endeavored to initiate relations between him and females connected to the group. The prevailing attitude seemed to be, as one member remarked, "he never gets laid so he must be a fag." S—— was able to deflect much of the punitive potential of these. . . slights using humor, but his apparent reluctance to seek out impersonal sex, to view women in purely objectifying ways, and to avoid physical confrontations nevertheless created a certain tension with regard to his place in the group.

Unsurprisingly, the kinds of roles females were expected to play in the Oi! skinhead subculture tended to be subservient and demeaning. . . .

It has been suggested that in working-class culture women tend to be excluded from the activities of men more often than in higher socioeconomic groups (Dunk, 1991:99). . . . For example, K—— made clothes such as braces for male members of the subculture and regularly organized mail-orders to England for skinhead clothing, albums and books. According to her, being a skinhead implied different things for males and females because, as she saw it, females had distinct interests. For instance, K—— noted that females tended to be Ska skins because:

> We like to dance, and you can't really dance to Oi! music. When skingirls are up, we wear our minis and our fishnets, our dress jackets, our Fred Perrys and our loafers. And you can't go out and mosh in a pit; there'd be no point to dressing up.

. . . All subjects identified key differences in the meanings and implications of being male or female in the skinhead subculture.

For example, R——, who had been living with K——. . . for three years, noted:

> Mentally, I think there are big differences. As much as skingirls are hanging out with the skinheads and things like that, they aren't as prone to be as violent. Women just aren't violent like men are, even when they're drinking. . . . Sometimes it's a good thing, sometimes it's a drawback. I haven't really fought much since I've been with K——, but any fights that I have really been in have been because of her. I mean, some person picking on her. . . .

There were also female participants who . . . occupied distinct roles within the subculture. These females included both long-term girlfriends of skinheads who had not adopted the skinhead look, as well as transitory females—"crew sluts"—who associated with the crew. Male skinheads' image of women, both inside and outside the group, tended to be congruous with patriarchal structures observed in Canadian working-class culture by Dunk (1991). For example, crew members with non-skinhead girlfriends contended that they treated "their" women well because they "brought them out" once in a while and because they avoided discussing graphic details about fights, sexual conquests and other practices in the presence of girlfriends.

By excluding them from such unpleasantness, male crew members believed they were showing their girlfriends respect. In fact, girlfriends . . . seemed to condone and justify the aggressive and flagrantly chauvinistic behavior of their boyfriends. For example, K—— argued that although she had several female friends who were non-members, they did not like to socialize with her skinhead friends:

> My girlfriends don't want to come out and hangout with the guys. They don't understand. A lot of the skinheads get aggressive and stuff and they fool around, but my girlfriends don't understand that they're just joking.

Rather than experiencing frustration with male members for providing an uncomfortable and often harassing and abusive atmosphere for her non-member female friends, K—— condoned skinhead behavior by explaining that her female friends failed to "understand," and argued that while the skinheads were sometimes crude and demeaning toward women, they were just "joking."

. . . Again, consistent with this view, the role of the transitory female in the skinhead subculture, according to veteran T——, was to "buy food, buy beer and have sex." Journeyman B—— emphasized that "crew sluts" would never be granted more than peripheral status in the group. Unlike most male and female members, "crew sluts" were usually middle-class, and lived with their parents in the suburbs. Most of them had met crew members while they were in high school.

Because of their often very obvious middle-class upbringing, and because they did not generally demonstrate loyalty to any particular member, male members treated "crew sluts" with very little respect—as their stigmatizing label would suggest. It was not uncommon for young women to be cut off and insulted ("Shut up, you little slut!") by a male skinhead when attempting to contribute to a conversation. There were clear distinctions between women who were eligible to become long-term girlfriends . . . and those who would remain "crew sluts." For example, once a female had been sexually intimate with more than one crew member, she was destined to remain on the margins of the subculture as a "crew slut.". . .

In brief, both male and female participants in the subculture embraced traditional gender roles and tended to replicate wider structures of gender inequality. Males constructed "performative" (Rutherford, 1992:186) identities based on displays of crudity, excess and physical dominance; there was little or no resistance by females within the group to the subordinate role they were expected to play.

'In Pride We Stride': Subcultural Identity and the Image of the Victimized Skinhead

Although none of the respondents claimed to be far-right at the time of the interview, all stated that one of the drawbacks to being a skinhead was being mistaken for a neo-Nazi skinhead. As one informant explained: "You can't go anywhere without people thinking 'wow man, there's one of them fascist-neo-Nazi-skinheads.'" Another respondent la-

mented the risks to reputation linked to being a skinhead: "You know, when you're a skinhead, everybody out there wants to kill you because everybody wants to be a hero. Everybody wants to say 'I beat up a skinhead.'"

Clearly, being continually mistaken for neo-Nazi skins frustrated Oi! members. . . . Because their position resulted in misunderstanding, even harassment, many Oi! skinheads found metaphoric significance in the image and plight of a "crucified skinhead." The representation of a skinhead hanging on a cross was found to be a popular tattoo among the subjects. . . .

. . . [S]kinheads find themselves in a contradictory social position. Having people regard them with trepidation is enabling. As one rather diminutive skinhead explained, being able to intimidate people had a certain appeal: "A lot of people back down from you. . . when they see you're a skinhead. It's just a mystique." While special interest groups monitoring the behavior of skinheads acknowledge that not all skinheads are neo-Nazis, they also tend to assume that membership in the skinhead subculture serves the function of shocking mainstream society. . . .

While Oi! skinheads enjoy the attention they often elicit from mainstream society, shock value is certainly not the only incentive to join up. In addition to winning power through intimidation, just being a member of a group with obscure traditions, rules and meanings provided the subjects with a strong sense of identity not shared by the general population. And despite concerns with public perception, all respondents described their "inside" knowledge of the skinhead way of life as empowering.

The so-called "prestige" associated with being a skinhead was clearly illustrated in the case of J——, who was discussing how he had been "given the finger," spat on, and had objects thrown at him because he was a skinhead. When asked why he thought people reacted to him in these ways, he replied:

Because they're uneducated, they don't know. They're doing just what they think we do. By generalizing us that way, they are doing exactly what Nazis do. So those kind of people are just totally uneducated. They should wake up.

Similarly, when asked how non-members re-acted to skinheads, S—— remarked: "They hate us. They're fascinated by it, but on the other hand they despise us because a lot of them are very ignorant of what we're about." Despite having to constantly qualify outsiders' impressions of Oi! skinheads, crew members' dedication to the subculture did not falter. In fact, terminating involvement with the subculture to avoid such public misunderstanding was seen by some as failing to meet the "skinhead challenge." As C——, a relatively recent member, explained:

> I'm a skinhead; that's just the way it is, I don't want to change it. I'm not going to let somebody else tell me what to do by saying "Oh, I'll give it up, I'll let my hair grow out." It's just letting them win. It's exactly what they want you to do, and what they want every other skinhead to do.

In sum, public anxiety stemming from skinheads' often daunting physical appearance and their notoriety was a cornerstone element in the construction of subcultural identity, and was actively pursued. On the other hand, the confirmation phase of the identity process often brought disadvantages, specifically in the form of public mislabelling of Oi! members as far-right or neo-Nazi skins.

Discussion

Both domestically and abroad, the skinhead subculture receives extensive public and media attention, especially with regard to the activities of some of its more militant members. Despite this interest and concern, little academic attention has been given in Canada to the subculture or to the meanings associated with its various branches. . . .

For present-day Canadian Oi! skinheads, as for earlier British subcultures (Clarke et al., 1976), while the sense that "special knowledge" regarding what it meant to be a skinhead was empowering to the group, any power was transitory or "magical" (P. Cohen, 1972:23) in that it did little to alter existing social relations. In effect, through their incorporation of the traditional skinhead value system, subjects showed evidence of repro-ducing dominant cultural practices and ideologies. . . . Whether in the United Kingdom or in Canada, the skinhead subculture has traditionally adopted an anti-intellectual stance. Consistent with other research on working-class groups, intellectual labor, such as that conducted in the academy, was viewed as meaningless and impractical in its contribution to economic growth (Willis, 1977; Dunk, 1991). As N—— remarked:

> There are the people that just want to go to school and that's it. I feel that if they just worked at any job like a restaurant job for three years before they did that, then it would put more into the economy and it would do more for the community.

In sum, working-class manual labor was seen to be that which helped the economy grow and was therefore perceived to be the most productive and honourable form of work.

As far as the gender order is concerned, the data from the study strongly suggest an unambiguous reproduction of patriarchy. Practicing and demonstrating heterosexual masculinity was, in the eyes of both male and female members of the group, compulsory, and was articulated in terms of a so-called clean-cut style, a willingness to "prove" oneself physically, an aggressive pursuit of the opposite sex, an open rejection of homosexuality, and chauvinistic attitudes toward all things perceived as "feminine." Field experience with our respondents indicated strictly segregated gender roles that empowered men and marginalized women.

"Non-political," to crew members, meant that they were not directly or formally involved in the political arena. As one veteran member explained: "I'm not out there protesting anything. If I beat someone up it's not because I'm trying to change the way they think; it's just because I don't like them." In other words, although subjects expressed such views with clear political implications (for example, the victims of Oi! skinhead violence are far from random), they considered themselves removed from any well-defined political agenda. . . .

In general, the (albeit weakly acknowledged) conservative ideologies and goals of these self-defined "non-political" skinheads were aggressively articulated and defended. This was particularly evident in their contempt for groups perceived (accurately or inaccurately) to harbor liberal or left wing values, such as hippies, punks, university students and "overly liberal" governments, whose policies on multiculturalism and immigration were held responsible for current economic retrenchment in Canada. . . .

While the right-wing ideologies of this particular branch of Canadian Oi! skinheads may not be surprising given that traditional focal concerns of the skinhead movement have included xenophobia and territoriality, it is important to note that many of their attitudes regarding race, immigration and employment can also be found in mainstream Canadian society. . . .

In a number of crucial respects, then, rather than inverting dominant values—as the early deviancy literature might have predicted—the values of the Canadian skinhead subculture, including members of its confusingly self-defined "non-political" Oi! branch, appear to be congruous with them, and even a caricature of them. Far from being resistant in any significant way, it is in these respects that Oi! skinhead values and identities contribute to the reproduction of dominant hegemonic ideology.

Finally, the study brought into focus a number of internal tensions and contradictions in the Canadian Oi! skinhead subculture. While professing to be part of a non-political group, members were, in several cases, former members of neo-Nazi skinhead gangs, espoused clearly racist and otherwise intolerant attitudes, adopted much of the same menacing style (tattoos of swastikas and Celtic crosses, nationalist insignia and emblems on clothing) and shared the same musical tastes (White Power music) as their self-confessed ultra-right counterparts; they operated on the basis of crude stereotypes of groups (punks, hippies, university students), many of which were identified in only the vaguest of ways, while at the same time deriding stereotypes that blurred their own attempts to distance themselves from more extremist branches of the subculture. In brief, while we acknowledge that the Canadian skinhead subculture is complex and potentially heterogeneous in the meanings it can carry for its members, the study suggests that the ideologies and goals of its various branches are far from mutually exclusive.

References

Baron, S. W. 1989. "The Canadian west coast punk subculture: A field study." *Canadian Journal of Sociology*, Vol. 14, pp. 289–316.

Baron, S. W. 1994. "Street youth and crime: The role of the labor market." Doctoral dissertation, University of Alberta.

Berg, B. L. 1989. *Qualitative Research Methods for the Social Sciences*. Boston: Allyn and Bacon.

Boyd, N. 1995. *Canadian Law: An Introduction*. Toronto: Harcourt Brace Canada.

Brake, M. 1974. "The skinheads: An english working class subculture." *Youth and Society*, Vol. 69, pp. 179–200.

Brake, M. 1985. *Comparative Youth Culture: The Sociology of Youth Culture and Youth Subcultures in America, Britain, and Canada*. London: Routledge and Kegan Paul.

Burr, A. 1984. "The ideologies of despair: A symbolic interpretation of punks' and skinheads' usage of barbiturates." *Social Science and Medicine*, Vol. 19, No. 9, pp. 929–38.

Centre for Democratic Renewal. 1986. "Nazi youth gangs inspire alarm." *The Monitor*, June.

Clarke, J., S. Hall, T. Jefferson, and B. Roberts. 1976. "Subcultures, cultures and class: A theoretical overview." In *Resistance Through Rituals: Youth Subcultures in Post-War Britain*. S. Hall and T. Jefferson (eds.). London: Hutchinson, pp. 9–74

Cloward, R. and L. Ohlin. 1960. *Delinquency and opportunity: A theory of delinquent gangs*. Chicago: The Free Press.

Cohen, A. K. 1955. *Delinquent boys: The culture of the gang*. New York: The Free Press.

Cohen, P. 1972. "Sub-cultural conflict and working class community." *Working Papers in Cultural Studies*, Vol. 2 (Spring), pp. 5–51.

Cohen, S. 1980 [1972]. *Folk Devils and Moral Panics: The Creation of the Mods and Rockers*. London: MacGibbon & Kee.

Coplon, J. 1988. "Skinhead nation." *Rolling Stone*, Dec. 1, pp. 59–65, 94.

Creechan, J. and R. Silverman (eds.). 1995. *Canadian Delinquency*. Scarborough, Ont.: Prentice- Hall.

Downes ,D. 1966. *The Delinquent Solution: A Study in Subcultural Theory*. London: Routledge and Kegan Paul.

Dunk, T. W. 1991. *It's a Working Man's Town: Male Working-Class Culture in Northwestern Ontario*. Montreal and Kingston: McGill-Queen's Univ. Pr.

Friesen, B. K. 1990. "Powerlessness in adolescence: Exploiting heavy metal listeners." In *Marginal Convention: Popular Culture, Mass Media and Social Deviance*. C. R. Sanders (ed.). Bowling Green, Ohio: Bowling Green State Univ. Popular Pr., pp. 65–77

Gold, R. L. 1958. "Roles in sociological field observations." *Social Forces*, Vol. 36, pp. 217–23.

Gordon, R. M. 1995. "Street gangs in Vancouver," In *Canadian Delinquency* R. A. Silverman and J. H. Creechan (eds.). Scarborough, Ont.: Prentice-Hall, pp. 311–21

Hamm, M. S. 1993. *American Skinheads: The Criminology and Control of Hate Crime*. Westport, Conn.: Praeger.

Marshall, G. 1991. *The Spirit of '69: A Skinhead Bible*. Dunoon, Scotland: S.T. Publishing.

Miller, W. B. 1958. "Lower-class culture as a generating milieu of gang delinquency." *Journal of Social Issues*, Vol. 14, pp. 5–19.

Moore, D. 1990. "Drinking, the construction of ethnic identity and social process in a western Australian youth subculture." *British Journal of Addictions*, Vol. 85, No. 10, pp. 1265–78.

Morgan, D. 1992. *Discovering Men*. New York: Routledge.

O'Bireck, G. 1996. *Not a Kid Any More: Canadian Youth, Crime, and Subcultures*. Toronto: Nelson.

Rutherford, J. 1992. *Men's Silences: Predicaments in Masculinity*. New York: Routledge.

Suall, I. and D. Lowe. 1988. "Shaved for battle: Skinheads target American youth." *Political Communication and Persuasion*, Vol. 5, pp. 139–44.

Suall, I. and T. Halpern. 1993. *Young Nazi Killers and the Rising Skinhead Danger*. New York: Anti-Defamation League.

Tanner, J. 1992. "Youthful deviance." In *Deviance: Conformity and Control in Canada*. 2d ed. V. Sacco (ed.). Scarborough, Ont.: Prentice-Hall, pp. 203–35.

Tanner, J. 1996. *Teenage Troubles: Youth and Deviance in Canada*. Toronto: Nelson.

Veltmeyer, H. 1986. *Canadian Class Structure*. Toronto: Garamond.

Walker, I. 1980. "Skinheads: The cult of trouble." *New Society*, Vol. 52, pp. 344–48.

Willis, P. 1977. *Learning to Labor: How Working Class Kids Get Working Class Jobs*. New York: Columbia Univ. Pr.

Willis, P. 1980. "Notes on method." In *Culture, Media, Language: Working Papers in Cultural Studies, 1972–1979*. S. Hall, D. Hobson, A. Lowe and P. Willis (eds.). London: Hutchinson, pp. 88–96.

32

Queer[1] Punk Fanzines: Identity, Community, and the Articulation of Homosexuality and Hardcore

Mark Fenster

This article examines the ways in which individuals who have identities based in two subcultures—homosexuality and punk—manage these identities. The authors focus on how publications addressing the combination of these subcultures provide individuals with a sense of community and support for their beliefs and values. This article shows that not only can individuals have more than one identity based in deviance, but sometimes these pieces of identity also introduce dissonance and confusion to their lives. Fanzines provide individuals with a basis for understanding themselves and a way to know that others like them exist in society.

As for homopunk stuff going on, forget it. Philomath is a logging town, full of rednecks. Corvallis is a college town, full of frat boys. Lots of punks but none would admit to being homo. As far as I can tell, no one in Corvallis does.
—letter in *Homocore* 6, May 1990.

Rock and roll is, has been and always will be the driving force in my life, more so than my sexuality. Reading *Homocore* has helped me to begin to bridge the gap be-

tween these two seemingly mutually exclusive aspects of my life. For this I thank you.
—Letter in *Homocore* 7, Winter/Spring 1991

These statements, and similar ones published in punk fanzines published by young gays and lesbians, seem to note this: To be a *queer* punk or fan of hardcore means, in many local music scenes, being outside the dominant sexual orientation articulated to a musical practice; to be a queer *punk* means having a taste and style that lies outside dominant notions of what music mainstream adult gays and lesbians perform, listen and dance to. There seems, these writings imply, to be no possibility for the linking of homosexuality and punk, no established or identifiable set of identities for the queer punk.

However, the increasing number of queer punk fanzines in which these kinds of writings have been published have themselves begun to establish possibilities and identities in their descriptions of the difficulties, pleasures, and empowerments involved in being a homosexual punk and in finding and communicating with others. As recently as four years ago, both the local scenes and national institutions of American hardcore music, which have an audience—and musician-base of middle- and lower-middle class white teenagers and post-adolescents, were articulated almost exclusively to a notion of the music as performed for an by heterosexuals. This does not mean that there were no gays or lesbians in bands or audiences; rather, there was little space for outward displays of homosexuality in the main sites of American hardcore. Queer punks describe themselves as feeling forced to stifle expression of their sexual preference in these sites for fear of both physical assault ("fag bashing" has been and remains a real danger in some scenes) and the more generalized and symbolic violence of homophobia. More recently, however, the issue of homosexuality has been confronted in punk and hardcore sites on a number of fronts: in bands, in particular "scenes" (most notably in San Francisco and Toronto), in "mainstream" hardcore publications like *Maxi-*

mum RocknRoll, and particularly in a proliferation of gay and lesbian fanzines.

The act of producing or writing to a fanzine (a small, self-produced, and more or less non-profit publication which circulates among the fans and musicians of a particular form of music) is one which both structures and is structured within these articulations of music and sexuality, within fields of musical meaning and identity. To call oneself a homopunk (along with others who do the same) is both to define a set of positions within these fields, and to attempt to define the fields themselves. Fanzines and the letters published within them represent attempts to communicate among fans and to communicate a particular set of constructions of the queer punk and her or his musical taste and practices. To be a homopunk is not simply to resist dominant meanings but to attempt to articulate and circulate a set of different identities, meanings and representations of specific positions within social space, as well as to construct some form of community within which such identities can exist.

In this sense, these fanzines are part of an ongoing process of producing, within forms of representation, a range of possible identities for gay participants in hardcore—to work within the play of identity and representation in order to construct and re-construct a space for the articulation of hardcore and homosexuality within a locality and across a burgeoning community of queer punk fanzines dispersed across North America. Thus they represent a double movement of radical sexual and cultural politics: first, the confrontational sexual politics that these fanzines undertake with respect to both the hardcore and gay and lesbian communities; and second, their cultural politics of constructing an alternative community for marginalized groups around popular musical practices.

Two important points need to be made to contextualize this movement. First, there is no singular collective identity circulated within these fanzines: gay and lesbian fanzines are somewhat different in their concerns and their modes of address; each fanzine has its own specific style, structure, and content; and within each fanzine, a range of different

voices and identities emerge. And second, the process of the construction of such identities is neither part of an ongoing set of individual decisions nor social/biological/psychoanalytic encodings that dictate sexuality and/or musical taste, but is instead an example of the ongoing articulation and "meshing" of individual and collective identities in cultural practices (King, 1988).

This essay is structured in order to detail the specific social, cultural, and musical contexts within which these fanzines have emerged; the operations of, as well as the identities and representations articulated within, these fanzines; and the fanzines' significance within contemporary musical, sexual and cultural practices. I will begin with a brief discussion of the most important cultural contexts within which queer punks have emerged, the North American hardcore community and mainstream gay and lesbian cultural practices. Then I will describe and analyze three different fanzines, focusing on one of the most popular and important sections in these fanzines, the letters section in *Homocore*. Queer punks and their fanzines have been re-articulated within the publications of both the hardcore and dominant gay and lesbian communities, and I will briefly discuss this process and its effects upon the social construction of "queer punks" before concluding with a discussion of the significance of these practices for critical communication studies.

Contexts: The Emergence of American Hardcore and of Mainstream Gay and Lesbian Culture

In order to analyze the emergence of queer punks, it is necessary to discuss the cultural contexts of the hardcore and gay and lesbian communities within which (and, to a large extent against which) this emergence has occurred. The current wave of activity of gay and lesbian punks in the American hardcore scene has arisen within a period that has seen the waning of hardcore's (and, before it punk's) reaction against bourgeois notions of sexuality and a much stronger articulation of punk and hardcore to a male-oriented hetero-sexuality. British punk brought together a number of different musical, stylistic, cultural and political elements at work throughout the history of Anglo-American rock music[2]. A relatively diverse musical, cultural and political[3] phenomenon, punk was and continues to be constructed as a "purified" and unmediated form of rock, an immediate and realistic communication between anti- (rather than simply un-) professional musicians and audiences[4], and opposed to the political and cultural values and practices of bourgeois parent culture. Punk sexuality could be quite ambiguous: punk fashion often borrowed from deviant sexual practices, such as sadomasochism and pornography[5], while its privileging of style as cultural politics and its playing with gender, fashion, and sexual roles both challenged bourgeois norms and opened space for alternative sexualities.[6]

British punk did not last very long, and most commentators consider its "death," through mainstream incorporation of many of its musical and stylistic elements, to have occurred in 1978, two years after it had begun. Contemporary American hardcore tends to see itself as the true off-spring of punk while it sees other types of music that claim some musical or stylistic heritage as having "sold out" or as not true to the punk tradition[7]. According to Tim Yohanna, editor of the important hardcore fanzine *Maximum RocknRoll* (*MRR*):

[The American punk scene] blossomed in '77 or '78. Then by around '80 or so it started losing its vitality—it became more commercialized and a lot of the original ethic of it was lost. Then around '80 or '81 or so hardcore started as a reaction against what punk had become, against the wimping out of punk to its values. And those people who said they were into "hardcore" punk were referring to the harder- edged [style] of both the music and ideals. So it was sort of a rejuvenation that a younger crop of kids were spearheading, and the music was even shorter and louder than before.[8]

The rise of local and national punk, and later, hardcore scenes retained an emphasis on certain cultural values articulated within British punk, specifically its aesthetics, its independent, participatory practices, and its oppositional position in relation to dominant culture and music.

As in British punk, the politics of American hardcore as a set of cultural practices are not unified, and include struggles over racism, gender, sexuality, and general political activism. And as in British punk, the individuals and institutions involved in hardcore have built a system of alternative channels for the production and distribution of, as well the participation in, musical practices on a local and national level. The cyclical rise, decline and survival of such scenes, the incredible number of bands forming, records being released, and fanzines being sent through the mail are a testament to the continuing viability of hardcore as a musical form, despite the ongoing battles within the music and its various scenes over the aesthetic, cultural/political and institutional basis of hardcore and the general lack of recognition that the music receives from the mainstream media and musical institutions[9].

The historical legacies and contemporary community of punk and hardcore constitute one context within which the articulation of a set of queer punk emerged; the social practices articulated within the construction of fluid and multiple gay and lesbian cultures represent another. By fluid and multiple, I am referring to the impossibility of a singular gay and lesbian culture, community or identity because of the diverse gender, race, ethnicity and generational positions of gays and lesbians, as well as to the fact that the notion of "homosexuality" as a singular site of regulation, contestation, and identity is itself a relatively recent construction[10]. Yet the ongoing attempt to articulate such a culture and community is historically and politically crucial[11]; as John D'Emilio (1983) demonstrates, the construction of homosexual identity in difference is one of the most important and difficult articulations in the history of gay and lesbian political and cultural activities. However, the construction of a dominated, minority gay and lesbian community making demands for rights itself posits a series of dominant homosexual cultural practices;

those middle class adult homosexuals who are more assimilated within dominant economic and social structures and who are better able to represent themselves and circulate those representations thus have relatively dominant positions within gay and lesbian communities.

Dominant gay and lesbian identities and cultural practices, whether represented in films or novels, described in periodicals, or on display in bars, music clubs, parties or on the street[12], constitute and display a series of historically changing identities, roles, and styles available to individuals and collectivities of homosexuals. This "set" also serves as a point of reference from or against which an individual or group can articulate emergent practices and alliances. As the excerpts from fanzines at the beginning of this chapter demonstrate, becoming a queer punk forces one to problematize not only punk music practices but also the set of available, dominant practices and identities associated with dominant, adult gay and lesbian cultures — to question and challenge those periodicals and musical forms and practices that constitute the "dominant" of gay and lesbian culture.

Perhaps the most significant recent development within gay and lesbian culture and political practices has been the increased radical politicization of many (particularly but by no means exclusively) homosexuals in the wake of the outbreak of AIDS and continuing oppression of gays and lesbians. The rise and success of ACT-UP in helping to foment and coordinate activity to protest the lack of appropriate medical, governmental, media and corporate responses to the disease has helped lead to the growth of radical political activity from the late-1980s to the present. The establishment in April 1990 of Queer Nation, a coalition that extends the political activity of ACT-UP into a confrontational struggle for gay and lesbian rights[13] is somewhat more significant in relation to queer punks, whose fanzines, while certainly not ignoring AIDS, focus more on a range of medical gay and lesbian cultural practices than on AIDS information and activism. The conjunctural rise of this activity cannot be explained, as Alisa Solomon has rightly argued, in terms of simple developments such as the rise of a "new, young generation" of gays and lesbians, but instead needs to be placed in the context of health crises, conservative political backlashes against previous and current gains in homosexual civil rights, the political and cultural conservatism of some middle class assimilationist homosexuals, as well as other developments (Solomon, 1991)[14]. While the connection between the growth of radical gay and lesbian activism and the dispersed queer punk community should not be seen as a direct causal relationship, the kinds of confrontational cultural practices, forms of representation, and styles and tastes that cross over between ACT-UP and particularly Queer Nation and the pages of *Homocore* and other queer punk fanzines mark the articulation of some common elements. Indeed, some queer punks have participated in ACT-UP and Queer Nation actions, and queer punk fanzines are finding a growing audience among gay and lesbian activists.

These cultures, along with the cultural practices of American hardcore, serve as the reference points and provide the central elements from which queer punk practices and identities have been articulated. I will now turn to a historical account and analysis of the fanzines that have operated at the center of this articulation.

Homocore and the Construction of a Queer Punk Community

While J.Ds (see below) was the first queer punk fanzine of the late 1980s, *Homocore* has been crucial in informing gays and heterosexuals in and outside the hardcore scene of the existence of gay fans and participants in the scene. *Homocore* shares a number of elements, concerns, and modes of representation with other similar (gay and straight) fanzines, yet its distinguishing and arguably most important act has been the facilitating of a dispersed community of queer punks—a group of individuals dispersed across space with shared interests in alternative musical practices—who are brought together within the pages of fanzines. The fanzine began through the efforts of one person, Tom Jennings, who started *Homocore* in September 1988.[15] As he describes it, the 'zine has been an attempt to "co-opt" the word punk and to give it some new sexual meanings, as well as to reject what he calls the "disco-consumptive" aspects of dominant gay culture (Jennings, 1990:35), for those gays and lesbians who have tastes and who participate in cultural practices which are tied more closely to hardcore and punk. *Homocore*'s content and design were inspired by certain conventions of hardcore fanzines,[16] but were adapted for a publication that concentrates more on written communication among readers about sexuality (through letters, reviews and articles) than about music—usually less than three pages (of the twenty-four to forty in the six issues through May 1990) are devoted to music reviews or band interviews.

Given the conventional fanzine format and layout of *Homocore*, it is the information that the 'zine passes along which makes it distinct. Jennings' declaratory, "What the Fuck Is *Homocore*?" section, placed at the front of the first issue and reproduced in all of the subsequent numbers, clearly demarcates the fanzine's editorial position. The statement begins:

You don't have to be a homo to read or have stuff published in *Homocore*. One thing everyone in here has in common is that we're all social *mutants*; we've outgrown or never were part of any of the "socially acceptable" categories. You don't have to be gay; being different at all, like straight guys who aren't macho shitheads, women who don't want to be a punk rock fashion accessory, or any other personal decision that makes you an outcast is enough. Sexuality is an important part of it, but only part.

It's obvious that there's gay punks and other people in the various scenes we hang out and work and live in. You'd almost never know it though, from the way people behave. It's usually just too scary to be open and honest when you hear supposedly cool and politically aware people and bands say or do sexist or homophobic shit, especially if you don't know any other homo punks or other people (*Homocore* #1).

Homocore's mission, then, is to construct a space (note the powerful image of "everyone in here") for the problematizing of sexuality within the hardcore scene rather than to create a new and radically different "scene"—as he clearly states, this is not intended to be simply a "gay" magazine but a homo punk fanzine. A direct attempt to articulate homosexuality to hardcore without completely disarticulating other sexualities, *Homocore* confronts the hardcore scene on the latter's own terms—keep the scene, keep the fanzine and its look and format, keep your own sexuality, just let gays and lesbians be "open and honest" and allow them to "behave" as they want (the section states, "Gay issues aren't just for same-sex friends and lovers; the freedom to do or behave as you want is important for everybody.")

By 1990, *Homocore* had become relatively successful within the limited commercial horizons of hardcore fanzines[17], and had received mention in gay and straight non-hardcore publications as well. Jennings has also produced live *Homocore* benefit shows, some solely through his own efforts and the efforts of others associated with the fanzine, and some with other independent producers and organizations. These shows, which have been held in different community spaces in San Francisco, have attempted to quite literally establish an alternative performance and gathering place, as well as a local community, for gay, lesbian, and interested straight punks. But for others dispersed across the country, without access to the facilities, homosexual community, and the degree of political and social acceptance that gays and lesbians in San Francisco have struggled to achieve, *Homocore* has been particularly important in the construction of a dispersed North American community of queer punks and is usually the first queer punk fanzine that its readers throughout the U.S. and the world hear about and read.

The letters section is arguably the most important section in *Homocore*; it appears in the front of the fanzine, it comprised nearly one-third of the total pages by issue #6, and it is the most important site for the discussion of the pleasures and difficulty of constructing viable identities for queer punks. *Homocore* claims to publish every letter it receives which asks to be published, and the letters share experiences of frustration with both the mainstream gay community and the hardcore scene: they express a sense of not belonging, of wanting to share musical and cultural tastes with others without being able to find those others in a local community. The overarching narrative that emerges within the 'zine, however, is a positive one; while the letters speak of the difficulty of operating as both a gay and a punk, they exalt in the emancipatory possibility of *Homocore* itself as a focal point for a dispersed community, and they express feelings of empowerment in the recognition that they have learned, through the letters section, that there are many queer punks across the country who have shared similar experiences. The letters thus operate in ways similar to declarations of coming out; as Martha Gever writes, "Coming out has always meant more than an individual declaration; it is also a fundamental social process that defies social disapprobation and infuses conventional representations of sexual deviance and moral degeneracy embodied by lesbians and gay men with new meanings" (1990:194). Like the act of coming out, the letters that declare the connections, on both individual and group levels, of punk and homosexuality attempt to construct empowering social identities that can operate within and be articulated to the hardcore scene. *Homocore*, then, in addition to its wide variety of articles, graphics, comics, and occasional erotic photography and images, privileges the "authentic" human voice of the individual, the letter writer who tells his or her story. This connects with—though is obviously distinct from—the format and mode of representation of both the hardcore fanzine (from which Jennings' notion of an extended letters section originated) as well as the affirmative political and cultural practices of the post-Stonewall gay liberation movement.

The letters often begin with the problems of the local, of the inability to freely participate in the cultural and sexual activities that the letter-writers desire to. The descriptions of the local are sometimes quite blunt:

> There is a small scene up here but homophobic to the extremes. There are 2 gay bars but we don't have much in common.—S.G., Anchorage, Alaska (Issue #6).

> Unfortunately the Cleveland scene is either nonexistent or so underground that it is impossible to locate. This makes it difficult to find others with the same social/ sexual attitudes.—S., Cleveland, OH (#4).

They speak of the isolation that results from operating within restraining physical and emotional places in which you are isolated as either a punk or a "homo," spaces that are so strongly connected to a particular sexuality and/or a particular set of musical and cultural practices that a de- and re-articulation either within them (i.e., a more open hardcore or gay scene) or in an alternative space (i.e., a *Homocore* show) seems impossible. Similarly, many letters describe this as not merely a problem of location; it is also a problem of taste and identification with cultural practices, and common complaints focus upon not fitting in with either punks or gays.

While many letters describe this problem of being stuck between two competing and unsatisfactory worlds, some concentrate on the particularities of one or the other world. While a number of letters construct the gay community as an often stifling set of stifling cultural and social practices, some of them concentrate specifically on problems of identification:

> Anyway, as I'd half expected, I'm the only punk (well, call me hardcore or maybe postcore) (how 'bout that for an alternative) member of the LBGA [Lesbian, Bisexual, and Gay Alliance] [at my college]. I've met some great people, but nobody I can immediately relate to—similar attitudes and tastes. Alone in a crowd again (any of this sound familiar?).—L., Amherst, MA (#2).

In addition, many of them specifically reject dominant gay periodicals like *Christopher Street* (N.Y.) and *The Advocate*, and many more strongly complain about their gay and lesbian friends' musical tastes, which are mostly described as disco, Women's Music, and mainstream pop.

Similarly they describe the hardcore scene as incomplete and unfulfilling—as a set of physical spaces and a community that limits the ability of gays and lesbians to feel comfortable and to participate fully in musical practices. This is particularly true of letters from or about musicians who write to describe how gay members of bands get "hassled all the time" (e.g., M., Harrisburg, PA, [#4]) and how one musician fears that if he comes out he would "lose band members, gigs, and furthermore be ostracized and ridiculed by this so-called 'scene'" (H., Chicago, [#4]). And a number of lesbian hardcore fans have described the physical space of the punk club as particularly threatening or alienating (e.g., T., Boulder, CO [#5] and D., Baltimore, MD [#6]).

These letters do not, however, reject all of the hardcore scene or dominant gay cultures; rather, they show an obvious desire to retain the cultural practices and sexual freedom that those respective communities represent. In many letters there is regard for the particularities of gay history and politics, whether in the form of the gay liberation movement or, more recently, ACT-UP. In their criticisms, the letters harshly criticize what are seen as conservative political strains within mainstream gay politics, as well as dominant gay cultural practices and the consumption of particular types of clothes, cars and music, but they give silent consent to the ability, within dominant gay cultural spaces and practices (i.e., the gay disco or gay "ghettos" like Castro Street in San Francisco) to openly express homosexuality. A similar respect for the punk and hardcore scenes is at work in the large number of letters that describe the individual's devotion to the music and excitement of the hardcore scene. This is most often apparent in lists of the bands to which the letter writer listens and the clubs which he or she attends despite discomfort or fear because or his or her sexuality.

The letters in *Homocore* ultimately spin an emancipatory narrative of the construction of community for gay fans of hardcore through the communication made possible by the fanzine:

Y'know, if it's done right, *Homocore*, as an entity, could be a movement as well as a magazine.—N., Livingston, NJ. (#3)

I personally would like to see the *Homocore* scene spread across this state and country, and I would like you to continue your publication.—D., Rio Rancho, NM (#4)

By the later issues, some letters express the belief that the fanzine has begun to lay the groundwork for a community of queer punks; one letter writer stated that,

I've never felt a sense of belonging to either the punk community or the mainstream gay community. Maybe things will start to change now, thanx to *Homocore*.—R., Watertown, MA (#6).

And by issue #6, the fanzine had indeed helped to establish a network of queer punks, becoming a tool that could be used to help create alternative spaces (a lesbian wrote to praise the fanzine as a "great tool for networking" that was informing lesbians of a San Francisco collective) as well as a space in which queer punks could read about and meet each other, forming a national network of correspondents, friendships and, ultimately, a community:

I got your magazine (#4). . .and it has helped me. I've met some neat people across the country and it's helped me realize that I'm not alone, or bad.—T., Creswell, OR (#6)

I'm alone . . . but not alone by a long shot among some 2000 *Homocore* readers—right? Damn poor substitute for friends to hang out with (and be comfortable around) and you can't fuck a letter or a zine, but maybe if I can shift my orientation to being part of a larger community (in my own, anti-social, fucked up way) I can wake up parts of my brain that've been dragging me through semi-lobotomized zombiehood here.—D., IL (#6)

P.S. I have met a lot of cool pen pals through your classifieds, the network is growing.—S., OH (#6).

Over the course of six issues, *Homocore* has come to represent a sense of belonging and identification through the formation of a printed space within which communities of homopunks can exist and communicate, and which can tie together a widely dispersed and different group of people with similar musical interests and sexualities. The letters and the fanzine as a whole construct an emancipatory narrative, detailing the problems of both mainstream adult gay culture and the hardcore scene and establishing a community in which the articulation of homosexuality and hardcore within a set of potential individual and collective identities is not only possible but is celebrated. As with a hardcore fanzine like *Maximum RocknRoll*, *Homocore* constructs a participatory, affirmative community of hardcore fans, and is in the cultural politics of gay and lesbian affirmation, *Homocore* presents and constructs a participatory, affirmative community of homosexual identities. More than any other fanzine, *Homocore* establishes and circulates a wide range of queer punk identities, and the efficacy of its efforts is apparent in its important contribution to the production of a dispersed community of homopunks.

. . . Throughout the period of its emergence, this community has itself been discussed within periodicals of straight hardcore fanzines and mainstream gay periodicals. This re-articulation has occurred in two ways: queer punks have been both identified and recognized as Other by the hardcore and gay communities, as things outside the boundaries of normal activity and social positions, and they have been (at times uncomfortably) incorporated within the structures and discourses of these communities. This is particularly evident in the ways in which queer punk fanzines have been discussed in *Maximum RocknRoll* and *The Advocate*.

In *MRR*, homosexuality has been incorporated within the magazine's established structure, becoming another issue (like sexism, racism, and politics) for discussion within the radical politics of the fanzine. While a minority of the leaders' letters published in *MRR* on gays and lesbians has been overtly homophobic, more have been from either accepting straights (whose acceptance ranges from begrudging to supportive) or gays and lesbians writing to complain about

homophobia or affirm gay and lesbian participation in the scene. In addition, the magazine ran a special issue on sexuality (April 1989, #71) which, like other such special issues, deviated slightly from the regular format in order to focus on sex and to a larger extent on the importance of accepting homosexuality within the hardcore scene. And a few regular *MRR* columnists, who are generally well-known and respected members of the hardcore scene, have come out as lesbian or bisexual in the past few years, often commenting on the similarities between the nonconformity of alternative sexuality and the non-conformity of the punk ethos.

Yet as some homophobic readers' letters published in *MRR* demonstrate, while this is the view sanctioned by the magazine's editors and columnists, the presence and participation of gays and lesbians remains contested. So when the questioning of assumed sexual roles and practices has entered the community constructed around *MRR*, it has done so as an issue that needs wider recognition and acceptance within the structures of the hardcore scene, and not as a radically different or separatist movement (i.e., one that needs its own separate scene). Ultimately, the varied discussion of queer punks in *MRR* problematizes the articulation of punk and sexuality —the queer punk represents a "problem" that needs to be eradicated (for homophobes), a "problem" for straights uneasy with the notion of an empowered homopunk, a "problem" that needs to be confronted (the concerned straight participant's rhetoric of "let's make the scene safe for gays"), and a "problem" of possibility (for gays and lesbians who express displeasure or discomfort in the hardcore scene).

Just as queer punk fanzines have had an impact on the hardcore community, they have also entered into the discourse of gay publications, most notably the mainstream gay male publication *The Advocate*. This is at least partially due to the efforts of Adam Block, the rock critic for the magazine, whose regular column ("Block on Rock") has covered queer punk fanzines a number of times. Block's treatment of these fanzines have emphasized the difference between what he calls the "acceptable" face of gay culture and "the rude, rowdy, radical, or dreamy delinquents" who produce and read fanzines like *J.D.*s and *Homocore* (Block, 1988 and Block, 1990a). But in addition, the participants in the queer punk scene are also presented to *The Advocate*'s readers as objects of gay male desire. This is apparent in Block's reviews of the fanzines, in which no lesbian fanzines are discussed and women's participation in *J.D.*s is never mentioned[18]. Block's review of the first *Homocore* live show similarly ignores the women participating in the bands and in the audience, focusing instead upon the "bare-chested" crowd in the slam pit, and a "humpy Hispanic in black Levi's, tank top, cowboy boots, and hat, who trotted and bobbed his fist around a gargantuan plastic cock and balls that hung from his waist" (Block, 1989). Queer punks are thus re-articulated within the mainstream gay male culture of *The Advocate* as participants in a different and resistant cultural practice who can serve as objectified sexual objects.[19]

This somewhat tense reaction by the relatively assimilationist *Advocate* to the radical sexual and cultural practices of queer punks is quite similar to the magazine's reaction to Queer Nation, and marks the attempt to understand and place within social space such emergent groups and political alliances among non-assimilationist gays and lesbians. As Randy Shilts, one of the most widely recognized writers on gay issues in the straight and assimilationist press and author of *And the Band Played On*, described in an article on the "resurrection of the Gay Movement," "older gay activists" (with which he presumably identifies himself) privately ask themselves about these new queer activists, "What do these people want?" (Shilts, 1990:34). He answers by concluding that what he terms "the queering of America" "is about the gay generation gap and the age-old rebellion of the young against the old." He goes on to argue that this new activism among the young started with "fashion statements" (leather jackets, body piercing, "menacing" haircuts, "fierce" attire, etc.) and then moved into politics, although "as in all things based on fashion, the message of this movement is more in pose than in language." Shilts is thus attempting to limit the possible

meanings of the radical cultural politics of groups like Queer Nation and queer punks: they are young, their rebellion is based upon their age differences from other older gays and lesbians, and their political effectivity is based upon and limited by their activism's basis in "pose," rather than in the more powerful and authentic discourse of language.

By arguing that this new queer "militancy" has been produced by and is limited to age difference, Shilts and *The Advocate* are attempting to represent these (and the representation of this as a singular militancy is also an attempt to limit the set of alliances among heterogeneous groups that constitute Queer Nation, queer punks and others) as inauthentic political movements that are relatively powerless to represent themselves in any coherent or persuasive way in order to demand rights or change the meanings and possibilities of social positions. As I will argue in the concluding section, this attempt to de-legitimate a "younger" generation of gay and lesbian groups like queer punks and Queer Nation ignores the cultural politics involved in the articulation of individual and group identities and the construction of community in these groups' very active engagement in cultural practices.

Queer Punks, the Construction of Community, and the Articulation of Emergent Identities in Cultural Practice

In closing, I want to identify the significance for critical communications studies of the two most significant aspects of the historical development of organized gay and lesbian punk practices: the struggle over identity and the construction of community in cultural practice. In particular, these practices represent the articulation of oppositional cultural politics through engagement with cultural practices—that is, they demonstrate the building of alliances among individuals and groups in relatively dominated social positions through engagement in popular cultural practices. By attempting to legitimate and demand rights for certain cultural forms, practices, and tastes, gay and lesbian punks demonstrate the ways in which culture remains a contested terrain in which relatively dominated groups challenge social and cultural hierarchies through the formation of identity and the building of community.

By identity I mean the recognition and representation by the self, group and others of the often shifting and multiple social positions of the individual and group. It does not simply exist; it is produced in the process by which one recognizes or is recognized as operating from a certain position or set of positions, and in the processes by which those recognitions are themselves objectified through some form of representations (e.g., language, visual symbols, music, etc.). As Stuart Hall argues, "Instead of thinking of identity as an already accomplished fact, . . .we should think instead, of identity as a 'production', which is never complete, always in process, and always constituted within, not outside, representation" (1989:68). In this sense, the discourses of queer punk fanzines are attempting to produce a set of identities for individuals and groups that had previously been invisible, unrepresented and unable to represent themselves. As the letters cited in the beginning of this essay declared, practicing as a gay or lesbian punk—indeed the fact of being a queer punk—was virtually impossible and remains quite difficult in many places. The public articulation[20] of a set of queer punk identities constitutes an attempt to make gay and lesbian punk practices possible. These identities can then be taken up or struggled against by individuals and groups, thus further articulating the meaning and possibility of queer punks. While a set of identities are articulated within the fanzines and other practices of queer punks, their meanings and their possible effectivity are contested as these identities are re-articulated within the hardcore scene and mainstream gay and lesbian culture.

The struggle over the formation and meaning of identity, then, is literally a politics of position, a fight to constitute a meaningful group and individual group identity that enables self-definition and, if constructed at the group level, political efficacy in the ability to

gain recognition, represent itself, and make demands for rights. This is particularly important for dominated groups whose cultural practices are marginalized. For queer punks, the struggle to define and gain recognition for themselves, as well as to demand the ability to attend hardcore shows and to enact their cultural tastes, are struggles to publicly represent and objectify a certain set of cultural positions—to declare and enact the possibilities of queer punks. In addition, this process is a struggle to change the categories of perception and evaluation of the social worlds, to effect the ways in which that position is constituted in social space and the logic by which potential articulations can be made (Bordieu, 1990:134)—in other words, to allow for the existence of and to legitimize queer punks within the hardcore and gay and lesbian communities. The articulation of identity, then, is crucial in the emergent cultural practices of a group in relatively dominated social positions.

The second significant production in these practices is the construction of a form of community based both on locality and the space of the circulated texts of the fanzines. By community I mean a highly symbolized and objectively manifested construct based upon some relatively formal group relationship in which individuals invest (Cohen, 1985:108–110). While the articulation of a set of cultural identities allows for the recognition and representation of specific social positions, the construction of a community of queer punks allows for the formation of social relationships based upon shared practices and tastes and the spaces within which those relationships and practices can form and take place. A crucial aspect of this formation is difference —difference from the dominant sexual practices of the hardcore scene, as well as from the dominant tastes, styles and cultural politics of mainstream gay and lesbian culture.

In this sense, taste and cultural practice play crucial roles in the formation of alliances among individuals and between groups. By participating in a practice (e.g., producing, writing to, or even simply reading a fanzine, playing in a punk band or attending a punk show) and identifying others in similar situations who do so, a particular population can recognize and construct itself as a group. Clearly, because these individuals are in relatively dominated cultural positions as gays and lesbians within the hardcore community and as punks within the gay and lesbian community, the importance of these alliances lie in allowing individuals to represent themselves in fanzines, to establish physical and emotional spaces for themselves in clubs and in the public communication of the letters section of *Homocore*, and to demand rights in the communities in which they are dominated. In this sense, queer punks are attempting to articulate a form of local—or more accurately, locally dispersed—community. By this I mean that in addition to operating at the local level (e.g., San Francisco, Toronto or other places where queer punks might meet), this community also operates in the sense that Tom Jennings invokes, in the opening section of every issue of *Homocore*, "What everyone in *here* has in common" [my emphasis]: the local community of an internationally circulated fanzine and community of fanzines. The constitution of the local, with its connotations of interpersonal relationships, safe borders and shared culture, is thus crucial in the construction of a community of individuals dispersed across space who identify themselves through their engagement in alternative cultural practices.

Having something in "common," then, proves to be a central notion for oppositional cultural practices—in articulating a set of identities and a sense of community, queer punk fanzines and practices help in the ongoing struggle by groups in relatively dominated positions to contest and re-configure their positions in social space and to enhance their possibilities to engage in cultural practice. At stake in the continuing struggle over the re-articulation of these identities within hardcore, dominant gay discourses and dominating social structures are the future meanings and efficacy of these identities and practices and their ability to continue to re-construct the possible meanings for positions and practices in social space.

References

Adam, Barry. 1987. *The rise of a gay and lesbian movement.* Boston: Twayne

Belsito, Peter and Bob Davis. 1983. *Hardcore California: A history of punk and new wave.* San Francisco: Last Gasp.

Ben is Dead. 1989. 'Zine Editors Speak! 8 (9 December 9): 37.

Block, Adam. 1990a. 'Scanning the zine scene. *The Advocate*,30 January,54–55.

———. 1990b. The queen of 'Zine. *The Advocate*, 20 November, 75.

———. 1989. Of Grammys, godheads, and dry dreams.*The Advocate*, 28 March, 47.

———. 1988. In search of the homo-core underground. *The Advocate*, 10 October, 52–53.

Bronski, Michael.1984. *Culture clash: The making of gay sensibility.* Boston: South End.

Cohen, Anthony. 1985. *The symbolic construction of community.* New York: Tavistock.

D'Emilio, John. 1983. *Sexual politics, sexual communities.* Chicago: University of Chicago Press.

Dyer, Richard. 1979. In defence of disco. *Gay Left* #8: 20–23.

Foucault, Michel. 1978. *The history of sexuality: An introduction.* Trans. Robert Hurley. New York: Vantage.

Frith, Simon. 1981. *Sound Effects.* New York: Pantheon.

Gever, Martha. 1990. The names we give ourselves. In *Out there: Marginalization and contemporary Cultures*, eds. Russell Ferguson, Martha Gever, Trinh T. Minh-ha, and Cornel West, 191–202. New York: New Museum of Contemporary Art.

Hall, Stuart. 1989. Cultural identity and cinematic representation." *Framework*, 36: 68–81.

———. 1986. On postmodernism and articulation: An interview with Stuart Hall." *Journal of Communication Inquiry*, 10: 45–60.

Halperin, David M. 1990. *One hundred years of homosexuality.* New York: Routledge.

James, David. 1988. "Hardcore: Cultural resistance in the postmodern." *Film Quarterly*, 42(2): pp. 31–39.

Jennings, Tom. 1990. Tom Jennings" In *Threat by example*, ed. Martin Sprouse, 34–36. San Francisco: Pressure Drop.

King, Katie. 1988. Audre Lord's Lacquered Layerings: The lesbian bar as a site of literary production." *Cultural Studies*, 2(3): 321–342.

Kozak, Roman. 1988. *This ain't no disco: The story of CBGB.* Boston: Faber and Faber.

Laing, Dave. 1985. *One chord wonders*. Milton Keynes: Open University.

Lont, Cynthia A. 1984. *Between a rock and a hard place: Subcultural persistence and women's music*. Unpublished Ph.D. Dissertation, University of Iowa.

Marcus, Greill. 1980. Anarchy in the U.K." In *The Rolling Stone Illustrated History of Rock & Roll*, ed. Jim Miller, 451–463. New York: Random House.

OUT/LOOK. 1991. Birth of a queer nation (special section). 11 (Winter), 12–23.

Robert, Gary, Rob Kulakofsky, and Mike Arrendondo. 1984. *Loud 3D*. San Francisico: IN3D

Robinson, Tom. 1989. A conversation about rock, politics and gays. In *Coming on Strong*, ed. Simon Shepherd and Mick Wallis, 275–286, London: Unwin and Hyman.

Shilts, Randy. 1990. The queering of America: Looking back at 1990 and the resurrection of the gay movement." *The Advocate*, 20 November, 32–39.

Solomon, Alisa. 1991. In whose face? *Village Voice*, 2 July, 28–29,

Stamps, Wickle. 1990. Queer girls with an attitude." *The Advocate* 20 November, 56–57.

Taylor, Lori Elaine. 1990. Positive force of punk: The role of music in creating community and political responsibility. Paper delivered to American Folklore Society Conference, Washington, D.C., October 1990.

Trebay, Guy. 1990. IN YOUR FACE! *Village Voice*, 14 August, 34–39.

Weeks. Jeffrey. 1981. *Sex, Politics, and Society*. London: Longman.

Widgery, David. 1986. *Beating Time*. London: Chatton & Windus.

Notes

1. I am using the term *queer punk* to refer to gay and lesbian punks in the sense that the word *queer* has been re-articulated by Queer Nation and radical gay and lesbian activists because: (1) "queer" notes the coalition of gay and lesbians in homopunk fanzines, and (2) like the fanzines themselves, "queer" celebrates and proclaims the marginality of gay and lesbian punks' social and sexual position. Since the term's re-articulation and its circulation, many of the fanzines have begun to use it. See below for more on Queer Nation.

2. The best single historical account of punk is Laing 1985.

3. The politics of punk were not marked by a unified (or for that matter fully articulated) set of positions or values; indeed, the work that Rock Against Racism had to perform in order to construct such a set (see Widgery, 1986) displays this lack of fit. As Greil Marcus writes, "Punk was an aesthetic and political revolt based in a mass of contradictions that sustained it aesthetically and doomed it politically" (Marcus, 1980: 451).

4. As Simon Frith (1981: 158–59) has argued, this "realism" is punk's central construction and is based as much upon formal conventions as the music against which it was a reaction.

5. In particular, punk fashion greatly influenced lesbian style for both butch and femme roles: for the butch, the erasing of gender differentiation in some punk fashions allowed for a more public display of the role, while for the femme, it "inject[ed] a kind of violent aura into femme chic that made it trashy and threatening instead of submissive and vulnerable to wear a skirt" (cited in Blackman and Perry, 1990: 71).

6. As Sue Steward writes, "Both the hippy idea of free 'permissive' love and the straighter conventions of love, romance and engagement rings were attacked, undermined and repudiated outright. In every way, punk sexuality was angry and aggressive, implicitly feminist" (Steward and Garratt, 1986: 157–58). Yet we should not exaggerate; Tom Robinson, the only self-identified "gay punk" whose music explicitly discussed his sexuality, hardly even considered himself to be in the punk movement (see Robinson, 1989).

7. British punk's direct effects on American rock music have been downplayed in most historical accounts. See, for example, Laing (1985: 115), and Stokes et al (1986: 365). American punk and hardcore are only important to rock historians to the degree to which certain "stars" or "great bands" have arisen from the masses (e.g., L.A.'s X in the late-seventies and Washington, D.C.'s Fugazzi in the early nineties).

8. Tim Yohanna, author's interview, San Francisco, 8/2/90. Kozak (1988: 117) also places 1980–81 as the period in which hardcore began to be used as the label for the newer and younger punk bands.

9. It would be hard, if not impossible, to figure the exact size of the American punk/hardcore community, particularly given its amorphous qualities, but I would estimate that the number of people in the United States who might identify themselves as members of that com-

munity would probably number in the tens of thousands. For accounts of individual scenes, see Belsito and Davis (1983) on California; Taylor (1990) on Washington D.C.; and Kozak (1988) on New York. Robert, Kulakofsky and Arrendondo (1984) and James (1988) attempt to describe and explain the national hardcore scene.

10. See, among others, Foucault (1978), Weeks (1981), Halperin (1990), and Adam (1987).

11. See Weeks (1981) (esp. 185–187) for a fuller discussion of the conditional fixing of continually changing meanings of sexuality and homosexual practices.

12. For more on the role of periodicals from the early homophile organizations of the fifties on, see Bronski (1984). For the importance of dance music and clubs for gays, see Dyer (1979), while for the importance of Women's Music for lesbians, see Lont (1984).

13. For more on Queer Nation, see various articles in *Out/Look* (1991). Solomon (1991), Trebay (1990), and various articles in *Outweek* throughout mid-and late-1990.

14. Interestingly, as Solomon (1991) and a "Homo time line" comic accompanying her article note, radical queer fashion (which includes black leather, Doc Maarten combat boots, and body piercing)—which is very close to punk fashion — has itself become a kind of dominating style on display in gay and lesbian urban ghettos.

15. The history of *Homocore* is based upon the following: author's interview with Jennings, 8/2/90, San Francisco; Walmsley n.d.; Jennings (1990); and *Ben is Dead* (1989).

16. Author's interview, op cit.

17. The first issues have sold out, and Jennings has steadily increased the number of copies in each issue's press run (between 2500 and 3000 copies of #6 were printed).

18. A letter from the New Lavender Panthers to *The Advocate* critically responding to this erasure of lesbian participation was never published there but did appear in *Homocore* #3; Tom Jennings' note accompanying the letter in *Homocore* notes that this "is typical of the usual sexist 'gay community' publications."

19. Interestingly, more recent articles on lesbian fanzines, including a profile of G.B. Jones by Adam Block, have provided more sympathetic representations of lesbian punks than those of gay male punks in Block's earlier reviews of queer punk fanzines. In these more sympathetic articles, being a lesbian punk is presented as possible, though difficult and controversial (they are described as "ostracized," "militant," and "anarchist," and these articles were both included as part of a cover story on the "new militancy" among young homosexuals—all rather charged adjectives and subjects for *The Advocate*). See Stamps (1990) and Block (1990b).

20. As Stuart Hall defines it, articulation is the linkage of social practices within a social field at a specific historical moment just as a speaker links thought and language in order to make a statement (1986: 53–55).

33

The Magazine of a Sadomasochism Club: The Tie That Binds

Rick Houlberg

Houlberg discusses the ways in which a monthly magazine published by a sadomaso-chist club addresses the issues, concerns, and interests of its members. He describes how the magazine provides readers with a sense of community and a way to identify others with similar interests. Moreover, the magazine provides a framework for helping people under-stand themselves. This article demonstrates how a marginalized community of individuals can achieve a greater understanding of their own activities and identities while providing explanations for behaviors that are generally socially disapproved.

The study of sadomasochism has only re-cently emerged as a legitimate endeavor for social researchers. Weinberg (1987:51) stated: "It was not until the late 1970s that a body of sociological research on S&M began to appear." Weinberg goes on to note that ear-lier published research focused on sadism and masochism as individual pathologies and not as interactions between people. Re-cent publications Weinberg argues, differ in issues addressed and in methods used but have as a unifying theme that S/M is "depen-dent upon meanings, which are culturally produced, learned, and reinforced by partici-pation in the S&M subculture" (pp. 51–52). It is the social subcultures of S/M that are now receiving some study (Breslow, Evans and Langley, 1985; 1986; and Naerseen, Hoogveen and Zessen, 1987).

The S/M social subculture of this study is a West Coast sadomasochism club. The Club has over 700 members in two West Coast chapters, and almost 100 other members scattered across the United States, Europe and Australia. The Club produces a monthly magazine, and in each issue the Club's mani-fest is detailed. In addition to educating the public in the "understanding, interpretation, and appreciation of erotic art by providing commentary and literary review of eroticism in the arts," the Club will conduct lectures and group discussions in order to foster "the development of understanding and apprecia-tion of erotic art" and the improvement of communication between erotic artists and the public. Finally, the Club provides instruc-tion in the use of interpersonal erotic "psy-chodrama as a means to explore, share, and express erotic fantasy.". . .

The only "cardinal" rules which the Club's membership insists each member must up-hold are that all S/M activities must be con-sensual, non-exploitative, and safe. All chil-dren are not considered to be able to consent, all activities must be between adults. The consensual and safety rules of the Club are constantly being reinforced. Safety and eti-quette issues, including restrictions on overt and heavy drug use, are strongly stressed at new-member orientations and in all written materials produced by the Club. . . .

The Club's Magazine

This study focuses on the Club's Magazine as a means of understanding the subculture represented within the Club. The Magazine is a periodic, primarily monthly, print publi-cation which contains letters, stories, re-ports, poems, and photographs from Club members; financial, membership, and busi-ness meeting actions; reports from Club offi-cers; and material from non-members such as reprints of newspaper articles and reports from other S/M organizations.

The publication was selected for study be-cause: (a) The Magazine is the only recorded organizational history containing records as membership reports and business meeting actions; (b) the publication provides a medi-ated forum for reflecting the S/M interests of

Club members (stories, poems, photographs, interviews, etc.); (c) major conflicts within the Club, such as resource allocation and the dominance of one chapter over another, are played out in the Magazine; (d) approximately 15% of the Club's members reside more than one hour's drive from the two West Coast chapters and the publication is their *only* contact with the Club; and (e) the Magazine's editor is an important gatekeeper and an officer of the Club. . . .

Definitions

Some definitions will be helpful in understanding this report. A "scene" is an event in which two or more people engage in some type of "erotic power transference" for a predetermined period of time. The terms S/M (sadomasochism), B/D (bondage and discipline), and D/S (dominance and submission) will be used somewhat interchangeably. "Vanilla" is a term used to indicate heterosexual, middle-of-the-road, generally accepted sexual activity sanctioned by a majority of the general population and devoid of experimentation. The person engaged in a "scene" who is "in control" is called a "top," "master," or "mistress"; the person being controlled is termed a "bottom," "submissive," or "slave" (although, in fact, both actors are engaged in control, power transference, and the direction of the "scene").

Method

A descriptive content analysis by theme (Stempel and Westley, 1981; Wimmer and Dominick, 1986) was completed on 47 issues of the Magazine published by the Club between October 1983 and January 1988. The somewhat discontinuous nature of this monthly publication, which published 47 issues over a 52-month period, is due to its dependence totally on a volunteer production staff. Utilizing descriptive categories, a numeric analysis was completed on the contents of the 47 issues. . . .

The December 1987 issue of the Magazine contained a 26-question survey as a means of gathering information about the publication's future. The survey was initiated by the Club in response to internal organizational conflict between the two West Coast chapters. The January 1988 issue of the publication contained the survey results as 358 readers responded (representing 44% of the 812 dues-paying members). The survey results are used to support the content analysis.

As a supplement to the content analysis and the readership survey, this report includes information gathered by the author as a nonparticipant-observer of the Club's activities during the period covered by this study. The author attended a mandatory orientation session and approximately four program meetings each calendar year. The author discussed the Club and the Magazine with Club members during the orientation and programs.

Magazine Format

From October 1983 to January 1987, 35 issues of the Magazine were produced in a magazine format sized 7 inches by 8 inches. In this format, the issues averaged 27.5 pages per issue, with a range of 22 pages to 46 pages. In February 1987, the Magazine's editor adopted a new format to allow for the easy use of desk-top publication computer software. The editor claimed the new format would be cost effective and would allow for a "more glitzy" publication. From February 1987 through January 1988, the format size changed to 8 inches by 11 inches, the issues averaged 16 pages, and the range was from 8 to 20 pages. All issues were black ink on white paper stock.

Readership Survey Results

Almost the entire content of the January 1988 issue of the Magazine was dedicated to the results of the December 1987 readership survey. . . .

The first seven questions of the readership survey were concerned with the Magazine's continuation and format. When asked if the Magazine should be eliminated, 10 readers marked "yes" and 339 marked "no." Four format questions elicited similar response patterns as the elimination question, with the vast majority of responses supporting the magazine format adopted in February 1987. . . .

Content Analysis Results

The content analysis results of the 47 issues are reported under seven subject content areas: media reviews, poetry, S/M issues, how-to articles, photography, stories, and organizational reports. The seven areas are reported starting with the smallest amount of space utilized per category and continuing to the largest amount of space used.

Media Reviews

Reviews of books, films and videos with S/M themes appeared in about every second issue of the Magazine, averaged .5 items per issue, and accounted for about 2% of the space in the Magazine. Included in this category were reviews of S/M related story lines on "Hill Street Blues" (February 1986—all reference dates for materials from the Magazine refer to the publication date of that issue) and the "Oprah Winfrey Show" (August 1987), and the best locations near the two Club chapters to purchase books, movies and other S/M media materials. The readership respondents overwhelmingly indicated the media reviews category should be retained by a vote of 304 to 13.

Poetry

Poems appeared an average of 1.2 times per issue, with a range of no poems in several issues to six poems in one issue, and accounted for about 5% of the Magazine's space. Poems tended to concentrate on the feelings (both physical and emotional) expressed by a "top" or "bottom" with regard to a "scene." Several poems were written by "slaves" to their "masters" or "mistresses." The readership respondents indicated poems were least favored content area with 139 votes for continuation, while 131 voted against continuation.

S/M Issues

Several types of S/M issue related articles appeared in the Magazine between 1983 and 1988. S/M issue articles and columns averaged 1.5 items per issue, ranged from a low of none in three issues to a high of six in two issues, and accounted for about 10% of the Magazine's space. Among the various discussions included in this category were long-term S/M relationships (June 1985), different levels of dominance (November 1985), masochistic "survival" (February 1985), a definition of torture (June 1985), and definitions of S/M terms (June 1985).

One recurring interest area was the concept that D/S was a more inclusive term than S/M. As noted in an October/November 1984 article:

> D/S is a broader term inclusive of S/M just as both are included in a still broader category of 'creative sexuality.' While inclusive of S/M, D/S is not higher or better than S/M. On the contrary, S/M is a special (some feel 'elite') subgroup within the broader context of D/S.

In July 1985 another writer agreed to the ideas expressed in the October/November 1984 article and added: "D/S doesn't have to be physically rough, nor does it require pain, fetishes—or even sex!"

Legal action against people engaged in S/M activities were reported. Information about a Sacramento, California, professional dominant who had been arrested for prostitution was included in issues starting with October 1983 and running until the middle of 1985. The cases of a Pennsylvania couple and a Michigan couple who ran into problems with the legal authorities were included in 1985 and 1986.

When asked about reporting legal actions, 289 respondents marked "yes," while 22 respondents marked "no." The readers also responded they wanted "reprints of S/M materials from non-members" by a 244 to 37 margin, and they responded with 280 "yes" and 18 "no" when asked about inclusion of "clippings of relevant S/M materials."

How-to Information

How-to information appeared in virtually every issue. This category averaged 2.4 items per issue, ranged from no items in one issue to seven items in six issues, and took up about 12% of the Magazine's space. How-to article titles indicated the subject matter, including: "Building Clothes Pins with a Screw Device" (October/November 1983) for attaching to a "bottom's" body, "Fur Braiding" (January 1985) for braiding rope in pubic hair, and "An Example of a Slavery Contract" (November 1986). In the how-to category, safety and health issues received a great deal of attention. The health problems related to AIDS received the most attention.

A readership survey question asking if how-to articles "doing S/M" articles should be included received an overwhelmingly positive response with 320 readers marking "yes" and 15 respondents marking "no."

Photography

Over the 47 issues which were content analyzed, the average was 7.5 photographs per issue, the range was no photographs in nine issues to 39 photographs in the October/November 1984 issues, and these images accounted for 14% of the Magazine's space. The photographs were primarily of erotic images by members and of local and national S/M events.

Accounting for almost half of all photographs, erotic images included one or more individuals tied in tight bondage with various devices attached to their bodies. Other photographs included both the "top" and the "bottom" at play in either private or public settings. Facial expressions ranged from the exhibitionist who seemed pleased that his or her picture was being taken, to the grimaces of "bottoms" who were in some type of painful scene.

Results of the readership survey indicated members wanted "erotic photographs by members" by a rate of 283 "yes" to 23 "no," and "photos of local or national S/M events" by a margin of 229 "yes" to 52 "no."

Stories

Stories, both real and fantasy, averaged 1.5 per issue, ranged from no stories in five issues to three stories in three issues, and accounted for 17% of the Magazine's space.

Fantasy stories tended to fall into those with "vanilla" titles and with very explicit titles. The first group included stories titled "Wednesday Afternoon" (May 1985) and "The Plan" (May 1987). More explicit titles included "Nocturnal Emissions from a Submissive" (August 1984) and "Scat'n Shower Delights" (October 1987) focusing on scatological and "golden shower" interests.

Stories of real scenes tended to be forthright in their titles, subject matter, and accompanying photographs. One real column, titled "A Slave Girl Writes," was included in five 1985 issues and was written by female "slaves." "Viola's Slave Diary" was included in the October through December 1987 issues. As noted earlier, all the stories were copyrighted with 93% including an author's name and 7% indicating the Club held the copyright.

"Erotic fiction" should be included by a vote of the readers of 297 to 25, and "real-life S/M experiences" should be continued by a response of 297 "yes" to 25 "no."

Organization

The largest content category, both in terms of space and number of items was devoted to Club organizational activities. Organizational items accounted for an average of 6.5 items per issue, ranged from 3 items in four issues to 12 items in 9 issues, and accounted for 40% of the Magazine's space.

Among the most common organization reports were: Complete monthly statements from the Club's treasurer, a column from the reports from the editor, reports from the Club's coordinator(s), membership reports, and extensive reports from the Communication Secretary (July 1984 to November 1987) or "Comm Sexy" as the column was signed. . . .

The Magazine reported on Club sponsored meetings. Approximately two theme programs were presented by the Club each month during the period of this study. The subjects of these programs, as presented in the Magazine's coverage, included: an ask-a-lawyer discussion (October/November 1984), a flagellation discussion/demonstration (December 1984), a founders' panel (February 1985), a body piercing demonstration (October/November 1984), a use of electricity demonstration (December 1985), an ask-a-chiropractor discussion (January 1987), a male genital torture discussion/demonstration (April 1987), and various panels by and about dominance and submission (March 1985, July 1985, and August/September 1985).

Several readership survey questions asked about organizational presentations in the Magazine. When asked if the readers wanted to read about "local club events and programs," 296 marked "yes" and 22 marked "no." When asked about the inclusion of the "Treasurer's reports and other club business reports," the respondents marked "yes" 171 times and "no" was checked by 86 readers. Even "classified or display advertising" should be kept in the Magazine according to 295 respondents who marked "yes" as opposed to the 12 readers who marked "no.". . .

Editors

All four of the Magazine's editors who worked during this study called for contributions to the Magazine by the Club's members, and they all stressed the participatory nature of the publication. One editor called in June 1985 for more members' input and then promised to "remain aware of the printed word's iconic powers and to remain sensitive to members' feelings." Another editor called in 1987 for material which was not mediocre but was "brought to life by being handled with verve, originality and some skill." The problem, that editor continued, was trite storylines and "doggerel" poetry that tended to make the contributions less interesting.

One editor indicated in October 1986 his editorial stance by writing that the Magazine was a tool for communicating. In a particularly lucid moment, this editor wrote about the worth of the publication:

[The Magazine] brings the membership an arena of common experience and concern. Each month of appearance is evidence of our energy and our pride—and our power. Because it is controlled by us, [the Magazine] can tell the evolving truth: no advertisers, governmental agencies, or professional practitioners! . . .We know the feelings of guilt, bewilderment, and isolation; we also know freedom and happiness when we can admit, discuss and demonstrate those feelings. [The Club] and [the Magazine], if you will, smooth a few steps on the road to happiness

This editor went on to explain the publication operates as the only legacy and historical document of the organization, and about half of the yearly dues go into the support of the publication.

Discussion

. . .In addition to being the only repository of the Club's history and the importance of the Magazine to individual members, the publication may serve to help create "shared meaning" for Club members. . . .As stated by one Magazine editor, "Through [the Magazine], we share experiences which few people in the world understand, and develop new vocabulary and concepts. Shared, our experiences become a legacy for every newcomer" (October 1986). The Magazine's editors and readers seem to agree that the publication is vital and provides opportunities to explain and explore their sadomasochistic experiences.

The "shared" experiences of Club members which is chronicled in the Magazine is a legacy to increasing numbers of Club members. During the period of this investigation, October 1983 to January 1988, the Club's membership increased by over 400%. The change in membership was of type as well as number. During the author's discussions with long-time members and through the author's nonparticipant observations of the audience composition for Club programs, the Club's membership was primarily male homosexuals at the end of 1983. Indeed, members' comments indicated, male gays comprised virtually the entire membership between Club's founding in 1974 and the early 1980's. From 1983 to 1988, a dramatic increase of both gay and heterosexual women was witnessed at program meetings. Male-female couples were at the end of this study about one third of all participants at program meetings. By the start of 1988, a majority of the Club members were heterosexual men, women and couples; of course, many members were still homosexual men and women. . . .

An issue highlighted through this research concerns the forces acting on an organization dedicated to alternative sexual practices. Contained in the Club's purpose statement is that the organization should attempt to help the public understand the S/M subcultures.

Yet access to the Club and its Magazine is restricted. Only dues-paying Club members receive the publication, copyright and confidentiality statements are prominent in the Magazine, entrance into programs and meetings is granted to card-carrying members and their guests only, and most members use either an S/M "name" or are called by their first names. Personal questions about a member's employment and residence, even in the most general terms, are greeted with some suspicion. The call for public education is clearly restrained by the need for individual members to retain some measure of privacy as a means of escaping scorn. . . .

References

Breslow, B., Evans, L., and Langley, J. (1985). "On the prevalence and roles of females in the sadomasochistic subculture: Report of an empirical study. *Archives of Sexual Behavior,* 14(4), 303–317.

Breslow, B., Evans, L., and Langley, J. (1986). "Comparisons among heterosexual, bisexual, and homosexual male sado-masochists. *Journal of Homosexuality,* 13(1), 83–107.

Naerseen, A.X. van, Dijk, M. van, Hoogveen,G., and Zessen, G. van (1987). Gay SM in pornography and reality. *Journal of Homosexuality,* 12(2/3), 111–119.

Stempel, G.H. and Westley, B.H. (Eds.), (1981). *Research methods in mass communication.* Englewood Cliffs, NJ: Prentice-Hall.

Weinberg, T.S. (1987). Sadomasochism in the United States: A review of recent sociological literature. *The Journal of Sex Research,* 23(1), 50–69.

Wimmer, R.D., and Dominick, J.R. (1986). *Mass media research: An introduction.* Belmont, CA: Wadsworth.

34

'Just Every Mother's Angel': An Analysis of Gender and Ethnic Variations in Youth Gang Membership

Karen A. Joe
Meda Chesney-Lind

Joe and Chesney-Lind consider the pressures that compel minority teenagers to join youth gangs. Contrary to popular stereotypes, the authors find that juveniles turn to gangs to find the security and sense of belonging they lack in their lives. Although crime and violence do exist within youth gangs, members think of these groups as family. This article shows how the social context in which they live can compel people to engage in deviant behaviors, just to survive. Moreover, the authors explain how actions that might appear deviant to outsiders are often engaged in by individuals trying to achieve some normalcy in their lives.

Official estimates of the number of youth involved in gangs have increased dramatically over the past decade. Currently, more than 90 percent of the nation's largest cities report youth gang problems, up from about half in 1983. Police estimates now put the number of gangs at 4,881 and the number of gang members at approximately 249,324 (Curry et al. 1992). As a result, public concern about the involvement of young men in gang activity, and the perceived violence associated with this lifestyle, has soared. The role of young men of color in these official estimates of gang activity, to say nothing of the public stereotypes of gangs, can hardly be overstated. Indeed, with nearly half (47 percent) of African American males between the ages of 21 and 24 finding their way into the police gang database in Los Angeles (Reiner 1992), *gang* has become a code word for race in the United States (Muwakkil 1993).

But what of girls and young women? The stereotype of the delinquent is so indisputably male that the police, the general public, and even those in criminology who study delinquency, rarely, if ever, consider girls and their problems with the law. Connell (1987) describes this process as the "cognitive purification" of social cleavages. Moore (1991), writing about the impact of this process on the public perception of gang activity, notes that media images of gangs "sharpen and simplify" middle-class notions of what constitutes lower-class maleness (p. 137).

Occasionally, girls and women do surface in media discussions of gangs and delinquency, but only when their acts are defined as either very bad or profoundly evil. The media's intense interest in "girls in gangs" (see Chesney-Lind 1993), which actually revisits earlier efforts to discover the liberated "female crook" (Adler 1975, 42), is lodged within the larger silence about the situation of young women of color on the economic, political, and judicial margins. The absence of any sustained research on these girls means there is often little with which to refute sensationalistic claims about their involvement in violence and gangs, as well as very little understanding of why they are in gangs.

There is a clear need, then, to balance, sharpen, and focus our analytical lenses on gender and ethnic variations in youth gang participation. Toward this end, this article first examines the place of gender in theoretical discussions on gangs and delinquency, and suggests that the most immediate task is to understand the role of masculinities and femininities in gang involvement. We then provide a general overview of the geographical setting of our current gang study, particularly in relation to ethnicity, economy, and crime. Next we report the findings from our in-depth interviews with 48 boys and girls from a number of ethnic gangs in Hawaii. We found that although boy and girl members faced common problems, they dealt with these in ways that are uniquely informed by both gender and ethnicity; moreover, consistent with previous ethnographic research, we found that delinquent and criminal activities in boys' gangs have been so exaggerated that it has prevented an understanding of the many ways that the gang assists young women and men in coping with their lives in chaotic, violent, and economically marginalized communities.

Masculinity and Gangs

Historically, the gang phenomenon and its association with youth violence has been defined and understood as a quintessentially male problem. This analytical focus first emerged in the pioneering work of Thrasher (1927) and continued in the same fashion with subsequent generations of gang researchers. During the second wave of research on gangs in the 1950s and early 1960s, the "gang problem" as "male" was even more clearly articulated (Cloward and Ohlin 1960; Cohen 1955; Miller 1958). The only point of difference among these researchers was found in their explanation as to why such delinquent peer groups and their distinctive subculture emerged among boys living in poor communities.

According to Cohen (1955), boys in lower-class communities suffer from "status frustration" because of their inability to succeed by middle-class standards. Ill-equipped to compete in school with their middle-class counterparts, they reject middle-class values and develop a delinquent subculture that emphasizes nonutilitarianism, malice, and negativism. These alternative values justify their manly aggression and hostility and become the basis for group solidarity. Miller (1958) contends, however, that the value gang boys place on "toughness, smartness, excitement, and cunning" is part of lower-class culture where boys and men are constantly struggling to maintain their autonomy in

households dominated by women. Cloward and Ohlin (1960) counter this "culture of poverty" explanation and adopt a structural framework for understanding gang subculture in lower-class communities. Lower-class boys are blocked from legitimate, and in some cases, illegitimate opportunities, and as a result, rationally choose from among their limited options to engage in particular types of crime. Again, though, all these researchers assume gangs to be a uniquely young men's response to the pressures and strains of poverty.

After this work, research on the gang phenomena fell out of fashion, even though the few studies done during that period document the fact that gangs continued to be a feature of life in poor, minority communities (Moore 1978; Quicker 1983). The economic dislocation of these communities during those decades of silence meant that gang cliques gradually found a place in the underclass (Hagedorn 1988; Moore 1991). In this context, a number of researchers attribute the involvement of young men in gangs and crime (as in organized drug sales) primarily to the material advantages a collective can bring in an environment with fewer and fewer legitimate options (Jankowski 1991; Skolnick et al. 1989; Taylor 1990). Others (Hagedorn 1988; Moore 1991; Waldorf 1993), however, have found little evidence to support the notion that gangs are lucrative business enterprises. In other words, the reasons for membership are far more complex and varied, because gangs flourish while clearly failing to provide their members with a ticket out of poverty.

In this connection, how are we to interpret the role of violence and the subcultural emphasis on toughness and bravado in boys' gangs described by earlier as well as later generations of researchers? Jankowski (1991) believes that gang violence and the defiant attitude of these young men is connected with the competitive struggle in poor communities.

The violence associated with members of gangs emerges from low-income communities where limited resources are aggressively sought by all, and where the residents view violence as a natural state of affairs. There the defiant individualist gang member, being a product of his environment, adopts a Hobbesian view of life in which violence is an integral part of the state of nature (p. 139).

In the end, Jankowski's argument is actually little more than a revisiting of the culture of poverty arguments of the late 1950s, with all of the flaws associated with that perspective (Ryan 1972). Of greater concern, though, is the fact that such characterizations "totalize" a range of orientations toward violence found among gang youth (Hagedorn 1992). Such generalizations are not only insensitive to the critical differences among individuals and groups, but they also result in a one-sided, unidimensional understanding of the lives of gang members; moreover, policymakers, the police. And the media are likely to interpret these findings precisely in that way, and the notion that "one bad ass is just like the next" becomes a justification for repressive, and ultimately racist, social control policies.

A far more promising theoretical avenue is found in recent discussions about masculinities and crime that examine the "varieties of real men" in relation to their differential access to power and resources (Connell 1987; Messerschmidt 1986, 1993). These authors move beyond the culture of poverty thesis, recognizing that manly displays of toughness are not a rebellious reaction to "the female-headed household" nor an inherent value of lower-class culture (Miller 1958). Instead, they have widened the lenses by adopting a structural approach, which locates such acts of manliness within the broader economic and social class context. Specifically, Messerschmidt (1993) argues that social structures situate young men in relation to similar others so that collectively they experience the world from a specific position and differentially construct cultural ideas of hegemonic masculinity»that is, dominance, control, and independence. Young minority males living in economically dislocated communities, "are typically denied masculine status in the educational and occupational spheres, which are the major sources of masculine status available to men in white middle class communities and white working class communities" (Messerschmidt 1993,

112). This denial of access to legitimate resources creates the context for heightened public and private forms of aggressive masculinity.

As Katz (1988) calls it, "street elite posturing" (e.g., displays of essential toughness, parading) represents one cultural form of public aggressiveness and is a gender resource for young minority men to accomplish masculinity. Similarly, acts of intimidation and gang violence by marginalized young men are not simply an expression of the competitive struggle in dislocated neighborhoods, but a means for affirming self-respect and status. These are cultural forms that celebrate man-hood and "solve the gender problem of accountability" in increasingly isolated poor communities (Messerschmidt 1993, 111). The "street," then, becomes both a battleground and a theater dominated by young minority men doing gender (Connell 1987).

Girls, Femininity, and Gangs

Gang research generally has assumed that delinquency among marginalized young men is somehow an understandable, if not "normal," response to their situations. How are we to understand the experience of girls who share the same social and cultural milieu as delinquent boys? Despite seven decades of research on boys' gangs and crime, there has been no parallel trend in research on girls' involvement in gang activity. As Campbell (1990) correctly points out, the general tendency to minimize and distort the motivations and roles of girl gang members is the result of the gender bias on the part of male gang researchers, who describe the girls' experience from the boy gang member's viewpoint. The long-standing "gendered habits" of researchers have meant that girls' involvement with gangs has been neglected, sexualized, and oversimplified. Girl members typically are portrayed as maladjusted tomboys or sexual chattel who, in either case, are no more than mere appendages to boy members of the gang. Collectively, they are perceived as an "auxiliary" or "satellite" of the boys' group, and their participation in delinquent activities (e.g., carrying weapons) is explained in relation to the boys (see Brown

1977; Flowers 1987; Miller 1975, 1980; Rice 1963).

This pattern was undoubtedly set by Thrasher (1927), who spent about one page out of 600 discussing the five or six female gangs he found. A more recent example of the androcentrism of gang researchers comes from Jankowski's (1991) widely cited *Islands in the Streets*, which contains the following entries in his index under "Women":@BL = "and codes of conduct"

- individual violence over
- as "property"
- and urban gangs

One might be tempted to believe that the last entry might refer to girl gangs, but the "and" in the sentence is not a mistake. Girls are simply treated as the sexual chattel of male gang members or as an "incentive" for boys to join the gang (because "women look up to gang members") (Jankowski 1991, 53). Jankowski's work as well as other current discussions of gang delinquency actually represents a sad revisiting of the sexism that characterized the initial efforts to understand visible lower-class boy delinquency decades earlier.

Taylor's (1993) work *Girls, Gangs, Women and Drugs* goes a step further to provide a veneer of academic support for the media's definition of the girl gang member as a junior version of the liberated female crook of the 1970s. It is not clear exactly how many girls and women he interviewed for his book, but the introduction clearly sets the tone for his work: "We have found that females are just as capable as males of being ruthless in so far as their life opportunities are presented. This study indicates that females have moved beyond the status quo of gender repression." (Taylor 1993, 8). His work then goes on to stress the similarities between boys' and girls' involvement in gangs, despite the fact that when the girls and women he interviews speak, it becomes clear that such a view is oversimplified. Listen, for example, to Pat in answer to a question about "problems facing girls in gangs":

If you got a all girls crew, um, they think you're "soft" and in the streets if you soft,

it's all over. Fellas think girls is soft, like Rob, he think he got it better in his shit cause he's a fella, a man. It's wild, but fellas really hate seeing girls getting off. Now, some fellas respect the power of girls, but most just want us in the sack (Taylor 1993, 118).

Presently there are a small but important number of studies that move beyond stereotypical notions about these girls as simply the auxiliaries of boy gangs to more careful assessments of the lives of these girls (Campbell 1984, 1990; Fishman 1988; Harris 1988; Lauderback, Hansen, and Waldorf 1992; Moore 1991; Quicker 1983). Of particular significance are those elements of girl gangs that provide them with the skills to survive in their harsh communities while also allowing them to escape at least for a while, from the dismal future that awaits them.

These ethnographies document the impact of poverty, unemployment, deterioration, and violence in the communities where these young women live. The girls share with the boys in their neighborhoods the powerlessness and hopelessness of the urban underclass. . . .

Their situation is further aggravated by the patriarchal power structure of their bleak communities. They find themselves in a highly gendered community where the men in their lives, although not traditional breadwinners, still act in ways that dramatically circumscribe the possibilities open to them. . . .

None of these accounts confirm the stereotype of the hyper-violent, amoral girls found in media accounts of girls in gangs. Certainly they confirm the fact that girls do commit a wider range of delinquent behavior than is stereotypically recognized, but these offenses appear to be part of a complex fabric of "hanging out," "partying," and the occasional fight in defending one's friends or territory. These ethnographies also underscore that although the "streets" may be dominated by young men, girls and young women do not necessarily avoid the "streets," as Connell (1987) suggests. The streets reflect the strained interplay between race, class, and gender.

For those with the conventional criminological perspective on gender, girls engaged in what are defined as "male," activities such as violent crime or gang delinquency are seen as seeking "equality" with their boy counterparts (see Daly and Chesney-Lind 1988). Is that what is going on? A complete answer to that question requires a more careful inquiry into the lives of these girls and the ways in which the gang facilitates survival in their world. Their lives are more complex than simple rebellion against traditional notions of femininity, and are heavily shaped by an array of economic, educational, familial, and social conditions and constraints. A focus on the meaning of the gang in girls' lives also means that comparisons with the experiences of the young men in their neighborhoods who are also being drawn to gangs will be possible. Our intent, then, is to move beyond the traditional, gender specific analyses of contemporary gangs to a more nuanced understanding of the ways in which gender, race, and class shape the gang phenomenon.

Social Setting

Ethnicity

Hawaii is probably the most ethnically diverse state. The largest population groups are Japanese American (25 percent), European American (33 percent), Filipino American (13.9 percent), and Hawaiian/part-Hawaiian (17 percent); other non-Caucasian ethnic groups compose the rest of the population (Department of Business and Economic Development and Tourism 1993). Although Hawaii is ethnically diverse, it is not without racial or ethnic tensions. Class and ethnic divisions tend to reflect the economic and political power struggles of the state's past as a plantation society as well as its current economic dependence on mass tourism. In this mix, recent immigrants as well as the descendants of the island's original inhabitants are among the most dispossessed; consequently, youth actively involved in gangs are drawn predominantly from groups that have recently immigrated to the state (Samoans and Filipinos) or from the increasingly marginalized Native Hawaiian population.

Crime in Hawaii

Despite its image, Hawaii has many of the same crime problems as other states. In 1991, Hawaii ranked fortieth out of the fifty states in overall crime, but eighth in terms of property crime victimization. In the city and county of Honolulu, the nation's eleventh largest city (Federal Bureau of Investigation 1992, 79–106), where three quarters of the state's population lives and the state's capital of Honolulu is located, the pattern is much the same. Oahu's total crime rate is slightly more than half the national average for cities between 500,000 and 1 million (6,193 per 100,000 versus 9,535.1 per 100,000 nationally), but the state's property crime rate is considerably closer to the national average (Crime Prevention Division 1993). Previous research (Chesney-Lind and Lind 1986) has linked part of the property crime problem in the state to the presence of tourists.

Like other major cities, Honolulu has witnessed a rapid growth in police estimates of gang activity and gang membership. In 1988, the Honolulu police (HPD) estimated that there were 22 gangs with 450 members. In 1991, the number of gangs climbed to 45 with an estimated membership of 1,020. By 1993, the number of gangs reached 171 with 1,267 members (Office of Youth Services 1993).

Methodology

Hawaii policymakers, concerned about the trends in gang membership reported by the HPD, enacted legislation to develop a statewide response to youth gangs. Previous evaluations of this system included a quantitative assessment of the youth included in HPD's gang database, and it also compared arrest patterns among officially labeled gang members with those of, non-gang members. The results of that study, which are reported elsewhere (Chesney-Lind et al. 1992), suggest that stereotypes regarding gang members' involvement in serious criminal behavior are just that. Both boys and girls labeled by police as gang members are chronic, but not necessarily violent, offenders; moreover, the research raised serious questions about the assumed criminogenic character of gangs and underscored the need for a more qualitative understanding of gang membership among boys and girls.

Toward this end, in-depth interviews with 48 self-identified gang members were conducted from August 1992 through May 1993. The sample included interviews with 35 boys and 13 girls. Respondents were recruited through a snowball sampling technique (Watters and Biernacki 1989) from referrals provided by the interviewers' personal contacts as well as agency and school staff who work closely with high-risk youngsters. Four young people refused to be interviewed. Interviews were conducted in a wide variety of locations, and none were held in closed institutions. Interviewers were selected based on their knowledge about local culture and the streets and, when possible, matched according to gender.

The interview instrument was derived from similar research efforts in San Francisco (Waldorf 1993) and modified for use in Hawaii. The interview consisted of two parts in which the youth first responded to social survey questions regarding personal and familial characteristics, self-reported delinquency, and contact with the juvenile justice system. The second half of the interview was more qualitative in nature. Here, the informant responded to a series of open-ended questions regarding his or her gang's history, its organization, activities, membership roles, and his or her involvement with the group, and interaction with family, community, and police.

Gangs, Ethnicity, and Culture in Hawaii

The respondents are predominantly male (although we specifically sought out female gang members), and they are from "have-not" ethnic groups: the males are largely of Filipino (60 percent) or Samoan (23 percent) background. Slightly less than half of the boys were born in another country. The majority of the girls are Samoan (61 percent) or Filipino (25 percent) and born in the United States. The boys in the interview sample are slightly older than the girls; the mean age is 16.7 years for the boys interviewed, and 15.3 years for the girls. The average age of our sample is younger than the young adults found in HPD's gang database, partially because of our reliance on agency and school-based referrals. Most of the boys (94 percent) and all of the girls said they were attending school.

The majority of boys (60 percent) and girls (69 percent) live with both parents and are dependent on them for money-though about a third of the boys also work. About one fourth of the boys and girls report stealing to obtain money. Their family lives are not without problems—over half (55 percent) of the boys and three quarters of the girls report physical abuse. In addition, 62 percent of the girls state that they have been sexually abused or sexually assaulted.

Over 90 percent of the boys and three quarters of the girls were arrested, some many times. Indeed, more than a quarter of the boys and almost the same proportion (23 percent) of girls report being arrested 10 or more times. Boys committed a wider range of offenses than girls, with the most frequent being property offenses, vandalism, violent offenses, and weapons offenses. Girls were as likely to report status offense arrests as criminal offenses, but about a third of the girls were arrested for a violent crime. Both boys and girls say peer pressure was a major reason for their involvement in criminal activities, but boys were more likely than girls to mention needing money as a reason for their illegal activities.

All respondents described the visible presence of gangs in their neighborhoods, and in most cases, a family member could provide them with firsthand knowledge about gangs. Virtually all of the girls (90 percent) and boys (80 percent) had a family member, usually a sibling, who belonged to a gang. In terms of their own experiences with the gang, boys tended to be slightly older than the girls when they joined (respectively, 14 compared to 12), and despite popular conceptions, few respondents said that "joining" involved "initiation" or "jumping in." The boys' gangs were larger than the girls' groups, with 45 percent of the boys indicating that their group included 30 or more members. By contrast, almost half of the girls said their gangs had between 10 and 20 members, compared to only 23 percent of the boys.

Although the interviews were done with individual gang members, it is important to know that gangs in the Islands tend to be ethnically organized and generally exclusively male or female. Filipino youth and Samoan youth tend to share the stresses of immigration; these include language difficulties, parentalization, and economic marginality. Beyond this, though, the cultures are very different. Samoan culture is heavily influenced by the Polynesian value system of collective living, communalism, and social control through family and village ties. In Samoa, although contact with the West has been present for a considerable period, there is still a clear and distinct Samoan culture to be found (unlike Hawaii). Samoan adults drawn from this traditional, communal society experience cultural shock upon immigration when poverty forces isolation, frustration, and accommodation to a materialistic, individualistic society. As their children begin to feel caught between two very different systems of values, and as the village system of social controls weakens, the pressures and problems in Samoan families multiply. Gender relations in traditional Samoan families are heavily regulated by Polynesian traditions of separation, obligation, and male dominance, while girls and women have always found ways to circumvent the most onerous of these regulations (Linnekin 1990).

In contrast, Filipino immigrants come from a culture that has already been affected by centuries of colonialism. As a consequence, the Philippines is a myriad of discrete ethnic cultures that have been reshaped by Spanish and U.S. conquest and occupation. Of the many costs attending colonialism, one of the most insidious is that many Filipinos feel ambivalent about the value of their own culture. In addition, although pre-Hispanic women in the Philippines were dynamic and vital members of their ethnic groups, girls in modem Filipino families are affected by the impact of colonial cultural and religious (largely Catholic) norms that stress the secondary status of women, a girl's responsibility to her family, and a concern for regulating female sexual experimentation (Aquino 1994; Lebra 1991). Boys, on the other hand, are given considerable freedom to roam, though they are expected to work hard, do well in school, and obey their parents. The downward mobility, over employment, and cultural shock experienced by many adult Filipinos put special pressures on the cultural values of filial obligation and strains relationships with both sons and daughters.

Native Hawaiians have much in common with other Native American groups as well as with African Americans. Their culture was severely challenged by the death and disease that attended contact with the West in the eighteenth century. Until very recently, Hawaiian was a dying language, and many Hawaiians were losing touch with anything that resembled Hawaiian culture. Hawaiians, like urbanized Native Americans and low-income African Americans, have accommodated to poverty by normalizing early motherhood; high rates of high school dropout; and welfare dependency for girls and high rates of drug dependency, crime, and physical injury for Hawaiian boys.

Living in Chaotic Neighborhoods: Common Themes in Gang Membership

A number of interrelated themes surfaced in the interviews with our respondents, which provide a framework for understanding youth involvement in gangs. The following discussion focuses on how everyday life in marginalized and chaotic neighborhoods sets the stage for group solidarity. At one level, the boredom, lack of resources, and high visibility of crime in their neglected communities create the conditions for turning to others who are similarly situated, and consequently, it is the group that realistically offers a social outlet. At another level, the stress on the family from living in marginalized areas combined with financial struggles creates heated tension and, in many cases, violence in the home. It is the group that provides our respondents with a safe refuge and a surrogate family. Although the theme of marginality cuts across gender and ethnicity, there were critical differences in how girls and boys, and Samoans, Filipinos, and Hawaiians express and respond to the problems of everyday life.

The "Hood"

One distinctive geographical factor about Hawaii is that many neighborhoods are class stratified rather than class/ethnic stratified. This is partly related to the history of the state's political economy (i.e., plantation, tourism) and the limited space of the island. These factors mean that a variety of low-income ethnic groups will live in proximity to each other.

Our respondents reside in lower-middle- and working-class neighborhoods. About a third (29 percent) of our respondents live in the central urban area of Oahu in the Kalihi district. This is a congested, densely populated area with a large Filipino population. It is filled with single family residences, housing projects, local small businesses, hospitals, and churches. Hawaiians and Samoans live along the fringes of the central district of Kalihi-Palama. This is an area that the police have targeted as being a high-crime neighborhood, particularly for drug sales, and this impression was confirmed through the observations and experiences of our respondents. Given law enforcement interest in this area, it is not surprising that several of our interviewees reported being tagged, harassed, and stopped by patrol units.

By contrast, similar ethnic groups are concentrated on the west end of the island, in what local residents refer to as the "plantation areas" and the "country." In some pockets of these rural neighborhoods, crime and drug transactions are visible as our respondents reported. Overall, however, neighborhoods in these rural areas are less crowded and relatively quiet; consequently, law enforcement surveillance operates differently in these areas than in the central district. Several of our respondents indicated that they were treated fairly by the police. In a few instances when youths were caught for a crime, the police sternly issued a warning and returned them home.

Despite differences in the density of and police attitudes toward these communities, these areas are similar to those described in recent gang ethnographies where the ongoing presence of crime combined with high rates of unemployment have resulted in a bleak and distressed environment (Rockhill et al. 1993). Not surprisingly, some of our respondents recognize that there has been little government investment in their neighborhoods, and all of them are quick to point out that there are few resources available for young people in their communities. They describe their lives in their neighborhoods as "boring." Simply put, being poor means being bored; there are few organized recreational activities, no jobs, no vocational training opportunities, no money to pay for entertainment, nowhere to go, and nothing happening for long stretches of time. Boys and girls alike echo this view: "there is nothing to do." How then do they cope on a daily level with having no money, no employment opportunities, and little to occupy their time?

Gang Provides a Social Outlet

Generally boys and girls have found the gang to be the most realistic solution to boredom. Our respondents uniformly state that their group provides a meaningful social outlet in an environment that has little else to offer. A sense of solidarity develops among those who face a similar plight, and as our respondents describe, their group provides a network of reliable friends who can be "counted on"; consequently, a large number of hours in school and outside of school are spent "hanging out" together and "wanting to have fun." How do they define "hanging out and having fun"? Much of their time together is spent in social activities, particularly sports. Both boys and girls indicate that they routinely engage in a variety of sports ranging from basketball to football to volleyball (mostly girls), and understandably, given the state's beaches, swimming, boogie boarding, and body surfing. Because program resources are either limited or nonexistent in their communities, our respondents are left on their own to organize their own activities. In many instances, they develop makeshift strategies to fill the time void. Because the local community center's hours are restricted, the girls from a Samoan group in the

Kalihi area find themselves waiting for nightfall when they can climb the fence unseen, and swim in the center's pool.

Beyond sports, however, the social dimension of the group and the specific solutions to boredom operate differently in the lives of the girls as compared with the boys and, in many ways, is tied to traditional and cultural gender roles. For example, several of our female respondents, particularly our Samoan girls, indicate that they spend a great deal of their time together "harmonizing, going to dances and competitions and all that." Singing, dancing, and learning hula from family members are time honored activities within Pacific cultures, and the integration of these activities into gang life signifies an interface between traditional culture and the culture of the streets.

By contrast, the boys relieve the boredom and find camaraderie in the traditional sport of "cruising." Cruising in an automobile is a regular part of their life with the group, allowing them more mobility than our girl respondents, who are largely confined to the gym or park in their neighborhoods or who ride with boys or take the bus to other areas. For those girls who live in the more rural areas of the island, mobility is simply not an option. Not surprisingly, cruising for the boys is often accompanied by other expressions of masculinity, specifically "drinking," "fighting," and "petty thieving," including "ripping off tourists." All our male respondents state that they drink, usually beer, and the majority report regular use. The combination of boredom along with the limited avenues to express their manliness cuts across ethnic and community lines. Trip, an 18-year-old Samoan from Waipahu, describes his daily routine;

> After school there is nothing to do. A lot of my friends like to lift weights, if there was someplace to lift weights. A lot of my friends don't know how to read, they try to read, but say they can't, and they don't have programs or places for them to go. . . .
> There are no activities, so now we hang around and drink beer. We hang around, roam the streets. . . . Yesterday we went to a pool hall and got into a fight over there.

A 14-year-old Filipino boy from the Kalihi area recounts a similar experience to Trip's:

> Get up at 1:00 in the afternoon. Then take a shower, then at three o'clock, go with my friend to Pearlridge [shopping mall], look for girls, and then cruise in Tantalus, and we almost got into a fight. We was gonna drop off the girls and go back but they had too many guys so we turned around. We had 4 guys and they had 20.

Interestingly, although cruising is also connected for many of the boys with "looking for girls," girls responded that although they sometimes talk about boys in their gangs, they do not see the group as a vehicle for "looking" for boys. This is not to say that girls are not involved in drinking or fighting like their boy counterparts; however, fighting and drinking are less frequent among the girls, with a few indicating that when they party, "they don't drink, smoke, or nothing," and "can't stand that stuff." Significantly fewer girls talked explicitly about getting into fights. Their fights usually have been because of "rumors" as Quente, whose group The Meanest Crew consists of a group of girls living in one of the city's largest and most densely populated housing projects in Oahu, explains:

> Yes they say rumors they saw this person. The first day of school, they say my sister wanted to beat up this girl, but my sister never knew who this girl was. . . . Then my other sister, they was fighting, and then my sister her nose was bleeding, and my sister and my cousin started fighting, and I came and beat up this eighth-grade girl. She was big and fat. She was taller than me. Then after that we went to the office, and they say my sister and I gang up on that girl. Those Kuhio girls they say my sister wanted to fight but my sister didn't know them. . . . Those SOK started it.

We are told that members of The Meanest Crew and the SOK live in the same neighborhood, attend the same high school, and consider themselves rivals. SOK member Anna Marie, who is also from Kalihi and 15 years of age, reports that her group too gets in fights. Her first arrest for assault occurred three years ago when she was "mobbed" by another group, and she has since been arrested six to seven times for assault. All 16 of the members have been picked up for assault, fighting, stealing, and running away.

As our girls suggest, their involvement in fights has less to do with an attempt to gain an egalitarian position to their male counterparts, but instead is directly related to the desperate boredom they experience. In this way, their situation is similar to their male counterparts. One 17-year-old Samoan girl explained her group's attempts to deal with boredom in the Kalihi district:

> Before it got worse? [Then] after school everybody would meet at Brother Brian's Bar, drink, dance, talk story, then when the sun was going down that's when all the drug dealing started. And then [later] couple times we would go out and look for trouble. Some of use just felt hyped and would go out and beat up people. We went up to this park and had this one couple, and so for nothing we just went beat em up.

Gang Serves as Alternative Family

The impact of distressed communities is felt not only by young people but by their families as well. Our respondents come from several different types of family situations. In many cases their parents are "overemployed," holding two jobs in working class and service industry occupations. They are, for example, laundry workers, hotel maids, and construction workers. Given the high cost of living in Hawaii, this is a common practice among working-class families. Unfortunately, when both parents are struggling to stay afloat in this economy, supervision is absent in the home. A few youth indicated that they are essentially on their own because their single parent, who is consumed by his or her job, is rarely home to supervise. In some instances, parents have difficulty keeping a steady job and are either unemployed or underemployed for periods of time. As their children recognize and describe to us, supervision may be present, but it is filled with tension as parents try to cope with financial problems. In a small but important number of cases, the cultural and familial ties of parents required either the mother or the father to remain in their native land. This was true among a few of our Samoan and Filipino

respondents. In light of family financial pressures and limited time for parental involvement or supervision, it is not surprising that these young people feel a sense of isolation and consequently find support and solace among members of their group. As one Samoan girl plainly puts it:

> [It's] good to just kick back and relax and have fun, but not get into trouble. We tell each other our problems. . . . I don't like to be a loner or feel isolated.

In sharing their problems at home with each other, the members of the group take on the role of a surrogate family. A common theme in the lives of our female and male respondents is that the gang serves as an alternative family. As Tina, a 15-year-old Samoan explains, "We all like sistas all taking care of each other." The symbolic kinship of the group is even reflected in the name of one female Samoan group called JEMA, which stands for Just Every Mother's Angel. Seventeen-year-old Daniella recounts the origins of her group's name.

> We chose that because all the girls I hang out with, yeah, all their mothers passed away, and during elementary days, we all used to hang out and all our mothers were close yeah, so that's how we came up with that name.

The males express similar views to those of the "sistas." Kevin, a 17-year-old Hawaiian, likens the leader of his group to "like the father of the house." On meeting the leader, he reports that "[the] first time I saw him I felt like bowing. I didn't though. He said if I respected him, he would respect me." Or as Ricky, a 17-year-old Filipino states, "The gang is a closer family than my parents because they are there to help me everyday. . . . unlike my parents."

The tension on the family is amplified by other factors. As noted earlier, among Samoan and Filipino families, the immigrant experience is frequently one of alienation because of differences in language and culture. The marginalization of the native Hawaiian people and their culture has a long history and has left them in an ambiguous cultural position. These ethnically diverse pressures on the family heighten the conflict at home and, in many instances, erupt into violence.

In this way, the group's surrogate family role takes on an even greater significance for the young people who report physical, emotional, and sexual abuse by a family member. As indicated earlier, 75 percent of the girls (6 out of 8 who were asked) and 57 percent of the boys (12 out of 21 who were asked) report "lickings" by one or both of their parents. In the midst of financial tension, physical abuse appears to be connected to the violation of cultural and gender role expectations. The girls, for example, indicate that their lickings were because of violations of a traditional sexual double standard: "not calling home," "coming home late," and "not coming home for the night." Staying out all night is interpreted differently for girls than for boys. When girls engage in these behaviors, this is "running away" and is often connected with "promiscuity." When boys don't come home for the night, this is normal adolescent behavior for working-class boys.

By comparison, all four of the Hawaiian boys and four of the nine Samoan boys reported that they were physically struck by one of their parents for delinquent behaviors such as "fighting," "stealing," and "smoking pakalolo (marijuana]." Kevin, a 17-year-old Hawaiian boy, described how his mother threw him down the stairs, cracking his ribs and bruising his spinal disc, when she found a bag of marijuana in his room. For two boys and one Samoan girl, their father's beatings were aggravated by alcohol and drug use, respectively. The experience of the four (out of eight) Filipino boys who stated that they received lickings differed from the South Pacific Islanders. According to the Filipino boys, the beatings were related to a wider range of behavior that their parents believed to be intolerable, such as a "bad attitude" and "poor grades." Dwane, a 17-year-old Filipino, recalled that his lickings stopped as he got older.

These young people's response to the abuse is usually one of reluctance and resistance to report the abuse, and must be viewed in a cultural context. Family loyalty is important among Filipino youth, where strong cultural pressures, language problems, and an understandable reticence to involve external agencies (and perhaps jeopardize immigration status) depress reporting of abuse. The Hawaiian and Samoan boys and girls who reported being physically abused also refused to call or permit official intervention (unless detected by school authorities). Despite child abuse education in the classrooms at all age levels, these young people viewed their loyalty to their parents as paramount. One 17-year-old Samoan male's loyalty to his father took precedence over his own victimization:

> Since my grandma passed away, I don't get along with my father. He comes home drunk and beat us up. He beats us up with those weight-lifting belts. The police never come, I don't tell nobody. I don't want nobody that's why, I don't want nobody butting in now. I run away when I can't stand it. . . .

Although the "sistas" and "brothers" of the gang offer some level of support it is understandably difficult for many to cope with everyday life. One 18-year-old Samoan girl who has been severely abused, physically and emotionally, by her parents, finds that her group provides "someone to talk to." In this particular case, the group has been especially important as she is fiercely loyal to her parents and rationalizes the beatings as a feature of the Samoan ways. "My parents aren't understanding. They are Samoan, and everything you do you get lickings"; moreover, she refuses to tell school and child protective services authorities because they will intervene. She must consequently contend with "wanting to kill myself because I'm tired of getting beat up." Many of them view their lives as "hopeless" and their future as being "jammed up." Their options seem limited as nearly half of them had contemplated suicide. Suicidal thoughts were more prevalent among the girls (71 percent or 5 of the 7 females asked) compared to the boys (33.3 percent or 6 of 18 males asked).

Differences in Crime and Delinquency

Boy and girl gang members differ in the area of crime and delinquent behavior. Although girls commit more crime and engage in more fights than their stereotype would support, they are certainly less involved in this behavior than the boys. They are also far less involved in drug selling, robbery, and other types of criminal behavior.

As noted earlier, for boys, fighting—even looking for fights—is a major activity within the gang. If anything, the presence of girls around gang members depresses violence. As one 14-year-old Filipino put it, "If we not with the girls, we fighting. If we not fighting, we with the girls." Many of the boys' activities involved drinking, cruising, and "looking for trouble." Looking for trouble also meant being prepared for trouble—though guns are somewhat available, most of the boys we interviewed used bats or their hands to fight. Some of this is cultural—as one respondent explained:

> My friend had a gun, one of our boys had a gun, but one of our gang members said put it somewhere else, cause we're Samoans and Samoans fight with hands.

Another Samoan youth who lives in the country adds, "down here we no more guns, just fist fight." Some of this may also be strategic, because some respondents mentioned knowing where to get their hands on guns, but not carrying them regularly. The hiding of guns and carrying of baseball bats, for example, avoids arrest for possession of an illegal firearm because a bat can always be a piece of sporting equipment.

Another major difference between the girls and the boys was involvement in drug dealing. Although girls drink and use drugs in the gang, a number (though not all) of male gangs are involved in selling drugs. As a 17-year-old Filipino male who was in a leadership position with his gang noted, the gang is important because it provides "opportunities to make money and use drugs." The gang helps you "find drugs faster. . . . [and] buy and sell drugsfaster."

The boys' gangs did demonstrate a range of orientations to drug use and selling. Some only sold drugs ("Guys in my group don't do drugs, sell yea, but only weed"); other groups did not use drugs ("We don't sell no drugs, we cruise, we used to paint graffiti, but not any

more"). For most of the boys, though, the gang was the site of drinking and doing drugs in a social way, "We do sports together, parties, we party every day, some guys do drugs and shit." One or two gang members belonged to groups that focused exclusively on drug selling. Logically, those most seriously involved in drug selling had moved to Waikiki and were selling to tourists. These gang members "sit on the wall and talk, look for vices, if a deal comes up, go and make the deal. [We] don't get into that much trouble, most people in Waikiki know us." This variation in delinquent and criminal involvement of different gangs is consistent with other male gang studies (Fagan 1989).

As alluded to earlier, the violence associated with boys' gang life is largely an outgrowth of the violence in their neighborhoods, which explains why in many of the boys' interviews, protection was mentioned as a major reason to join the gang. As one young man put it, the gang gives "protection for when you go to school, some guys tough and that's your power. . . . the gang's that power. . . . you don't get picked on or beat up."

The violence that fuels membership in gangs, though, spills over into more general "trouble" as groups of young men begin to hang out, "Yeah, we have fights with other groups, sometimes when it is getting close to the weekend, there are fights. Sometimes one on one fights or the whole group against another group. . . . [we] just collide into each other and fight."

Experience with this kind of violence and drug use combined with the fact that almost all of these youth had relatives in gangs occasionally produces a reflective voice:

> Sometimes when my friends are in trouble, we go help my friends. . . . that is how we get into fights and stuff. We play sports together, party. look for women, go to concerts, when we party sometimes my friends drink, but me I only drink a little … chill out. . . . cruise. . . . cause one of my uncles he used to drink and smoke a lot he died last year. . . . when I think of him I think it is going to happen to me.

Only infrequently are non-gang members the targets of violence; when they are, they are tourists assaulted for their money. As one 14-year-old Hawaiian youth puts it, "When we no more money, me and my friends walking around and get hungry, the first Jap[anese tourist] we see, we knock and take his money and go to McDonalds lidat [like that], eat and go home after." This behavior, though, was the exception. Most of the youths who engaged in gang behavior did drugs, sold drugs, and engaged in petty thefts—again chiefly as a group activity. As one 17-year-old Filipino puts it, "If one person go steal car, we all go steal car. . . . they don't have to, but everybody go for watch." Another 17-year-old Samoan youth says, "I've been gang banging since I was fifth grade, I've been hitting (stealing?] cars and all kinds of shit."

For girls, fighting and violence are part of life in the gang—but not something they necessarily seek out. Instead, protection from neighborhood and family violence is a major theme in girls' interviews. One girl simply states that she belongs to the gang to provide "some protection from her father." Through the group she has learned ways to defend herself physically and emotionally. "He used to beat me up, but now I hit back and he doesn't beat me much now." Another 14-year-old Samoan put it, "You gotta be part of the gang or else you're the one who's gonna get beat up." Though this young woman said that members of her gang had to "have total attitude and can fight." She went on to say, "We want to be a friendly gang. I don't know why people are afraid of us. We're not that violent." Fights do come up in the lives of these girls, "We only wen mob this girl 'cause she was getting wise, she was saying 'what, slut' so I wen crack her and all my friends wen jump in." Later this young women explained that the gang and its orientation to violence changed:

> At first [I] thought of the gang as a friendship thing, but as I grew into the gang, it just started to change. I started seeing it as, I guess, I don't know, I guess as trying to survive in the streets and everything, and that about it. . . . protection, cause at the time I was scared, cause my sister and cousin used to beat me up and before I even joined the gang, you know how you would threaten your sister. . . . my sister

stole my mom's car and her money and my cousin use to steal her dad's money, and I knew all these things, and my sister would say, "We're going to beat you up if you tell dad."

In general, the girls talk about the trouble the gang gets into as a tonic for boredom. "Sometimes we like cause trouble yeah cause boring, so boring. So we like make trouble ah, for make scene, so we just call anybody, if they looking at us." Girls rarely carry weapons ("No, I don't carry weapons, but I can get it if I want to."). In fact, one girl said in answer to a question about knives, "I have knives, but only for food." This same 13-year-old girl saw some of the pointlessness of their violence:

> I think the girls and boys that don't join gangs are smart, but girls like me who are in gangs are stupid, they are just wasting their time cause dumb fighting over color, just for a stupid color. . . .

Conclusion

This article has stressed the need to explore gangs in their social context and to avoid totalizing notions of either boys' or girls' gangs. Previous research as well as our own interviews clearly suggest that such an approach is needed. One of the major conclusions one draws from listening to these young women and men is that the gang is a haven for coping with the many problems they encounter in their everyday life in marginalized communities. Paradoxically, the sense of solidarity achieved from sharing everyday life with similarly situated others has the unintended effect of drawing many gang youth—both boys and girls—into behaviors that ultimately create new problems for them.

On the broadest level, both the girls and boys are growing up in communities racked by poverty, racism, and rapid population growth. The gang is clearly a product of these forces. Shaped by the ethnicity, race, and gender of its participants, the gang takes on different shapes depending on its composition. Clearly, for both males and females, the gang provides a needed social outlet and a tonic for the boredom of low-income life. The gang provides friends and activities in communities where such recreational outlets are pitifully slim. . . .

The violence that characterizes their family lives and their communities is another prod into the gang for most of these youth. Gangs provide protection for both girls and boys. Many youth are drawn from families that are abusive, and, particularly for girls, the gang provides the skills to fight back against the violence in their families. . . .

The marginalization of working- and lower-working-class communities has specific meaning for young men as well. The displays of toughness and risk-taking described by the boys in our study are a source for respect and status in an environment that is structurally unable to affirm their masculinity. Their acts of intimidation and fighting are rooted in the need for protection as well as the need to validate their manliness. Police harassment of gangs, particularly in the cities, further strengthens their group solidarity and, at the same time, increases their alienation from conventional others (like store owners) in their neighborhoods.

Abuse and neglect shape experiences with their families as well, but here there are rather stark ethnic differences in the ways both the boys and girls experience abuse. First, girls are more likely to experience abuse, with problems of sexual victimization and sexual abuse appearing in their accounts of family life. For boys, the violence is further mediated by culture. . . .

Gangs, though, do produce opportunities for involvement in criminal activity. Especially for boys from poor families, stealing and small time drug dealing make up for a lack of money. These activities are not nearly as common among the girl respondents. Instead, their problems with the law originate with more traditional forms of girl delinquency, such as running away from home. Their families still attempt to hold them to a double standard, which results in parental tensions and disputes that have no parallel among the boys.

Media constructions of gang behavior, then, which stress the violence done by gang members, need to be countered by far richer assessments of the role played by gangs in the lives of these young people. Gang participation and gang structure is clearly shaped by both gender and race. Products of distressed neighborhoods, the gangs emerge to meet many needs that established institutions—schools, families, communities—do not address. Many of the impulses that propel youth into gangs are prosocial and understandable—the need for safety, security, and a sense of purpose and belonging. For boys, violence is certainly a theme in gang life, but it is as much a product of violent neighborhoods as it is a cause of the phenomena. Boys' experiences of violence and abuse within the family, although kept from official agencies by cultural norms stressing the centrality of the family, certainly provide an additional and powerful perspective on the violence of boys. For girls, violence (gang or otherwise) is not celebrated and normative; it is instead more directly a consequence of and a response to the abuse, both physical and sexual, that characterizes their lives at home. Girls' participation in gangs, which has been the subject of intense media interest, certainly needs to be placed within the context of the lives of girls, particularly young women of color on the economic and political margins. Girl gang life is certainly not an expression of "liberation," but instead reflects the attempts of young women to cope with a bleak and harsh present as well as a dismal future. One 15-year-old Samoan girl captured this sense of despair when in response to our question about whether she was doing well in school, said, "No, I wish I was, I need a future. [My life] is jammed up."

Attempts to totalize these youth as amoral and violent must be seen as part of a larger attempt to blame them for their own problems in a culture where gang has become synonymous with race. As young women are demonized by the media, their genuine problems can be marginalized and then ignored. Indeed, they and their boy counterparts have become the problem. The challenge to those concerned about these youth is, then, twofold. First, responsible work on gangs must make the dynamics of this victim blaming clear. Second, research must continue to build an understanding of gangs that is sensitive to the contexts within which they arise in an era that is increasingly concerned about the intersection of class, race, and gender, such work seems long overdue.

References

Adler, Freda. 1975. *Sisters in Crime*. New York: McGraw Hill.

Aquino, Belinda. 1994. Filipino women and political engagement. The Office for Women's Research, working paper series. Volume 2 (1993–1994). Honolulu: University of Hawaii, Manoa.

Bowter, Lee, and Malcolm Klein. 1983. The etiology of female juvenile delinquency and gang membership: A test of pyschological social structural explanations. *Adolescence 18:739–51.*

Brown, W. 1977. Black female gangs in Philadelphia. *International Journal of Offender Therapy and Comparative Criminology* 21:221–8.

Campbell, Ann. 1984. *Girls in the gang*. Oxford: Basil Blackwell.

——. 1990 Female participation in gangs. In Gangs in America, edited by C. Ronald Huff. Newbury Park, CA: Sage.

——. 1992 Female gang members' social representations of aggression. Paper presented at the Annual meeting, American Society of Criminology, New Orelans, LA.

Chesney-Lind, Meda. 1993. Girls, gangs and violence: Reinventing the liberated female crook. *Humanity and Society* 17:321–44.

Chesney-Lind, Meda, and Ian Lind. 1986. Visitors as victims: Crimes against tourists in two Hawaii counties. *Annals of Tourism Research* 13:167–91.

Chesney-Lind, Meda, Nancy Marker, Ivette Stearn, Allison Yap, Valerie Song, Howard Reyes, Yolanda Reyes, Jeffrey Stearn, and JoAnn Taira. 1992. Gangs and delinquency in Hawaii. Paper presented at the Annual Meetings, American Society of Criminology, New Orleans, LA.

Cloward, Richard, and Lloyd Ohlin. 1960. *Delinquency and opportunity: A theory of delinquent gangs*. New York: Free Press.

Cohen, Albert. 1955. *Delinquent boys: The culture of the gang*. Glencoe, IL: Free Press.

Connell, R. W. 1987. *Gender and power*. Stanford, CA: Stanford University Press.

Crime Prevention Division. 1993. *Crime in Hawaii. Honolulu: Department of the Attorbey General.*

Curry, G. David, Robert J. Box, Richard A. Ball, and Darryl Stone. 1992. *National Assessment of law enforcement anti-gang information resources: Draft 1992 final report*. West Virginia University: National Assessment Survey 1992.

Daly, Kathleen, and Meda Chesney-Lind. 1988. Feminism and criminology. *Justice Quarterly* 5:497–538.

Department of Business and Economic Development and Tourism. 1993. *Hawaii State Datebook, 1992*. Honolulu: Author.

Fagan, Jeffrey. 1989. The social organization of drug use and drug dealing among urban gangs. *Criminology 27:633–67.*

Federal Bureau of Investigation. 1992. *Uniform crime reports 1991*. Washington, DC: U.S. Government Printing Office.

Fishamn, Laura. 1988. The vice queens: An ethnographic study of Black female gang behavior. Presented at the Annual Meetings, American Society of Criminology, New Orleans, LA.

Flowers, R.B. 1987. *Women and criminality. New York: Greenwood.*

Hagedorn, John. 1988. *People and folks*. Chicago: Lake View.

Hagedorn, John. 1992. Homeboys, dope fiends, legits and new jacks. Paper presented at the Annual Meetings, American Society of Criminology, New Orleans, LA.

Harris, Mary. 1988. *Cholas: Latino girls and gangs*. New York: AMS Press.

Jankowski, Martin Sanchez. 1991. *Islands in the street: Gangs and American urban society*. Berkeley: University of California Press.

Katz, Jack. 1988. *Seduction of crime*. New York: Basic Books.

Lauderback, David, Joy Hansen, and Daniel Waldorf. 1992. Sisters are doin' it for themselves: A Black female gang in San Francisco. *The Gang Journal* 1:57–72.

Lebra, Joyce. 1991. *Women's voices in Hawaii*. Niwot: University Press of Colorado.

Linnekin, Jocelyn. 1990. *Sacred queens and women of consequence*. Ann Arbor: University of Michigan Press.

Messerschmidt, James. 1986. *Capitalism, patriarchy, and crime*. Totowa, NJ: Rowman & Littlefield.

——. 1993. *Masculinities and crime*. Lanham, MD: Rowan &Littlefield.

Miller, Walter. 1958. Lower Class culture as a generating milieu of gang delinquency. *Journal of Social Issues* 3:5–19.

——. 1975. Race, sex, and gangs: The Molls. *Trans-Action* 11:32–5.

——. 1980. The Molls. In *Women, crime, and justice*, edited by S.K. Datesman and F.R. Scarpitti. New York: Oxford University Press.

Muwakkil, Salim. 1993. Ganging Together. *In These Times,* 5 April.

Office of Youth Services, State of Hawaill. 1993. *An interim report to the Legislature on the Gang Response System Act 300. 1992 SLH.* Honolulu: Author.

Ostner, Ilona. 1986. Die Entdeckung der Madchen. Neue Perspecktiven fur die. *Kolner-Zeitschrift-fur Soziologie und Sozialpsychologie* 38:352–71.

Quicker, John. 1983. *Homegirls: Characterizing Chicana gangs.* Los Angeles: Internation Univeristy Press.

Reiner, Ira. 1992. *Gangs, crime and violence in Los Angeles. Findings and proposals from the Sitrrict Attoney's Office, executive summary.* Los Angeles: District Attorney, County of Los Angeles.

Rice, R. 1963. A reporter at large: The Persian queens. *New Yorker,* 19 October.

Rockhill, Anna, Meda Chesney-Lind, Joe Allen, Nestor Batalon, Elise Garvin, Karen Joe, and Michele Spina. 1993. *Surveying Hawaii's youth: Neighborhoods, delinquency, and gangs.* Honolulu: Social Science Research Institute, University of Hawaii.

Ryan, William. 1972. *Blaming the victim.* New York: Vintage Books.

Skolnick, Jerome, Theodore Correl, Elizabeth Navarro, and Roger Rabb. 1989. *The social structure of street drug dealing.* Sacramento, CA: Office of the Attorney General, State of California.

Taylor, Carl. 1990. *Dangerous society.* East Lansing: Michigan State University Press.

Taylor, Carl. 1993. *Girls, gangs, women and drugs.* East Lansing: Michigan State University Press.

Thasher, Frederick. 1927. *The gang.* Chicago: University of Chicago Press.

Waldorf, Daniel. 1993. *Final report on crack sales, gangs and violence to the National Institute on Drug Abuse.* San Francisco: Institute for Scientific Analysis.

Watters, John K., and Patrick Biernaki. 1989. Targeted sampling: Options for the study of hidden populations. *Social Problems* 36:416–30.
